DICTIONARY OF
AMERICAN HISTORY

DICTIONARY OF
AMERICAN HISTORY

FROM 1763 TO THE PRESENT

Peter Thompson

SERIES EDITOR · CHRIS COOK

Checkmark Books®
An imprint of Facts On File, Inc.

For Alexander, James, Marlis, Robert – and, above all, Walter.

Dictionary of American History: From 1763 to the Present

First published in Great Britain by Cassell as Cassell's Dictionary of Modern American History.

Copyright © 2000 by Peter Thompson

Facts On File, Inc.
11 Penn Plaza
New York, NY 10001

Library of Congress Cataloguing-in-Publication Data

A CIP catalog record for this book is available from Facts on File.

ISBN 0-8160-4462-7 hb
ISBN 0-8160-4463-5 pb

Facts On File books are available at special discounts when purchased in bulk quantities for businesses, associations, institutions or sales promotions. Please call our Special Sales Department in New York at 212/967-8800 or 800/322-8755.

You can find Facts On File on the WorldWide Web at http://www.factsonfile.com

Designed by Gwyn Lewis

Cartography by Lovell Johns Limited

Printed and bound in Great Britain by MPG Books Ltd, Bodmin, Cornwall

CONTENTS

Introduction   7

The Dictionary   13

Maps   471

APPENDIX 1
Constitutional documents   475

APPENDIX 2
The Presidents of the United States   495

APPENDIX 3
Membership of the United States
Supreme Court   519

APPENDIX 4
Subject index   523

APPENDIX 5
Further reading   537

INTRODUCTION

THIS DICTIONARY has been designed and written by a professional historian whose working life revolves around the use of techniques of historical anthropology to investigate social relations in colonial America. I did not come by my interest in the mores of taverngoing in eighteenth-century Philadelphia by reading a dictionary of the subject. Rather, in learning to understand the basic shape of American history, I discovered a topic for further investigation. It is my hope that *Cassell's Dictionary of Modern American History* will offer readers the opportunity to come to their own understanding of basic issues and developments in American history and perhaps even encourage them to pursue specialist interests. Since even the most arrogant academic would hesitate to claim complete and exhaustive knowledge of American history since 1763, there is also an excitement in writing a work of this kind that I hope is reflected in the main body of the text. For the writer, as for the reader, a dictionary is a companion on a voyage of discovery and recollection.

If 'dictionary,' 'American,' and 'history' were ever self-explanatory terms, they are not now. I have tried to write a dictionary, not a companion or encyclopedia. I do not claim to cover every aspect of my chosen topic, but I aim at something other than a work that embellishes knowledge acquired elsewhere. In selecting material for inclusion I have tried to balance an obligation to provide specific information on particular topics against the need to provide entries enabling the reader to come to an understanding of American history as a whole. A particular feature of *Cassell's Dictionary of Modern American History* is its appreciation that readers will approach this text with a variety of questions and must therefore be provided information in a varied format. In addition to short definitive entries, readers will also find a number of longer interpretive essays. Among the topics covered by these longer essays are the American Revolution, the Civil War, Reconstruction, the Women's Suffrage movement, Progressivism, the New Deal, the Cold War and the Civil Rights movement. Each of these essays provides the reader with an overview of the subject and cross-references to entries providing more specialized information. In addition, the Dictionary contains appendices in which are reproduced the Declaration of Independence, the US Constitution and Bill of Rights, results of presidential elections from 1789 to 1996 and details on the composition of the Supreme Court and presidential administrations. As a further aid to the reader, an appendix cross-references over 1200 entries by simple subject headings.

This book seeks to foster a historical understanding of the American nation. I have therefore attempted to confine my coverage to people, institutions, events and ideas of national historical significance. However, some national events are of little *historical* significance, as can be demonstrated by two examples, one from the domain of mass culture, one from the 'higher' ground of politics. Heavyweight boxing championships or World Series baseball games temporarily rivet the nation's attention, but have yet to change its history. (On the other hand, the development of major professional sports and the careers of a small number of individual sportspeople, such as Muhammad Ali and Jackie Robinson, are of considerable sociological significance and are included in these pages accordingly.) Similarly, despite the claims of candidates down the years, presidential elections have *not* always changed the course of American history. I have therefore included in the main text entries only for those elections, such as that of 1860 which elevated Lincoln to the White House, that form landmarks in the nation's history. (The candidates standing in and votes recorded in every presidential contest between 1789 and 1996 are, however, detailed in a separate appendix.)

The treatment of 'minority' groups in a work purporting to illustrate a national history is always the subject of scrutiny and comment. As will become evident, I believe that any appreciation of American history must be informed by an understanding of the role played by immigrants, native peoples and African-Americans in the nation's development. However, I have attempted to draw a distinction, which must of necessity remain uneasy, between understanding the role played by 'minority' groups in America's past and celebrating the achievements of such groups. My coverage of jazz or the Harlem Renaissance attempts to explain the historical significance of these topics. I leave to other works the task of assessing their cultural merit.

I should also note that this work is intended to help readers understand the domestic history of the United States of America. That history was of course shaped by events in faraway places, and topics such as the My Lai massacre, the Berlin Wall Crisis and the Spanish-American War receive their due attention. However I have not attempted to chronicle in exhaustive detail the United States' changing role in world affairs, and my coverage of events such as the Second World War is designed with the needs of a student of American history in mind.

Historians are opinionated people, and although dictionaries are supposed to be dispassionate texts, the process of selecting material for inclusion in a historical dictionary inevitably prompts larger questions about the nature of the discipline itself. The proposition that there is more to 'history' than battles, treaties and great men now commands near universal assent. Most historians would also agree that in America, as perhaps in no other modern industrialized nation, phenomena such as the rise of a fast-food industry do not just reflect historical developments but are themselves agents of historical change. I therefore make no apology for including in this dictionary an entry on McDonalds. However, in a work which does not claim to be an encyclopedia, the selection of historically significant cultural forms involves some tough choices. I believe that jazz is rooted in American history (and I include an entry on it), but that an entry on rock and roll would be more appropriate to a volume with a global focus. In the case of religion, I include entries on denominations that originated in America, and on religious issues specific to American history, but leave to other volumes the task of assessing the American religious experience in a global context. Readers will find in the pages that follow entries on, for example, *Uncle Tom's Cabin*, Elvis Presley and Route 66. I believe these cultural topics say something about American history. However, I have not attempted to build into this dictionary biographies of major American artists or appreciations of great works of art and literature.

Researching and writing the dictionary raised the knotty issue of what belonged in its pages and what did not. I hoped, in the spirit of US Supreme Court Justice Potter Stewart, to 'know it when I saw it.'

The resulting coverage and content may not satisfy the demands of every potential reader but will, I believe, help a broad cross-section of users come to their own understanding of America's past.

Cross-references to related entries are announced in the main text and appendices by small capital letters, for example NULLIFICATION CRISIS within the entry on Andrew Jackson. Common or frequent cross-references, to, for example the US Supreme Court or individual states, are not announced if the reader's understanding of a particular subject does not depend upon the cross-reference.

Cassell's Dictionary of Modern American History is unusual in that has been written by a single author rather than a dispersed team. However the readability, accuracy and utility of this dictionary have been enhanced enormously by the editorial advice and labors of Chris Cook, Jenny Cranwell, Ian Crofton and Richard Milbank. Richard and Jenny deserve particular thanks for defining, and then helping me realize, the 'vision thing'. When writing a dictionary, particularly a volume with no end date, one finds oneself praying 'may no new thing arise.' Many thanks are due to my wife, Alex Franklin, for providing continuity and reassurance in the form of support upon which I come to rely but have no right to expect. This book is dedicated to my son Walter and to my niece, nephew and godchildren.

Peter Thompson
Oxford, June 2000

THE DICTIONARY

A

AAA, *see* AGRICULTURAL ADJUSTMENT ADMINIS-
TRATION.

ABC-1 agreement, the product of secret
negotiations (codenamed ABC-1) between
US and British military planners conducted
in Washington DC between January 27 and
March 29 1941. The USA and Britain agreed
that if both Japan and Germany declared
war on the USA, the latter would seek to
defeat Germany first. The USA stuck to the
agreement after PEARL HARBOR, with incal-
culable consequences for the outcome of
WORLD WAR II.

Abelman vs. Booth (March 7 1859), US
Supreme Court ruling concerning runaway
slaves. The Supreme Court ruled unanimously that northern states could not use
PERSONAL LIBERTY LAWS to transfer from
federal to state courts the prosecution of
runaway slaves apprehended under the
FUGITIVE SLAVE ACT (1850). The Court also
forbade states from hindering federal officials implementing the Fugitive Slave Act,
and it gratuitously affirmed the constitutionality of that statute.

Abernathy, Reverend Ralph David
(1926–90). Often overshadowed by Martin
Luther KING, Abernathy was one of the
founding fathers of the CIVIL RIGHTS MOVE-
MENT. Following the MONTGOMERY BUS BOY-
COTT, Abernathy, a Baptist minister, helped
to found the SOUTHERN CHRISTIAN LEADERSHIP
CONFERENCE (SCLC) in 1957 and served as

its first treasurer and secretary. Abernathy
fought for the traditional values of the Civil
Rights Movement during the turmoil that
afflicted it in the 1960s. In 1968 he led an
interracial march of poor southerners to
Washington DC and, echoing the BONUS
ARMY, established a semi-permanent protest
settlement named Resurrection City in the
vicinity of the Lincoln Memorial. From
1968 to 1977 he served as president of the
SCLC.

ABM treaty, *see* DÉTENTE.

abolition, the emancipation of slaves in the
USA. Slavery was abolished in some states
during the AMERICAN REVOLUTION, but continued to be legal in other areas until the
end of the CIVIL WAR in 1865. As the movement for the complete abolition of slavery
gained strength after 1800, the constitutional question of who had the power to
outlaw slaveholding became a central issue
in American politics.

In 1777 Vermont became the first American territory to abolish slavery completely.
Other northern states, led by Pennsylvania
in 1780, passed GRADUAL EMANCIPATION laws
freeing children born to slave parents.
Many southern states amended their legal
codes to make the MANUMISSION of slaves by
their masters easier. The NORTHWEST ORDI-
NANCE (1787) stipulated that slavery would
not be legal in new states to be formed
north of the Ohio river and east of the

Mississippi. The US CONSTITUTION allowed Congress to charge a duty on slaves imported into the USA, and to completely bar the import of slaves after 1808. These developments deceived many Americans into believing that slavery would soon die out.

Hopes that this would transpire faded after the development of Eli WHITNEY's cotton gin in 1793. This device sparked a boom in cotton production in the lower south that fueled a renewed demand for slaves. Anticipating a congressional ban on the import of slaves, cotton planters invested heavily in slaves while they were still able to do so. Moreover, as the southern economy recovered from the REVOLUTIONARY WAR, demand for labor rose. This made slaves more valuable and masters less willing to manumit.

Economic concerns aside, white southerners doubted that former slaves could live among them. Thomas Jefferson's NOTES ON THE STATE OF VIRGINIA was the first of many texts written by southerners predicting that abolition would be followed by a race war. A pro-slavery petition submitted to the Virginia state legislature in 1785 argued that the abolition of slavery would be 'exceedingly impolitic' because it would produce 'want, poverty, and distress' for the white population, and expose them to 'rape, murder, and outrage' at the hands of 'revengeful and remorseless' former slaves. In 1806 the Virginia legislature responded to these concerns by placing restrictions on manumission and requiring newly freed slaves to leave the state. Even in northern states support for the abolition of slavery did not translate into a commitment to extend civil rights to free blacks. Only five northern states allowed blacks to vote. Some passed laws prohibiting the inward migration of free blacks. In most states north of the MASON–DIXON LINE free blacks were barred from school systems and subjected to harassment.

The most conservative approach to abolition was adopted by the AMERICAN COLONIZATION SOCIETY (ACS), which was founded in 1816. The ACS raised funds to resettle free blacks in the west African country of Liberia in the hopes that, by removing former slaves from America, slave owners might be persuaded to voluntarily manumit their bondsmen. Many prominent southern politicians (among them Henry CLAY and James MONROE) and several state legislatures gave their blessing to the Society's endeavours. But by 1831 the ACS had resettled just 1420 freed blacks in Liberia.

On March 2 1807 the US Congress passed legislation prohibiting the importation of slaves into the USA after January 1 1808. But thereafter it did little to effect the abolition of slavery. Congressmen such as John Quincy ADAMS who formed the moderate wing of the abolition movement believed that Congress could not impose antislavery legislation on the states. Campaigners who favored immediate abolition bombarded Congress with petitions demanding that it take action. Yet nothing better indicates the strength of pro-slavery sentiment within Congress than the GAG RULE adopted on May 26 1836. Congress refused to discuss antislavery petitions on the grounds that it possessed no power to interfere with slavery where it was already legal. Southern congressmen, many of whom were themselves slave owners, took the position that the right to own slaves was guaranteed by the FIFTH AMENDMENT, and that legislation interfering with this right represented an unconstitutional infringement of southern liberties. Many congressmen from northern and western states reflected their constituents' hostility to free blacks and their indifference to the morality of slavery. The one area where Congress could take action against slavery was the DISTRICT OF COLUMBIA. From the 1830s onwards abolitionists campaigned for Congress to take the symbolic step of outlawing slavery in the nation's capital. As part of the COMPROMISE OF 1850 Congress did outlaw the slave trade in the District of Columbia, but residents retained the right to own slaves. Despite gaining some influence within the WHIG PARTY, abolitionists found that the SECOND PARTY SYSTEM was impervious to their concerns.

The roots of that broad-based popular opposition to slavery that helped characterize the REPUBLICAN PARTY in the 1850s can be traced back to the activities of the AMERICAN ANTISLAVERY SOCIETY (AAS) and its charismatic leader William Lloyd GARRISON. Founded on December 4 1833, the AAS coordinated the presentation of antislavery petitions to Congress and developed a national campaign in support of abolition. Through Garrison's newspaper the *LIBERATOR* and public meetings addressed by former slaves such as Frederick DOUGLASS, the AAS gradually reduced the number of northerners who were neutral toward, or uninterested in the issues of slavery and abolition. Most members of the AAS had been 'awakened' during the Protestant fundamentalist religious revivals of the 1820s and 1830s and supported Garrison's call for the immediate uncompensated abolition of slavery. A minority within the AAS, led by James Birney (1792–1857), took the line that this should be achieved gradually and by constitutional amendment. In 1840 Birney and his followers left the AAS to found the LIBERTY PARTY, which campaigned to end slavery by constitutional amendment.

Meanwhile, Garrison adopted ever more radical positions. He toyed with secession, arguing that northern states should leave a Union that permitted slavery. In 1843, in keeping with this logic, Garrison persuaded the Massachusetts Antislavery Society to resolve that the US Constitution was 'a covenant with death and an agreement with hell'. On 4 July 1854 he burned a copy of the Constitution at a public meeting, proclaiming, 'so perish all compromises

with tyranny'. In the 1850s, inspired in part by Garrison's rhetoric, radical abolitionists began taking direct action against slavery. The UNDERGROUND RAILROAD helped slaves escape from southern states. Following passage of the KANSAS–NEBRASKA ACT (1854), armed abolitionists battled pro-slavery forces for control of the Kansas territory. On October 16 1859 John BROWN and a party of 21 men seized the US federal arsenal at HARPER'S FERRY as the prelude to what they hoped would become a general slave uprising in the south.

The radical wing of the abolitionist movement was perhaps more successful in uniting southerners than it was in persuading northerners of the immorality of slavery. Although the Republican Party was more sympathetic to the cause of abolition than any previous political party had been, leading Republican politicians, including Abraham LINCOLN, were more concerned by the threat posed to the northern way of life by SLAVE POWER than they were by the immorality of slavery itself. During the Civil War Lincoln proceeded toward abolition with extreme caution. He justified the EMANCIPATION PROCLAMATION (1863) by reference to military necessity, not to higher morality. He sent the THIRTEENTH AMENDMENT (abolishing slavery) to the states for ratification in February 1865, only when (February 1865) it was obvious that the south had been defeated and that public opinion in the north would accept the abolition of slavery. RADICAL REPUBLICANS in Congress pushed through rather more vigorous measures in the form of two Confiscation Acts. The first, passed on 6 August 1861, allowed Union military commanders to free any slave captured while aiding the Confederate war effort. The second, enacted on 17 July 1862, permitted the Union Army to free all slaves belonging to active supporters of the Confederacy. The fact that an abolition movement existed in antebellum America shows the better side of the US political system. The limitations of that movement reveal the limitations of America's political culture in the period.

abortion. Debate over the morality of abortion has shaped the cultural and political landscape of America since 1973. On January 22 1973 the US Supreme Court ruled by 7–2 in the case of ROE VS. WADE that state laws preventing a woman from choosing to abort a foetus during the first trimester of pregnancy represented an unconstitutional abridgement of a right to privacy implied by the FOURTEENTH AMENDMENT. The Court's decision was consistent with its finding, in the case of Griswold vs. Connecticut (June 7 1965), that the US Constitution implies a right to privacy which is abridged by state laws banning the sale of birth-control devices. The Roe verdict was also consistent with the values espoused by the emerging WOMEN'S MOVEMENT.

But for a sizeable minority of Americans, who continue to view the morality of abortion from a conservative Christian perspective, the Roe verdict represented an alarming and unprecedented imposition of 'permissive' values on an otherwise godly country. Even neutral observers struggled to locate the verdict within American history and culture. At its peak the WOMEN'S SUFFRAGE movement had shown little interest in reproductive-health issues; indeed movement leaders had joined conservatives in criticism of Margaret SANGER's birth-control campaign. In the 1930s, and again during the BABY BOOM of the 1950s, liberals in most states had tacitly accepted the conservative assumption that single mothers should either marry or give their babies up for adoption. Few regarded abortion as a value-neutral 'choice' that women had a right to make. A considerable stigma was attached to abortion, and this was reinforced by state laws that drove women seeking abortion to back-street practitioners. For all these reasons, many Americans found the Roe verdict surprising.

The effects of the Roe verdict were immediate. It invalidated abortion law in 46 states, and led to a sharp rise in the number of abortions performed in the USA: in 1973 615,000 legal abortions were performed, in 1979 1.25 million.

The REPUBLICAN PARTY and conservative Christian groups such as the MORAL MAJORITY soon formed a coalition built around opposition to liberalized abortion law. In 1976 Republican congressmen pushed the HYDE AMENDMENT (withholding MEDICAID funding for abortions) through Congress. The jubilant religious right turned out in force for Ronald REAGAN in 1980 and 1984. As the influence of religious conservatives within the GOP grew, liberal Republicans, notably George BUSH, were driven to the right, and the abortion issue became yet more polarized. President Reagan sought to appoint conservatives likely to overturn Roe to the Supreme Court, although Democrats rallied to block this strategy, and scored a notable success in the BORK CONFIRMATION HEARINGS. Republicans forced bills chipping away at the Roe verdict through state legislatures. The Supreme Court struck down the main features of a Pennsylvania law restricting access to abortion (by making it difficulty for a woman to demonstrate that she had given prior 'informed consent') in its ruling on THORNBURGH VS. AMERICAN COLLEGE OF OBSTETRICIANS (1986). But 'pro-life' activists scored a major victory when the Supreme Court, in its ruling on WEBSTER VS. REPRODUCTIVE HEALTH SERVICES (1989) found that an unborn child possessed rights. In 1990, in its ruling on HODGSON VS. MINNESOTA, the Court upheld the constitutionality of state laws establishing a waiting period prior to abortion and requiring underage girls to obtain parental or judicial consent before undergoing the procedure.

In the early 1990s, anti-abortion activists adapted the tactics of the CIVIL RIGHTS MOVEMENT to mount mass demonstrations outside abortion clinics. Thousands of arrests were made outside a clinic in Witchita, Kansas, in the summer of 1992. The gruesome placards and extreme rhetoric that became features of these demonstrations may have alienated uncommitted observers, but they forced women seeking abortions, or even advice about abortion, to fight their way through highly hostile crowds. Fringe elements of the anti-abortion movement began threatening and attacking doctors and nurses willing to perform abortions.

Although Congress made it a federal offence to threaten a health-care worker and passed legislation preventing demonstrators from blocking the entrance to clinics, fewer and fewer doctors or clinics in the midwest and Bible Belt are now willing to offer abortions. Many American women seeking an abortion must now travel to the northeast, the west coast or abroad to obtain one. The Supreme Court has announced that it may review the Roe verdict in the future.

Abraham Lincoln Battalion, a volunteer force of US socialists, communists and anti-fascists that participated in the Spanish Civil War on the side of the Republic. The battalion formed part of the International Brigades organized by the Comintern. The battalion eventually totaled 3200, and 1600 US members of the Lincoln Battalion and similar units (such as the John Brown Artillery Battery) were killed.

Abrams vs. US (November 10 1919), US Supreme Court ruling on freedom of speech. In 1919 the Supreme Court reviewed a conviction under the Sedition Act (*see* ALIEN AND SEDITION ACTS) made against the author of a pamphlet criticizing US intervention in SIBERIA during the Russian Civil War. The Court declared that FIRST AMENDMENT guarantees of freedom of speech do not extend to criticism of the US government during war. Therefore the Sedition Act's restrictions on freedom of expression were constitutional.

In a dissenting opinion Justice Oliver Wendell HOLMES, who had argued in SCHENCK VS. US that Congress could place limits on freedom of expression, criticized the Sedition Act and pleaded for the value of ideas to be judged in a 'free market'.

Acheson, Dean (Gooderham) (1893–1971), secretary of state (1949–53) in TRUMAN's administration, in which position he played a crucial role in the creation of America's COLD WAR policy of CONTAINMENT. Acheson was one of the chief architects of the MARSHALL PLAN and of the NORTH ATLANTIC TREATY ORGANIZATION. He was often the subject of RED-BAITING attacks for supposedly being 'soft on communism', and he defended Alger HISS at great political cost. Ironically, Richard NIXON, who had been one of Acheson's chief tormentors, turned to him for advice on how to secure 'peace with honor' in the VIETNAM WAR.

ACLU, *see* AMERICAN CIVIL LIBERTIES UNION.

Adair vs. US (January 27 1908), US Supreme Court ruling concerning the rights of workers to join a trade union. In a major defeat for the US labour movement, the Supreme Court ruled 6–2 that a section of the Erdman Act (1898) was unconstitutional. The section concerned had forbidden railroad companies from compelling employees to sign YELLOW-DOG CONTRACTS which would prevent them from joining a trade union. The Court reasoned that the FIFTH AMENDMENT gave companies the broadest possible latitude to protect their property. It also asserted that the federal government's power to regulate interstate commerce did not imply that it could enact laws that might encourage the creation of trade unions. This argument was eventually overturned in NATIONAL LABOR RELATIONS BOARD VS. JONES AND LAUGHLIN STEEL (1937).

Adams, John (1735–1826), FEDERALIST statesman, 1st vice president (1789–97) and 2nd president (1797–1801) of the USA. John Adams was second cousin of Samuel ADAMS, and his son, John Quincy ADAMS, was elected to the presidency in 1824 – a unique family achievement.

John Adams came to prominence as defense counsel for the British troops tried for murder following the BOSTON MASSACRE. Addressing the Boston trial jury he characterized the crowd into which the soldiers fired as a 'motley rabble of saucy boys, Negroes ... Irish teagues and outlandish jack tars'. Service in the Massachusetts legislature (1770–4) and CONTINENTAL CONGRESS (1774–7) followed. Although lacking charm, he served as a US minister to France (1777–9), the Netherlands (1780–2) and Britain (1785–8). His diplomatic career was marked by the negotiation of a substantial loan from the Netherlands and a prominent role in drafting the treaty of PARIS (1783) ending the REVOLUTIONARY WAR. An obvious choice to serve as WASHINGTON's vice president, Adams had a fussy regard for the dignity of the office which led opponents to brand him a closet monarchist.

Decisively elected as Washington's successor, Adams served as president from 1797 to 1801. By resisting calls for war with France during the QUASI-WAR, he alienated fellow federalists enraged by the XYZ AFFAIR. His willingness to sign the ALIEN AND SEDITION ACTS convinced his vice president, Thomas JEFFERSON, to take active leadership of DEMOCRATIC- REPUBLICAN opposition to Adams's administration. Adams pardoned the leaders of FRIES'S REBELLION against his administration's taxation policies. However, on the eve of his departure from office, he stacked the judiciary and federal bureaucracy with FEDERALISTS, thereby creating the MARBURY VS. MADISON case. Adams's death received less than due commemoration because it occurred on the same day (July 4) as Jefferson's.

Adams, John Quincy (1767–1848), NATIONAL REPUBLICAN statesman and 6th president of the USA (1825–9). The son of John ADAMS, he is the only son of a former president to be elected to the presidency.

Adams was elected to the US Senate from Massachusetts in 1803. He soon offended his predominantly FEDERALIST constituents by voting in favor of the LOUISIANA PURCHASE and by supporting Jefferson's position on the EMBARGO ACT. In 1808 he resigned his seat to practice law. President MADISON appointed Adams head of the US team that negotiated the treaty of GHENT (1815), which ended the WAR OF 1812. As secretary of state (1817–25) in MONROE's administration, he brokered the ADAMS–ONIS TREATY (1821) and formulated the MONROE DOCTRINE (1823).

In 1824 Adams stood for the presidency as a conservative Democrat. Although Andrew JACKSON outpolled Adams in the POPULAR VOTE, no candidate achieved a majority in the ELECTORAL COLLEGE. With the support of Henry CLAY, Adams was elected president by the House of Representatives. Jacksonians alleged the pair had made a CORRUPT BARGAIN.

Adams, whose administration lasted from March 4 1825 to March 4 1829, was a high-minded president, and he declined to reward Jacksonian Democrats with patronage appointments. Congress refused to fund Adams's programme of internal improvements, and Georgia defied his opposition to the treaty of INDIAN SPRINGS (1825). Adams, caricatured as an aloof and quasi-aristocratic figure, was the subject of partisan attacks by Jacksonians throughout his presidency. When Adams declined to veto the TARIFF OF ABOMINATIONS (1828), the Democratic party nominated Andrew JACKSON as its candidate in the presidential election of 1828. Jackson defeated Adams by 178 to 83 in the electoral college.

Adams served subsequently as a congressman (1831–48) and remains the only former president to do so. With Henry Clay he led the National Republican faction of the Democratic Party, a precursor of the WHIG PARTY. He opposed the annexation of TEXAS and the GAG RULE. In 1841 Adams defended the *AMISTAD* mutineers before the Supreme Court.

Adams, Sam(uel) (1722–1803), politician who played an important role in the AMERICAN REVOLUTION. Born in Boston, Adams was a second cousin of John ADAMS, the future president of the USA. He attended Harvard before taking over his father's brewery. When it failed he became a tax collector.

Adams achieved prominence as an instigator and coordinator of opposition to the SUGAR ACT, STAMP ACT and TOWNSHEND ACT in Boston. Adams helped found Boston's SONS OF LIBERTY, created Massachusetts's COMMITTEE OF CORRESPONDENCE, organized the city's non-importation association and the BOSTON TEA PARTY – all while serving in the lower house of the Massachusetts assembly (1765–74). He was elected a delegate to the CONTINENTAL CONGRESS in 1774, where he supported immediate independence.

In Adams's political thought the citizen's responsibilities to the state were emphasized with as much vigour as the rights and liberties of the individual. Dubbed the 'last Puritan', Adams supported the conservative Massachusetts state constitution of 1780. He was an uncompromising opponent of SHAYS'S REBELLION. He served as governor of Massachusetts (1794–7).

Adamson (Eight-Hour) Act (September 3 1916), legislation that mandated an eight-hour working day for railroad workers. The act was passed in order to preempt a national strike. The eight-hour day gradually became the norm in other industries.

Adams–Onis treaty, (February 22 1819) agreement made between the USA and Spain concerning their respective territories in North America. John Quincy ADAMS's discussions with Spanish ambassador Luis Onis settled the boundaries of the LOUISIANA PURCHASE, brought EAST and WEST FLORIDA under American jurisdiction, placed most of TEXAS under Mexican control and established the 42nd parallel as the northernmost boundary between the USA and Mexico. The USA agreed to assume responsibility for settling $5 million worth of claims against the Spanish government. The treaty was ratified by the Senate on February 19 1821.

Addams, Jane (1860–1935), a leading reformer of the PROGRESSIVE era. Addams is chiefly remembered for her role in founding and running Hull-House, a settlement house on Halsted Street, Chicago, founded in 1889 in imitation of Toynbee Hall in London's East End. In 1910 Addams published *Twenty Years at Hull-House*, a widely read memoir of her pioneering attempt to establish Hull-House as an uplifting community center in a large, ethnically heterogeneous American city. She was an enthusiastic supporter of Theodore ROOSEVELT's PROGRESSIVE PARTY in the PRESIDENTIAL ELECTION OF 1912. But during WORLD WAR I Addams broke with Roosevelt and in 1915 helped to found the Women's International League for Peace and Freedom and the WOMEN'S PEACE PARTY. Her work on behalf of international peace occupied the remainder of her life, and was recognized in 1931 when she shared the Nobel Peace Prize with Nicholas Murray Butler (1862–1947), who had helped to inspire the KELLOGG-BRIAND PACT. Addams was the first American woman to be awarded a Nobel prize. She donated her share of the prize money to the Women's Peace Party.

Administration of Justice Act (May 20 1774), legislation passed by the British Parliament that permitted cases involving soldiers or crown officials accused of capital crimes in Massachusetts to be transferred to Britain, or to another colony, if the governor believed a fair trial was unobtainable in Massachusetts. The law, one of the INTOLERABLE ACTS, was dubbed the 'Murder Act'. It was particularly offensive to Bostonians, who were proud of their impartial response to the BOSTON MASSACRE.

AEC, *see* ATOMIC ENERGY COMMISSION.

affirmative action, controversial concept that assumes that the economic effects of the systematic and deep-seated discrimination endured by African-Americans and other minority groups can only be overcome by preferential government policies.

The concept divided the CIVIL RIGHTS MOVEMENT, some of whose leaders foresaw that any government attempt to compensate for the past mistreatment of blacks would provoke a white backlash. However, President Lyndon B. JOHNSON believed that the CIVIL RIGHTS ACT OF 1964 (which bans racial discrimination in employment) would become a dead letter unless the government acted to promote African-American entry into areas of employment such as the construction industry or the fire service. On September 24 1965 Johnson established by executive order an Office of Federal Contract Compliance (OFCC) to enforce Title VI of the 1964 act. In conjunction with the Equal Employment Opportunities Commission, the OFCC began compiling statistics to make a prima facie case that the under-representation of African-Americans in certain trades was attributable to active racial discrimination. Employers were quick to recognize that they would have to hire more black workers to remain eligible for federal contract work.

White workers, especially in the construction industry, were encouraged by Republicans, especially President NIXON, to view the developing policy as one that promoted blacks at the expense of whites. As unions, employers and government officials struggled to define fair 'quotas' of African-American employment in US workforces, they created enormous workplace unrest, and fueled charges that affirmative action amounted to reverse discrimination against whites. In REGENTS OF THE UNIVERSITY OF CALIFORNIA VS. BAAKE (1978) the US Supreme Court outlawed the use of inflexible racial quotas by college admissions offices. But in UNITED STEEL WORKERS OF AMERICA VS. WEBER (1979) the Supreme Court upheld the legality of voluntary programs to correct the past under-representation of racial minorities in particular jobs. Affirmative-action policies prompted many white working-class males to abandon the Democrats and vote Republican in the 1970s and 1980s.

AFL, *see* AMERICAN FEDERATION OF LABOR.

African Methodist Episcopal (AME) church, homegrown African-American religious denomination. Formed in 1816 under the leadership of ex-slave and charismatic preacher Richard Allen (1760–1831), the AME was America's first independent African-American church.

During the colonial era, itinerant Methodist preachers converted several thousand free blacks and slaves, often in the face of obstruction from local authorities and white Protestants. African-Americans were attracted by Methodist preaching emphasizing the equality of all men before God and the immorality of slavery. By the close of the eighteenth century, many Methodist congregations in northern towns and cities possessed a sizeable African-American component. Yet black Methodists did not always receive equal treatment from their co-religionists. Attempts by the white elders of St. George's Methodist Church in Philadelphia to confine African-American worshippers to a separate gallery and to deny them access to the altar rail prompted Richard Allen to organize a separate congregation (the Bethel Church) in 1793. The AME united such independent congregations within a single church whose first bishop was Richard Allen.

The AME took a prominent role in the ABOLITION movement and supported the aims of the AMERICAN COLONIZATION SOCIETY. The church also directed aid to black communities in the West Indies and Canada. Overcoming opposition from slave-owners, the AME gained a growing number of converts among enslaved southerners. In 1865 the church had over 50,000 members and more than 2000 congregations. Along with other independent black Methodist and Baptist churches, the AME experienced a surge in membership after the Civil War. During the 20th century the AME adopted a non-political stance, although individual congregations furnished support for Marcus GARVEY's United Negro Improvement Association, the NAACP and the CIVIL RIGHTS MOVEMENT. In 1990 2.2 million Americans identified themselves as members of the AME.

Agent Orange, chemical defoliant sprayed over forested regions of Southeast Asia by US planes during the VIETNAM WAR. Some 100 million pounds (45 million kg) of Agent Orange were used in an attempt to deprive the Viet Cong and North Vietnamese army of cover. The systematic use of the chemical destroyed half of Vietnam's forests, and created long-term health problems for civilians and US servicemen, but made no decisive impact on the fighting.

Agnew, Spiro T(heodore) (1918–1996), Republican statesman and vice president of the USA (1969–73). On October 10 1973 Agnew became only the second man in US history to resign from the vice presidency, leaving office to avoid prosecution for receiving kickbacks and bribes while governor of Maryland and, allegedly, while vice president of the USA.

A native of Baltimore, Agnew began practicing law in the city in 1947. He was elected to serve as executive of Baltimore County (1963–7) and in 1966, running as a Republican, was elected governor of Maryland. Agnew won fleeting national celebrity for adopting tough measures to prevent the residents of Maryland from joining the rioting that swept America following the assassination of Martin Luther KING. Richard NIXON chose Agnew to be his running-mate in the PRESIDENTIAL ELECTION OF 1968. Agnew served as vice president from January 20 1969 until his resignation. He was known chiefly for ferocious attacks on enemies of the administration and especially on journalists, whom he labeled 'nattering nabobs of negativism'.

Agricultural Adjustment Administration, NEW DEAL agency established to combat the effects of the GREAT DEPRESSION on US agriculture. The Agricultural Adjustment Administration was established through the Agricultural Adjustment Act (May 12 1933). It set limits on crop production and established price supports. There had been previous bills attempting similar goals, namely the McNAURY–HAUGEN BILL (1927) and the AGRICULTURAL MARKETING ACT (1929). However, the 1933 act went further than these: it covered a wide range of crops and livestock; it provided financial compensation to farmers who limited production; and it established a central administrative agency (the Agricultural Adjustment Administration). The act helped create the GREAT MIGRATION, as southern landowners took land farmed by SHARECROPPERS out of production in order to claim subsidies. The Supreme Court ruled the act unconstitutional in UNITED STATES VS. BUTLER (1936).

Agricultural Marketing Act (June 15 1929), legislation brought in by the HOOVER administration to tackle collapsing crop prices. The act was intended to encourage farmers to form cooperatives to take land out of cultivation, and established a federal board to purchase surpluses. However, few farmers volunteered to take land out of cultivation. In fact, most increased production in an attempt to maintain income, leaving the US government holding huge surpluses. The failure of this program made the AGRICULTURAL ADJUSTMENT ACT (brought in four years later as part of the NEW DEAL) all the more devastating in its impact.

Alabama, southeastern state on the Gulf of Mexico, bordered by Georgia to the east, Tennessee to the north and Mississippi to the west. Alabama was originally part of the

French colony of Louisiana. American settlement began in 1805 but proceeded slowly until after the CREEK WAR. Alabama became a territory on March 3 1817 and the 22nd state on December 14 1819. Cotton produced by slave labor dominated its ANTE-BELLUM economy and on January 11 1861, Alabama became the fourth state to secede from the Union and join the CONFEDERACY. During RECONSTRUCTION, Alabama was placed under military government, but congressional representation and self-government were restored to the state on June 25 1868. Over the next 40 years the Alabama legislature passed numerous JIM CROW laws denying African-Americans their civil rights. By 1901 most African-Americans had been disenfranchised and public facilities were segregrated. In the 1950s and 1960s The MONTGOMERY BUS BOYCOTT and BIRM-INGHAM DESEGREGATION CAMPAIGN placed the state at the center of the CIVIL RIGHTS MOVEMENT. Police violence and Governor George WALLACE's stand against desegregation gave the state a reputation for bigoted conservatism. In 1990 Alabama had 4,040,587 residents and was the 22nd most populous state in the Union.

Alabama claims, compensation demanded from Britain by the USA for the damage caused by the *Alabama* and ten other Confederate warships built in British shipyards during the CIVIL WAR. These British-built warships had captured or sunk 257 Union ships and destroyed 100,000 tons of cargo. At the end of war the US government put in a claim for $19 million compensation. In 1872, following arbitration by an international panel, the British government agreed to pay $15.5 million.

Alamo, battle of the (March 6 1836), engagement in Texas in which Mexican forces defeated a small band of Americans. As the movement to detach TEXAS from Mexican rule and establish it as an independent republic gathered force, 183 men, predominantly American, occupied a forti-fied mission called the Alamo, near San Antonio. Mexican President Antonio Santa Anna personally oversaw the siege, bombardment and final assault on the insurgents. During the engagement, 175 of the defenders were killed, and 7 more were executed after capture. The one survivor was a black slave named Joe who was owned by the commander of the US insurgents, Colonel William Travis. Mexican losses were at least three times greater. The action inspired Texan reprisal in the battle of SAN JACINTO. Davy CROCKETT's death at the Alamo entered popular legend, serving as an inspiration for the idea of MANIFEST DESTINY.

Alaska, state in the far northwest of the American continent, separated from the rest of the USA by Canada. Russia founded the first permanent European settlement in Alaska on Kodiak Island in September 1784. Further Russian settlement proceeded slowly in the face of severe resistance from the native Tlinglit Indians. On October 18 1867 Russia sold Alaska to the United States for $7,200,000. The deal was the brainchild of Secretary of State William H. SEWARD and the state was popularly known as 'Seward's Folly.' The United States did not appoint a governor to the region until 1884 and Alaska did not become a US territory until August 24 1912. Major gold deposits were discovered at Nome in 1899 and Fairbanks in 1902. Inward migration was also stimulated by miners seeking to take part in Canada's Klondike gold rush. Alaska became the 49th state on January 3 1959. The discovery of vast oil reserves in Prudhoe Bay in 1968 prompted a surge in economic development. In 1990 Alaska's population numbered 550,043, making it the 49th most populous state in the Union.

Albany desegregation campaign, unsuccessful civil rights campaign in the town of Albany, Georgia, in 1961–2. Its failure provided a number of lessons for the CIVIL RIGHTS MOVEMENT. In November 1961 a coalition of civil rights groups, chief among them the STUDENT NON-VIOLENT COORDINATING COMMITTEE (SNCC), began a campaign of boycotts and peaceful mass protest to desegregate transportation services and businesses in Albany. On December 15 Martin Luther KING and Ralph ABERNATHY took part in a downtown rally designed to produce mass arrests that would clog the court system. White civic leaders stymied this protest by releasing protesters without bail, and by promising to create a biracial commission to examine means of desegregating the town. In the absence of police brutality, and given that white civic leaders had announced a willingness to discuss desegregation, the federal government refused to push the demonstrators' demands. Once King and Abernathy had left town, Albany's civic leaders reneged on their deal.

The campaign demonstrated the vulnerability of the Civil Rights Movement to factional disputes among its component organizations. It also showed that the KENNEDY administration would act on behalf of civil rights campaigners only in municipalities that set their face against integration and employed violence against protesters. Luckily for civil rights activists, violent white resistance to the BIRMINGHAM DESEGREGATION CAMPAIGN forced federal action, and thereby maintained the movement's momentum.

Albany Regency, informal name of an organization that used patronage and favors to keep New York state government in Democratic hands between 1820 and 1850. The Regency was marshalled by Martin VAN BUREN, and took its name from the city of Albany, the state capital of New York. Regency support helped ensure Andrew JACKSON's victory in the 1828 presidential election. In later life Van Buren edged towards abolitionist reform. He and his BARNBURNER supporters broke with the Regency in 1848, arguing that it had no agenda beyond retaining power.

Albright, Madeleine (Korbel) (1937–), secretary of state under President CLINTON since 1996, the first woman ever to hold the post. She was born in Czechoslovakia but was educated at Wellesley College and Columbia University. She served on the NATIONAL SECURITY COUNCIL during CARTER's administration, and was the US representative at the UNITED NATIONS when appointed to head the State Department by Clinton.

Alger, Horatio, Jr (1832–99), writer of stories for boys, who had an enormous influence on the cultural landscape of late 19th-century America. His bestselling but formulaic boys' stories – starting with *Ragged Dick* (serialized in 1867) – featured the rags-to-riches progress of their heroes, and were read as demonstrating the inevitable triumph of perseverance, thrift and moral probity over poverty.

Ali, Muhammad (1942–), African-American boxer, whose sporting exploits and snappy comments on civil rights and BLACK POWER have made him one of the world's most famous living Americans. Born Cassius Marcellus Clay, in Louisville, Kentucky, Ali won the gold medal in the light-heavyweight division at the 1960 Olympic Games in Rome. On his return home he was denied service in a Louisville restaurant under JIM CROW laws. In protest he hurled his Olympic medal into the Ohio river. As a young professional, Clay traded one-liners as fast as punches. He was dubbed the 'Louisville Lip', and white Americans watched his fights in the hopes that he would get his comeuppance. In 1964 he beat Sonny Liston (previously regarded as near invincible) to win the world heavyweight championship for the first time. Before the fight, Ali had begun his association with the NATION OF ISLAM. With the help of MALCOLM X, Ali converted to the Islamic faith and found himself thrust into the limelight of the CIVIL RIGHTS and ANTIWAR MOVEMENTS. In 1967 Ali was ordered to report for military service in the VIETNAM

WAR under the terms of the DRAFT. Citing his faith, he refused to be inducted into the armed services and was promptly stripped of his boxing titles. Although threatened with imprisonment, Ali was unrepentant. His case attracted international attention, as did his ad-libbed remark 'I ain't got no quarrel with them Vietcong.' He was allowed to resume his career in 1970, and over the next eight years regained, lost, regained and finally lost his title in a series of extraordinary bouts with 'Smokin' Joe' Frazier, George Foreman and Leon Spinks. Many of these fights were held, on Ali's insistence, in Third World locations. Ali's descriptions of these fights, for example 'the Rumble in the Jungle' or 'the Thrill-a in Manila', made world headlines. So too did his poetic predictions, prefiguring the rap-music style, that he would, for example, 'Float like a butterfly, sting like a bee'. In 1996 Ali, now suffering from Parkinson's disease, made an emotional appearance at the Atlanta Olympic Games.

Alien and Sedition Acts (1798), the collective term for four partisan measures passed by a FEDERALIST-controlled Congress at the height of the QUASI-WAR with France. The Naturalization Act (June 18 1798) increased from 5 to 14 years the period of residence required for eligibility for US citizenship. The Alien Act (June 25 1798) authorized the president to expel from the USA aliens who were deemed subversive. The Alien Enemies Act (July 6 1798) authorized the president, in time of war, to arrest and imprison any subject of an enemy power resident in the USA. The Sedition Act (July 14 1798) forbade any person, including US citizens, from conspiring to oppose the execution of the law or to in any way aid 'any insurrection, riot, unlawful assembly or combination'.

The acts were aimed against DEMOCRATIC-REPUBLICAN journalists. The Sedition Act, in particular, threatened to make Democratic-Republican campaigning in the PRESIDENTIAL ELECTION OF 1800 unlawful. JEFFERSON urged passage of the KENTUCKY and VIRGINIA RESOLUTIONS in protest. All save the Alien Enemies Act lapsed or were repealed by 1802.

Allen, Ethan (1738–89), the founder of the state of VERMONT, and an able American commander in the REVOLUTIONARY WAR. Allen moved to VERMONT in 1772. He organized a militia, the Green Mountain Boys, which protected land grants issued by NEW HAMPSHIRE from seizure by NEW YORK. At the start of the Revolutionary War, Allen's militiamen captured FORT TICONDEROGA (1775). He himself was captured by British troops during an unsuccessful assault on QUEBEC (1775). Exchanged in May 1778, Allen continued to press for independent statehood for Vermont, which was achieved shortly after his death.

Altgeld, John Peter (1847–1902), Democratic politician of the PROGRESSIVE era. Altgeld was born in Germany, raised in Ohio and served in the Union army during the CIVIL WAR. In 1875 he moved to Chicago to open a law office. In 1892 he was elected governor of Illinois, the first foreign-born man to occupy the post. Altgeld's strength in the state's industrialized north also ensured that he was the first Democrat elected to the governorship since the Civil War. During the DEPRESSION OF 1893, Altgeld promoted social reform. He broke with President CLEVELAND over the use of federal troops in the PULLMAN STRIKE and pardoned three anarchists convicted for murder in the HAYMARKET RIOT. He was an influential supporter of William Jennings BRYAN's bid for the White House in the PRESIDENTIAL ELECTION OF 1896 – a position which cost Altgeld his governorship.

American Antislavery Society (AAS), ABOLITION organization founded on December 4 1833 by a group of 61 leading abolitionists, chief among them William Lloyd GARRISON.

The AAS aimed to complement the work of state abolitionist societies and coordinate the presentation of anti-slavery petitions to

Congress (although the petition campaign was thwarted when Congress adopted the GAG RULE in 1836). Garrison's newspaper, *The Liberator*, promoted the society's anti-slavery message. Women, among them such pioneers of the WOMEN'S SUFFRAGE movement as Lucretia MOTT, and African-Americans, notably Frederick DOUGLASS, played a prominent role in the society's campaigns.

Most members of the AAS followed Garrison in calling for the immediate abolition of slavery. However, in 1840 James Birney (1792–1857), one of the founders of the AAS, led some of its members into the newly formed LIBERTY PARTY to campaign for a gradual emancipation by constitutional amendment.

American Board of Customs Act (June 29 1767), legislation passed by the British Parliament that created a customs board with headquarters in Boston. Parliament hoped that the new board would aid the fair and efficient collection of the TOWNSHEND REVENUE ACT (passed on the same day), and prevent smuggling. The act's extension of the VICE-ADMIRALTY COURT system and its erosion of the power of colonial assemblies and courts led Americans to oppose the measure on principle. Clumsy and insensitive customs officials provoked crowd actions such as the *LIBERTY* riot and the burning of the *GASPEE*.

American Civil Liberties Union (ACLU), America's most prominent and effective civil liberties pressure group. It was founded to assist Americans prosecuted for opposing US involvement in WORLD WAR I. Among the ACLU's founders were the social reformer Jane ADDAMS, the lawyer Clarence Darrow (1857–1938) and Norman THOMAS, leader of the SOCIALIST PARTY OF AMERICA. During the RED SCARE that followed passage of the Sedition Act (*see* ALIEN AND SEDITION ACTS) of 1918, the ACLU helped to provide legal defense for thousands of Americans imprisoned for speaking their minds. The ACLU has always taken an expansive view of the right to free speech guaranteed by the First Amendment to the US Constitution. It has been prepared to defend unpopular speech acts, famously arguing for the right of a group of US Nazis to hold a parade in a predominantly Jewish district of Skokie, Illinois. No private organization has represented more clients in cases heard by the US Supreme Court. In the late 1980s George BUSH was widely derided for campaign speeches in which he portrayed the ACLU as a deviant 'liberal' fringe group.

American Colonization Society (ACS), organization established in 1816 that sought to promote the ABOLITION of slavery by resettling free blacks in the west African state of Liberia. The Society's members believed that their resettlement plan would encourage the MANUMISSION of bondsmen by allaying fear amongst whites that former slaves resident in southern states would burden public welfare rolls or exact revenge on their former masters. The Society's first president was Bushrod Washington (1762–1829), a US Supreme Court justice and nephew of George WASHINGTON. Its backers included Henry CLAY, Thomas JEFFERSON and James MONROE. The state legislatures of Virginia, Maryland, Kentucky, North Carolina and Mississippi also endorsed the Society's efforts. By 1831, 1420 free blacks had been resettled in Liberia through the auspices of the ACS.

American Federation of Labor (AFL), large federation of US trade unions. The AFL was formed by 13 CRAFT UNIONS at a meeting in Columbus, Ohio, held on December 8 1886. They elected Samuel GOMPERS president. Member unions could call on support for strikes and boycotts from the AFL, but they remained self-governing bodies. Membership increased during the DEPRESSION OF 1893, as skilled workers struggled to defend their position. During the depression Gompers presided over a decisive break with radicalism and independent political activity, establishing higher wages for skilled workers and the betterment of workplace conditions as the AFL's priorities. In July 1894, Gompers contributed to the defeat of the PULLMAN STRIKE by ordering AFL members on strike in support of railroad workers to return to work. In addition, the AFL voted only a miserly $1100 to the fund established to help rail-union leader Eugene DEBS appeal his conviction for conspiring to obstruct the US mail during the strike. In December 1894 Gompers defeated attempts by socialists to commit the AFL to campaign on behalf of the PEOPLE'S PARTY and the social ownership of the means of production, but he lost the presidency of the AFL for one year as a result. By 1904 the thoroughly respectable AFL had over 1,676,000 members, and Gompers was touting it as 'labor's business organization' – the equivalent of the National Association of Manufactures.

A setback came in 1908 when the Supreme Court's decision in LOEWE VS. LAWLER threatened the ability of trade unions to act in support of pay claims or work-related grievances: in reaching its decision the Court argued that secondary boycotts constituted conspiracies to restrain trade in contravention of the SHERMAN ANTI-TRUST ACT. Nevertheless Gompers rejected appeals for the AFL to throw its weight behind Debs's SOCIALIST PARTY. Instead he secured a commitment from the Democrats to exempt unions from anti-trust legislation. WILSON rewarded AFL support for him during the 1912 election with the CLAYTON ANTI-TRUST ACT (1914). Gompers hailed this as 'labor's Magna Carta'. Unlike the SOCIALIST PARTY and the INDUSTRIAL WORKERS OF THE WORLD (IWW or Wobblies), the AFL supported US entry into WORLD WAR I.

By 1920 the AFL had 3,250,000 members, and its past record of respectability afforded it protection during the RED SCARE. During the NEW DEAL, advocates of INDUSTRIAL UNIONISM – organized in the Committee for Industrial Organization (CIO), forerunner of the CONGRESS OF INDUSTRIAL ORGANIZA-

TIONS – demanded that the AFL take a more active role in unionizing mass-production workers. Tensions between AFL stalwarts and CIO activists boiled over at the 1935 AFL convention in Atlantic City, New Jersey. Ten CIO unions were suspended from the AFL and, in 1936, expelled. The rift endured until 1955, when the two groups merged to form the AFL-CIO. During the COLD WAR the AFL and CIO strove to limit the influence of communists and socialists within their ranks and to disown the corruption associated with Teamsters' boss Jimmy HOFFA. However, in the post-war USA, trade union membership declined. In 1945 33% of US workers belonged to a trade union, the vast majority of them to affiliates of the AFL. By 1990 less than 20% of US workers belonged to a trade union. Declining membership has been attributed to the conservatism displayed by the AFL-CIO during the Cold War and CIVIL RIGHTS era, and also to aggressive anti-union drives organized by employers with the encouragement of the Republican party.

American Indian Movement (AIM), group founded in 1968 that soon established a reputation for militant campaigns on behalf of the civil rights and social welfare of the Native American population. In 1972 AIM organized the 'Trail of Broken Treaties' caravan, a series of traveling exhibitions and demonstrations publicizing grievances and demanding a renegotiation of treaties through which Native Americans had ceded land to the US government. The demonstrators reached Washington DC on November 1 1972 and occupied the headquarters of the Bureau of Indian Affairs. During the week-long occupation, demonstrators stole or destroyed much of the Bureau's paperwork. The negative publicity generated by the protesters' lawlessness gave the federal government a mandate to mount a massive operation to suppress AIM's subsequent WOUNDED KNEE PROTEST (the armed seizure of a federal Oglala SIOUX reservation in South Dakota). AIM's leaders were indicted on a variety of conspiracy and public-order charges and the movement collapsed. The USA has not renegotiated treaties with native peoples, but AIM met its general objective of raising public awareness of issues relevant to Native Americans.

American Party, *see* KNOW NOTHING PARTY.

American Railway Union (ARU), trade union for railroad workers formed in 1893 by Eugene DEBS. The ARU pioneered INDUSTRIAL UNIONISM. Any white railroad worker was eligible to join the union, regardless of his skill level or job description. By 1894 membership stood at 150,000. On June 26 1894, the ARU entered the PULLMAN STRIKE by ordering its members to boycott trains containing Pullman coaches. This brought the nation's rail system to a standstill. But the strike, and with it the union, was smashed when employers obtained injunctions outlawing boycotts under the SHERMAN ANTI-TRUST ACT, and persuaded the CLEVELAND administration to deploy federal troops to enforce these injunctions.

American Revolution, term applied to the sequence of events that led up to the DECLARATION OF INDEPENDENCE (1776), the actual achievement of independence through American victory (1783) in the REVOLUTIONARY WAR (known in Britain as the American War of Independence) and the social and political change in America during the years preceding the ratification of the federal Constitution (1788). The American Revolution has been described by the historian J. Franklin Jameson as a movement for home rule that turned into a debate over who should rule at home.

The crisis that produced America's Declaration of Independence from Great Britain originated in Britain's response to the SEVEN YEARS' WAR (known in America as the French and Indian Wars) and PONTIAC'S WAR. In the wake of these conflicts, crown officials and parliamentarians considered ways of reducing the cost and increasing the benefit to

Britain of an American empire which, since the treaty of PARIS (1763), not only included the THIRTEEN COLONIES, but also Canada and virtually all land east of the Mississippi. The British introduced a number of measures that assumed that the colonies did not contribute sufficiently to either the British treasury or its military garrison. These measures included the PROCLAMATION OF 1763, prohibiting settlement west of the Appalachians; the CURRENCY ACT (1764), forbidding colonies to issue legal-tender paper money; the SUGAR ACT (1764), lowering duties but tightening collection mechanisms; and the QUARTERING ACT (1765), requiring five colonies to provide material support for British troops. This legislation also affronted the authority of elected assemblies in each of the colonies.

The STAMP ACT, passed on March 22 1765 and due to take effect from November 1, brought differences between Britain and America to boiling point. Designed to raise £100,000, the act required colonists to buy specially watermarked or stamped paper upon which to print newspapers, property titles, legal documents, pamphlets, playing cards and even college degrees. To collect duties, Britain set about creating within America a new, intrusive and intrinsically corrupt bureaucracy. America's assemblymen opposed the measure on the grounds that they alone had the right to initiate the taxation of their constituents. America's small farmers and artisans opposed the measure because it added to the cost of living and because its collection mechanism (crown appointees to be paid a percentage of tax collected and VICE-ADMIRALTY COURTS to hear cases of evasion) threatened cherished liberties. A 'Declaration of Rights and Grievances' produced by the STAMP ACT CONGRESS meeting in New York in October 1765 argued that America already contributed 'very largely' to the British treasury, that Americans could not be taxed without their consent, and that since Americans were not represented in the British Parliament the power to raise direct taxes on the colonies rested with colonial legislatures. Meanwhile artisans, tradesmen and lesser merchants in the seaport cities, associated as the SONS OF LIBERTY, organized street demonstrations and a NON-IMPORTATION AGREEMENT to prevent implementation of the act.

The Stamp Act never was implemented. Parliament repealed it on March 18 1766 but, on the same day, passed the DECLARATORY ACT reasserting its right to tax the colonies. Parliament revisited the appropriation and collection of revenue in the TOWNSHEND REVENUE ACT (1767) and the AMERICAN BOARD OF CUSTOMS ACT (1767). The Townshend Act required Americans to pay a duty on the import into the colonies of certain 'enumerated' commodities. Its supporters argued that the act did not contravene the exclusive right of colonial legislatures to tax their constituents since it was designed to regulate trade, not to raise revenue. A number of American pamphleteers attacked this argument. LETTERS FROM A FARMER IN PENNSYLVANIA, published in 1767 and written by John DICKINSON, made an especially well-reasoned case against the new duties.

Meanwhile, a politicized citizenry – drawing on ideas about the workings of government in general and the British constitution in particular, ideas described collectively as REPUBLICAN IDEOLOGY – expressed their opposition to British legislation in terms that posited the duty of the man of VIRTUE to venerate and defend liberty. This ideology informed both crowd actions, such as the LIBERTY RIOT, and organized campaigns, such as the NON-IMPORTATION AGREEMENT, which forced repeal of all Townshend duties, save that on tea, on April 12 1770. The prominence of 'liberty' and the notional 'rights of freeborn Englishmen' in popular rhetoric helped push colonial assemblies to adopt radical positions they might otherwise have avoided (the contro-versial MASSACHUSETTS CIRCULAR LETTER being a case in point). The REGULATOR movements of North and South Carolina applied the language of principled opposition to unjust legislation in a local, American, context. Nevertheless – despite the BOSTON MASSACRE (1770), the formation of inter-colonial COMMITTEES OF CORRESPONDENCE to discuss remaining American grievances, and the burning of the GASPEE (1772) – the imperial crisis eased following repeal of the Townshend duties.

The passage of the TEA ACT (1773) suggested to many Americans that Parliament had ignored, mistaken or dismissed the character of their opposition to earlier measures. The passage of the INTOLERABLE ACTS (1774), a heavy-handed response to the BOSTON TEA PARTY (1773), confirmed this belief. Republican ideology told Americans that their liberties were both rare and vulnerable. Hence, although the Intolerable Acts were directed primarily at Massachusetts, patriots throughout the colonies enforced a boycott on trade with Britain designed to force repeal of the acts. This was because the measures directed against Massachusetts represented to patriots the threat of 'tyranny', whose thrust it was the duty of every virtuous man to resist.

In September 1774 all colonies save Georgia sent representatives to a CONTINENTAL CONGRESS held in Philadelphia to coordinate measures designed to force Britain to repeal the Intolerable Acts. Congress approved the SUFFOLK RESOLVES, which called for an interim self-government. It adopted the CONTINENTAL ASSOCIATION, transferring some de facto governmental powers to extra-legal committees. It also rejected a plan of union between Great Britain and the American Colonies proposed by Joseph Galloway (1729–1803). Congress's last concerted attempt at reconciliation (the OLIVE-BRANCH PETITION of 1775) was rendered irrelevant by news of the outbreak of armed conflict at LEXINGTON

AND CONCORD and BUNKER HILL – the beginning of the Revolutionary War.

Yet a second CONTINENTAL CONGRESS, including delegates from Georgia, waited almost a year before adopting the DECLARATION OF INDEPENDENCE. Fear of military defeat and the hope of last-minute reconciliation played a part in creating this delay. But there was also the question – which a bravura defence of the republican form of government in Tom PAINE's best-selling pamphlet *COMMON SENSE* raised but did not settle – of what governmental forms would suit an independent nation. This latter question suggested itself with growing force because within each colony the question 'who should rule at home?' became irresistible, as local governments established under British rule were superseded. No colony was bound to create a government that recognized any or all of the 'certain inalienable rights' alluded to in the Declaration of Independence. Southern colonies kept slavery, whereas in 1780 Pennsylvania became the first of several northern states to enact ABOLITION, through GRADUAL EMANCIPATION laws. Rhode Island, Georgia and especially Pennsylvania created state governments reflecting a more expansive view of human rights than that inherent in the LOCKEAN language utilized in the Declaration of Independence.

Throughout the Revolutionary War each of the thirteen colonies was engaged in an internal revolution. In each, pressure from the 'common man' eroded legal, economic and cultural impediments to the wider ownership of land. Each colony engaged in fierce debate over how to include in government a greater number of representatives from back-country regions, how to balance the interests of debtors against those of creditors and how to treat LOYALISTS and lukewarm patriots. Republican ideology provided the framework and symbolism of these debates, but no standard solution.

While individual states wrestled with their own political futures, each sought to avoid delegating powers to an overarching central authority. As a result, between 1776 and 1788 the United States of America had a weak central government. Neither the second Continental Congress (which served as America's national government until ratification of the ARTICLES OF CONFEDERATION in 1781) nor its successor, the CONFEDERATION CONGRESS, possessed the power of taxation. Funding for national expenditure was provided, often tardily, by the individual states. The national currency became grossly inflated, angering the army and alarming foreign creditors. The states squabbled with one another over western land claims and economic policy. Confederation Congress proved able to exploit the windfall gains of the treaty of PARIS (1783), which ended the Revolutionary War, by establishing an orderly system for the disposal of western lands through the ORDINANCE OF 1785 and the NORTHWEST ORDINANCE of 1787. But it was less successful in resolving economic issues. Meetings such as the MOUNT VERNON CONFERENCE in 1785 between representatives from Maryland and Virginia went some way to harmonizing economic policies, but they did so outside the framework of Confederation government.

During the 1780s a growing number of political leaders became convinced of the necessity to create a stronger national government, and of weakening the sovereignty of the individual states. Yet those who sought to revise the Articles of Confederation faced the daunting prospect of securing the consent of all thirteen states. Alexander HAMILTON used the ANNAPOLIS CONVENTION (1786) to launch an attack on the defects of the Articles, which he implied should be superseded, not amended. A majority of delegates to the Annapolis Convention contented themselves with issuing a call for a subsequent meeting to be held in Philadelphia in May 1787 to consider revising the Articles. With the blessing of

Confederation Congress, the CONSTITU-TIONAL CONVENTION began its deliberations on May 25 1787.

The Constitutional Convention met in closed session and did not publish its proceedings. Personal notes on its debates compiled by James MADISON show that one of the first steps taken by delegates was to abandon the attempt to revise the Articles of Confederation and to write instead an entirely new framework of government. SHAYS'S REBELLION, a major agrarian insurrection in the winter of 1786–7, lent urgency to the delegates' deliberations, and strengthened the hand of ardent nationalists such as Hamilton. Madison's notes also reveal substantial disagreements among the delegates. Some rallied behind the Virginia Plan, which would have stripped states of their authority and left them resembling British county councils. Representatives from smaller states rallied behind the New Jersey Plan in a bid to retain state sovereignty. The institution of slavery was seldom discussed, but the question of whether a state's slave population should be factored into the apportionment of representation within the proposed legislature was heavily debated. The CONNECTICUT COMPROMISE resolved representation in the House and Senate by endorsing the THREE-FIFTHS COMPROMISE on the apportionment of representation to states where slavery remained legal. With the issue of representation for slave states settled, the convention moved speedily to finalize a constitution in which power and sovereignty were balanced between the three branches of government (executive, legislature and judiciary, *see* SEPARATION OF POWERS), the states and the people. The idea that checks and balances on power should be built into governmental arrangements was long established. The application of this idea to a republic as large as the USA was novel, even daring. Delegates rejected the idea of attaching a BILL OF RIGHTS to the constitution, but agreed to submit the finished document to the states for RATIFICATION.

During the ratification process some opponents of the new constitution, dubbed ANTIFEDERALISTS by the Constitution's supporters, questioned the legitimacy of the new constitution and demanded a second convention. Many antifederalists feared that the new government would be too powerful, too remote and likely to be dominated by the wealthy. Over the winter of 1787–8 James Madison, Alexander Hamilton and John JAY sought to refute these fears in the *FEDERALIST PAPERS*. They were only partially successful, but by agreeing to the main antifederalist demand, that a Bill of Rights be appended to the Constitution, FEDERALIST supporters of the Constitution were able to secure its ratification.

The adoption of the US Constitution in 1788 marked the end of the American Revolution. The 1790s saw intense factional rivalry develop between DEMOCRATIC-REPUBLICANS and Federalists. Each group claimed to be guarding, or even advancing, the goals of the American Revolution, but their dispute revolved around conflicting interpretations of the Constitution rather than around radically new political agendas. Although the American Revolution proved an inspiration to political reformers outside the USA, it is unlike other revolutions in at least one respect: it did not produce a period of counter-revolutionary reaction, or a subsequent dictatorship. This outcome reflects the extent to which sentiments such as 'all men are created equal' or 'we, the people' appealed to the unprecedentedly egalitarian and democratic political culture of America's colonial past. The American Revolution sought to preserve and clarify liberties that Americans had once enjoyed at least as much as it sought to invent or broaden future freedoms. For this reason, in most periods of American history the US Constitution and Bill of Rights have been regarded as the American Revolution's greatest legacy. This tendency to see the most important achievement of the Revolution as being its peaceful constitutional settlement was a contributory cause of the CIVIL WAR. It has also meant that ideologies seen as being outside the constitutional tradition, such as communism and fascism, have made only a limited impact on American political culture.

Americans for Democratic Action, organization that lobbies for government action to combat poverty and promote social democracy. It was founded in 1947 by a group of prominent liberals including Hubert HUMPHREY and Eleanor ROOSEVELT. The group was influential within the DEMOCRATIC PARTY during the 1950s, and campaigned enthusiastically on behalf of Adlai STEVENSON. However, it had little influence in the country at large. The prosperity brought to the newly emerging suburbs by the COLD WAR defense build-up made a continuation of NEW DEAL or FAIR DEAL social-welfare programmes pointless in the eyes of many voters.

American System, a national economic programme which was devised by the WHIG statesman Henry CLAY during the Andrew JACKSON administration. Clay's idea was that each region of the USA should serve as an internal market for the others. In pursuit of this goal he sought to introduce a sound currency (through a national bank), to establish a road and canal network to encourage internal trade and to protect American manufacturers via TARIFFS on imported manufactured goods.

American War of Independence, *see* REVOLUTIONARY WAR; AMERICAN REVOLUTION.

American Woman Suffrage Association (AWSA), organization formed in 1869 to campaign for WOMEN'S SUFFRAGE. Middle-class Protestant women, most of them resident in New England, formed the backbone of ABOLITION campaigns and the vanguard of the women's suffrage movement. Lucy STONE and Julia Ward HOWE

(author of the 'Battle Hymn of the Republic') were among a group of men and women who formed the AWSA in Cleveland in 1869. Outraged that Congress had not included a guarantee of women's right to vote in the FIFTEENTH AMENDMENT, Susan Brownell ANTHONY and Elizabeth Cady STANTON formed the rival NATIONAL WOMAN SUFFRAGE ASSOCIATION (NWSA) in the same year.

In contrast to the NWSA, the AWSA welcomed the Fifteenth Amendment as a step in the right direction. It concentrated on persuading individual states to grant women the vote rather than confronting Congress with demands for a constitutional amendment to extend the franchise to women. The AWSA persuaded several western states to ballot voters on the question of women's suffrage. But in no case did an AWSA-sponsored referendum directly produce a change in state law. The AWSA regarded obtaining the vote as an end in itself, and made little attempt to build links with other social-reform groups. It merged with the NWSA in 1890 to create the NATIONAL AMERICAN WOMAN SUFFRAGE ASSOCIATION.

Amistad **mutiny,** incident in which 53 Africans, led by Joseph Cinque, took over the Spanish slave ship *Amistad* in which they were sailing in Cuban waters on July 1 1839 and set course for the USA. This incident produced one of the most celebrated legal cases in US history. The *Amistad* was seized by the USS *Washington* off Montauk, Long Island, and escorted into New London, Connecticut. The Spanish authorities demanded the return of the ship and insisted that the Africans on it were slaves. ABOLITIONISTS argued that the *Amistad* captives had not been legally enslaved and should not be returned to Cuba. Former president John Quincy ADAMS represented the mutineers before the US Supreme Court, which decided on March 9 1841 that the captives were free men entitled to return to their homelands.

Andersonville, location in Georgia of a notorious Confederate prisoner-of-war camp. During the CIVIL WAR inadequate and unhealthy prisoner-of-war camps were operated by both sides. However, the appallingly high death rates suffered by Union prisoners held at Andersonville became notorious, and prompted America's first war-crimes trial. Opened in February 1864, at its peak capacity Andersonville held 32,000 Union soldiers on a 26-acre (10.5-ha) site. The prisoners suffered from malnutrition, inadequate medical care and diseases caused by contaminated drinking water. At least 12,000 prisoners died during the 14 months that the Andersonville camp was operational (3000 prisoners died in August 1864 alone). The camp's commander, Henry Wirz, was hanged on November 10 1865 after a court-martial concluded that he failed to take adequate steps to safeguard the prisoners' health. Wirz was the only Confederate officer hanged for his part in the war.

Annapolis Convention, meeting held in 1786 by representatives from five states to discuss trade and commercial concerns. Nine states accepted an invitation issued by Virginia to the meeting, but only five delegations (from New York, New Jersey, Pennsylvania, Delaware and Virginia) arrived in Annapolis, Maryland, in time to participate in the discussions, held September 11–14, They approved a proposal, made by Alexander HAMILTON, to call a further convention dedicated to the task of revising the ARTICLES OF CONFEDERATION. The CONFEDERATION CONGRESS endorsed the suggestion on February 21 1787, legitimizing the CONSTITUTIONAL CONVENTION.

antebellum, Latin phrase meaning 'before the war', used adjectivally by historians to describe the period between ratification of the US Constitution and the outbreak of the CIVIL WAR.

Anthony, Susan B(rownell) (1820–1906), campaigner for WOMEN'S SUFFRAGE, and social reformer. Anthony was raised as a Quaker and trained as a schoolteacher. In 1849 she gave up a position at Canajoharie Academy, New York, to devote her energies to social reform. She founded the Women's State Temperance Society of New York, and campaigned for the abolition of slavery. During the CIVIL WAR she advocated extending suffrage to FREEDMEN. Anthony campaigned unsuccessfully to persuade RADICAL REPUBLICAN leaders to include women's right to vote in the FOURTEENTH or FIFTEENTH AMENDMENT. Angered by what she regarded as the scant recompense women activists had received for their labors on behalf of abolition, in 1869 Anthony founded the NATIONAL WOMAN SUFFRAGE ASSOCIATION (NWSA). This body accepted only women as members. It saw voting not as an end in itself but as part of a larger set of issues. Working closely with Elizabeth Cady STANTON, Anthony forged links with other social-reform groups, while campaigning tirelessly for a constitutional amendment securing the right to vote. After the rival AMERICAN WOMAN SUFFRAGE ASSOCIATION merged with the NWSA in 1890 to form the NATIONAL AMERICAN WOMAN SUFFRAGE ASSOCIATION, Anthony served as its president from 1892 to 1900.

Antiballistic Missile Treaty, *see* DÉTENTE.

Antietam, battle of (September 17 1862), engagement in Maryland during the CIVIL WAR in which Union forces claimed victory. Emboldened by their success at the second battle of MANASSAS and the capture of the federal arsenal at Harper's Ferry (September 15 1862), 40,000 Confederate troops under General Robert E LEE pushed north into Maryland. On September 17 1862 a Union force of 70,000 under General George McCLELLAN stopped this advance at Antietam creek near the town of Sharpsburg. 4900 soldiers were killed at Antietam, more than twice the number killed in the War of 1812, Mexican War and Spanish-American War combined. Lee retreated, allowing the

Union to claim victory. President LINCOLN, who fired McClellan for not exploiting the Union victory, interpreted the bloodshed as a divine judgment, and on September 22 issued a preliminary EMANCIPATION PROCLAMATION. News of Antietam persuaded Britain and France to delay recognizing the Confederacy.

antifederalists, proponents of antifederalism, a political philosophy that emerged during the RATIFICATION of the US Constitution (1787–90). Antifederalists rejected the Constitution in its then current form, and called for substantial revision and amendment. Some argued that this should be carried out by a second constitutional convention. Antifederalists feared the proposed national government was too powerful and too remote. They believed that sovereignty should reside with state governments, since these predated national government and were more likely to protect the rights and liberties of the people. Above all else, antifederalists demanded that a BILL OF RIGHTS guaranteeing fundamental rights be appended to the Constitution.

MADISON, HAMILTON and JAY offered detailed rebuttals of antifederalist arguments in the *FEDERALIST PAPERS*. Nevertheless, five state ratifying conventions (including those in Massachusetts, New York and Virginia) approved the US Constitution only on the understanding that it be amended to include a bill of rights. When the first federal Congress agreed to this demand, antifederalism was robbed of its main unifying theme. State officeholders tended to be antifederalist, as did small farmers and others who traded in local rather than regional markets. During the 1790s the DEMOCRATIC-REPUBLICANS drew the bulk of their support from former antifederalists.

Anti-Masonic Party, political party formed in New York in 1830 to combat the supposed influence of Freemasons within government. A witch-hunt against Freemasons had been triggered in New York State by the disappearance in 1826 of a bricklayer named William Morgan, who was widely believed to have been murdered by members of the order for betraying their secrets. In the presidential election of 1832 the party's election nominee William Wirt (1772–1834) gained 8% of the POPULAR VOTE, and by carrying the state of Vermont gained 8 votes in the ELECTORAL COLLEGE. The party dissolved thereafter, with most of its supporters joining the WHIG PARTY. The Anti-Masons were the first American political party to choose their presidential candidate at a national nominating convention, and the first to issue an election manifesto.

Anti-Saloon League of America, organization that lobbied for the passage of state laws enacting PROHIBITION. The League was the brainchild of Congregational minister Howard Hyde Russell (1855–1946), and was organized on a national basis in 1895. It drew its support primarily from devout Protestants and former members of the WOMEN'S CHRISTIAN TEMPERANCE UNION. The League's uncompromising hostility to the sale of alcohol helped secure passage of the EIGHTEENTH AMENDMENT, which brought in Prohibition across the USA, and the defeat of 'wet' politicians, notably 'Al' SMITH.

Antiwar Movement, mass movement of protest against the VIETNAM WAR. The Antiwar Movement lay at the heart of the social upheaval that shook America from the mid-1960s to the early 1970s. The scale of domestic opposition to the war ultimately made its continuation impossible. Antiwar protest also convinced Lyndon B. JOHNSON not to seek re-election, and persuaded the NIXON administration to mount a disastrous and illegal counteroffensive against its internal 'enemies'.

Although church groups, leaders of the CIVIL RIGHTS MOVEMENT (notably the Reverend Martin Luther KING) and prominent

African-Americans (notably Muhammad ALI) expressed opposition to the war, the main source of support for the Antiwar Movement came from white middle-class college students. The first 'teach-in' against the war was held on the campus of the University of Michigan in March 1965 soon after Johnson announced the bombing of North Vietnam (OPERATION ROLLING THUNDER). The organizers of 'teach-ins' sought to educate students in the history of Vietnam and of US involvement in Southeast Asia, as well as to counter the influence of 20 years of COLD WAR anticommunism. The teach-in campaign spread across America's college campuses and gave rise to one of the Antiwar Movement's least attractive features, a propensity for self-righteous moralizing.

At the same time the Catholic priests Philip and Daniel Berrigan began organizing what became a national network of local committees that took direct action against DRAFT boards. This network also assisted young men who refused to obey the draft. Few antiwar protesters followed the example set by Muhammad Ali, who accepted the loss of his boxing titles rather than serve in Vietnam. Many more young men – principally middle-class whites – feigned insanity or disability, enrolled in full-time education, fled to Canada or, like future Vice President Dan QUAYLE, pulled strings to get out of active service. Ronald REAGAN was the first of a number of right-wing politicians to attempt to exploit the class tensions produced by the Antiwar Movement when, as governor of California, he dismissed protesting students as motivated by nothing more than a fondness for 'sex, drugs and treason'.

The numbers attending antiwar rallies gradually rose. On April 15 1967 an umbrella group, the Spring Mobilization Committee, organized demonstrations in New York that drew 200,000 and in San Francisco that drew 50,000. On October 21–22 1967, 50,000 protesters marched from the Lincoln Memorial to the Pentagon, where they attempted to 'levitate' the headquarters of the US military. Nevertheless, until the TET OFFENSIVE of 1968, 'hawks' (who argued that President Johnson's war strategy was insufficiently aggressive) tended to outnumber 'doves' (advocates of peace) in Congress. In a major congressional debate on the war held in 1967, for example, Representative Gerald FORD urged Johnson to unleash the full might of the US military against the North Vietnamese. On November 30 1967 Democratic Senator Eugene McCARTHY announced that he would run against Johnson for the Democratic nomination in the PRESIDENTIAL ELECTION OF 1968. On March 12 1968 McCarthy polled 42% of the vote in the New Hampshire primary. This strong showing convinced Senator Robert KENNEDY to enter the race (March 16) and led President Johnson to announce that he would not seek re-election (March 31). Opposition to the war in Vietnam now became a major political issue, and the passions aroused by it burst out in the CHICAGO CONVENTION RIOTS of August 26–29.

During the 1968 presidential campaign Republican candidate Richard NIXON announced that he had a secret plan to end the war and secure 'peace with honor'. Although Nixon began withdrawing US troops from Vietnam, the PARIS PEACE TALKS stalled. In November 1969 some 700,000 'peaceniks' gathered in Washington to call for an immediate withdrawal. (Nixon made headlines by wandering among the demonstrators in the early hours of the morning.) A further wave of protest erupted following Nixon's announcement (April 30 1970) that the USA had conducted a 'limited' invasion of CAMBODIA. A protest rally at KENT STATE (May 4 1970) led to the deaths of four student demonstrators. On May 14 1970, two students at Jackson State University in Mississippi were shot dead while protesting against the Kent State shootings.

Lyndon B. Johnson had been angered and embittered by antiwar slogans such as 'Hey, hey, LBJ, how many kids did you kill today?' Richard Nixon was determined to take action to prevent this kind of abuse from his 'enemies'. Following publication of the PENTAGON PAPERS in 1971 Nixon authorized a smear campaign against Daniel Ellsberg, the man suspected of leaking the document. The FEDERAL BUREAU OF INVESTIGATION (FBI) and the CENTRAL INTELLIGENCE AGENCY (CIA) conducted intelligence operations against peace protesters; the CIA's OPERATION CHAOS was mounted in violation of its charter. Nixon also made a strong play to enlist the support of the 'silent majority' of Americans who loathed antiwar protesters almost as much as the continuing US presence in Vietnam.

The Antiwar Movement succeeded in making continued US military involvement in Vietnam politically unacceptable. However, in the process it shattered the Democratic Party and opened a class division in America that has never quite healed. The Antiwar Movement was carried forward by predominantly middle-class college students and radicalized African-Americans. Younger working-class males, as well as veterans of WORLD WAR II and the KOREAN WAR, found it difficult to accept that Draft Evasion was motivated by principle and were alienated by 'unpatriotic' acts of protest such as burning the American flag. Conscripts who served in Vietnam bitterly resented the treatment they received on their return to America from sections of the Antiwar Movement. These tensions help explain the emergence of REAGAN DEMOCRATS in the 1980 election and the breakup of the NEW DEAL COALITION.

Anzus treaty (August 4 1951), agreement concluded during the early years of the COLD WAR, pledging Australia, New Zealand and the USA (hence 'ANZUS') to guarantee each other's security. During the VIETNAM WAR the USA invoked the treaty to demand military assistance from Australia and New Zealand in its fight against the North Vietnamese and Viet Cong. In 1985 New Zealand barred US ships and submarines carrying nuclear weapons from entering its ports. This action led the USA and New Zealand to abrogate their portion of the mutual defense treaty in 1986.

Apache, name applied to a number of Native American peoples in the southwest USA. Mexican and US authorities designated at least six different peoples living in Arizona and New Mexico as 'Apache' (the name derived from the ZUNI word for enemy). These peoples include the Jicarillos, Mescaleros, Chiricahuas, Western Apache, Lipan and Kiowa-Apache. They all speak an Athabascan language, and it is thought that they originally came from Canada, around 1000 years ago.

Until 1846 Mexican authorities pursued the subjugation of the Apache peoples by enslaving their women and children and paying bounties for warriors' scalps. For this reason the Apache initially welcomed US victory in the MEXICAN WAR (1846–8). But in 1850 the USA created the territory of New Mexico (stretching west to the current Arizona–California boundary and north into Colorado). As the Apache began attacking mining settlements and wagon trains bound for California, tensions in the territory mounted. Its third governor recalled, 'I well knew that when the Indians and the whites once commenced fighting, the Indians would never make peace until whipped, and, therefore necessity compelled me to whip them.'

From 1862 to 1886, under COCHISE and later GERONIMO, bands of Apache resisted confinement on reservations, and mounted raids in New Mexico, Arizona and northern Mexico. Large numbers of US and Mexican troops were deployed to retaliate for these raids, which were only effectively suppressed when US military commanders began hiring Apache scouts to track 'hostiles'.

Following Geronimo's final defeat in 1886, the Chiricahua were held as prisoners of war until 1913, in Florida, Alabama and Oklahoma. The other Apaches were confined to reservations in New Mexico and Arizona. There are now about 11,000 Apache on these reservations.

Apollo program, the US space program to land a man on the Moon. The genesis of the $35 billion investment by the NATIONAL AERONAUTICS AND SPACE ADMINISTRATION (NASA) in manned lunar exploration came in a speech given by John F. KENNEDY on May 25 1961. Stung by the success of the Soviet space program, Kennedy announced that within the decade the USA would land men on the Moon and return them safely. At the time he made the speech no American had even orbited the Earth.

In 1961, 50,000 Americans worked for NASA. By 1966, 420,000 people were employed on the Apollo program. At its peak in 1969 the program absorbed 1% of the gross national product of the USA. While a team led by Wernher Von Braun developed the giant Saturn V rocket that would power the three-man Apollo spacecraft out of Earth's orbit and toward the Moon, NASA launched a series of unmanned lunar probes and perfected manned space-flight techniques through the Mercury and Gemini programs. The first simulated launch of an Apollo spacecraft ended in disaster on January 27 1967 when a wiring fault caused a launch-pad fire that killed astronauts Virgil 'Gus' Grissom, Edward White and Roger Chafee. Between January 21 and 27 1968 *Apollo 8*, commanded by Jim Lovell, successfully left Earth's orbit, circled the Moon and returned home safely. In 1969 *Apollo 9* and *Apollo 10* refined the navigational and lunar-orbit techniques necessary for a manned landing.

Apollo 11, carrying Neil Armstrong, Ed 'Buzz' Aldrin and Michael Collins, left Cape Canaveral on July 16 1970. On July 20 Armstrong and Aldrin became the first men to walk on the surface of the Moon, while Collins orbited above them in the command module. Stepping onto the lunar surface Armstrong said, 'That's one small step for [a] man, one giant leap for mankind.' The astronauts left behind an American flag, messages of peace and a diagram that might help alien life forms understand the human form and humanity's position in the universe. Five more manned landings were completed. The mission of *Apollo 13*, which was to have included a lunar landing, had to be curtailed in dramatic circumstances when a vital fuel cell exploded. The last Apollo astronauts to land on the Moon returned to Earth on July 19 1972.

Appomattox Court House, site in Virginia of the main Confederate surrender in the CIVIL WAR. General Robert E. LEE surrendered his remaining forces in Virginia to General Ulysses S. GRANT at a ceremony in the court house which took place on April 9 1865. Grant offered rations to Lee's troops and permitted officers to retain their side arms. Fighting continued in North Carolina and Georgia until April 26. On May 26 Confederate troops in New Orleans surrendered, bringing the war to a close.

Arapaho, Native American people whose language belongs to the Algonkian group. In 1780 approximately 3000 Arapaho inhabited lands in Minnesota shared with their linguistic and cultural cousins the CHEYENNE. Encroachment from white settlers and elements of the SIOUX NATION forced the Arapaho south and west to the plains of Nebraska and Wyoming. These new lands straddled routes used by US citizens moving west, principally the OREGON TRAIL, and this lead the Arapaho to split into northern and southern bands.

The northern Arapaho harassed US settlers and wagon trains in the 1860s and fought in the third SIOUX WAR. They finally accepted confinement on the SHOSHONI reservation in Wyoming established by the first treaty of FORT LARAMIE (1851). The southern Arapaho were the subject of a prolonged campaign to drive them from the Arkansas river valley in Colorado and Kansas. The SAND CREEK MASSACRE (1864) was the bloodiest incident in this campaign, which culminated in the creation, via the treaty of MEDICINE LODGE (1867), of an Arapaho reservation in Oklahoma. Some southern Arapaho participated in the last-ditch RED RIVER WAR against US expansion.

Arizona, southwestern state, bordered on the north by Utah, on the west by Nevada and California, to the south by Mexico and to the east by New Mexico. The first permanent European settlement was founded by Spanish missionaries at San Javier del Bac, near Tucson, in 1700. The USA acquired Arizona from Mexico through the treaty of GUADELUPE-HIDALGO (1848) and added to its territory through the GADSDEN PURCHASE (1853). US settlement was stimulated by the discovery of silver deposits near Tubac in 1856. APACHE peoples resisted further US settlement until their final defeat in 1886. In 1862 Confederate troops briefly occupied Arizona. The US Congress awarded territorial status to Arizona (by separating it from New Mexico) on February 24 1863. Arizona became the 48th state on February 14 1912. One of its legislature's first actions was to grant women the right to vote.

Arizona was among the 'sunbelt states' to benefit from internal migration and the relocation of business headquarters in the second half of the 20th century. It had 3,665,228 residents in 1990, making Arizona the 24th most populous state in the Union. The uncompromising conservative Republican Barry GOLDWATER (born in Phoenix, Arizona) achieved national prominence in the presidential election of 1964. Associate Justice of the US Supreme Court Sandra Day O'CONNOR is a native of Arizona, and the current Chief Justice William Rehnquist (1924–) began his legal career in the state. However, the state's most famous 'native sons' are probably COCHISE and GERONIMO.

Arkansas, southern state, bordered by the Mississippi river to the east, Louisiana to the south, Texas and Oklahoma to the west and Missouri to the north. Permanent European settlement was begun by the French in 1686. The USA acquired Arkansas from France through the LOUISIANA PURCHASE. It became a US territory on March 2 1819 and the 25th state on June 15 1836. Cotton production using slave labor provided the initial spur to the state's development. Later a distinctive regional culture, often characterized perjoratively, began to develop among white settlers in the state's Ozark Mountain range. On May 6 1861, Arkansas became the ninth state to secede from the Union and join the CONFEDERACY. In 1862, Union forces regained control of the state and in 1864, a provisional state government abolished slavery. During RECONSTRUCTION the state was placed under military rule (March 2 1867), but self-government and congressional reconstruction were restored on June 22 1868. The Arkansas legislature passed JIM CROW laws denying African-Americans their civil rights and establishing racial segregation in the state. Over a million African-Americans left the state for jobs in the north during the GREAT MIGRATION that began in the 1920s.

In 1917 Arkansas became the first state in the south to grant women the right to vote. In 1931 Arkansas appointed Hattie Caraway (1878–1950) to replace her husband (who died in office) as one of the state's US Senators. Caraway, a Democrat, thereby became the first woman to sit in the US Senate. She was subsequently reelected and served until 1945. Arkansas' racially segregated school system became the focus of national attention during the LITTLE ROCK SCHOOL DESEGREGRATION BATTLE, when state governor Orval Faubus led whites determined to resist the implementation of the US Supreme Court's decisions in BROWN VS. BOARD OF EDUCATION. Complete desegregation of the state's school system was not achieved until the later 1960s. In 1990 Arkansas had 2,350,725 residents and was the 33rd most populous state in the Union. The state's most famous native son is former Governor Bill CLINTON.

Arnold, Benedict (1741–1801), American army officer, the most famous traitor of the REVOLUTIONARY WAR. Arnold had pursued careers as a druggist, bookseller and West India merchant before he led, in May 1775, a small force of Connecticut militiamen that helped to capture FORT TICONDEROGA. With Ethan ALLEN, he led an unsuccessful American assault on QUEBEC (1775). Promoted for his bravery, he helped lead resistance to a British invasion of upper New York State in 1776. Promoted once more, he played a leading role in the campaign leading to the British surrender at SARATOGA (1777).

In 1778 Arnold was made military commander of Philadelphia. Here he met and married Margaret Shippen, a LOYALIST sympathizer. Court-martialled for abuse of his powers, he was effectively demoted by transfer to command of West Point Military Academy. He plotted to surrender the fort to the British, was discovered, and fled to British lines on September 25 1780. He re-entered the war on the British side, with the rank of brigadier general. He later received from Britain an honorarium of £6315.

'Arsenal of Democracy' speech, one of the FIRESIDE CHATS given by President Franklin ROOSEVELT (broadcast on December 29 1940), in which he justified his decision to boost defence spending and military preparation with the argument that the USA should serve as 'a great arsenal of democracy'. Opinion polls showed the US public remained strongly opposed to American involvement in WORLD WAR II. Germany denounced US aid to Great Britain as 'moral aggression'.

Arthur, Chester A(lan) (1829–86), Republican statesman and vice president (1881), who became the 21st president of the USA (1881–5) following the assassination of President GARFIELD.

Raised in Vermont, Arthur became a lawyer in New York. His abolitionist principles made him an early convert to the REPUBLICAN PARTY, and he became a key figure in its New York state organization. In 1868 Arthur raised money and votes for GRANT's successful presidential bid, and, in 1871, received his reward – the post of collector of the port of New York City. Arthur used the post's immense patronage powers to rally support for Grant's re-election bid and for HAYES's successful campaign in 1876. But in 1878 Hayes forced Arthur to resign, following 'revelations' that he had used his powers to promote Republican loyalists and to coerce contributions to Republican campaigns.

In 1880 HALF-BREED nominee James Garfield balanced the Republican ticket by naming Arthur as his running mate. The vice presidency was the only office Arthur occupied by election. He automatically took over the presidency on September 20 1881 following the death of President Garfield from shots fired by Charles GUITEAU. Thought to epitomize corruption in public life, President Arthur signed the PENDLETON (CIVIL SERVICE REFORM) ACT. He thereby alienated STALWART Republicans, who blocked his bid for re-election in 1884, and his term as president ended on March 4 1885.

Articles of Confederation, the first constitutional framework for a union between the independent states of America, drafted during the AMERICAN REVOLUTION. On June 12 1776 the second CONTINENTAL CONGRESS authorized John DICKINSON to draft 'Articles of Confederation and Perpetual Union'. Dickinson's draft was discussed and amended in Congress before being sent to the states for ratification on November 17 1777. Led by Connecticut, the smaller states withheld ratification in an attempt to force the larger states to renounce their claims to western lands. Adoption of the Articles was delayed until March 1 1781.

Under the Articles each state delegated to a unicameral national assembly (CONFEDERATION CONGRESS) the minimum authority necessary for it to conduct diplomacy, war and the supervision of the national finances. Confederation Congress was left dependent for revenue upon contributions from the individual states. The Articles did not permit the creation of national governmental departments or a national judiciary. Diplomatic affairs, for example, were conducted by committees drawn from the membership of Confederation Congress. The presidency of the Confederation Congress rotated among the states, and did not confer upon its incumbent the executive powers associated with the role of head of state. Major legislation required the approval of nine states. Amendment of the Articles could be achieved only by unanimous consent.

Dissatisfaction with the Articles grew during the 1780s. The CONSTITUTIONAL CONVENTION chose not attempt a revision of them, but wrote instead the US Constitution, which in 1788 superseded the Articles of Confederation as the basis of the union between the states.

Atlanta, battle for (1864), protracted campaign by Union forces during the CIVIL WAR to capture Atlanta, Georgia, the south's largest city. The campaign marked the beginning of the end of the war.

Following the battle of CHATTANOOGA, Union General William SHERMAN spent the winter of 1863–4 in southeastern Tennessee, assembling a 100,000-strong army for an assault on Atlanta. Opposing him were 60,000 Confederate troops led by Joseph E. Johnston (1807–91). Sherman began his advance in May 1864. Johnston utilized the defensive advantages of the terrain of northeastern Georgia, ceding territory but preserving his army. On June 27 1864 SHERMAN, losing patience with 'a big Indian war', ordered a frontal assault on Confederate trenches at Kennesaw Mountain, Geor-

gia. It was repulsed at the cost of 3000 Union casualties.

Confederate leaders believed this victory repudiated Johnston's defensive strategy. On July 17, with Sherman only eight miles from Atlanta and the PRESIDENTIAL ELECTION OF 1864 looming, Jefferson DAVIS replaced Johnston with the fire-eating General John Bell Hood (1831–79). Robert E. LEE described Hood, who had lost an arm and a leg to Union bullets, as 'all lion and none of the fox'. On July 20 and 22 Hood ordered open field attacks that cost 15,000 Confederate casualties and compelled him to withdraw within Atlanta's perimeter defenses. When Sherman outflanked these defenses, Hood abandoned Atlanta to preserve his army for the field. On September 2 SHERMAN telegraphed 'Atlanta ours and fairly won.' The resulting boost to northern morale helped ensure LINCOLN's re-election. On November 15 1864 Sherman authorized the burning of Atlanta, before initiating his MARCH TO THE SEA.

Atlanta Exposition speech, speech given in 1895 by the leading African-American educator Booker T. WASHINGTON, in which he tacitly accepted racial segregation. In the speech, given to guests attending an exhibition celebrating southern industrial and agricultural progress, Washington argued that 'In all things purely social [black and white southerners] can be as separate as the fingers, yet one as the hand in all things essential to mutual progress.' Washington's speech, made in an era when LYNCHING went unchecked and on the eve of the Supreme Court's PLESSY VS. FERGUSON ruling, was acclaimed by whites but condemned by African-American activists such as W.E.B. DU BOIS.

Atlantic Charter, a non-binding statement of postwar aims drawn up in August 1941 by President Franklin D. ROOSEVELT and British Prime Minister Winston Churchill. The Charter was the outcome of meetings held by the two leaders on August 9–12

1941 aboard US and British warships anchored in Placentia Bay, Newfoundland. Bearing similarities to Woodrow WILSON's FOURTEEN POINTS, it renounced territorial aggression and supported the right of people to choose their own forms of government. Other provisions called for freer trade and global economic cooperation. The Charter's references to a permanent postwar peace structure foreshadowed the creation of the UNITED NATIONS and NATO.

Atomic Energy Commission (AEC), federal agency established by act of Congress on August 1 1946. The act gave the AEC complete control over research into and development of atomic materials, and charged it with developing the peaceful use of atomic technology. In a departure from the organization of the MANHATTAN PROJECT, which built America's first atomic bombs, the AEC was headed by a five-man civilian board. Nevertheless the Commission spent 90% of its budget on research into military applications of atomic technology.

Aztlan, name given to southwestern North America by CHICANO activists to popularize the notion that the USA conquered and still occupies a distinctive Hispanic–Native American homeland. The ideological implications of this concept were developed in 1969 by the Chicano Youth Liberation Conference's *El Plan Espiritual de Aztlan*. In practice, emotional attachment to the concept of Aztlan among Hispanic-Americans has served to bolster expressions of Mexican and Mexican-American solidarity (such as *LA HUELGA*) directed at improving their position within the USA.

B

baby boom, the surge in the birth rate in the USA in the period following World War II. This was the prime cause of a huge and unprecedented increase in the country's population, which rose from 141 million in 1947 to 181 million in 1960.

The preconditions for the population surge were laid during World War II and the early years of the Cold War. During World War II the Office of Price Management held down prices while wages rose. Postwar defense expenditure helped maintain full employment. As a result between 1947 and 1960 Americans' real disposable income rose by 17%. Many Americans therefore had the necessary savings or job prospects to make marriages delayed by wartime service feasible. The GI BILL encouraged a spirit of self-advancement in American men, while strong cultural pressure was placed on American women to leave the workforce and become 'homemakers'. The boom affected every aspect of American life, and, as the 'boomers' age and require health care, will continue to do so.

Bailey vs. Drexel Furniture Company (May 15 1922), US Supreme Court ruling concerning child labor. The Child Labor Act (1919) imposed a 10% tax on the profits of companies that used child labor to manufacture goods sold across state lines. The Supreme Court, Chief Justice TAFT presiding, ruled 8–1 that the tax constituted an improper use of federal power and an illegitimate means of raising revenue. It deemed the law a selective penalty. This decision, which made federal action to curb child labor almost impossible, was reversed in US vs. Darby Lumber Company.

Baker, Ella (1903–86), a stalwart of the CIVIL RIGHTS MOVEMENT, who played a leading role in the creation of the STUDENT NON-VIOLENT COORDINATING COMMITTEE (SNCC) and the MISSISSIPPI FREEDOM DEMOCRATIC PARTY (MFDP). Baker moved to New York City during the GREAT MIGRATION. In 1930 she co-founded the Young Negro's Cooperative League in Harlem, and ran that organization while also working in a public library on 135th Street. In 1938 she moved south to spearhead NATIONAL ASSOCIATION FOR THE ADVANCEMENT OF COLORED PEOPLE (NAACP) campaigns against JIM CROW laws. During the 1950s she urged the NAACP's conservative and largely male leadership to sponsor campaigns of direct action, such as the MONTGOMERY BUS BOYCOTT, and to work more closely with the newly formed SOUTHERN CHRISTIAN LEADERSHIP CONFERENCE. She played a crucial role at the two conferences held in 1960 in the wake of the GREENSBORO SIT-IN from which the SNCC emerged. Baker urged the students to lift their sights higher than the desegregation of lunch counters by effecting a radical transformation of American society. Irritated by the patronizing manner of Martin Luther KING and other leaders of the SOUTHERN CHRISTIAN LEADERSHIP CONFERENCE (SCLC), Baker told the students that truly strong movements do not rely upon strong leaders. She was a forceful advocate of the need to build campaigns from the grass roots. The MFDP (at whose convention she gave the keynote address) represented the fullest expression of Baker's beliefs and influence.

Baker vs. Carr (March 26 1962), US Supreme Court ruling concerning the apportionment of seats within state legislatures. The case arose from a legal challenge to apportionment in the Tennessee legislature. Tennessee had not redrawn the boundaries of its election districts for over 60 years and, as a result, they did not reflect the distribution of population within the state. This outdated apportionment worked to diminish the electoral influence of city-dwellers and ethnic minorities and to protect the power of incumbents representing rural constituencies with a dwindling number of white voters. The US Supreme Court had, in the case of Colegrove vs. Green (1946), taken the position that apportionment was a 'political question' best left to the states. Overturning this verdict, the Court now ruled, by 6–2, that it could review apportionment in order to protect civil rights. The decision allowed the CIVIL RIGHTS MOVEMENT to mount legal challenges to state apportionment schemes that discriminated against minority voters.

Bancroft, George (1800–91), government official and historian. Bancroft attended Harvard and Göttingen universities. In 1831 he began work on what turned into a ten-volume *History of the United States*. Published between 1834 and 1876, this established Bancroft as the pre-eminent historian of his age. A keen Jacksonian Democrat (*see* JACKSONIAN DEMOCRACY), Bancroft was one of the earliest supporters of James POLK's dark-horse bid for the Democratic nomination in 1844. He supported whole-heartedly Polk's expansionist policies, and, as Polk's acting secretary of war, in May 1845 signed the orders that sent General Zachary TAYLOR's US task force south of the Texas border, prompting the MEXICAN WAR. Bancroft also helped facilitate California's independence through the BEAR FLAG REVOLT. As secretary of the navy (1845–6), Bancroft founded the US Naval Academy at Annapolis, Maryland. He later served as US ambassador to Great Britain (1846–9) and Germany (1867–74).

Bank Holiday (March 1933), temporary closure of US banks by presidential decree in order to restore confidence in the banking system during the GREAT DEPRESSION. In the last days of President HOOVER's administration Americans made panic withdrawals from the nation's banks. President ROOSEVELT used his inaugural address (March 4 1933) to assert 'the only thing we have to fear is fear itself'. Roosevelt took the advice of Treasury Secretary William H. Woodin (1868–1934) and Jesse Jones (1874–1956), director of the RECONSTRUCTION FINANCE CORPORATION (RFC), and used the Trading with the Enemy Act (1917) to close all banks by presidential decree.

The closure began on Monday March 6, and was extended until Monday March 13. During this period Congress passed the EMERGENCY BANKING RELIEF ACT, and Woodin and Jones decided which banks should reopen and which should remain closed. On Sunday March 12, Roosevelt broadcast a FIRESIDE CHAT in which he explained to the nation the terms on which banks would reopen and the measures being taken to ensure their solvency. The policy worked. On Monday March 13 deposits exceeded withdrawals as Americans returned cash hidden under mattresses to the custody of the nation's banks. Banks that remained closed were assisted by the RFC. By the end of June 1933, 90% of US banks were open.

Banking Act (June 16 1933), legislation designed to restore confidence in the banking system during the GREAT DEPRESSION. The act followed in the wake of the BANK HOLIDAY called in March 1933. The act created the FEDERAL DEPOSIT INSURANCE CORPORATION, which insured deposits up to a maximum of $2500 (later $5000) against a bank failure. By encouraging the 'little guy' to leave his money in banks, the measure made a repeat of the panic withdrawals witnessed in February 1933 unlikely. The act also prohibited banks from underwriting stock issues for corporations, and placed limits on banks' involvement in sponsoring bond issues.

Bank of the United States, first, the first US national bank (1791–1811). A key component of Alexander HAMILTON's economic programme was a national bank akin to the Bank of England. The Bank was designed to hold federal surpluses, extend credit to government and entrepreneurs and issue reliable notes. The US government would hold a fifth of its stock. DEMOCRATIC-REPUBLICANS led by JEFFERSON argued that the Constitution did not delegate to Congress the power to incorporate a bank. Hamilton responded with an IMPLIED POWERS reading of the Constitution, arguing that Congress was empowered to regulate trade and the Bank was designed to achieve that end. Congress chartered the Bank for 20 years on February 25 1791. In 1811 it declined to recharter the bank, largely because much of its stock was held by British investors.

Bank of the United States, second, the second US national bank, chartered for 20 years on March 14 1816. The Bank paid the government $1,500,000 for its charter privileges in lieu of future interest on government funds held on deposit. Congress retained the exclusive right to suspend SPECIE payment. This led the Bank to adopt a hard-money policy which contracted credit and which southerners and westerners blamed for a recession in 1819. The Bank's constitutionality and independence were protected by the Supreme Court decision in McCULLOCH VS. MARYLAND (1819).

President JACKSON's first inaugural address (1829) announced opposition to the Bank's recharter. Its director, Nicolas Biddle (1766–1844), decided to apply for renewal in advance of the 1832 presidential election. Congress approved the recharter, but on July 10 1832 Jackson vetoed the bill. He reasoned that the Bank was unconstitutional, dismissing the McCulloch ruling on the grounds that each branch of government had to be guided by its own interpretation of the Constitution. Following his re-election Jackson removed federal funds from the Bank and deposited them in state banks dubbed 'pet banks' by WHIGS. The US Senate passed a motion censuring Jackson, which Jackson's supporters later expunged. The Bank was rechartered in Pennsylvania, and eventually failed in 1841. The DEPOSIT ACT (1836) provided for the continuation of some of the Bank's former functions. However, America's banking system operated without the supervision of a central bank until the creation of the FEDERAL RESERVE SYSTEM in 1913.

Banneker, Benjamin (1731–1806), African-American intellectual, whose achievements challenged the contemporary wisdom that blacks were intellectually inferior to whites. Banneker, a free black from Maryland, was educated at a Quaker school in Joppa. In 1761, after seeing a clock for the first time, he built a functioning replica from wooden components. Banneker's interests included astronomy and mathematics. In the 1780s he compiled a series of best-selling almanacs. Following an exchange of letters in 1791, JEFFERSON appointed Banneker to survey the boundaries of the DISTRICT OF COLUMBIA. Despite Banneker's achievements, Jefferson refused to retract the racial views he had espoused in his *NOTES ON THE STATE OF VIRGINIA*.

barbed wire. On October 27 1873 an Illinois farmer, Joseph E. Glidden (1813–1906), applied to patent wire fencing whose barbs could be machine-twisted. Barbed wire was expensive, but its effectiveness was immediately apparent. Production rose and retail prices fell as imitators circumvented Glidden's patent by designing fancy barbs of their own. The cost and impracticality of fencing land on the Great Plains with wooden rails had previously deterred settlement by homesteaders and encouraged open-range grazing. Low-cost barbed wire stimulated a surge of settlement on the Great Plains and in west Texas, and made the range-riding COWBOY redundant.

Barnburners, supporters of Martin VAN BUREN'S attempt to reform the ALBANY REGENCY (the DEMOCRATIC PARTY's New York State machine). They acquired their name when they were derided by the HUNKERS (their opponents) as the kind of men who would burn their own barn to kill the rats in it. Barnburners supported Van Buren's FREE SOIL candidacy in 1848.

Barnum, Phineas Taylor (1810–91), showman and co-founder of the renowned Barnum and Bailey Circus. Barnum entered show business, following the collapse of several more orthodox business ventures, when he agreed to manage Joice Heth, a former slave who claimed to be over 160 years old and to have nursed George Washington in his youth. Barnum attracted audiences for Heth's lectures by inviting the public to judge for themselves the veracity of his claims. He developed this technique by organizing national tours in which curiosities and celebrities (among them the midget Tom Thumb and the soprano Jenny Lind), were exhibited to the paying public. Branching out, he opened Barnum's American Museum in New York City (an exhibition of oddities and dubious historical artifacts) and organized tours through which American curios were displayed to credulous European audiences. During the 1850s Barnum, who was an abolitionist and temperance campaigner, stood unsuccessfully for election to Congress as a Republican. He organized his first circus in 1871. Buying up such attractions as the famous 'White Elephant' of Siam to trump rivals, Barnum went into partnership with James A. Bailey and in 1881 sent out on tour the 'Greatest Show on Earth': an unprecedented three-ringed circus. During his lifetime, Barnum made and lost several fortunes while establishing mass entertainment formats and procedures that continue to influence cultural tastes.

Barton, Clara Harlowe (1821–1912), pioneering nurse and humanitarian reformer. Barton was born in Massachusetts and trained as a schoolteacher. In 1854 she moved to Washington DC to take up a post as a clerk in the US patent office. At the outbreak of the CIVIL WAR she abandoned her job and began distributing medicine, food and small luxuries to Union casualties in field hospitals. The care with which she recorded the names of the Union dead so that their next-of-kin could be notified was particularly appreciated by the troops, who dubbed her 'the angel of the battlefield'. In 1869 she moved to Europe to recuperate from illness, but during the Franco-Prussian War (1870–1) worked on behalf of the International Red Cross. On her return to America she established the US branch of the Red Cross and served as its first president (1881–1904). Barton led the lobbying effort that in 1882 induced the US government to sign the Geneva Convention governing the conduct of war.

baseball, the oldest distinctively American SPECTATOR SPORT. Exported to Cuba, Puerto Rico and the Dominican Republic by US troops in the 1900s, it is also an important part of a regional American culture.

During the colonial and early national periods America's most popular organized ball game was cricket. Baseball, a variant on the British game 'rounders', evolved in the industrialized cities of the north. The first baseball club in the USA, the New York Knickerbocker Base Ball Club, was founded in 1845 and it was a Knickerbocker's official, Alexander Cartwright, a member of the New York City Fire Department, who codified the rules on which the modern game is based. Journalists quickly dubbed baseball 'America's pastime' in a bid to distinguish it from cricket. However, like cricket clubs, the first US baseball clubs tended to reflect rather than transcend divisions of class, race and residence. By bringing together crowds of young men, often from working-class neighborhoods, baseball games were associated with 'rowdyism' in the minds of many respectable city burghers. (For this reason cricket remained popular among the middle classes.) However, precisely because baseball was rooted in urban neighborhoods, politicians sought to associate themselves with popular teams. The TWEED RING, for example, sponsored the New York Mutuals and in the game's early days, a fan's baseball club affiliation often mirrored his political affiliation.

In 1866 the Philadelphia Athletics admitted to paying its team members. In 1869 a professional club, the Cincinnatti Red Stockings, undertook a nationwide exhibition tour in which they went undefeated. A National League of Professional Base Ball Clubs, the forerunner of the present-day National League, was founded in 1876. The National League sought to attract an up-market audience by charging fifty cents for admission, banning the sale of liquor at ballparks and, at least initially, by refraining from staging games on Sundays. The National League, whose constituent teams were required to be run on business lines, also pioneered the techniques that eventually made the game profitable for owners. It controlled the number of professional teams in a city through the franchise system, and bound professional players to clubs through the use of the 'reserve clause.' (Developed in 1879, the 'reserve clause' prevented at first the best five players, and later any squad member, from switching teams

without the permission of the club that 'reserved' the player's services. The US Supreme Court subsequently exempted these restrictive contracts from antitrust legislation). A 'gentleman's agreement' among team owners excluded African-American players from team rosters. Owners operated blacklists to exclude troublesome players, and justified paying their stars less than the market rate with the argument that many players were of such poor moral character that they couldn't be trusted with large sums of money. (The prevalence of alcoholism and suicide among players, as well as a series of betting scandals, seemed to bolster the owners' case.)

Players bitterly resented the reserve system and made repeated attempts to organize the professional game in a format which might give them, and a club's fans, greater reward. The American League, founded in 1901 and descended from earlier syndicates of player-controlled clubs, permitted the sale of alcohol, played on Sundays and, from 1882, charged spectators a quarter for admission. The players mounted a national strike in 1889–90 during which they organized a rival player-controlled league. The strike was broken when National League backers bought out the most profitable franchises in the Players' League. In the final third of the 19th century, membership of both the National League and the American Association (forerunner of the American League) changed almost yearly. 850 professional franchises were created in the period 1869–1900 and 650 of these went out of business within two years. However, the mass production of baseball equipment, especially balls and the glove used by fielders, reflected and further promoted interest in playing the game. The 1880s and 1890s saw the creation of a bewildering variety of 'minor leagues' below the main professional baseball leagues and also the development of an amateur version of baseball – softball.

The first 'World Series' between the champions of the National League and the champions of the American League was staged in 1903. The creation of a national championship format generated even greater interest among fans and increased revenue for club owners. The greatest scandal in baseball history involved the 1919 World Series and was indirectly caused by the players' alienation from the revenues generated by the game.

In 1917, the Chicago White Sox emerged as the best team in the USA. Over the next two years, the White Sox's star players grew increasingly frustrated by the refusal of the team's owner, Charlie Comiskey, to recognize their worth. (Late in the 1919 season, for example, Comiskey ordered the team's coaches to drop star pitcher Eddie Cicotte, winner of 29 games, in order to escape paying a performance bonus in Cicotte's contract.) On September 21 1919, White Sox first baseman Chick Gandil, representing seven other team members, met with professional gamblers at the Ansonia Hotel, New York, to arrange to throw the upcoming World Series against the Cincinnati Reds. The players' price was $100,000. The Sox duly walked the Reds to a World Series victory and rumors of a fix reverberated throughout the USA. Eight members of the Sox team were tried on the charge of conspiracy to defraud the public but all were acquitted on September 28 1920. Club owners had created the office of Commissioner of Baseball in response to the scandal and, following the players' acquittal, Commissioner Kennesaw Mountain Landis (1866–1944) barred all eight players from professional baseball for life.

George Herman 'Babe' RUTH has been credited with single-handedly restoring the battered reputation of the sport in the 1920s. However the spread of RADIO ownership was probably as important (the 1922 World Series was the first broadcast to a national audience). Ruth himself was a throwback to an earlier age and from the 1930s, fans increasingly identified with players who exuded application, for example, 'Iron Horse' Lou Gehrig (1903–41) of the New York Yankees, or consistency, for example 'The Yankee Clipper' Joe Di Maggio (1914–99), who also played for the Yankees.

An important first step in the integration of black players within professional baseball was, paradoxically, the formation of the Negro League in 1920. The League provided a stable showcase for talented black professionals. It proved popular with fans because general standards of play were as high as those in the white majors and because players employed stratagems, notably base-stealing, that made the game more exciting to watch. Nevertheless, many white fans and most white newspapermen continued to adduce spurious racial reasoning to argue that African-Americans made inferior baseball players. At the end of World War II Branch Rickey (1881–1965), general manager of the Brooklyn Dodgers, asked Negro League star Jackie ROBINSON to become the first African-American to play in the majors. Robinson, who had seen active service in World War II, kept his cool through the firestorm of abuse and controversy that followed his major-league debut for the Dodgers in 1947. During the 1950s the Dodgers, who remained popular despite losing several big games in the most agonizing circumstances, demonstrated the existence of links between teams and communities that transcended success on the field. The sudden sale of the team and its relocation to Los Angeles therefore took on a huge metaphorical significance.

Televised coverage of baseball increased interest in the game still further and generated vast revenues for owners. In 1969, Curt Flood mounted a successful legal challenge to the 'reserve clause' contract system that resulted in players being granted a modicum of 'free agency'. Players' salaries soared immediately. To meet payrolls, owners adopted quality control and revenue boosting techniques pioneered by firms such as McDONALDS. Fans castigate the greed and arrogance of the players (especially during strikes and contract hold-outs) almost as much as they despise the sterility and commercialism of the modern ballpark. However, precisely because they are products of the culture they are criticizing, Americans continue to attend baseball games or, more frequently, watch them on TV.

basketball, *see* SPECTATOR SPORTS.

Bataan, battle of (1941–2), defeat of US-Filipino forces in the Philippines by the Japanese. The Japanese raid on PEARL HARBOR was accompanied by a major assault on the Philippines, and by December 23 1941, 65,000 Filipino and 16,000 US troops, under the command of General Douglas MACARTHUR, had been confined to the Bataan peninsula of the main Philippine island of Luzon. By the January 28 they held just 10 square miles (26 square km), but resisted until 9 April 1942. In what was dubbed the 'Bataan Death March', the 45,000 Filipino and 11,500 US troops who had surrendered were force-marched 60 miles (100 km) to prison camps. Starved and beaten, some 10,000 Filipinos and 2,000 GIs died en route. Many more died in the prison camps. US-Filipino resistance to the Japanese occupation of the Philippines ceased following the battle of CORREGIDOR.

Bay of Pigs invasion (1961), landing on Cuba by 1500 armed Cuban exiles, trained and equipped by the CIA, in the hope of creating a popular insurrection that would overthrow Fidel Castro. The landing occurred on April 17, and the attackers encountered immediate Cuban resistance. On April 20, 1100 survivors surrendered. The invasion had been planned under the EISENHOWER administration but President KENNEDY gave it the go-ahead and accepted responsibility for its failure. The failed invasion helped to push Castro more firmly into the Soviet camp, contributing to the CUBAN MISSILE CRISIS of the following year.

Bayonne decree, announcement by Napoleon on April 17 1808 that he would seize US ships and goods in ports under his control. This was on the grounds that, following the EMBARGO ACT (1807), vessels trading with European ports under a US flag must be doing so under false pretences.

Bear Flag Revolt (1846), revolt against Mexican rule by US settlers in California, who adopted a flag featuring a black bear. In 1846, at the height of the OREGON BORDER CRISIS and with a US-Mexican war over TEXAS imminent, John FRÉMONT led a US Army scientific expedition into northern California. Concluding, erroneously, that President POLK favored the immediate annexation of California, Frémont's troops encouraged a revolt by US settlers. At a meeting in Sonoma on June 14 1846 American rebels declared California an independent republic. On July 7 the US annexed the recently established republic of California. Mexican inhabitants mounted a rebellion against US rule, but this ended following the battle of San Gabriel (January 8–9 1847) and the US occupation of Los Angeles, resulting in the treaty of CAHUENGA.

Bell, Alexander Graham (1847–1922), inventor and teacher of the deaf. Bell was born in Scotland and emigrated to Canada in 1870. He joined the faculty of Boston University in 1873, as Professor of Speech and Vocal Physiology. Here he began experiments that would lead him to patent the telephone in 1876. Bell's patent was immediately disputed but ultimately upheld. The Bell Telephone Company, organized to exploit his invention, made Bell an immensely rich man. Bell helped found the journal *Science* and served as president of the National Geographic Society (1898–1904). Through the Alexander Graham Bell Association for the Deaf, founded in 1890, he promoted lip-reading and other techniques to assist the deaf. On the day of his funeral,

Americans were asked to pay silent tribute to Bell by refraining from using their phones.

Bell, John, *see* CONSTITUTIONAL UNION PARTY.

Bemis Heights, battle of (1777), American victory in New York State during the REVOLUTIONARY WAR. The centerpiece of Britain's military campaign in the summer of 1777 was an invasion of New York, launched southward from Lake Champlain by General John Burgoyne's column of 8500 redcoats. American victories at ORISKANY, FORT STANWIX and BENNINGTON denied Burgoyne reinforcement and resupply. Desperate to maintain his advance, Burgoyne ordered two separate attacks (September 19, October 7) on fortified American positions commanding the Hudson river and the northern approaches to Albany. Both were repulsed, at the cost of some 1000 British casualties. The remnants of Burgoyne's force surrendered at SARATOGA on October 17.

Bennington, battle of (August 16 1777), American victory in Vermont during the REVOLUTIONARY WAR. In August 1777 Lieutenant Colonel Friedrich Baum led a detachment of 600 HESSIANS on an expedition to seize supplies for General John Burgoyne's invasion of New York State. Baum's force was met at Bennington by 2500 New Hampshire militiamen under General John Stark (1728–1822). On August 15, Stark's troops killed or captured three-quarters of Baum's detachment, and the next day severely mauled a column sent to reinforce it. The action contributed to Burgoyne's eventual surrender at SARATOGA.

Berlin airlift, *see* BERLIN BLOCKADE.

Berlin blockade (1948–9), blockade of West Berlin by Soviet forces. The blockade crystallized the geopolitical confrontation at the heart of the COLD WAR.

The city of Berlin lay within the eastern part of Germany occupied by Soviet forces from the end of World War II. The city itself was divided, with US, British and French forces occupying zones in its western half.

On June 24 1948 the Soviet Union closed all land routes to Berlin through eastern Germany in protest at the US, British and French decision to create a unified federal state out of their occupation zones in western Germany. The Western powers used transport aircraft to supply the 2 million inhabitants of Berlin who lived in areas under their control. This 'Berlin Airlift', which began in June 1948, eventually necessitated 272,000 sorties. The Soviets announced the lifting of their blockade on May 5 1949.

Berlin Wall crisis, COLD WAR crisis provoked in 1961 by Soviet Premier Nikita Khrushchev in an attempt to force President KENNEDY to accept Soviet proposals for the future governance of Berlin and Germany. It produced the most evocative symbol of the Cold War – the Berlin Wall.

Repeated Soviet threats to give formal recognition to the Soviet satellite regime in East Germany led millions of East Germans to seek refuge in the West. Many chose to escape through Berlin, where the western sectors were under US, British and French control. On August 13 1961 Soviet troops began building a wall separating Soviet-controlled East Berlin from the western part of the city. East Germans attempting to escape over the wall were shot by Soviet guards, while US, British and French troops were denied access to the eastern sector of the city. Kennedy sent troop reinforcements to Berlin. On October 10 1962 Congress authorized the use of force to re-establish the free access of western troops to the eastern half of the city. On June 26 1963 Kennedy visited West Berlin and told a crowd that the USA was willing to risk nuclear war to protect Berliners' freedom. His speech famously ended with the words, *'Ich bin ein Berliner.'* A stalemate developed, which lasted until the wall was destroyed by joyous Berliners in November 1989.

Beveridge, Albert J(eremiah) (1862–1927), influential member of the REPUB-

LICAN PARTY's imperialist wing, Beveridge represented Indiana in the US Senate from 1899 to 1911. His maiden speech in the Senate chamber defended the occupation of territory acquired during the SPANISH–AMERICAN WAR with the argument that God had been preparing the 'English-speaking and Teutonic people' to 'serve as the master organizers of the world'.

Bill of Rights, the collective term used to describe the first ten amendments to the US Constitution. During the AMERICAN REVOLUTION many states attached statements known as 'bills of rights' to their constitutions. These bills of rights specified fundamental liberties that government might never abridge or infringe. ANTIFEDERALIST opponents of the federal Constitution argued that it too should contain a bill of rights in order to guarantee basic liberties. In some states ratification of the Constitution was made contingent on the addition of such a bill.

FEDERALISTS and, initially, James MADISON argued that a bill of rights was unnecessary, since the Constitution itself specified what federal government could and could not do. However, bowing to popular pressure, Madison drafted twelve amendments to the Constitution in the first session of Congress. These were sent to the states on September 25 1789. By December 15 1791 ten had been ratified. These became known as the Federal Bill of Rights. Most famous are the First Amendment (guaranteeing freedom of speech and worship), the Fifth Amendment (providing freedom from self-incrimination) and the Second Amendment (which many Americans interpret as establishing their right to own handguns and assault rifles). For the full text of the original Constitution, and of the first ten amendments (the Bill of Rights), *see* Appendix 1; *see also* dictionary entries on the first ten amendments.

bimetallism, *see* SILVER–GOLD CONTROVERSY *and* GOLD STANDARD.

Birmingham City Jail, Letter from, *see* LETTER FROM BIRMINGHAM CITY JAIL.

Birmingham desegregation campaign, one of the high points of the CIVIL RIGHTS MOVEMENT, launched in the winter of 1962. The campaign made Martin Luther KING an international figure.

Birmingham, Alabama, was home to a declining steel industry and had a long history of white supremacist violence. But the SOUTHERN CHRISTIAN LEADERSHIP CONFERENCE (SCLC) had strong support among the city's black churches, and some members of the local white elite favored an accommodation with civil rights protesters as a means of generating inward economic investment. The SCLC obeyed a state court injunction banning protest marches in the city in order to encourage white moderates to enter meaningful negotiations over the desegregation of the city. The talks stalled, and on Good Friday 1963 Martin Luther KING and Ralph ABERNATHY broke the injunction against marching. They, and 50 other volunteers and onlookers, were arrested and jailed. King was placed in solitary confinement. He spent nine days in prison, writing the *LETTER FROM BIRMINGHAM CITY JAIL* before his release. SCLC activists organized daily marches on City Hall, resulting in mass arrests. They were running short of volunteers for jail when James Bevel hit on the idea of organizing a march by schoolchildren. King approved this plan.

On May 3, Birmingham's police chief Eugene 'Bull' Connor unleashed water cannon and Alsatian dogs on the marching schoolchildren, generating sensational television pictures. These forced the KENNEDY administration to announce its intention to prepare comprehensive federal civil rights legislation. King called off the marches on May 7, in return for promises to desegregate city lunch counters, a commitment from white stores to hire black workers, and the creation of a biracial commission to resolve tensions.

On May 11 bombs exploded at the SCLC's meeting hall and at the home of King's brother. The city's black population rioted, strengthening O'Connor's hand. White civic leaders delayed implementing the May agreements until, on September 15, a bomb exploded at the 16th Street Baptist church, killing four black children and creating an atmosphere of national revulsion that made further white resistance in Birmingham untenable.

black codes, laws developed in 1865–6 by southern states, led by Mississippi, restricting FREEDMEN's civil rights, freedom of movement and access to an open labor market. These codes enumerated criminal offences that applied to blacks only. Most forbade interracial marriage, and they prevented blacks from arming in self-defense. On April 9 1866 Congress enacted, over President JOHNSON's veto, a CIVIL RIGHTS ACT in an attempt to safeguard the liberties of former slaves.

Black–Connery Bill, bill formulated by Democratic congressmen to reduce unemployment as the GREAT DEPRESSION worsened during the dying days of President HOOVER's administration. Their bill, backed by the AMERICAN FEDERATION OF LABOR, called for a 30-hour working week. Enforcement would be achieved by banning the interstate shipment of goods made in factories that did not comply. The bill cleared the US Senate on April 6 1933, but the newly elected President ROOSEVELT vetoed it in favor of the more ambitious NATIONAL INDUSTRIAL RECOVERY ACT.

Black Friday (1869), a crash in the price of gold following a period of fevered speculation. The events leading up to the crash arose out of the 'hard-money' position of the GRANT administration, which insisted that the government repay its debts in gold. In 1869 James Fisk (1834–72) and Jay Gould (1836–92) attempted to profit from this policy by launching a speculative bid to corner the US gold market. In four days of frantic buying they raised the price of gold by 20%. By entertaining Grant aboard Fisk's yacht they created the impression that the president would not order intervention in the market. Speculators, and even some businesses, scrambled to buy gold, only to be ruined when, on Friday September 24 1869, Grant ordered a massive sale of federal gold reserves.

Black Hawk War (1832), conflict in the midwest between Native Americans led by Chief Black Hawk (1767–1838) and US forces and their allies. In 1804 the Fox and Sauk peoples had ceded their lands in northeastern Illinois and southeastern Wisconsin to the USA in return for reservations in Iowa. However, some Sauk remained east of the Mississippi. In 1831 Black Hawk urged these diehards to defy the 1804 treaty and resist further white settlement. In the summer of 1832 Illinois militiamen (among them Abraham Lincoln), US army regulars (among them Zachary Taylor) and Dakota Indians conducted a campaign against Black Hawk's followers. On August 2 1832 around 500 Sauk were killed at the battle of Bad Axe River, Illinois, and Black Hawk was captured. This ended Native American resistance to white settlement in Illinois and Wisconsin.

blacklist, list of individuals deemed to hold 'subversive' views. During the RED SCARE of 1917–21, but especially during the early years of the COLD WAR, American industry bosses collaborated to draw up such lists, naming people whom they sought to bar from employment. In the later 1940s and 1950s HOLLYWOOD studio bosses blacklisted directors, actors and screenwriters suspected of communist sympathies. Ronald REAGAN (head of the Screen Actors' Guild 1947–52) and Elia Kazan (director of the classic *On the Waterfront*) cooperated with this policy. In 1947 ten filmmakers were blacklisted by studio bosses for refusing to disclose their political beliefs to the House Un-American Activities Committee (*see* DIES COMMITTEE).

Among them was Edward Dmytryk (1908–99), who, in Britain, went on to direct *The Caine Mutiny*. Other victims of industry blacklists include the film director Joseph Losey (1909–84), who directed *The Servant*, and the actor-singer Paul ROBESON. In 1999, amidst much controversy, Elia Kazan received a 'Lifetime Achievement' award from Hollywood's Academy of Motion Picture Arts and Sciences. Ronald Reagan went on to become president of the USA.

Black Muslims, *see* NATION OF ISLAM.

Black Panther Party, political party that promoted black nationalism and radical community action. It was set up in Oakland, California, in October 1966 by Bobby Seale (1937–) and Huey Newton (1942–89). They were inspired by the LOWNDES COUNTY FREEDOM ORGANIZATION (whose symbol was a black panther), established in Alabama in the summer of 1965 by Stokeley CARMICHAEL. The Black Panther Party for Self-Defense, as it was formally known, attempted to protect the black community by 'monitoring' the police to prevent oppression. Armed party members shadowed police patrols in black neighborhoods, ready to intervene on behalf of local residents. The party also established schools and community centers. By the summer of 1967 Black Panther 'chapters' had been established in most major US cities. Party leaders made unapologetic use of the slogan BLACK POWER, and delighted in publicity stunts such as posing with their guns or demanding reparations from white businesses. These activities helped to create a backlash from the police and public prosecutors, and this limited the party's influence even within black neighborhoods. The Panthers also helped to create a more general white backlash against the CIVIL RIGHTS MOVEMENT.

black power, radical African-American slogan that emerged in the later 1960s. The concept of 'black power' was popularized by Stokeley CARMICHAEL, chairman of the STUDENT NON-VIOLENT COORDINATING COMMITTEE (SNCC), at a rally on May 14 1966. As interpreted by the BLACK PANTHERS it suggested the necessity of armed self-defence by African-Americans. The more moderate NATIONAL ASSOCIATION FOR THE ADVANCEMENT OF COLORED PEOPLE (NAACP), taking this to be Carmichael's meaning, criticized the slogan. Carmichael claimed that he was not calling on African-Americans to detach themselves from white society. The CONGRESS OF RACIAL EQUALITY (CORE), taking Carmichael at his word, endorsed the slogan as a legitimate expression of self-esteem at their annual convention (July 4 1966). The concept alarmed and angered many whites. Carmichael was held responsible for a fracas between local police and residents of a black district of Atlanta, Georgia, and was arrested on charges of inciting a riot. At the 1968 Olympic Games several African-American members of the US team, notably Tommie Smith, winner of the gold medal in the 200 metres, gave black-power salutes during the playing of the American national anthem. The furore surrounding the slogan encapsulated growing divisions within the CIVIL RIGHTS MOVEMENT.

Black Republicans, term of opprobrium used by southern Democrats to describe white Republicans, and especially those elected during RECONSTRUCTION through the support of FREEDMEN.

Blackwell, Elizabeth (1821–1910), the first American woman to earn a medical degree. Blackwell was born in England. Her family emigrated to the USA in 1832 but was left in poverty following the death of her father in 1838. Blackwell sought a medical training to support her mother and sisters. Numerous medical schools turned her application down, but she was finally admitted to medical training in Geneva, New York, and graduated in 1849. She pursued her training in Paris and London, before returning to the USA in 1851. Settling in New York City she founded a hospital for indigent women and children. In

April 1861 Blackwell organized a meeting of women at the Cooper Institute in New York to discuss ways in which they might aid the Union war effort. This meeting marked the start of a campaign, headed by Blackwell, to recruit women volunteers for nursing duties. It also gave rise to the creation of the Women's Central Association for Relief, a forerunner of the US Sanitary Commission that saved hundreds of lives during the CIVIL WAR by improving conditions and care in Union hospitals.

Blaine, James G(illespie) (1830–93), Republican politician and twice secretary of state (1881, 1889–92). The leader of the Republican Party's HALF-BREED faction, Blaine was one of only two Republican presidential nominees to be defeated by a Democrat between 1860 and 1908. Blaine was raised in Maine. He was elected to the US House of Representatives (1862–76), serving as its Speaker between 1869 and 1876. After a period in the Senate (1877–81), James GARFIELD appointed him secretary of state in 1881, but he resigned soon after when the STALWART Republican Chester ARTHUR succeeded Garfield. Blaine's bid for the presidency in 1884 was derailed by allegations that he had delivered political favors in exchange for railroad stock. Democrats assailed him as 'Blaine, Blaine, James G. Blaine – the continental liar from the state of Maine'. Blaine lost the state of New York (and with it the presidency) by 600 votes. He would have won had he disassociated himself from a taunt made by a supporter that Irish-Americans were devotees of 'rum, Romanism, and rebellion', and had he not attended a sumptuous feast with New York's industrial magnates in a period of high unemployment. Blaine later served as secretary of state (1889–92) in Benjamin HARRISON's administration, and did his best to improve relations with Latin America.

Bland–Allison Act (1878), legislation concerning the use of silver in the US coinage, emerging out of the SILVER–GOLD CONTRO-VERSY. In 1876 Representative Richard Bland (1835–99) sponsored a bill calling for the unlimited minting of silver dollars at a ratio to gold of 16–1. Supported in the House by western mining interests and farmers seeking a debtor-friendly 'soft-money' regime, the bill was amended in Senate. In its final version the US Treasury was given the discretion to purchase for coinage between $2 and $4 million worth of silver every month. Congress passed the bill over President HAYES's veto on February 28 1878. The Treasury used its discretionary powers to make minimal purchases, keeping the silver–gold controversy alive.

bleeding Kansas, the period of violence between advocates of slavery (BORDER RUFFI-ANS) and abolitionists (including John BROWN) that engulfed the Kansas territory in the years before the Civil War. The violence followed the KANSAS–NEBRASKA ACT (1854), which disturbed the MISSOURI COMPROMISE by allowing residents north of 36° 30' to decide for themselves whether to permit slavery.

Using fraud and intimidation, pro-slavery forces seized control of the Kansas territory's first legislature and in 1855 applied for admission to the Union as a slave state. On January 15 1856 anti-slavery settlers elected their own government, a move denounced by President PIERCE. Congress, whose bitter divisions were encapsulated in the BROOKS–SUMNER INCIDENT on the Senate floor, refused to seat representatives from either government. Incoming President BUCHANAN encouraged Kansans to settle matters by calling a new constitutional convention. Battles over the selection of that convention and ratification of its LECOMPTON CON-STITUTION delayed Kansas's admission as a free state until 1861.

bloody shirt. During the IMPEACHMENT hearings against President Andrew JOHNSON, Representative Benjamin Butler (1818–93) exhibited on the floor of the House the blood-stained shirt of a Republican killed by the KU KLUX KLAN. Thereafter, any rhetorical onslaught by Republicans on Democrats – pictured as defenders of the Confederacy and opponents of enlightened RECONSTRUCTION – was referred to as 'waving the bloody shirt.'

Bloomer, Amelia Jenks (1818–94), campaigner on behalf of the women's suffrage movement, temperance and a relaxation of oppressive social conventions. Arising from the last-named interest, she designed special trousers for women, and this distinctive garment became synonymous with her name.

bodycount, a measure of military success dependent upon the number of enemies killed. Before the TET OFFENSIVE, US military commanders were generally successful in persuading Washington that the difference between American and Vietnamese casualties – the 'bodycount' – demonstrated the overall success of the SEARCH AND DESTROY strategy adopted during the VIETNAM WAR. Although official figures were inflated, it seems clear that US servicemen killed Vietnamese soldiers at ten, or even twenty, times the rate that they themselves were killed. But Viet Cong and North Vietnamese commanders were able to frustrate US attempts to wage and win a war of attrition by attacking or lying dormant as they saw fit.

Bonus Army, demonstration in the summer of 1932, in which 15,000 veterans of WORLD WAR I marched on Washington to demand immediate payment of benefits guaranteed by the BONUS BILL. Their protest quickly captured national attention. On July 28 1932 President HOOVER ordered that a camp set up by the 'Bonus Expeditionary Force' in Washington DC be dispersed by the US Army. General Douglas MACARTHUR commanded the operation (in which EISENHOWER and PATTON also participated), and the encampment was broken up amidst accusations of heavy-handed brutality. Newsreel footage of the Army operation against the protesters fueled a catastrophic decline in Hoover's popularity.

Bonus Bill (May 15 1924), legislation, passed over President COOLIDGE's veto, that granted WORLD WAR I veterans an endowment. The value of the endowment varied according to an individual's length of service and region of deployment. Individuals could borrow a portion of the value of the endowment. If they left it untouched for 20 years they would receive a 300% bonus. During the GREAT DEPRESSION a BONUS ARMY occupied Washington to demand immediate payment of veterans' endowed accounts.

Boone, Daniel (1734–1820), hunter and frontiersman who achieved legendary status, and who helped to found the modern state of KENTUCKY. He began his exploration of the Kentucky country in 1767, and in 1771 founded what he hoped would be a permanent settlement. Following a Native American attack in which one of Boone's sons was scalped, he abandoned his projected settlement and joined forces with the TRANSYLVANIA COMPANY. He helped broker the treaty of SYCAMORE SHOALS (1775), through which the company purchased from native peoples 26,000 square miles (67,000 square km) of Kentucky land. In the same year he blazed the WILDERNESS ROAD to facilitate settlement of the region. Boone's desire to live and hunt on lands where he would not see the smoke of a neighbour's fire led him into frequent conflict with Native American nations. He was twice captured, and once formally adopted by SHAWNEE warriors, but escaped on each occasion. He also fell foul of the American legal system. When Virginia asserted control over the Kentucky country in 1776, Boone served in a number of minor state government posts. However, he lost all his land claims through legal chicanery, and eventually retired westward to the Missouri country in disgust.

Booth, John Wilkes (1838–65), the assassin of Abraham LINCOLN. The assassination took place during a performance of *Our*

American Cousin at Ford's Theatre, Washington DC, on April 14 1865. On the same night a co-conspirator attacked Secretary of State William SEWARD. Booth was a Shakespearean actor, born and raised in Virginia. In 1859 he served in the Virginia militia unit that recaptured HARPER'S FERRY from John BROWN. He spied for the CONFEDERACY during the CIVIL WAR. His motive for shooting Lincoln was hatred of northern abolitionists and anger at the destruction of the southern way of life during the war. Immediately after he had shot Lincoln, he leapt from the presidential box onto the stage, declaiming 'Sic semper tyrannis! The South is avenged!' Booth fled Washington following the assassination, but on April 26 he was cornered in a barn in Virginia. Here he was shot, either by a soldier or by his own hand.

border ruffians, armed gangs, recruited in Missouri, that sought to terrorize settlers in Kansas into adopting a constitution permitting slavery, following the passage of the KANSAS–NEBRASKA ACT (1854). On May 22 1856 border ruffians sacked Lawrence, Kansas. They burned down the governor's mansion, pillaged homes and destroyed the presses of two antislavery newspapers, the *Herald of Freedom* and the *Kansas Free State*. Antislavery forces organized armed gangs, known as JAYHAWKERS, to retaliate. *See also* BLEEDING KANSAS.

border states, the four slave states (DELAWARE, MARYLAND, KENTUCKY and MISSOURI) that remained within the Union during the CIVIL WAR. Delaware's legislature voted unanimously against secession, but significant support for the Confederacy existed in Maryland, Kentucky and Missouri. Had these three states joined the Confederacy, they would have increased its white population and military manpower by 45%, its manufacturing capacity by 80% and its supply of horses and mules by 40%. By moderating Union war aims LINCOLN was able to keep the border states loyal and

thereby force the Confederacy to disperse its troops in a perimeter defense.

Bork confirmation hearings (1987), US Senate hearings culminating on October 23 1987 when President REAGAN's nominee, Robert Bork (1927–) was rejected for a vacancy on the US Supreme Court. This was only the fifth time in its history that the Senate had rejected a president's nominee for such a vacancy. (The first rejection occurred in George WASHINGTON's administration, the second in the John J. PARKER CONFIRMATION HEARINGS, and the third and fourth in Richard NIXON's administration.)

Bork had impeccable conservative credentials. In 1973 he accepted promotion to attorney general in order to carry out President NIXON's request that the congressionally appointed special prosecutor charged with investigating the WATERGATE SCANDAL be summarily dismissed. President Reagan nominated him for the Supreme Court in 1987 in the belief that Bork would use his seat to erode or overturn the ROE VS. WADE verdict liberalizing ABORTION law. Bork's abrupt refusal to discuss his judicial philosophy during televised confirmation hearings (September 15–19) convinced three Republicans to join the Democrats in voting down his nomination 58–42. Reagan then nominated Douglas Ginsburg, who withdrew after revelations that he used marijuana while teaching law at Harvard. The Senate unanimously approved Anthony Kennedy (1936–) on February 3 1988.

Boston massacre (March 5 1770), shooting of a number of American civilians by British troops during the AMERICAN REVOLUTION. Tensions between British troops and Bostonians boiled over on the morning of March 5 1770 when a crowd began harassing soldiers guarding the headquarters of the American customs service. A soldier knocked down by a snowball discharged his musket into the crowd, sparking a volley that claimed five lives. The troops stood trial for murder, but their counsel, John

ADAMS, persuaded a Boston jury to acquit all bar two. These defendants were convicted on the lesser charge of manslaughter. The incident, and the measured response to it by the Bostonians, made British legislation such as the ADMINISTRATION OF JUSTICE ACT (1774) all the more intolerable.

Boston Port Bill (March 13 1774), legislation passed by the British Parliament that closed the port of Boston to all trade, save that necessary to prevent starvation. This INTOLERABLE ACT, which came into force on June 1 1774, was an attempt to force reparations following the refusal of the Boston town meeting to compensate the East India Company for the BOSTON TEA PARTY.

Boston Tea Party (1773), incident during the AMERICAN REVOLUTION in which a cargo of cut-price East India Company tea, subject to a new British import duty, was dumped in Boston harbor by disgruntled colonists.

The first ship bearing East India Company tea to arrive in America after passage of the TEA ACT docked in Boston on November 27 1773. Bostonians vowed to prevent its cargo from being unloaded. Massachusetts Governor Thomas Hutchinson (1711–80) insisted that the tea be unloaded and import duty paid. Acting on orders from Samuel ADAMS, a group of men disguised as MOHAWK Indians boarded the ship on the night of December 16 and dumped 342 chests of tea valued at £9000 into Boston harbor. No other property was disturbed. The incident demonstrated that the TEA ACT was essentially unenforceable, but prompted the retaliatory INTOLERABLE ACTS.

Bourbons, nickname applied by populists to wealthy southern conservatives who, during the 1880s and 1890s, played on racial tensions to defeat reform of the region's economic and political system. The nickname derived from the name of the deposed French royal family. By harping on their role in the south's REDEMPTION from the horrors of RECONSTRUCTION, the conservatives reminded populists of the French royalists, who were said to have learned nothing and forgotten nothing.

Boynton vs. Virginia (December 1 1960), Supreme Court ruling that outlawed the provision of racially segregated facilities in bus terminals serving interstate passengers. Even terminals that primarily served intrastate travel were ordered to dismantle segregated facilities. In May 1961 John Lewis (1940–), an interstate FREEDOM RIDER, attempted to act on this ruling and was beaten brutally outside a 'white-only' waiting room at the Greyhound terminal in Rock Hill, South Carolina.

Bozeman Trail, trail blazed in 1862 by John M. Bozeman (1835–67) to the goldfields of southwestern Montana. The trail began in Fort Laramie, Wyoming, and lead northwest, through the Powder river country, to Virginia City, Montana. Local SIOUX and CHEYENNE harassed users of the trail, and fought the second SIOUX WAR to prevent the USA from fortifying it.

braceros (work hands), name given to Mexican agricultural laborers in California and the southwest who had been encouraged by the USA to migrate north of the border during WORLD WAR II. Trade unionists opposed the program because employers were permitted to pay the migrants less than the minimum wage. Allegations that braceros were taking American jobs contributed to the ethnic tensions that produced the ZOOT SUIT RIOTS.

Bradley, Omar (1893–1981), US Army general. A career soldier, who was a contemporary of EISENHOWER's at West Point Military Academy, Bradley exercised command over the American contingent of ground troops during the D-DAY LANDINGS. At the height of the Normandy campaign Bradley had over one million men under his command. He said of his troops, 'Every GI to me was the son I never had.'

Brady Bill, see GUN CONTROL.

Brains Trust, nickname given to a team of advisers first assembled by Franklin D.

ROOSEVELT while he was governor of New York (1929–33). Following his election to the presidency Roosevelt reassembled the team, and relied heavily on it for advice and speech-writing as he set about formulating and enacting the NEW DEAL. Prominent members included Adolph Berle (1895–1971), Hugh Johnson (1882–1942), Raymond Moley (1886–1975), Donald Richberg (1881–1960) and Rexford Tugwell (1891–1979).

Brandeis, Louis (Dembitz) (1856–1941), Supreme Court justice. In 1916 Brandeis became the first Jewish man to be appointed to the Supreme Court, and is regarded as one of the most distinguished jurists to have served on it. He retired in 1939 to devote the remainder of his life to philanthropic work.

Brandeis received his law degree from Harvard at the age of 21. He recorded the highest grade-point average ever obtained at Harvard Law School, and established a practice in Boston. He specialized in defending the rights of trade unions and consumers, earning the nickname 'the people's attorney'. In 1906–7 he helped to persuade the Massachusetts legislature to enact a law that established low-cost pensions. In 1908 he presented arguments to the US Supreme Court in the case of MULLER VS. OREGON that helped to persuade the Court to uphold an Oregon state law limiting the hours of female workers. In this case he pioneered the use of what became known as the 'Brandeis brief': the use of compelling statistical data to demonstrate the injurious social effects of the freedom from government regulation at that time granted to big business under an expansive reading of the FOURTEENTH AMENDMENT. His nomination to the Supreme Court was opposed by the American Bar Association (on the grounds of his religion) and by big business (on the grounds of his political beliefs). Brandeis often joined Oliver Wendell HOLMES in the Court's dissenting minority.

Brandywine Creek, battle of (September 11 1777), American defeat in Pennsylvania during the REVOLUTIONARY WAR. On August 25 1777 a 12,500-strong British force landed in Maryland and marched northeast on PHILADELPHIA. On September 11, 11,000 American regulars and militiamen, commanded by WASHINGTON, attempted to prevent the British from crossing the Brandywine in the vicinity of Chad's Ford. Surprised by an outflanking maneuver, Washington's army was mauled and withdrew in disarray. Congress fled Philadelphia on hearing the news. British troops entered Philadelphia on September 26 1777.

Brant, Joseph or **Thayendnaegea** (1742–1807), anglicized member of the MOHAWK nation, and an influential leader within the IROQUOIS CONFEDERACY. During the REVOLUTIONARY WAR, Brant led many members of the confederacy in a last-ditch stand against American expansion in western New York, Pennsylvania and Ohio.

In PONTIAC'S WAR (1763–4) the Iroquois Confederacy had allied itself with Anglo-American forces fighting Ottawa, SHAWNEE and renegade SENECA warriors in the Ohio country. However, the confederacy received scant recognition for its services, and after 1776 Brant persuaded most of its members to ally themselves with Britain in a bid to halt American encroachment on their territory. In 1778 Brant led a party of mainly Mohawk warriors on a series of raids into central New York and Pennsylvania's Wyoming valley. American forces mounted SULLIVAN'S CAMPAIGN in retaliation. American troops were ordered by George WASHINGTON to destroy Brant's army and lay waste to the confederacy's settlements. Defeated in battle, Brant fled to Canada with the remnants of his army.

Breadbasket, Operation, *see* OPERATION BREADBASKET.

Breckinridge, John C(abell) (1821–75), vice president of the USA (1857–61), unsuccessful presidential candidate in 1860 and

Confederate Army officer. Born in the BORDER STATE of Kentucky, Breckinridge was a staunch defender of slavery. He served as President BUCHANAN's vice president from March 4 1857 to March 3 1861. During the PRESIDENTIAL ELECTION OF 1860 he led southern Democrats in revolt against the DEMOCRATIC PARTY's official nominee, Stephen DOUGLAS. Breckinridge campaigned as a 'National Democrat' on a platform that offered the complete protection of slaveholders' interests. He won 11 slave states and 18% of the popular vote. He joined the Confederate Army in November 1861 and fought with distinction before entering exile at the end of the Civil War.

Breedlove vs. Suttles (December 6 1937), US Supreme Court ruling that upheld unanimously the constitutionality of a Georgia law disenfranchising any adult who did not pay a poll tax. It found that poll taxes, used by southern states to prevent blacks from voting, did not contravene the FOURTEENTH or FIFTEENTH AMENDMENTS. The Court finally reversed itself in HARPER VS. VIRGINIA BOARD OF ELECTIONS (1966).

Bretton Woods Conference (July 1–22 1944), international conference held in New Hampshire that established the financial structures that governed the economies of the Western world until 1973. The influence of two of the bodies that it created – the World Bank and the International Monetary Fund – continue to this day.

The delegates to the conference, drawn from 44 nations, agreed mechanisms through which the exchange rates of the world's major currencies could be set and, if necessary, readjusted. The central feature of the system was that the relative value of each currency was assessed by reference to its individual value against gold. Gold was deemed to be worth $35 an ounce (28.3495 grams), an assessment that meant that the dollar replaced sterling as the world's strongest currency. The dollar thereby became the reserve currency in which international loans were calculated. To ensure confidence in the dollar, the US Treasury restored the convertibility of dollars to gold.

This de facto return to the GOLD STANDARD by the USA was welcomed by economists on the grounds that currency earned or expended in international trade would possess a stable and objectively determined value, and therefore the value of currency offered in repayment of debt would be secured. Without this agreement the USA would have been reluctant to lend money to finance postwar reconstruction.

The conference also established the International Bank for Reconstruction and Development (popularly known as the World Bank) to help countries rebuild their economies, participate in international trade and earn dollars. To protect currencies against speculation and instability the conference established another body, the International Monetary Fund.

Although the Soviet Union refused to participate, the Bretton Woods system worked effectively until, in 1971, President NIXON halted a run on US gold reserves by suspending the right to convert dollars to gold. This called the value of the dollar into question and threw the system into crisis. On November 12 1973 Western finance ministers agreed to let the dollar float against other major currencies at rates ultimately determined by the money markets. The US FEDERAL RESERVE Board currently attempts to control the dollar's value by adjusting US interest rates.

Brooks–Sumner incident (1856), violent confrontation in the US Senate arising out of the conflict between pro- and anti-slavery factions in Kansas. On May 19 1856 Republican Senator Charles Sumner (1811--74) made a speech in the Senate describing the 'rape' of BLEEDING KANSAS by pro-slavery BORDER RUFFIANS. His speech included personal remarks directed against Senator Andrew P. Butler of South Carolina, who was absent from the chamber. On

May 22 Butler's nephew, Representative Preston Brooks (1819–57) of South Carolina, beat Sumner savagely with a cane as he sat in the Senate chamber. Brooks escaped censure and became a hero throughout the south. Sumner's injuries kept him from Congress until December 1859. Abolitionists were outraged by the attack.

Brown, John (1800–59), radical and emotionally disturbed abolitionist. In May 1856, during the BLEEDING KANSAS upheaval, Brown took it upon himself to avenge the BROOKS–SUMNER INCIDENT by disemboweling five unarmed advocates of slavery at Pottawatomie, Kansas. Convinced of the need to 'fight fire with fire', in 1859 Brown led an ill-conceived raid on the federal arsenal at HARPER'S FERRY. This was defeated, and Brown was hanged, together with six of his companions. Many northerners and most abolitionists disavowed Brown, although a minority exulted that his soul went 'marching on'. Brown's actions united the south in condemnation. *See also* ABOLITION.

Brown vs. Board of Education of Topeka (May 17 1954), unanimous US Supreme Court ruling that segregating pupils in public school systems by race contravened a citizen's right to equal protection under the law. The ruling reversed PLESSY VS. FERGUSON (1896), which had permitted 'separate but equal' provision in racially segregated public institutions. Attempts to enforce the Brown ruling in LITTLE ROCK, Arkansas, prompted white resistance, which attracted national and international attention. Returning to the case on May 13 1955, the Court now directed lower courts to oversee the desegregation of public school systems 'with all deliberate speed'.

Both rulings provoked outrage in southern states. Alabama's Senate passed a 'nullification' resolution on January 19 1956, and Virginia's legislature pledged on February 1 1956 to interpose its authority to prevent enforcement of the order. 'White citizens' councils' were formed in many southern towns to defend segregation. Groups within the CIVIL RIGHTS MOVEMENT, notably the NATIONAL ASSOCIATION FOR THE ADVANCEMENT OF COLORED PEOPLE (NAACP), campaigned to ensure that the order was enforced, and brought legal actions against recalcitrant school districts.

Bryan, William Jennings (1860–1925), Democratic politician and lawyer, with strong populist tendencies, who ran three times for the presidency, and was later secretary of state (1913–15) in Woodrow WILSON's administration. He is also remembered for his anti-evolution stance in his role as prosecutor in the SCOPES TRIAL.

Bryan, who was born in Illinois and trained as a lawyer at Union College, Chicago, moved to Lincoln, Nebraska, in 1887. He joined the DEMOCRATIC PARTY but sympathized with the main goals of POPULISM. After two terms in the US House of Representatives (1891–5), he was defeated in a bid to be elected to the US Senate because he opposed repeal of the SHERMAN SILVER PURCHASE ACT. National speaking tours explaining the benefits and justice of FREE SILVER made Bryan a household name. His 'CROSS OF GOLD' SPEECH at the Democratic convention in Chicago (July 8 1896) brought the SILVER–GOLD CONTROVERSY to boiling point and secured him the Democratic nomination to run for president. During the 1896 campaign Bryan (who was also endorsed by the PEOPLE'S PARTY) traveled 18,000 miles (29,000 km) in three months and addressed an estimated 5 million people. He came within 600,000 votes of McKINLEY, but shrewd spending by the REPUBLICANS in key midwestern states secured them a handy victory in the ELECTORAL COLLEGE.

The Democrats nominated Bryan again in 1900. Running on a platform that called for the return of territory acquired during the SPANISH-AMERICAN WAR, Bryan was soundly beaten – even his home state of

Nebraska went for McKinley. From 1901 Bryan broadcast his views to the party faithful through the pages of *The Commoner*. For western and southern Democrats he remained the conscience of their party. In 1908, to the consternation of party managers, Bryan stampeded the Democratic convention in Denver into nominating him for a third presidential bid. He was trounced by William H. TAFT by 321 to 162 in the electoral college.

In 1913 Woodrow WILSON made Bryan secretary of state. Bryan had supported Wilson for the presidency, despite the fact that at the 1912 Democratic convention Wilson had hoped to see Bryan and his views 'knocked into a cocked hat'. Bryan, a life-long pacifist, resigned on June 7 1915 because he believed Wilson's response to the sinking of the *Lusitania* would drag the USA into WORLD WAR I.

Bryan's stern Protestantism led him to embrace the SOCIAL GOSPEL and reject SOCIAL DARWINISM. He was a staunch defender of the account of the creation revealed in the Bible and an opponent of Charles Darwin's theory of evolution. Bryan's rejection of Darwinian thought culminated shortly before his death in the famous SCOPES trial, in which he prosecuted a Tennessee schoolteacher for teaching the theory of evolution. He won a conviction, but was made to look out of touch and scientifically ignorant by defense attorney Clarence Darrow (1857–1938). Among the other causes Bryan supported were PROHIBITION, WOMEN'S SUFFRAGE and a progressive INCOME TAX.

Buchanan, James (1791–1868), Democratic statesman and 15th president of the USA (1857–61). His compromises on slavery failed to prevent the secession of the southern states. He is unique among presidents in that he never married.

Buchanan began his political career as a FEDERALIST congressman from Pennsylvania. He became a JACKSONIAN Democrat after 1828. Buchanan served as minister to Russia

(1832–3), secretary of state (1845–9) and minister to Britain (1853–6). In 1844, 1848 and 1852 he failed to secure nomination as the Democrats' presidential candidate. He was ultimately nominated and elected because his temporizing style was thought likely to prevent southern secession. He served as president from March 4 1857 to March 3 1861.

Buchanan believed slavery to be immoral: but he helped draft the OSTEND MANIFESTO, approved of the Supreme Court's ruling in DRED SCOTT VS. SANDFORD, and was prepared to resolve the BLEEDING KANSAS issue by accepting the LECOMPTON CONSTITUTION. These compromises did not prevent southern secession following Abraham LINCOLN's victory in the 1860 presidential election, but they did lead fellow Pennsylvanian and RADICAL REPUBLICAN Thaddeus STEVENS to describe Buchanan as 'a bloated mass of political putridity'.

Buena Vista, battle of (February 22–23 1847), engagement in Mexico during the MEXICAN WAR in which US forces were victorious. Prior to the battle, General Zachary TAYLOR – his force reduced to some 600 regulars and 4000 volunteers by order of President POLK – had waged a skillful campaign in northern Mexico. This ultimately drew a Mexican force of 15,000 into a carefully chosen defensive site in the La Angostura mountains. On February 22–23 Taylor's troops repulsed repeated Mexican attacks. The broken Mexican army retreated southwards, but Taylor lacked the force to follow up. He asked to be relieved of command soon after the victory and returned to the USA a national hero.

Buffalo Bill, nickname given to William Fredrick Cody (1846–1917), frontiersman and showman. Cody was born in Iowa, but grew up in Kansas. During his life on the Great Plains he served as a scout for the US army (and later for private hunters), carried messages for the forerunners of the Pony Express and hunted buffalo to feed railroad workers constructing the transcontinental link. He also tried his hand at mining, ranching and real estate development. In 1872, Cody was hired to play a frontiersman in a western melodrama staged in Chicago. He worked as an actor for several years before organizing his own, open-air, 'Wild West' show in 1883. This show, and spin-offs from it, established the buckskin-clad 'Buffalo Bill' as a mythic figure across the industrialized world. The Wild West Show, which featured practical demonstrations of frontiersmens' skills and re-enactments of historic events such as the battle of LITTLE BIG HORN, exerted an influence on popular culture comparable to that of the FRONTIER THESIS on academic culture. In later years, the SIOUX leader SITTING BULL was among the show's most popular attractions. Cody died broke, following an unwise mining investment.

buffalo soldiers, name given by Native American warriors to African-American soldiers, organized in four segregated US Army units (the 9th and 10th Cavalry, and the 24th and 25th Infantry regiments), who fought against them in nearly 200 engagements on the Great Plains. As the 9th Cavalry's actions following the massacre at WOUNDED KNEE showed, African-American soldiers could be just as uncompromising and vengeful toward Native Americans as their white colleagues.

Bulge, battle of the (December 16–26 1944), the largest and most important battle between US and German forces in the European theatre during WORLD WAR II.

As Allied forces advanced on Germany, the British Seventh and US Ninth Armies (campaigning through the Netherlands and northern Belgium) became detached from both the US First Army (operating in central-southern Belgium) and General PATTON's Third Army even further to the south. The Germans committed 25 divisions to a massive counter-attack through the Ardennes forest whose objective was to split the First Army from the Seventh and Ninth and ultimately recapture the vital deep-water port of Antwerp.

Exploiting surprise, bad weather, the inexperience of many First Army units and imaginative sabotage by elite commandos, the Germans drove US troops back and created a 'bulge' 50 miles (80 km) deep into Allied lines. Between December 22 and 26 the 101st Airborne Division mounted a suicidal defense of Bastogne, Belgium, which delayed the German advance long enough for reinforcements from Patton's Third Army to steady the line. When German officers asked the 101st's commander General Anthony McAuliffe (1898–1975) to surrender Bastogne he replied, 'Nuts.' During the battle of the Bulge 19,000 US soldiers died and 47,000 were wounded. However, the failure of their last counteroffensive made German defeat inevitable.

Bull Moose campaign, see PRESIDENTIAL ELECTION OF 1912.

Bull Run, battles of, see MANASSAS, BATTLES OF.

Bunker Hill, battle of (June 17 1775), engagement near Boston during the REVOLUTIONARY WAR in which the Americans claimed victory over the British. It was the first major battle of the war, and also the bloodiest.

On June 17 1775, 2400 British troops under Sir William Howe dislodged 1600 American soldiers under the command of William Prescott (1726–95) from fortified positions overlooking Boston. Although the British secured their objective, the Americans claimed victory because they inflicted 1054 casualties while suffering 367. News of the engagement prompted George III to reject the OLIVE-BRANCH PETITION.

Burgoyne, John (1722–92), British general during the REVOLUTIONARY WAR. In the spring and summer of 1777 Burgoyne led a column of 6000 British regulars and Hessian mercenaries in an invasion of New York State. His surrender at SARATOGA transformed the war by convincing France to ratify the FRANCO-AMERICAN ALLIANCE.

Burnside, Ambrose (Everett) (1824–81), Union Army general in the CIVIL WAR. A career soldier, Burnside led the Army of the Potomac to defeat at FREDERICKSBURG (1862). During the battle Burnside dissipated an overwhelming numerical superiority over Confederate forces in a series of six head-on charges against fortified positions. In January 1863 he was reassigned to the Ohio theater of operations, but in 1864 he was brought back to the Virginia front, this time under the direct supervision of Ulysses GRANT. Burnside exercised operational command over Union troops at the disastrous battle of PETERSBURG (1864), and was censured by a subsequent court of investigation. He resigned his command in 1865. Burnside is chiefly famous for his distinctive facial whiskers, and such adornments have ever since been known as 'sideburns'.

Burr, Aaron (1756–1836), Democratic statesman and vice president of the USA (1801–5). While vice president, Burr mortally wounded Alexander HAMILTON in a duel fought at Weehawken, New Jersey, on July 11 1804. This incident curtailed a political career in which Burr had helped define the DEMOCRATIC PARTY and shape the conduct of presidential politics.

Burr studied theology and law at Princeton. With the outbreak of the REVOLUTIONARY WAR, in 1775 he participated in Benedict ARNOLD's ill-fated attack on QUEBEC. Promoted to lieutenant colonel and assigned to WASHINGTON's staff, Burr organized a valuable spy network. At the conclusion of the war, Burr moved to New York City to practice law. He served as New York's attorney general (1789–91), as one of the state's US senators (1791–7) and as a state assemblyman (1797–9). During this period, Burr distanced himself from the state's DEMOCRATIC-REPUBLICAN societies while maintaining working relations with the state's ascendant FEDERALIST leadership. In the presidential election of 1796 he received 30 votes in the ELECTORAL COLLEGE.

Concluding that with Burr he could carry New York State, JEFFERSON chose Burr as his running-mate in the PRESIDENTIAL ELECTION OF 1800. Enlisting the support of the Sons of St TAMMANY, Burr duly delivered the state. But although Jefferson and Burr out-polled their opponents, tactical voting in the ELECTORAL COLLEGE, designed to deny Jefferson the presidency, resulted in the Democratic running-mates each receiving 73 electoral votes. To Jefferson's fury, Burr did not step quietly into the vice presidency. Thus, in accordance with the Constitution, the election was resolved in the US House of Representatives. After 35 ballots, Jefferson was declared president and Burr his deputy.

Alexander Hamilton's role in swinging New York's congressional delegation against Burr during the adjudication of the election of 1800 marked an intensification of the long-standing political rivalry between the two men. Hamilton's subsequent campaign to discredit Burr and regain control of New York politics led him to accuse Burr of gross immorality – the proximate cause of their celebrated duel. Following Hamilton's death in the duel, warrants were issued for Burr's arrest and he was dumped by Jefferson although he was still technically vice president.

Burr fled to Philadelphia and became involved with quixotic western expansionists. He was the alleged mastermind behind a rumored secession of western states and invasion of Mexico. Arrested in Alabama in 1806, he was tried for treason in Richmond, Virginia, with Chief Justice MARSHALL presiding. Acquitted on March 30 1807, Burr went into exile. On his return from Europe in 1812, he resumed the practice of law in New York City.

Bush, George (Herbert Walker) (1924–), Republican statesman, vice president to Ronald REAGAN (1981–9) and 41st president of the USA (1989–93). He was the first sitting vice president since Martin VAN BUREN to be elected to the presidency.

Raised in an affluent WASP family, Bush volunteered for service as a US Navy pilot during WORLD WAR II before attending Yale. In 1948 he moved to Texas to begin a career in the oil business. Here he became active in Republican circles and planned his political future. In 1964 he unsuccessfully sought election to the US Senate from Texas. His campaign endorsed Barry GOLD-WATER's uncompromising conservatism. Bush was elected to the US House of Representatives, in which he sat from 1967 to 1971, by running as a moderate with enlightened views on CIVIL RIGHTS.

After another unsuccessful Senate bid, he persuaded NIXON to appoint him US ambassador to the UNITED NATIONS (1971–3). In this role he served as Nixon's unofficial spokesman on the New York party circuit. Nixon made him chairman of the Republican Party in 1973, and Bush defended Nixon throughout the WATERGATE SCANDAL. President FORD declined to nominate Bush for the vice presidency and instead designated him as the USA's representative in China (1974–5). Ford then leant on Bush to accept the directorship of the CENTRAL INTELLIGENCE AGENCY (1975–7).

From 1977 Bush campaigned for the Republican presidential nomination. He was beaten by Reagan, who chose Bush as his running-mate in the 1980 presidential election despite the fact that Bush had derided his tax-cutting proposals as 'voodoo economics'. Bush spent two terms as Reagan's vice president (1981–9). He claimed misleadingly that he played no part in the IRAN–CONTRA SCANDAL because he was 'out of the loop'.

Chosen as the Republican presidential candidate in 1988, Bush struggled to define or articulate his beliefs beyond stating that he wished to create a 'kinder, gentler' America. Political commentators described him as a 'wimp'. Nevertheless, Bush's glitzy and often negative campaign, during which he repeatedly said 'Read my lips – no new taxes,' gave him a decisive victory over Michael DUKAKIS. Bush took 54% of the POPULAR VOTE to Dukakis's 46%, and 426 ELECTORAL VOTES to Dukakis's 111.

Bush's presidency (January 20 1989– January 20 1993) would have been remembered for the failure of his 'War on Drugs', the SAVINGS AND LOANS SCANDAL and a widely condemned invasion of PANAMA, were it not for the PERSIAN GULF WAR. Although he was criticized for not ordering allied troops into Baghdad, Bush received credit for the success of the war. But this was not enough to prevent his defeat by Bill CLINTON in 1992.

bussing, a policy, beginning in the 1960s, of transporting black students to schools in predominantly white areas, and sometimes white students to 'black' schools, in an attempt to provide equal opportunities in education.

Federal courts began ordering US school districts to implement bussing in the 1960s in a bid to observe the letter and spirit of the Supreme Court's BROWN VS. BOARD OF EDUCATION ruling (1954). In the PRESIDENTIAL ELECTIONS OF 1968 and 1972 both Richard NIXON and George WALLACE sought the votes of whites angered by this policy. The Supreme Court upheld the constitutionality of bussing in SWANN VS. CHARLOTTE-MECKLENBERG BOARD OF EDUCATION (1971). But, in its 1974 ruling on Milliken vs. Bradley, it outlawed the most politically sensitive aspect of the policy – bussing white suburban children into predominantly black inner-city schools. However, unease continued among white parents who objected to the bussing of black students into 'their' schools. In the spring of 1976, white parents in South Boston mounted a major protest against bussing, which was closely watched by officials in other cities. This event forced a radical overhaul of the policy.

C

Cahuenga, treaty of (January 13 1847), treaty ending organized Mexican resistance to US rule in CALIFORNIA, following the US capture of Los Angeles. Mexican residents were afforded the rights of US citizens, and their property was safeguarded. A more general peace ending the MEXICAN WAR was established by the treaty of GUADALUPE-HIDALGO (February 2 1848).

cajuns, shorthand term used to describe descendents of French settlers ('Acadians') exiled from Canada during the SEVEN YEARS' WAR, who settled in LOUISIANA.

Some 6000 French Catholics in Nova Scotia and New Brunswick (known to the French as Acadia) refused to swear allegiance to the British forces that occupied the region in 1755. They were forcibly deported and many eventually made their way to Louisiana, which was then under Spanish jurisdiction. The 'cajun' people founded a sub-culture which still flourishes in rural sections of the state. Cajun culture boasts a distinctive cuisine (featuring spicy and 'blackened' dishes), an infectious music known as zydeco and a distinctive French patois.

Calhoun, John C(aldwell) (1782–1850), Democratic statesman who held various government posts, including vice president of the USA (1825–32). A champion of the southern slave states, he became a notable defender of STATES' RIGHTS, and was the chief advocate of NULLIFICATION (the theory that states had the right to nullify any federal law they believed to be unconstitutional). Calhoun was a leading member of that political generation (whose other luminaries were Henry CLAY and Daniel WEBSTER) that shaped and maintained the SECOND PARTY SYSTEM, but lived to see it torn apart by conflict between the slave states of the south and the 'free' states of the north.

Born in South Carolina, Calhoun was educated at Yale and trained as a lawyer. His earliest political positions reflected a nationalist perspective. He applauded the US decision to fight Britain in the WAR OF 1812 and supported the protective TARIFF of 1816. He served as secretary of war under President MONROE (1817–25) and as US vice president under both John Quincy ADAMS and Andrew JACKSON (1825–32). In 1826 Calhoun was charged with committing corruption while secretary of war, but was exonerated by a select committee of the House of Representatives in 1827.

Meanwhile Calhoun expressed increasing opposition to tariff policies that protected northern manufacturers at the expense of southern planters. President Jackson's role in formulating the TARIFF OF ABOMINATIONS alienated Calhoun, while the role of Calhoun's wife in the Peggy EATON affair angered Jackson. In December 1832 Calhoun resigned the vice presidency (one of only two men to do so) to accept a Senate seat representing South Carolina.

By this time Calhoun was known to be the author of the SOUTH CAROLINA EXPOSITION AND PROTEST, and was accepted as the chief theorist of nullification. Calhoun's subsequent career was dominated by the defense of states' rights and of slavery, themes which he addressed powerfully in debate over the WILMOT PROVISO. Although as secretary of state in President TYLER's administration (1844–5) Calhoun had presided over the annexation of TEXAS, he opposed the MEXICAN WAR, CALIFORNIA statehood and the COMPROMISE OF 1850 on the grounds that northerners would use the expansion of the Union to attack slaveholders' interests.

Although Calhoun sought to contain the effects of the positions he had developed through the theory of a CONCURRENT MAJORITY, his career helped create an uncompromising and suspicious southern faction within the DEMOCRATIC PARTY, and thus made CIVIL WAR more likely

California, large state on the Pacific coast of the USA, bordered by Oregon to the north, Nevada and Arizona to the east and Mexico to the south. Permanent European settlement began in 1769 and Los Angeles was founded in 1781. In 1846 US settlers mounted the BEAR FLAG REVOLT against Mexican rule. Mexican resistance was ended by the treaty of CAHUENGA (1847) and the USA secured title to California through the treaty of GUADALUPE-HIDALGO (1848). At this time the territory's combined Mexican and American population totalled 14,000. On January 24 1848 gold was discovered at Sutter's Mill in northern California. Newspaper reports of the discovery sparked a gold rush in 1849 and by 1852, despite the departure of thousands of disappointed 'forty-niners,' the state's population exceeded 250,000. California's prompt admission to the Union was achieved through the COMPROMISE OF 1850: it became the 31st state on September 9 1850.

Over the next century California continued to receive immigrants and internal migrants. 75,000 Chinese and Japanese men settled in California between 1850–1880. This prompted a NATIVIST backlash. Congress barred further immigration from China through the CHINESE EXCLUSION ACT (1882) while Japan limited emigration through the 'Gentleman's Agreements' with the USA (1900, 1906–7). (Following PEARL HARBOR, President Franklin D. ROOSEVELT authorized the RELOCATION OF JAPANESE-AMERICANS resident in California and other Pacific coast states). In the 1930s California received reluctantly some 400,000 'Okies' fleeing the DUST BOWL. During WORLD WAR II Californian employers recruited hundreds of thousands of Mexican workers through the BRACERO programme. These influxes created further nativist anxieties among the established population which flared up during the ZOOT SUIT RIOTS.

The state has always enjoyed robust and diverse economic development, with major strengths in mining, manufacturing, agricultural production and, more recently, the entertainment industry centered on HOLLYWOOD. It became the most populous state in the Union in 1964 and in 1990 had 29,760,021 residents.

California has also enjoyed a turbulent political history, partly because state law allows residents to petition to place legislative initiatives, known as 'propositions', before the electorate. (The most famous use of this system occurred in 1978 when Californians approved a tax cut by voting in favor of Proposition 13.) California's decision to grant women the vote in 1911 was a major turning point in the struggle for WOMEN'S SUFFRAGE. In 1934 Upton Sinclair (1878–1968), running on a ticket that promised to End Poverty in California (EPIC), narrowly failed to be elected governor of California. During the COLD WAR Hollywood pioneered the use of BLACKLISTS and Californian native Richard NIXON's victory in a 1950 Senate race showed the popularity of RED-BAITING rhetoric with the state's voters. During the 1960s Californians helped define cultural trends that influenced the nation and much of the world. The state was a major center of the ANTIWAR MOVEMENT. Activists Cesar CHAVEZ, Ernesto GALARZA and the BLACK PANTHER PARTY introduced new themes to the CIVIL RIGHTS MOVEMENT. The WATTS RIOT (1965) gave warning of the alienation felt by minorities living in US cities. The WOMEN'S MOVEMENT and GAY RIGHTS MOVEMENT have enjoyed strong support in the state. Partly as a consequence, many Californians, especially the elderly and males living in southern California became uncompromising opponents of AFFIRMATIVE ACTION and supporters of tax-cutting SUPPLY-SIDE ECONOMICS. Former Governors who achieved national prominence include Hiram JOHNSON (1911–17), Earl WARREN (1945–53) and Ronald REAGAN (1967–75).

Cambodia, US operations in. During the VIETNAM WAR the USA destroyed the rule of law in Cambodia, and indirectly facilitated the creation of Pol Pot's genocidal Khmer Rouge regime.

Cambodia was officially a neutral country when in March 1969 incoming US President NIXON ordered a campaign of bombing raids against suspected Viet Cong and North Vietnamese bases and supply lines inside Cambodian territory. This decision was illegal because Nixon had no congressional authorization to mount the campaign, and he went to extraordinary lengths – even devising clandestine methods of Pentagon bookkeeping – to keep the existence of the bombing campaign from public or congressional scrutiny. 3630 B-52 sorties were flown against Cambodian targets before Operation Menu was halted in June 1970.

A coup on March 18 1970 brought a pro-Western warlord, Lon Nol, to power in Cambodia. Nol appealed for US assistance and Nixon responded by ordering 32,000 US and 50,000 South Vietnamese troops to invade the Parrot's Beak and Fishhook areas of Cambodia in a bid to capture the supposed nerve center of North Vietnamese operations against South Vietnam. Nixon announced the invasions on April 30 1970, ten days after they had begun and long after communist forces had fled their Cambodian 'sanctuaries'.

Nixon's invasion came as the USA was publicly committed to withdrawing troops from Vietnam. Major ANTIWAR MOVEMENT protests, including the tragic KENT STATE demonstration, erupted across the USA. Although Nixon withdrew the troops in June, Congress, furious at Nixon's secrecy, repealed the TONKIN GULF RESOLUTION in a bid to prevent him from mounting a further escalation of the war.

North Vietnam concluded from Nixon's actions that it needed a pro-communist Cambodia to protect the flanks of a unified Vietnam. After the USA withdrew from Vietnam in 1973, Cambodia was plunged into civil war from which the communist Khmer Rouge emerged victorious in 1974, although it was later to clash with the Vietnamese, who took over the country in 1978. The tragedy was that Nixon, acting on the logic of the 'MAD DOG' STRATEGY, felt he had to wage war against Cambodia to convince Hanoi that he was serious about peace in Vietnam.

Camden, battle of (August 16 1780), American defeat during the REVOLUTIONARY WAR. In the summer of 1780 General Horatio GATES led a force of 1000 American regulars and 1100 militiamen on a mission to capture British supplies at Camden, South Carolina. Under the command of Lieutenant General Charles CORNWALLIS 2100 British troops surprised and comprehensively defeated Gates's men. It was the heaviest American defeat of the war: 250 Americans were killed, 800 wounded and 800 captured.

Cannon, Joseph Gurney (1836–1926), Republican politician and staunch opponent of reform. Cannon entered the US House of Representatives in 1872 and served 46 years in Congress. As Speaker of the US House of Representatives (1903–11) 'Uncle Joe' Cannon appointed 'Old Guard' Republican opponents of reform to crucial committees. His motto was, 'This country is a hell of a success. Don't muck with it.' His hostility to reform and his defense of the Speaker's prerogatives led him into a conflict with the liberal wing of his own party and with presidents Theodore ROOSEVELT and Robert TAFT. (Cannon once said of Taft that if he were Pope he would want to appoint some Protestants to the college of cardinals.) Cannon's stranglehold on the House of Representatives was broken by the progressive Republican George NORRIS.

Capone, Alphonse 'Al' (1899–1947) notorious gangster. Capone was born in an Italian neighbourhood of Brooklyn, New York. While working as a bartender and bouncer he was slashed by a razor in a street fight and became known as 'Scarface' in underworld circles. He moved to Chicago and, following the adoption of PROHIBITION, made a fortune from bootlegging, gambling and prostitution. Capone bought off local law enforcement officials and ruthlessly suppressed rival gangs. Capone's arrogance, and the violence of events such as the St Valentine's Day Massacre (1929), fascinated America and made his headquarters on the outskirts of Chicago, the town of Cicero, Illinois, a byword. Capone's activities also contributed to the WICKERSHAM REPORT's conclusion that prohibition was unenforcable. Capone was indicted on charges of income tax evasion in 1931. He was eventually sentenced to an eleven-year prison term. He was released from prison in 1939 on the grounds of ill-health and died of syphilis eight years later on his Florida estate.

Caraway, Hattie (Ophelia Wyatt), *see* ARKANSAS.

Carlisle Indian School, the first educational establishment for Native Americans built outside the confines of a reservation, established with federal assistance in a former military barracks in Carlisle, Pennsylvania, in 1879. The school's first director, Richard Henry Pratt (1840–1924), summed up its philosophy as 'kill the Indian and spare the man'. Among the school's inmates were younger members of GERONIMO's band. Few of its pupils underwent the cultural transformation Pratt sought to achieve. The school's most famous alumnus was Jim THORPE.

Carlisle peace commission (1778), delegation, headed by the Earl of Carlisle, dispatched to America by the British Parliament during the REVOLUTIONARY WAR to offer peace terms that met most American demands save recognition of US independence. The strategic aim of the commission was to avert a FRANCO-AMERICAN ALLIANCE. Congress decreed (April 22 1778) that any American negotiating with the commissioners would be branded a traitor. The commission offered bribes to congressmen, and also published an appeal to the American people threatening a war of destruction if US resistance continued. News of the Franco-American alliance rendered the commission redundant.

Carmichael, Stokeley (1941–98), African-American activist. Born in Trinidad and raised in Harlem, Carmichael popularized the slogan BLACK POWER, and in the process transformed the CIVIL RIGHTS MOVEMENT. After participating in the FREEDOM RIDER campaign, Carmichael joined a voter-registration project in Mississippi organized by the STUDENT NONVIOLENT COORDINATING COMMITTEE (SNCC). He became a leading light within the SNCC, and in 1966 was elected its president. Carmichael helped to found the LOWNDES COUNTY FREEDOM ORGANIZATION (LCFO) (1966), and it was in the context of speeches defending the LCFO that Carmichael spoke of 'black power'. Although Carmichael initially opposed expelling SNCC's white members, as its president he implemented the policy. He also developed close links with the BLACK PANTHER PARTY. Carmichael was a fast-talking character who once joked bitterly that he could only ever pronounce 'three-fifths' of the word 'Constitution' (*see* CONNECTICUT COMPROMISE). His remark to the effect that women could best further the cause of black power by gratifying the sexual needs of male activists was seized upon by the WOMEN'S MOVEMENT. In 1973, acting on the teachings of Marcus GARVEY, Carmichael emigrated to Uganda and assumed the name Kwame Ture. He never resumed permanent residence in the USA.

Carnegie, Andrew (1835–1919), Scottish-born industrialist and philanthropist. An industrial titan of the GILDED AGE, Carnegie achieved lasting fame in his retirement for giving over most of his personal fortune to philanthropic projects.

Carnegie emigrated to the USA from Scotland in 1848. He worked in the Pittsburgh offices of the Western Union Telegraph Company before becoming the personal telegrapher and private secretary of Thomas Scott, the general superintendent of the Pennsylvania Railroad Company. In this post Carnegie learnt the value of a constant attention to costs. He also augmented his salary by shrewd stock-market investments. During the CIVIL WAR Scott, who served as assistant secretary of war, appointed Carnegie superintendent of the eastern division of the Union Army's telegraph network. He performed ably.

At the end of the war Carnegie branched out on his own, founding the Union Iron Mills in 1868. He concentrated on steel production from 1873 and set about building a vertically integrated production network. Carnegie refused all pleas from rival steelmakers to join cartels or TRUSTS, and by driving down costs through rigorous accounting procedures and constant investment in new technology forced his competitors to sell out to him. He expected his workers to share his philosophy, and in 1892 provoked the bitter HOMESTEAD STEEL STRIKE to smash a union standing in the way of business efficiency. Carnegie became the world's dominant steelmaker. America's skyscrapers, New York's Brooklyn Bridge and a new US Navy were all built from Carnegie steel. In 1900 the annual profits of the Carnegie Steel Company were estimated at $40 million. In 1901 Carnegie sold his entire holdings to J.P. MORGAN's US Steel Corporation for $447 million and retired.

As early as 1886 Carnegie had argued that while it was acceptable to make money it was morally unacceptable to die without having given to the community. He developed these ideas in the widely read *The Gospel of Wealth* (1900). Carnegie founded New York's Carnegie Hall for the performing arts in 1892. After his retirement he established a network of institutions and agencies including the Carnegie Institution (1902), the Carnegie Foundation for the Advancement of Teaching (1906) and the Carnegie Endowment for International Peace (1910). A financial report issued on Carnegie's death showed that he had given $350 million to various philanthropic projects.

Carolinas, *see* NORTH CAROLINA, SOUTH CAROLINA.

***Caroline* affair,** diplomatic episode arising from an incident in 1837 when the US steamer *Caroline*, carrying supplies for a movement seeking to overthrow British rule in Canada, was seized by Canadian militia in American waters and burnt. One American died. The resulting furore complicated and prolonged negotiations with Britain concerning the Canadian border, which led ultimately to the WEBSTER-ASHBURTON TREATY.

carpetbaggers, pejorative term which was applied by white southern REDEEMERS to northerners who went south to assist in RECONSTRUCTION. 'Carpetbaggers' were presumed to be motivated by a desire for personal enrichment, a misplaced affection for blacks, or by pure mischief. They were often targets of mob violence.

Carson, Rachel (1907–64), biologist and environmentalist. While working as a marine biologist in the US Bureau of Fisheries, Carson published articles, pamphlets and two bestselling books, *The Sea Around Us* (1951) and *The Edge of the Sea* (1955), alerting the US public to the destruction of aquatic environments. Her final work, *Silent Spring* (1962), has been credited with kick-starting the modern environmental movement in the USA. In it Carson assailed the unsupervised use of pesticides such as DDT. She suggested that a demonstrable decline among certain bird species could be traced to the effect of chemicals on birds eggs. The dystopic metaphor of a future world without birdsong captured the public imagination, while Carson's scientific hypotheses were officially endorsed by President Kennedy's Science Advisory Committee. In 1973 the USA banned the agricultural use of DDT.

Carter Doctrine, policy announced in President CARTER's State of the Union address on January 23 1980 asserting that the USA would repel, by 'any means necessary including military force', all attempts by 'outside' powers to gain control of the Persian Gulf. The doctrine identified Gulf oil reserves as vital to US interests, and it was cited by President BUSH as a justification for the PERSIAN GULF WAR.

Carter, Jimmy (James Earl Carter) (1924–), Democratic statesman and 39th president of the USA (1977–81). His idealistic presidency foundered under the weight of international crises over which he had little control.

Carter attended the US Naval Academy at Annapolis, Maryland, and between 1946 and 1953 was a career naval officer, participating in the development of America's nuclear submarine fleet. When his father died Carter resigned his commission and returned to Plains, Georgia, to manage the family peanut farm. He served in the state Senate (1963–7), and had one term as governor of Georgia (1971–5).

Carter was the darkest of dark horse candidates for the Democrats' nomination in the presidential election of 1976. Running on a platform that stressed restoring trust in government following the WATERGATE SCANDAL, Carter narrowly defeated incumbent President FORD by 297 to 240 in the ELECTORAL COLLEGE. His ill-fated presidency began on January 20 1977 and lasted until January 20 1981.

Carter's domestic program called for full employment, the creation of a national energy policy and the deregulation of major transportation industries. In foreign policy he stressed human rights, continued DÉTENTE and returned the PANAMA CANAL zone to Panama. But pressured to respond forcefully to the IRANIAN HOSTAGE CRISIS and the Soviet invasion of Afghanistan, Carter abandoned much of the idealism he had brought to foreign policy. For example, the CARTER DOCTRINE, announced in January 1980, applied traditional CONTAINMENT strategy to the Persian Gulf. Some of Carter's presidential pronouncements, notably the 'CRISIS OF CONFIDENCE' SPEECH, reflected an introspective Christianity that irritated many Americans. Although he again secured the Democrats' nomination in 1980, he was decisively defeated in the presidential election by Ronald REAGAN. However, his work with the underprivileged and in various international conflict-resolution missions since 1981 has contributed to a partial rehabilitation of his reputation.

Casablanca Conference (January 14–24 1943), summit meeting between Allied leaders Franklin ROOSEVELT and Winston Churchill in Morocco during WORLD WAR II. Stalin had been invited to attend, but declined on the grounds that the Stalingrad campaign was in a critical phase. Roosevelt and Churchill agreed that the Allies would demand the 'unconditional surrender' of Germany, but failed to agree on the best site for a joint invasion of Nazi-occupied Europe.

Catt, Carrie Chapman (1859–1947), formidable campaigner for WOMEN'S SUFFRAGE, who favored the tactic of persuading states to enfranchise women as a means of building pressure for a constitutional amendment. As Susan B. ANTHONY's successor as president (1900–4) of the NATIONAL AMERICAN WOMAN SUFFRAGE ASSOCIATION (NAWSA), Catt committed the organization to action at state level. In 1911 she led pro-suffrage forces to a narrow victory in a California state referendum, which revitalized the entire women's suffrage movement. She resumed the presidency of NAWSA in 1915 and masterminded its final triumphant campaigns. Following passage of the NINE-TEENTH AMENDMENT (1919), which gave women the vote, Catt became the first president of the League of Women Voters. Catt was a pacifist. In 1915 she formed the WOMEN'S PEACE PARTY to campaign against US entry into WORLD WAR I and chaired the Commission on the Cause and Cure of War between 1925–32. During the 1930s Catt came to the conclusion that Hitler's Nazi regime had to be opposed by force.

Cedar Falls, Operation, *see* OPERATION CEDAR FALLS.

CENTO, *see* CENTRAL TREATY ORGANIZATION.

Central Intelligence Agency (CIA), the USA's most prominent intelligence-gathering organization. It was established on July 26 1947 as part of an omnibus National Security Act, which also created the NATIONAL SECURITY COUNCIL. During the COLD WAR the CIA mounted covert operations around the world in support of US CONTAINMENT policy. CIA agents were particularly active in Southeast Asia prior to, and during, US involvement in the VIETNAM WAR.

The agency's enormous budget and secret status allowed it to mount an extraordinary range of sometimes bizarre operations. For example, in a bid to demonstrate to the world that American culture was not dominated by mindless materialism, the CIA in the 1950s helped to create a market for the work of abstract expressionist painters such as Jackson Pollock. Hoping to discredit Cuban revolutionary leader Fidel Castro, CIA agents attempted to feed him drugs that would cause his distinctive beard to fall out. More damagingly, the CIA trained and bankrolled the army of Cuban exiles that unsuccessfully attempted to overthrow Castro in the BAY OF PIGS invasion of 1961. In 1973 the agency helped to overthrow a democratically elected socialist regime in Chile and install in its place a military dictatorship led by General Augusto Pinochet. In the 1980s the CIA conducted covert operations against the left-wing Sandinista regime in Nicaragua, and was involved in the IRAN–CONTRA SCANDAL.

The CIA's remit to conduct intelligence gathering and covert action extends only to operations mounted outside the borders of the USA. The agency has violated this charter, most notoriously in the case of OPERATION CHAOS, a domestic surveillance operation mounted against members of the Vietnam-era ANTIWAR MOVEMENT. In 1974 Congress imposed tougher oversight procedures on the agency, and has sought since to prevent the CIA from using assassination as a tool to influence world affairs.

Central Treaty Organization (CENTO), mutual defense alliance between Turkey, Iraq, Iran, Pakistan and Britain, created by the Baghdad Pact in 1955 as the Middle East Treaty Organization. In 1959 Iraq left, the organization became CENTO and the USA became an associate member as part of its COLD WAR policy of CONTAINMENT. Iran left in 1979 following the fall of the Shah, and the organization was dissolved.

Chae Chan Ping vs. US (May 13 1889), US Supreme Court ruling that unanimously upheld the constitutionality of the CHINESE EXCLUSION ACT (1882). The Court argued that control over IMMIGRATION was a fundamental component of national sovereignty. In 1893 the Court ruled (in Fong Yue Ting vs. US) that Chinese residents could be deported without due process.

Challenger disaster, the destruction of the NASA space shuttle *Challenger* by an in-flight explosion at 11:40 EST on January 28 1986. The explosion, captured on TV and visible from the ground, killed seven astronauts instantly and led to a major public investigation during which all shuttle flights were suspended. Among those killed was Christa McAuliffe (1948–86), a teacher at Concord High School, New Hampshire, who had beaten 11,000 other applicants to become NASA's first 'teacher-in-space'. During the subsequent investigation, physicist Richard Feynman established that insufficiently robust rubber sealants had caused the explosion. The investigation also revealed that NASA had cut safety corners to retain public funding. The agency subsequently rebranded its manned space-flight program under the logo 'Nice and Safe Attitude'.

Chambers, Whittaker, *see* HISS, ALGER.

Champlain, Lake, battle of, *see* LAKE CHAMPLAIN, BATTLE OF.

Chancellorsville, battle of (May 2–4 1863), bloody but inconclusive engagement in Virginia during the CIVIL WAR. In April 1863 a Union force of 130,000, commanded by General Joseph HOOKER, marched into northern Virginia determined to avenge the defeat at FREDERICKSBURG. Confederate General Robert E. LEE split his force of 60,000 in a series of risky but successful outflanking manoeuvres. After three days of fighting, Hooker's forces retreated. But Confederate forces suffered 13,000 casualties, including General Thomas 'Stonewall' JACKSON.

Chaos, Operation, *see* OPERATION CHAOS.

Chapultepec, battle of (September 13 1847), engagement at the climax of the MEXICAN WAR in which US forces broke through the defenses of Mexico City.

General Scott's US force of 7000 regulars and volunteers assaulted 15,000 Mexican troops occupying fortified positions on the outskirts of the city. Overcoming fierce Mexican resistance, including a suicidal stand by 100 military cadets ('Los Ninos'), US troops secured the gateways to the Mexican capital. Ulysses S. GRANT was promoted on the field for his bravery in the attack. That night US Marines hoisted the Stars and Stripes over the National Palace, ensuring 'the Halls of Montezuma' their place in US military legend.

Charles River Bridge vs. Warren Bridge (1837), US Supreme Court ruling that allowed closer state regulation of corporate activity. The case arose when the Massachusetts legislature chartered the Warren Bridge Company to build a second toll bridge over the Charles river. The Charles River Bridge Company (which owned an existing bridge over the river) sued, citing DARTMOUTH COLLEGE VS. WOODWARD to argue that the state's action was an unconstitutional infringement of the contract established in its charter. The Supreme Court ruled 4–3 that the Charles River Bridge Company's charter had not granted an exclusive right to monopolize traffic across the river, and so a second bridge might be built. The Court reasoned that business charters granted corporations only those privileges inherent in an obvious reading of specific terms, and that states could interpret ambiguous terms to the detriment of a corporation's 'rights' or the value of its stock.

Charleston, siege of (1780), engagement in South Carolina during the Revolutionary War, ending in the surrender of the American garrison to the British.

On June 28 1776 a British force of 3000 troops had been prevented from capturing Charleston (or Charles Town) by 435 American soldiers who, withstanding a fierce bombardment, held Sullivan's Island in Charleston's harbour. On February 11 1780, developing their attempt to win the war by exploiting the strength of LOYALISM in the southern colonies, British commanders committed 13,000 soldiers and marines and ten warships to a successful siege of the city. Charleston's garrison of 5400 men, commanded by General Benjamin Lincoln (1733–1810), surrendered on May 12. This was the heaviest loss suffered by US forces during the war. British commander in chief Major General Henry Clinton sent Lieutenant General Charles Cornwallis to complete the task of subjugating the south, but stripped him of 6000 troops. This decision fatally undermined British strategy.

Chase, Salmon P(ortland) (1808–73), antislavery leader, lawyer, politician and chief justice of the US Supreme Court (1864–73). A hero of the ABOLITION movement for his work in defending runaway slaves, Chase was a thorn in Abraham LINCOLN's side. Lincoln appointed Chase secretary of the treasury in 1861 and he performed ably, utilizing the LEGAL TENDER ACTS to issue paper currency (GREENBACKS) bearing his portrait to finance the Civil War. However, Chase imagined he would make a better president than Lincoln, and on at least three occasions tendered his resignation in protest at Lincoln's handling of the war. In 1864 Lincoln accepted Chase's resignation and appointed him chief justice of the US Supreme Court. Chase presided over the IMPEACHMENT trial of Andrew JOHNSON. The workings of Chase's tortured conscience were typified during the Supreme Court's deliberations on the LEGAL-TENDER CASES (1870–1), when Chase, who as secretary of the treasury had issued paper currency to the value of $450 million, ruled the Legal Tender Act unconstitutional. Chase, who once left a dollar bill as a calling card, is today featured on the reverse of the $10,000 note.

Chattanooga, battle of (November 23–25 1863), this marked the culmination of a successful campaign mounted in central and southeastern Tennessee by Union forces during the CIVIL WAR. In the summer of 1863 the Union Army of the Cumberland, under the command of General William Starke Rosencrans (1819–98), drove Confederate forces from Tennessee and, on September 9, captured the important rail junction of Chattanooga. 'We are don [sic] gone up the spout,' wrote one Confederate deserter after the defeat. However, under the skillful command of General Braxton Bragg (1817–76), Confederate troops lured Rosencrans's army from Chattanooga and defeated it at the battle of CHICKAMAUGA. Union forces retreated to Chattanooga and Bragg's Confederate army besieged the town. Major General Ulysses GRANT assumed command of Union forces and broke the siege of Chattanooga through victories at the battle of Lookout Mountain (November 24) and Missionary Ridge (November 25). These victories allowed Union commander William T. SHERMAN to use Chattanooga as the base for his campaign against ATLANTA in the spring of 1864.

Chavez, Cesar (1927–93), CHICANO (Mexican-American) leader who dedicated his life to adapting the non-violent protest techniques of the CIVIL RIGHTS MOVMENT to the task of defending the rights of migrant farm workers. In 1962 Chavez founded the National Farm Workers' Association (NFWA). In 1965 the union joined a strike mounted by Filipino grape-pickers in California's San Joacquin valley. This marked the start of LA HUELGA, a ten-year campaign of strikes and boycotts designed to improve the pay and working conditions of migrant workers. In 1968 Chavez launched a nationwide boycott of Californian grapes harvested by non-union labor that proved so effective that an estimated 17 million Americans stopped buying grapes altogether. That year Chavez mounted a 25-day hunger strike in protest against escalating violence between strikers and fruit company goons. However, the campaign was so successful that by 1970 two-thirds of the California grape crop was harvested by workers who possessed a standardized union contract. In 1972 the AFL–CIO extended affiliate status to the renamed United Farm Workers. By 1975 Chavez's UFW had 50,000 members.

'Checkers' speech (September 23 1952), speech on national television in which Richard NIXON (EISENHOWER's running-mate in the 1952 presidential election) answered charges that he had received secret campaign contributions from Californian businessmen. In an emotional speech Nixon stressed his poverty and his probity, but admitted accepting, on behalf of his children, a dog named Checkers. Positive reaction to the speech persuaded Eisenhower to keep Nixon on the REPUBLICAN ticket. The incident established the power of television, and led Nixon to the belief – which may have cost him the PRESIDENTIAL ELECTION OF 1960 – that he understood the new medium. *See also* RADIO AND TELEVISION.

Cherokee, Native American people who speak an Iroquoian language. Some 20,000 Cherokee lived on the eastern slopes of the southern Appalachians when Europeans began settlement of Georgia and the Carolinas.

During the REVOLUTIONARY WAR the Cherokee sided with the British, and in its aftermath retreated from the Carolinas to homelands in northwestern Georgia. Some Cherokee fought with the USA in the first CREEK WAR, yet the Cherokee nation became the primary target of Andrew JACKSON's policy of INDIAN REMOVAL. Cherokee autonomy was consistently eroded following the discovery of gold in northern Georgia. In 1835, despite favorable Supreme Court judgments in CHEROKEE NATION VS. GEORGIA and WORCESTER VS. GEORGIA, the Cherokee elders ceded (through the treaty of NEW ECHOTA) the nation's land claims in the region in return for a reservation in Oklahoma. Cherokee resisters were forcibly marched west on the TRAIL OF TEARS.

The USA regarded the Cherokee as one of the FIVE CIVILIZED TRIBES, because they employed a written language and were governed by a formal constitution (drafted by John ROSS). The Cherokee permitted slavery on their western reservations, and many sided with the Confederacy during the CIVIL WAR.

The Cherokees' tolerance of 'mixed' marriages has helped rebuild the nation's population to the point where (measured by self-identification on census forms) there are now more than twice as many Cherokee alive in the USA as existed at the moment of first contact with European settlers.

Cherokee Nation vs. Georgia (March 18 1831), US Supreme Court ruling in which it declined 4–2 to intervene in a suit brought by the CHEROKEE alleging that an attempt by Georgia to extend its state law to their territory was unconstitutional. Chief Justice John MARSHALL argued that the Cherokee were a 'domestic dependent nation' whose relationship to the USA resembled that of a 'ward to a guardian'. The Supreme Court could not 'interpose' on state laws regulating the self-government of Native Americans living within a state's borders. However, Native Americans possessed an 'unquestionable right' to the land they occupied, unless and until they ceded it to the federal government. This verdict (and a subsequent ruling in WORCESTER VS. GEORGIA) came even as the implementation of the INDIAN REMOVAL ACT (1830) was destroying the autonomy of the Native American nations of the southeast.

Chesapeake Capes, battle of (September 5 1781), the largest naval engagement of the REVOLUTIONARY WAR, fought off the coast of Virginia. A 24-ship French fleet commanded by Admiral François de Grasse prevented 19 British ships commanded by Admiral Thomas Graves from relieving the siege of YORKTOWN.

***Chesapeake*, USS,** US warship lost in an engagement with the British during the WAR

OF 1812. During the war, the US Navy won four victories in single-ship actions against the Royal Navy. Perversely, the loss of the USS *Chesapeake* to HMS *Shannon* on June 1 1813 did as much as these victories, if not more, to inspire Americans. This was because the engagement stemmed from a challenge to battle issued to the *Chesapeake*'s captain, James Lawrence (1781–1813), by the *Shannon*'s commander, Philip Broke, and because Lawrence, facing defeat and dying from his wounds, reputedly told his crew, 'Don't give up the ship.' American sailors were reminded of Lawrence's words prior to the battle of LAKE ERIE.

Cheyenne, Native American people belonging to the Algonkian linguistic group. In 1780 approximately 3500 Cheyenne inhabited lands in northeastern Minnesota shared with their linguistic and cultural cousins the ARAPAHO. Retreating from white settlement and the SIOUX, the Cheyenne moved south and west to the Great Plains. As increasing numbers of US pioneers and settlers impinged on their new territory, some Cheyenne moved further south, while others buried traditional enmities with the Sioux to resist US encroachment.

In the 1860s the northern Cheyenne under Red Cloud (1822–1909) joined with the Sioux to resist fortification of the BOZEMAN TRAIL. They later joined SITTING BULL's warriors in the last-ditch third SIOUX WAR (1876–7) before accepting confinement on a reservation on the Montana–Wyoming border. Following the SAND CREEK MASSACRE the southern Cheyenne resisted US attempts to force them out of Colorado and Kansas. The treaty of MEDICINE LODGE (1867) created a Cheyenne reservation in Oklahoma, but militants resisted relocation until finally defeated in the RED RIVER WAR (1874–5).

Chicago convention riots (August 26–29 1968), riots resulting from ANTIWAR MOVEMENT protests outside the DEMOCRATIC PARTY convention in Chicago. The party had gathered in a divided and embittered mood to nominate a candidate for the PRESIDENTIAL ELECTION OF 1968. Despite the strong showing of peace candidates Eugene McCARTHY and George McGOVERN in PRIMARY ELECTIONS, party bosses were united behind Hubert HUMPHREY. Humphrey had liberal credentials but, because he was pledged to continue Lyndon JOHNSON's prosecution of the VIETNAM WAR, was regarded by democratic activists as a turncoat. Thousands of antiwar protesters gathered in Chicago in an attempt to persuade Humphrey to write a peace plank into the Democrats' election manifesto. Several hundred YIPPIES campaigned to 'dump the Hump', and nominated a pig ('Pigasus') for president. Humphrey was nominated on the first ballot, but this event was overshadowed by a police riot in which several hundred policemen chanting 'Kill, kill, kill' clubbed protesters gathering outside the Conrad Hilton hotel. These scenes were relayed on national television. The mayor of Chicago, Richard J.Daley (1902–76), was a delegate at the convention and exploded in anger when Senator Abraham Ribicoff denounced from the podium the 'Gestapo tactics' used by his police force. Humphrey's response to continuing street fighting was to blame TV networks for showing it. Humphrey and Daley were forced to retract their criticism of the demonstrators and media when the police began beating McCarthy delegates. By the end of the week National Guardsmen had to be deployed to restore order in the city. A subsequent commission of investigation blamed the violence on the police.

chicano, a term used to celebrate the unique ethno-cultural roots of Mexican-American people living in the USA. Its usage was popularized in the 1970s in an attempt to replace derogatory collective nouns and adjectives. *See* AZTLAN; CHAVEZ, CESAR; LA RAZA UNIDA PARTY.

Chickamauga, battle of (September 20 1863), Confederate victory in Tennessee during the CIVIL WAR.

On September 9 1863, 58,000 Union troops, advancing through southeastern Tennessee, captured the important rail junction of Chattanooga. Before they could strike at northeastern Georgia (and deliver a fatal blow to Confederate morale weakened by defeat at GETTYSBURG and the loss of VICKSBURG), a reorganized Confederate army of 66,000 severely mauled the Union army in two days of fighting at Chickamauga Creek (September 19–20). Only staunch Union defense by the 'Rock of Chickamauga', General George Thomas (1816–70), prevented total rout. But the victory cost 20,000 Confederate casualties. To the fury of his subordinates, Confederate General Braxton Bragg (1817–76) declined to order an assault to recapture Chattanooga, and instead ordered his army to high ground overlooking the town (Lookout Mountain and Missionary Ridge) in preparation for a siege.

Chickasaw, Native American people belonging to the Muskogean linguistic family. The Chickasaw's ancestral lands lay in southwestern Tennessee and northern Mississippi.

In the mid-18th century the Chickasaw were harassed by French and CHOCTAW neighbors, and, after allying themselves with the British during the REVOLUTIONARY WAR, the Chickasaw accepted confinement on a reservation in central Tennessee. Protestant missionaries developed a written language for the Chickasaw (based in fact on the similar language of their enemies, the Choctaw). This led US authorities to regard the Chickasaw as one of the FIVE CIVILIZED TRIBES. The Chickasaw did not resist removal to Oklahoma. Currently some 12,000 Chickasaw survive on an Oklahoma reservation.

Chinese Exclusion Act (May 6 1882), federal legislation barring Chinese immigration. By 1880 Chinese immigrants constituted 9% of the population of California. In 1879 Congress, pandering to nativist bigotry, passed a law barring Chinese immigrants. This was vetoed by President HAYES, who authorized negotiation of a treaty with China limiting, but not ending, Chinese immigration. In 1882 Congress broke this treaty by enacting a bill, vetoed by President ARTHUR, suspending all Chinese immigration for 20 years. Arthur signed a subsequent act (the Chinese Exclusion Act) suspending immigration for 10 years and forbidding US courts to grant citizenship to Chinese already resident in the USA. The law, renewed in 1892 and 1902, was not repealed until 1943. Its constitutionality was upheld in CHAE CHAN PING VS. US. *See also* NATIVISM.

Chippewa, battle of (July 5 1814), US victory in Ontario, Canada, during the WAR OF 1812. A US force of 1900 regulars, militia and Native American allies under the command of Winfield SCOTT defeated a British force of equal strength. This was the first US victory in the war that was not dependent on numerical superiority. It marked the US Army's coming of age: thereafter no force of US regulars was defeated by the British.

Chisholm vs. Georgia (1793), US Supreme Court ruling concerning the right of states to confiscate property. Georgia had refused, on the grounds of sovereign immunity, to hear a case of unlawful confiscation of TORY property brought against it by residents of South Carolina. In 1793 the Supreme Court ruled against Georgia 4–1. Anger at the ruling prompted the ELEVENTH AMENDMENT.

Chivington massacre, *see* SAND CREEK MASSACRE.

Choctaw, Native American people belonging to the Muskogean linguistic family. Dubbed one of the FIVE CIVILIZED TRIBES by US authorities, the Choctaw's homelands were in southern Mississippi and western Alabama. Pressure from French settlement in Louisiana led the Choctaw to encroach upon, and wage war with, the CHICKASAW to the north and the CREEK to the west. In

1830 the Choctaw ceded their reservation lands in Mississippi for $5 million and a new reservation in Oklahoma, where today some 17,500 Choctaw still live.

Christiana riot (1851), violent incident in Christiana, Pennsylvania, arising from the attempt by a slave owner to recapture two fugitive slaves. 'Civil War – The First Blow Struck!' was the headline in a local paper following the armed confrontation.

On September 11 1851 a Maryland slave owner, accompanied by members of his family and US marshals, rode into the remote community of Christiana to search for two fugitive slaves. The fugitives were sheltered by 24 armed black men, and two local Quakers advised the slave owner to retreat. When he refused, shooting broke out. The slave owner was killed, and his son, two local whites, and two blacks were wounded.

President FILLMORE used the incident to show his determination to enforce the FUGITIVE SLAVE ACT (1850). US Marines seized six local Quakers and 30 black men, who were tried for treason. The government's attempt to depict the accused as insurrectionaries quickly collapsed, but it provided abolitionists with a propaganda coup.

Christian Science, homegrown American religious movement. The founder of the Church of Christ, Scientist was a New Englander, Mary Baker (1821–1910).

In 1866, Mary Baker cured herself of a life-threatening injury through contemplation of the Bible, prayer and the use of 'mental healing' techniques popularized by Phineas Pankhurst Quimby (1802–66). Baker later published *Science and Health* (1875), the founding text of the Christian Science Movement. Baker's creed, which entered popular culture through the simplified slogan 'mind over matter,' suggested that sickness and death are illusions to be overcome through an understanding of God's perfection. Operating through the Christian Scientists' Association (1876), she attempted to bring Americans to appreciate God's healing power. In 1877 she married one of her students, Asa Gilbert Eddy, and in 1879 chartered the Church of Christ, Scientist. Mary Baker Eddy was appointed first minister of the Church in 1881. The first Christian Science reading room was opened in 1888. From its inception the movement was riven with schism and wracked by lawsuits challenging its claims. In 1892, Eddy and her followers established the breakaway First Church of Christ, Scientist in Boston, known subsequently as the 'mother church'. During the 20th century, the movement attracted thousands of adherents around the world and its newspaper, the *Christian Science Monitor*, first published in 1908, is well-respected and remains widely read.

Christmas bombing (December 18–30 1972), intensive US bombing campaign against North Vietnam. At the close of US involvement in the VIETNAM WAR, President NIXON, pursuing his 'MAD DOG' STRATEGY to secure 'peace with honor', ordered around-the-clock sorties by B-52 bombers against targets in the Hanoi and Haiphong areas. Nixon had ordered a halt to the bombing of North Vietnam on October 23 1972 in a bid to boost the chances of the KISSINGER INITIATIVE. The renewed campaign was prompted by last-minute hitches in Kissinger's negotiations with his North Vietnamese opposite number, Le Duc Tho, and by Nixon's desire to appear 'credible' in Soviet eyes. The campaign was the most ferocious of the war, and brought near-universal condemnation. However, Nixon maintained that it 'persuaded' North Vietnam to include a release of US prisoners of war in the final peace treaty he signed on January 27 1973.

CIA, *see* CENTRAL INTELLIGENCE AGENCY.

Cincinnati, Society of the, a fraternal organization for Continental Army officers formed on May 13 1783. It was named after Cincinnatus, a Roman farmer turned soldier who exemplified VIRTUE. Its first two presidents were George WASHINGTON and Alexander HAMILTON, and its members were staunch supporters of the FEDERALISTS. Each member's oldest living male descendant was eligible to join, leading to fears that the society might form the basis of an order of nobility. Following the CIVIL WAR the order nearly collapsed. It was revived in 1902, since when it has flourished.

CIO, *see* CONGRESS OF INDUSTRIAL ORGANIZA- TIONS.

citizens' councils, bodies of white community leaders determined to offer 'massive resistance' to desegregation campaigns backed by the CIVIL RIGHTS MOVEMENT. Such bodies were formed in the core states of the former Confederacy in the immediate aftermath of the US Supreme Court's ruling on BROWN VS. BOARD OF EDUCATION (1954).

Council members used intimidation and obfuscation to prevent the NATIONAL ASSO- CIATION FOR THE ADVANCEMENT OF COLORED PEOPLE (NAACP) from bringing court suits to desegregate school districts. They also rallied white voters behind candidates dedicated to a defense of JIM CROW by espousing a version of STATES' RIGHTS rhetoric.

Civilian Conservation Corps (CCC), public-works organization set up in 1933 under the NEW DEAL to provide work for the unemployed.

During the first HUNDRED DAYS of President Franklin ROOSEVELT's administration Congress passed the Reforestation Relief Act (March 31 1933), which created the CCC. At that time a quarter of the US workforce was idle, and the CCC enrolled over 250,000 men aged between 18 and 25. The men were sent to work camps, run by army officers, where they planted trees or built fire breaks, roads and flood-control barriers. In addition to their board and lodging the men received a stipend of $30 a month, the bulk of which was sent by the Corps directly to relatives. Four government departments (Agriculture, Interior, Labor and War) ran the Corps in a spirit of interdepartmental cooperation that was seldom achieved in the administration of other NEW DEAL programmes.

Civil Rights Act of 1866, legislation passed on April 9 1866 (over President JOHN- SON's veto) that invalidated the DRED SCOTT ruling by conferring citizenship on all black Americans, and by specifying their rights with regard to property and access to the protection of the court system. The act was amended in the House of Representatives to prevent a conflict with state SEGREGATION statutes. The FOURTEENTH AMENDMENT (1868) was subsequently formulated to protect the act from legal challenge. However, the CIVIL RIGHTS CASES weakened the act's protection against civil-rights violations committed by private individuals.

Civil Rights Act of 1875, legislation (signed by President GRANT on March 1 1875) that prevented blacks from being excluded from juries, from bars and hotels and from trains and trolley cars. It established federal jurisdiction in cases arising from infringements of the right of access to public accommodation and amenities. The Supreme Court's ruling in the CIVIL RIGHTS CASES (1883 and 1896) seriously weakened the protection offered against violations of civil rights committed by private individuals.

Civil Rights Act of 1957, legislation that created a six-man Civil Rights Commission, and a civil rights division within the Department of Justice, empowered to investigate the use of intimidation and obstruction to prevent a citizen from voting. The act was signed by President EISENHOWER on September 9, despite a 24-hour FILIBUSTER from Senator Strom Thurmond (the longest on record).

Civil Rights Act of 1960, legislation (signed by President EISENHOWER on May 6) that built on the 1957 act by providing further aid to African-American voter registration and polling. The act required states to keep and preserve accurate records of registered voters, and it allowed courts to appoint referees to ensure that African-Americans were given access to the registration and voting procedures.

Civil Rights Act of 1964, legislation that aimed to outlaw all aspects of racial discrimination and that also addressed other forms of discrimination. President Lyndon JOHNSON signed this massive omnibus bill on July 2. Its provisions shape US workplace relations to this day, long after the blatant racial discrimination that was the original target of the CIVIL RIGHTS MOVEMENT has disappeared from American life.

President KENNEDY sent a civil rights bill to Congress on July 1 1963. Despite mounting pressure for its passage generated by the MARCH ON WASHINGTON and Kennedy's assassination, Congress swamped the bill with amendments. But Johnson's mastery of congressional politics, and pressure applied to wavering congressmen by groups such as the NATIONAL ASSOCIATION FOR THE ADVANCEMENT OF COLORED PEOPLE (NAACP), ensured that a comprehensive bill passed through the Senate despite a FILIBUSTER mounted by southern conservatives.

The act has eleven titles. Title II requires open access to public accommodation, bus and train stations, movie theaters, bars, theaters and the like. This finally dismantled the network of racially segregated facilities that had been a feature of southern life under JIM CROW. Title VI bars the federal government from funding any program that discriminates on the grounds of race, gender or religion. Title VII outlaws discrimination in employment on the grounds of race, color, religion, sex or national origin. In the 1970s and 1980s women used this provision, and the Equal Employment Opportunity Commission it spawned, to gain access to occupations previously reserved for men.

Furthermore, the act authorizes the US attorney general to instigate court suits to enforce the desegregation of school systems and of public amenities. It also prevents states from using literacy tests to deny residents voting rights, and it ended the practice whereby some southern states excluded African-Americans from voting on the grounds that they had made minor mistakes on their registration forms.

The Supreme Court upheld the constitutionality of Title II in HEART OF ATLANTA MOTEL VS. US. It took a broad view of Title VII in MERITOR SAVINGS BANK VS. VINSON, and made unexpected use of Title VI in REGENTS OF THE UNIVERSITY OF CALIFORNIA VS. BAAKE. The act served as the basis for a number of quasi-academic doctrines applied to race and gender relations in the 1970s and 1980s, including AFFIRMATIVE ACTION and COMPARABLE WORTH.

Civil Rights Act of 1968, legislation (signed by President JOHNSON on April 11) that outlawed racial discrimination in the housing market and offered federal protection for CIVIL RIGHTS MOVEMENT activists. Delayed in Congress for two years, the act was hurriedly passed following the assassination of Martin Luther KING (April 4).

Civil Rights Act of 1970, legislation (signed by president NIXON on June 22) that renewed the protections laid out in the VOTING RIGHTS ACT (1965), forbidding for a further five years the use of literacy tests in voter-registration procedures. The act also established 30 days as the maximum residency requirement for voting in presidential elections, and stipulated that the minimum voting age in local, state and federal elections should be 18. The act's provisions were reviewed by the Supreme Court in OREGON VS. MITCHELL.

civil rights cases, two notable cases brought before the US Supreme Court that revolved around the constitutionality of the CIVIL RIGHTS ACT OF 1875 which had outlawed racial segregation in public transport and accommodation.

On October 15 1883 the Supreme Court gutted the provisions of the 1875 Act by ruling 8–1 that neither the THIRTEENTH nor the FOURTEENTH AMENDMENT gave Congress the power to prohibit private citizens or companies from providing racially segregated amenities. This ruling, coupled with the Court's subsequent judgment in PLESSY VS. FERGUSON (1896), provided legal protection for segregation that was not breached until passage of the CIVIL RIGHTS ACT OF 1964.

Civil Rights Movement, mass movement to end racial discrimination in the USA. The movement emerged in the 1950s, and by 1970 had secured the passage of several important civil rights acts through Congress.

African-Americans had been struggling for full equality of citizenship long before events such as the MONTGOMERY BUS BOYCOTT (1955–6) captured the attention of the wider American public. The NIAGARA MOVEMENT and the NATIONAL ASSOCIATION FOR THE ADVANCEMENT OF COLORED PEOPLE (NAACP) had made limited progress in the fight against the south's JIM CROW caste system in the first half of the 20th century. But the impact of the movement that developed in the mid-1950s was all the more profound for drawing on frustrations that had been generated in over a century of injustice.

Several structural changes in American social and political life lay behind the emergence of the Civil Rights Movement of the 1950s and 1960s. The GREAT MIGRATION had seen millions of African-Americans leave farms to work in southern towns or northern cities. White elites in southern cities were less able and, to some extent, less willing to enforce the rigid racial segregation practiced by their paternalistic counterparts in rural areas. (In contrast, urban white laborers, who stood to lose status in direct proportion to black gains, proved all too willing to use violence and intimidation to defend the Jim Crow system.)

Changing voting patterns were also important. Those blacks who could vote in the 1930s responded to the NEW DEAL by switching allegiance from the REPUBLICAN PARTY (the party of Lincoln) to the DEMOCRATIC PARTY (the party of Franklin Roosevelt). Democratic Party leaders recognized the importance of African-American votes to the maintenance of the NEW DEAL COALITION forged by President Roosevelt. Over opposition from reactionary southern Democrats (DIXIECRATS), the TRUMAN administration of the later 1940s began to push a civil rights agenda in order to keep black voters in the Democratic fold. Moreover, during the New Deal and the COLD WAR federal government became bigger and stronger, and the capacity of state governments to resist federal policies weakened accordingly. (Although, as a counter-weight to this, seniority rules in the US Senate gave southern conservatives considerable scope to block civil rights legislation by the use of parliamentary tactics such as the FILIBUSTER.)

Finally, under Presidents Roosevelt, TRUMAN and EISENHOWER the US Supreme Court was rejuvenated by the appointment of justices prepared to listen to the claims the Civil Rights Movement would lay before it. The BROWN VS. BOARD OF EDUCATION verdict (1954) ordering the desegregation of elementary and secondary school systems gave fair warning of the change a thoughtful Supreme Court could effect.

The reasoning the Court employed in its Brown verdict raised issues that would dog the developing Civil Rights Movement, and upon which it would ultimately founder. The Court relied heavily on scientific arguments suggesting that educational segregation inflicted psychological harm on black children. As Chief Justice Earl WARREN put it, segregation 'generates [in black children] a feeling of inferiority'. Warren stressed this argument in order to achieve unanimity on the bench and to maximize support for the verdict among liberal-minded whites. But for many African-Americans it was the fundamental injustice and inherent absurdity of segregation – rather than the effects of it – that made it intolerable in a nation whose constitution guaranteed equal rights and protection under the law to all citizens regardless of race. Simply put, the energy African-Americans devoted to dismantling Jim Crow originated in an affirmation of their humanity as much as in a consciousness of injury or psychological damage. (The Montgomery bus boycott and the GREENSBORO SIT-IN, both very much the product of grass-roots activism, captured this mood among African-Americans.) As the furore over the term BLACK POWER would demonstrate, many white northerners and some conservative southern blacks supported the movement only insofar as it righted past wrongs. Yet the historical significance of the movement lies precisely in the fact that it generated a debate over what it means to be a black or a white citizen of the USA – a debate that continues to this day.

Of more immediate significance to the creation of the movement was the response of southern whites to the Brown verdict. The first of dozens of white CITIZENS' COUNCILS pledged to defend segregation was formed in Indianola, Mississippi, in the summer of 1954. Southern congressmen wrote a 'southern Manifesto' reassuring their white constituents that they would offer 'massive resistance' to desegregation. (Lyndon B. JOHNSON was one of three southern senators who refused to sign the document.) This posturing produced the LITTLE ROCK SCHOOL DESEGREGATION BATTLE and a later battle over the admission of James MEREDITH to the University of Mississippi.

White resistance to the Brown verdict, coupled with the success of the Montgomery bus boycott, revitalized moribund civil rights groups and led to the creation of new organizations. The CONGRESS OF RACIAL EQUALITY (CORE) had been founded in Chicago in 1942, but had lain dormant during the anticommunist witch-hunt launched by Senator Joe McCARTHY. CORE members, early exponents of non-violent direct action, now resurfaced to popularize the sit-in tactic and organize the FREEDOM RIDER campaign. The Montgomery boycott also moved Baptist ministers Martin Luther KING and Ralph ABERNATHY to found the SOUTHERN CHRISTIAN LEADERSHIP CONFERENCE (SCLC) in 1957. The STUDENT NON-VIOLENT COORDINATING COMMITTEE (SNCC), whose members would furnish youthful energy and fervor to the movement, emerged in the wake of the GREENSBORO SIT-IN protest mounted by North Carolina A&T students in February 1960.

In their separate ways the ALBANY DESEGREGATION CAMPAIGN of 1961–2 and the BIRMINGHAM DESEGREGATION CAMPAIGN of 1963 convinced movement leaders to throw their weight behind a campaign for federal legislation to break Jim Crow. The campaign in Albany, Georgia, was weakened by disagreements among the major civil rights organizations, but ultimately defeated by white civic leaders who announced a willingness to meet protesters' demands but dragged their feet in subsequent negotiations. It showed that in the absence of pictures of demonstrators being beaten by policemen, the KENNEDY administration would not intervene to force white civic leaders to desegregate their communities. The SCLC-led campaign in Birmingham, Alabama, produced a plethora of newsworthy images, including the use of watercannon to disperse protesting schoolchildren and the bombing of the 16th Street Baptist Church.

Martin Luther King, arrested during the Birmingham protest, used the LETTER FROM BIRMINGHAM CITY JAIL and the 'I HAVE A DREAM' SPEECH at the climax of the MARCH ON WASHINGTON to increase the pressure on Congress to pass the civil rights bill Kennedy sent to Congress on July 1 1963. The killing of Medgar EVERS, the NAACP's field secretary in Mississippi, also brought home to Americans the scale of the challenge facing the movement in the deep south.

Thanks largely to the managerial skills of President Lyndon B. JOHNSON, the CIVIL RIGHTS ACT OF 1964 passed Congress despite a Senate FILIBUSTER. It outlawed the segregation of public facilities and discrimination by employers on the grounds of race, color, religion, sex or national origin. The act gave the federal government enhanced powers to act against segregation, and indicated a clear commitment on the part of federal government to end Jim Crow. However, the act did little to secure voting rights. The SELMA FREEDOM MARCH and the MISSISSIPPI FREEDOM SUMMER of 1964 presented contrasting approaches to this problem. The Selma march demonstrated the caution of the SCLC, and its reliance on moral persuasion and the charisma of Martin Luther King. The Freedom Summer demonstrated the enthusiasm and energy of SNCC and CORE, and their willingness to risk provoking white supremacist violence through civil disobedience. Where King worked with the Johnson administration, the Freedom Summer campaign produced the MISSISSIPPI FREEDOM DEMOCRATIC PARTY (MFDP), which, to Johnson's intense irritation, rocked the Democratic Party boat in a presidential election year.

By the spring of 1965 the Civil Rights Movement was beginning to disintegrate. SNCC and CORE activists saw in Johnson's suppression of the MFDP confirmation of the analysis presented by militants such as MALCOLM X. Although Johnson pushed the VOTING RIGHTS ACT of 1965 through Congress and made good his promise to wage a WAR ON POVERTY, he was angered by CORE and SNCC's criticism of the VIETNAM WAR and their increasing propensity to dismiss the entire US political system as being corrupt and racist. Moderates such as Martin Luther King were under fire from the Johnson administration for being insufficiently grateful for the initiatives it had launched, and under attack from grass-roots activists for being too close to 'the system'. The

WATTS RIOT, which erupted five days after Johnson signed the Voting Rights Act, suggested the difficulty of addressing the civil rights problems of urban America through non-violent campaign techniques. Nevertheless, on September 1 1965 the SCLC launched a year-long campaign designed to desegregate public housing in Chicago. Parts of this campaign, notably OPERATION BREADBASKET, produced results. But Chicago's mayor, Richard J. Daley (1902–76), ultimately bought off the protest by agreeing a reform package which, in the absence of pressure from the federal government, he proved in no hurry to enact.

SNCC and SCLC made one last cooperative gesture when in the summer of 1966 they united to complete the protest 'pilgrimage' through Mississippi that James Meredith had been forced to interrupt after he was wounded by a white supremacist. But by this time the slogan 'BLACK POWER' had divided the movement and the USA at large. In December 1966 SNCC's governing body overrode the advice of Fanny Lou HAMER and Stokeley CARMICHAEL and voted to expel its white members. CORE followed suit in 1967. These decisions alienated SNCC and CORE from their major source of funding – white liberals living in northern cities. SNCC's ability to push a black nationalist agenda was hampered by the unavoidably diffuse nature of the agenda itself and by their growing involvement in the ANTI-WAR MOVEMENT. Attempts by the leadership of the NAACP to put a moderate spin on 'black power' were ignored by many local activists and by black militants such as the BLACK PANTHER PARTY who had never had much time for the Association's reformist stance.

Martin Luther King made a more significant accommodation with the spirit of the times when, in the spring of 1967, he began criticizing the Vietnam War. But he was by now under increasingly intrusive FBI surveillance and struggling to find a way of linking blacks and whites in a unified campaign against poverty and economic hardship. His hold on what he dubbed 'the vital center' was slipping, and as it did so the influence of the movement as whole waned. King's assassination (April 4 1968) galvanized Congress into passing the CIVIL RIGHTS ACT OF 1968, which retroactively recognized the aims of the SCLC's earlier campaign in Chicago. But the rioting that broke out in the wake of King's shooting played into the hands of Richard NIXON as growing numbers of Americans became alienated by black activism, antiwar protest, and the crime and disorder they associated with these phenomena. In the run-up to the PRESIDENTIAL ELECTION OF 1968 the Democratic Party atoned for its refusal to recognize the MFDP in 1964 by seating black delegates at its convention, but at the cost of opening wounds within the party that made it incapable of defining a focused civil rights agenda.

During Nixon's presidency the US government began to push AFFIRMATIVE ACTION policies. The Democratic Party rallied behind an EQUAL RIGHTS AMENDMENT proposed by a WOMEN'S MOVEMENT that drew much of its energy from the frustrations experienced during the civil rights struggle. Meanwhile the NAACP continued to mount legal challenges to discriminatory practices. But by 1968 a unified civil rights movement no longer existed.

The Civil Rights Movement can claim three lasting achievements. It destroyed the Jim Crow system in southern states. It finally opened America's political process to African-American participation. And it began to address the DE FACTO SEGREGATION that characterized life in northern cities.

Civil War (1861–5), conflict between the northern states, who wished to preserve the United States of America (the Union), and the southern states, who had seceded from the Union in 1861 to form the Confederate States of America (the CONFEDERACY). The institution of SLAVERY, legal in southern states and condemned by many northerners, was a significant, but not the sole, factor in the outbreak of hostilities between the two sides. Northern victory in the war, achieved through superior manpower and industrial and economic might, resulted in restoration of the Union and total abolition of slavery.

In his 'HOUSE DIVIDED' SPEECH, given to a Republican Party convention in June 1858, Abraham LINCOLN prophesied that the USA could not permanently endure 'half slave and half free.' This speech illustrates one cause of the Civil War, a growing conviction among Americans that, as Lincoln put it: '… [America] will cease to be divided. It will become all one thing or all the other.' As Lincoln feared, it took the bloodiest conflict in American history, the Civil War, to resolve the intractable divisions within American society caused by slavery.

However, the impending crisis over slavery identified and defined by politicians in the 1850s had deeper roots in three features of America's development as a nation: the compromise over slavery reached at the CONSTITUTIONAL CONVENTION (1787), the separate and unequal growth of northern and southern economies, and the popular belief that a large and expanding nation could and should provide opportunities for the advancement of all its citizens whether they wished to own slaves or not. During the Civil War, the morality of slavery and the future status of African-Americans moved to the top of the political agenda. However, the Civil War was waged neither primarily nor exclusively out of a desire to free America's slaves.

On July 12 1787 delegates to the Constitutional Convention began discussing what became known as the CONNECTICUT COMPROMISE. They eventually agreed that a state's representation in the US House of Representatives should be based on the total of its white population plus three-fifths of its slave population. (This Three-fifths compromise, enshrined in Article I Section 2 of the US Constitution, remained operative until ratification of the FOUR-TEENTH AMENDMENT.) The compromise gave the southern states (in which slave owners were the dominant interest) the upper hand in the House of Representatives and in the ELECTORAL COLLEGE. Since the House was charged with initiating economic legislation, and since the US president possessed a veto on legislation, slave owners could be assured that the federal government was unlikely to enact financial policies injurious to their interests. The Constitution made several other concessions to slave owners' interests. It provided for the return of fugitive slaves, and bound the federal government to assist in the suppression of slave revolts. Article I Section 9 stipulated that Congress could not consider any law banning the import of slaves into the USA until 1808.

Many Americans accepted these concessions in the belief that slavery might soon die. The NORTHWEST ORDINANCE had already barred slavery from future states formed north of the Ohio river and east of the Mississippi. Slavery was thought unlikely to prove suitable or profitable in the remainder of the west. Thomas JEFFERSON optimistically predicted that white yeomen farmers would in time form the backbone of the nation. However, the cotton gin, a machine for separating seeds from cotton which was patented in 1794 by Eli WHITNEY, gave slavery a new lease of life in southern and southwestern states. The cotton gin allowed a single slave to produce 50 pounds (23 kg) of market-quality cotton a day. To meet the expanding demands of textile mills in New England and Great Britain, southern planters bought slaves to maximize production on cotton plantations established in Georgia, Alabama and Mississippi. A northerner described the investment cycle of the southern economy as consisting of selling cotton 'to buy negroes to make more cotton to buy more negroes'. Although in time southern investors established railroads, banks and manufacturing plants, the southern economy, and therefore the economic and political interests of the region's dominant classes, diverged from northern patterns of development over the course of the 19th century. The ANTEBELLUM south always contained a preponderance of small farmers who did not employ slaves to grow staple crops, but the most valuable sector of the southern economy was dependent on slave labor. As a result any threat to slavery, however remote, could be characterized by slave owners as a threat to a distinctively southern way of life.

The equally distinctive development of northern society led residents of this region to see in SLAVE POWER a threat to *their* way of life. During the 19th century the white population of states north of the MASON-DIXON LINE and the Ohio river expanded far more rapidly than in the south. The population of new states like Indiana was augmented by the migration of white families from the slave south (among them Abraham Lincoln's) as well by an influx of pioneers from the east. Northern and western states received 84% of the influx of foreign-born migrants to the USA in the first half of the 19th century. Over 90% of America's manufacturing capacity was located in northern states. Despite the best efforts of the ABOLITION movement, the bulk of the northern population remained indifferent to the plight of African-Americans held in slavery in southern states. However, the movement successfully exploited the furore over the GAG RULE and the passions aroused by the *AMISTAD* MUTINY to create a vague but growing sense that the institution of slavery was incompatible with American values.

Ideology as well as demography led northern families west into territories formed from land acquired through the LOUISIANA PURCHASE. FREE-SOIL IDEOLOGY contrasted the 'wage slavery' of the factory system with the virtuous independence of the yeoman farmer. From the free-soil perspective, core American values, threatened by foreign immigration and the factory system, could only be protected and nurtured on land free from slavery. Free-soilers opposed the expansion of slavery into western territories not out of sympathy for the slave but because they feared the political power of the slave owner. The MISSOURI COMPROMISE of 1820 (which allowed slavery in new territories organized south of a line extended westward from the Missouri-Arkansas border, but barred slavery in future states to the north of it) appeared to guarantee prospective homesteaders an adequate supply of land on which to establish family farms. However, during and after the MEXICAN WAR, free-soilers sought to bar slavery from new western lands acquired by the USA while slave owners insisted on being able to exercise what they took to be their FIFTH AMENDMENT right to transport slaves into newly acquired territory. Thus by 1848 slave owners and free-soilers had begun the struggle over America's future that would lead to secession and the Civil War.

The COMPROMISE OF 1850 appeared to resolve the tensions created by America's acquisition of enormous tracts of land formerly under Mexican jurisdiction. California entered the Union as a free state, the territories of New Mexico and Utah were given the option of entering the Union with constitutions permitting slavery, and the terms of the Fugitive Slave Act (1793) were strengthened to protect the interests of slave owners. Stephen DOUGLAS played a crucial role in shepherding this package through Congress, only to undermine it in 1854 by sponsoring the KANSAS–NEBRASKA ACT. This abrogated the Missouri Compromise and created the BLEEDING KANSAS crisis: a civil war fought in the territory of Kansas between slave-owning settlers bent on writing a state constitution permitting slavery

and free-soil settlers bent on barring slavery.

The crisis in Kansas led northern free-soil and abolitionist opponents of 'slave power' to form the REPUBLICAN PARTY in a bid to halt the expansion of slavery. As a result the DEMOCRATIC PARTY fell under the control of southern supporters of slavery, who viewed opposition to the Kansas–Nebraska Act and northern support for the UNDERGROUND RAILROAD, PERSONAL LIBERTY LAWS and John BROWN's raid on HARPER'S FERRY as indicative of a desire to use unconstitutional means to destroy slavery. In 1857 the Supreme Court's verdict on DRED SCOTT VS. SANDFORD, which held the Missouri Compromise unconstitutional and ruled that slaves were not US citizens, heightened partisan tensions. The BROOKS–SUMNER INCIDENT – the savage beating of a leading abolitionist by a FIRE-EATING congressman in the chamber of the US Senate – illustrated the extent to which the political system could no longer contain the passions associated with the future status of slavery in the Union. After this incident congressmen carried firearms to protect themselves from attack. Lincoln's victory in the PRESIDENTIAL ELECTION OF 1860 convinced seven southern states to secede (*see* SECESSION). Four more left the Union after the attack on FORT SUMTER (April 12 1861). These eleven states formed the CONFEDERACY. Following the bombardment of Fort Sumter, Lincoln declared an 'insurrection' in those states that had already seceded, and called for 75,000 volunteers to suppress it.

The Confederacy was poorly placed to fight a war against the Union. The north could draw on a pool of men of fighting age twice the size of its southern equivalent. Most of the USA's industrial capacity, including its munitions plants, was located in northern states. The south's main source of revenue, cotton sales, was vulnerable to interdiction by naval blockade. As a result the Confederacy adopted draconian measures. In April 1862 it adopted the first

DRAFT law in US history. In 1863 it authorized an income tax and by the end of the
war had resorted to the impressment of livestock, farm produce and transportation
equipment. Generous exemptions protected
the interests of the major slaveowners: land
and slaves, for example, were never taxed.
These lent substance to the charge that the
war represented 'a rich man's struggle but a
poor man's fight.' Southern war aims – the
preservation of STATES' RIGHTS and of slavery
– held only limited appeal for the majority
of the Confederacy's population. Nevertheless, during the war southern soldiers
were asked to defend 'their' territory against
an invading force, and many fought with
great bravery over four years to do just that.
They were greatly aided by a Pennsylvanian, Josiah Gorgas (1818–83), who as
the Confederacy's chief of Ordnance performed logistical miracles to keep the
south's armies supplied with munitions.

Realizing the potential superiority of the
north presented an enormous political challenge to Lincoln. His first priority was to
prevent the BORDER STATES from joining the
Confederacy. Strong support for secession
existed in Maryland, Kentucky and Missouri. Had these three states left the Union,
the Confederacy's military manpower
would have been increased by 45% and its
manufacturing capacity by 80%. By defining moderate war aims (the preservation of
the Union rather than the destruction of
the southern way of life), Lincoln kept the
border states in the Union, but provoked
criticism from the radical wing of the
Republican Party. On the other hand,
throughout the war many northerners
favored a speedy peace, and the NEW YORK
CITY DRAFT RIOT provided a lurid example
of the reluctance of northern men to fight
to 'free the slaves.' (In contrast, 220,000
African-Americans fought for the Union
during the war, but they received at best
grudging recognition for their service.) To
quell opposition, Lincoln was forced to take

measures that threatened to destroy the
Constitution he held so dear. The war,
which cost $2 million per day, brought
the USA close to bankruptcy, and made
necessary the introduction of an INCOME
TAX. Most vexing of all, Lincoln was
beset by divisions within the high comm-
and of the US Army that threatened to
thwart a coordinated military campaign.

Lincoln believed that the Union should
concentrate on destroying the Confederacy's armies. However, until Ulysses S.
GRANT assumed overall command in March
1864, the US Army built its strategy around
capturing cities, especially Richmond, Virginia, the capital of the Confederacy. In July
1861 Confederate troops defeated a thrust
against Richmond at the first battle of MAN-
ASSAS. In the same month a Union victory
at the battle of RICH MOUNTAIN secured
northern control of WEST VIRGINIA. However,
following the defeat at Manassas, General
George McCLELLAN emerged as commander
of the Union's main eastern army, and
McClellan's strategy was to build up a
massive army for a second assault on Richmond. Union forces in the east remained
inactive while McClellan prepared.

In desperation Lincoln ordered his western commanders to initiate offensive operations. They in turn authorized a campaign
led by Grant, which in February 1862 produced the surrender of FORT DONNELSON AND
FORT HENRY in western Tennessee. 'Unconditional Surrender' Grant, the Union's first
war hero, consolidated Union control over
western Tennessee and Kentucky by defeating a Confederate counteroffensive at the
battle of SHILOH (April 1862). These actions
gave the Union control of the upper Mississippi and Ohio river systems.

McClellan finally launched his PENINSU-
LAR CAMPAIGN against Richmond in March
1862. McClellan's innate caution, and a successful Confederate counteroffensive in the
first SHENANDOAH VALLEY CAMPAIGN, led to
the assault fizzling out 6 miles (10 km) from

Richmond. Confederate forces, now under the command of Robert E. LEE, counterattacked, driving Union troops from Virginia at the second battle of MANASSAS (August 1862). Lee's subsequent invasion of Maryland, which threatened Washington DC, was turned back at the battle of ANTIETAM (September 1862).

On April 25 1862 the US Navy captured New Orleans. Following the unprecedented naval battle between the MONITOR AND VIRGINIA in May 1862, the US Navy also seized the important naval base of Norfolk, Virginia. These victories contributed to an increase in the effectiveness of the US blockade of the southern coastline and a consequent decrease in the revenue the Confederacy could derive from sales of cotton. To tighten the economic screw and to placate the radical wing of the Republican Party, Lincoln issued a preliminary EMANCIPATION PROCLAMATION on September 22 1862. A belated attempt by Union forces to exploit the victory at Antietam ended in defeat at the battle of FREDERICKSBURG.

The year 1863 proved to be the turning point of the war. The Emancipation Proclamation took effect on January 1 1863. Its immediate military impact was negligible but its propaganda value, especially in Great Britain where the TRENT AFFAIR had swung public opinion against the Union side, was enormous. In April 1863 Lee defeated yet another Union thrust against Richmond at the battle of CHANCELLORSVILLE, and mounted a Confederate invasion of western Maryland and south-central Pennsylvania. This was ultimately defeated at the battle of GETTYSBURG (July 1863). Gettysburg was the bloodiest battle ever fought on US soil. The ground gained briefly by Confederate forces has been dubbed 'the highwater mark of the Confederacy.' Although Union forces failed to exploit their victory, Confederate losses were so great that Lee was forced to adopt an essentially defensive strategy for the remainder of the war. An equally impor-

tant victory was achieved in the west, where on July 4 1863 Grant accepted the surrender of the Confederate garrison at Vicksburg, Mississippi, thereby consolidating Union control of the Mississippi river. The capture of Vicksburg meant that Confederate states west of the Mississippi (Louisiana, Arkansas and Texas) could no longer communicate with states to the east. Meanwhile the Union regained access to the most valuable trade route in the west. The loss of Vicksburg prompted recriminations and despair within the Confederacy. Grant sought to exploit this by paroling the town's garrison in the hopes that emaciated Confederate troops would return to their homes and spread defeatist gloom. Even so, Confederate resolve proved strong enough to defeat the next stage of Grant's campaign, an offensive through eastern Tennessee whose ultimate aim was the capture of Atlanta, Georgia. Union troops captured CHATTANOOGA, an important rail junction in southeastern Tennessee, on September 9 1863. But a subsequent Union advance into northwestern Georgia was repulsed at the battle of CHICKAMAUGA.

On March 9 1864 Grant was made commander in chief of the Union Army. He began building the Army of the Potomac to a strength of 100,000 in preparation for an all-out assault on Confederate forces defending Virginia. This campaign, initiated at the battle of the WILDERNESS and developed at SPOTSYLVANIA, COLD HARBOR and PETERSBURG, produced unprecedented casualties. Grant failed to capture Richmond but bled Lee's Army of Northern Virginia to the point of exhaustion. In July 1864 a Confederate column under General Jubal Early (1816–94) conducted a raid on Maryland designed to relieve pressure on Lee's main army. Early's troops came within 5 miles (8 km) of Washington DC, but were driven back by Union troops under General Philip SHERIDAN in the second Shenandoah valley campaign. Sheridan employed scorched-earth tactics to ensure that the valley could no longer supply Confederate forces. To the south and west, General William T. SHERMAN began the campaign that would culminate in the battle for ATLANTA and the MARCH TO THE SEA. On November 30 1864 the strongest Confederate army remaining outside Virginia was routed at the battle of FRANKLIN.

Lincoln used his second INAUGURAL ADDRESS and the *RIVER QUEEN* PEACE TALKS (February 1865) to offer the Confederacy lenient surrender terms. But even after Lee surrendered the Army of Northern Virginia to Grant at APPOMATTOX COURT HOUSE on April 9 1865, Confederate President Jefferson DAVIS called for continued resistance. A final surrender of Confederate forces was not achieved until May 26 1865.

During the Civil War, 359,000 Union soldiers died: 110,000 were killed in battle and 275,000 were wounded. On the Confederate side, 258,000 soldiers died (this represented 25% of the male population of military age in the eleven states of the Confederacy): roughly 94,000 were killed in battle, and at least 100,000 were wounded. In both armies death from disease was more common than death in combat. Conditions in prisoner-of-war camps were especially grim; the suffering experienced by Union prisoners in the Confederate camp at ANDERSONVILLE, Georgia, prompted a war-crimes trial. Civilians on both sides suffered from the destruction and appropriation of property by regular army units (as in the second Shenandoah Valley campaign and Sherman's March to the Sea) and from irregular guerrilla groups such as QUANTRILL'S RAIDERS. Southern civilians suffered disproportionately: 40% of the south's livestock was destroyed during the war, and by its end the south was threatened with famine.

Lincoln was assassinated by the Confederate sympathizer John Wilkes BOOTH on April 14 1865. Had Lincoln served out his second term he might have been able to preside over the harmonious RECONSTRUCTION of the nation. But in the event Reconstruction would prove almost as divisive as the Civil War itself.

Civil Works Administration (CWA), agency created under the NEW DEAL in 1933 to create jobs by undertaking public works. The history of the CWA provides a good example of conflict between New Deal bureau and within ROOSEVELT's cabinet. Title II of the NATIONAL INDUSTRIAL RECOVERY ACT (June 16 1933) appropriated $3.3 billion for a PUBLIC WORKS ADMINISTRATION (PWA). But Harold Ickes (1874–1952), director of the PWA, was reluctant to fund job-creation schemes unless and until they met stringent standards. On November 9 1933, with around 25% of America's workforce idle, Roosevelt created the CWA by executive order and funded it from the PWA's budget. Within three months the CWA had set 4 million men to work building roads and schools. In March 1934 the CWA was subsumed within the FEDERAL EMERGENCY RELIEF ADMINISTRATION.

Clark, George Rogers (1752–1818), American military leader who, during the REVOLUTIONARY WAR, led Kentucky militiamen on an expedition to wrest control of the NORTHWEST TERRITORY from Britain and its Native American allies. Clark's force marched as far west as the Mississippi, establishing forts at Vincennes (Indiana) and Kaskaskia (Illinois). In February 1779 Clark captured the regional commander of British forces at Vincennes. He reinforced this success with the ritual slaughter of four Algonkian-SHAWNEE leaders, thereby temporarily establishing America as the strongest power in the region. The treaty of PARIS (1783) reflected this dominance, contributing greatly to the TERRITORIAL EXPANSION of the USA. In 1793 Clark was implicated in a plot to detach western territories from the USA hatched during GENÊT'S MISSION.

Clark, Mark (Wayne) (1896–1974), US Army general. A career soldier, who was a contemporary of EISENHOWER's at West

Point military academy, Clark served as a major general in World War I, and, with the rank of lieutenant general, as commander of the US Fifth Army in the North African and Italian campaigns of WORLD WAR II. Clark led the force that captured Rome on June 4 1944, and revelled in the publicity. Clark pioneered the US Army's amphibious-landing techniques. At the close of the war he commanded US ground troops in the occupation of Austria (1945–7).

Clay, Cassius, *see* ALI, MUHAMMAD.

Clay, Henry (1777–1852), influential politician, initially a Democrat, then a National Republican, and finally a Whig, who ran three times for president (1824, 1832, 1844). He was the chief promoter of compromise between north and south in the decades prior to the Civil War, earning him the nickname 'the great compromiser'. Clay was a leading member of that political generation (whose other luminaries were John C. CALHOUN and Daniel WEBSTER) that shaped and maintained the SECOND PARTY SYSTEM but lived to see it torn apart by conflict arising from the future status of slavery within the USA.

Born in Virginia, Clay trained as a lawyer. In 1797 he took up practice in Lexington, Kentucky. After service in the Kentucky legislature (1803–6, 1807–9) and US Senate (1806–7, 1809–10) Clay was elected to the US House of Representatives, serving as Speaker (1811–20, 1823–5).

Clay's instincts were toward a pragmatic nationalism. He supported the WAR OF 1812, but was a chief negotiator of the treaty of GHENT (1815) that ended the war. He helped devise the MISSOURI COMPROMISE (1820), accommodating slavery within the westward expansion of the Union. Clay ran unsuccessfully for president in 1824, but the successful candidate, John Quincy ADAMS, appointed him secretary of state, provoking talk of a 'CORRUPT BARGAIN'. Clay held this position until 1829.

Increasingly uncomfortable within the DEMOCRATIC PARTY, Clay, promoting an AMERICAN SYSTEM of internal improvements, touted a NATIONAL REPUBLICAN alternative to Andrew JACKSON's populism and John C. Calhoun's defense of STATES' RIGHTS. Clay worked with Jackson and against Calhoun to defuse the NULLIFICATION CRISIS by proposing the compromise TARIFF of 1833. He opposed Jackson by supporting the BANK OF THE UNITED STATES. The WHIG PARTY nominated him for president in 1832 and 1844. Both bids failed because Clay (who declared after the 1844 campaign 'I would rather be right than be president') misjudged public opinion on the Bank in the first campaign, and on the annexation of TEXAS in the second. While serving in the US Senate (1831–42, 1849–52), Clay led the Whig Party and, by providing moderate southerners with an alternative to the Democrats, maintained the viability of the second party system. He played a crucial role in securing southern support for the COMPROMISE OF 1850, which temporarily averted civil war.

Clayton Anti-trust Act (October 15 1914), legislation that outlawed specific restrictive or monopolizing corporate practices – unlike the vaguely worded SHERMAN ANTI-TRUST ACT (1890). The practices outlawed included the use of discriminatory pricing to force competitors out of business; 'tying contracts' binding purchasers to shun competitors' goods; and the use of interlocking directorships to stifle competition among corporations capitalized at over $1 million.

The act gave the FEDERAL TRADE COMMISSION the power to issue cease-and-desist orders to corporations whose business practices contravened the act. Officers in corporations found guilty of persistently restricting competition were held individually accountable, and could be liable to pay damages to competitors who brought successful actions through the civil courts.

The Clayton Act also reversed the Supreme Court ruling IN RE DEBS, leading Samuel GOMPERS to hail it as 'labor's Magna

Carta'. It specified that trade unions were legal, and that they could not be considered illegal combinations in restraint of trade under antitrust laws. The law forbade employers from applying to the courts for injunctions to prevent strikes or secondary boycotts, except in cases where irreparable property loss might ensue. However, subsequent Supreme Court verdicts (especially DUPLEX PRINTING PRESS COMPANY VS. DEERING) weakened the protection afforded to secondary boycotts by the act.

clear and present danger, *see* SCHENCK VS. US.

Cleveland, (Stephen) Grover (1837–1908), Democratic statesman, and 22nd (1885–9) and 24th president (1893–7) of the USA. The only president to serve two non-consecutive terms, Cleveland was also the only Democrat elected to the White House between 1860 and 1908.

Born in New Jersey and raised in New York state, Cleveland opened a law office in Buffalo in 1859. He exploited the terms of the CONSCRIPTION ACT (1863) to buy himself out of service in the Civil War. He served as mayor of Buffalo (1881–2) and governor of New York (1882–4). In both positions he fought corruption, arguing, 'Public office is a public trust.' In 1884 his reputation for rectitude secured him the DEMOCRATIC PARTY's presidential nomination over the objections of TAMMANY HALL, the New York party machine. In a brutal election campaign Cleveland admitted fathering an illegitimate child, but was elected with 49% of the popular vote.

President Cleveland vetoed more bills than any previous incumbent, but presided over the passage of the DAWES SEVERALTY ACT (1887) and the INTERSTATE COMMERCE ACT (1887). On June 2 1886 Cleveland became only the second man to marry while serving as president. His bride Frances Folsom (1864–1947) was 28 years his junior, and his decision to conduct the ceremony in the White House is unparalleled.

In the 1888 presidential election Cleveland outpolled his Republican opponent Benjamin HARRISON by 60,000 votes but lost in the ELECTORAL COLLEGE. But in 1892 Cleveland's commitment to lower tariffs led to his nomination once more by a Democratic Party determined to exploit the unpopularity of the McKINLEY TARIFF. Despite his support for the GOLD STANDARD, Cleveland was elected president because he lost fewer votes to POPULIST James WEAVER than did the Republican incumbent Harrison. Cleveland's orthodox fiscal response to the DEPRESSION OF 1893 (he demanded repeal of the SHERMAN SILVER PURCHASE ACT) split the Democratic Party.

Clinton, Henry (1738–95), British military officer who held a variety of commands in the British army during the REVOLUTIONARY WAR, and served as its commander in chief from March 1778 to May 1782. Major General Clinton fought at the battle of BUNKER HILL (1775) and took part in an unsuccessful attempt to capture CHARLESTON (1776) before taking up occupation duties in New York City. He commanded the British army defeated by Washington at MONMOUTH COURT HOUSE in July 1778. Following the successful capture of Charleston, he took part with CORNWALLIS in the British attempt to capitalize on the strength of LOYALIST sentiment in the southern colonies. Following the battle of CAMDEN (1780), Clinton ordered Cornwallis to join him in New York, but Cornwallis refused and invaded Virginia instead. Irked, Clinton withheld reinforcements from Cornwallis. This dispute between the two men allowed Washington to isolate Cornwallis's force, and ultimately led to Cornwallis's surrender at YORKTOWN. Clinton was replaced as commander in chief in May 1782.

Clinton, Hillary, *see* RODHAM CLINTON, HILLARY.

Clinton, William ('Bill') Jefferson (1946–), Democratic statesman, and 42nd president of the USA (1993–). In January

1999 Clinton became the first elected president to face an IMPEACHMENT trial in the US Senate.

Clinton grew up in a poor and unhappy family. His natural father, William Jefferson Blythe, died in a freak accident before Clinton was born. His stepfather Roger Clinton was an abusive alcoholic. Nevertheless, the young Clinton tried to get along with his stepfather, changing his name by deed poll at the age of 16. He graduated in international affairs from Georgetown University, and won a Rhodes Scholarship to Oxford. He studied politics, philosophy and economics, but left in 1970, without graduating, to take up a scholarship at Yale University Law School. It was at Yale that he met his future wife Hillary RODHAM CLINTON. They married in 1975.

One year after graduating from Yale in 1973, Clinton made an unsuccessful bid to be elected to Congress from Arkansas's Third District. He was defeated, but two years later, in 1976, was elected the state's attorney general. In 1978 he was elected governor of Arkansas, and at 32 became the youngest governor in the country. At this stage in his career Clinton was on the liberal wing of the DEMOCRATIC PARTY. As state governor he raised taxes to improve the educational system and, as a result, was defeated in the 1980 gubernatorial election. Begging the state's voters for another chance, he was re-elected in 1982, 1984 and 1986. In 1988 Clinton was asked to give the keynote address nominating Michael DUKAKIS at the Democrats' national convention. He ran 30 minutes over his allotted time, raising applause only when he said 'and finally'. Typically, he turned this disaster to his advantage by appearing on TV talk shows to joke about it. He also set about transforming himself into the moderate's moderate.

With George BUSH's approval rating sky-high in the wake of the PERSIAN GULF WAR, many prominent Democrats chose not compete for their party's nomination in the 1992 presidential election. Clinton, overcoming early revelations of sexual infidelity, ridicule for his claim that as a student he had smoked cannabis without inhaling, and criticism of efforts to avoid the DRAFT during the VIETNAM WAR, emerged as the Democratic candidate, and won the election on a minority share of the POPULAR VOTE. He took up office on January 20 1993.

Much of Clinton's first year in office was spent battling Congress on the issue of reducing the federal deficit. However, he did persuade Congress to endorse the NORTH AMERICAN FREE TRADE AGREEMENT in 1993. An ambitious and complicated overhaul of the nation's health service devised in collaboration with his wife Hillary was blocked by Congress in 1994. The Republican Party made much of the Clintons' alleged involvement in the WHITEWATER AFFAIR and, touting a CONTRACT WITH AMERICA, gained control of both houses of Congress in the 1994 mid-term elections. Clinton finished his first term as a virtual lame duck, and yet still gained a convincing victory over Bob DOLE in the presidential election of 1996. Clinton's second term was entirely overshadowed by allegations of sexual impropriety, which led to his eventual impeachment trial on charges of perjury and obstruction of justice arising from the LEWINSKY SCANDAL. On February 12 1999 the Senate voted 55–45 against impeaching Clinton for perjury and 50–50 against impeachment for obstructing justice.

coal strike of 1902, strike by 140,000 members of the UNITED MINE WORKERS OF AMERICA in pursuit of an eight-hour day, a pay rise and union recognition. The strike began on May 12 . Mine owners sought to starve the miners back to work. Centered in western Pennsylvania, a region which had seen decades of labor activism and careful union planning, the strike held.

In October President Theodore ROOSEVELT intervened to protect the nation's coal supply. He was shocked when the employers' chief negotiator told him that God 'in his infinite wisdom' had given control of property interests to capitalists, among them mine owners, who were solely qualified to protect the rights and interest of the laboring man. Roosevelt threatened to place the mines under federal control unless owners agreed to binding arbitration by a presidential commission. Miners returned to work while the commission deliberated. On March 22 1903 it awarded miners a cut in hours and a modest pay rise, but withheld union recognition. Roosevelt, who claimed that his intervention showed his commitment to a 'square deal' for the working man, gained votes in the 1904 presidential election.

coal strike of 1946, strike by 400,000 members of the UNITED MINE WORKERS OF AMERICA (UMWA) for higher pay and better conditions. The strike began in April. On May 21 President TRUMAN authorized the US government to take over the mines and ordered the miners back to work while negotiations were conducted. On November 21 the UMWA ordered its members to resume the strike in protest at the mine owners' intransigence. This action broke a court injunction and led to the UMWA being fined $3.5 million and its leader, John L. LEWIS, being convicted of contempt. The miners returned to work on December 7 1946 and, as part of as of the deal returning the mines to private ownership negotiated by the federal government, secured a generous pay settlement and a health and pension plan that were the envy of other workers.

Coca-Cola and Pepsi. The elevation of these two products to the status of global cultural icons began with campaigns for Temperance and PROHIBITION in the USA. In 1886 an Atlanta druggist, John Styth Pemberton, synthesized a blend of extract of coca leaf and juice from cola nuts. In 1887 he sold Coca-Cola to Asa Griggs Chandler for $283.29. Chandler took advantage of the recently invented crown seal cap to increase production and the availability of what he dubbed 'The Great National Temperance Drink'. Chandler sold the company for $25 million in 1919.

During the 1920s Harrison Jones created a sales team driven by an almost evangelical desire to make Coca-Cola available in every conceivable outlet. Consumption rose during PROHIBITION, but it rose again following passage of the TWENTY-FIRST AMENDMENT ending Prohibition. During WORLD WAR II, General EISENHOWER ordered ten mobile bottling plants to accompany US troops on the D-DAY campaign. In 1985 Coca-Cola committed one of the worst public-relations blunders in US corporate history when it tried to wean the public onto a 'new and improved' blend.

Pepsi-Cola was synthesized by a North Carolina druggist, Caleb D. Bingham, in the 1890s. It was thought to relieve suffering caused by peptic ulcers. Pepsi was usually cheaper than Coca-Cola. Its increase in market share in the 1930s and 1940s was largely due to the efforts of a sales force directed by Alfred N. Steele. Pepsi went to great lengths to exploit Coca-Cola's 1985 formula change. But the incident highlighted a truth about the soft-drinks industry that had been apparent for almost thirty years: that consumer interest in the rivalry between the two companies stimulates sales for both.

Cochise (*c*.1824–74), Chiricahua-APACHE leader who waged war against the USA in the territory of New Mexico from 1862 to 1872. Like many Apache, Cochise initially befriended US settlers on the grounds that they were enemies of the Mexicans. But in February 1862, Cochise and eight followers were imprisoned following false accusations that they had abducted a Mexican-Irish boy named Mickey Free. Cochise and three others escaped, but the rest of his followers were hanged. Cochise killed an equal number of US settlers in retaliation. A war of mutual revenge ended only in 1872, when the Chiricahua-Apache were promised that their homelands in southeastern Arizona would be granted reservation status. The USA later broke this treaty, resulting in a second Apache insurrection led by GERONIMO.

Cody, William, *see* BUFFALO BILL.

Coeur d'Alene miners' strike (1892), unsuccessful strike in northern Idaho by miners protesting at a pay cut and in support of improved working conditions. Gold, lead and large deposits of silver had been discovered in the area in the 1880s. The strike, by miners in the Coeur d'Alene silver fields, began on July 14 1892. Mine owners lobbied successfully for a declaration of martial law and the deployment of US soldiers and state militiamen to protect imported strikebreakers. State and federal authorities connived in the creation of impromptu detention centers in which strikers were held without trial. These tactics broke the strike. Coming soon after the suppression of the HOMESTEAD STRIKE, and in the midst of the DEPRESSION OF 1893, this defeat marked the lowest point in the fortunes of organized labor in US history.

Cold Harbor, battle of (June 1–3 1864), engagement in Virginia, one of the worst Union defeats in the CIVIL WAR. On June 1 1864, developing a campaign initiated at the battle of the WILDERNESS, a Union army under GRANT tried and failed to capture Cold Harbor, a crossroads 7 miles (11 km) from Richmond. (Union forces had previously attempted to capture Gaines Mill, near Cold Harbor, during the SEVEN DAYS' BATTLE of 1862.) Grant's army had suffered 44,000 casualties in less than a month, but reinforcements maintained its strength at 100,000. Nevertheless, LEE's Confederate army of 60,000 held their positions. On

June 3 a desperate Union assault against Confederate trenches produced 7,000 Union casualties against 1,500 Confederate losses. On 12 June Grant broke the stalemate that developed after this assault by ordering an outflanking march against PETERSBURG. During the fighting Union troops took to pinning their names and addresses to their tunics so that they could be identified after they had been killed.

Cold War, period lasting from the end of WORLD WAR II in 1945 until the break-up of the USSR and the Soviet bloc in the late 1980s, in which the USA and the Soviet Union engaged in a global economic and political struggle without actually going to war with each other. At various moments, notably during the CUBAN MISSILE CRISIS, the Cold War threatened to boil over, threatening the world with nuclear devastation.

The origins of the Cold War can be traced to US and Soviet perceptions of one another's aims. The founding fathers of the Soviet Union believed that capitalist nations sought, and would always seek, the destruction of communism. Soviet leaders interpreted President Wilson's decision to send US troops to SIBERIA in 1918 as a thinly disguised attempt to undermine the Bolshevik regime. The USA refused to grant diplomatic recognition to the Soviet Union until 1933, heightening the latter's sense that the USA regarded it as a pariah. During WORLD WAR II the Soviet Union and the USA were thrown together as allies in the fight against Nazism. However, Stalin suspected that American capitalists secretly hoped that Hitler would destroy the Soviet Union. The delayed opening of a 'second front' in Europe, finally achieved by the D-DAY LANDINGS of 1944, was a major source of tension in the wartime relationship between the USA and the Soviet Union. While 50 Soviets died for every American killed during the war, and much of the western part of the USSR was devastated, the USA emerged from the war as the world's strongest industrial nation, and the sole possessor of atomic weapons. From a Soviet perspective a weakened USSR now faced isolation and confinement within a global capitalist system dominated by the USA.

US attitudes towards the Soviet Union were governed by negative responses to the uncompromising atheism of communism and its critique of American capitalism, and by hostility to the activities of Soviet agencies such as the Comintern, founded to foment revolutions abroad. As the RED SCARE of 1917–20 demonstrated, many Americans almost immediately linked Soviet communism with a threat to their distinctive way of life. In the wake of the GREAT DEPRESSION, hostility towards the Soviet Union softened. American intellectuals argued that elements of the Soviet-programme were progressive, and the COMMUNIST PARTY OF THE USA experienced a surge in membership during the 1930s. The Nazi-Soviet Pact of 1939, Stalin's desperate attempt to buy time to prepare for war, led most Americans to the conclusion that the Soviets were duplicitous, and that their American supporters were dupes. But by the time the USA entered the war, Germany had invaded the USSR, and the USA and the Soviets were thrown together as allies. President Franklin ROOSEVELT extended LEND-LEASE aid to the USSR, and Vice President Henry WALLACE urged closer cooperation with the Soviets. However, Roosevelt had justified US entry into the war through the universalist rhetoric of the FOUR FREEDOMS, and as early as the TEHERAN CONFERENCE in 1943 it was obvious that Stalin did not share, and would not lightly accept, American definitions of the freedoms that should inform the postwar world. Roosevelt tried harder than most subsequent American statesmen and politicians to understand the Soviet world view and explain it to the American public. However, after Roosevelt's death, American perceptions of Soviet aims centerd on the threat they posed to

democracy within the USA and in the world at large. Assuming the mantle of 'the leader of the 'free world', the USA embarked on the CONTAINMENT of a Soviet regime it believed was bent on spreading totalitarian communism around the world.

The opening exchanges in the Cold War centered on Eastern Europe. At the YALTA CONFERENCE the Western Allies attempted to recognize Stalin's demand that regimes friendly to the Soviet Union be established in countries in Eastern Europe occupied by the Nazis, while at the same time insisting that democratic elections be held in Poland. At the POTSDAM CONFERENCE the Allies agreed to the division of Germany, while attempting to moderate Stalin's demands for reparations. It was soon clear that the Soviet Union would not tolerate the creation of non-communist regimes in territories controlled by the Red Army. On March 15 1946 Winston Churchill gave a speech in Fulton, Missouri, in which he suggested that an 'iron curtain' had descended across Europe. As Stalin consolidated Soviet control over areas occupied by the Red Army, local communist parties made gains in elections held in France and Italy. In Greece a communist-led coalition gained the upper hand in a civil war fought against a right-wing government backed by Britain. In February 1947 Britain informed the USA that it could no longer afford to aid the Greek government. Washington responded by formulating the TRUMAN DOCTRINE.

President Harry S TRUMAN announced his eponymous doctrine in a speech to Congress delivered on March 12 1947. The USA would, he declared, support 'all free people who are resisting attempted subjugation by armed minorities or by outside pressures'. The Senate approved this policy (67–23) on April 23, and the House of Representatives followed suit (287–107) on May 9. At the end of May Truman announced a $400 million aid package for Greece and Turkey. Later that year, the Truman administration unveiled the MARSHALL PLAN, a program of economic aid to Europe. The Soviet Union and its Eastern European satellites were invited to apply for Marshall aid. They denounced the program as an imperialist plot. The process of creating two mutually antagonistic power blocs in Europe was speeded by the BERLIN BLOCKADE (1948–9), the creation in 1949 of NATO (the NORTH ATLANTIC TREATY ORGANIZATION), and the acquisition of atomic weapons by the Soviets, also in 1949. In 1950 the USA endorsed NATO's FORWARD STRATEGY, and, over Republican opposition, Truman ordered a substantial increase in the number of US troops in Europe.

Soon after Truman's surprise victory in the PRESIDENTIAL ELECTION OF 1948 the focus of the Cold War shifted to eastern Asia. In 1949, after years of civil war, Mao Zedong's Chinese Communist Party consolidated its control over mainland China and exiled the pro-Western nationalist Chiang Kai-shek (Jiang Jie Shi) to the island of Formosa (Taiwan). Democrats and Republicans blamed each other for 'the loss of China'. Republicans alleged that Truman had directed too much aid to Europe and too little to Chiang Kai-shek. They criticized Truman's refusal to enact NSC-68, a policy document recommending the tripling of US defense expenditure. Senator Joseph McCARTHY injected a sinister sub-theme into this partisan wrangling when, in February 1950, he announced that at least 57 card-carrying communists in the State Department were shaping US foreign policy. The McCARTHY HEARINGS, the ROSENBERG TRIAL and the COMMUNIST CONTROL ACT fed on the idea that communist advances abroad could be explained by 'subversion' at home. In February 1950 China and the USSR concluded an alliance, which many US commentators presented as the first step in a concerted program of global communist expansion — a program that it was the duty of the 'free world' to resist. In June 1950 North Korean

troops, allegedly acting on Soviet orders, invaded South Korea. Truman ordered US intervention in the KOREAN WAR under the auspices of the UNITED NATIONS, and a massive defense build-up.

The Korean War eventually produced a military and diplomatic stalemate. Republicans criticized Truman's conduct of the war, and some of them even sympathized with General Douglas MACARTHUR's view that the USA should have used nuclear weapons against China in pursuit of a conclusive victory in Korea. The EISENHOWER administration, the first Republican administration for 20 years, was determined to avoid any appearance of being 'soft on communism'. Its NEW LOOK DEFENSE POLICY sought to move beyond the 'negative, futile and immoral policy of containment' by building up America's nuclear arsenal in a bid to force concessions from the USSR and China. Eisenhower's secretary of state, John Foster DULLES, even spoke of ROLLBACK — the use of military force to liberate areas of the world already under communist control. Eisenhower was a good deal more cautious than Dulles and, by describing nuclear war as 'unthinkable', gave the USSR reason to suspect that the USA would not in fact use nuclear weapons to deter Soviet expansion. Nevertheless, Eisenhower endorsed the DOMINO THEORY and the EISENHOWER DOCTRINE, both of which committed the USA to a simplified yet broadened containment strategy. The USA would henceforth use economic and military aid to prevent the formation of communist governments in areas of the world, such as Vietnam, which had previously been considered of little strategic value or, as in the case of the Middle East, outside the USA's traditional sphere of influence. Meanwhile US policymakers, backed by the emerging MILITARY-INDUSTRIAL COMPLEX, peddled the notion of a 'missile gap' in order to maintain and increase the USA's nuclear arsenal. (There *was* a missile gap in the late 1950s: the USA possessed a far great number of nuclear warheads and delivery systems than the USSR.)

Events exposed the limitations of US strategic policy. Containment strategy and Dulles's commitment to 'rollback' failed to deter the Soviet Union from invading Hungary in 1956 in order to crush an embryonic democracy. Neither did containment policy deter Fidel Castro from overthrowing the corrupt but pro-American Batista regime in Cuba in 1959 and turning to the Soviet Union for support in 1960. The Soviets concluded that the Americans would not fight a nuclear war to protect Hungarian democracy, and Castro doubted that they would use nuclear weapons to defend Cuban corruption. But these events, as well as the USSR's success in launching *Sputnik*, the world's first space satellite, in 1957, and the U-2 INCIDENT in 1960, inflamed US public opinion. The more assertive US strategic policy became, the more pressure was exerted on US presidents to demonstrate that the threats and commitments implicit in US policy were credible. This vicious circle began to take shape at precisely the moment when Soviet Premier Nikita Khrushchev embarked on a quest for propaganda victories overseas to deflect attention from the failure of his domestic policies. In 1961 the Cold War entered its most dangerous phase.

During the PRESIDENTIAL ELECTION OF 1960 both John F. KENNEDY and Richard NIXON made a series of speeches announcing their determination to resist the spread of communism. One of President Kennedy's first acts in office was to approve an invasion of Cuba, sponsored by the Central Intelligence Agency (CIA), designed to overthrow the Castro regime. The BAY OF PIGS INVASION was a military disaster. It strengthened Castro's hold on power and encouraged him to align Cuba with the USSR. Khrushchev immediately sought to exploit this debacle by provoking the BERLIN WALL CRISIS and by ordering the construction of Soviet missile

sites on Cuba. The destruction of these Soviet bases on Cuban soil was a non-negotiable US demand, and Kennedy announced that the USA would do 'whatever must be done' to achieve it. Kennedy's first act was relatively cautious, the creation of a 'quarantine' around Cuba to prevent the delivery of missiles and warheads. This allowed Khrushchev time to reconsider. The world held its breath. In major US and European cities schoolchildren practiced evacuation drills in preparation for a global nuclear war. On October 26 1962 Khrushchev announced his readiness to negotiate. In the final analysis the USSR was not willing to risk the destruction of Moscow to preserve Marxist-Leninism in Cuba. After the frightening brinksmanship of this crisis, the USSR and the USA adopted a policy of 'peaceful coexistence', and strove to improve communications between the leaderships of both countries (this was when the telephone 'hotline' linking the White House and the Kremlin was set up). A further marker of reducing tension was the signing of the Nuclear Test Ban treaty in 1963.

One unfortunate consequence of the peaceful resolution of the Cuban crisis, however, was the fostering of a sense of hubris within the Kennedy administration. This led it to commit a growing number of US 'advisers' to the VIETNAM WAR. Many of Kennedy's team served in the subsequent JOHNSON administration, and advised President Johnson to escalate US military involvement. Johnson, who did not want to be remembered as the 'the man who lost Vietnam', complied. Johnson's successor, Richard NIXON, had made his name as a RED-BAITING anti-communist. Yet, ironically, Nixon's desire to secure 'peace with honor' for America in Vietnam led him to pursue DÉTENTE with the USSR and a rapprochement with China that lowered Cold War tensions.

Nixon's decision to seek better relations with the USSR and China was not motivated by a desire to abandon the policy of containment. On the contrary, Nixon's national security adviser, and later secretary of state, Henry KISSINGER, described détente as a 'philosophical deepening' of containment doctrine. Nixon and Kissinger sought to exploit the rift in Soviet-Chinese relations that had developed in the 1960s. They hoped to use the USSR's need for improved trade links with the West to stabilize the arms race and to force concessions from the Soviet Union on human rights. Détente was attacked in Congress both by 'hawks' (who argued that it made too many concessions to the Soviets) and by 'doves' (who argued that it did not go far enough). It enjoyed little support among an American public sickened by Vietnam and distrustful of foreign-policy experts. In the end, détente did not deter the Soviet Union and Cuba from seeking to take full advantage of the USA's post-Vietnam malaise by intervening in the Angolan civil war, in Yemen, in Ethiopia and in Somalia.

Middle Eastern affairs contributed a further source of superpower friction in the détente era. The USA contributed billions of dollars of military and economic aid to Israel. Meanwhile, during the 1960s and 70s the Soviet Union sought to expand its influence in the Arab world, offering extensive military assistance to Egypt and Syria. The Arab–Israeli war of 1973 demonstrated that neither superpower exercised complete control over their client states. During the war Arab countries imposed an embargo on oil exports to the US in retaliation for America's support for Israel. Following the war, in a move which hit the US economy hard, the Arab-dominated Organization of Petroleum Exporting Countries raised world oil prices to unprecedented levels. The USA sought to build bridges with the Arab world and especially with the oil-producing countries of the Persian Gulf. The Soviet Union sought to maintain or increase its influence in the Gulf for similar reasons.

The détente experiment ended, and US strategic policy reverted to a more familiar form, following the Soviet invasion of Afghanistan in December 1979. President CARTER described the invasion as the 'biggest threat to world peace since World War II'. He withdrew from trade agreements with the Soviet Union, denounced its leadership and sought to persuade other nations to treat the USSR as a pariah. Carter's successor, Ronald REAGAN, also made the invasion the pretext for a series of hawkish policy decisions. In 1983 Reagan famously described the Soviet Union as an 'evil empire'. He also believed that arms-control agreements had given the Soviets a military advantage over the West. From this perspective a stable, businesslike relationship with the USSR was undesirable and in any case impossible. To the delight of US arms manufacturers, Reagan induced Congress to pass a $180 billion program to modernize US strategic forces. He authorized the development of the MX and cruise missiles, the B-2 bomber and a navy capable of fighting 'two and a half wars' at once. At one point during Reagan's first administration Congress had appropriated more money than there were programs on which to spend it, and the inevitable result was that defense contractors padded their profits by charging the government $500 for a hammer and $2000 for a toilet seat. Yet for all the waste associated with this program, it still produced technological advances that the Soviet Union could not match. After struggling throughout the 1960s and 1970s to achieve and maintain a rough strategic parity with the USA, the Soviet Union was now faced with the intensification of an arms race it could no longer afford. For this reason Soviet premier Yuri Andropov warned in 1984 that Reagan's build-up made war more, not less, likely.

Yet Reagan's support for the STRATEGIC DEFENSE INITIATIVE (dubbed 'Star Wars'), and the position he adopted at the REYKJAVIK

CONFERENCE, seemed to indicate a willingness to end, or at least greatly diminish, the nuclear stand-off between the USSR and the USA. At the same time, as arguments defending and attacking the Reagan administration's position in the IRAN–CONTRA SCANDAL made clear, the American public now identified terrorism sponsored by fundamentalist Islamic states, not Soviet communism, as the number-one threat to their way of life. The election of Mikhail Gorbachev as General Secretary of the Soviet Communist Party in March 1985, and his policy of *perestroika* (restructuring), marked the beginning of the end of the Cold War. Gorbachev did not embark on *perestroika* with the intent of dismantling the Soviet Union or its hegemony in Eastern Europe. However, once it became clear that the Soviet satellite states would use Gorbachev's restructuring to assert their independence, he did not stand in their way. Moreover, Gorbachev's policies set in motion events within his own country that led to the break-up of the Soviet Union in 1991.

Experts continue to argue over whether the USA 'won' the Cold War, and whether indeed it is in fact over. The Cold War reflected, and further encouraged, a tendency within American culture to see the world in manichean terms: as divided unambiguously between good and evil. Asked to supply the 'vision thing' following the collapse of the Soviet Union, President BUSH spoke tentatively of America's opportunity to lead a 'new world order'. However, the policies adopted by the USA during and after the PERSIAN GULF WAR were shaped as much by the desire to protect vital American interests, such as oil, as by a commitment to bring a new spirit of idealism to international relations. The domestic consequences of the Cold War have often been viewed as uniformly retrograde. Yet for all the ugliness of McCarthyism, the Cold War did produce positive developments within America. Primed by defense spending, the US econ-omy boomed. The CIVIL RIGHTS MOVEMENT benefited from the reluctance of successive presidents to be seen to be acquiescing in the subjugation of African-Americans while claiming America's leadership of the free world. The NATIONAL DEFENSE EDUCATION ACT (1958), passed amid fears that the USA was losing the 'space race', contributed to an enormous expansion in the American university system. The APOLLO PROGRAM was funded out of a desire to surpass Soviet achievements in space. More controversially, modern American art, especially the abstract expressionism associated with Jackson Pollock, benefited from subsidies and purchases discreetly funded by the CIA in a bid to demonstrate to the world that Americans were not mindless consumers.

Colfax massacre (1873), massacre of black activists by white supremacists in the town of Colfax, Louisiana. This incident was the bloodiest manifestation of white rage during RECONSTRUCTION.

Armed FREEDMEN, drilled by black Union veterans, had built a system of trenches around the town, in an attempt to prevent white supremacists from occupying the courthouse and falsifying election results. Following a three-week siege, 200 armed whites overran the town on Easter Sunday, and 50 black citizens were massacred after their surrender. In UNITED STATES VS. CRUIK-SHANK the Supreme Court quashed murder convictions obtained against the ringleaders of the white violence.

Collier, John (1884–1968), founder of the American Indian Defense Association (1922), and commissioner of Indian affairs during ROOSEVELT's presidency, in which capacity he fashioned the 'Indian NEW DEAL'.

Collier became fascinated by Native American culture during a period spent living among the PUEBLO peoples near Taos, New Mexico, and campaigned against government policies that eroded those cultures by breaking up tribal structures. Collier's most important legislative achievement, the

WHEELER–HOWARD ACT (1934), reversed previous policy by encouraging native peoples to reinvigorate tribal government and by banning further sales of Native American lands to white homesteaders. Collier welcomed the creation of an INDIAN CLAIMS COMMISSION (1946) to investigate grievances against the US government.

Colorado, western state, encompassing the eastern slope of the Rocky Mountains and bordered to the north by Wyoming, to the east by Kansas and Nebraska, to the south by Oklahoma and New Mexico and to the west by Utah. The USA acquired most of Colorado through the LOUISIANA PURCHASE (1803), and secured title to the remainder in the treaty of GUADELUPE-HIDALGO (1848). The first permanent white settlement in the territory was established on the banks of the San Luis river in 1851. The discovery of gold near Pike's Peak in 1858 boosted settlement and Colorado became a US territory on February 28 1861. CHEYENNE resistance to further settlement by miners and ranchers was overcome through the treaty of MEDICINE LODGE (1867) and the RED RIVER WAR (1874–5). Colorado became the 38th state in the Union on August 1 1876. It granted women the right to vote in 1893.

The early history of the state was dominated by conflict between farmers and ranchers and mine-workers and owners. Farmers in the state were enthusiastic supporters of the POPULIST movement. Tensions in the state's mining industry boiled over following the LUDLOW MASSACRE (1914), the brutal suppression of a strike against a mining company owned by John Davison Rockefeller Jr (1874–1960). The INDUSTRIAL WORKERS OF THE WORLD, a syndicalist union, gained numerous supporters within the state during this period. In the 1930s many farms in southeastern Colorado were devastated by the DUST BOWL

The growth of urban centers, chiefly Denver, and the development of new industries, chiefly tourism, in the second half of the 20th century have diversified the state's economy. In 1990 Colorado had 3,294,394 residents, making it the 26th most populous state in the union.

Comanche, Native American people, whose language belongs to the Uto-Aztecan family and is closely related to that of the SHOSHONI, of whom they are an offshoot. The Comanche's original homelands were in Montana, close to lands occupied by the Shoshoni. The Comanche migrated south in the 17th century and settled in northern Texas, eastern New Mexico and southern Colorado.

The Comanche were particularly hostile toward interlopers. During the 18th century they fought protracted campaigns against the Spanish in Texas. Although their numbers dwindled in the 19th century following epidemics of smallpox and cholera, they still put up bitter resistance to US settlement in the region. So feared were Comanche horsemen that during the CIVIL WAR the CONFEDERACY signed a generous treaty of non-aggression (April 12 1861) with them in order to prevent further raids on Texan settlers and cattle. In 1865 the Comanche and the KIOWA signed a treaty with the US government granting them a large part of western Oklahoma. However, the government reneged on the treaty, and fighting broke out again. This was ended by the treaty of MEDICINE LODGE (1867), and many of the Comanche settled on a reservation in Oklahoma. But inroads by white settlers, and the refusal of militant Comanches to settle on reservations, led to the RED RIVER WAR. The supposed 'treachery' of the Comanche in having signed the 1861 treaty with the Confederacy inspired US troops to prosecute this war with extraordinary savagery. After the war the Comanche were confined to their reservation. Today about 3000 Comanche live in western Oklahoma.

Commission on Industrial Relations, congressional inquiry into labor violence set up in 1913. President WILSON appointed Frank Walsh (1864–1939), a Kansas City social worker, to head the commission. Walsh sharply cross-examined John D. Rockefeller Jr (1874–1960) on the LUDLOW MASSACRE. In a report unprecedentedly sympathetic to labor unions, the commission denounced 'industrial feudalism', autocratic management and dangerous working conditions. It called for federally funded social-welfare and education programs, laws restricting child labour and establishing equal pay and further protection for collective-bargaining rights. Congress ignored the report.

Committee on Public Information, propaganda machine established by President WILSON on April 14 1917, one week after US entry into WORLD WAR I. Under the chairmanship of journalist George Creel (1876–1953), the committee peddled crude anti-German propaganda and whipped up war hysteria in the USA. Creel created a network of 75,000 'four-minute men', who gave short talks on US war aims and German ghastliness in movie theaters, theaters and other public places. The committee encouraged Americans to refer to hamburgers as 'liberty sandwiches' and sauerkraut as 'liberty cabbage'. Among the films it produced was *The Kaiser: Beast of Berlin*. To the horror of educated liberals, the committee's work was popular, and it unleashed forces that underpinned the hunt for undesirables and subversives during the RED SCARE.

Committee on Un-American Activities, House, *see* DIES COMMITTEE.

committees of correspondence, committees set up in most of the 13 colonies to discuss American grievances with patriots in the other colonies. The first such committee was set up in Boston in November 1772, at the behest of Sam ADAMS. By 1774 every colony except Pennsylvania and North Carolina had formed committees, and these coordinated American resistance to the INTOLERABLE ACTS.

Commodity Credit Corporation (CCC), NEW DEAL agency that allowed farmers to use harvested crops as collateral for federally funded loans. The CCC was established on October 18 1933, and run within the AGRICULTURAL ADJUSTMENT ADMINISTRATION. The idea was that if producers were relieved of the economic pressure to market their crop as soon as it was harvested, they would withhold their produce from the market and cause prices to rise. Most CCC loans were made to southern cotton farmers. Marginal rises in the value of agricultural crops were offset by the contraction in world trade caused by high American TARIFFS.

Common Sense, radical anti-monarchical pamphlet by Tom PAINE. Published anonymously in Philadelphia on January 9 1776, the pamphlet became a best seller. At a time when many Americans still balanced opposition to ministerial measures with professions of loyalty to the king, Paine's sustained attack on the legitimacy of monarchical government was sensational. Arguing that George III (the 'Royal Brute') supported the subjugation of America, Paine called for an immediate declaration of independence. Paine argued that Americans should create a republic that would offer an asylum for liberty, and serve as a beacon for the rest of humanity.

communes, *see* ONEIDA COMMUNE.

Communist Control Act (August 24 1954), legislation passed during the COLD WAR that invoked 'national security' to deprive members or supporters of the COMMUNIST PARTY OF THE USA of their civil rights. The act allowed the government to dismiss individuals deemed as security risks from positions in the federal civil service. Trade unions thought to have been infiltrated by communists were stripped of the recognition due to them under the WAGNER ACT.

Communist Party of the USA (CPUSA), political party formed following the merger of two rival factions in 1924. The CPUSA's influence peaked during the 1930s: in 1930 it had 7000 members; by 1939 membership had reached 100,000. During this period hundreds of thousands of Americans attended party meetings or took part in campaigns sponsored by the party.

The CPUSA was particularly successful in recruiting African-Americans. In 1928 the 6th Communist Congress, held in Moscow, had called for the creation of a separate African-American state within America. Communist trade-union organizers did not discriminate against African-American workers, and the party supported civil rights causes, such as the case of the SCOTTSBORO BOYS, that mainstream groups, such as the NATIONAL ASSOCIATION FOR THE ADVANCEMENT OF COLORED PEOPLE (NAACP), were slow to take up. James Ford (1893–1957), the CPUSA's candidate for vice president in the PRESIDENTIAL ELECTION OF 1932, was the first African-American to be nominated by any party for election to the executive branch of government.

The CPUSA initially opposed the NEW DEAL on the grounds that it would prop up capitalism. In 1935 it switched to support for President Franklin D. Roosevelt in keeping with the Comintern's Popular Front strategy. From 1939 to 1941, following the Soviet line, it opposed US entry into WORLD WAR II, changing its policy when the Nazis invaded the USSR in June 1941. CPUSA members were subject to BLACKLISTING, and targeted by the DIES COMMITTEE, the SMITH ACT, the McCARRAN ACT, the TAFT–HARTLEY ACT and the COMMUNIST CONTROL ACT. The party's influence declined dramatically during the COLD WAR. Prominent members of the CPUSA included William Z. Foster, W.E.B. DU BOIS and Paul ROBESON.

comparable worth, concept developed by feminist lawyers in the 1970s in a bid to utilize Title VII of the CIVIL RIGHTS ACT OF 1964 to force employers to raise women's wages. The concept assumes that conscious sexual discrimination among employers explains why women often earn less than men, even when they are comparably qualified and performing essentially the same functions. If this could be proven, a prima facie case under the 1964 act would exist. In 1981 the US Supreme Court examined the concept in the case of County of Washington vs. Gunther. It found that an intent among employers to discriminate against women could not be inferred from aggregate statistics suggesting that women were paid less than men for doing the same job.

Compromise of 1850, package of measures agreed between moderate northern and southern interests in Congress that put limits on the expansion of slavery, but protected it where it already existed. The fragile agreement was torn apart four years later by the KANSAS–NEBRASKA ACT.

Debate over the WILMOT PROVISO (1846) demonstrated that the questions of whether and how slavery should be extended to newly acquired territories held the potential to split the Union. These issues became unavoidable following the conclusion of the MEXICAN WAR (1848), when the USA acquired vast areas of new territory. On November 13 1849 California, one of the newly acquired territories, adopted a constitution banning slavery and sought immediate admission to the Union. California's entry would tip the balance between free and slave states in the former's favor. Proslavery partisans believed that their opponents would then exploit this imbalance; either by prohibiting slavery in newly acquired territories, or by making a territory's admission into the Union conditional on its renunciation of slavery. Anti-slavery partisans, such as William SEWARD, argued that a 'higher law' dictated Congress should do both, since slavery was 'radically wrong and essentially vicious.'

Hence southern Congressmen attempted to block California's admission, and some argued for pre-emptive secession, on the grounds that a Congress in which free states formed the majority would inevitably attack slavery where it already existed. Meanwhile, growing numbers of northerners, concerned less with the injustice of slavery than with the power of slave states to block legislation favorable to non-slaveholding interests, demanded California be admitted without concession to the south. The FREE SOIL PARTY was among the groups that took this line.

Debate in the Senate over the admission of California and the organization of other land acquired from Mexico in the treaty of GUADALUPE-HIDALGO (1848) centered on a package of measures, suggested by Henry CLAY, designed to restore to the south 'the power she possessed of protecting herself before the equilibrium between the sections was destroyed by the action of this government.' Daniel WEBSTER – speaking as 'an American ... for the preservation of the Union,' and imploring colleagues to 'hear me for my cause' – rallied crucial northern support for Clay's package.

Nevertheless southerner senators, led by John CALHOUN and, after March 31 1850, Jefferson DAVIS, engineered the defeat of Clay's 'Omnibus Bill.' Stephen DOUGLAS then suggested that the components of Clay's package be presented to the Senate as individual measures. By presenting their plan in this way, Clay and Douglas skillfully manipulated shifting coalitions of sectional interests within the Senate. Their achievement was subsequently hailed as a great compromise. Supporters of the package presented its component elements to Congress in three distinct stages. California was admitted as a free state on September 9 1850. The boundaries of Texas (where slavery was permitted) and New Mexico were settled. The settlement gave Texas less new territory than pro-slavery interests – keen to increase congressional representation – would have liked. New Mexico was granted territorial status on September 9 1850 and its inhabitants were left to decide whether they would permit slavery without preju-

dice to their future admission to the Union. (Little support for slavery existed in New Mexico, which became a state in 1912.) Utah was organized as a territory on the same terms at the same time. (Here too there was little support for slavery. Statehood was granted in 1896.) On September 18 1850 Congress passed a FUGITIVE SLAVE ACT that placated southern slave owners by providing federal aid for the capture and return of fugitives. Abolitionists assailed the Act, because it hindered the operation of the UNDERGROUND RAILROAD and contradicted PERSONAL LIBERTY LAWS that had been enacted by many northern states. In the final stage of the compromise Congress took the symbolic step of abolishing the slave trade in the District of Columbia (September 20 1850). The carefully constructed compromise was shattered by the subsequent KANSAS–NEBRASKA ACT (1854).

Compromise of 1877, agreement between northern and southern politicians that ended RECONSTRUCTION and inaugurated the THIRD PARTY SYSTEM. On February 26 1877 a meeting of southern Democrats agreed not to contest the verdict of an extraordinary electoral commission that the PRESIDENTIAL ELECTION OF 1876 be awarded to Republican candidate Rutherford HAYES. In return, Republicans pledged to withdraw remaining federal troops from the south, signaling the south's REDEMPTION.

concurrent majority, conservative political doctrine that a simple numerical majority should not be sufficient to pass legislation. The various minority interests concerned should also be taken into account, according to the doctrine, and the legislation passed only if it is supported by a majority within each of these interests; this would then constitute a 'concurrent majority.'

Just before his death in 1850, John C. CALHOUN completed 'A Disquisition on Government.' Its theme was the protection of minority interests within constitutional government. Modifying the STATES' RIGHTS arguments he had proposed during the NULLIFICATION CRISIS, Calhoun argued for the 'restoration' of the doctrine of a concurrent majority within the US Constitution and government. Significant national interests – such as those of slave owners – should be permitted a veto on the enactment or implementation of laws hostile to them, even where such laws were supported by numerical majorities. To achieve this goal, Calhoun proposed a constitutional amendment to create a dual executive, with one president elected by northern states and one by southern states. Legislation would require the signatures of both presidents. Most northern politicians regarded Calhoun's doctrine as a thinly disguised defence of SLAVE POWER. The COMPROMISE OF 1850 resolved sectional tensions without accepting the principle of concurrent majority.

Confederacy, the, informal name for the Confederate States of America (CSA), the confederation of eleven southern slave-owning states formed following their SECESSION from the Union between December 20 1860 and May 20 1861, precipitating the CIVIL WAR. It was formally established on February 8 1861, and was at war with the USA (the Union) from April 12 1861 to May 26 1865, when it finally surrendered and was dissolved.

At a meeting held on February 8 1861 in Montgomery, Alabama, delegates from six seceded states (Alabama, Florida, Georgia, Louisiana, Mississippi and South Carolina) approved a provisional constitution creating the Confederate States of America. On February 9, Jefferson DAVIS was elected to a six-year term as president. Georgian Alexander H. Stephens (1821–82) was named vice president on February 18. Texas's delegation signed the constitution as soon as it arrived, and the four states that seceded after the surrender of FORT SUMTER (Arkansas, North Carolina, Tennessee and Virginia) also quickly approved. On May 20 1861 Rich-

mond, Virginia, became the Confederacy's capital. Both Missouri (admitted October 31 1861) and Kentucky (December 10 1861) had dual status as US and CSA states.

The Confederacy's constitution followed the wording of the US Constitution but inserted guarantees of states' and slaveholders' rights at every point where these might be in question. It also prohibited secession. Alexander Stephens defended the constitution's punctilious regard for states' rights when he denounced those who called for 'independence first and liberty afterwards'. However, the political organization of the Confederacy hindered its ability to fight a total war. In 1864, for example, Georgia's governor refused to send state militiamen to defend Richmond, because they represented his state's 'only remaining protection against the encroachment of centralized power'. A disillusioned southerner suggested 'Died of a theory' as the Confederacy's epitaph.

The theoretical issues raised by the fact of secession troubled northern politicians and foreign governments. Abraham LINCOLN argued that since the Union was permanent and indivisible the Confederacy had not legally left the United States of America. He regarded the leaders of the Confederacy as insurrectionists and took the position that their confederation of southern states could not be recognized under international law as co-belligerents in a civil war. (He opposed RADICAL REPUBLICAN demands to declare the states of the confederacy to be in rebellion, on the grounds that this would amount to a tacit admission of the constitutionality of secession.)

Britain (the primary purchaser of the South's cotton) responded to Lincoln's announcement that the USA would enforce a naval blockade of the Confederacy by declaring neutrality on May 13 1861. Whether by accident or design, this had the effect of challenging Lincoln's position by suggesting that the Confederacy was a co-belligerent in a civil war. It followed from this that Britain could, if it wished, grant diplomatic recognition to the Confederacy. In fact Britain and other European nations, although tempted to recognize the Confederacy, declined to take this step. Union victories, especially that at ANTIETAM, coupled with overseas support for the goal of abolishing slavery meant that no foreign nation recognized the Confederacy. This lack of diplomatic support was an important factor in the Confederacy's eventual defeat.

Following the final surrender of Confederate forces (May 26 1865) President JOHNSON angered Radical Republicans by offering the eleven states which had seceded lenient terms for re-admission into the Union. The questions of when and how former Confederate states might resume self-government within the USA dominated RECONSTRUCTION.

Confederate States of America (CSA), *see* CONFEDERACY, THE.

Confederation Congress, unicameral legislature, established by the ARTICLES OF CONFEDERATION, that governed America from 1781 to 1788. It replaced the second CONTINENTAL CONGRESS and was in turn superseded upon RATIFICATION of the US CONSTITUTION.

Each state was represented in Confederation Congress by no less than two and no more than seven delegates. The method of selection of delegates was left up to the individual states. Each state delegation cast a single vote in debates, and the approval of nine state delegations was required to enact legislation.

The effectiveness of Confederation Congress was compromised by the terms of the Articles of Confederation, which withheld from it crucial powers such as the right to levy taxes on the inhabitants of the USA. Confederation Congress was also often inquorate. Its inefficiency contributed to the growing support for a stronger national government that became associated with the FEDERALIST political philosophy.

Confederation Congress enacted two measures of long-term significance: the ORDINANCE OF 1785 and the NORTHWEST ORDINANCE (1787). These laid out the procedure by which lands to the north of the Ohio and east of the Mississippi would be surveyed, formed into territories and, ultimately, admitted into the Union.

Confiscation Acts, *see* ABOLITION.

Congress, collective term properly used to describe both chambers of the legislative branch of the federal government established following RATIFICATION of the US CONSTITUTION in 1788, but more commonly used in reference to the lower chamber – the US House of Representatives.

Article I, Section 2 of the Constitution describes the process by which seats in the House of Representatives are apportioned and filled. The number of representatives a state may send to the House is determined by its population. The Constitution stipulates that a census be held every ten years to determine the distribution of seats in the House. The CONNECTICUT COMPROMISE adopted at the CONSTITUTIONAL CONVENTION allowed states to include three-fifths of their enslaved population in calculations determining their representation in the lower chamber. This provision, an indirect cause of the CIVIL WAR, was repealed by the FOURTEENTH AMENDMENT in 1868. Article I Section 7 of the Constitution specifies that revenue bills must originate in the House. The House is also charged with framing charges in IMPEACHMENT cases

The composition and duties of the upper chamber of Congress, the Senate, are described in Article I Section 3 of the US Constitution. Each state is entitled to elect two members to the Senate. Until ratification of the SEVENTEENTH AMENDMENT in 1913, senators were chosen by state legislatures rather than by direct election. Article II Section 2 of the Constitution stipulates that the 'advice and consent' of two-thirds of the US Senate must be obtained before treaties with foreign powers may be ratified. The Senate is also charged with confirming the appointment of Supreme Court justices, senior government officials and ambassadors. When a president is impeached, the Senate acts as a court of judgment. The vice president acts as the presiding officer of the US Senate and may cast a deciding vote when senators are evenly divided. The procedural rules governing debate in the Senate allow senators to attempt to talk a bill to death by mounting a FILIBUSTER.

congressional Reconstruction, those aspects of RECONSTRUCTION initiated and controlled by Congress. Frustrated by the leniency towards the south shown by Presidents LINCOLN and, especially, JOHNSON, Congress began challenging for control of Reconstruction policy in December 1865. The fruits of congressional reconstruction included the CIVIL RIGHTS ACT (1866), the RECONSTRUCTION ACTS (1866–7) and the formulation of the FOURTEENTH and FIFTEENTH AMENDMENTS. Congressional commitment to Reconstruction began to wane following passage of the ENFORCEMENT ACTS (1870–1).

Congress of Industrial Organizations (CIO), federation of US trade unions, formed in 1935 as the Committee for Industrial Organization. The CIO was generally more militant and politicized than its rival, the AMERICAN FEDERATION OF LABOR (AFL), although the two organizations merged in 1955.

During the 1930s various union leaders, including John L. LEWIS of the mine workers and Sidney Hillman (1887–1946) of the clothing workers, pressured the AFL to commit resources to the organization of INDUSTRIAL UNIONS among workforces in mass-production businesses. On November 9 1935, in the wake of the WAGNER ACT (1935), the AFL reluctantly recognized a Committee for Industrial Organization. Industrial unions formed by this commit-

tee employed militant tactics, including SIT-DOWN STRIKES, which prompted the AFL to suspend, and in 1936 expel, its newly formed industrial affiliates.

In 1938 the Committee for Industrial Organization changed its name to the Congress of Industrial Organizations, adopted a constitution and elected John L. Lewis president. Membership in CIO-affiliated unions grew rapidly, although some unions were penetrated by communists and others corrupted by organized crime. In 1943 the CIO formed a committee to mobilize its 5 million members to vote as a bloc for pro-labor candidates, whereas the AFL had always eschewed political endorsements. Hostility between the AFL and CIO diminished following passage of the anti-union TAFT–HARTLEY ACT (1947), and on December 5 1955 the two groups merged to form the AFL-CIO.

Congress of Racial Equality (CORE), unstable coalition of white intellectuals and African-Americans dedicated to non-violent protest against racial discrimination. CORE was founded in Chicago in 1942, and played a major role in the CIVIL RIGHTS MOVEMENT of the 1960s.

In the summer of 1942 CORE mounted a sit-in protest at Jack Spratt's, a segregated Chicago restaurant, which led a sympathetic but puzzled labor leader to conclude that its members were 'Quaker-like kookies'. Some CORE members were communist sympathizers, and the organization almost folded during the McCARTHY witch-hunts. But, under James Farmer (1920–), CORE organized the FREEDOM RIDER campaign desegregating interstate bus travel, and played a crucial role in the MISSISSIPPI FREEDOM SUMMER. As African-Americans came to dominate the leadership and membership of CORE, the organization endorsed the militancy associated with the slogan BLACK POWER and the oratory of MALCOLM X.

Connecticut, New England state, northeast of New York City; it is bordered to the north by Massachusetts, to the east by Rhode Island, to the south by Long Island Sound and to the west by New York State.

The first permanent European settlements in the territory were established by Dutch traders and Anglo-American Puritans in 1633. Following the suppression of local Indians in the Pequot war of 1636–7, the Puritan towns of the Connecticut river valley agreed on a common system of government entitled the Fundamental Orders of Connecticut. In 1662 Charles II recognized Connecticut's independent existence. The river towns then annexed a settlement centered on New Haven in the southwest of what would become the state's territory. Connecticut shared the same general characteristics as its neighbor Massachusetts, although lacking a major seaport its population and economy grew at a slower rate. As in Massachusetts the Congregational church enjoyed established status (and was not disestablished until 1818). Connecticut was a follower rather than a leader during the AMERICAN REVOLUTION. However, Connecticut's delegation to the CONSTITUTIONAL CONVENTION made a significant contribution to the future history of the USA by proposing the CONNECTICUT COMPROMISE on the apportionment of seats in the proposed federal assembly. Connecticut became the 5th state when it ratified the Constitution on January 9 1788. Connecticut abolished slavery in 1784.

In 1800, Connecticut had 251,000 residents and was the eighth most populous state. For much of the 19th century, the state's population retained its colonial characteristics in that it was overwhelmingly white, Protestant, rural and of British descent. This gave the state a distinctive 'Yankee' identity. Gradually, the state's textile and firearm factories began to attract internal migrants and immigrants. The state's population doubled between 1860 and 1900 as a result of industrial development. In 1900, Connecticut had 908,420 residents. In the second half of the 20th century, its economy and population grew again as a COLD WAR defense expenditure created jobs in Connecticut's munitions factories and shipyards, and the city of Hartford emerged as a major corporate headquarters. In 1990, Connecticut had 3,287,116 residents and was the 27th most populous state in the Union. Prominent 'native sons' of Connecticut include Benedict ARNOLD, Phineas T. BARNUM and John BROWN.

Connecticut Compromise (1787), agreement reached in the FEDERAL CONVENTION regarding the representation of each state in the lower house of the proposed federal assembly. The Convention had came close to deadlock on the issue of whether each state should have an equal number of representatives, or whether representation should reflect the unequal distribution of population among the states. On July 12 1787 Connecticut delegate Roger Sherman (1721–93) introduced a compromise proposing that a state's representation in the lower chamber should be based on the sum of its white population plus three-fifths of its black population, but that each state should send an equal number of senators to the upper house. This compromise informed Article 1 Section 2 of the Constitution until ratification of the FOURTEENTH AMENDMENT.

Conscience Whigs, *see* WHIG PARTY.

Conscription Act (March 3 1863), legislation passed during the CIVIL WAR that made all males aged 20–45 liable for service in the Union Army. The act, which aimed to harness the north's manpower advantage over the CONFEDERACY, proved enormously contentious. Each state was asked to supply a quota of draftees, adjusted to take account of the state's population and previous record of enlistment. Conscripts were to be chosen by lottery. However, a man could avoid service by paying $300 or by providing a substitute willing to serve for three years. In the event, 52,000 men paid the fee, while 110,000 supplied a substitute. Anger at this loophole was a major cause of the NEW YORK CITY DRAFT RIOT.

Constitution of the United States, document that, with its subsequent amendments, defines the nature and power of the government of the USA, and establishes the rights of its citizens. The original Constitution was written at the CONSTITUTIONAL CONVENTION held in Philadelphia in 1787. It was sent to the states for RATIFICATION before it took effect on March 4 1789. The US Constitution superseded the ARTICLES OF CONFEDERATION as the basis of national government in the USA. Although it has been amended 27 times, it continues to provide the foundation of US government. Written in the name of the people of the USA, and with the intent of forming 'a more perfect union', the Constitution weakened the power of the states formed after the DECLARATION OF INDEPENDENCE by the original THIRTEEN COLONIES. It created new national institutions, notably the presidency, CONGRESS and the SUPREME COURT. Following the doctrine of SEPARATION OF POWERS, intended to avoid tyrannical government, the Constitution attempts to balance the power of the executive, legislature and judiciary by assigning separate functions to them.

During debate over the adoption of the Constitution, ANTIFEDERALISTS argued that the separation of powers inherent in the Constitution provided an insufficient guarantee of popular liberty, and campaigned successfully for a BILL OF RIGHTS to be added by amendment. In the 19th century STATES' RIGHTS theorists were also critical of the power granted to central government by the Constitution. They argued that the individual states were ultimate guarantors of the people's liberty, and that the states could therefore 'interpose' their authority between the federal government and the people, or even declare laws passed by the US Congress under the Constitution null and void (*see also* NULLIFICATION CRISIS).

Several sections of the Constitution – notably Article I Section 8 describing the power of Congress to regulate commerce, Article II Section 1 describing the working of the ELECTORAL COLLEGE, and Article II Section 4 describing crimes that might lead to the IMPEACHMENT of the president of the USA – were quite deliberately left open to interpretation by the FOUNDING FATHERS. Disputes over the meaning of these and other passages occasioned political partisanship as early as 1790, when Alexander HAMILTON used an IMPLIED POWERS reading of the Constitution to justify the creation of a BANK OF THE UNITED STATES. The legality and implications of a strict versus a loose construction of the US Constitution have informed American politics ever since (*see* STRICT CONSTRUCTIONISM and LOOSE CONSTRUCTIONISM). In 1803 the US Supreme Court asserted in its verdict on MARBURY VS. MADISON the right of JUDICIAL REVIEW; that is the right to review the constitutionality of state and federal legislation. When the Supreme Court has exercised this function, as in its verdict on DRED SCOTT VS. SANDFORD (1857), the Court has often intensified rather than quelled dispute.

For the full text of the original Constitution, and of the first ten amendments (the Bill of Rights), *see* Appendix 1. All subsequent amendments (from the Eleventh to the Twenty-seventh) have their own entries.

Constitutional Convention, special assembly that met in secret session in Philadelphia from May 25 to September 17 1787 to draw up the US Constitution. The convention consisted of 55 delegates representing all THIRTEEN COLONIES except Rhode Island.

Authorized by CONFEDERATION CONGRESS to revise the ARTICLES OF CONFEDERATION, delegates began by considering the Virginia Plan, which scrapped the existing confederate form of government in favor of a strong national government with pre-eminent authority over the states. Delegates from smaller states, and those who sought to provide a check on central authority, rallied to a counter-proposal known as the New Jersey Plan. This retained elements of the confederate structure, particularly with regard to representation in Congress.

The issue of how seats in the new Congress should be apportioned was complicated by slavery. If slaves were counted among a state's population for the purposes of representation, then southern states would dominate the new federal legislature. If they were not, southern states would form a permanent minority. The CONNECTICUT COMPROMISE protected the voice of both slaveholding and smaller states in the new government, by counting slaves as three-fifths of a person for the purpose of apportioning seats in the lower house, and by granting each state, regardless of size, the same number of senators. Throughout these discussions James MADISON proved highly influential.

The convention made two other important decisions before adjourning. The first was to omit a BILL OF RIGHTS. The second was to stipulate that the Constitution would become effective when nine state conventions had ratified it. The first decision became the axle around which opposition to the Constitution turned. The significance of the second became apparent when, in the key moment of the RATIFICATION process, the powerful state of New York was presented with a choice between accepting a Constitution that already had requisite approval, or enduring isolation from the Union.

Constitutional Union Party, shortlived political party that fought the PRESIDENTIAL ELECTION OF 1860 on a platform that ignored the crisis over slavery. The party drew its support from former WHIGS and KNOW NOTHINGS, and was led by John Bell (1797–1869). The ticket ran well in the BORDER STATES, and gained 13% of the POPULAR VOTE. The party dissolved following SECESSION.

containment, strategy that dominated US geopolitical thought during the COLD WAR. As originally articulated by George Kennan (1904–) in 1947, containment required the USA to use non-military aid to block the USSR's 'expansive tendencies' in a limited number of strategically important regions around the world. The MARSHALL PLAN, directing economic aid to Western Europe, reflected the limited goals of early containment strategies. The TRUMAN DOCTRINE, which committed the USA to support free peoples resisting attempted subjugation throughout the world, represented a substantial broadening of the policy. With the formation of the NORTH ATLANTIC TREATY ORGANIZATION and the outbreak of the KOREAN WAR, the USA committed itself to use military force to contain communism. The DOMINO THEORY and the EISENHOWER DOCTRINE expanded US commitments. Proponents of ROLLBACK even envisioned liberating territory then controlled by communist regimes. The VIETNAM WAR discredited containment strategy. The experiment in DÉTENTE, initiated by President NIXON and Secretary of State Henry KISSINGER in the 1970s, attempted to reformulate the doctrine on more manageable lines. What ultimately contained the USSR's 'evil empire', as President Reagan described it, was the inability of the Soviet economy to support overseas expansion.

Continental Association, one of the most remarkable documents produced during the AMERICAN REVOLUTION, adopted by the first CONTINENTAL CONGRESS on October 18 1774 in response to the INTOLERABLE ACTS. Through it Congress sanctioned the creation of extralegal local committees to enforce a ban on the import of British goods from December 1 1774, the export of goods to Britain on September 1 1775, and an eventual ban on the purchase of slaves from overseas. Where the majority of a local committee judged that merchants or others had broken the Association, they were authorized to brand the offender an enemy of American liberty. However, the Association also sought to foster VIRTUE within the THIRTEEN COLONIES by asking Americans to forgo all forms of extravagance and dissipation, to trade with one another at fair prices and to promote domestic manufactures. In many regions of New England and the middle colonies, and especially in the city of Philadelphia, the committee system sanctioned through the Association brought into power artisans and craftsmen who had not previously held office. The Association thereby helped to turn a movement for home rule into a struggle over who should rule at home.

Continental Congress, first (1774–5), gathering during the AMERICAN REVOLUTION of representatives from all of the THIRTEEN COLONIES except Georgia, called to discuss a coordinated trade boycott to force repeal of the British Parliament's INTOLERABLE ACTS.

The Congress first met in Philadelphia on September 5 1774. It endorsed the SUFFOLK RESOLVES (calling for the colonies to assume temporarily some powers of self-government) on September 17, and rejected a plan of union between Great Britain and the American colonies proposed by Joseph Gallaway (1729–1803) on September 28. On October 14 it approved a Declaration of Grievances, and resolved to levy economic sanctions until American rights, including life, liberty and property, were acknowledged by Parliament. The CONTINENTAL ASSOCIATION, adopted on October 18, bound the colonies to gradually end trade links with Britain, to cease consuming luxury goods (especially tea), to promote domestic manufactures and to discontinue the slave trade. Congress sanctioned the creation of local committees to enforce the Continental Association, a first step towards self-government. Congress adjourned on October 26 1774.

A second session, opening on May 10 1775, reacted to news of the battles of LEXINGTON AND CONCORD (the opening engagements of the REVOLUTIONARY WAR) by authorizing the creation of an army and the invasion of Canada. On July 5 it endorsed a declaration, written by Thomas JEFFERSON, justifying these steps on the grounds that Americans would rather die than live as slaves. It adopted the OLIVE-BRANCH PETITION the next day. Congress adjourned on August 2 1775.

Continental Congress, second (1775–81), gathering of colonial delegates during the REVOLUTIONARY WAR phase of the AMERICAN REVOLUTION. Unlike the first CONTINENTAL CONGRESS, the second Continental Congress included representatives from all the THIRTEEN COLONIES.

The Congress first met on September 12 1775, in Philadelphia. It created a navy (October 13), and authorized diplomatic initiatives to seek foreign aid (November 29). It was this body that commissioned and approved the DECLARATION OF INDEPENDENCE (1776), adopted the ARTICLES OF CONFEDERATION (1777) and served as America's national governing body until the ratification of the Articles in 1781.

contrabands, term applied to runaway slaves during the CIVIL WAR. The owners of slaves who fled to Union lines during the war actually argued that their property should be returned to them under the terms of the FUGITIVE SLAVE ACT. Led by General Benjamin Butler (1818–93), Union military commanders declared runaways to be 'contrabands of war' and refused to return them. President LINCOLN, reluctant to alienate the BORDER STATES, disavowed RADICAL REPUBLICAN attempts to arm escaped slaves and attempted to restrict the 'contraband' designation to male slaves who had been directly contributing to the Confederate war effort. However, on May 13 1862 Congress passed a formal amendment to its Articles of War to prohibit Union officers from returning any fugitive slave.

Contract Labor Act (February 26 1885), legislation to restrict the immigration of Chinese laborers on short-term contracts. The CHINESE EXCLUSION ACT (1882) had barred Chinese laborers from entering the USA with the intention of establishing permanent residence. However, many Chinese workers in the mining and railroad industries were recruited on short-term contracts that provided for their return to China. The Contract Labor Act, for whose passage Terrence POWDERLY and the KNIGHTS OF LABOR lobbied hard, closed this loophole. Its anti-Chinese bias can be gauged from the fact that exemptions were granted to permit contract work by domestic servants, usually Mexican, and professionals, generally European.

Contract with America, ten-point legislative program devised by Representative Newt Gingrich (1943–) and endorsed by REPUBLICAN candidates in the 1994 congressional elections.

The highly partisan program committed Republicans to present within the first 100 days of the new congressional session laws toughening prison sentences, cutting capital-gains taxes, cracking down on child pornography, tightening eligibility for welfare, balancing the federal budget and reforming the system of awards in criminal-liability law suits. The contract proved popular with voters, and gave the Republicans a majority in both houses of Congress for the first time since the 1948 midterm elections. Gingrich, who became Speaker of the House in 1995, enjoyed a brief period of immense political influence. However, attempts to implement the program led to a stand-off between Republican congressmen and President CLINTON that produced a federal government shut-down for which voters blamed Gingrich.

Conway Cabal, supposed group of plotters, allegedly intent on removing George WASHINGTON from overall command during the REVOLUTIONARY WAR.

Washington's conduct of the opening stages of the war attracted criticism from some congressmen and from rival generals. In the autumn of 1777 Brigadier General Thomas Conway (1735–c.1800), an Irishman who had previously served in the French army, wrote a letter highly critical of Washington's leadership to Horatio GATES, Washington's closest rival for overall command. The leaking of this letter prompted speculation that congressmen and generals were plotting to oust Washington. Gates was forced to disavow Conway, who resigned his commission in April 1778. The British surrender at SARATOGA (1777) ended talk of replacing Washington.

Coolidge, (John) Calvin (1872–1933), Republican statesman, vice president (1921–3) and 30th president of the USA (1923–9) following the death of the incumbent Warren HARDING.

Coolidge was trained as a lawyer. His political instincts were conservative but, as a Republican in industrialized Massachusetts, he showed some sympathy for PROGRESSIVE causes. He was elected or appointed to various posts in Massachusetts before coming to national prominence when, as governor (1919–21), he suppressed a strike by police in the city of Boston. Coolidge declared, 'There is no right to strike against the public safety by anybody, anywhere, any time.'

As vice president, Coolidge automatically succeeded to the presidency following Harding's death in office (August 2 1923). Re-elected on the slogan 'Keep Cool with Coolidge' with 54% of the vote in 1924, he served until March 4 1929. He decided not to run again in 1928, and Herbert HOOVER became the successful Republican candidate.

The fiscal orthodoxy that marked Coolidge's presidency was encapsulated in a remark he made in 1924: 'The chief business of America is business.' Coolidge cut top rates of INCOME TAX, thereby making federal taxation a national political issue for the first time. Congress overrode his veto of the BONUS BILL (1924), but Coolidge successfully blocked a price-support program for farmers contained in the McNAURY–HAUGEN BILL. He has been criticized for failing to do anything about the stock-market speculation that culminated in the WALL STREET CRASH.

Coolidge was not known for his conversational gifts, and earned the nickname 'Silent Cal'. When a White House guest told Coolidge she had just made a bet that she could get more than three words out of him, he replied, 'You lose.' It was said that Dorothy Parker (1893–1967), on being told that Coolidge was dead, remarked, 'How could they tell?'

Copperhead, nickname given to any northerner in the CIVIL WAR suspected of subversive activities on behalf of the CONFEDERACY. The ranks of PEACE DEMOCRATS, who called for an armistice and a negotiated settlement of the CIVIL WAR, included a small number of northern pro-Confederate sympathizers prepared to initiate acts of civil disobedience and even insurrection. Loyal Unionists believed clandestine networks of subversives, who identified themselves by showing the copper head of a one-cent coin, existed in southern Indiana and Ohio. The real or imaginary activities of Copperheads became issues in the PRESIDENTIAL ELECTION OF 1864.

Coral Sea, battle of the (May 4–8 1942), naval engagement in the Pacific theater during WORLD WAR II, in which US forces, under the command of Rear Admiral Frank Fletcher, prevented a Japanese invasion fleet from capturing Port Moresby, New Guinea. Had the Japanese fleet got through, Allied supply lines would have been cut, and Australia threatened with invasion. The US aircraft carrier *Lexington* was sunk in the action. It was the first naval battle in history fought entirely by carrier-based planes.

CORE, *see* CONGRESS OF RACIAL EQUALITY.

Cornwallis, Charles, 1st Marquess and 2nd Earl (1738–1805), the most distinguished British battlefield commander in the REVOLUTIONARY WAR. His disobedience of his superior Henry CLINTON led to the British surrender at YORKTOWN in 1781. Major General Cornwallis was transferred to the American station in 1776. He fought at the battle of LONG ISLAND and helped to secure the British capture of NEW YORK CITY on September 16 1776. After two periods of leave in Britain he returned to America as a lieutenant general, and presided over the British strategy of attempting to capitalize on the strength of LOYALIST sentiment in the southern states. At the battle of CAMDEN (1780) Cornwallis inflicted on American troops their heaviest defeat of the war. However, buoyed by this success, Cornwallis disobeyed Clinton's orders and launched an invasion of Virginia. Although this nearly resulted in the capture of Thomas JEFFERSON, Cornwallis's force was eventually besieged at Yorktown and, denied reinforcement, was forced to surrender, bringing hostilities to an end.

Corregidor, battle of (April–May 1942), engagement during WORLD WAR II that marked the completion of the Japanese conquest of the Philippines. Japan invaded the Philippines three days after PEARL HARBOR. US troops were isolated and, defeated at the battle of BATAAN, retreated to Corregidor island ('the Rock') in Manila Bay. Following a 27-day siege, the US and Filipino garrison of 11,500 men surrendered to the Japanese on May 6 1942.

correspondence, committees of, *see* COMMITTEES OF CORRESPONDENCE.

'corrupt bargain' of 1824, alleged deal by which Henry CLAY was supposed to have been awarded the position of secretary of state in return for obtaining the presidency for John Quincy ADAMS.

Four candidates – Adams, Clay, William Crawford (1772–1834) and Andrew JACKSON – contested the 1824 presidential election.

Jackson achieved pluralities in the POPULAR VOTE and in the ELECTORAL COLLEGE. But since the electoral college failed to produce an outright majority, the election was turned over to the House of Representatives. Clay instructed his supporters to vote for Adams. On February 9 1825, 13 state delegations in the House voted for Adams, 7 for Jackson and 4 for Crawford. Thus Adams became president despite finishing second in the popular vote. When Adams appointed Clay as secretary of state, Jacksonians alleged there had been a 'corrupt bargain' to thwart the people's will.

Cotton Gin, *see* WHITNEY, Eli.

Coughlin, Charles E(dward), Father (1891–1979), Roman Catholic priest who in the 1930s emerged as one of the most vocal and offensive critics of Franklin ROOSEVELT and the NEW DEAL. From studios in Detroit, Coughlin ran a syndicated radio show called the 'Golden Hour of the Little Flower'. During the GREAT DEPRESSION he began lambasting President HOOVER, while raking over the embers of the SILVER–GOLD CONTROVERSY with calls for the remonetization of silver and the creation of a central bank (Coughlin's company invested heavily in silver futures). When Roosevelt took office, the 'radio priest' had a weekly audience of 45 million. Coughlin gave Roosevelt a year to prove himself before denouncing the New Deal as the creation of a bizarre coalition of communists and Wall Street bankers. Coughlin's personal and anti-Semitic attacks, together with his obsession with imagined conspiracies, led Catholic leaders to disown him in 1937. His broadcasts were suppressed in 1942 for criticizing US involvement in WORLD WAR II.

court-packing controversy, furore arising from the attempt by President Franklin ROOSEVELT to increase the number of justices in the US Supreme Court.

Many within Roosevelt's administration were convinced that conservative justices on the Supreme Court were willfully obstructing the NEW DEAL by striking down key statutes. New Dealers were especially angered by the Court's decision (in SCHECTER POULTRY CORPORATION VS. US) that Title 1 of the NATIONAL INDUSTRIAL RECOVERY ACT was unconstitutional.

On February 5 1937, fresh from his triumph in the 1936 presidential election, Roosevelt presented to Congress a Judiciary Reorganization Bill. This reformed procedure in lower courts, and expedited the process of hearing constitutional challenges to the enforcement of laws. The bill's most controversial feature, however, was a proposal to increase membership of the Supreme Court from 9 to 15. Critics charged that the measure would allow Roosevelt to 'pack' the court by appointing up to 6 new justices. Roosevelt stuck by the proposal even as Congressional opposition mounted. In a speech made on March 4 he alleged that justices were acting on their 'personal economic predilections' to thwart a popularly elected government. In a FIRESIDE CHAT broadcast on March 9 he told the American people that an unreformed Supreme Court threatened the ability of a democratically elected government to react to 'modern social and economic conditions'.

Roosevelt dropped the planned reorganization following the retirement of the arch conservative Justice Willis Van Devanter (1859–1941) and Court decisions upholding the constitutionality of the WAGNER ACT and the SOCIAL SECURITY ACT. Nevertheless, the Republicans, joined by some Democrats, denounced Roosevelt and opposed subsequent legislation thought likely to disturb the balance between the branches of government. Ironically, a series of deaths and retirements allowed Roosevelt to appoint liberals, notably Felix Frankfurter (1882–1965) to the Court.

cowboys, mounted cattle herders whose working lives have come to symbolize within popular culture the rugged individualism of the American west.

Cowboys were not always viewed as noble or glamorous figures. In colonial and early national America, cattle herders were regarded as unskilled transient workers and were seldom welcome in established communities. Since many family farms raised cattle or hogs of their own, the market price of beef remained low and the services of cowboys were seldom required. In the 19th century, immigration to northern cities fueled demand for beef. Demand rose still further during the CIVIL WAR, as Confederate and Union armies severely depleted existing cattle herds. Beef became a valuable commodity. Increased demand was met in the first instance by Texans, and it was in Texas that the 'golden age' of the cowboy (1866–86) began. An estimated 5 million prime longhorn steers roamed wild in the 'Lone Star' state. Worth around four dollars a head in Texas, these steers fetched around forty dollars when sold to northern slaughterhouses. From the conclusion of the Civil War, cowboys, around a quarter of whom were black, began rounding up Texan cattle and driving them to railheads in more northerly states. The routes followed in such drives, for example, the Chisholm trail from San Antonio, Texas, to Abilene, Kansas, became famous. 'Cow towns,' such as Abilene (which by 1871 was handling 300,000 steers a year), Sedalia, Missouri and, later, Wichita and Dodge City, Kansas, enjoyed boom times. The great cattle drives often trespassed on Indian territory and on the water rights of established farmers. Cattle theft – 'rustling' – was also common. For these reasons, cowboys were generally armed and, especially when paid off at the end of a drive, often violent.

Cowboys were also required to manage the open-range herds of the great plains states. As family farmers began to settle on the great plains following passage of the HOMESTEAD ACT (1862), disputes between ranchers and farmers over crop damage and water rights grew increasingly intense. Although their interests were well-represented within state legislatures, the cattle rancher's presumed right to graze and water herds on the public domain free of charge, depleting resources as he did so, became increasingly hard to defend. The commercial production of BARBED WIRE made it easier for farmers and ranchers to co-exist, but, once herds were fenced in, cowboys gradually became mounted farm hands. In 1886–7, a severe drought followed by a hard winter destroyed many thousands of open-range cattle and hastened the reorganization of the cattle industry. The expansion of the nation's network of RAILROADS rendered great cattle drives – and many cowboys – redundant.

Owen Wister's (1860–1938) bestselling novel *The Virginian* (1902) sparked an avalanche of literary celebrations of the cowboy's life. William S. Hart (1872–1946), star of such silent movies as *The Return of Draw Egan* (1916) and *The Covere Wagon* (1923), was the first actor to profit from HOLLYWOOD's interest in cowboy movies.

Coxey's Army, one of a number of 'armies' of unemployed men that marched on Washington to demand relief following the DEPRESSION OF 1893, which left a sixth of the American workforce unemployed.

'General' Jacob S. Coxey (1854–1951) was a wealthy POPULIST whose commitment to currency reform led him to name his youngest son 'Legal Tender'. Setting out from Massillon, Ohio, on March 25 1894, Coxey's army, formally known as the 'Commonweal of Christ' in newspaper accounts, reached Washington on April 30. When Coxey attempted to read an address calling for a $500 million public-works program on the grounds of the Capitol he was arrested for walking on the grass, and his supporters were dispersed in a police baton charge. Coxey's followers, joined by sympathizers, camped out in Washington. They were dispersed by police in August.

craft unions, trade unions formed by workers who possessed a skill that gave them bargaining power in negotiations with employers. Craft unions, such as Samuel GOMPER's Cigar Makers International Union, avoided involvement in political campaigning and sought to exclude socialists and others bent on fundamental economic reform from their ranks. Links between skilled and unskilled workers were not unknown, however. In the Homestead steel plant, unionized skilled workers secured an agreement that raised pay rates for unskilled workers. In return, unskilled workers stood by the craft unionists during the HOMESTEAD STRIKE. But the fundamental imperative of craft unionism, the preservation of status differentials and gains won, limited the power of the trade-union movement as a whole. Craft unions formed the core of the AMERICAN FEDERATION OF LABOR.

Crazy Horse or **Ta-Sunko-Witko,** *see* LITTLE BIG HORN, BATTLE OF; SIOUX WARS.

Crédit Mobilier scandal (1872), financial scandal involving prominent politicians, including the future president James GARFIELD.

Crédit Mobilier was a holding company formed by the Union Pacific Railroad, with the assistance of a French bank, to 'manage' federal construction subsidies granted to it by the PACIFIC RAILROAD ACT (1862). Inevitably, the Union Pacific's directors used Crédit Mobilier to line their own pockets. To insure against congressional investigation, the company 'sold' (at purely nominal prices) shares in its stock to influential politicians such as Schuyler Colfax (1823–85) and James Garfield. The scandal broke during the 1872 presidential election. Colfax went on to became GRANT's vice president, and Garfield was elected president in 1880.

Creek, Native American people whose language belongs to the Muskogean family. There are two groups of Creek: the Muskogee, originally living in Georgia, and the Hitchiti, originally living in Alabama.

In the 18th century the Creek developed a lucrative trade in deerskins with white colonists. They fought on the British side in the Revolutionary War, but through Alexander McGILLIVRAY's diplomacy deflected US encroachment until the CREEK WAR of 1813–4. The punitive treaty of FORT JACKSON (1814) opened much of their territory to US settlement. With other members of the FIVE CIVILIZED TRIBES, the Creek were forcibly removed to Oklahoma following the passage of the INDIAN REMOVAL ACT (1830). Today, about 20,000 Creek live in Oklahoma.

Creek War (1813–4), conflict between the CREEK and the USA. Enthused by the oratory of TECUMSEH and encouraged by news of US defeats in the WAR OF 1812, Red Sticks (younger Creek opposed to accommodationist tribal elders) massacred Creek enemies and American settlers at Fort Mims, Alabama, on August 30 1813. The news left Andrew JACKSON 'panting for vengeance' and brought comprehensive US retaliation. A six-month campaign, in which 'friendly' and 'hostile' Creeks suffered alike, ended in March 1814 when Jackson slaughtered some 800 Red Sticks at the battle of HORSESHOE BEND. The Creek ceded land to the USA by the subsequent treaty of FORT JACKSON (1814). Davy CROCKETT was one of few Americans not to acclaim Jackson as a hero.

Crime of '73, nickname given by its opponents to the Coinage Act (passed on February 12 1873), which withdrew silver from use as currency by ordering the US Treasury to cease minting silver dollars. The act effectively placed the USA on the gold standard. Western mining interests, together with FREE SILVER activists seeking to take advantage of US silver reserves to run a 'soft' monetary policy, alleged the measure was part of a 'gold conspiracy'. The measure ignited the SILVER–GOLD CONTROVERSY.

'Crisis of confidence' speech (July 15 1979), speech delivered by President CARTER that encapsulated the USA's post-VIETNAM

WAR malaise. Carter argued that a 'crisis in confidence' posed 'a fundamental threat' to US democracy. 'We can see this crisis,' he told his audience, 'in the growing doubt about the meaning of our own lives and in the loss of unity of purpose for our nation.' The 'social and political fabric of America' was, he said, under threat from a lack of optimism. Such downbeat rhetoric contributed to Carter's defeat by Ronald REAGAN in the presidential election of 1980.

Crockett, Davy (David) (1786–1836), frontiersman and congressman. Raised in eastern Tennessee, Crockett served as a sergeant under Andrew JACKSON in the CREEK WAR. This was the beginning of a bitter enmity between the two men that Crockett (who styled himself 'half horse, half alligator') pursued first as a DEMOCRATIC (1827–31) and later as a WHIG (1833–5) congressman during Jackson's presidency. Crockett regarded Jackson's hatred of Indians as a moral flaw, and questioned his manliness. Defeated in the congressional elections of 1835 by a comparably virile Jackson loyalist named Huntsman (who had a wooden leg), Crockett left Tennessee saying, 'Since you have chosen to elect a man with a timber toe to succeed me, you may all go to Hell and I will go to Texas'. His subsequent death at the ALAMO (1836), fighting for the independence of TEXAS from Mexico, captured the nation's attention. Crockett's maxim ('Be sure you're right, then go ahead') prefigured MANIFEST DESTINY and was used by expansionists to justify the annexation of Texas and the west.

crop lien, claim on a farmer's future crop as surety for goods bought on credit. Crop liens were widely used in the south when its credit and banking system collapsed following the CIVIL WAR. White southern hill farmers, who lacked the cash to buy seed and provisions, were forced to purchase them on credit and at inflated prices from 'furnishing agents' funded by northern banks. The agent placed a lien or claim on the farmer's future crop to cover his investment. Merchants pressured farmers into growing cotton, since that crop had the highest cash value. By doing so they contributed to a collapse in cotton prices, and dragged many small farmers into crippling indebtedness.

'Cross of gold' speech (July 8 1898), speech delivered in Chicago to the DEMOCRATIC PARTY convention by William Jennings BRYAN. The speech marked the high point of the SILVER–GOLD CONTROVERSY. Bryan attacked the GOLD STANDARD, favored by the REPUBLICANS, in a speech whose imagery reflected his Protestantism: 'Having behind us the producing masses of this nation and the world, supported by the commercial interests, the laboring interests and the toilers everywhere, we will answer their demand for a gold standard by saying to them: you shall not press down upon the brow of labor this crown of thorns, you shall not crucify mankind on a cross of gold.' Although the speech secured for Bryan the party's presidential nomination, some eastern 'gold bug' Democrats defected. The PEOPLE'S PARTY nominated Bryan as its candidate on the strength of the speech, and was subsequently torn apart by wrangling over this decision following his defeat.

CSA, the Confederate States of America; *see* CONFEDERACY.

Cuba, US attempts to annex. In 1848 Jefferson DAVIS, then US senator from Mississippi, declared 'Cuba must be ours.' President POLK supported the acquisition of Cuba, the largest Spanish colony remaining in the Americas. Polk saw such an acquisition as a means of defusing the tense question of whether slavery should be allowed in territory acquired through the treaty of GUADALUPE-HIDALGO.

Spanish adventurer Narciso López asked Davis to lead an expedition to capture the island for the USA. Davis refused and suggested Robert E. LEE, who also declined.

López led an invasion force of Cubans and southerners that captured the town of Cárdenas in May 1850 before withdrawing. López returned to Cuba in August 1850 but was captured and publicly garrotted in Havana's central square (August 16). Both expeditions were organized in New Orleans, where the execution of López was greeted with anti-Spanish riots.

The OSTEND MANIFESTO, made public in March 1855, committed the USA to the acquisition of Cuba, by force if necessary. President PIERCE disowned this project, ending attempts to incorporate Cuba as a slave state within the Union. A period of de facto annexation followed the SPANISH-AMERICAN WAR at the end of the 19th century.

Cuban missile crisis (October 22–November 20 1962), confrontation between the USA and the USSR, in which the COLD WAR posturing of both sides came close to causing a nuclear war.

In the aftermath of the BAY OF PIGS INVASION, and a US-inspired declaration by the ORGANIZATION OF AMERICAN STATES that Cuba's refusal to repudiate communism had placed it outside the 'inter-American system', Cuba accepted economic and military aid from the Soviet Union.

On October 16 1962 President KENNEDY was shown evidence that the Soviets were building sites in Cuba from which missiles could be launched against the USA. On October 22 Kennedy demanded that the Soviets dismantle the sites, and announced that the USA would enforce an air and sea 'quarantine' around Cuba to prevent further Soviet missiles, planes or military hardware from reaching Cuba. The quarantine went into effect on October 24. The first Soviet ship that was stopped carried oil, and was eventually allowed to proceed to Cuba. Other Soviet ships changed course to avoid inspection. Soviet bombers en route to Cuba turned back, but not before one of them shot down a US plane.

The world hung on the Soviet response to the quarantine. On October 26–27 Kennedy received two messages from Moscow. The first indicated a willingness to compromise by offering to remove the missiles in exchange for a US guarantee that it would not invade Cuba. The second message linked withdrawal of the missiles to the removal of US missiles in Turkey. Kennedy ignored the second message and responded to the first. This allowed Soviet premier Khrushchev to back down, and he signed an agreement to dismantle the bases on October 28. In return Kennedy agreed that the US would never invade Cuba. On November 20 Kennedy verified the Russian response and lifted the quarantine.

Currency Act (April 19 1764), legislation passed by the British Parliament barring the American colonies from issuing legal-tender paper money. The measure was put through at the behest of British merchants seeking a hard-money regime. The act threatened to fine any governor who assented to issues of paper money approved by a colonial assembly — a provision indicative of the balance of power in colonial government. Colonies were allowed to appeal for emergency issues, without which their economies would have collapsed. Colonial resentment arising from the act helped cause the AMERICAN REVOLUTION.

Custer, George Armstrong (1839–1876), US Army cavalry officer. In 1861 Custer graduated from West Point Military Academy – bottom of his class. He achieved martyrdom as the commander of a detachment of 225 men of the Seventh Cavalry who were slaughtered by SIOUX and CHEYENNE warriors at the battle of LITTLE BIG HORN (1876), a débâcle that entered into folklore as 'Custer's Last Stand.' Custer's previous service in the CIVIL WAR and RED RIVER WAR did little to temper the over-confidence that was the ultimate cause of his death.

D

Dakota, *see* NORTH DAKOTA, SOUTH DAKOTA. The name is also applied to the SIOUX collectively, and in particular to the Santee-Sioux.

Danbury hatters' case, case that eventually came before the US Supreme Court, whose ruling in 1908 threatened to strip unions of their capacity to strike.

In 1901 workers at Dietrich Loewe's hat factory in Danbury, Connecticut, went on strike for union recognition. The hatters' union ordered its members to boycott the company's suppliers and customers. Loewe, financed by a manufacturers' association, appealed through the courts to lift the boycott. The case went to the Supreme Court, which on February 3 1908 ruled unanimously that the boycott, by now in its sixth year, was a conspiracy to restrain trade in contravention of the SHERMAN ANTI-TRUST ACT (1890).

The union was ordered to pay court costs and damages of more than $250,000. Local courts were ordered to seize union members' homes and savings accounts as security against payment. However, Herculean efforts by the AMERICAN FEDERATION OF LABOR ensured that the court costs were met with the minimum of suffering to the hatters. By applying antitrust legislation and personal financial liability in this way, the Court made strikes and boycotts all but unsustainable.

Dartmouth College vs. Woodward (February 2 1819), US Supreme Court ruling on the power of state legislatures to interfere with existing contracts.

In 1816 the New Hampshire legislature appointed a new board of trustees to manage Dartmouth College, thereby violating the royal charter of 1769 that had established the college. The original trustees sued William Woodward, secretary of the college, arguing that the state legislature's action had contravened the protection afforded to contractual obligations by the Constitution. The state supreme court ruled for the new board; holding that the college charter had established a public, not a private, corporation and that, therefore, constitutional protections did not apply.

On February 2 1819 the US Supreme Court, Chief Justice MARSHALL presiding, ignored the public–private distinction and overturned the state court's verdict 5–1. The Court's judgment that a charter to a private corporation constituted a form of contract beyond impairment by state legislatures was welcomed by businessmen. The questions of whether and how the state might regulate the economic activities of existing corporations was revisited in CHARLES RIVER BRIDGE VS. WARREN BRIDGE (1837).

Davis, David (1815–86), US Supreme Court justice and politician. Davis was almost single-handedly responsible for ensuring that the PRESIDENTIAL ELECTION OF 1876 was awarded to the Republican candidate Rutherford HAYES.

Davis practised law in Illinois in the 1840s and 1850s. He abandoned the WHIG PARTY for the Republicans at same time as another Illinois lawyer, Abraham LINCOLN. Davis went on to make the speech nominating Lincoln for president at the Republicans' 1860 convention. In 1862 Lincoln appointed him to the Supreme Court. Despite their past friendship, Davis's opinion in EX PARTE MILLIGAN explicitly criticized Lincoln's use of wartime powers. Davis further distanced himself from mainstream Republicanism by expressing sympathy for the GREENBACKER movement, although when the NATIONAL LABOR UNION nominated Davis as their presidential candidate in 1872 he declined to accept the honor.

The extraordinary commission created to resolve the disputed 1876 presidential election was deadlocked along party lines when the Supreme Court chose Davis to complete the judiciary's representation on the commission. It was assumed that Davis would vote to award the election to Democratic nominee Samuel Tilden (1814–86). To general astonishment Davis declined to serve on the commission, and instead resigned from the Supreme Court to take up an invitation from the Illinois legislature to sit in the US Senate as a Democrat. He was replaced on the commission by a Republican appointee, and the Democrats were robbed of their presidential election victory.

Davis, Jefferson (Finis) (1808–89), southern statesman who became the first and only president of the Confederate States of America (the CONFEDERACY).

Raised in Mississippi, the last of ten children (hence his middle name), Davis attended West Point Military Academy and fought in the BLACK HAWK WAR. He was elected, as a DEMOCRAT, to represent a Mississippi district in the US House in 1845, but resigned his seat to fight in the MEXICAN WAR. Despite the fact that he was married to Zachary TAYLOR's daughter, he was passed over for promotion and in 1846 resigned his commission to take over the management of a model plantation in Mississippi owned by his eldest brother.The relatively humane treatment of slaves on this plantation led Davis to dismiss as abolitionist propaganda reports detailing the cruelty of slavery.

Elected to the US Senate as a Democrat in 1847, he opposed the COMPROMISE OF 1850 on the grounds that it infringed slave owners' rights. He modernized the US Army as secretary of war (1853–7) in President PIERCE's administration. Returning to the Senate, he offered the DAVIS RESOLUTIONS (1860). When Mississippi seceded from the Union he resigned his Senate seat.

Davis was elected provisional president of the Confederacy on February 9 1861. He was confirmed for a six-year term in November 1861. A short-tempered man, Davis was unable to persuade the Confederate states to work together. He failed to exploit the diplomatic opportunity presented to the Confederacy by the TRENT AFFAIR because he disliked Britain. He also interfered with military appointments and planning. Davis was captured by Union troops at Irwinsville, Georgia, on May 10 1865 and spent two years in prison under indictment for treason before his release in 1867.

Davis, Richard (1864–1900), the most prominent African-American trade unionist of the 19th century. Raised in North Carolina, he migrated to the coalfields of West Virginia and Ohio in search of higher wages. Mining companies used black miners to break strikes, creating racial tensions between workers that limited the effectiveness of trade unions. Throughout the 1890s Davis organized miners from both races on behalf of the UNITED MINE WORKERS OF AMERICA, helping to make the union the largest multiracial organization of any kind in

19th-century America. He was elected to the union's national executive in 1896, but died a discredited figure following an unsuccessful strike campaign in Alabama.

Davis Bend experiment (1864–6), short-lived experiment in land redistribution in the south at the end of the CIVIL WAR.

In 1864 US military governors seized six plantations (including that of Jefferson DAVIS) located on the east bank of the Mississippi river just south of Vicksburg, Mississippi. The land was turned over to 75 FREEDMEN who, assisted by government credits, raised crops and turned a profit. In 1865 a further subdivision brought in 1800 landless African-Americans, who organized production under a variety of cooperative programs. By year's end the black farmers had made a net profit of over $150,000.

Some RADICAL REPUBLICANS saw in the experiment a blueprint for land reform under RECONSTRUCTION. However, in 1866 President JOHNSON returned the land to its former white owners, ending the experiment.

Davis Resolutions, a staunchly pro-slavery package presented to the US Senate by Jefferson DAVIS on February 2 1860. Davis suggested that Congress should implement ABELMAN VS. BOOTH by forbidding northern states from evading the FUGITIVE SLAVE LAW (1850), and implement DRED SCOTT VS. SANDFORD (1857) by removing the right of citizens in a US territory to ratify a constitution outlawing slavery. The Senate adopted these resolutions on May 24 1860. Some Democrats in the House of Representatives broke ranks and voted against the resolutions, splitting the DEMOCRATIC PARTY and defeating the package. Southern Democrats regarded the resolutions as entirely reasonable, and saw their rejection as evidence of a northern hostility to slavery that justified SECESSION.

Dawes Severalty Act (February 8 1887), legislation that divided Native American reservations into private holdings. The existence of large Native American reservations troubled both reformers such as Helen Hunt JACKSON (who believed that reservation life fostered indolence and hindered assimilation), and land-hungry westerners alike. Under the act, each head of family was offered title to 160 acres (64 hectares) of reservation land, single adults were offered 80 acres (32 ha), and minors 40 acres (16 ha). Native Americans who accepted the deal were eligible for US citizenship. 'Excess' reservation land was sold to white settlers. In 1887, 138 million acres (56 million ha) of land lay within Indian reservations. By 1934, 62% of this total had been transferred to white ownership. Unconditional US citizenship was granted to Native Americans in the Snyder Act (1924).

DC, *see* DISTRICT OF COLUMBIA.

D-Day landings (June 6 1944), Allied invasion of Nazi-occupied France during WORLD WAR II. Operation Overlord (as the landings were officially designated) was the largest air and sea operation in the history of warfare, and proved the turning point of the fighting in Europe.

After spending months attempting to deceive German forces into believing they would attack the area around Calais, the Allies landed on five beaches in Normandy. Utah beach on the Cotentin peninsula was the most westerly landing site. It was attacked by the Seventh US Army Corps. To its east was OMAHA BEACH, attacked by the US Fifth Army Corps. Still further east, Gold beach was attacked by British troops, Juno beach by Canadians and Sword beach, near the mouth of the Orne river, by British and Free French troops. US General Dwight D. EISENHOWER exercised overall command of the operation. He demonstrated his courage by postponing the landings for 24 hours, then ordering them to go ahead despite bad weather forecasts.

Except at Omaha beach, casualties were relatively light. Within 48 hours the Allies were able to land 176,000 front-line combat troops. Within three weeks 1 million troops, 171,000 vehicles and 566,648 tons of supplies (including ten mobile COCA-COLA bottling plants) had passed through the beachhead. US Army Chief of Staff George C. MARSHALL played a crucial role in coordinating this vital logistical support. As the Normandy campaign developed, it confronted stiffening German resistance. In July 1944 the US Third Army under General George PATTON broke a developing stalemate around the Normandy beachhead with the ST LÔ OFFENSIVE. Nearly 3 million Allied soldiers, sailors and airmen served in the Normandy campaign. Securing and opening the Normandy beachhead cost 122,000 Allied casualties, and 15,000 French civilians died in the fighting.

Debs, Eugene (Victor) (1855–1926), labor leader and Socialist politician. A pioneering advocate of INDUSTRIAL UNIONISM, a cofounder of the INDUSTRIAL WORKERS OF THE WORLD and standard-bearer of the SOCIALIST PARTY OF AMERICA, Debs dominated radical politics in the early years of the 20th century.

Born in Indiana, Debs began work in the railroad industry at 15. He helped organize a footplatemen's union, and in 1880 became its national secretary. He served one term in the Indiana state legislature (1884–6). Frustrated by CRAFT UNIONS' emphasis on defending the status of skilled workers, Debs was an eager participant in the creation of the industry-wide AMERICAN RAILWAY UNION (ARU), and in 1893 became its first president. He led the ARU in the PULLMAN STRIKE of 1894 and was jailed for six months for obstructing the mail service. (The Supreme Court's IN RE DEBS verdict upheld the conviction.)

The strike, and his jail sentence, converted Debs to socialism. He played a leading role in the creation of the Socialist Party of America in 1901 and in the foundation of the syndicalist Industrial Workers of the

World in 1905. He stood as an independent socialist in the presidential election of 1900, and as the Socialist Party of America's nominee in 1904, 1908, 1912 and 1920. In 1912 he gained 6% of the POPULAR VOTE. His 1920 campaign (in which he gained 900,000 votes) was remarkable in that it was conducted from Atlanta penitentiary, where he was serving a ten-year sentence for violating the ESPIONAGE ACT of 1917. Debs's conviction, which also resulted in his being stripped of US citizenship, stemmed from a speech he gave in June 1918 in which he defended three socialists who had refused to serve in WORLD WAR I. The US Supreme Court upheld his conviction, but President HARDING released Debs, without restoring his citizenship, in 1921. His citizenship was restored posthumously in 1976.

decimal currency. The USA established a decimal currency system, and outlawed all others, via the Mint Act of April 2 1792.

Declaration of Independence (1776), document by which the THIRTEEN COLONIES declared their independence from British rule. The Declaration was written at the behest of the second CONTINENTAL CONGRESS by a committee whose dominant member was Thomas JEFFERSON. Congress debated Jefferson's draft Declaration on June 23 1776. It made several changes, the most notable of which was the deletion of a lengthy passage blaming George III for forcing Americans to adopt slavery. Congress approved the amended draft on July 4, and it was made public on July 8. The Declaration carries no force in US law, but Jefferson's elegant use of LOCKEAN THOUGHT ensured that the document has been widely quoted. On September 2 1945, for example, Ho Chi Minh incorporated sections of the US Declaration of Independence into a text declaring Vietnam independent of France; an event that helped trigger the VIETNAM WAR. For the full text of the Declaration of Independence approved by Congress, *see* Appendix 1.

Declaratory Act (March 18 1766), legislation passed by the British Parliament that reasserted its power over the American colonies, so defining the crisis in imperial relations that would produce the AMERICAN REVOLUTION. The act specifically denied the claims of American assemblies to 'the sole and exclusive right of imposing duties and taxes in the colonies'. Instead Parliament asserted through the act the 'full power and authority to make laws and statutes' within the colonies 'in all cases whatsoever'. The act was passed on the same day that Parliament repealed the controversial STAMP ACT. The TOWNSHEND REVENUE ACT (1767) and the INTOLERABLE ACTS (1774) were justified by reference to the Declaratory Act.

de facto segregation, term applied to implicit racial segregation and discrimination in northern states. During the GREAT MIGRATION hundreds of thousands of African-Americans moved to northern and western cities. Although these cities did not possess JIM CROW laws, African-Americans tended to be confined to particular residential districts, schools and job grades. The novelist James Baldwin quipped, '*De facto* segregation means that negroes are segregated but nobody did it.' White residents of cities such as Chicago and Boston reacted angrily to policies such as BUSSING and AFFIRMATIVE ACTION designed to change this situation.

Delaware, small northeastern state, bordered to the north by Pennsylvania and New Jersey and to the west by Maryland.

The first permanent European settlement in the territory was established by Swedish settlers at Fort Christina (near modern Wilmington) in 1638. The colony was subsequently subsumed within the Dutch colony of New Netherland and came under British dominion by conquest in 1664. Delaware was placed under the jurisdiction of the new colony of Pennsylvania by royal charter in 1682. Delaware was permitted to convene its own assembly from 1704 and in 1775 became an independent colony.

On December 7 1787, Delaware became the first state to ratify the US Constitution. Its constitution permitted slavery and from 1820 it was the most northerly slave state in the Union. Delaware was one of four BORDER STATES that LINCOLN sought to keep within the Union during the CIVIL WAR. In 1861, Delaware's state legislature voted unanimously against SECESSION. The state supplied troops and munitions to the Union army but, after the war, the state legislature refused to emancipate slaves or to ratify the THIRTEENTH, FOURTEENTH or FIFTEENTH AMENDMENTS. The state also enacted some of the most draconian JIM CROW laws passed outside the deep south. Changes to the state's laws on incorporation in the 1950s prompted an economic boom which has seen Wilmington, Delaware, emerge as a major center for corporate finance. In 1990 Delaware had 666,168 residents and was the 46th most populous state in the Union. Delaware's most famous statesman is John DICKINSON.

Democratic Party, one of the two main political parties in the USA, the other being the REPUBLICAN PARTY. The Democratic Party has claims to be considered the oldest continuously functioning political party in the world.

The origins of the Democratic Party lie in the DEMOCRATIC-REPUBLICAN movement marshalled by Thomas JEFFERSON, James MADISON and Aaron BURR in the 1790s to oppose the FEDERALISTS. A feature of this movement was its use of partisan newspapers and societies such the Sons of St TAMMANY to link congressional politicians with grass-roots activists. The defection of a die-hard Democratic-Republican faction known as the QUIDS during the presidencies of Jefferson and Madison, and the collapse of the Federalist Party following the WAR OF 1812, left the remainder of the fledgling Democratic Party with a loose consensus on a broad range of issues.

Democrats inclined toward a STRICT

CONSTRUCTION of the Constitution, together with a defense of STATES' RIGHTS to protect the people from government tyranny. They viewed themselves as the champions of laboring men, especially small farmers. Democrats opposed central economic planning (especially the BANK OF THE UNITED STATES). They also opposed any involvement of the federal government in the slavery issue, favoring TERRITORIAL EXPANSION as a means of defusing its associated tensions. These broad positions were clarified during JACKSON's administration.

Democrats who believed that central government had a role to play in directing the economic and financial policy of the nation left to join the WHIGS. So too did those Democrats who believed that there were limits to slaveholders' rights, and that central government could legitimately establish the future status of slavery within the Union. The mainstream Democratic Party remained relatively unmoved by the religious revivals and moral crusades of the 1830s and 1840s; providing a further point of contrast with the Whigs, and adding to the party's appeal to immigrants in northern cities, especially the Irish. These distinctions formed the basis of the SECOND PARTY SYSTEM.

The Democratic Party that emerged from the Jacksonian era was markedly southern in complexion, increasingly pro-slavery, and aggressively expansionist. It was enormously successful. Between 1800 and 1860 every president except HARRISON and TAYLOR was elected on a Democratic ticket. Over the same period the Democrats controlled the Senate, with the exception of 1841–4, and the House of Representatives, with the exception of 1841–2, 1847–8 and 1855–60. Despite the rise of the REPUBLICAN PARTY, and the increasingly uncompromising defense of slaveholders' rights by southern Democrats, the party retained significant support in midwestern states right up to the outbreak of the CIVIL WAR as witnessed

by Stephen DOUGLAS's defeat of Abraham LINCOLN in the 1858 Illinois race for the US Senate.

But the Democrats entered a long period of opposition after the war. Their support was heavily concentrated in the former Confederate states and the immigrant districts of the great northern cities. Democrats made some gains in the midwest and west by championing the causes of agrarian reform, trade unionism and FREE SILVER. The western wing of the party produced the charismatic leader William Jennings BRYAN. But even Bryan could not overcome the national perception that the Democratic Party was mired in southern racism and urban corruption. Only two Democrats sat in the White House between 1860 and 1933 – Grover CLEVELAND and Woodrow WILSON (and Wilson owed his election to splits in the Republican ranks).

Franklin ROOSEVELT's victory in the PRESIDENTIAL ELECTION OF 1932 cemented the NEW DEAL COALITION, and led to a renewed period of Democratic hegemony. Between 1933 and 1994 the Democrats held control of both houses of Congress, with the exception of 1947–9, 1953–5 and 1981–6, when the Republicans controlled the Senate. The Democrats have fared less well in presidential elections since 1952, winning only five out of twelve. This is partly because the Republicans, dusting off an old Whig Party strategy, have nominated charismatic candidates, notably EISENHOWER and REAGAN, and presented them to voters as being above the hurly-burly of congressional politics. But the Democrats' failure in presidential elections can also be traced to the fact that, for the past 30 years, working-class and middle-class white males, especially in the south, have begun voting Republican. This shift in voting behavior reflects the bitterness caused by the VIETNAM WAR as well as opposition to AFFIRMATIVE ACTION, feminism and the ROE VS. WADE verdict liberalizing ABORTION. By a curious twist Republicans have wooed white males by borrowing an old Democratic theme: opposition to 'big government'. In 1998 President CLINTON brilliantly manipulated the Democrats' remaining support among minorities, 'pro-choice' women, the recipients of federal expenditure and government employees to become the first Democrat since Franklin Roosevelt to win two presidential elections.

Democratic-Republicans, political faction, the forerunner of the DEMOCRATIC PARTY, that emerged in the 1790s. Democratic-Republicans were united by a distrust of central government, and staunchly opposed the FEDERALIST PARTY.

Despite the adoption of the BILL OF RIGHTS, Democratic-Republicans believed that the US Constitution had created an overly powerful government. They demanded a STRICT CONSTRUCTION of the Constitution, and were appalled by the IMPLIED POWERS defense of the first BANK OF THE UNITED STATES put forward by Alexander HAMILTON. They believed that a citizen's liberties were ultimately guaranteed by the individual states. (This view found its fullest expression in the VIRGINIA and KENTUCKY RESOLUTIONS.)

Led by JEFFERSON, the party venerated independent small producers as the backbone of the republic, and demanded a return to what John Taylor (1753–1824) dubbed 'genuine republicanism'. Grassroots Democratic-Republicans were pro-French. They welcomed Citizen GENÊT and denounced the NEUTRALITY PROCLAMATION and JAY'S TREATY. During the QUASI-WAR with France, John Adams's Federalist administration passed the ALIEN AND SEDITION ACTS in an attempt to crush the Democratic-Republicans. Despite this, Adams was decisively defeated in the PRESIDENTIAL ELECTION OF 1800. Yet in his first INAUGURAL ADDRESS (March 4 1801) President Jefferson blithely stated, 'Every difference of opinion is not a difference of principle. We are all Republicans, we are all Federalists.' This signalled the

abandonment of 'genuine republicanism'.

Over the next quarter century the Democratic-Republicans metamorphosed into the DEMOCRATIC PARTY, although John Randolph (1773–1833) led a faction, known as QUIDS, that continued to press for strict construction of the Constitution and the creation of an agrarian republic.

Dependent Pension Act (June 27 1890), legislation granting a pension to any Union veteran of the Civil War who had served at least 90 days and who was unable to work owing to physical or mental incapacity.

The 'old soldier' vote, marshalled by the GRAND ARMY OF THE REPUBLIC, was instrumental in securing congressional approval for the measure. The act extended previous provisions by making dependants (wives, widows and children) eligible for pensions. By 1895, 970,000 pensions had been awarded. This cost $135 million per annum.

Deposit Act (1836), legislation requiring the Treasury secretary to designate at least one bank in each state and territory as a place of public deposit. Federal surpluses in excess of $5 million were distributed equally among the states and placed in the designated banks. The act exacerbated the DEPRESSION OF 1837.

Depression, Great, *see* GREAT DEPRESSION.

Depression of 1837. In 1836, for the first time in its history, the US government made more from land sales than it did from TARIFFS and duties. It amassed a $40 million surplus. President JACKSON sought to curb land speculation and manage its effects via the SPECIE CIRCULAR and the DEPOSIT ACT. The circular slowed land sales to the point where, by 1843, the US government deficit had reached $46 million.

The government began recalling deposits distributed among the states, just as British banks began recalling American loans. A collapse in cotton prices added to the pressure on banks. When eastern banks could not meet their depositors' demands for gold and silver, and suspended SPECIE payment in May 1837, paper money became worthless in many cities.

President VAN BUREN called Congress into special session on September 5 1837. It repealed the Specie Circular in May 1838, restoring some value to paper currency. Real-estate values and the price of cotton remained depressed, while land sales were stagnant. Van Buren's response was to push Congress to adopt the INDEPENDENT TREASURY ACT (1840), detaching custody of federal funds from private banks chartered by the states. This long-term, hard-money approach – which did little to alleviate suffering – was opposed by some Democrats and most WHIGS.

Depression of 1893. The underlying cause of the USA's second-worst depression was instability in the bullion, security and stock markets. The SHERMAN SILVER PURCHASE ACT (1890) bound the US Treasury to purchase silver using notes redeemable in gold. Later that year European holders of US government securities began redeeming their notes for gold in a bid to limit liabilities generated by the failure of the Baring Brothers bank in London. The protectionist McKINLEY TARIFF (1890) reduced the volume of US imports and with it the value of US tariff revenue, further pressuring US gold reserves. In April 1893 these fell below $100 million.

On June 27 1893, in the aftermath of three major business failures, nervous investors triggered a major stock-market crash, and the depression began. Between June and December 1893, 8000 businesses, 360 banks and 156 railroad companies failed. A further 318 railroad companies, controlling 33% of the nation's track, went into receivership. Unemployment reached crisis proportions, with 20% of the workforce jobless. Protests such as that mounted by COXEY'S ARMY demanded government-funded public-works programs.

President CLEVELAND, a staunch defender of the GOLD STANDARD, addressed the depression by attempting to bolster gold reserves. At his persuasion, a special session of Congress narrowly approved (October 30) the repeal of the Silver Purchase Act. This 'victory' split the Democratic Party, and brought the SILVER–GOLD CONTROVERSY to boiling point. Further drains on reserves led Cleveland to order the purchase of gold by four separate bond issues. The third of these (February 1895) was floated only by cooperation with a banking syndicate, headed by J. Pierpoint MORGAN, which took massive commissions. Enraged POPULISTS, led by Democrat 'Champ' Clark (1850–1921), compared Cleveland to Judas Iscariot. The bonds used to purchase bullion were themselves redeemable in gold. This helped prolong fiscal contraction.

The depression fueled a surge in activism by labor unions, and led imperialists to argue that the acquisition of foreign territory was vital to the USA's domestic well-being.

Depression of 1929, see GREAT DEPRESSION.

Desert Storm, Operation, see PERSIAN GULF WAR.

détente, policy of improving relations between two previously hostile nations (the word is French for 'loosening'). The term is particularly applied to the policy towards the USSR and communist China pursued enthusiastically by President NIXON and his national security adviser, later secretary of state, Henry KISSINGER. This contributed to an easing of COLD WAR tensions, although both men denied that it represented an abandonment of CONTAINMENT.

Nixon and Kissinger sought to exploit the growing rift between the USSR and China that had developed in the 1960s. Nixon visited China in February 1972, and on February 27 announced that the USA now accepted communist China's claim to the island of Taiwan, controlled by the Nationalist Chinese, and would abandon its opposition to communist China's membership of the UNITED NATIONS. (Formal diplomatic relations were established in January 1979.) This initiative was designed to broaden the focus of US policy towards Asia, which had been narrowed by the USA's preoccupation with the VIETNAM WAR.

Nixon also hoped to use his China policy, and the USSR's need for Western trade links and technology, to force concessions from the Soviet Union. On March 26 1972 Nixon and Soviet leader Leonid Brezhnev brought two years of detailed negotiation to fruition by signing a first Strategic Arms Limitation Treaty (SALT). This stabilized the offensive nuclear capabilities of the USSR and the USA at a level of rough parity. On the same day they signed an Antiballistic Missile (ABM) Treaty, which allowed each country to build a limited number of defensive missile sites but preserved the concept of 'mutually assured destruction' that lay at the heart of nuclear deterrence. Thereafter, détente produced warmer relations between the USA and Soviet leaders, but little substantive progress. The policy enjoyed little public support, and was attacked in Congress by 'hawks' (who argued that it made too many concessions to the Soviets) and by 'doves' (who argued that it did not go far enough). The USSR's determination to expand its influence in Africa and the Middle East obstructed progress on a second SALT treaty. SALT II was signed in 1979, but never ratified, and the USA repudiated it in 1986. The discovery of Soviet combat troops in Cuba and the Soviet invasion of Afghanistan in 1979 brought to a premature close the experiment in détente.

Nevertheless, arms-control talks between the USA and the Soviet Union resumed in 1982. The Strategic Arms Reduction Talks (START) proposed by President REAGAN on May 9 1982 included discussion of intermediate-range nuclear missiles and the STRATEGIC DEFENSE INITIATIVE. At the talks, held in Geneva, US negotiator Kenneth Adelman and his Soviet counterparts broke new ground by attempting to reduce both countries' stockpiles of nuclear weapons rather than define ceilings on the deployment of warheads as in the earlier SALT treaties. START produced a treaty in which both sides agreed to dismantle and destroy intermediate-range land-based nuclear missiles stationed in western Europe. (The US Senate ratified this on May 27 1988.) However, Soviet demands that the USA abandon research into the SDI hindered agreement on a reduction in the number of long-range nuclear missiles. At the REYKJAVIK CONFERENCE (1986) president REAGAN and Soviet premier Mikhail Gorbachev considered total nuclear disarmament but could not reach agreement on SDI. In the event START produced an agreement reducing by 50% stockpiles of long-range nuclear weapons. President BUSH signed this on June 2 1992 and Senate ratification followed on October 2. However, Kazakhstan and the Ukraine, independent nations following the break-up of the Soviet Union, refused to ratify the agreement.

Detroit riot (July 23–30 1967), the worst domestic insurrection in the USA since the NEW YORK CITY DRAFT RIOTS in 1863: 43 people were killed, 2000 injured and 5000 were left homeless. A subsequent presidential commission found that the riot was caused by social deprivation. Before the riot the white population had deserted central Detroit for the suburbs, and the remaining predominantly African-American population faced declining social-service expenditure, poor schools and rising unemployment. Rioters targeted white-owned ghetto businesses for destruction, suggesting the economic frustrations that led normally law-abiding residents to participate in the destruction.

Dickinson, John (1732–1808), author of *LETTERS FROM A FARMER IN PENNSYLVANIA* (1767), one of the most influential pamphlets published during the AMERICAN REVOLUTION. In it Dickinson, a lawyer by training, made the characteristically balanced argument that while the British Parliament might legislate to regulate trade, it had no right to levy internal taxes on the colonies. During the second CONTINENTAL CONGRESS Dickinson drafted the OLIVE-BRANCH PETITION (1775) to King George III which suggested a peaceful means of resolving the crisis in Anglo-American affairs based on repeal of the INTOLERABLE ACTS. As late as 1776 Dickinson argued against immediate adoption of the DECLARATION OF INDEPENDENCE and urged further negotiation with Britain. In 1777 he wrote the first draft of the ARTICLES OF CONFEDERATION. These were adopted, in a heavily revised form, in 1781.

Dies Committee, committee established on May 26 1938 by the House of Representatives to investigate 'un-American activities' attributed to American communists and Nazis. The committee's first chairman was Representative Martin Dies of Texas (1901–69). The committee gained influence during WORLD WAR II, and was given permanent status by a House vote on January 3 1945. The House Un-American Activities Committee (HUAC), as it became known, took a leading role in the furore sparked by Senator Joseph McCARTHY's allegations of communist subversion.

Dingley Tariff (July 7 1897), increase in TARIFFS on imported goods to a record average of 57%. The measure was introduced by the REPUBLICANS, who were able to exploit their control of both houses of Congress. The tariff was popular with large corporations, but DEMOCRATS attacked its effects on consumer prices, while PROGRESSIVES bemoaned its tendency to encourage the creation of cartels. Rates were reduced in the Payne–Aldrich Act (1909).

Disney, Walt(er) Elias (1901–66), pioneering film-maker and successful entrepreneur. During the 1930s, Disney's cartoon characters (especially Mickey Mouse) became American icons recognized throughout the world.

Disney was born in Chicago and grew up in rural Illinois. His parents were strict Presbyterians who inveighed against time 'wasted' on play and leisure. Disney worked as a commercial artist in Kansas City before moving to HOLLYWOOD in 1923 to establish a small studio dedicated to making cartoons. Disney's first animated feature film *Steamboat Willie* (1928) featured the character, Mickey Mouse, who would make him famous. Disney's feature *Flowers and Trees* (1935) was the first film produced in the USA to feature the three-color Technicolor process. The use of color in his animated feature *Snow White and the Seven Dwarfs* (1937) bewitched audiences. *Fantasia* (1940), also featuring Mickey Mouse, took the animated film format to new heights of sophistication through its use of action matched to a classical music score.

During the 1950s, Walt Disney, and his brother Roy, produced documentaries, notably *The Living Desert* (1953), live action movies, notably *Treasure Island* (1959) and television programs, notably a series based on the life of Davy CROCKETT. The Disney Corporation virtually invented the concept of the 'family movie' – of which *Mary Poppins* (1964) is an outstanding example. Disney received 31 Academy Awards during his lifetime, and movies produced by the Disney Corporation since his death continue to garner critical and commercial acclaim.

In 1955, Disney opened a theme park (Disneyland) in Anaheim, California, that he believed represented the culmination of his life's mission. It was hugely popular, but it celebrated a view of the USA (spotlessly clean, eternally innocent, devoid of trade unionists, homosexuals, ethnic minorities or mature appreciation of the outside world) that was at odds with the nation's history and a source of embarrassment to progressive opinion. Following Disney's death, even more ambitious parks were opened in Florida (1971), Japan (1983) and France (1992).

District of Columbia (DC), a ten square mile (26 square km) tract of land bordered by Maryland and Virginia that has, since November 17 1800, been the site of the USA's capital city, Washington. (New York and Philadelphia had previously served as the headquarters of the federal government.) The decision to relocate the nation's capital to a district outside the jurisdiction of an existing state was made on July 19 1790 and justified on the grounds that it would distance government from lobbyists. It has also been alleged that the District of Columbia was created as part of a bargain which saw Virginian congressmen drop their opposition to key features of Alexander HAMILTON's economic program in return for an agreement to relocate the federal capital to the south. The city of Washington was incorporated on May 3 1802. Most government buildings were destroyed in a British raid during the WAR OF 1812.

The status of slavery in the District of Columbia proved particularly contentious. Abolitionists urged Congress to take the symbolic step of using its jurisdiction over the District to outlaw the slave trade in the nation's capital. Proslavery congressmen were equally determined to prevent Congress from using its power in this way. The slave trade was eventually outlawed in the District of Columbia through the COMPROMISE OF 1850 and slavery itself was abolished in 1862. Residents of the District of Columbia are not represented in the US Congress and were not granted the right to vote in presidential elections until 1964. Washingtonians were granted the right to elect a mayor and city council in 1973. Both J. Edgar HOOVER and John Foster DULLES were born and died in Washington DC.

Dix, Dorothea Lynde (1802–87), pioneering social reformer. At the age of 19 Dix established a school for girls in Boston which she ran (1821–35) until she was stricken with tuberculosis. In 1841 she visited a Massachusetts prison and was shocked by the general brutality inflicted on the prisoners and the particularly inhumane treatment of insane inmates, who were confined alongside the prisoners. She began a lifelong campaign to improve conditions in prisons and to provide specialist treatment for the mentally ill. During the CIVIL WAR Dix was appointed Superintendent of Female Nurses and charged with training the women volunteers who responded to the recruitment campaign spearheaded by Elizabeth BLACKWELL. With Clara BARTON Dix developed an orderly system for notifying the Union war dead's next-of-kin.

Dixiecrats, nickname given to southern conservatives who left the DEMOCRATIC PARTY in protest at President Harry S TRUMAN's support for desegregation. In July 1948 they founded the States' Rights Party, and Strom Thurmond, their presidential nominee, won 1,169,063 votes in the PRESIDENTIAL ELECTION OF 1948. In 1954 all bar three of the south's Democratic congressmen signed a manifesto pledging 'massive resistance' to federal legislation dismantling JIM CROW.

Dole, Robert ('Bob') J(oseph) (1923–), Republican politician. A party hack, Dole realized a long-cherished dream when in 1996 he ran as the Republicans' presidential nominee against the incumbent Bill CLINTON. Dole served with distinction as an infantry officer in World War II, and sustained an arm injury while fighting in the Italian campaign. This injury has caused him pain ever since, and is said to account for his occasional outbursts of ill-humor. Dole served in the Kansas state legislature (1951–3), before election to the US House of Representatives in 1960, and to the US Senate in 1968. Between 1984 and 1996 he led the Republicans in the Senate, twice serving as majority leader. Dole was chosen as Gerald FORD's running-mate in the presidential election of 1976. During a vice-presidential debate he made a spectacularly offensive speech blaming the Democratic Party for the ills of the 20th century. He made determined efforts to seize the presidential nomination in 1980 and 1988. George BUSH torpedoed Dole's 1988 campaign with a barrage of negative TV advertisements that left Dole barely in control of his temper. Dole's 1996 presidential campaign never really caught fire. Recently Dole has gained celebrity of a kind by appearing in advertisements extolling the virtues of the anti-impotence drug Viagra.

dollar diplomacy, doctrine that the goal of US diplomacy should be the promotion and protection of US business interests abroad. Dollar diplomacy was devised by William Howard TAFT's Republican administration (1909–13), developing OPEN DOOR rhetoric and the ROOSEVELT COROLLARY.

The doctrine was applied with particular rigor in Central America. Taft genuinely believed that what was good for US business was good for Central Americans. When in 1912 Nicaragua threatened to install a government unpalatable to US investors, Taft sent Marines to 'restore order'. Franklin ROOSEVELT's GOOD-NEIGHBOR POLICY attempted to establish more equal trading relationships.

Dominican Republic, US interventions in (1916–24, 1965–66). The USA has twice intervened militarily in this Caribbean country, which forms the eastern part of the island of Hispaniola.

(1) On May 26 1916 President Woodrow WILSON ordered US Marines to occupy Dominica in order to enforce US control over the country's customs house. The USA had been claiming control of Dominica's custom revenue since 1905, arguing that American stewardship was necessary if Dominica was to repay international debts. Following the occupation of 1916, the USA placed the island under a US military government. Dominican guerrillas clashed periodically with US troops until the occupation was lifted on September 16 1924.

(2) On April 28 1965 President Lyndon JOHNSON sent US troops to Dominica to prevent a return to power by former president Juan Bosch. US analysts regarded Bosch as pro-communist. Johnson justified the intervention, which involved 30,000 troops at its peak, with the argument that the USA had a right to block the establishment of 'communist dictatorships' in the western hemisphere. The action was widely criticized, and in May 1965 the USA acquiesced in the 'internationalization' of the occupation by agreeing to act in concert with other members of the ORGANIZATION OF AMERICAN STATES (OAS). A multinational OAS force supervised free elections held in March 1966, which returned an authoritarian but pro-American government to power. The last US troops left Dominica on September 20 1966.

domino theory, COLD WAR doctrine that held that successful communist subversion in one country would lead neighboring states to 'topple' into communist control like a line of dominos. The metaphor was first used by President TRUMAN to justify military and financial aid to Greece and Turkey. President EISENHOWER described the consequences of a communist take-over in Vietnam in similar terms (although Eisenhower declined to act on the theory by sending military aid to the French colonial government in Indo-China). Presidents KENNEDY and JOHNSON used the domino theory to justify US involvement in the VIETNAM WAR.

double jeopardy, the retrial of a defendant on a criminal charge of which he or she has already been found innocent. Double jeopardy is prohibited by the Fifth Amendment. In 1937 the US Supreme Court interpreted the Fifth Amendment in such a way as to permit retrials in some cases within the jurisdiction of the state court system. The Court reversed this decision in 1969. *See* Appendix 1.

doughface, term of abuse applied to northern congressmen who acquiesced in the expansion of slavery. It was coined by John Randolph (1773–1833) of Virginia to describe northern supporters of the MISSOURI COMPROMISE. The 1848 Democratic presidential nominee Lewis Cass (1782– 1866) was dubbed a 'doughface' for arguing that the federal government should let the residents of territories acquired through the MEXICAN WAR decide for themselves whether they wished to permit slavery. The Democrat Franklin PIERCE, elected in 1852, was the first doughface president.

Douglas, Stephen A(rnold) (1813–61), Democratic politician who argued for the right of new territories to decide for themselves on the slavery issue. He was defeated by LINCOLN in the PRESIDENTIAL ELECTION OF 1860.

Born in Vermont, Douglas settled in Illinois, where he practiced law. Elected to the House of Representatives in 1843 as a Democrat, Douglas supported the MEXICAN WAR. Between 1847 and 1861 he sat in the US Senate. He helped assemble the COMPROMISE OF 1850, but in 1854 introduced the KANSAS–NEBRASKA ACT, which effectively destroyed it. Douglas justified this act on the grounds that it was for the inhabitants of a territory to decide whether to permit slavery. His energy and eloquence in defense of this position earned him the nickname 'little giant,' although opponents alleged he was courting southern support for a future presidential bid.

In 1858 Abraham Lincoln stood against Douglas for the US Senate in Illinois. The pair staged the LINCOLN–DOUGLAS DEBATES, during the course of which Douglas formulated the FREEPORT DOCTRINE. This reassured Illinois voters, but cost him any future support in the south. Nominated as Democratic candidate for the presidency in 1860, Douglas polled 29% of the popular vote, but could make no inroad on Lincoln's command of the ELECTORAL COLLEGE. Following the attack on FORT SUMTER he pledged support to the Union and castigated the CONFEDERACY. He died an exhausted man in June 1861.

Douglass, Frederick (1817–95), exslave who became a leading campaigner for ABOLITION, and later served as a government official. In the 1840s Douglass electrified abolitionist meetings by recounting his escape from slavery.

Douglass's mother was an African-American slave, and his white father was his mother's owner. Douglass learned to read and write while working as a household slave in Baltimore, Maryland. His owner, suspecting Douglass was insufficiently submissive, sold him into service as a plantation field hand in 1833. After an unsuccessful escape attempt in 1835, on September 3 1838 Douglass, posing as a sailor, successfully reached Philadelphia. Dropping his given surname, Bailey, he worked as a laborer in New York City, before moving to New Bedford, Massachusetts.

Douglass drifted into the abolitionist circle centered around William Lloyd GARRISON, and in 1841 gave his first address to the Massachusetts Antislavery Society. An immediate success, he was hired to conduct a regional speaking tour. He published a best-selling *Narrative* of his life in 1845; defenders of slavery asserted that Douglass could not possibly have written so moving a tract. During the CIVIL WAR Douglass helped recruit African-Americans into the Union Army. He subsequently held a number of government positions, ending his career as US consul general to Haiti (1889–91).

draft, the, conscription of civilians into the US armed forces. Conscription has always been unpopular in the USA, and for that reason US politicians and military leaders have sought whenever possible to man the nation's armed forces with volunteers.

During the REVOLUTIONARY WAR bounties were paid to recruits who agreed to serve as foot soldiers in the Continental Army. US militiamen signed on for fixed terms, which they observed regardless of the military situation that prevailed at the moment their enlistment expired. The voluntary system proved adequate for the demands of the WAR OF 1812 and the MEXICAN WAR, but wholly inadequate during the CIVIL WAR. The first draft in US history was enacted by the CONFEDERACY on April 16 1862. The exemptions in the act concerned gave rise to the southern saying that the Civil War was 'a rich man's war, but a poor man's fight'. The Union matched the Confederacy's initiative through the CONSCRIPTION ACT of March 3 1863. This too allowed wealthy men to evade service by furnishing a substitute or paying a $300 bounty, and provoked the NEW YORK CITY DRAFT RIOTS.

Mindful of these precedents, following the USA's entry into WORLD WAR I the Wilson administration was careful to call its conscription act the SELECTIVE SERVICE ACT. This act, which was passed in May 1917, inducted 2.8 million American men into the armed forces, of whom 16% failed to report for duty or immediately deserted. The first peacetime draft in US history was instituted through the Selective Training and Service Act of 1940. During WORLD WAR II some 10 million American men were inducted into the armed forces under the terms of the act. It expired on March 31 1947 but, amid rising COLD WAR tensions, was revived by President TRUMAN on June 24 1948. In the KOREAN WAR the majority of US Army personnel were draftees.

During the 1950s resistance to the draft was relatively uncommon. Prominent figures, among them Elvis PRESLEY, cooperated with the system. However, during the VIETNAM WAR some 136,000 draftees failed to report for duty, and many more evaded active service by enrolling on graduate degree courses, moving to Canada, or registering for service in the National Guard. The boxer Muhammad ALI famously brought together the concerns of the CIVIL RIGHTS MOVEMENT and the ANTIWAR MOVEMENT by refusing to be drafted on the grounds that 'I ain't got no quarrel with them Vietcong.' President CLINTON and former Vice President J. Danforth QUAYLE are among a bevy of BABY BOOM politicians who used legal means to escape being drafted into active service in Vietnam.

From January 27 1973 the US Department of Defense announced that it would no longer induct draftees into the armed forces, and Congress allowed the Selective Service Act to expire on June 30 1973. On January 21 1977 President CARTER issued an executive pardon to all men who had evaded the Vietnam draft. In January 1980, following the Soviet invasion of Afghanistan, Carter revived draft registration procedures. These were quietly shelved by President REAGAN.

Dred Scott vs. Sandford (March 6 1857), US Supreme Court ruling that favored the rights of slave owners. The ruling further polarized the positions of the pro- and anti-slavery factions in the years leading up to the CIVIL WAR.

In 1846 Dred Scott, a slave, sued for freedom in Missouri, his former master's home state. Between 1834 and 1838 Scott and his then master had resided in Illinois, and Wisconsin: states wherein slavery was prohibited by the NORTHWEST ORDINANCE and MISSOURI COMPROMISE.The Missouri state court of appeal overturned an earlier verdict granting Scott freedom on the basis of his residence on free soil.

The case was ultimately decided in the US Supreme Court, Chief Justice Roger Taney presiding. On March 6 1857 the Court ruled by 7–2 that since Scott (and all slaves and their descendants) were not citizens of the USA they could not sue through federal courts. By 6–3 it ruled that temporary residence on free soil did not impart freedom. Most controversially of all, the Court declared the Missouri Compromise to be an unconstitutional infringement of slave owners' rights under the FIFTH AMENDMENT. (This was only the second occasion on which the Court ruled an act of Congress unconstitutional.)

The Court's rulings, issued during the BLEEDING KANSAS struggle, led many northerners to conclude that their way of life was threatened by SLAVE POWER. The REPUBLICAN PARTY immediately gained fresh support. The FREEPORT DOCTRINE espoused by Stephen DOUGLAS was an attempt to evade the verdict's implication that neither national government nor an existing state could bar slavery without infringing slave owners' Fifth Amendment rights. The citizenship rights of black Americans were not guaranteed until adoption of the FOURTEENTH AMENDMENT (1868).

Du Bois, W(illiam) E(dward) B(urghardt) (1868–1963), civil rights activist. Du Bois was the pre-eminent African-American intellectual of his generation, and a founding father of American sociology.

A native of Massachusetts, Du Bois was educated at Fisk (1885–88) and Harvard (1888–95) universities, from where he was the first African-American to earn a doctorate. Between 1891 and 1894 he studied with the great German sociologists at Heidelberg and Berlin. His classic sociological study, *The Philadelphia Negro*, was published in 1899. It was not until he attempted to secure an academic post appropriate to his abilities that Du Bois fully grasped the pervasive injustice of racial discrimination in the USA.

At the time, many African-American leaders were prepared to follow the compliant stance on segregation outlined in Booker T. WASHINGTON's ATLANTA EXPOSITION SPEECH. Du Bois rejected this position and, in his book *The Souls of Black Folk* (1903), criticized the emphasis on black self-improvement and vocational training expressed in Washington's *Up from Slavery* (1901). In 1905 Du Bois helped found the NIAGARA MOVEMENT, dedicated to securing for African-Americans 'by every civilized

and peaceful method the rights which the world accords men'. Outraged by the SPRINGFIELD LYNCH RIOT, he played a leading role in the creation of the NATIONAL ASSOCIATION FOR THE ADVANCEMENT OF COLORED PEOPLE (NAACP) in 1909, and for 24 years edited its journal *The Crisis*.

The GREAT DEPRESSION deepened Du Bois's conviction that attempts to integrate African-Americans within white economic and political structures were futile. In 1934 he published an article in *The Crisis* calling on African-Americans to distance themselves from white society and pursue a strategy of independent and cooperative economic development. Heavily criticized, he resigned from the NAACP. He subsequently urged closer cooperation between the USA and the Soviet Union. Summoned before the McCARTHY HEARINGS, Du Bois became increasingly disillusioned with the USA. In 1961 he renounced his citizenship and took up exile in Ghana.

Dukakis, Michael S(tanley) (1933–), the Democratic Party's nominee in the presidential election of 1988. After one of the most negative campaigns in recent memory, he was soundly defeated by Republican nominee George BUSH.

Dukakis, the son of Greek immigrants, had previously been elected governor of Massachusetts in 1974, 1982 and 1986. After enduring an interminable speech from Bill CLINTON, delegates to the Democrats' 1988 convention (held in Atlanta) warmed to a passionate acceptance speech from Dukakis, in which he promised to throw out the 'cramped ideals and limited ambition' of the REAGAN era. Political pros admired the manner in which Dukakis handled Jesse JACKSON. Dukakis's poll ratings were good. However, these advantages were dissipated by Dukakis's decision to campaign on the issue of 'competence', and Bush's relentless negative attacks on the supposed liberalism symbolized by Dukakis's membership of the AMERICAN

CIVIL LIBERTIES UNION (ACLU). The Bush campaign released pictures of Willie Horton, a menacing African-American criminal, whom they claimed was free to walk the streets as a result of a parole program which was adopted in Massachusetts while Dukakis was governor. Dukakis did not help his cause when, in an attempt to highlight the fact that he had complied with the DRAFT while Bush's running-mate Dan QUAYLE had dodged service in the US Army, he staged an ill-advised photo opportunity posing in a combat helmet and business suit at the controls of a tank. Just 57% of the electorate bothered to vote. Of those that did, 54% voted for Bush and 46% for Dukakis. Bush received 426 votes in the ELECTORAL COLLEGE to Dukakis's 111.

Dulles, John Foster (1888–1959), secretary of state in President EISENHOWER's administrations (1953–9). In this capacity Dulles promoted assertive US policies that raised the temperature of the COLD WAR. Arguing that the CONTAINMENT policies pursued by the previous TRUMAN administration had made too many concessions to communism, Dulles called for the 'liberation' of territory already under communist control. On January 23 1953 he told 'captive' peoples behind the Iron Curtain, 'you can count on us.' This speech helped foment an uprising in East Berlin, which the USA did not assist and which was crushed by Soviet troops. Unshaken, Dulles continued to propound what became known as the doctrine of ROLLBACK. He was a staunch defender of the nuclear-weapons build-up announced in the NEW LOOK DEFENSE POLICY, and the main author of the EISENHOWER DOCTRINE (1957), which committed the USA to use force to assist any Middle Eastern nation resisting communist aggression. Dulles was an inveterate traveler, clocking up over 500,000 miles (800,000 km) of air travel during his tenure in office. The main international airport servicing Washington DC is named after him.

Dumbarton Oaks Conference (August 21 –October 7 1944), conference held on the outskirts of Washington DC that established the basic structure of what was to become the UNITED NATIONS. The meeting was attended by representatives of the main Allied powers in World War II: the USA, the USSR, Britain and China. The organization of the Security Council reflected Franklin ROOSEVELT's belief that the great powers ought to act as the policemen of the new world order. In a harbinger of COLD WAR tensions, the USSR's negotiators refused to accept the US position that a nation should not vote on, or veto discussion of, issues to which it was party. This impasse was finally resolved at the San Francisco Conference establishing the United Nations Organization.

Dunmore's Proclamation (November 17 1775), offer made by the royal governor of Virginia, John Murray, Earl of Dunmore, to free any slave who would take up arms on behalf of King George III in the REVOLUTIONARY WAR. The formation of a Royal Ethiopian Regiment of 800 former slaves followed. This alienated Virginia's planter class, and led JEFFERSON to include in the DECLARATION OF INDEPENDENCE an indictment of George III for raising 'domestic insurrection'.

Duplex Printing Press Company vs. Deering (January 3 1921), US Supreme Court ruling outlawing secondary boycotts in industrial disputes. The CLAYTON ANTITRUST ACT (1914) specified that most secondary boycotts organized by unions against the suppliers and customers of a company involved in a strike action were legal. Seven years later the Supreme Court ruled (6–3) that secondary boycotts constituted an illegal restraint of trade, and permitted companies to apply for court injunctions to lift them. This reaffirmation of the Court's ruling in the DANBURY HATTERS' CASE (1908) stifled a surge in labor militancy ushered in by the Clayton Act.

dust bowl, term coined by an Associated Press reporter to describe the effects of soil erosion in the plains regions of Oklahoma, Kansas, northern Texas and eastern Colorado. Between 1933 and 1937, a series of storms accompanying a severe drought blew much of the region's topsoil away, ruining farmlands and forcing at least 300,000 OKIES to migrate to the Pacific coast in search of work. Newspaper reports and John Steinbeck's novel *The Grapes of Wrath* (1939) contributed to the popular impression that the 'dust bowl' was an unavoidable natural disaster. In fact, as agricultural prices fell during the GREAT DEPRESSION, plains farmers removed the hedges, trees and ditches that sheltered their land from the wind in a desperate bid to increase the acreage under production, and with it their revenue. The inability of Congress and the HOOVER administration to produce effective price-support and production-limitation programs exacerbated the problem. The inevitable storm, which deposited up to 9 feet (2.75 m) of dust on some areas and darkened the skies of east-coast cities, ruined prudent and imprudent farmers alike. During the NEW DEAL, the Department of Agriculture under Henry WALLACE spent millions of dollars on teaching the remaining farmers about soil-conservation techniques and the building of 'shelterbelts'.

E

East Florida, former territory comprising most of the modern state of FLORIDA, except the northwestern 'panhandle', which formed part of the territory of WEST FLORIDA.

In 1763 Britain created a royal colony in the territory, bounded by Georgia to the north and the Apalachicola river to the west. SEMINOLE migrants outnumbered European settlers, and Britain ceded the territory to Spain in the treaty of PARIS (1783). Following US occupation of WEST FLORIDA, and the first SEMINOLE WAR, Spain ceded EAST FLORIDA to the USA in the ADAMS–ONIS TREATY (1819).

Eaton, Peggy (1796–1879), woman whose marriage to President Andrew JACKSON's secretary of war resulted in a split in Jackson's cabinet.

In 1828 Peggy O'Neale, the recently widowed daughter of a Washington innkeeper, married John Henry Eaton (1790–1856). John Eaton became Jackson's secretary of war soon after. Washington society, led by the wife of John C. CALHOUN, Jackson's vice president, ostracized Mrs Eaton as it was believed that prior to the marriage she and Eaton had been conducting an adulterous affair, which had driven Mrs Eaton's first husband to suicide. Washington wives also looked down on Mrs Eaton's lowly social background.

Jackson, who maintained that his own wife's death had been hastened by snide social comment, ordered his cabinet to treat Mrs Eaton with respect and courtesy. With the exception of Martin VAN BUREN, a widower, they refused. The affair strained relations between Jackson and Calhoun, and prompted a major cabinet reshuffle in 1831. Calhoun resigned as vice president in 1832, while Jackson nominated Van Buren as his running mate in the presidential election of that year.

Edison, Thomas Alva (1847–1931), the USA's greatest inventor. As a boy Edison was dubbed a slow learner and taken out of school after just three months. He sold newspapers and candy on trains and in 1863 became a telegraph operator. After a year with the Western Union Telegraph Company in 1869 he moved to New York to form the Pope and Edison Electrical Engineering Company. The company built an improved electric stock-market ticker to Edison's design, and within a year was bought out by rivals. Edison received $40,000 in the buyout and established the world's first industrial research laboratory, which from 1876 was based in Menlo Park, New Jersey, and from 1887 in Orange, New Jersey.

Edison worked flat out, sleeping just six hours a night on the floor beneath his bench, and at his peak filing a fresh patent application every eleven days (when he died he held 1328 patents). In 1877 he developed the phonograph, and in 1879 invented the world's first practical electric light bulb (the giant General Electric Corporation evolved from the spin-off company Edison formed to produce the bulbs). He went on to invent the vitaphone movie projector, the dictaphone, the alkaline battery and the electric train. In 1881 Edison built an electric power station in New York that advertised his faith in the new energy source by lighting the famous Tiffany Theater and much of lower Manhattan. Other cities soon clamored to have their downtown districts lit by electric light.

Edison loathed bankers and lawyers but, by paying attention to the commercial application of his inventions, was able to fund a research laboratory that gave unparalleled freedom to its staff. He also established a company ethos that attracted like-minded men. Henry FORD built his first car while working for the Edison Illuminating Company in Detroit, and the two men became friends in later life, taking family vacations together. By the 1920s most major US corporations were creating research-and-development units in imitation of Edison's lab. Unlike most inventors, Edison enjoyed wealth and influence in his own lifetime.

Eighteenth Amendment, amendment to the US Constitution that imposed a PROHIBITION on the sale and transportation of alcohol within the USA. The amendment was sent to the states on December 18 1917, and proclaimed on January 29 1919. The ban took effect, through the VOLSTEAD ACT, on January 16 1920. The WICKERSHAM REPORT (1933) recognized that Prohibition was unenforceable, and the TWENTY-FIRST AMENDMENT (ratified December 5 1933) lifted the constitutional ban on the sale of alcohol within the USA.

Eighth Amendment, amendment to the US Constitution prohibiting excessive bail and punishments. It was one of the ten amendments making up the BILL OF RIGHTS. For the full text, *see* Appendix 1.

eight-hour movement, campaign to secure a maximum eight-hour day for all workers. The campaign began in the later 19th century, but its goal was not realized until just before World War II.

In 1868 Congress passed a law limiting laborers employed by, or on behalf of, the federal government to an eight-hour day. Both the NATIONAL LABOR UNION and, later, the KNIGHTS OF LABOR demanded that the eight-hour day be extended to all workers. Late 19th-century labor activists invested the eight-hour day with an almost religious significance. On May 1 1886, for example, workers in Chicago mounted a general strike in support of this goal, creating a fevered atmosphere that helped cause the HAYMARKET RIOT. Employers were no less adamant that the eight-hour movement infringed their liberties and threatened them with bankruptcy.

The employers' position was favored by Supreme Court verdicts, such as LOCHNER VS. NEW YORK (1905), which struck down state laws limiting workers' hours – although the Court's decision in MULLER VS. OREGON (1908) limited the working day for some women. Faced with a national rail strike in 1916, President WILSON pressured Congress to pass the ADAMSON ACT, which established an eight-hour day for workers on interstate railroad lines. But it was not until the NEW DEAL, and passage of the FAIR LABOR STANDARDS ACT (1938), that an eight-hour day became the norm for most industrial workers.

Eisenhower, Dwight D(avid) (1890–1969), US Army general, Republican statesman and 34th president of the USA (1953–61). Eisenhower was Supreme Allied Commander in western Europe in the closing phase of WORLD WAR II. As president he continued the COLD WAR while presiding over a dramatic growth in domestic prosperity.

Eisenhower graduated from West Point Military Academy in 1915 and began a career in the US Army. Until 1941, this career was undistinguished – he remained a major from 1920 to 1936. In 1932 he helped General Douglas MACARTHUR disperse the BONUS ARMY from Washington DC, and he served on MacArthur's staff in the Philippines from 1935 to 1939. Following Pearl Harbor, Eisenhower assisted the war planning division of the chiefs of staff. He was promoted rapidly, and in July 1942 he achieved the rank of lieutenant general.

Eisenhower's appointment (in September 1942) as commander of US forces in Europe was something of a surprise, since he had not served in Europe during World War I. Yet as Allied commander in chief he oversaw the successful invasions of North Africa (November 1942), Sicily (July 1943) and Italy (September 1943). In December 1943 he was named Supreme Allied Commander and charged with mounting the D-DAY landings in Normandy (June 1944). During this operation Eisenhower demonstrated his courage by first postponing the landings (on June 5) and then ordering them to proceed on June 6 despite unfavorable weather forecasts. During the final assault on Germany, and throughout the war, Eisenhower displayed considerable patience and tact in his dealings with subordinate commanders and Allied nations. After receiving Germany's surrender (May 7 1945), Eisenhower returned to the USA as the Army's chief of staff. He resigned from the Army in February 1948.

Both main parties sought Eisenhower as their candidate in the PRESIDENTIAL ELECTION OF 1948. However, Eisenhower preferred to remain in his new post as president of Columbia University. In December 1950 President TRUMAN asked Eisenhower to leave Columbia to serve as Supreme Commander of NATO forces, a position he held until May 1952. The beneficiary of a 'Draft Eisenhower' movement at the 1952 Republican Party convention, Eisenhower

resigned his NATO command to run for the presidency. He pledged that, if elected, he would go to Korea to secure a negotiated end to the KOREAN WAR, and in November he achieved a sweeping victory over the Democratic nominee Adlai STEVENSON.

Eisenhower began his presidency on January 20 1953. Re-elected in 1956, he served until January 20 1961. His folksy charm (commemorated in campaign buttons proclaiming 'I like Ike') masked considerable independence of thought. He criticized the excesses of the McCARTHY HEARINGS. He took advice to accept Richard NIXON as his running-mate, but declined to promote Nixon's career. By sending paratroopers to quell the LITTLE ROCK SCHOOL DESEGREGATION VIOLENCE, and overseeing passage of the CIVIL RIGHTS ACTS of 1957 and 1960, he advanced the cause of civil rights. At the same time he built links between the Republican Party and African-American voters.

Eisenhower popularized the DOMINO THEORY and warned of the influence of the MILITARY-INDUSTRIAL COMPLEX. Yet he sent US advisers to Vietnam, ordered a massive build-up of US nuclear weaponry and enunciated the EISENHOWER DOCTRINE, which he used to justify US intervention in LEBANON. The U-2 INCIDENT ended his hopes of decreasing Cold War tensions.

Eisenhower Doctrine, policy propounded by President EISENHOWER in 1957 that US forces should aid any country in the Middle East threatened by communist aggression.

Prompted by concerns that the USSR might seek to enlarge its influence in the Middle East, on January 5 1957 Eisenhower asked Congress for discretionary powers to use financial, and if necessary military, resources to prevent Soviet expansion. In a remarkable resolution enacted on March 7 1957, Congress granted to the president the unilateral right to use US military force to aid any Middle Eastern country 'requesting assistance against armed aggression from any country controlled by international communism'. In 1958 Eisenhower used this generous suspension of congressional oversight to send Marines to LEBANON.

electoral college, body that chooses the president and vice president in two separate ballots. The college was established under Article II Section 1 of the US Constitution, and modified by the TWELFTH and FOURTEENTH AMENDMENTS.

Each state contributes to the college a number of electors equal to its representation in the House of Representatives and Senate; in 1964 the DISTRICT OF COLUMBIA was awarded the right to contribute three electors to the college. The means by which electors are selected is a matter for the states. There are currently 538 votes available in the electoral college.

After the POPULAR VOTE has been cast in the presidential election, a state's electors meet to apportion their state's votes in the electoral college. The college does not meet as a whole. A state's electors have the constitutional right to ignore the outcome of polling in their state, or to split votes between candidates. However, the controversy surrounding the election of John Quincy ADAMS in 1824 convinced most states to instruct their electors to award all of their votes to the leading candidate in their state. The candidate gaining a majority of votes in the electoral college (the 'electoral vote') is elected. By doing well in populous states a candidate may gain a majority in the electoral college – and with it the presidency – while polling a minority of the popular vote. When no candidate for the presidency achieves a majority in the electoral college, the election is decided by the House of Representatives. This procedure was used to resolve the PRESIDENTIAL ELECTION OF 1800 and the presidential election of 1824. Inconclusive balloting for a vice president within the electoral college is resolved by the Senate. (In 1837 Richard Mentor JOHNSON became the only vice president to be chosen by this procedure). Disputed electoral college returns led Congress to create an extraordinary commission to resolve the PRESIDENTIAL ELECTION OF 1876.

Electoral Count Act (February 3 1887), legislation, inspired by the disputed PRESIDENTIAL ELECTION OF 1876, that gives each state sole responsibility for determining to which presidential candidate it will award its votes in the ELECTORAL COLLEGE. Congress may intervene only if a state cannot decide which candidate should receive its electoral votes, or if a state decides illegally. In the event that Congress cannot resolve a dispute, determination reverts to the state governor.

electoral vote, *see* ELECTORAL COLLEGE.

Eleventh Amendment, amendment to the US Constitution that exempts state governments from being sued without their consent in federal courts by non-resident citizens or foreigners. Drafted in response to CHISHOLM VS. GEORGIA, the amendment was submitted to the states on March 5 1794, received the requisite support on December 4 1797 and took effect on January 8 1798.

Elkins Act (February 19 1903), legislation that made it illegal for rail companies to offer rebates on their published freight charges to customers who shipped high volumes of freight across state lines. Low-volume shippers were delighted. But rail companies also welcomed the measure, because it allowed them to charge all freight customers a standard rate, which was generally higher than that in effect when rebates were legal.

Emancipation Proclamation (January 1 1863), edict issued during the CIVIL WAR by President LINCOLN freeing all slaves in Confederate-controlled territory. The proclamation was more strategic than idealistic in intent, and slavery was not completely abolished in the USA until ratification of the THIRTEENTH AMENDMENT in 1865.

On August 6 1861 Congress passed a bill emancipating any slave fighting or laboring against the Union. On April 16 1862 it abolished slavery in Washington DC, and on July 17 emancipated all slaves owned by supporters of the Confederacy. Lincoln hesitated to go further, citing the likelihood of secession among the slaveholding BORDER STATES if emancipation were applied to Union soil. Nevertheless, in the summer of 1862 Lincoln began to link emancipation with the preservation of the Union. He told the *New York Tribune*, 'If I could save the Union without freeing any slaves, I would do it; and if I could save it by freeing all slaves, I would do it.'

Union victory at the battle of ANTIETAM emboldened Lincoln to issue a preliminary Emancipation Proclamation on September 22 1862. In the final Proclamation (issued on January 1 1863) Lincoln, appealing to military necessity (i.e. the need to weaken the Confederacy), freed all slaves in Confederate-controlled territory and authorized Union commanders to enroll them as soldiers. The proclamation did *not* apply to slaves resident in Union territory where slavery was legal, or in Confederate territory under Union control. Thus 800,000 slaves were unaffected until freed when the Thirteenth Amendment took effect on December 18 1865.

Embargo Act (December 22 1807), legislation passed during the Napoleonic Wars that barred US ships from sailing to foreign ports and foreign ships from carrying goods out of US ports. The act was in-tended to gain French and British recognition of the neutrality of US shipping, which had been repeatedly violated by French and especially British warships.

Congress passed the act at the behest of President JEFFERSON, who hoped that the ensuing disruption of trade would force Britain and France into a recognition of US neutrality. In fact ships already at sea evaded the law, while Napoleon, acting on the BAYONNE DECREE, seized US ships in ports under his control. FEDERALISTS and QUIDS assailed Jefferson's action. In 1809 the embargo was redefined to cover only trade with Britain and France. The act's failure helped cause the WAR OF 1812.

Emergency Banking Relief Act (March 9 1933), legislation that retroactively approved ROOSEVELT's declaration of a BANK HOLIDAY to stem panic withdrawals and bank closures during the GREAT DEPRESSION.

Owing to the urgency of the situation, the measure was introduced into Congress, debated, passed and signed into law in one day. The act laid out the terms on which banks would be permitted to reopen, authorized the RECONSTRUCTION FINANCE CORPORATION to acquire stock in solvent banks against which it could extend credit to ailing banks and established stiff penalties for hoarding and speculating. The emergency act restored public confidence. The BANKING ACT, passed later that year, initiated fundamental reforms.

Emergency Quota Act (May 19 1921), legislation which limited European IMMIGRATION. Passed amid fears that immigrants from eastern and southern Europe were 'debasing' the USA's population, the act limited yearly immigration from any European nation to 3% of the number of persons born in that country and resident in the USA in 1910. It specified that no more than 357,000 Europeans were to be admitted to the USA in any year. Canadian and Latin American immigration was not affected. This landmark restriction on immigration was refined in the NATIONAL ORIGINS ACT (1924).

Emergency Relief and Construction Act (July 21 1932), legislation that expanded the role of the RECONSTRUCTION FINANCE CORPORATION (RFC) and took a modest step towards a federally funded public-works program. Congress appropriated $500 million to the RFC with the proviso that it be directed at bailing out state agencies engaged in supporting the poor. It made available $1.5 billion in loans for states and municipalities to build roads, bridges and dams. The PUBLIC WORKS ADMINISTRATION (1933) expanded federal support for construction projects.

Emergency Relief Appropriation Act (April 8 1935), legislation that appropriated an unprecedented $4.8 billion to fund social-improvement programs. Passage of this bill marked a second phase in the NEW DEAL.

President ROOSEVELT used the appropriation granted by Congress to create agencies (such as the RESETTLEMENT ADMINISTRATION and the RURAL ELECTRIFICATION ADMINISTRATION) whose primary purpose was social improvement rather than the delivery of direct aid to the victims of the GREAT DEPRESSION. Nearly a third of the appropriation was used to fund the WORKS PROGRESS ADMINISTRATION. This put the unemployed to work on slum clearance, road-building and the construction of public amenities such as hospitals and schools.

Enforcement Acts (1870, 1871), three acts passed during the RECONSTRUCTION era aimed at preventing violations of civil and political rights by states or individuals.

(1) The first Enforcement Act (May 31 1870) made it illegal to intimidate voters or interfere with balloting, so strengthening the protections offered to black voters by the FIFTEENTH AMENDMENT. The act authorized the Army to prevent intimidation. The Supreme Court undermined the law's intent in UNITED STATES VS. REESE (1876), but affirmed Congress's right to pass such legislation in EX PARTE YARBOROUGH (1884). In 1879 President HAYES vetoed an attempt to nullify the measure.

(2) The second Enforcement Act (February 28 1871) supported the FOURTEENTH AMENDMENT by providing for federal supervision of elections in cities with populations over 20,000. In 1879 President HAYES vetoed an attempt to nullify the measure. But in United States vs. Harris (1883) the Supreme Court, building on the logic of its ruling in UNITED STATES VS. CRUIKSHANK (1876), undermined the bill by ruling that it did not offer

black voters protection from acts of discrimination and intimidation perpetrated by individuals.

(3) For the third Enforcement Act (April 20 1871), *see* KU KLUX KLAN ACT.

ENIAC (Electronic Numerical Integrator and Computer), the world's first truly automated electronic computer, developed between 1940 and 1946 by Dr John Mauchly and Dr John P. Eckert of the Moore School of Electrical Engineering at the Unversity of Pennsylvania, Philadelphia. ENIAC, which utilized 18,000 vacuum tubes, could multiply two ten-decimal numbers in three-thousandths of a second and complete 5000 additions in a second. The building that housed ENIAC is preserved on the University of Pennsylvania campus.

Equal Rights Amendment (ERA), proposed amendment to the US Constitution that would outlaw discrimination against women. The adoption of the amendment was one of the major aims of WOMEN'S MOVEMENT campaigns during the 1960s and 1970s. Women's groups had lobbied previously for the passage of such an amendment in the 1870s, when the FOURTEENTH AMENDMENT was adopted, and again in the 1920s, following adoption of the NINETEENTH AMENDMENT giving women the vote.

On March 22 1972 Congress passed a draft amendment to the Constitution stipulating that equal rights under the law should not be abridged or denied on account of a person's sex. To take effect the amendment needed the support of 38 states. Pressure from supporters of the amendment, especially the NATIONAL ORGANIZATION FOR WOMEN, persuaded 22 state legislatures to ratify the ERA within a year. However, as opponents rallied, the amendment stalled. By July 30 1982 only 30 states had voted for ratification, and 5 states that had originally favored the amendment had reversed their decision. The amendment lapsed. Nevertheless, many of its objectives have been achieved through a more vigorous enforcement of Title VII of the CIVIL RIGHTS ACT OF 1964.

Equal Rights Party, labor-oriented political party. The Equal Rights party was a short-lived successor to the WORKINGMEN'S PARTY which had split amidst factional dispute in 1831. The party, formed in 1833, had few members outside New York City and its dominant figure was George Henry Evans, publisher of the *Working Man's Advocate*. During its short existence the party called for legislation to enact a ten-hour working day and better educational opportunities for working men. The party took the significant step of linking the advancement of the interests of free laborers with the destruction of SLAVE POWER. 'We are now convinced,' Evans wrote, 'that Equal Rights can never be enjoyed, even by those who are free, in a nation which contains slaveites enough to hold in bondage two million human beings.' Most of Evans's supporters soon returned to the DEMOCRATIC PARTY fold.

ERA, *see* EQUAL RIGHTS AMENDMENT.

Erie, Lake, battle of, *see* LAKE ERIE, BATTLE OF.

Espionage Act (June 15 1917), legislation aimed at countering subversion and sedition during WORLD WAR I. The strength and variety of previous opposition to US entry into the war, together with publication of the ZIMMERMANN TELEGRAM and a series of mysterious explosions at east-coast factories, unleashed patriotic and paranoid forces within the USA. The strength of these feelings was reflected in the terms of Espionage Act, passed two months after Congress had declared war on Germany.

The act provided stiff penalties for aiding the enemy, interfering with the draft or suborning members of the US armed forces. The postmaster general was empowered to exclude from the mails materials he deemed seditious or treasonable. The socialist and labor activist Eugene DEBS was jailed under the terms of the act in 1918. The constitutionality of the act was upheld in SCHENCK VS. US (1919).

European Recovery Program, *see* MARSHALL PLAN.

Evers, Medgar (1925–63), hero of the CIVIL RIGHTS MOVEMENT whose murder touched the conscience of the nation. In July 1946, following active service in World War II, Evers led a group of black ex-servicemen who attempted to register to vote in Decatur County, Mississippi. Rebuffed by white officials, Evers began organizing on behalf of the NATIONAL ASSOCIATION FOR THE ADVANCEMENT OF COLORED PEOPLE (NAACP), and eventually became field secretary of the NAACP in Mississippi. In 1963, frustrated by the caution of NAACP chiefs, Evers forged links with the STUDENT NON-VIOLENT COORDINATING COMMITTEE (SNCC) and the CONGRESS OF RACIAL EQUALITY (CORE) to create a major campaign against JIM CROW laws, centered on Jackson, Mississippi. He was murdered outside his front door by a white supremacist on the night President KENNEDY promised to pass a civil rights act. Kennedy arranged for Evers to be buried at Arlington National Cemetery with full military honors. Evers's killer, Byron De La 'Delay' Beckwith (1920–), was initially acquitted of murder, but was sentenced to life imprisonment following a retrial in 1994.

Everson vs. Board of Education of Ewing Township, New Jersey (February 10 1947), US Supreme Court ruling concerning the involvement of the state in religion. In one of the great tests of JEFFERSON's doctrine that a 'wall of separation' should exist between church and state, the Supreme Court considered the question of whether the use of state government funds to help transport children to parochial schools by bus constituted a violation of the FIRST AMENDMENT. The Court reaffirmed that states may not make laws establishing religion, before ruling (5–4) that the expenditure in question constituted a subsidy to parents rather than state support for Catholic education.

exodusters, nickname given to an estimated 20,000 former slaves who migrated to Kansas from southern states in 1879. The out-migration of FREEDMEN from the south was primarily a response to the creation of white supremacist regimes in former slave states during the later stages of RECONSTRUCTION. Black clergymen across the south promoted a 'Kansas fever' by depicting the state as a new Promised Land wherein good farms could be had on easy terms. Most exodusters possessed little working capital and were unable to purchase land. Many became destitute, overwhelming charitable agencies in Kansas and prompting the state legislature to bar the further in-migration of African-Americans.

Ex Parte Merryman (1861), case concerning the authority of the president to suspend habeas corpas.

John Merryman was a wealthy landowner and Confederate sympathizer. In April 1861 he sabotaged rail and telegraph lines in Maryland. He was among a number of suspected saboteurs and Confederate sympathizers arrested on the orders of Union Army commanders in Maryland.

Merryman sued for a writ of habeas corpus in a federal court, and on May 26 1861 Judge Roger TANEY (author of the DRED SCOTT verdict) ordered Union commanders to appear in court to explain their action. The officers refused, arguing that they were acting on presidential authority. Article I Section 9 of the constitution appeared to permit the president to suspend habeas corpus, but Taney ruled that this power lay with Congress alone and that Merryman's arrest was therefore unconstitutional. Union officers ignored Taney's ruling, while Republicans denounced it.

Ex Parte Milligan (1866), US Supreme Court ruling regarding the power of military tribunals over civilians. The case arose from an appeal lodged by four civilians, among them Lambdin P. Milligan (1812–99), who had been tried by a military tribunal and convicted of attempting to foment a pro-Confederate insurrection in Indianapolis in 1864.

On April 3 1866 the Supreme Court ruled unanimously that it was unconstitutional to try civilians under martial law if civilian courts capable of hearing the case existed. A majority of the Court added that neither Congress nor president possessed the authority to create military tribunals in areas remote from actual fighting. Milligan subsequently sued for damages: but future president Benjamin HARRISON, representing the officers of the military tribunal that had convicted Milligan, persuaded an Indianapolis jury to award Milligan just $5. These verdicts had a profound influence on the shape of RECONSTRUCTION. RADICAL REPUBLICAN Congressmen had favored treating the former members of the CONFEDERACY as conquered territories to be ruled by martial law. By declaring this strategy unconstitutional the Court encouraged Congress to pass the CIVIL RIGHTS ACTS OF 1866 AND 1875 and to formulate the FOURTEENTH AMENDMENT to protect the legal rights of African-Americans living in Reconstructed states.

Ex Parte Yarborough (1884), US Supreme Court ruling that the KU KLUX KLAN ACT (1871) was constitutional. The act made it a federal crime for individuals (such as Klansmen) to interfere with a citizen's right to vote in a federal election.

F

Fair Deal, the slogan that President TRUMAN attached to his domestic program. He hoped to supplement and extend the NEW DEAL by raising the minimum wage, broadening social security coverage, establishing a national health-insurance program, increasing spending on education and science and taking action to secure the civil rights of African-Americans. Between 1946 and 1948 the Republicans controlled both houses of Congress and Truman made little headway. In his second administration he was able to secure congressional approval for the Housing Act (1949), which directed federal funds to slum clearance and urban-renewal programmes. He also established the National Science Foundation. However, he failed to win support for a repeal of the TAFT–HARTLEY ACT or the creation of a national health-insurance program.

Fair Labor Standards Act (June 25 1938), NEW DEAL legislation that exemplified the emphasis President Franklin ROOSEVELT's second administration placed on social justice rather than economic management. It mandated a minimum wage of 40 cents per hour, a 40-hour working week and time-and-a-half overtime for 63 million workers in enterprises involved in interstate commerce. It also banned employment of under 16s, thereby ending most forms of child labor. Domestic servants, professionals, agricultural workers and some small businesses were exempted from these provisions. The act's constitutionality was tested, and affirmed, in US VS. Darby Lumber Company (1941).

Fallen Timbers, battle of (August 20 1794), engagement near the southwestern tip of Lake Erie in Ohio, in which US troops led by Anthony Wayne (1745–96) defeated the Native American nations of the NORTH-WEST TERRITORY, forcing them to negotiate the treaty of GREENVILLE (1795).

Fard, Wallace D., *see* NATION OF ISLAM.

Farm Credit Administration (FCA), NEW DEAL agency that brought together various bureaux offering loans and grants to farmers. Franklin ROOSEVELT created the FCA by presidential decree on March 27 1933. The FCA went on to administer the Farm Mortgage Refinancing Act (January 31 1934), and removed millions of farmers from a mire of mortgage arrears. By lessening farmers' fears of foreclosure, the FCA contributed to the effectiveness of production-control programs established by the AGRICULTURAL ADJUSTMENT ADMINISTRATION. In 1939 the FCA was absorbed within the Department of Agriculture.

Farmer-Labor Party, political party established in Minnesota in 1924. It built on the concerns of the earlier POPULIST movement, but pursued a socialist agenda designed to appeal to factory workers as well as farmers. The party advocated the nationalization of banks, industrial plants and public utilities, the creation of a universal system of social welfare and the redistribution of wealth within the USA. During the 1930s the party supported the NEW DEAL, and thereby lost much of its independent identity.

farmers' alliances, *see* POPULISM.

Farrakhan, Louis, *see* NATION OF ISLAM.

fast food, *see* McDONALDS.

FBI, *see* FEDERAL BUREAU OF INVESTIGATION.

FCA, *see* FARM CREDIT ADMINISTRATION.

FDIC, *see* FEDERAL DEPOSIT INSURANCE CORPORATION.

Federal Bureau of Investigation (FBI), branch of the US Department of Justice responsible for the enforcement of federal laws. It investigates all federal crimes not covered by other agencies such as the Food and Drug Administration or the Internal Revenue Service. The FBI has been particularly involved in the investigation of organized crime and threats to internal security.

Tracing its origins to the Bureau of Investigation established within the Department of Justice in 1907, the FBI was founded in 1924. Under J. Edgar HOOVER (who headed the organization until shortly before his death in 1972) the Bureau nurtured a reputation for employing scientific techniques, such as fingerprinting, in the fight against crime. However, in the decades after World War II the FBI was not particularly effective in fighting the Mafia and other crime syndicates, and it proved extremely reluctant to protect CIVIL RIGHTS MOVEMENT activists from white supremacist violence. The FBI's public image was tarnished when, during the WATERGATE SCANDAL, it emerged that Hoover had used the Bureau to conduct politically motivated surveillance campaigns against private individuals.

Federal Deposit Insurance Corporation (FDIC), NEW DEAL agency created by the BANKING ACT (July 16 1933) to insure millions of low-value savings and checking (i.e. current) accounts. By convincing the 'little guy' that his savings or cash would continue to be available even if the bank in which they were held failed, the FDIC checked a wave of panic withdrawals that threatened to make the GREAT DEPRESSION catastrophic. The FDIC continues to insure Americans' savings and checking accounts, although it came close to bankruptcy during the SAVINGS AND LOANS CRISIS.

Federal Emergency Relief Administration (FERA), agency created by Congress as part of the NEW DEAL on May 12 1933 to provide direct grants to states to embark on public-works programs. FERA worked under the auspices of the RECONSTRUCTION FINANCE CORPORATION. Under Harry Hopkins (1890–1946) the agency also helped resettle farmers devastated by the DUST BOWL, and developed programs to help migrant workers. FERA's job-creation programs ran into political controversy, and this aspect of its remit was taken over by the WORKS PROGRESS ADMINISTRATION. FERA continues to function as the primary federal agency charged with assisting victims of earthquakes, floods and major fires.

Federal Farm Loan Act (July 17 1916), legislation that provided substantial subsidies to farmers by establishing twelve regional boards to which members of farmers' cooperatives could apply for long-term, low-cost loans, funded by the US Treasury. President WILSON felt he had to sign the act to gain reelection.

federalism, political movement in favor of strong central government. Those who urged unconditional RATIFICATION of the US Constitution in the late 1780s appropriated the label federalist, and dubbed their opponents antifederalists, in a largely successful attempt to portray themselves as men who believed that the several states retained an important if subordinate role within the new national government. Federalist beliefs were articulately outlined in the *FEDERALIST PAPERS*, authored by Alexander HAMILTON, James MADISON and John JAY.

In fact the federalist outlook was robustly

nationalist. Federalist readings of the Constitution (such as LOOSE CONSTRUCTIONISM and IMPLIED POWERS) stressed the powers it gave national government rather than the protections it afforded states and individuals. Federalists regarded state governments as overly 'democratic', beholden to small farmers and, as a consequence, infuriatingly narrow-minded. They dismissed the idea, put forward by JEFFERSONIAN DEMOCRATS, that state governments possessed a right and duty to review, and if necessary check, national legislation.

Federalists saw America's future security and prosperity as being linked to the development of a domestic manufacturing base and internal improvements. Federalists supported sound money, the interests of creditors over debtors and of merchants over farmers. Federalism found support among all classes and regions, but was especially strong in northern states and among men engaged in regional and international trade. The FEDERALIST PARTY, which coalesced during WASHINGTON's administration, sought to apply these principles to US national government.

Federalist Papers, the collective title given to 85 essays on government published as *The Federalist* under the pseudonym Publius in New York newspapers between October 27 1787 and May 28 1788. Alexander HAMILTON wrote 51 of the essays, James MADISON 26 and John JAY 5, while the remaining 3 were co-authored. The essays, widely reprinted, rallied support for RATIFICATION of the US Constitution.

The most celebrated of the essays are numbers 10 and 51, written by Madison. In these Madison analyzed the problem of faction – men's tendency to create interest groups that seek to subvert disinterested government. Breaking with conventional wisdom, Madison argued that in a large republic equipped with an adequate system of checks and balances (i.e. in an America that had ratified the Constitution), faction would clash against faction but no single interest could ever dominate government. This being the case, disinterested government could emerge from man's innate desire to pursue self-interest. Madison's description of the Constitution implied that the various interests within American society would compete on equal terms to influence government policy. In fact the Constitution safeguarded the interests of slaveholders, protecting them from the full effects of factional competition.

Federalist Party, former political party espousing the ideas of FEDERALISM, principally the belief in strong central government. The formation of the party in the late 1780s marked the beginning of the FIRST PARTY SYSTEM, in which the Federalists were opposed by the DEMOCRATIC-REPUBLICANS. It could be said that the Democratic-Republicans distrusted government, while the Federalists distrusted the people. John ADAMS, Washington's vice president (1789–97), was the first and only avowedly Federalist president (1797–1801).

Built around the coalition that endorsed Alexander Hamilton's *REPORT ON THE PUBLIC CREDIT* and the creation of the BANK OF THE UNITED STATES, the Federalist Party defined itself by veneration of George WASHINGTON, distrust of the French Revolution and a 'realistic' approach to diplomatic relations with Britain. Federalists castigated Democratic-Republicans for the enthusiastic reception they gave to Citizen GENÊT. They defended JAY'S TREATY (1795) on the grounds that there was little the USA could do to stop British warships from searching US vessels and seizing deserters. In the aftermath of the XYZ AFFAIR Federalist congressmen whipped up an anti-French hysteria, which produced the QUASI-WAR and pressured Adams into passage of the ALIEN AND SEDITION ACTS. Voters repudiated this illiberal package in the PRESIDENTIAL ELECTION OF 1800. Thereafter Federalist Party support was confined to New England, and it finally evaporated even there when, during the WAR OF 1812, die-hard Federalists called the secret HARTFORD CONVENTION.

Federal Reserve System (FRS), agency established in the second decade of the 20th century to exercise central control over the American banking system. There had been two previous US central banks, the first and second BANK OF THE UNITED STATES, but following passage of the DEPOSIT ACT (1836) the US banking system operated with little or no central supervision.

The FRS – the most influential and least understood government agency in the USA – traces its origins to the National Monetary Commission established under Senator Nelson Aldrich (1841–1915) in the aftermath of the PANIC OF 1907. In 1911 Aldrich's commission recommended the creation of a centralized banking system with absolute control over federal fiscal and monetary policy. However, his suggestion that the central bank be a private body was rejected following the PUJO HEARINGS.

The main features of the system were enacted in the Owen–Glass Act (1913). All national banks were required to join, and state banks were given an option to participate. Member banks were required to transfer 6% of their capital to one of twelve regional Federal Reserve banks. The activities of the regional banks were overseen by a Federal Reserve Board, whose members were appointed by the president and confirmed by the Senate. The system addressed the threat of localized liquidity problems, which had exacerbated the panic of 1907, by giving regional Federal Reserve banks the power to raise or lower interest rates, to raise or lower levels of reserves required of member banks (thereby expanding or contracting available credit) and to expand or contract money supply through the sale or purchase of Federal Reserve notes.

These powers, which effectively place control of national monetary and fiscal policy beyond interference from private banks or Congress, were removed from the regional Federal Reserve banks and vested in a seven-man central Federal Reserve Board via the BANKING ACT of 1935. Since November 12 1973, and the collapse of protocols agreed at the BRETTON WOODS CONFERENCE (1944), the Federal Reserve Board has also been entrusted with managing the US dollar's foreign exchange rate. The financial markets now regard the chairman of 'the Fed' as a more powerful figure than the Treasury secretary.

Federal Trade Commission (FTC), five-man agency, created by Congress on September 26 1914, that has the power to investigate and regulate corporate business practices. Creation of the commission, and passage of the CLAYTON ANTI-TRUST ACT (1914), signaled the WILSON administration's determination to regulate TRUSTS. The commission used 'cease-and-desist' orders to attack business practices such as price-support agreements among corporations, and the mislabeling and adulteration of products.

FERA, *see* FEDERAL EMERGENCY RELIEF ADMINISTRATION.

Ferguson, Patrick (1744–80), British army officer, the inventor of the Ferguson flintlock rifle. At the outset of the REVOLUTIONARY WAR, Ferguson organized a volunteer corps of riflemen within the British army. Armed with an extremely accurate and rapid-firing breech-loading rifle designed by Ferguson himself, the corps performed effectively at the battle of BRANDYWINE CREEK. During the battle Ferguson trained a rifle on an unsuspecting WASHINGTON, but declined to shoot a 'sitting bird'. Ferguson was wounded soon afterwards, and British commanders took the opportunity to disband Ferguson's corps and return his rifles to storage. He returned to service, but was killed at the battle of King's Mountain, North Carolina.

Ferraro, Geraldine (Anne) (1935–), Democratic politician, who was chosen by presidential nominee Walter MONDALE as his running mate in the presidential election of 1984, making her the first woman thus nominated by a major political party. Ferraro pursued a career as a lawyer in New York before entering the House of Representatives (1979–84). Soon after the Democratic convention in 1984, Ferraro became embroiled in a controversy regarding her failure to comply with a legal requirement to disclose details of her husband's finances. Dark rumors, reflecting prejudice against Italian-Americans, suggested that her husband had links to organized crime. Ferraro never really recovered, though her treatment of George BUSH in a lively debate between the vice-presidential candidates prompted Barbara Bush to dub her a 'witch'. Mondale must have hoped that Ferraro would attract women voters, but most women voted for REAGAN in 1984.

Fetterman massacre (December 21 1866), the crucial engagement of the second SIOUX WAR. Captain William J. Fetterman, based at Fort Phil Kearny, Wyoming, had boasted that with 80 cavalrymen he could defeat the entire Sioux nation. When a foraging party from the fort was attacked, Fettermen rode out with 78 troopers. His party was ambushed by Sioux and annihilated. Resisting calls for a retaliatory war of extermination, US officials negotiated the second treaty of FORT LARAMIE in the aftermath of the massacre.

Field Order 15, measure redistributing land in part of the south in the closing phase of the Civil War. On January 16 1865 General William T. SHERMAN designated Georgia's Sea Islands and a 30-mile (48-km) strip of the Carolina coastline as sites for the resettlement of FREEDMEN. Each head of family was to be given 'possessory title' to 40 acres (16 ha) of land confiscated from slave owners. This order was obeyed enthusiastically by military commanders on the Sea Islands. By the summer of 1865, 40,000 freedmen were growing crops on land they had once

tilled as slaves. Sherman's lead was followed in the bill establishing the FREEDMEN'S BUREAU. *See also* DAVIS BEND EXPERIMENT.

Fifteenth Amendment, amendment to the US Constitution that stipulates that a US citizen's right to vote cannot be denied or abridged on the grounds of race or previous condition of servitude. The amendment was sent to the states on February 26 1869 and proclaimed on March 30 1870.

Passage of the amendment, and of three ENFORCEMENT ACTS designed to protect its intent, marked the high-water mark of RADICAL REPUBLICAN commitment to the RECONSTRUCTION of the south after the Civil War. However, southern states used literacy tests, grandfather clauses and poll taxes to evade the amendment's intent. Subsequent US Supreme Court decisions upholding the constitutionality of these evasions (especially in UNITED STATES VS. REESE and BREEDLOVE VS. SUTTLES) reduced the amendment's protection of black male voting rights.

The amendment's wording prompted renewed agitation for WOMEN'S SUFFRAGE. Outraged by a constitutional innovation that secured the vote for 'Patrick, Sambo, Hans, and Ung Tung' but excluded educated women, Elizabeth Cady STANTON and Susan Brownell ANTHONY formed the NATIONAL WOMAN SUFFRAGE ASSOCIATION.

Fifth Amendment, amendment to the US Constitution prohibiting any person from being retried for the same offense; deprivation of life, liberty or property 'without due process of law'; forced self-incrimination; and seizure of property without compensation. It was one of the ten amendments making up the BILL OF RIGHTS. For the full text, *see* Appendix 1.

filibuster, (1) term used to describe a parliamentary procedure whereby by a US Senator holds the floor, speaking continuously, in an attempt to prevent a bill from being brought to a vote. The procedural rules of the US Senate allow its members unlimited speaking time unless they vote for 'cloture' (closure). The longest filibuster on record (24 hours and 18 minutes) was mounted by arch-conservative Strom Thurmond (1902–) of South Carolina in an unsuccessful attempt to prevent passage of the CIVIL RIGHTS ACT OF 1957.

(2) term applied to individual adventurers who sought to use military force to annex Central American and Caribbean countries to the USA. In 1850 Narcisco Lopez made two attempts to foment a rebellion in Cuba designed to bring the island into the USA as a slave state. In 1855 William Walker (1824–60) seized much of Nicaragua in a bid to create a slave state and to guarantee US control over the route of the proposed Pacific canal. Lopez and Walker received backing from US citizens but were disavowed by the federal government. The OSTEND MANIFESTO (1854) suggested that the US government shared some of the filibuster's goals.

Fillmore, Millard (1800–74), WHIG statesman, vice president (1849–50) and 13th president of the USA (1850–3) following the death of incumbent Zachary TAYLOR.

Fillmore, who joined the Whigs in 1834, served as congressman from New York between 1833 and 1843. Fillmore was an accommodationist in the slavery debate. He reluctantly supported the COMPROMISE OF 1850, which was opposed by Taylor, and after the latter's death he assumed the presidency on July 10 1850. As president he enforced the FUGITIVE SLAVE ACT, and purged radical Whigs from government posts, thereby alienating northerners and precluding his renomination in 1852. He served until March 4 1853. His most lasting achievement was to authorize Commodore PERRY to open links with Japan. Fillmore was the presidential nominee of the anti-immigrant KNOW NOTHING PARTY in 1856.

films, *see* HOLLYWOOD.

fire-eaters, term applied to southern politicians who, believing that the north was conspiring to attack slavery where it already existed, saw in the nomination and election of Abraham LINCOLN justification for immediate SECESSION.

fireside chats, informal radio addresses made by Franklin ROOSEVELT. Roosevelt began making such broadcasts while governor of New York. On Sunday March 12 1933 President Roosevelt adapted past practice by broadcasting to the American people from a White House fireside. This first fireside chat, explaining why he had ordered a BANK HOLIDAY, was well received. Roosevelt subsequently broadcast carefully scripted but homey addresses on NEW DEAL policies and, memorably, on the LEND-LEASE program throughout his presidency. Later presidents lost interest in the format, especially when they could address the nation by television. However, President REAGAN made enthusiastic and effective use of weekly radio addresses. *See also* RADIO AND TELEVISION.

First Amendment, amendment to the US Constitution vouchsafing freedom of religion, speech, the press, petition and peaceful assembly. It was one of the ten amendments making up the BILL OF RIGHTS. For the full text, *see* Appendix 1.

First New Deal, term applied by some historians to the first two years (1933–5) of the NEW DEAL. When President Franklin D. ROOSEVELT came to power (March 4 1933), his first priority was to direct federal aid to the victims of the GREAT DEPRESSION. Approaching the depression as a temporary national emergency, Roosevelt and his cabinet sought to enlist the cooperation of businessmen and large farmers in the federal management of a planned economic recovery through detailed regulation of the USA's rural and industrial economies. The NATIONAL RECOVERY ADMINISTRATION and the AGRICULTURAL ADJUSTMENT ADMINISTRATION were founded on this principle. Although Roosevelt and his cabinet never abandoned their interest in economic planning (especially in the agricultural sector), in 1935 Roosevelt backed away from previous attempts to regulate supply, demand, prices and wages. Some historians argue that Roosevelt's subsequent emphasis on the creation of a social-security system within a free-market economy constitutes a SECOND NEW DEAL.

first party system, term referring to the close involvement of the country at large in the struggle for control of Congress and the presidency waged by DEMOCRATIC-REPUBLICANS and FEDERALISTS between 1788 and 1817.

Party divisions emerged during WASHINGTON's administration (1789–97), reached fever pitch during ADAMS'S administration, lost some of their force during JEFFERSON's first administration (1801–5), but re-emerged in the run-up to the WAR OF 1812. Federalist support evaporated following the war, and in 1820 James MONROE initiated a period of DEMOCRATIC PARTY hegemony when he was elected president with just one dissenting vote cast against him in the ELECTORAL COLLEGE. A SECOND PARTY SYSTEM began to take shape during Andrew JACKSON's administration as opponents of JACKSONIAN DEMOCRACY formed the WHIG PARTY.

Five Civilized Tribes, term applied in the early 19th century by white Americans to the CHEROKEE, CHICKASAW, CHOCTAW, CREEK and SEMINOLE nations of the southeast. The agricultural and trade practices of these Native American peoples supported large towns and a partial acceptance of black slavery. The Cherokee had begun to adopt print culture and they used the court system in an attempt to protect their lands. Despite US perception that these nations were 'civilized', they were the primary subjects of the INDIAN REMOVAL ACT (1830).

Fletcher vs. Peck (March 16 1810), US Supreme Court ruling that a land grant was a contract, and that Article I Section 10 of the Constitution forbade a state from inter-fering with the obligations inherent in a contract. The case arose from the YAZOO LAND FRAUD, a land grant by the state of Georgia to four companies, which had been obtained by bribery and rescinded in a subsequent legislative session. The Supreme Court dismissed arguments based on the corruption used to obtain the contract, arguing that the judiciary could not inquire into legislators' motives. The verdict strengthened the position of corporations in the USA.

Florida, southeastern state, comprising a large peninsula separating the Atlantic Ocean from the Gulf of Mexico, plus a 'panhandle' along the Gulf coast. The state is bordered to the north and west by Georgia and Alabama respectively. St. Augustine on Florida's Atlantic coast, founded by the Spanish in 1585, is the oldest continuously occupied settlement in the USA. British settlers and adventurers coveted the territory. In 1702 South Carolinian militiamen briefly occupied St. Augustine. Britain acquired Florida from Spain through the first treaty of PARIS (1763) and organized the territories of EAST FLORIDA and WEST FLORIDA (the latter extending beyond the boundaries of the modern state along the Gulf coast as far as the Mississippi river). During the REVOLUTIONARY WAR US forces made several attempts to annex these crown colonies. Florida reverted to Spanish control through the second treaty of PARIS (1783). The USA annexed West Florida during the WAR OF 1812. East Florida, site of the SEMINOLE WARS, was acquired permanently by the USA through the ADAMS–ONIS treaty of 1819. On March 3 1845 Florida became the 27th state.

During the 19th century Florida's population grew slowly. Prior to the CIVIL WAR the state's economy was heavily dependent on the production of cash crops using slave labor. On January 10 1861 Florida became the third state to secede from the Union and join the CONFEDERACY. During RECON-

STRUCTION a provisional government installed by President Andrew JOHNSON wrote strict BLACK CODES and refused to ratify the FOURTEENTH AMENDMENT. The state was placed under military rule in 1867, but self-government and congressional representation were restored on June 25 1868. Florida was one of four states at the center of the disputed PRESIDENTIAL ELECTION OF 1876. Following the COMPROMISE OF 1877 the state legislature introduced racial segregation through a series of JIM CROW laws and disenfranchised most African-American voters through a poll tax.

During the 1920s Florida was transformed by one of the largest internal migrations in US history. Throughout the state, cities and towns boomed. In 1920 Miami had 30,000 permanent residents; five years later the figure stood at 75,000. Over 2000 real estate businesses catered for the frenzied speculation in developments in and around Miami. The developer Carl G. Fisher made $40 million by burying a mangrove swamp under millions of tons of sand and then selling lots on the newly created Miami Beach. Elsewhere, in a promotion typical of the boom, a retired congregational minister named George Albert Merrick hired William Jennings BRYAN to give lectures 'selling' God-fearing sun-seekers on the idea of buying houses in Merrick's Coral Gables development. The real estate boom collapsed following a devastating hurricane in September 1926, but by then Florida was firmly established as a tourist and retirement destination much favored by northern urbanites. A renewed wave of in-migration which began in the 1950s further augmented the state's population. IMMIGRATION from Cuba, Haiti and other locations in the Caribbean basin gave south Florida, in particular, distinctive Latino and Afro-Caribbean sub-cultures. In 1990 Florida had a permanent population of 12,937,926 and was the fourth most populous state in the Union.

Flynn, Elizabeth Gurley (1890–1964), labor organizer, radical and prominent communist. Flynn was a lifelong dissident, celebrated in left-wing circles of the PROGRESSIVE era as the 'rebel girl'. During the LAWRENCE TEXTILE STRIKE (1912), Flynn, at that time a member of the INDUSTRIAL WORKERS OF THE WORLD, organized the evacuation of the children from Lawrence in protest at the violence unleashed against strikers by company guards. A year later she played a prominent role in a strike by silk-workers in Paterson, New Jersey. In both settings Flynn popularized techniques of passive resistance that would later be utilized by the CIVIL RIGHTS MOVEMENT. She helped to found the AMERICAN CIVIL LIBERTIES UNION (ACLU) and joined the COMMUNIST PARTY OF THE USA (CPUSA) in 1937. In 1951 she was sentenced under the SMITH ACT to 28 months in prison for her membership of the CPUSA. She became the party's president in 1961, a move that led to her expulsion from the ACLU. She died while on vacation in the Soviet Union.

football, *see* SPECTATOR SPORTS.

Ford, Gerald (Rudolph) (1913–), Republican statesman, vice president (1973–4) and 38th president of the USA (1974–7). Ford became president following the resignation of Richard NIXON. He is the only man to occupy the White House without having previously won a national vice-presidential or presidential election.

As the REPUBLICAN representative from Michigan's Fifth District in the US House of Representatives (1949–73), Ford established a record of moderate conservatism. He disliked McCARTHY's witch-hunts but declined to criticize him, and he opposed the nomination of the right-wing Barry GOLDWATER as Republican presidential candidate in 1964, although he ultimately supported him. He went on to describe Lyndon B. JOHNSON's WAR ON POVERTY as nothing more than 'a lot of washed-up old programs'. Ford was House minority leader between

1965 and 1973, and in 1967 he urged Johnson to throw the entire US military arsenal into the VIETNAM WAR.

Following the forced resignation of Vice President Spiro AGNEW, Nixon nominated Ford for the vice presidency under the terms of the TWENTY-FIFTH AMENDMENT. He was sworn in on December 6 1973. Following Nixon's own resignation, Ford became president on August 9 1974. Throughout the WATERGATE SCANDAL Ford had defended Nixon and, on September 8 1974, one month after Nixon's resignation, granted him a much-criticized pardon for 'all offenses against the US, he has committed or may have committed or taken part in'. On taking office Ford declared 'our long national nightmare is over'. Ford's self-deprecating style – he once said 'I am a Ford, not a Lincoln' – and his physical clumsiness helped Americans accept this proposition. Ford won the Republican nomination in 1976, despite a strong challenge from Ronald REAGAN, but was defeated in the presidential election by Jimmy CARTER. Ford served until January 20 1977.

Ford, Henry (1863–1947), automobile engineer and industrialist. By developing the Model T automobile, Ford revolutionized transportation in the USA, and helped to create an entirely new industry.

Ford was born on an isolated Michigan farm. He had little formal education before beginning an apprenticeship as a machinist in 1879. He later repaired farm machinery and operated a sawmill. In 1893 he built a functional 4-horsepower gas-driven car. He named a modified version of this the Model T, and in 1903 set up the Ford Motor Company to produce it. The Model T went on sale in the winter of 1908–9 for $850, a price beyond the means of the isolated farmers Ford saw as his natural customers. To bring down the cost of the car he utilized standardized components that could be assembled using production-line techniques. By 1916 he had made 577,036

Model Ts and lowered the retail price to $360. By the time production of the Model T ceased in 1927, 15 million had been manufactured. The Model T was extremely basic – Ford once joked that customers could have one in any colour they liked, provided it was black – but it was durable. Other companies, notably General Motors, produced a range of vehicles often more alluring than the Model T, but Ford's simple design propelled his company to a 55% share of the automobile market in 1921.

Ford's management techniques were equally influential. He distrusted trade unions, and to discourage his workers from seeking union recognition he paid them the unparalleled rate of $5 for an eight-hour day. Associating his car and his company with the American Dream, he encouraged foreign-born workers to take out US citizenship and staged lavish pageants at his plants designed to 'Americanize' his workers. In 1915 Ford campaigned to broker a cease-fire in WORLD WAR I, but once the USA joined the war he converted his plants to the production of military materiel. In 1918 he made an unsuccessful attempt to gain election to the US House of Representatives. In 1919 he handed management of the Ford Motor Company to his son Edsel, but when Edsel died in 1943 he resumed control of the company and ran it until his own death. In 1936 father and son established the Ford Foundation, which is currently one of the largest philanthropic institutions in the USA. In later life Ford expressed reactionary and anti-Semitic views. He was the only American 'honored' with an approving reference in the pages of Adolf Hitler's *Mein Kampf*.

Fort Donnelson and Fort Henry, battles of (February 1862), two engagements in Tennessee during the CIVIL WAR, in which Union forces captured Confederate forts.

During the winter of 1861–2 LINCOLN urged reluctant Union generals to stage an offensive against western Kentucky and central Tennessee. Eventually General Ulysses S. GRANT was appointed to lead a force of 25,000, supported by gunboats, up the Tennessee and Cumberland river valleys. Fort Henry, on the Tennessee, surrendered to Grant on February 6 1862. Confederate forces at Fort Donnelson (on the Cumberland) fought effectively, but early successes were negated by divided command. On the morning of February 16, Confederate commander Simon Bolivar Buckner proposed terms for the surrender of the fort. Although Buckner had lent him the fare home when Grant resigned his commission in 1854, Grant replied that the only terms he would accept were 'immediate and unconditional surrender'.

These victories boosted northern morale, and made 'Unconditional Surrender' Grant a national hero. He went on to lead a strengthened force southwards into central Tennessee in a campaign that saw Union forces capture Nashville (February 26 1862), and that climaxed in the battle of SHILOH.

Fort Fisher, capture of (1865), successful Union operation in North Carolina during the CIVIL WAR. As long as Confederates held Fort Fisher on the Cape Fear River, blockade-runners from the Carolinas could assist in the supply of LEE's Army of Northern Virginia. On December 24 1864 Major General Butler (1818–93) presided over an unsuccessful Union assault on the fort, a failure that provided the pretext for Butler's dismissal. A second attempt on January 13–15 1865 succeeded. Confederate desertion rates now reached 'epidemic' proportions: in February alone Lee lost 8% of his army. Confederate politicians urged President DAVIS to sue for peace.

Fort Jackson, treaty of (August 9 1814), treaty that ended the CREEK WAR. Although some Creeks had fought with the US forces during the war, the treaty stripped their nation of 34,000 square miles (88,000 square km) of land west of the Coosa river and north of the Alabama river. Andrew

JACKSON justified the cession on the grounds that all Creeks 'wanted flogging'.

Fort Laramie, treaties of (1851, 1868), two treaties arising out of conferences between Native American elders and US authorities at a US Army fort in Wyoming.

(1) In a treaty signed on September 17 1851 Native American leaders representing the nations of the Great Plains agreed to confine their peoples within clearly defined territory and to accept responsibility for attacks on US citizens using the OREGON TRAIL. In return the USA offered signatories $50,000 in trade goods and a pledge that it would deter its citizens from entering Native American territory. Congress later refused to appropriate funds for the trade goods. The treaty marked the first step toward extension of the reservation system to the Great Plains.

(2) On November 6 1868 CHEYENNE leader Red Cloud (Mahpiua Luta, 1822–1909) signed a treaty with the USA that brought the second SIOUX WAR to a conclusion. The USA abandoned attempts to fortify the BOZEMAN TRAIL, and recognized Sioux land rights in western South Dakota.

Fort Stanwix, battle of (August 4–22 1777), successful American defense during the REVOLUTIONARY WAR of a fort commanding the headwaters of the Mohawk river, New York state. In August 1777 its garrison, 750 US regulars commanded by Colonel Peter Gansevoort (1749–1812), resisted a three-week siege by 2000 redcoats, Tories and Iroquois. Stubborn US resistance here, and at ORISKANY, prevented British forces from reinforcing General Burgoyne's advance in the Hudson valley, thereby contributing to his eventual surrender at SARATOGA.

Fort Stanwix, treaties of (1768, 1784), two treaties involving the IROQUOIS CONFEDERACY signed at Fort Stanwix, New York.

(1) On November 5 1768, in an attempt to protect their homelands in western New York state from encroaching white settlement, the Iroquois Confederacy sold their

claim to lands south of the Ohio river (encompassing most of modern Kentucky) for goods worth £10,000. This violated the PROCLAMATION OF 1763 and angered the Native American nations of the NORTHWEST TERRITORY.

(2) Weakened by SULLIVAN'S CAMPAIGN, the Iroquois Confederacy were eventually forced to cede their claim to lands in north-central Pennsylvania in the second treaty, signed on October 23 1784.

Fort Sumter, attack on (1861), the opening engagement of the CIVIL WAR, in which Confederate troops captured a Union strongpoint on a man-made island, at the entrance to Charleston harbor, South Carolina.

On December 31 1860 President BUCHANAN rejected a demand from South Carolina that federal troops be withdrawn from Charleston harbor, and incoming President LINCOLN insisted on provisioning the Fort Sumter garrison. On April 12 1861 South Carolinian artillery began a bombardment that forced the federal garrison to surrender on April 13. This bloodless action began the Civil War.

Fort Ticonderoga, US capture of (1775), engagement in New York state during the REVOLUTIONARY WAR. On the night of May 10 1775, 83 New Englanders, commanded by Ethan ALLEN and Benedict ARNOLD, captured this British fort at the southern end of Lake Champlain for the loss of one man. Henry KNOX transported captured British artillery and materiel to Boston, where US forces under WASHINGTON used it to force the British evacuation of the city (March 7–17 1776). The fort's strategic significance, commanding waterways south of Quebec, led Britain to commit a force of 8500 soldiers to its recapture. Although the British reoccupied the fort (July 5 1777) the American garrison escaped. The diversion of resources involved in the campaign was a contributory cause of the eventual British surrender at SARATOGA.

Fort Toronto, US capture of (1813), engagement in Canada during the WAR OF 1812. In an attempt to gain control of Lake Ontario, a US raiding force of 1700 men led by Zebulon PIKE seized Fort Toronto on April 27 1813. They destroyed British shipping but ignited the fort's magazine, causing an explosion that killed Pike and over 300 others. Ill-disciplined US troops ransacked York (modern Toronto), burning the town's public buildings before retreating back across the lake on May 8. British forces later destroyed Buffalo, New York and Washington DC in retaliation.

forty acres and a mule. In the spring of 1865 Sherman's FIELD ORDER 15 and congressional discussion of the FREEDMEN'S BUREAU led to a rumor that the federal government was about to grant ex-slaves 40 acres and a mule in order to aid their transition to a free labor system. In the event very little direct economic assistance was offered to former slaves during RECONSTRUCTION.

Forward Strategy, policy, developed in 1950, that bound the USA to resist immediately, and as far east as possible, any Soviet attack on Western Europe. The policy was developed by the USA in conjunction with the Council of the NORTH ATLANTIC TREATY ORGANIZATION. To ensure that the USA had sufficient troop strength to achieve this, President TRUMAN ordered a 200% increase in the number of US servicemen stationed in West Germany. The strategy clarified COLD WAR defense planning. Its assumption that the USA should continually maintain high troop levels in Germany was criticized by Republicans, who believed that European nations should contribute more toward the cost of their own defense.

Founding Fathers, term applied to the 55 delegates to the CONSTITUTIONAL CONVENTION of 1787, and, more broadly, to the delegates to the first and second CONTINENTAL CONGRESS and CONFEDERATION CONGRESS, as well as to the signatories of the DECLARATION OF INDEPENDENCE.

Four Freedoms, US aims in the event that it joined WORLD WAR II, defined on January 6 1941 by President Franklin D. ROOSEVELT in his annual message to Congress. The aims were to secure freedom of speech and expression, freedom of worship, freedom from want and freedom from fear.

Fourteen Points, President Woodrow WILSON's plan to establish a just and lasting settlement of WORLD WAR I, published on January 8 1918. Cynics jeered that it had four more elements than the Ten Commandments.

The plan called for open diplomacy, freedom of navigation, free trade, multilateral arms reductions, decolonization, impartial adjustment of colonial claims, the restoration of territory in France, Belgium and Russia occupied by German troops, the transfer of Alsace-Lorraine to France, new borders for Italy, ethnic self-determination for peoples within Austria-Hungary, the recreation of Romania, Serbia and Montenegro, the dismemberment of the Ottoman empire, the creation of an independent Poland with access to the sea and the creation of a LEAGUE OF NATIONS.

Wilson drew up the plan in the hope of convincing Russia's Bolshevik government to stay in the war and fight for a progressive peace. They ignored it and concluded a separate peace with Germany. At the PARIS PEACE CONFERENCE Wilson acquiesced in punitive Anglo-French interpretations of his plan in return for a commitment to establish a League of Nations.

Fourteenth Amendment (1868), amendment to the US Constitution that specifies that all persons born in the USA (including former slaves but excluding Native Americans), and all naturalized citizens, are US citizens and guaranteed due process and equal protection under state and federal law. The amendment also specifies how the congressional representation from each state was to be calculated. The amendment was inspired by the DRED SCOTT verdict and by doubts over the constitutionality of the CIVIL RIGHTS ACT OF 1866.

Section II of the amendment abrogated the CONNECTICUT COMPROMISE reached by the FEDERAL CONVENTION whereby slaves had counted as three-fifths of a person when determining congressional representation. With future representation to be based on the total of qualified voters within a state, southern states that enfranchised former slaves stood to gain additional seats in the House of Representatives.

A third clause barred from state and federal office men who had sworn allegiance to the Constitution and then aided the Confederacy. The amendment also prohibited the repayment of Confederate war debt.

Southern opposition to the amendment was overcome only when ratification was made a condition of readmission to the Union. The amendment took effect on July 18 1868. In the SLAUGHTERHOUSE CASES and PLESSY VS. FERGUSON the US Supreme Court took a narrow view of the amendment's guarantee of civil rights. Citizenship was extended to Native Americans born in the USA by act of Congress in 1924. For the full text, *see* Appendix 2.

Fourth Amendment, amendment to the US Constitution prohibiting unreasonable searches and seizures by the authorities. It was one of the ten amendments making up the BILL OF RIGHTS. For the full text, *see* Appendix 1.

fragging, term that emerged in the VIETNAM WAR, referring to the murder or maiming of US officers by enlisted men under their command – often accomplished by use of a fragmentation grenade. The vast majority of combat soldiers in Vietnam were draftees, not volunteers, and they often took violent exception to orders issued by 'spit and polish' officers to carry out high-risk patrols. In 1970 the US Army admitted 2000 fragging incidents in that year, and estimated that 65,000 servicemen were using drugs.

Franco-American Alliance (1778), treaty that proved crucial to US victory in the REVOLUTIONARY WAR. The alliance was ratified by Congress on May 4 1778. The USA and France exchanged most-favored-nation trade status. Each pledged the other support in the war with Britain. France recognized the independence of the USA, its existing borders and its aspirations for the conquest of Canada. Both parties forswore concluding a separate peace with Britain. Unsuccessful Franco-American military operations at SAVANNAH (1779), for example preceded successful collaboration in the war's most significant action – the battle of YORKTOWN (1781).

Franklin, short-lived state in what is now eastern Tennessee. In 1784 a convention meeting at Jonesboro voted to establish a separate state in eastern Tennessee and to apply for recognition from CONFEDERATION CONGRESS. Inhabitants named their state after Benjamin Franklin. They wrote a state constitution, collected taxes and elected John Sevier (1745–1815) governor. Under pressure from North Carolina, which claimed the region formed part of its territory, Congress withheld recognition. In 1788 this 'lost state' ceased independent existence.

Franklin, battle of (November 30 1864), engagement in Tennessee during the CIVIL WAR in which the Confederates won a Pyrrhic victory over Union forces. As SHERMAN prepared for the MARCH TO THE SEA, Confederate General John Bell Hood (1831–79) led the last significant Confederate army outside of the Virginia theater on a quixotic raid into Tennessee. 15 miles (24 km) south of Nashville, he ordered his 27,000 soldiers to mount a frontal assault on an entrenched Union army of comparable size. At the cost of 7000 casualties, including five generals, the Confederates forced a Union retreat. But Hood's shattered army was subsequently smashed in a Union counterattack on the outskirts of NASHVILLE.

Franklin, Benjamin (1706–90), statesman, printer, scientist and diplomat. Franklin almost personified American national identity, and played a major role in the AMERICAN REVOLUTION.

Franklin was born in Boston, the 15th of 17 children. At the age of 12 he was apprenticed to his brother James, a printer. In 1721 he broke his apprenticeship, running away to Philadelphia and finding work in a printer's shop. After an unprofitable sojourn in London (1724–6), Franklin returned to Philadelphia and established his own printing business. From 1729 he published a weekly newspaper, the *Pennsylvanian Gazette*, and, from 1732, *Poor Richard's Almanac*. He launched numerous civic initiatives in Philadelphia, including the creation of a debating club for young artisans that was a forerunner of the American Philosophical Society, and of an academy that later became the University of Pennsylvania. In 1746 he began a series of experiments investigating electricity. By flying a kite in a thunderstorm he demonstrated that lightning contains an electrical charge, and he later developed a conductor to protect buildings from lightning strikes.

Franklin was elected repeatedly to the Pennsylvania Assembly, and in 1764 negotiated a peaceful settlement of the PAXTON BOYS crisis. Franklin sought to remove Pennsylvania from the control of the Penn family and place it under a royal administration and for this reason initially favored compliance with the STAMP ACT. However, from 1766 to 1775 he represented the interests of Pennsylvania (and later Georgia and Massachusetts) in London. On his return he was elected to the second CONTINENTAL CONGRESS, and in 1775 was appointed postmaster general. During debate over the DECLARATION OF INDEPENDENCE Franklin warned fellow delegates, 'We must indeed all hang together or, most assuredly, we shall all hang separately.' Franklin served as a US minister to France from 1776 to 1785. He helped to negotiate the FRANCO-AMERICAN ALLIANCE and the treaty of PARIS (1783) concluding the REVOLUTIONARY WAR. He was a delegate to the CONSTITUTIONAL CONVENTION (1787) that drafted the US Constitution. Between 1771 and 1789 he worked on an *Autobiography* that was not published in its entirety until 1868. This reveals an irreverent and self-deprecatory character, and immortalizes Franklin as the most approachable of America's FOUNDING FATHERS.

Fredericksburg, battle of (December 11–13 1862), Confederate victory in Virginia during the CIVIL WAR. Belatedly seeking to exploit their tactical victory at ANTIETAM, 114,000 Union troops under General Ambrose BURNSIDE launched an attack on 72,000 Confederates under LEE, but were bloodily repulsed. Burnside resigned following the defeat, to be replaced by General 'Fighting Joe' HOOKER.

freedmen, term applied to former slaves during the CIVIL WAR and RECONSTRUCTION by the US government and many white northerners. The term's patronizing overtones encapsulated the scale of the mental adjustment that even well-intending whites would have to undertake in order to recognize the humanity and citizenship rights of black Americans.

Freedmen's Bureau, federal agency that, during its brief existence, played a unique role in the RECONSTRUCTION of the south. The Bureau of Refugees, FREEDMEN and Abandoned Land, to give it its full title, was established on March 3 1865, and run within the War Department. The bureau was designed to provide temporary humanitarian assistance to displaced former slaves, white refugees and devastated communities. Congress rechartered the bureau over President JOHNSON's veto on July 16 1866 and encouraged bureau chief Major General Oliver Howard (1830–1909) to adopt an expansive view of the agency's brief.

The bureau handed out rations, operated 46 hospitals and spent $5 million on build-

ing schools for African-Americans. It helped former slaves settle on abandoned lands, regulated labor contracts and, after 1866, established special courts in areas where African-Americans were denied access to a fair trial. Thus the bureau was the only federal agency willing and able to take direct action to combat the social and economic effects of BLACK CODES and other measures discriminating against African-Americans in the postwar south. Yet a REPUBLICAN-controlled Congress concluded that the bureau's activities constituted unacceptable social engineering and, in 1869, voted to wind up its programs.

Freedom of Information Act (July 1966), legislation that makes it illegal for federal agencies to withhold from US citizens information on them held by federal agencies except in cases where that information bears on national security, current criminal investigations or the regulation of business. In 1974 the law was strengthened to make it harder for bureaucrats to withhold information on the grounds of national security. Since 1966 hundreds of thousands of Americans have filed freedom-of-information suits to gain access to information held on them by government agencies.

freedom riders, participants in a civil-disobedience campaign organized by the CONGRESS FOR RACIAL EQUALITY (CORE) in 1961. The campaign was aimed at testing compliance with the Supreme Court verdict in BOYNTON VS. VIRGINIA ordering the desegregation of interstate bus travel. It was one of the most successful campaigns of the CIVIL RIGHTS MOVEMENT.

On May 4 1961 CORE sent seven black and six white volunteers on two scheduled buses from Washington DC to New Orleans. Outside Anniston, Alabama, a white mob forced a bus carrying freedom riders off the road and set it ablaze. Freedom riders were beaten up in bus terminals in Birmingham and Montgomery, Alabama. Reinforced by volunteers from the STUDENT NON-VIOLENT

COORDINATING COMMITTEE (SNCC), the protest was carried into Mississippi. Here freedom riders were arrested for violating state and local segregation laws. Hundreds more freedom riders poured into Mississippi in response. On September 22 1961 the KENNEDY administration pressured the Interstate Commerce Commission into issuing an order barring interstate bus companies from using segregated facilities, ensuring the success of the campaign.

Freeport Doctrine, policy on the legality of slavery in the territories, enunciated by Stephen DOUGLAS during the second LINCOLN DOUGLAS DEBATE, held in Freeport, Illinois, on August 27 1858. During the debate, Abraham LINCOLN asked Douglas whether, in the light of the DRED SCOTT verdict, residents of a territory possessed a constitutional right to ban slavery. In what became known as the Freeport Doctrine, Douglas replied that residents could bar slavery prior to the creation of a state constitution because slavery could not exist unless a territorial legislature chose to support it through necessary local policing regulations. This position cost Douglas southern support and nomination as Democratic presidential candidate in 1860.

free silver, slogan of those interests that supported the unlimited minting of silver dollars at a ratio to gold of 16–1, following the CRIME OF '73 (the decision to cease production of silver coinage in 1873). Those in favor of 'free silver' included western mining interests and farmers seeking a soft-money fiscal regime. Advocates of free silver battled supporters of the GOLD STANDARD during the ensuing SILVER–GOLD CONTROVERSY.

free-soil ideology, belief espoused by many Americans in the decades before the CIVIL WAR that the new western territories should be open to development by small-scale white homesteaders, and that the importation of the slaveowners' 'peculiar institution' should be barred.

Congressional discussion of the WILMOT PROVISO (1846) – that slavery should be outlawed in any territory acquired as a result of the MEXICAN WAR – initiated a national debate in which latent assumptions about American development came together to form a distinctive ideology. Northerners, midwesterners and some southerners regarded themselves as possessing what amounted to a right to establish homesteads on western lands and better their condition. Permitting slave owners to establish plantations on western lands contravened this presumptive right.

As Wilmot made clear, free-soil opposition to the expansion of slavery was not grounded in 'morbid sympathy for the slave'. Northerners and midwesterners who formed free-soil clubs and supported the FREE SOIL PARTY objected to slavery because it depressed the wages and restricted the political power of white workers. Their goal was the creation of a region devoid of slave owners, slaves and even free blacks. Only on 'free soil' might the industrious white worker escape wage slavery and prosper.

It was in accordance with these precepts that state legislatures in Iowa, Indiana and Illinois passed bills banning all blacks from settling in their states. Free-soilers explained national legislation such as the KANSAS–NEBRASKA ACT (1854), and even the COMPROMISE OF 1850, by reference to SLAVE POWER – the capacity of wealthy slave owners to exploit or pervert the political system to further their own interests to the detriment of the independent small producer.

Ultimately, free-soil ideology led many Americans to the conclusion that the destruction of slave power could be achieved only by attacking slavery where it already existed. Some of those who reached this conclusion took comfort from the thought that their self-interest coincided with the destruction of a morally indefensible institution. Few free-soilers had the betterment of blacks in mind.

Free Soil Party, political party formed at a national convention held in Buffalo, New York, in 1848, drawing support from abolitionist DEMOCRATS, 'Conscience' Whigs (*see* WHIG PARTY) and proponents of FREE-SOIL IDEOLOGY. The party opposed the further expansion of slavery and sought to promote the interests of homesteaders and the industrious poor. In 1848 its first presidential nominee, Martin VAN BUREN, won 10% of the POPULAR VOTE and ran particularly well in New York State. The effect of this was to swing the election to WHIG candidate Zachary TAYLOR, who was thought to favor the expansion of slavery. In 1852 the party only took 5% of the popular vote. It dissolved following the formation of the REPUBLICAN PARTY (1854).

Frémont, John C(harles) (1813–90), US Army officer, explorer and Republican politician, who played a key role in the US conquest of California.

The illegitimate son of a refugee from the French Revolution, Frémont joined the Army and achieved a national reputation as 'the Pathfinder' for his exploration of the Mississippi, Missouri and Des Moines river valleys (1838–41). In 1846 Frémont offered encouragement and leadership to California's BEAR FLAG REVOLT. His involvement led to court-martial and his resignation from the army in 1848.

Frémont was the REPUBLICAN PARTY's first presidential nominee, polling 33% of the popular vote in 1856. The CIVIL WAR saw Frémont reinstated to military command. Ordered to keep Missouri in the Union, Frémont placed the state under martial law and issued an emancipation proclamation. LINCOLN disavowed this action and dismissed him (November 2 1861). He declined an invitation from RADICAL REPUBLICANS to challenge Lincoln for the Republican nomination in 1864. He later made and lost a fortune in railroad ventures, and served as territorial governor of Arizona (1878–83).

French and Indian Wars, name applied by Americans to fighting in North America during the SEVEN YEARS' WAR.

Fries's Rebellion, mass protest in southeastern Pennsylvania against the implementation of a federal property tax levied by President John ADAMS to finance an arms build-up during the QUASI-WAR with France. In February 1799 several men imprisoned in Bethlehem, Pennsylvania, for non-payment of the tax were freed by militiamen led by John Fries (1750–1818). Fries was captured, twice convicted of treason, sentenced to hang, but pardoned by Adams.

frontier thesis, thesis originally expounded in a talk entitled 'The Significance of the Frontier in American History', delivered in Chicago to the annual meeting of the American Historical Association by Professor Frederick Jackson Turner (1861–1932) on July 12 1893.

Turner used the 1890 census report to lament that the USA no longer had a region of substantially unsettled land – the 'frontier'. He argued that the passing of the frontier marked the end of a distinct epoch in US history, because hitherto most Americans had at one time lived in a frontier environment and had there acquired distinctively American traits. In Turner's formulation settlers were drawn to the free land of the frontier, but were initially overwhelmed by the environment they found there. To survive and prosper they had to shed inappropriate cultural baggage brought over from Europe (for example a fondness for titles of nobility and other forms of social snobbery), and adopt instead a 'rugged individualism' better suited to their new environment. Eventually, as settlers tamed the wilderness, they formed local governmental institutions that were distinctively democratic and uniquely American because they reflected the shared experience of living in an environment where the ideas and opinions of the 'Old World' had little relevance. Those who were unhappy living in these newly settled areas moved further west, where, joined by new arrivals, the frontier process began again.

Turner's frontier thesis reflected the then current PROGRESSIVE concern that new waves of immigration, which were at the time fueling the massive growth of cities such as Chicago, might dilute core American values. Historians have since questioned the extent to which settlers on western lands abandoned inherited cultural values, and have pointed out that Turner's thesis has little to say about slavery or Native Americans. However, a diluted version of the frontier thesis informed the world-view of countless HOLLYWOOD westerns, and this has helped ensure that Turner's ideas continue to be discussed.

FRS, *see* FEDERAL RESERVE SYSTEM.

FTC, *see* FEDERAL TRADE COMMISSION.

Fugitive Slave Act (September 18 1850), legislation favoring the rights of slave owners, passed as part of the COMPROMISE OF 1850. The act created federal commissioners empowered to issue warrants for the arrest and return of runaways on no more evidence than an affidavit from their owner. Fugitives and wrongly arrested free blacks could not testify in their own defense, and were denied trial by jury. US citizens aiding fugitives were made subject to heavy fines and imprisonment. Abolitionists were outraged.

Fulbright, J(ames) William (1905–95), Democratic politician and early critic of the VIETNAM WAR. Fulbright was educated at the University of Arkansas and Oxford University. He was elected to the House of Representatives in 1942 and to the US Senate, from Arkansas, in 1944. In 1946 Fulbright shepherded a bill through Congress creating a federally funded higher-education exchange program that continues to this day. He was a critic of Senator Joseph McCARTHY's anticommunist witch-hunts. In 1964 Fulbright helped to steer the TONKIN GULF RESOLUTION through Congress. This gave President JOHNSON the authorization he needed to escalate US involvement in the Vietnam War. However, in February 1966 Fulbright chaired the Senate Foreign Relations Committee hearings that aired criticism of Johnson's strategy. In retaliation Johnson took to deriding 'Senator Halfbright'. Fulbright lost his Senate seat in 1974.

G

Gadsden Purchase, purchase of land in northern Mexico (now incorporated within the states of Arizona and New Mexico) by the US government, finalized in 1854. James Gadsden (1788–1858), a South Carolina railroad promoter and the US minister to Mexico, negotiated the sale of 29,000 square miles (75,000 square km) of Mexican territory for $10,000,000 on December 30 1853. An intended corridor for a transcontinental railroad, the Gadsden Purchase was blocked in the Senate by proponents of a northern route until June 29 1854.

Gag Rule, decision taken by both houses of Congress on May 26 1836 to refuse to discuss, or enter into their records, petitions demanding the ABOLITION of slavery, or of slave sales, either in WASHINGTON DC (where Congress had jurisdiction), or in the nation at large. The House of Representatives also resolved (182–9) that it had no power to interfere with slavery where it already existed. House rules required that the measure be renewed each year. Representative John Quincy ADAMS earned the sobriquet 'Old Man Eloquent' for his opposition to the rule. It lapsed in 1844.

Galarza, Ernesto (1905–1980), Mexican-American labor organizer and educator. Born in Mexico, Galarza moved with his family to Sacramento, California, in the aftermath of the Mexican Revolution of 1910. An exceptional student, Galarza nevertheless experienced educational and occupational discrimination in California that he would later explore in his classic memoir *Barrio Boy* (1971). Galarza attended Occidental College and Stanford University, before obtaining a PhD in History from Columbia University. In 1936, he returned to California to unionize migrant farm workers and expand their educational opportunities. His book *Merchants of Labor* (1964) drew on these experiences to present a devastating critique of the mistreatment of BRACERO laborers by California's employers. During the 1960s, Galarza turned his attention to conditions in the barrios – Mexican-American districts in California's cities. His emphasis on education sometimes put him at odds with a younger generation of CHICANO activists but, with Cesar CHAVEZ, Galarza helped channel the momentum generated by the CIVIL RIGHTS MOVEMENT toward an alleviation of discrimination against Mexican-Americans.

Garfield, James (Abram) (1831–81), Republican statesman and 20th president of the USA (1881), who was assassinated a few months after taking up office.

Born and raised in Ohio, between 1857 and 1861 Garfield served as a classics instructor at, and then as president of, the Eclectic Institute, Hiram. He taught himself law, and was admitted to the Bar in 1860. A CIVIL WAR volunteer, he left the army in

1863 to sit as a REPUBLICAN in the US House of Representatives. Initially associated with his party's radical wing, during RECONSTRUCTION Garfield developed an interest in 'hard-money' finance. In 1866 he represented the plaintiff in EX PARTE MILLIGAN, becoming the first attorney to argue his case before the US Supreme Court. In 1873 Representative Garfield was implicated in the CRÉDIT MOBILIER scandal, but survived by denying any wrongdoing.

Nominated by the Republicans as a compromise candidate in 1880, Garfield won the presidential election with just 48.3% of the popular vote. During his brief tenure, beginning on March 4 1881, Garfield disagreed with the Republicans' STALWART faction. He was wounded by Charles J. GUITEAU on July 2 1881 and died on September 19 1881. He was succeeded by his vice president, Chester ARTHUR.

Garrison, William Lloyd (1805–79), passionate opponent of slavery, and leader of the radical wing of the ABOLITION movement.

Garrison was born in Newburyport, Massachusetts, and at the age of 13 was apprenticed to the local newspaper, the *Herald*. In 1826 he started his own paper but it failed within two years. In 1828 he moved to Boston where he became interested in reform causes. In 1829 he accepted an invitation to co-edit *The Genius of Emancipation*, an abolitionist newspaper printed in Baltimore, Maryland. A fiery editorial led to Garrison's arrest and imprisonment for libel. His fine was paid by a wealthy abolitionist, and he returned to Boston to found an abolitionist newspaper of his own: the LIBERATOR. He helped found the New England Antislavery Society (1832) and the AMERICAN ANTISLAVERY SOCIETY (1833).

Garrison's uncompromising support for immediate abolition, and the scorn he directed at all those who did not share his views, angered contemporaries. On October 21 1835 Garrison was dragged through the streets of Boston by a mob and almost killed. Undaunted, he continued his outspoken campaign, and by the late 1830s was suggesting that northern states ought to leave the Union unless and until the Constitution ceased offering protection to slavery. On July 4 1854 he burned a copy of the US Constitution at a public meeting in Framingham, Massachusetts, in protest against the application of the FUGITIVE SLAVE ACT (1850) declaring: 'So perish all compromises with tyranny.' Such was Garrison's fixation with abolition that, during the CIVIL WAR, he offered wholehearted support for the Union cause only after the EMANCIPATION PROCLAMATION (1863). Despite inviting former slaves such as Frederick DOUGLASS to address abolitionist meetings, Garrison took a patronizing attitude towards African-Americans, and had little interest in securing their civil rights during RECONSTRUCTION. He regarded his crusade as completed with ratification of the THIRTEENTH AMENDMENT (abolishing slavery) and closed the *Liberator* on the day it was ratified.

Garvey, Marcus (Mosiah) (1887–1940), founder of the first significant black nationalist organization, the Universal Negro Improvement Association (UNIA). Born in Jamaica, in 1916 Garvey conducted a wildly successful speaking tour in the USA on behalf of the UNIA. The UNIA sought to lead blacks from the Americas to Africa, where they would expel the colonial powers and build a model African nation. This message was couched in a rhetoric of black self-help and accompanied by ritual expressions of racial pride. In 1919 the UNIA claimed 500,000 members in the USA, and Garvey eventually collected some $10 million from his followers. His views were denounced by the NATIONAL ASSOCIATION FOR THE ADVANCEMENT OF COLORED PEOPLE (NAACP), W.E.B. DU BOIS, the AFRICAN METHODIST EPISCOPAL CHURCH and the trade unionist A. Philip RANDOLPH. Randolph called him the 'supreme Negro Jamaican Jackass' and 'an unquestioned fool and ignoramus'. Garvey was convicted of mail fraud in 1923, jailed, and deported from the USA in 1927.

Gaspee, burning of the (June 10 1772), an incident in the period leading up to the AMERICAN REVOLUTION. The revenue schooner *Gaspee*, commanded by Lieutenant Dudingston, ran aground near Providence, Rhode Island, on June 9 1772. Enraged by Dudingston's draconian enforcement of trade legislation, local men boarded the schooner (wounding Dudingston) and torched it. This action reflected and exacerbated the breakdown in Anglo-American relations that continued even after the repeal of the TOWNSHEND REVENUE ACT.

Gates, Horatio (*c*.1728–1806), Continental Army commander during the REVOLUTIONARY WAR, who led American forces to victory at SARATOGA and defeat at CAMDEN. He was born in Britain, and served with the British army in America during the SEVEN YEARS' WAR. During this tour of duty he met and befriended George WASHINGTON, and the two men remained friends after Gates emigrated to Virginia and established himself as a gentleman farmer. In 1775 Washington appointed Gates adjutant general of the Continental Army, and in 1776–7 he served as commander of FORT TICONDEROGA. On August 4 1777 he was appointed commander of the Northern Department and charged with ensuring the defeat of a British invasion of New York State led by General John Burgoyne. Gates received much of the credit for the British surrender at Saratoga in October 1777, and he was compared favorably with Washington in congressional circles. Gates denied complicity in the CONWAY CABAL, a short-lived plot to replace Washington as commander of the Continental Army. Following the British capture of CHARLESTON, South Carolina (1780), Gates was appointed commander of the Southern Department. On August 16

1780 Gates led American forces at the battle of Camden, the most comprehensive defeat suffered by the Americans during the Revolutionary War. He was suspended from command while a lengthy investigation into his conduct was held. Reinstated in 1782, he spent the remainder of the war serving with Washington's headquarters staff.

gay rights movement, a coalition of organizations and individuals that emerged in the 1960s determined to end discrimination against gays and lesbians, and to secure for them equal treatment from employers, government agencies and the public. In the 1980s gay rights activists played a major role in highlighting the risk posed to public health by the AIDS virus.

As late as 1961 sodomy was illegal throughout the United States. Gays and lesbians were routinely subject to negative stereotyping, discrimination and occasionally violent harassment. Many gays and lesbians denied or disguised their sexuality. The emerging CIVIL RIGHTS MOVEMENT and established organizations such as the AMERICAN CIVIL LIBERTIES UNION distanced themselves from the concerns of pioneering gay organizations such as the International Bachelor's Fraternal Orders for Peace and Social Dignity (founded in Los Angeles in 1950) and the Daughters of Bilitis (founded in San Francisco in 1955). However by the mid-1960s gay activists in San Francisco were adapting the rhetoric of the Civil Rights movement to protest against the violence and discrimination their community faced. This issue achieved national prominence when on June 28 1969 a heavy-handed police raid on the Stonewall Inn, a gay meeting place in New York City's Greenwich Village, sparked a riot in which several policemen and gay men were injured. The riot prompted the formation of the Gay Liberation Front and the Gay Activists Alliance – organizations which developed the rhetoric of the civil rights movement to campaign against the 'oppression' of all minority groups within the USA. In 1970 gays and lesbians mounted a Gay Pride march in New York City to commemorate the Stonewall riot. The march became an annual event and similar demonstrations were mounted around the country. Mainstream politicians in major US cities, recognizing the political power of gay voters, began to address the issues raised by their gay and lesbian constituents. Nevertheless, in 1976 the US Supreme Court upheld the constitutionality of state laws prohibiting homosexual acts and in 1978 Harvey Milk (1931–78), an openly gay man who had been elected to San Francisco Board of Supervisors, and George Moscone, a heterosexual who as mayor of San Francisco had expressed a willingness to address gay concerns, were murdered by homophobes.

As the gay rights movement gathered momentum in the wake of these events it was also confronted with new problems. The AIDS virus was identified in 1981. Its deadly effects were soon apparent within the gay community. Gay activists criticized the tardiness with which governmental agencies and drug companies responded to the developing epidemic of AIDS cases. (Between 1985 and 1994 284,249 Americans are known to have died from AIDS.) Militant organizations, among them the AIDS Coalition to Unleash Power (ACT-UP), founded in 1987 in the aftermath of a massive protest march held in Washington DC, alleged that the official response to the AIDS epidemic in the USA was driven by the perception that its victims were deviant members of society. ACT-UP soon developed a reputation for vivid sloganeering. On January 22 1991, during the PERSIAN GULF WAR, one of its members interrupted a live CBS TV news bulletin to proclaim 'Fight AIDS – Not Arabs.' Organizations such as the Gay Men's Health Crisis pursued a more constructive approach and played a leading

role in the testing of new treatments to combat the AIDS and HIV viruses.

During the 1990s gay rights campaigners continued their struggle to secure from both the government and the public equality of esteem for gays and lesbians and have often engaged in polemic with the conservative Christian right. Activists have focused on two issues in particular: the rights of gay servicemen and the legitimacy of same-sex marriages. In 1991 three same-sex couples sued the state of Hawaii in a test case designed to force legal recognition of gay and lesbian marriages. They won a partial victory in 1996 when Hawaii's supreme court ruled that withholding a civil marriage license from same-sex couples might contravene federal legislation prohibiting sex discrimination. This ruling has implications for taxation, inheritance and child adoption law throughout the United States. Campaigns to end discrimination against gays and lesbians in the US armed forces have been less successful. President CLINTON initially backed demands that the services be prevented from dismissing, demoting or transferring homosexuals. In 1993 however, Clinton agreed an uneasy compromise – the so-called 'Don't Ask, Don't Tell' policy. This prevents the overt forms of discrimination against gays in the armed forces without ensuring full equality of treatment.

Genêt's mission (1793), mission to the USA from revolutionary France, led by Citizen Edmond Charles Genêt (1763–1834). The French Revolution was greeted with fraternal enthusiasm by DEMOCRATIC-REPUBLICANS and with disquiet by FEDERALISTS. The new French republic sent Genêt to America with instructions to reinvigorate the FRANCO-AMERICAN ALLIANCE (1778), to secure immediate repayment of America's debt to France, and to encourage Spanish Louisiana and Florida and British Canada to adopt French republicanism.

Genêt arrived in Charleston, South Carolina, on April 6 1793. Here, and on his journey north to Philadelphia, he was greeted warmly. This encouraged him to make undiplomatic criticisms of Washington's NEUTRALITY PROCLAMATION. He secretly granted US vessels charters as French privateers (a move that would result in Britain seizing over 250 US ships in retaliation), and plotted with George Rogers CLARK to launch an assault on New Orleans from US soil. Learning of these developments, Washington's cabinet demanded Genêt's recall. JEFFERSON secured him asylum in the USA.

Georgia, southeastern state, bordered to the north by Tennessee, North Carolina and South Carolina, to the west by Alabama and to the south by Florida. The most southerly of the original THIRTEEN COLONIES, British settlement in Georgia dates from a charter granted to 21 trustees by George II in 1732. Under James Oglethorpe (1696–1785) Georgia was developed as a refuge for the persecuted and the indigent. Its first legal code barred slavery. The colony languished until 1750, when slavery was legalized and Caribbean and South Carolinian planters established rice plantations on the Atlantic seaboard. During the REVOLUTIONARY WAR the British captured Georgia's chief settlement (SAVANNAH) and occupied much of the state. Georgia ratified the US Constitution on January 2 1788 and became the fourth state. CREEK peoples, led by Alexander McGILLIVRAY, opposed the westward expansion of American settlement. However in 1800 the Creek and CHEROKEE agreed land cessions in a bid to accommodate planters seeking to establish cotton plantations on Georgia's rich soil. Hunger for land helped produce the YAZOO LAND FRAUD and led to the full implementation of the INDIAN REMOVAL ACT (1830) through which most of Georgia's remaining native peoples were relocated on RESERVATIONS in Oklahoma.

The production of cotton using slave labor dominated the economy of ANTEBELLUM Georgia. Atlanta emerged as one of the south's most important banking and transportation centers on the strength of the industry. A special convention held at Milledgeville, Georgia, in December 1850 denounced the COMPROMISE OF 1850 and hinted that southern states would secede if Congress further encroached on slaveholders' rights. In 1860 44% of the state's population was enslaved. On January 19 1861 Georgia became the fifth state to secede from the Union and join the CONFEDERACY. The state was devastated in the latter stages of the CIVIL WAR by Sherman's assault on ATLANTA and the subsequent MARCH TO THE SEA.

During RECONSTRUCTION a provisional government installed by President Andrew JOHNSON wrote strict BLACK CODES and denied FREEDMEN the right to vote. The state was placed under military rule on March 2 1867, but self-government and congressional representation were restored on July 15 1870. The state legislature subsequently introduced racial segregation through a series of JIM CROW laws and in 1908 disenfranchised most African-American voters. Despite this many Georgians, black and white, believed that their state might become the cornerstone of a 'New South' of the sort outlined by Booker T. WASHINGTON in the ATLANTA EXPOSITION SPEECH (1895). In the late 19th century Georgia's SHARECROPPERS embraced many of the tenets of POPULISM and, under the leadership of Tom WATSON, it seemed that poor white and African-American farmers might unite to promote social reform. These hopes faded in the early 20th century amidst a wave of LYNCHINGS and the re-emergence of the KU KLUX KLAN. During the GREAT MIGRATION over one million African-Americans left Georgia for northern cities and the state gained a deeply conservative reputation. Nevertheless Georgia was the first southern state to fully desegregate its school system and, under Governor Jimmy CARTER, it attracted new economic investment. In

1990 Georgia had 6,478,216 residents and was the eleventh most populous state in the union.

Germantown, battle of (October 4 1777), failed American attempt to take PHILADELPHIA, Pennsylvania, from the British during the REVOLUTIONARY WAR. The main body of the British force that had captured Philadelphia in September 1777 (some 9000 men) stationed itself on the city's outskirts. On October 4, WASHINGTON launched an ambitious attack on British positions at Germantown (now a suburb of Philadelphia). Hampered by dense fog, and lacking discipline sufficient to execute Washington's complicated battle plan, the American attack collapsed in confusion. The British were left in secure command of America's largest city, and Washington's army was forced to take winter quarters at VALLEY FORGE.

Geronimo or **Goyathlay** ('He who yawns') (1829–1909), Native American leader who led a final wave of APACHE resistance to US authority in Arizona and New Mexico. Along with SIOUX leader SITTING BULL, he went on to become familiar through books and personal appearances to large numbers of Americans in the late 19th century.

Between 1881 and 1886, accompanied by a small band of followers, Geronimo raided US and Mexican settlements while evading some 9000 troops on both sides of the Mexican border. He surrendered in 1886 and, along with his followers, was imprisoned in Florida. Many of the young men in his party were sent to the CARLISLE INDIAN SCHOOL. Geronimo and his remaining followers were eventually imprisoned in Oklahoma. He took up farming, became a member of the Dutch Reformed Church in 1903, rode in President Theodore ROOSEVELT's inaugural parade and in 1906 published a best-selling autobiography.

gerrymandering, the redrawing of political constituencies to secure a partisan advantage. The first scheme of this kind was initiated in 1810 by the governor of Massachusetts, Elbridge Gerry (1744–1814). To ensure that DEMOCRATIC–REPUBLICANS dominated the state legislature, Gerry redrew the electoral map of Massachusetts. One of the new districts resembled a salamander, prompting the editor of the FEDERALIST Boston *Centinel* to coin the verb to 'gerrymander.' The US Supreme Court announced its intent to investigate gerrymandering in its ruling on BAKER VS. CARR (1962).

Gettysburg, battle of (July 1–3 1863), Union victory in Pennsylvania that proved to be the turning point of the CIVIL WAR. The battle ended Confederate invasion of the north, and threw the Confederacy onto the defensive for the remainder of the war.

Confederate commander LEE followed up the hard-won victory at CHANCELLORSVILLE by marching his 75,000-strong army north through Maryland into central Pennsylvania. President LINCOLN issued an emergency call for volunteers, and appointed General George MEADE to command the 88,000-strong Union Army of the Potomac sent to repulse the invasion.

The three-day battle of Gettysburg began on July 1 1863. Initial Confederate gains had the effect of drawing Lee's forces onto strong Union defensive positions. The valor with which Confederate troops attempted to secure these was encapsulated in Pickett's Charge, in which a 15,000-strong Confederate column suffered 10,000 casualties in an unsuccessful attempt to capture Cemetery Ridge (July 3). The ridge became known as the 'high water mark of the Confederacy' because Lee's shattered troops were forced to retreat following their failure to capture it. In the bloodiest battle ever fought on US soil, immortalized in Lincoln's GETTYSBURG ADDRESS, a total of 46,000 soldiers were killed or wounded, or went missing. To Lincoln's fury, Union commanders allowed Lee's broken army to retreat unmolested.

Gettysburg Address, 286-word address delivered by President LINCOLN on November 19 1863, dedicating the military cemetery at GETTSYBURG, Pennsylvania. Received with indifference at the time, it came to define the Union's purpose in fighting the CIVIL WAR. The full text of the address follows:

'Four score and seven years ago our fathers brought forth on this continent, a new nation conceived in Liberty, and dedicated to the proposition that all men are created equal.

Now we are engaged in a great civil war, testing whether that nation, or any nation so conceived and so dedicated, can long endure. We are met on a great battlefield of that war. We have come to dedicate a portion of that field as a final resting place for those who here gave their lives that that nation might live. It is altogether fitting and proper that we should do this.

But in a larger sense we can not dedicate, we can not consecrate, we can not hallow this ground. The brave men, living and dead, who struggled here, have consecrated it far above our poor power to add or detract. The world will little note, nor long remember what we say here, but it can never forget what they did here. It is for us the living, rather, to be dedicated here to the unfinished work which they who fought here have thus far so nobly advanced. It is rather for us to be here dedicated to the great task remaining before us; that from these honoured dead we take increased devotion to that cause for which they gave the last full measure of devotion; that we here highly resolve that these dead shall not have died in vain; that this nation, under God, shall have a new birth of freedom; and that government of the people, by the people, for the people, shall not perish from the earth.'

Ghent, treaty of (December 24 1814), peace treaty concluding the WAR OF 1812, signed at Ghent in what is now Belgium by Britain and the USA. The latter was represented by John Quincy ADAMS, Henry CLAY and Albert Gallatin (1761–1849). The USA made no territorial concessions, but received no redress on IMPRESSMENT. The battle of NEW ORLEANS (1815) was fought after the treaty had been signed, but before it was ratified in Congress on February 17 1815.

Ghost Dance, name given by white Americans to two new Native American cults in the later 19th century. The first cult originated with Wodziwob, a Paiute seer in Nevada, in 1869. It spread to California and Oregon in the early 1870s, but soon died out. The second Ghost Dance, originating in 1889, was much more influential, and prompted cultural resistance among the Native American nations of the Great Plains – resistance that, in the case of the SIOUX, had tragic consequences.

The second Ghost Dance originated with Wovoka, another Paiute shaman. While witnessing a solar eclipse in the Nevada desert in 1889, Wovoka had a vision in which he died, talked to God and was reborn. God gave Wovoka rituals through which others might receive his message of peace. These rituals, which included Christian elements, were dubbed the 'ghost dance' by white observers. They seemed to the participants to allow communication with dead relatives, and even the possibility of their resurrection. Reinterpreted as it was taken up by peoples living east of the Rockies, the cult supposedly predicted the destruction of the white man. Sioux living on reservations in the Dakotas added to it a myth of invulnerability, symbolized through distinctive chest armor.

Alarmed by eyewitness accounts of the dance and by reports that SITTING BULL was leading a party of Teton-Sioux to a major religious site, US authorities in South Dakota began disarming bands of Sioux Indians. The massacre at WOUNDED KNEE (1890) was sparked when soldiers attempted to disarm Teton-Sioux enthused by the Ghost Dance.

Gibbons vs. Ogden (March 2 1824), US Supreme Court ruling on a case revolving around the question of whether the New York state assembly could grant a monopoly to a steamboat company trading between New York and New Jersey. The Supreme Court, presided over by Chief Justice MAR-SHALL, ruled unanimously that New York's legislature had acted unconstitutionally in granting the monopoly. In a markedly broad interpretation of Article 1 Section 8 of the Constitution (the 'commerce clause'), the Court argued that Congress alone has the right to regulate interstate commerce. The Court's verdict suggested that all forms of 'commercial intercourse' were covered by this regulatory power, and that therefore state-granted monopolies and other forms of excessive state regulation were unconstitutional. The verdict helped to ensure that the US economy developed along laissez-faire lines.

GI Bill of Rights (March 31 1944), legislation, formally known as the Servicemen's Readjustment Act, that guaranteed US troops (GIs) who served during WORLD WAR II loans and stipends to attend college or undertake vocational training. The act was later extended to cover veterans of the KOREAN WAR. Over 2 million former servicemen used the act to take bachelor's or graduate degrees, and a further 2 million used it to finance vocational training. Congress refused to make equally generous provision for veterans of the VIETNAM WAR.

Gilded Age, term used to identify a period roughly corresponding to the final quarter of the 19th century during which some US industrialists and financiers made vast fortunes while corruption and urban squalor became almost endemic. The term is taken from the title of a novel written by Mark Twain (1835–1910) and Charles D. Warner (1829–1900) satirizing the complacent materialism of the age. SOCIAL DARWINISTS defended the unregulated, laissez-faire economy that gave rise to vast fortunes.

PROGRESSIVES and proponents of the SOCIAL GOSPEL attacked the social effects of greed and corruption.

Gilman, Daniel Coit (1831–1908), influential university educator. As president of Johns Hopkins University from 1876 to 1901, Gilman popularized within US higher education an emphasis on rigorous postgraduate training that was modeled on German university procedures. Under Gilman, Johns Hopkins became the first US university to establish PhD programs, and it also pioneered the use of seminars rather than tutorials as the primary method of instruction.

Gingrich, Newt, *see* CONTRACT WITH AMERICA.

Goldman, Emma (1869–1940), Jewish refugee from Tsarist Russia who became the most notorious anarchist in the PROGRESSIVE-era USA. She arrived in New York aged 16 in 1885, and over the next 25 years campaigned on behalf of women's rights, free love, birth control and tolerance for homosexuals. Her views would have been ignored by mainstream Americans were it not for the fact that Leon Czolgosz (1873– 1901), who assassinated President McKINLEY on September 6 1901, claimed to have been influenced by Goldman. Goldman criticized the assassination, but said that Czolgosz possessed the 'beautiful soul of a child'. She was a fierce opponent of WORLD WAR I and was deported from the USA in 1919 for criticizing US involvement in the war. She and her lover Alexander Berkman settled in Russia, but fled after criticizing the Bolshevik regime. She died in England.

gold standard, a former international monetary system in which the value of a country's currency was based on the value of gold, and in which paper money could be converted to gold on demand.

The USA joined the gold standard on March 14 1900 at the height of the SILVER-GOLD CONTROVERSY. It valued each dollar at the price of 25.8 grains (1.67 grams) of 90% pure gold. The USA built a gold reserve of

$150 million to back its currency. Supporters of the gold standard saw it as a symbol of national probity and economic virility. Opponents believed that the move hurt farmers and favored Wall Street interests. The USA left the gold standard in 1935. After the BRETTON WOODS CONFERENCE (1944) the USA restored the convertibility of dollars to gold. The USA has refused to redeem dollars with gold since 1971.

Goldwater, Barry (Morris) (1909–), Republican politician. He was the REPUBLICAN PARTY's presidential nominee in 1964, the first Jewish-American to head a major party ticket.

Goldwater represented Arizona in the US Senate (1953–65, 1969–87). He was an unequivocal conservative who voted against the CIVIL RIGHTS ACT OF 1964, advocated a US withdrawal from the United Nations and pledged to escalate the VIETNAM WAR. He told delegates at the Republicans' 1964 convention: 'Extremism in the defense of liberty is no vice – moderation in the pursuit of justice is no virtue.' President Lyndon B. JOHNSON, running against him in the 1964 election, seized on Goldwater's extremism, running TV adverts suggesting that Goldwater had a casual approach to the use of nuclear weapons. Goldwater took just 39% of the POPULAR VOTE in the election.

Gompers, Samuel (1850–1924), trade union leader, the USA's leading exponent of CRAFT UNIONISM. Born in England, he emigrated to the USA in 1863 as an apprentice cigar-maker. He joined the cigar-makers' union in 1864 and by 1877 was its president. In 1886 he became president of the AMERICAN FEDERATION OF LABOR (AFL). He was re-elected each year, with the sole exception of 1895, until his death.

Gompers believed that only national unions of skilled workers possessed the discipline and bargaining power to ameliorate working conditions. These prejudices were shared by the vast majority of skilled workers, who had little desire to expend their advantages on improving the pay and conditions of unskilled workers. Gompers steered the AFL away from alliances with the PEOPLE'S PARTY and the SOCIALIST PARTY OF AMERICA. But, under his leadership, organized labor forged links with the DEMOCRATIC PARTY that endure to this day. During WORLD WAR I Gompers founded the War Committee on Labor, which worked to prevent labor disputes from damaging war production.

good-neighbor policy, policy of non-interference in other western-hemisphere nations, announced by President HOOVER, developed by President Franklin D. ROOSEVELT and enacted by his Secretary of State Cordell HULL. On entering office Franklin D. Roosevelt renounced Theodore ROOSEVELT's corollary to the MONROE DOCTRINE – the so-called ROOSEVELT COROLLARY, – which had asserted the USA's exclusive right to intervene in the affairs of Latin American nations. Franklin D. Roosevelt's inaugural address (March 4 1933) declared that the USA would be a 'good neighbor' and would respect the rights of other nations. On December 26 1933 the USA signed a treaty with western-hemisphere nations that stipulated that no state had a right to intervene in the internal or external affairs of another. The spirit of this agreement was sorely tested during the COLD WAR.

GOP (Grand Old Party), nickname for the REPUBLICAN PARTY.

Gore, Al(bert Arnold), Jr (1948–), Democratic statesman, and CLINTON's vice president since 1993. Gore, who served in the US House of Representatives (1977–84) and Senate (1985–93), first came to national prominence when challenging Michael DUKAKIS for the Democratic Party's nomination in the presidential election of 1988. His concern for the environment, and his wife Tipper's campaign against 'satanic' heavy-metal records, made headlines before a lack of support and therefore funding forced him from the race. Clinton's decision to make Gore his running-mate defied conventional wisdom in two respects. First, Gore's record of service in the VIETNAM WAR only highlighted the fact that Clinton had evaded the DRAFT. Second, Gore was from the same BABY BOOM generation and the same region as Clinton (Gore is from Tennessee, while Clinton comes from neighboring Arkansas), and therefore did not 'balance the ticket'.

President Clinton's IMPEACHMENT trial did not help Gore's chances of relaunching his political career and he struggled to gain the Democratic Party's nomination for the presidential election of 2000.

'Go West, young man, and grow up with the country.' Authorship of this stirring admonition has been variously attributed to the Indiana journalist J.L.B. Soule and to Horace GREELEY, editor of the *New York Tribune*. Reputedly the young man to whom it was offered in the 1840s founded Grinnell College, Iowa. The slogan helped encourage TERRITORIAL EXPANSION by building a belief in America's MANIFEST DESTINY to extend its territory from the Atlantic to the Pacific.

Goyathlay, *see* GERONIMO.

gradual emancipation, term applied to various measures that were intended to achieve the ABOLITION of slavery while minimizing its social and financial repercussions. The first gradual-emancipation law was enacted by Pennsylvania in 1780. It stated that henceforth all children born to enslaved parents would become free on reaching their 28th birthday. New York and New Jersey passed similar laws in 1799 and 1804 respectively. Such laws did not free anybody who was already enslaved.

graduate school cases, two cases concerning African-American access to professional training, brought before the US Supreme Court. On June 5 1950 the Court issued rulings on the cases that chipped away at the JIM CROW system.

In most southern states the provision of

legal or medical training for black students, if it existed at all, was manifestly unequal to that offered to whites. But rather than allow blacks to enroll at colleges training white professionals, many southern states offered black students bursaries to allow them to pursue their studies outside their home state. Such schemes allowed southern states to claim that they were providing equal access to professional training.

Ruling on the case of Sweatt vs. Painter, the Supreme Court outlawed the payment of bursaries, and stipulated that qualified black students could not be denied access to a 'white' law school if the segregated alternative within their state could be shown to offer inferior training. In its verdict on McLaurin vs. Oklahoma, the Court ruled that once admitted to a previously all-white college, a black student could not be confined to segregated facilities but must be allowed equal access to libraries, dormitories, sports facilities and the like. These verdicts partially vindicated the strategy of the NATIONAL ASSOCIATION FOR THE ADVANCEMENT OF COLORED PEOPLE (NAACP) of fighting racial segregation by challenging its application to educational opportunities.

Grand Army of the Republic (GAR), organization formed in 1866 to represent veterans of Union service in the Civil War. The GAR became a powerful lobbying organization and a semi-official arm of the REPUBLICAN PARTY. At its peak the GAR claimed 400,000 members. Pressure from it helped secure passage of the DEPENDENT PENSION ACT (1890).

Grand Old Party (GOP), nickname for the REPUBLICAN PARTY.

Granger laws, series of laws passed in midwestern states in the 1870s that sought to regulate the costs associated with transporting and storing grain. The laws were promoted by farmers organized in the GRANGER MOVEMENT, and supported by merchants and small businessmen in rural communities. The first of the Granger laws was an Illinois state law (April 7 1871) establishing a commission to set maximum rail freight and warehouse fees. The legislatures of Iowa and Wisconsin took similar steps. In its ruling on MUNN VS. ILLINOIS (1877) the Supreme Court defended such legislation. But later rulings, beginning with WABASH, ST LOUIS AND PACIFIC RAILROAD COMPANY VS. ILLINOIS (1886), severely restricted a state's ability to regulate corporations.

Granger movement, informal name for the secret Order of the Patrons of Husbandry, founded in Washington DC on December 4 1867. Its goal was to promote the interests of rural communities and to encourage cooperation between northern and southern farmers. By 1874, 20,000 lodges (or 'Granges') had been organized, and the movement claimed 800,000 members. It lobbied for legislative aid for rural interests, advocating a 'soft' fiscal policy and the regulation of rail freight fees and grain silo charges. These efforts produced GRANGER LAWS in many midwestern states. Individual members provided a key source of support for the GREENBACK PARTY and the PEOPLE'S PARTY, as well as for POPULISM as a whole. Grangers later became staunch supporters of the NEW DEAL. The National Grange continues to serve as a fraternal organization and lobbying group for US farmers.

Grant, Ulysses S(impson) (1822–85), US Army general, Republican statesman and 18th president of the USA (1869–77). Grant emerged from the CIVIL WAR as the Union's most revered general, making him an ideal Republican candidate for the presidency. His administration was dominated by RECONSTRUCTION, and was marked by a number of scandals.

Few would have predicted Grant's rise to power and fame. He attended West Point Military Academy and served with distinction in the MEXICAN WAR, but, passed over for promotion, he resigned his Army commission in 1854. He failed miserably in a number of civilian trades and took to the bottle. After FORT SUMTER he raised a volunteer infantry regiment in his home state of Illinois. In August 1861 he was promoted to brigadier general, but was assigned to a relatively obscure command in southeastern Missouri. From here he led an advance into Tennessee that captured FORT HENRY AND FORT DONNELSON in February 1862. At Fort Donnelson Grant demanded of his Confederate opponent 'immediate and unconditional surrender'. This demand made 'Unconditional Surrender' Grant a Union war hero. Grant further demonstrated his resolute and aggressive tactics at the battle of SHILOH (April 1862). Pressed to remove Grant by superiors fearful that he would divert resources from the PENINSULAR CAMPAIGN, LINCOLN replied, 'I can't spare this man – he fights.'

In 1863 Grant masterminded the capture of VICKSBURG, and on March 9 1864 he was appointed commander in chief of all Union armies. He prepared for a massive assault on the Confederate army defending Richmond, Virginia. The remorseless and bloody nature of this campaign, initiated with the battle of the WILDERNESS (May 1864), led newspapers to dub Grant a 'butcher' bent on a war of attrition. But in 1865 he had the satisfaction of receiving LEE's surrender at APPOMATTOX. In July 1866 Grant was promoted to general of the army, the first man since WASHINGTON to hold the rank.

Grant was nominated for the presidency unanimously on the first ballot held at the REPUBLICAN PARTY's convention in May 1868. Elected on the slogan 'Let us have peace,' he became president on March 4 1869. He easily defeated Horace GREELEY to win re-election in 1872, and served until March 4 1877. In the era of Reconstruction, Grant denounced southern attempts to deny blacks citizenship rights but, arguing that 'social equality is not a subject to be legislated upon', opposed all legislation to 'advance the social status of the colored man' except that giving 'equal access' to schooling and travel. Hence Grant authorized armed force to suppress the KU KLUX KLAN, but signed legislation to dismantle the FREEDMEN'S BUREAU. This distinction, popular with white voters, signaled the end of Radical Reconstruction. Although his administration was mired in corruption and scandal, Grant's personal popularity survived the BLACK FRIDAY, CRÉDIT MOBILIER and WHISKEY RING scandals. In retirement Grant wrote a best-selling memoir, which provided for his wife's security and made up for the losses he suffered through ill-judged speculation. Grant's tomb in northwestern Manhattan (dedicated by President McKINLEY in 1897) is seldom visited.

Great Depression, long-lasting economic depression, affecting most parts of the world, that began with the 1929 WALL STREET CRASH and continued up to World War II. In the USA its social effects were ameliorated from 1933 by the NEW DEAL policies of President Franklin D. ROOSEVELT.

The severity of the depression in the USA was a function of the variety of its causes. During World War I, US farmers had increased production to capitalize on increased overseas demand. In the 1920s European demand for US crops fell, but US farmers continued to produce huge surpluses that depressed prices. Measures such as the AGRICULTURAL MARKETING ACT (1929), which supported prices by seeking limits to production, were only partially successful. US industry was not growing fast enough to absorb surplus rural workers, and the US government was unwilling, and probably unable, to subsidize cuts in agricultural production on the level necessary to raise prices. Rural banks began accumulating bad debts.

Meanwhile the FEDERAL RESERVE BOARD kept US interest rates artificially low for most of the 1920s. This helped to create a consumer boom whose most visible mani-

festations were a huge increase in car-ownership and, in 1928–9, a surge in the value of the stock market fueled by small investors buying stock on low margins (or credit). From 1928 the Federal Reserve tried, but failed, to discourage speculation in the stock market by raising interest rates. Protected by high TARIFFS, US industry had made gains in productivity that outstripped demand in the US economy. For as long as low interest rates supported domestic consumption, US manufacturers had little incentive to seek out new export markets. Once the Depression hit, they lobbied successfully for the punitive HAWLEY–SMOOT TARIFF (1930), which helped bring international trade to a standstill.

Finally, World War I had made the USA the world's largest creditor nation. The USA insisted that Britain and France repay war debt (and they in turn demanded that Germany keep up reparation payments), but the USA lent money abroad to keep the cycle of repayment flowing. At the start of the Depression US banks called in overseas loans. This helped create a worldwide financial crisis.

The Depression was triggered on October 29 1929 by the Wall Street Crash. Many speculators were ruined. Banks, holding massive levels of bad debt, called in loans. Businesses, confronting falling demand, laid off workers or collapsed. By 1933, 10,000 banks had failed or merged, and the value of their remaining assets had declined by 29%. The US gross national product fell by over 25% between 1929 and 1933. Unemployment rose from 3.2% in 1929 to 25% in 1933. The Depression reached its nadir in 1933. In that year at least 30 million Americans were out of work.

President HOOVER's belated response, the creation of the RECONSTRUCTION FINANCE CORPORATION (February 2 1932), centered on stimulating business activity. Relief for the unemployed was left up to the states. In the last days of Hoover's presidency

Americans began making panic withdrawals from banks. To prevent a complete collapse of confidence, incoming President Franklin D. Roosevelt gambled, successfully, on the declaration of a week-long BANK HOLIDAY.

The human cost of the Depression was colossal. The USA had no federal welfare system. State, municipal and charitable relief agencies were overwhelmed. The national suicide rate jumped by 50% between 1929 and 1932. Millions of Americans lost their farms, their businesses or their family homes. Many households relied on wages earned by women. Yet 'selfish' women workers were blamed for causing male unemployment, and the federal government actively encouraged measures, such as banning married women from school teaching, which kept women from the labor market. Millions of southern blacks took part in a GREAT MIGRATION to search for work in northern cities. The New Deal tackled most of the social problems caused by the Great Depression. The SOCIAL SECURITY ACT (1935) – which laid the foundations of the USA's welfare state – provided vulnerable Americans with some protection against future depressions. However, despite the New Deal, the industrial and agricultural sectors of the USA's economy remained depressed until US entry into WORLD WAR II.

Great Migration, the movement of some 6.5 million African-Americans from the rural south to the urban north during the course of the 20th century. In 1910, 90% of American blacks lived in the south; by 1970 only 53% did so. A subsidiary feature of this great internal migration was the movement of African-Americans from southern farms to southern cities. A collapse in the price of cotton and the superior economic opportunities available in southern towns and northern cities were primarily responsible for creating this mass migration. Accomplished over opposition from southern legislatures and hostility from whites in northern cities, the Great Migration began to destabilize the south's JIM CROW caste system and helped generate the CIVIL RIGHTS MOVEMENT.

Great Society, phrase coined by President Lyndon B. JOHNSON to sum up his vision of prosperity, social improvement and civil rights reform in the USA. Johnson used the phrase in a commencement address given at the University of Michigan in May 1964, when he announced: 'We have the opportunity to move not only toward the rich and the powerful society, but upward to the Great Society.' In Johnson's view, 'The Great Society rests on abundance and liberty for all. It demands an end to poverty and racial injustice.' Johnson continued his WAR ON POVERTY, pushed the CIVIL RIGHTS ACT OF 1964 through Congress, and created MEDICAID and MEDICARE in pursuit of his vision. The VIETNAM WAR undermined it.

Greeley, Horace (1811–72), newspaperman of genius whose maverick opinions plagued the REPUBLICAN PARTY during the CIVIL WAR and RECONSTRUCTION. He stood unsuccessfully for the presidency in 1872 as a LIBERAL REPUBLICAN, and is today perhaps best remembered for the advice 'GO WEST, YOUNG MAN.'

Greeley had little formal education, but learned the rudiments of journalism as a printer's apprentice in New York City. He co-founded a weekly journal entitled the *New Yorker* in 1834 and seven years later merged this publication with the *New York Tribune*. As editor of the *Tribune*, Greeley championed the workingman, opposed slavery, denounced the MEXICAN WAR and criticized big business. In 1854 he helped found the Republican Party. During the Civil War he demanded a tough line against the Confederacy, and immediate emancipation. He published the WADE–DAVIS MANIFESTO (critical of LINCOLN) in 1864. But after the Confederate surrender Greeley sought reconciliation with the south, and even helped bail Jefferson DAVIS out of jail.

Greeley shared President GRANT's cautious approach to RECONSTRUCTION, but stood against him in 1872, as a Liberal Republican endorsed by the DEMOCRATS, on a platform denouncing administration corruption. He polled 44% of the POPULAR VOTE (to Grant's 56%), but died before the ELECTORAL VOTE was cast.

Greenback Party, political party, formed after the PANIC OF 1873 and strongest in midwestern states, that campaigned for a 'soft' financial regime favorable to debtors' interests. It sought to keep a large number of GREENBACKS (paper notes) in circulation, opposed the RESUMPTION ACT and supported the BLAND–ALLISON ACT. Fourteen Greenback-Labor congressmen were elected in 1878. Most supporters shifted their allegiance to the PEOPLE'S PARTY in the 1880s.

greenbacks, paper notes, named after their distinctive colour, which were issued to finance the Union effort in the CIVIL WAR. The issue of this paper currency, to the value of $450 million, was authorized by the Legal Tender Acts of 1862 and 1863. The viability of these paper notes rested ultimately on an INCOME TAX (1861). Creditors and vendors were required to accept the notes, which could not be exchanged for gold. The US Supreme Court ruled on the constitutionality of their issue in the LEGAL–TENDER CASES. Following the PANIC OF 1873 the GREENBACK PARTY campaigned against the premature withdrawal of notes from circulation. The RESUMPTION ACT (1875) allowed for the exchange of greenbacks for gold coin.

Green Mountain Boys, *see* ALLEN, ETHAN.

Greensboro sit-in (1960), protest against segregated dining facilities in Greensboro, North Carolina, that marked a new phase in the CIVIL RIGHTS MOVEMENT. The protest began on February 1 1960 when four African-American students from North Carolina A&T demanded service at a lunch counter in a Woolworth's store reserved by 'local custom' for whites only. Declaring, 'Fellows like you make our race look bad,' a black waitress refused to serve them. Although harassed by white customers, the students refused to leave the counter. Store managers and local police watched, uncertain whether they should intervene. By February 3, 85 students had joined the protest, occupying the counter in shifts to avoid missing classes. The Greensboro sit-in was copied by young African-Americans throughout the south, and eventually resulted in the formation of the STUDENT NON-VIOLENT COORDINATING COMMITTEE (SNCC).

Greenville, treaties of (1795, 1814), two treaties between the US government and Native American nations signed in Greenville, Ohio.

(1) Concluded on August 3 1795, the first treaty, reflecting US military superiority in the Ohio valley established at the battle of FALLEN TIMBERS (1794), brought two-thirds of the modern state of Ohio under US jurisdiction.

(2) In 1811 the battle of TIPPECANOE CREEK initiated a last-ditch attempt by Native American nations to resist US occupation of the NORTHWEST TERRITORY. Britain assisted this effort during the opening phases of the WAR OF 1812. On July 22 1814 the Native American nations, demoralized by the death of TECUMSEH at the battle of the THAMES RIVER, met at Greenville to broker an alliance with the USA. This treaty effectively ended Native American resistance to white settlement in Ohio, Indiana and Michigan.

Grenada, US intervention in (1983). Citing an implausible threat to the safety of 700 US medical students on the Caribbean island, President REAGAN sent 1900 US troops (and token forces from other islands in the West Indies) into Grenada on October 25 1983 to secure the formation of a pro-American government. From 1979 to 1983 Grenada had been ruled by Maurice Bishop, an eccentric leftist who believed in the existence of UFOs and was vehemently anti-American. Bishop was assassinated by rival Marxists on October 19 1983, prompting US security experts to call for pre-emptive action to prevent the creation of a Cuban-style regime. Grenada was a member of the Commonwealth whose head of state is Queen Elizabeth II. Britain was not informed or consulted in advance of the US action. This discourtesy prompted the British prime minister Margaret Thatcher to administer a severe tongue-lashing to Reagan.

Guadalcanal campaign (August 7 1942 –February 9 1943), the first major US counteroffensive in the Pacific theater in WORLD WAR II. Despite the US naval victory at the battle of the CORAL SEA (May 1942), Japanese troops continued to threaten Port Moresby in New Guinea and Allied supply routes to Australia. US Marines landed on Guadalcanal island at the southwestern tip of the Solomon archipelago on August 7 1942 in a bid to relieve pressure on the New Guinea front. They captured the island's airfield, renaming it Henderson Field. However, on August 9 the Japanese navy mauled the invasion's supply fleet and temporarily deprived the Marines on Guadalcanal of air and sea support. Bitter fighting ensued. On November 12 the US Navy intercepted a convoy carrying Japanese reinforcements to the island, but three months of further fighting were needed to establish US control.

Guadalupe-Hidalgo, treaty of (February 2 1848), treaty that ended the MEXICAN WAR. The treaty was negotiated by Nicholas Trist (1800–74) after the failure of the SLIDELL MISSION. Ignoring a recall order from President POLK, on February 2 1848 Trist secured from Mexico the cession of all or part of CALIFORNIA, NEW MEXICO, ARIZONA, UTAH, NEVADA, COLORADO and WYOMING. In return the USA agreed to pay Mexico $15 million and to assume responsibility for meeting $3.25 million in outstanding claims against Mexico made by US citizens. The US Senate ratified the treaty by a vote of 38–14 on March 10 1848. The treaty secured the TERRITORIAL EXPANSION of the USA, but raised debate over the future status of SLAVERY to a new intensity (*see* COMPROMISE OF 1850). The US–Mexican border was amended by the GADSDEN PURCHASE in 1853.

Guam, the largest of the Mariana Islands in the western Pacific. The island is an unincorporated territory of the USA, acquired in the settlement of the SPANISH–AMERICAN WAR. It was administered by the US Navy until August 1 1950. At that time residents were granted US citizenship. Since 1972 Guam has sent a non-voting delegate to Congress.

Guiteau, Charles J. (1842–82), the assassin of President GARFIELD. On July 2 1881 Guiteau shot Garfield in the back as he strolled with Secretary of State James Blaine (1830–93) in a Washington DC train station. Guiteau, who described himself as a STALWART Republican, became mentally unbalanced when he was denied a diplomatic post in Garfield's administration. Garfield died on September 19 1881. That day Guiteau wrote to new President ARTHUR explaining that the assassination was 'an act of God' and advising him on the selection of a cabinet. Guiteau was sentenced to hang. On June 30 1882 he sang, from the scaffold, a hymn he had composed that began 'I am going to the Lordy, I am so glad.' The incident discredited Stalwarts and encouraged passage of the PENDLETON ACT (the Civil Service Reform Act).

Gulf of Tonkin Resolution, *see* TONKIN GULF RESOLUTION.

Gulf War, *see* PERSIAN GULF WAR.

gun control. Throughout its history, America has offered its citizens comparatively easy access to gun ownership. In America, as in no other industrialized country, proponents of gun control must explain why their proposals do not infringe on a presumed constitutional 'right to bear arms.' A distinctive feature of US history, especially in recent years, has been the way in which the passionate debate over gun control that has followed a sequence of assassinations and shooting sprees keeps alive issues and arguments that were current during the creation of the republic.

Three arguments in favor of relatively unrestricted access to gun ownership took shape during the AMERICAN REVOLUTION. On the practical level, a large percentage of American men already owned guns and used them either for hunting or for protection against Indians and thieves. Disarmament was impracticable. On the political level, REPUBLICAN IDEOLOGY suggested to Americans that a population stripped of its weaponry would be vulnerable to subjugation by a tyrant. For similar reasons, Americans were suspicious of standing armies and hoped to defend their country through militias drawn from an armed and patriotic citizenry. (For this reason some states required free adult males to own a gun.) Gun ownership was thus seen as a protection against governmental oppression and external aggression. However, Americans also invested gun ownership with emotional qualities. Gun ownership suggested independence, responsibility and manliness. It suggested that a man's neighbors and governors respected and trusted him. (These associations took on greater force for free white laborers because the severely restricted access to guns offered to African-American slaves was an obvious symbol of degraded status.) For practical, political and emotional reasons, ANTIFEDERALISTS demanded a constitutional amendment safeguarding the right to bear arms during RATIFICATION of the US Constitution in 1787–8.

James MADISON was responsible for drafting, from suggestions proposed by state ratifying conventions, what became the SECOND AMENDMENT. The meaning and intent of the Second Amendment has proved enormously contentious. It is certainly possible to argue, by comparing the wording of

the eventual amendment with the wording of suggestions sent in by the states and rejected, that the Founding Fathers saw the Second Amendment as a response to the practical and political arguments in favor of gun ownership rather than to the emotional case for unrestricted access. In contrast, the main opponents of gun control legislation, the National Rifle Association, have argued that the Second Amendment gives citizens an open-ended right to bear arms regardless of whether they are members of a 'well-regulated militia.' Nineteenth-century Americans were well aware of the emotional issues associated with gun ownership and, perhaps for this reason, those few states or localities which enacted gun legislation, concentrated on proscribing concealed weapons or requiring saloon-goers to check their weapons, at the door.

The first laws that actually restricted an individual's right to purchase a gun were passed by southern states during RECONSTRUCTION and were designed to prevent African-Americans from acquiring firearms. In 1911, an attempted assassination of the mayor of New York City spurred the New York state legislature to pass the 'Sullivan Law' which required citizens to obtain a police permit to own and to carry a pistol. Even in New York, and the four other states which followed its lead, the grounds on which were the police could refuse or rescind a permit were narrowly drawn.

In 1934, responding belatedly to the violence associated with PROHIBITION-era gangsters like Al CAPONE, the federal government introduced restrictions on the sale and ownership of machine-guns and sawed-off shotguns. A generation passed before the Omnibus Crime Control and Safe Streets Act (1968) barred the purchase of weapons by mail order and required gun dealers to obtain a license. (Lee Harvey OSWALD had obtained the rifle he used to assassinate President KENNEDY through mail order.) In

1986 the Reagan administration diluted the 1968 act. From this moment on, Congress came under growing pressure to pass the so-called 'Brady Bill.' This measure, which became law on November 24 1993, was named after White House Press Secretary James Brady, who was wounded and paralyzed during an attempted assassination of President REAGAN in 1981. It requires a potential purchaser of a handgun to wait five days while the police verify that the purchaser is not a felon, fugitive, drug addict or illegal alien. In 1994, Congress banned the sale of 19 models of military assault rifle.

These modest restrictions have done little to slow the rate at which Americans purchase guns legally and they leave in circulation millions of guns purchased illegally or before restrictions came into force.

H

Half-Breeds, nickname given in the 1880s by MUGWUMP Republicans to those within their party who, led by James BLAINE, advocated cautious measures to check the SPOILS SYSTEM. Blaine's Half-Breeds sought to avoid an open split with STALWART party bosses on the issue of civil-service reform.

Hamer, Fanny Lou (Francis Lou Townsend Hamer) (1917–77), heroine of the CIVIL RIGHTS MOVEMENT. Hamer worked as a sharecropper and as a plantation timekeeper in Sunflower County, Mississippi, before attending her first STUDENT NONVIOLENT COORDINATING COMMITTEE (SNCC) meeting in 1962. Fired up with enthusiasm, she organized a voter-registration drive among a group of Sunflower County African-Americans. This was rebuffed, and Hamer was eventually sentenced to a term in Mississippi's toughest prison. In 1964 she played a leading role in the creation of the MISSISSIPPI FREEDOM DEMOCRATIC PARTY (MFDP), and gained national celebrity for a televised speech she gave at the Democratic Party's national convention criticizing the refusal of party bosses to seat MFDP delegates. (President Lyndon B. JOHNSON hastily organized a press conference in order to switch national TV coverage away from Hamer's speech.) Hamer traveled extensively in Africa before returning to Mississippi in 1969 to organize an experimental Freedom Farm Cooperative. She once said that she was 'sick and tired of feeling sick and tired'.

Hamilton, Alexander (1755–1804), FEDERALIST statesman and first secretary of the US Treasury (1789–95), who died in a duel with his political opponent, Aaron BURR. As coauthor of the FEDERALIST PAPERS, architect of the USA's financial system and spokesman for the FEDERALIST PARTY, Hamilton exercised an influence on the AMERICAN REVOLUTION that was a product of genius rather than advantages of birth.

Hamilton was born, out of wedlock, on Nevis, in the British West Indies, and orphaned at the age of 13. He worked as a clerk to a Nevis merchant until the age of 17, when relatives and friends paid for him to enroll at King's College (now Columbia University), New York City. In March 1776 Hamilton volunteered for service as an artillery officer in the Continental Army. Within a year he had been appointed to George WASHINGTON's staff. In 1780 he married into a grand New York family, and on retirement from the Army (December 1783) practiced law in New York City.

Hamilton submitted a report to the ANNAPOLIS CONVENTION (1786) that led that body to propose the CONSTITUTIONAL CONVENTION (1787). Hamilton's only major speech at the Constitutional Convention denounced the weakness of the ARTICLES OF CONFEDERATION and endorsed the

Virginia Plan, which transferred power from the states to the proposed new national government. At the convention, and in the *Federalist Papers*, Hamilton opposed the addition of a BILL OF RIGHTS to the US Constitution.

In 1789 President Washington appointed Hamilton secretary of the Treasury. Hamilton maintained that the future health and prosperity of the USA lay in the hands of manufacturers, financiers and merchants. These were unfashionable beliefs. Most Americans regarded merchants and financiers as self-interested. Many shared JEFFERSON's view that small farmers, not capitalists, were 'the chosen people of God'. However, Hamilton had experienced the disinterested benevolence of wealthy men and he felt no need to puff the vanity of the yeomen farmers who dominated electoral politics. Scornful of opposition, Hamilton pushed his *REPORT ON THE PUBLIC CREDIT* through Congress and committed the USA to a 'sound-money' fiscal regime. He used IMPLIED POWERS reasoning to create the BANK OF THE UNITED STATES. However, he failed to persuade Congress to adopt the protective TARIFF advocated in his *REPORT ON MANUFACTURES*. Hamilton's beliefs, his undisguised support for the emerging Federalist Party and his influence over President Washington (which was supposedly demonstrated in the NEUTRALITY PROCLAMATION and WHISKEY REBELLION) attracted political opposition and led to his resignation as Treasury secretary in 1795.

During John ADAMS's presidency, Hamilton advocated the prosecution of DEMOCRATIC-REPUBLICANS under the ALIEN AND SEDITION ACTS, and, during the QUASI-WAR with France, served as second-in-command of the Army (1798–1800). Hamilton helped break the deadlock resulting from the PRESIDENTIAL ELECTION OF 1800 by urging New York congressmen to support the election of Thomas Jefferson. This dashed the prospects of fellow New Yorker Aaron BURR, and was an indirect cause of the duel between the two men, fought at Weehawken, New Jersey, on July 11 1804, which claimed Hamilton's life.

Hampton Roads Conference, *see RIVER QUEEN PEACE TALKS.*

Harding, Warren (Gamaliel) (1865–1923), Republican statesman and 29th president of the USA (1921–3), who died in office. His administration included some notable men, but was tainted by corruption.

Harding, a REPUBLICAN PARTY hack, had edited the *Star* newspaper in his hometown of Marion, Ohio. He later served as a state senator (1899–1903), lieutenant governor of Ohio (1903–5) and US senator (1915–21), before emerging from the SMOKE-FILLED ROOM as Republican presidential nominee in the 1920 election. He avoided contentious campaign issues, and when, in a slip of the tongue, he pledged to return America to 'normalcy', he struck a chord with voters exhausted by issues arising from WORLD WAR I and the LEAGUE OF NATIONS fight. In the election Harding achieved one of the greatest POPULAR VOTE majorities in American history, polling 16,152,200 votes, 60.4% of the total. His opponent, Democrat James M. Cox (1870–1957), polled 9,147,353 votes, 35% of the total.

Harding embarked on his presidency on March 4 1921. He used his INAUGURAL ADDRESS to assure the American public, 'We seek no part in directing the destinies of the world.' On February 2 1923 he told Congress, 'The League [of Nations] is not for us.' Some of Harding's appointments were inspired. Secretary of State Charles Evans HUGHES (1862–1948) presided over the successful WASHINGTON NAVAL CONFERENCE in 1921–2. Charles Dawes (1865–1951) was an able director of the Budget Bureau, a body Harding created. However, the TEAPOT DOME SCANDAL and other instances of corruption arose from Harding's willingness to appoint greedy or incompetent cronies to high office.

Throughout his presidency Harding continued an extramarital affair with Nan Britton, by whom he had a daughter (Harding and Britton once had sex in a White House wardrobe). In June 1923 Harding began a 'Voyage of Understanding', which saw him become the first US president to visit Alaska. He died in a room at the Palace Hotel, San Francisco, on August 2 1923. His death was probably caused by an allergic reaction to tainted crab-meat, although rumors persisted that he was poisoned by his wife.

Harlan, John Marshall (1833–1911), associate justice of the US Supreme Court from 1877 till his death. Known as the 'Great Dissenter', Harlan wrote 380 dissenting opinions during his Supreme Court career, the best-known of which favored the civil rights of African-Americans.

A former Kentucky slave owner, who fought on the Union side in the CIVIL WAR, Harlan was appointed to the Court by President HAYES following the COMPROMISE OF 1877. Perhaps his most prescient dissent was that in PLESSY VS. FERGUSON. Harlan argued that 'state enactments which proceed on the ground that colored citizens are so inferior that they cannot be allowed to sit in public coaches occupied by white citizens' would 'arouse race hatred'.

Harlem Renaissance, term applied to an artistic movement, chiefly literary, centered on New York's Harlem district in the 1920s. During this period, writers and artists generated a new aesthetic within African-American culture, one that reflected the opportunities and challenges facing a younger generation that was moving away from the rural south to northern districts like Harlem as part of the GREAT MIGRATION.

The idea of a 'Harlem Renaissance' gained currency following the publication in 1925 of Alain Locke's (1886–1954) *The New Negro*. Locke, who was born in Philadelphia and studied at Oxford as the university's first African-American Rhodes Scholar (1907–10), identified in the work of Harlem's artistic

community 'a spiritual coming of age.' For Locke, and for other observers, the work of writers such as Langston Hughes (1902–67) and Zora Neale Hurston (1901–60) celebrated, and was itself a source of, 'race pride.' Like Locke, Langston Hughes had traveled extensively within the USA and Europe. He returned to the USA conscious of his heritage but distanced from both the 'social disillusionment' of an earlier generation of African-American intellectuals and the escapist pan-Africanist rhetoric of a figure such as Marcus GARVEY. Hughes, Hurston and other members of the loosely defined movement saw African-American districts like Harlem as viable communities (not pathological ghettoes) and set out to explore their new and distinctive cultures realistically, unapologetically and without reference to a rhetoric of self-improvement. The Renaissance attracted criticism from conservative black community leaders and, at least briefly, the interest of white intellectuals. Always primarily concerned with the aesthetics of self-expression, the Renaissance lost momentum in the Depression-era USA.

Harper's Ferry, raid on (October 16 1859), seizure of the federal arsenal at Harper's Ferry, Virginia, by a group of abolitionists led by John BROWN. The group comprised 18 men, including 5 free blacks, and their intention was to incite a slave rebellion and ultimately found a haven for African-Americans in the Allegheny Mountains. After a two-day siege, Brown's gang was captured by US Marines led by Robert E. LEE. Brown and six other insurgents were hanged in December 1859. Many southerners assumed that Brown's views were typical of the abolitionist movement as a whole and that northerners sought to destroy the institution of slavery by inciting a race war. Southern demands that northerners totally repudiate Brown and enact legislation offering cast-iron protection of slavery helped cause the CIVIL WAR.

Harper vs. Virginia Board of Elections
(March 24 1966), US Supreme Court ruling
that prohibits states from levying poll taxes,
or from using taxes to prevent an individual from exercising voting rights. Such laws
had previously been used in many southern states to evade the intent of the
FIFTEENTH AMENDMENT.

Harris, Patricia Roberts (1924–85), lawyer, diplomat and cabinet officer. Harris was
the first African-American woman to be
appointed to a US ambassadorship and the
first to hold a US cabinet post.

Harris was born in Illinois. She was
trained in law at Howard University and the
University of Chicago. President Lyndon B.
JOHNSON appointed her US ambassador to
Luxembourg in 1965. Replaced in 1969, she
became Dean of Howard University Law
School. In 1971 she became a director of
IBM. During President CARTER's administra-
tion, Harris served as Secretary of Housing
and Urban Development (1977–9) and
Secretary of Health, Education and Welfare
(1979–81).

Harrison, Benjamin (1833–1901), grandson of William Henry HARRISON, REPUBLICAN
statesman and 23rd president of the USA,
who served from March 4 1889 until March
4 1893.

Harrison was born and raised in Ohio but
moved to Indianapolis, Indiana, in 1854 to
begin a career in the law. During the CIVIL
WAR he attained the rank of brigadier-general in the Union Army. He saw active service in SHERMAN's ATLANTA campaign and
also helped swing the PRESIDENTIAL ELECTION
OF 1864 in favor of the incumbent by fur-
loughing enlisted men likely to vote for
President LINCOLN. After the war, Harrison
represented Union officers defending a suit
for civil damages arising from the US
Supreme Court's judgment in EX PARTE MIL-
LIGAN (1866). As a US Senator (1881–7), his
support for a pension for union veterans
earned him the nickname the 'soldier's
legislator.' He also supported high TARIFFS,

civil service reform and conservation measures. When he lost his Senate seat to a
Democrat, Harrison declared 'I am a dead
statesman but a living and rejuvenated Republican.' The slogan 'rejuvenated republicanism' helped propel Harrison to his
party's presidential nomination in 1888. He
was elected to the presidency with a minority share (49%) of the popular vote. Harrison's administration was notable chiefly for
the encouragement he gave Congress to
enact what became the SHERMAN ANTI-TRUST
Act (1890) and for the exacerbation of the
SILVER-GOLD CONTROVERSY that stemmed
from his decision to amend the operation
of the SHERMAN SILVER PURCHASE Act (1890)
by permitting Treasury notes to be
redeemed in gold. Harrison lost interest in
his re-election campaign when his first wife
Caroline died on October 25 1892. He also
lost votes to POPULIST candidate James
WEAVER. In retirement Harrison returned to
practice of law.

Harrison, William Henry (1773–1841),
soldier, WHIG statesman and 9th president
of the USA, who served only from March 4
1841 until his death on April 4 1841, the
first president to die in office.

Harrison was born in Virginia but raised
in the NORTHWEST TERRITORY. While governor of Indiana Territory, he won the battle
of TIPPECANOE CREEK (1811), and also led
forces to victory in the battle of THAMES
RIVER in the WAR OF 1812, an exploit celebrated by Whig supporters in his victorious
LOG CABIN AND HARD CIDER presidential
campaign of 1840. Harrison had served
previously as a US representative in the
House (1816–19), Ohio state senator
(1819–21), US senator (1825–8) and US
minister to Colombia (1828–9). His death
was attributed to pneumonia caught while
delivering the longest INAUGURAL ADDRESS
on record.

Hartford Convention (December 15 1814),
meeting in which 26 FEDERALIST delegates
from the New England states convened

to discuss in secret session 'public grievances and concerns' arising from the WAR OF 1812.

The convention developed the doctrine of interposition, the 'right and duty' of a state to protect its sovereignty from the unconstitutional actions of the federal government. It called for greater state control over the deployment of militias, and a congressional majority of two-thirds for any measure restricting commerce, declaring war or admitting new states. Delegates also demanded that the apportionment of taxation and of representation in the House should be determined by reference to a state's free population alone. They sought a single-term presidency and laws barring naturalized citizens from senior federal posts.

The Convention's existence became public knowledge when delegates elected a three-man committee to represent their views in Washington. The Federalist Party was immediately pilloried. New England merchants had long opposed war with Britain on the grounds that it would prove financially ruinous and strategically misguided. Outside New England the Convention's statement of STATES' RIGHTS principles was dismissed as special pleading. The DEMOCRATIC party seized upon the Convention's implicit threat that the New England states might secede if their demands were not met as evidence of disloyalty and demanded that Federalist leaders repudiate the meeting. Since the Convention's demands were made public after news of the Treaty of GHENT and Andrew JACKSON's victory at the battle of NEW ORLEANS reached the USA, its Federalist delegates were made to appear unpatriotic.

Hatch Act (August 2 1939), legislation that made it illegal for most federal employees to participate in political campaigns, to solicit contributions from welfare recipients or to use their authority to influence the outcome of elections. The act emerged out of Republican allegations that officials in the WORKS PROGRESS ADMINISTRATION had pressured workfare recipients to vote for Democrats in the 1938 Congressional elections.

Hawaii, state in the north-central Pacific Ocean, consisting of a chain of volcanic islands, including Oahu and Hawaii itself. In 1778 Captain Cook claimed the archipelago, which he renamed the Sandwich Islands, for Britain. The islands remained an independent kingdom until January 16 1894, when US citizens in Hawaii, assisted by Marines and encouraged by sugar planters, overthrew Queen Liliuokalani and established a republic. The USA annexed this republic on July 7 1898 and granted Hawaii territorial status on June 14 1900. The islands' chief value to the USA lay in their strategic location. The Japanese attack on the US Pacific Fleet's base at PEARL HARBOR on Oahu brought the USA into World War II. Hawaii became the 50th state in the union on August 21 1950. Since statehood Hawaii's population has boomed. In 1990 Hawaii had 1,108,229 residents and was the 41st most populous state in the union. Its chief industry is tourism. In 1987 Hawaii's US Senator Daniel Inouye (1924–) attracted national attention as the chair of a congressional investigation of the IRAN-CONTRA SCANDAL.

Hawley–Smoot Tariff (June 17 1930), legislation raising import duties on a range of farm produce and manufactured goods to an average level of 42%. The measure was passed by congressmen desperate to be seen to be doing something to aid constituents caught in the GREAT DEPRESSION. Predictably, European nations retaliated. International trade came to a virtual standstill, adding greatly to the severity of the depression and even convincing Congress to cede some of its power over tariff policy to the president through the Trade Agreements Act (1934).

An intriguing cultural aspect of the Hawley–Smoot Tariff was that Treasury Secretary Andrew W. Mellon (1855–1937) wrote into the bill a relaxation of obscenity laws, which permitted the import of works such as *The Arabian Nights*, *Memoirs of Casanova* and *The Decameron* for the first time.

Hayes, Rutherford B(irchard) (1822–93), Republican statesman and 19th president of the USA (1877–81). Under his presidency the remaining federal troops were withdrawn from the south, ending RECONSTRUCTION.

Hayes, a Cincinnati lawyer, joined the REPUBLICAN PARTY following the COMPROMISE OF 1850 to oppose the expansion of slavery. He fought with distinction in the CIVIL WAR and served two terms as governor of Ohio (1868–72, 1876–7). Ohio's importance within the ELECTORAL COLLEGE was such that Hayes beat James G. BLAINE for the Republicans' presidential nomination in 1876.

Following the controversial PRESIDENTIAL ELECTION OF 1876 Hayes announced, in the COMPROMISE OF 1877, his willingness to end Reconstruction. He took up office on March 4 1877. As president he vetoed the BLAND–ALLISON ACT, supported the RESUMPTION ACT, and used federal troops to crush a railroad strike. Honoring a pledge not to seek re-election, he served until March 3 1881. In retirement he chaired an educational charity that awarded a scholarship to W.E.B. DUBOIS.

Haymarket riot (May 4 1886), socialist protest in Chicago that ended in the deaths of eleven people. On May 1 1886, 40,000 workers in Chicago mounted a one-day strike in support of the EIGHT-HOUR MOVEMENT. On May 3 1886 a mass picket in support of strikers at the city's McCormick Reaper works ended in violence. Two demonstrators were shot. Local socialists called for a protest rally in Haymarket Square on May 4. About 300 workers attended. At its conclusion someone threw a bomb that killed a policeman and injured many protesters. The police opened fire, causing a stampede in which ten workers were killed and scores more injured. The

incident provoked a hysterical backlash against socialists, anarchists and the KNIGHTS OF LABOR. Four 'ringleaders' were hanged.

hayseed socialists, derogatory nickname for supporters of the PEOPLE'S PARTY.

Hearst, William Randolph (1863–1951), the USA's first media magnate and pioneer of YELLOW JOURNALISM. Hearst used his newspapers to inflame public opinion in advance of the SPANISH-AMERICAN WAR. His papers were also widely blamed for inciting the assassination of President McKINLEY. Hearst controlled 23 newspapers, owned gold and silver mines, had interests in movie production and owned magazines such as *Good Housekeeping*. Yet he also favored the EIGHT-HOUR MOVEMENT, public ownership of utility companies and the direct election of US senators. He served as a US representative (1903–7), but sought unsuccessfully to become the DEMOCRATIC PARTY's presidential nominee (1904), mayor of New York City (1905, 1909) and governor of New York State (1906).

Heart of Atlanta Motel vs. US (December 14 1964), US Supreme Court ruling that upheld the constitutionality of Title II of the CIVIL RIGHTS ACT OF 1964, prohibiting racial segregation in public accommodation. The decision was a landmark, and reversed the Court's finding in the CIVIL RIGHTS CASES (1883).

Henry, Patrick (1736–99), politician and orator. On March 23 1775, during the AMERICAN REVOLUTION, Henry reputedly closed a speech urging the Virginia House of Burgesses (assembly) to resist British authority by force with the famous words, 'Give me liberty or give me death.' As Virginia's first elected governor (1776–9), he authorized George Rogers CLARK's expedition. During a second spell as governor (1784–6) Henry clashed with MADISON and JEFFERSON on the separation of church and state. Henry opposed the VIRGINIA STATUTE FOR RELIGIOUS FREEDOM because he wished to use a state tax to support Christianity. He also opposed RATIFICATION of the US Constitution, on the grounds that it would weaken the powers of individual states. Henry later used his influence to ensure that Madison was denied a seat in the US Senate as a punishment for his support for the Constitution. The two men cooperated on the drafting of the BILL OF RIGHTS, but Henry ended his life an embittered FEDERALIST.

Hepburn Act (June 29 1906), legislation reinforcing the regulation of rail charges. The INTERSTATE COMMERCE ACT (1887) had created an Interstate Commerce Commission with powers to investigate whether rail charges were 'reasonable and just'. However, rail companies found it relatively easy to employ creative accounting to evade the act's intent. The Hepburn Act gave to the Commission the power to set maximum freight and passenger rates. It also established uniform book-keeping procedures. These were provisions that MUCKRAKERS had urged Congress to enact. The MANN–ELKINS ACT (1913) built on this regulatory base.

Hepburn vs. Griswold, *see* LEGAL-TENDER CASES.

Hessians, generic term applied to some 30,000 German mercenaries hired by Britain during the REVOLUTIONARY WAR. Hessians proved better at looting than fighting. At TRENTON and BENNINGTON Hessian units detached from British support were badly mauled. During the war 5000 deserted and took up residence in the USA.

Hiroshima and Nagasaki, bombing of. The use of atomic weapons on these two Japanese cities ended WORLD WAR II, vindicated the billions of dollars spent on the MANHATTAN PROJECT and helped foment the COLD WAR.

On July 29 1945 Japan rejected an ultimatum demanding its unconditional surrender. President TRUMAN – apprised of the successful test of an atomic bomb at Alamagordo Air Force Base, New Mexico, on July 16, and believing that a conventional assault on the Japanese home islands would incur 1 million Allied casualties – authorized the immediate use against Japan of four untested atomic bombs in various states of preparation.

On August 4 1945 US planes dropped leaflets over Hiroshima warning the inhabitants that their city would be obliterated. Just after 8:00 a.m. on August 6 bombardier officer Major Thomas Ferebee released an atomic bomb code-named 'Little Boy' from the *Enola Gay*, a B-29 warplane flying at 31,600 feet (9600 m) above Hiroshima. At least 78,000 inhabitants were killed instantly – some 250,000 others died days, months or years later from burns and radiation sickness. A slightly more advanced plutonium bomb, code-named 'Fat Man', was dropped on Nagasaki on August 9, with equally devastating results. Two more bombs were available and scheduled to be released on August 13 and 16. However on August 10 Emperor Hirohito ordered the immediate surrender of Japanese forces.

Hiss, Alger (1904–), former State Department official accused of being a communist spy during the early COLD WAR period. On August 3 1948 Whittaker Chambers (1901–61), a self-confessed former communist, testified before the House Un-American Activities Committee (See DIES COMMITTEE) that during the 1930s Hiss, then an official in the State Department, had sent secret documents to Moscow. Hiss denied the charge and filed suit for slander against Chambers.

A special HUAC subcommittee, chaired by Richard NIXON, grilled Hiss, who continued to maintain his innocence. Chambers produced a stash of microfilmed State Department papers hidden in a hollowed-out pumpkin on his Maryland farm. Hiss denied giving them to Chambers. Milking the case, Nixon alleged that the State Department was more interested in protecting the Harvard-educated Hiss than in ascertaining who stole the documents in Chambers's possession. Hiss was indicted for perjury and on November 17 1949, after two trials, was found guilty and sentenced to five years' imprisonment.

Hodgson vs. Minnesota (July 22 1990), US Supreme Court ruling that modified the unequivocal affirmation of a woman's right to choose an ABORTION established in ROE VS. WADE. The 5–4 verdict included two points. The Court ruled that states could require a woman seeking an abortion to wait 48 hours before obtaining one. The Court also upheld the right of states to pass laws requiring underage girls to obtain the permission of both parents, or a judge, prior to an abortion.

Hoffa, Jimmy (James Riddle) (1913–75), corrupt trade union leader. Hoffa was working in a grocery warehouse when, in 1931 he joined the International Brotherhood of Teamsters, Chauffeurs, Warehousemen and Helpers of America, (the Teamsters' Union). Over the next 26 years Hoffa rose through the ranks of the union, strengthening central control over its membership. He was elected president of the Teamsters in 1957. Hoffa immediately repudiated an ethics code drawn up by the AMERICAN FEDERATION OF LABOR and CONGRESS OF INDUSTRIAL ORGANI- SATIONS, leading the AFL-CIO to expel the Teamsters. Membership in the Teamsters' union remained buoyant despite allegations that Hoffa was embezzling its funds and using it as a cover for extortion rackets. Hoffa won a national contract for truck drivers belonging to the Teamsters in 1964. He began to recruit members among airline and railroad employees. However, Hoffa's management of the union and its funds was the subject of a massive Department of Justice investigation led by Robert KENNEDY. In 1967 Hoffa was convicted of jury-tampering, embezzlement and mail fraud, and sentenced to 13 years imprisonment. In 1971 President NIXON commuted Hoffa's sentence in the hope of gaining sup-

port from the Teamsters in the PRESIDENTIAL ELECTION OF 1972. Hoffa disappeared in 1975. He is believed to have been murdered by the Mafia and buried in concrete beneath the New Jersey turnpike.

Hollywood, district of Los Angeles, California, that for much of the 20th century served as the headquarters of the US film industry. 'Hollywood' became synonymous with production techniques and cultural values that have shaped US history throughout the 20th century.

Movies did not originate in the USA, but the business practices that turned a popular novelty into a mass entertainment industry were thoroughly American. On April 23 1896, the owners of Koster and Bial's Music Hall in New York City exhibited a motion picture to a paying public for the first time in US history. The experiment relied on film developed by Thomas EDISON and a projector designed by Thomas Armat. The combination came to be known as Vitascope. Edison was later to claim credit for inventing movies, but in fact rival systems were already in existence and were soon demonstrated to a paying American public. Edison's breakthrough lay in realizing the commercial possibilities of projecting a film onto a screen that could be viewed by a large audience. In 1896, much of the embryonic industry was still working on a formula modeled on the peepshow that produced viewing machines and films to be used by a single viewer at a time. There was more profit to be made from showing the same short film at regular intervals to a large audience than there was in waiting for audiences to take their turn at an individual viewer. By plowing a portion of their profits back into production, the makers of motion pictures aimed at large audiences were soon able to offer more ambitious and sophisticated films than the images available through a peepshow machine. The economies of scale inherent in the exhibition of motion pictures to a mass audience also drove down the price of admission. In 1905, Pittsburgh entrepreneurs John P. Harris and Harry Davis opened a movie house which charged a nickel for admission. By 1908 there were over 8,000 'nickelodeons' in operation in the United States. The Edison Vitascope company, the American Biograph company and numerous lesser rivals relentlessly sued one another in successive bids to establish their production, exhibition and distribution arrangements as the industry standard. In 1908, the rivals switched tack and formed a TRUST – the Motion Pictures Patent Company – which operated for seven years before being broken up by court order. During this period, independent producers like William Fox (1879–1952) fought the trust by publicizing their film stars and switching production facilities to Hollywood.

Movies grew inexorably in length and ambition. In 1899 Edwin Porter (1870–1941) produced the first US film whose narrative was created through editing: *The Life of an American Fireman*. In 1903, Porter filmed the first 'western': *The Great Train Robbery*. The first US director of genius, D.W. Griffith (1875–1948), began making movies in Hollywood in 1908. His highly contentious account of the Civil War and Reconstruction, *Birth of a Nation* (1915), is widely regarded as the first great American movie. Cecil B. DeMille (1881–1959), later synonymous with 'epic' movies, made his first Hollywood movie in 1913. Mack Sennett, who launched the careers of Charlie Chaplin (1889–1977) and Buster Keaton (1895–1966), began making two reel slapstick comedy features in 1911. Although the film industry was soon producing a diverse range of movies, those which proved most popular with audiences were usually excessively sentimental. The popularity of 'America's sweetheart,' the virginal Mary Pickford (1893–1979), symbolized for many educated Americans the shortcomings of the new medium.

Even before Hollywood cooperated with the US government's COMMITTEE ON PUBLIC INFORMATION to produce 'patriotic' features (such as *The Kaiser: Beast of Berlin*) that whipped up anti-German hysteria during World War I, moralists fretted over the effects of movies on public morals. In 1907, Chicago became the first US city to empower its police to suppress offensive movies. In 1915, the US Supreme Court ruled that movies were not forms of 'free speech' protected by the FIRST AMENDMENT. (It reversed this decision in 1952). In 1922, the film industry organized a voluntary regulatory agency, the Motion Picture Producers and Distributors of America, whose first director, former postmaster-general Will Hays (1879–1954), wrote a detailed code describing what could and could not be shown in Hollywood movies.

Industry moguls agreed to self-censorship partly to avoid the negative publicity associated with a series of sex and drug scandals involving major studio stars and partly because some of the most profitable movies of the early 1920s, such as *The Sheik* (1921) and *Blood and Sand* (1922) starring Rudolph Valentino (1895–1921), dealt with 'exotic' themes likely to trouble moralists. The construction of new 'picture palaces,' offering unparalleled amenities and class-segregated seating plans of the type found in theaters, helped attract a new, middle-class, audience to the movies in the 1920s. These developments encouraged producers to redouble their efforts to organize the production, distribution and exhibition of movies under a single umbrella. The 'studio system' began to take shape in 1912 with the creation of the Paramount studio. Paramount's chief, Adolph Zukor (1873–1976), pioneered the 'block booking' system whereby movie theaters not tied to a studio had to show that studio's flops in order to get their hands on its hits. Four other 'major' studios were organized along the same lines; Warner Brothers in 1923, Metro-Goldwyn-

Mayer and Radio-Keith-Orpheum (RKO) in 1924 and 20th Century-Fox in 1935.

The studio system proved a mixed blessing for the US film industry. Competition between studios initially helped to stimulate technical innovation. In 1926, for example, Warner Brothers, the studio with the weakest foothold in the distribution business, gambled on the production of movies which were accompanied by sound recorded on discs. *The Jazz Singer* (1927), featuring Al Jolson (1886–1950), was the first movie to feature snatches of spoken dialogue and singing. The other major studios soon responded with more sophisticated sound systems. 'Talkies' were popular, but they introduced a period of turmoil in which some stars found their careers at an end, new stars emerged and cinemas across the USA raced to install sound equipment. To ride out the GREAT DEPRESSION, the five major studios attempted to play to their strengths rather than risk artistic experiments. For example, MGM, which boasted of having more stars than the night sky, specialized in musicals. The major studios exercised ever closer supervision of actors and directors, especially after pressure from the Catholic Legion of Decency forced the industry to adopt an even stricter production code in 1934. Industry workers battled against the rigidities of the studio system by forcing bosses to recognize independent trade unions. (Many of the most militant unionizers were later BLACKLISTed during the COLD WAR). However many actors and actresses complained of being 'typecast.' Considerations of the 'bottom line' help explain why the major studios were slow to switch to making movies in color. (The Technicolor Corporation was founded in 1915 and made a feature film to demonstrate its product as early as 1922). Walt DISNEY was perhaps the most innovative filmmaker to emerge during the Depression era (he made his first technicolor feature in 1935), but Disney ran his independent company in the autocratic style of a major studio boss.

After this period of retrenchment, the industry entered a 'golden age' in the late 1930s. By 1939, Hollywood studios were producing over 400 feature films a year and over 80 million Americans a week went to the movies. Movies like *Gone with the Wind* and *The Wizard of Oz* (both 1939) were acclaimed as artistic as well as commercial successes. During World War II Hollywood made fewer movies, but revenue increased because audiences were starved of entertainment. In 1946 Hollywood enjoyed the most profitable year in its history.

The rise of TELEVISION, and the political imperatives of the COLD WAR, produced a divided response within Hollywood that harmed the industry as a whole. During World War II, millions of Americans took on unfamiliar work, moved to new neighborhoods and cities or saw military service overseas. The GI BILL contributed to a further broadening of horizons by encouraging Americans to take up a college education. Some talented industry professionals attempted to engage with this new climate by producing movies tackling themes that had been ignored in the escapist 30s. The naturalistic 'method acting' style associated with Marlon Brando and Rod Steiger, helped make socially conscious movies such as *On the Waterfront* critically acclaimed triumphs. Yet at the same time other Hollywood professionals used the Cold War to settle scores with 'progressive' actors, writers and directors by blacklisting them from employment. Ronald REAGAN, president of the Screen Actors' Guild (1947–52), was complicit in this cultural purge. During the 1950s, Hollywood produced relatively crude 'patriotic' productions with far greater frequency than it made socially conscious movies. The industry also made faltering attempts to fight the popularity of television by switching to production in color and by producing movies in the widescreen

Cinemascope format and even in 3-D. The 1950s also saw the popularization of a new exhibition concept, the 'drive-in' movie. However, at the same time the industry came under greater pressure from the courts to end 'block-booking' and to sever its links with chains. Desperate to retain its studio system of organization, the industry began to produce movies for television and tried to exploit trends, like rock and roll, that it neither understood nor controlled.

By 1968, the industry produced fewer than 200 movies annually and weekly audiences had fallen below 20 million. The costs associated with producing an entire movie in Hollywood led many producers to shoot overseas, using the former headquarters of the film industry for post-production work only. The major studios relied increasingly on television work or on sales of their back catalogs. However in 1968, the industry introduced a new system of film classification that broke the last vestiges of the puritanical Hays Code. Hollywood set itself on a road to partial recovery by making movies whose language, nudity, violence and attitude to drug-taking could never be replicated in a commercial television show. By providing a stable revenue stream, formulaic sex-initiation, violent revenge and softcore pornography, movies generated a pool of capital that allowed the industry to gamble on the production of big-budget summer 'blockbusters' and more experimental 'niche' movies. The improved financial health of the industry led to a wave of corporate takeovers in the 1980s that saw many famous Hollywood companies pass out of American control. Rupert Murdoch acquired 20th Century-Fox in 1985; Columbia and Universal passed into Japanese ownership in 1989 and 1990 respectively.

Hollywood is currently under attack for promoting immoral attitudes toward sex and violence. The relentless commercial packaging of Hollywood's major productions has led some moviegoers to seek out movies by independent or foreign filmmakers. However, despite the fact that widespread ownership of video-cassette players makes the private viewing of movies accessible to millions, the US film industry has succeeded in keeping the habit of going to the movies alive.

Holmes, Oliver Wendell (1841–1935), associate justice of the US SUPREME COURT from 1902 to 1932. Holmes is regarded as one of America's greatest jurists. Often outvoted by his colleagues on the Court, he wrote 173 dissenting opinions during his tenure. Many of these influenced subsequent Courts to reverse verdicts.

Holmes was raised in Massachusetts, and attended Harvard University. He served with distinction in the Civil War before returning to Harvard Law School to train as a lawyer. He taught constitutional law (at Harvard) and edited the *American Law Review* before joining the Massachusetts Supreme Court in 1882, of which he was chief justice from 1899 to 1902. During this period Holmes wrote over 1000 legal opinions.

Holmes was nominated to the US Supreme Court by President Theodore ROOSEVELT. Holmes's reasoning proved finely tuned to the point of apparent inconsistency. One of his first decisions was to dissent from the majority opinion in NORTHERN SECURITIES VS. US (1904), which dissolved a railroad holding company on the grounds that it restrained trade. Holmes reasoned that the action against the holding company constituted an improper use of the SHERMAN ANTI-TRUST ACT. However, in SWIFT AND COMPANY VS. US (1905), Holmes contributed eloquently to an expansive reading of the Sherman Act by arguing that the notion of a 'current of commerce' justified its use to regulate the intrastate activities of meatpacking and other corporations involved in interstate commerce. Equally finely reasoned was Holmes's position on free speech. In 1919 Holmes wrote the majority opinion in the case of SCHENCK VS. US, which upheld the conviction of DRAFT protesters convicted under the ESPIONAGE ACT (1917). Holmes argued that Congress could abridge the right to free speech in wartime (through such measures as the Espionage Act) if there was a 'clear and present danger' that the exercise of free speech would bring about 'substantive evils that Congress has a right to prevent'. In the same year Holmes dissented from the majority in the case of ABRAMS VS. US by arguing that 'harmless' free speech enjoys protection even in wartime. His opinion in the Abrams case championed the notion that the FIRST AMENDMENT protects a free trade in ideas and that 'the best test of truth is the power of thought to get itself accepted in the competition of the market'. Holmes resigned from the Supreme Court on his 90th birthday.

Homestead Act (May 20 1862), legislation, passed over opposition from Democrats and from the border states, that allowed any settler to claim 160 acres (65 ha) of public land provided that he or she had lived on and farmed it for five years. A later amendment allowed Union veterans to set military service against the residency requirement. Registration fees apart, the land was 'free'. By 1865, 25,000 settlers had staked claim to some 3 million acres (1.2 million ha).

Homestead steel strike (1892), violent industrial dispute that marked a defining moment in the struggle between labor and capital in the late 19th-century USA.

Homestead, Pennsylvania, was the site of a complex of steel mills and company homes built in the 1880s by Andrew CARNEGIE. In an 1889 agreement with the workforce Carnegie recognized a CRAFT UNION formed by skilled workers, paid its members higher wages than those offered by rival companies and pegged the pay of his unskilled, non-union workers below that of the skilled workers.

But in 1892 Carnegie ordered his deputy Henry Clay Frick (1849–1919) to break the union. Frick fortified the complex, then, on July 2 1892, locked out the existing workforce and announced that only non-union laborers would be allowed back to work. Unable to persuade Homestead's non-union unskilled workers to abandon their unionized colleagues by returning to work on these new terms, Frick brought in strikebreakers. To protect the strikebreakers from intimidation he hired 300 PINKERTON agents. On July 5 several hundred strikers intercepted a convoy of Pinkerton men. In a ferocious gunfight nine strikers and seven agents were killed. This prompted the intervention of state militia, who protected strikebreakers and helped company officials evict strikers from company houses. The strike was called off on November 20. Leading unionists were blacklisted from the reopened plant.

Labor activists concluded from the strike that organization by skills should give way to organization by industry. However, the PULLMAN STRIKE (1894) showed that even well-organized INDUSTRIAL UNIONS could be defeated by determined employers backed by the force of the state.

Hooker, Joseph (1814–79), Union Army general. A career soldier, during the CIVIL WAR Hooker schemed to obtain command of the Union's Army of the Potomac, but proved unable to defeat Robert E. LEE.

After graduation from West Point Military Academy Hooker served with distinction in the MEXICAN WAR. At the outbreak of the Civil War he was appointed a brigadier general of volunteers. He distinguished himself at the battle of Williamsburg in the PENINSULAR CAMPAIGN, earning the nickname 'Fighting Joe'. He was promoted to brigadier general of the US Army following the battle of ANTIETAM, during which he was wounded.

In the winter of 1862–3 Hooker maneuvered to replace BURNSIDE in command of the Army of the Potomac. He also let it be known to newspaper reporters that he thought the Union needed a military dictator. Appointing Hooker to command on January 26 1863, LINCOLN told him, 'Only those generals who gain military successes can set up as dictators. What I ask of you now is military success, and I will risk the dictatorship.' Hooker's appointment raised the morale of the Army of the Potomac, but he proved unable to halt Lee's invasion of Maryland and Pennsylvania in the spring of 1863, and following defeat at the battle of CHANCELLORSVILLE Hooker asked to be relieved of command. For the remainder of the war he served under George Henry Thomas (1816–70) and SHERMAN in the southeastern theater.

Hoover, Herbert (Clark) (1874–1964), Republican statesman and 31st president of the USA (1929–33). Hoover's presidency coincided with by the worst years of the GREAT DEPRESSION. He was the first president to be born west of the Mississippi, and the first millionaire to occupy the White House.

Hoover majored in geology at Stanford University. He worked as a manual laborer in a gold mine before travelling as a mining engineer to Australia and China. He made his fortune from a silver mine in Burma. During World War I he directed agencies supplying humanitarian relief to Europe and, although he was a Republican, served on a number of the councils that President WILSON established to direct the US war effort. Hoover supported US membership of the LEAGUE OF NATIONS but criticized Wilson's tactics during the Senate debate on entry.

Hoover's instincts and talents were managerial. He served as secretary of commerce (1921–8) in the administrations of HARDING and COOLIDGE, before being nominated as the Republican's presidential candidate in 1928. During the campaign he praised the 'American system of rugged individualism' over European systems of 'state socialism'. Nonetheless, his past commitment to hum-

anitarian concerns secured him the endorsement of welfare campaigner Jane ADDAMS. He began his presidency on March 4 1929, a few months before the WALL STREET CRASH. Hoover misjudged the severity of the GREAT DEPRESSION. Although he created the RECONSTRUCTION FINANCE CORPORATION to assist ailing businesses, he was thought insufficiently sensitive to the plight of the poor, and by the time his presidency ended on March 3 1933 he was a largely discredited figure.

Hoover, J(ohn) Edgar (1895–1972), director of the FEDERAL BUREAU OF INVESTIGATION (FBI) from its founding in 1924 until his death. Through careful publicity and cautious innovation he established a popular image of the FBI as an incorruptible, indefatigable and scientific crime-fighting organization. Hoover expended the enormous influence public veneration of the Bureau gave him on a hunt for 'subversives' – especially communists – in all walks of American life.

Hoover's obsession with subversion first became apparent during the RED SCARE when, as a special assistant to the US attorney general, he put together secret dossiers on 60,000 left-wing activists. During the 1940s, 50s and 60s Hoover directed the FBI to compile secret files detailing the sexual and financial misdemeanors of the USA's political leaders. By the late 1950s the Bureau's commitment to the enforcement of civil rights legislation and the fight against organized crime was suffering as a result of this diversion of resources. The USA's political leaders, conscious that Hoover might hold material on them that would ruin their careers, declined to criticize public investigations (such as that mounted against Martin Luther KING) they privately believed to be misguided and out of touch with the public mood. (Robert KENNEDY was one of the few politicians prepared to risk a feud with Hoover.) Hoover wrote two books whose titles – *Persons in*

Hiding (1938) and *Masters of Deceit* (1958) – made perhaps unconscious reference to his own homosexuality and penchant for cross-dressing.

Hoovervilles, name given to shantytowns of homeless and destitute people that sprang up in most major US cities during the early years of the GREAT DEPRESSION. President HOOVER's response to the depression emphasized the restoration of business confidence rather than the alleviation of poverty; the term 'Hooverville' was coined to shame him into action.

Hopi, Native American PUEBLO PEOPLE, who have lived in settlements in northeastern Arizona since the 13th century. Although they suffered at the hands of the NAVAJO, the Hopi's sedentary lifestyle and remote homelands protected them from harassment by US settlers. In 1962 they were ordered to share 75% of a reservation granted to them in 1882 with their traditional enemy the Navajo. Some 9000 Hopi now live in northeastern Arizona.

Horseshoe Bend, battle of (March 27 1814), massacre in Alabama that ended the first CREEK WAR. A force of 3000 Tennessee militiamen and several hundred CHOCKTAW warriors, led by Andrew JACKSON, assaulted a CREEK fort on the Tallapoosa river. During the fighting 800 Creek men were shot or drowned, and 350 women carried off; 50 whites were killed.

House Un-American Activities Committee (HUAC), *see* DIES COMMITTEE.

'House divided' speech (June 17 1858), speech in which Abraham LINCOLN appeared to anticipate the coming CIVIL WAR. The occasion of the speech was Lincoln's announcement to an Illinois REPUBLICAN convention of his intention to run for the US Senate against DEMOCRAT Stephen DOUGLAS.

Lincoln's speech made memorable use of a biblical metaphor: '[Slavery agitation] has not only not ceased, but has constantly augmented. In my opinion it will not cease until a crisis has been reached and passed. A house divided against itself cannot stand. I believe this government cannot endure permanently half slave and half free – I expect [the house] will cease to be divided. It will become all one thing, or all the other.' The implications of this analysis were explored in the subsequent LINCOLN–DOUGLAS DEBATES.

House of Representatives, *see* CONGRESS.

Howe, Julia Ward (1819–1910), abolitionist and campaigner for WOMEN'S SUFFRAGE. Julia Ward married Samuel Gridley Howe (1801–76) in 1843. The couple co-edited the abolitionist newspaper *The Commonwealth*. During the 1850s the Howes gravitated to the extremist wing of the abolitionist movement (*see* ABOLITION). They gathered secret funds to aid the slave rebellion that John BROWN hoped to create through his raid on HARPER'S FERRY. In 1862 Julia adapted the words of 'John Brown's Body' to create 'The Battle Hymn of the Republic' ('Mine eyes have seen the glory of the coming of the Lord / He is trampling out the vintage where the grapes of wrath are stored'). She went on to help found the AMERICAN WOMAN SUFFRAGE ASSOCIATION and was the first woman elected to the American Academy of Arts and Sciences.

Howe, Sir William (1729–1814), commander in chief of British forces in America in the first three years of the Revolutionary War (1775–8). A veteran of the SEVEN YEARS' WAR, Howe commanded British forces at the battle of BUNKER HILL, defeated WASHINGTON at the battle of LONG ISLAND, and presided over the occupation of NEW YORK and PHILADELPHIA. He resigned in 1778, and became 5th Viscount Howe in 1799. His brother Richard, Earl Howe (1726–99), commanded British naval forces between 1776 and 1778.

HUAC, *see* DIES COMMITTEE.

Huelga, La, strike which was organized by Cesar CHAVEZ against exploitative Californian grape growers, and that played a crucial role in the development of CHICANO (Mexican-American) self-consciousness in the 1960s.

The strike began in 1965. Chavez, acting through the United Farm Workers Organizing Committee, urged Mexican and Mexican-American migrant workers to pursue non-violent protest in the face of physical intimidation. This generated support for a national boycott of Californian grapes, which, by 1970, had forced employers to grant standard contracts to about two-thirds of the grape-picking workforce. The strike generated comparisons with the African-American CIVIL RIGHTS MOVEMENT, and led student activists to develop an ideology of Hispanic self-assertion built around the concept of AZTLAN.

Hughes, Charles Evans (1862–1948), eleventh chief justice of the US Supreme Court. Hughes is the only man who has resigned from, but later rejoined, the Court.

Hughes was educated at Brown and Columbia universities, and from 1884 established a practice dealing with big business and public utility cases. His political beliefs placed him in the PROGRESSIVE wing of the REPUBLICAN PARTY, and in 1906 he was elected governor of New York. He was nominated to the Supreme Court in 1910 by President TAFT, but resigned in 1916 to fight as the Republican nominee in the presidential election. He lost to Woodrow WILSON by just 23 votes in the ELECTORAL COLLEGE and returned to his legal practice. President HARDING appointed Hughes secretary of state in 1921. During a five-year term of office Hughes's main achievement was to sponsor the disarmament agreed at the WASHINGTON NAVAL CONFERENCE (1921). President HOOVER nominated Hughes to serve as chief justice, a post he held from February 13 1930 until his retirement in 1941.

Hughes' second period on the Court, as chief justice, was dominated by the NEW DEAL and the COURT-PACKING CONTROVERSY. Hughes spoke for a unanimous court in the case of SCHECTER BROTHERS POULTRY CORPORATION VS. UNITED STATES, which ruled much of Franklin D. ROOSEVELT's landmark NATIONAL INDUSTRIAL RECOVERY ACT unconstitutional. However, Hughes cast the deciding vote, and wrote the majority opinion, that upheld the constitutionality of the WAGNER ACT in the case of NATIONAL LABOR RELATIONS BOARD VS. JONES AND LAUGHLIN STEEL CORPORATION (1937). Precisely because he did not believe the Supreme Court was implacably opposed to the aims of the New Deal, Hughes campaigned vigorously against Franklin Roosevelt's attempt to reorganize the Court in 1937.

Hull, Cordell (1871–1955), secretary of state (1933–44) under Franklin ROOSEVELT. Hull's eleven-year tenure as secretary of state is the longest on record. He was trained as a lawyer and served as a judge in Tennessee (1903–7) before entering the US House of Representatives as a Democrat (1907–21, 1923–31). In 1913 Hull helped to draft the legislation that reintroduced an INCOME TAX to the USA. He served one term in the Senate (1931–3) before being appointed secretary of state. Hull implemented Roosevelt's GOOD-NEIGHBOR POLICY towards Latin America. Like Roosevelt he was concerned by Hitler's rise to power, but was constrained by the strength of ISOLATIONIST sentiment in the USA. Hull felt personally betrayed by the attack on PEARL HARBOR because he had been involved in negotiations with Japanese diplomats throughout the fall of 1941. He was awarded the Nobel Peace Prize in 1945 for his efforts to establish the UNITED NATIONS.

Humphrey, Hubert H(oratio) (1911–78), Democratic statesman, vice president under Lyndon B. JOHNSON (1965–9) and the Democratic Party's nominee in the bitter PRESIDENTIAL ELECTION OF 1968. Humphrey was elected mayor of Minneapolis in 1945, and was US senator from Minnesota (1948–64). In the PRESIDENTIAL ELECTION OF 1948 he pushed TRUMAN to include in the

Democratic platform the civil rights planks that prompted the DIXIECRAT rebellion. As vice president, Humphrey was a staunch supporter of the GREAT SOCIETY. Following Eugene MCCARTHY's strong showing in the New Hampshire primary of March 1968, Johnson announced he would not seek re-election and made way for Humphrey. Although Humphrey was popular with organized labor and party chiefs, liberal Democratic activists loathed him for his failure to condemn the VIETNAM WAR. His nomination was overshadowed by the CHICAGO CONVENTION RIOTS. Humphrey's share of the POPULAR VOTE held up well, but he was decisively defeated in the ELECTORAL COLLEGE. He returned to the US Senate in 1970 and died in office.

hundred days, the, the first three months of President Franklin ROOSEVELT's first administration. During the 'hundred days' Roosevelt pressed Congress into an aston-ishing burst of legislative activity that estab-lished the foundations of the NEW DEAL. In 1935 Roosevelt ordered Congress to sit in a special summer session. Some historians describe this as a second 'hundred days'. In the 1960s members of President KENNEDY's administration referred to the 'thousand days' of the Kennedy presidency in an attempt to suggest the scale of their chief's accomplishment and highlight the tragedy of his assassination.

Hunkers, nickname given by BARNBURNERS (New York Democrats who supported Martin VAN BUREN) to their rivals for control of the state party machinery, whom they alleged were motivated by nothing more than 'hunker' (hunger) for office.

Hyde Amendment (1976), amendment to an appropriation bill to establish a blanket ban on the use of MEDICAID to reimburse the cost of an ABORTION. The amendment was made by Republican congressmen, led by Representative Henry Hyde of Illinois, in response to religious opposition to the ROE VS. WADE verdict liberalizing abortion law. The amendment passed the House by 207–164 on July 24 1976. The Senate amended Hyde's measure to allow Medic-aid funding for abortions performed to save a woman's life. Overriding President FORD's veto, Congress enacted the measure on Sep-tember 30. Hyde later chaired the House prosecution team in the IMPEACHMENT trial of President CLINTON.

I

Ia Drang Valley, battle of (November 14–18 1965), the first, and one of the largest, clashes between US and North Vietnamese troops in the VIETNAM WAR. In the summer of 1965 North Vietnam responded to President JOHNSON's accelerated deployment of US troops with a pre-emptive invasion of South Vietnam. In November some 10,000 North Vietnamese regulars trapped units of the US Air Cavalry in mountainous terrain some 250 miles (400 km) north of Saigon. Marshalling their superior air power, US forces drove the North Vietnamese back, killing 1770 soldiers. The engagement convinced North Vietnamese commanders to shift their emphasis toward guerrilla tactics.

ICC, the Interstate Commerce Commission (*see* INTERSTATE COMMERCE ACT).

Idaho, Rocky Mountain state bordered by Montana and Wyoming to the east, Utah and Nevada to the south, Oregon and Washington to the west and Canada to the north. The USA claimed title to the territory through the LOUISIANA PURCHASE. The LEWIS AND CLARK EXPEDITION (1803–6) traveled through the SHOSHONI and NEZ PERCÉ's homelands in Idaho but the first permanent US settlement in the region was established by the Rocky Mountain Fur Company in 1834. Followers of Brigham YOUNG established MORMON communities in Idaho in 1860, but the region did not attract sub-

stantial American settlement until after the discovery of gold at the head of the Snake river in 1861. The USA granted territorial status to Idaho, by detaching it from the jurisdiction of neighboring Washington, on March 4 1860. Further settlement was promoted by the extension of the nation's railroad network and the discovery of lead and substantial silver deposits in the vicinity of Coeur d'Alene in 1884. Idaho entered the Union as the 43rd state on July 3 1890. It granted women the right to vote in 1896.

Labor militancy in the state's mining industry was crushed by the imposition of martial law during the COEUR D'ALENE MINERS' STRIKE (1892). Many embittered miners subsequently joined the INDUSTRIAL WORKERS OF THE WORLD. Idaho was one the chief beneficiaries of the NATIONAL RECLAMATION Act (1902). Since 1945 a growth in tourism has further diversified the state's economy. In 1990 Idaho had 1,006,749 residents and was the 42nd most populous state. The state's most influential politician was probably William Borah (1865–1940). As a US senator, Borah 'the Lion of Idaho,' sponsored the SIXTEENTH and SEVENTEENTH AMENDMENTS and led the fight against the LEAGUE OF NATIONS and WOMEN'S SUFFRAGE.

'I have a dream' speech (August 28 1963), speech given by Martin Luther KING that legitimated the aspirations of the CIVIL RIGHTS MOVEMENT in the minds of Middle

Americans. The speech was an extemporized peroration given to participants in the MARCH ON WASHINGTON gathered at the Lincoln Memorial. King told the crowd that he dreamed of the day when 'all of God's children, black man and white man, Jew and Gentile, Protestant and Catholic, will be able to join hands and sing in the words of the old Negro spiritual, free at last, thank God almighty, I'm free at last. '

Illinois, midwestern state bordered to the north by Wisconsin and Lake Michigan, to the east by Indiana, to the south by Kentucky and Missouri, and to the west by Iowa and the Mississippi river. The first permanent European settlement in the territory was founded in the environs of present-day Chicago by the French Jesuit missionary and explorer Fr Jacques Marquette (1637–75) in December 1674. Further French fur-trading settlements were incorporated within the colony of Louisiana. Control of Illinois passed to Britain via the first treaty of PARIS (1763) and to the USA through a military expedition mounted by George Rogers CLARK during the REVOLUTIONARY WAR. Illinois was part of the NORTHWEST TERRITORY whose admission into the Union was laid out in the NORTHWEST ORDINANCE (1787). It became a US territory on February 9 1809 and became the 21st state on December 3 1818.

From 1820 to 1850 the state's population increased by 1,442%. It doubled in the 1850s alone, and by 1860 Illinois had over 1,700,000 permanent residents – 99% of them white. (The family of the state's most famous statesman, Abraham LINCOLN, were among the first wave of this great in-migration.) Agricultural land in Illinois was prized because the Mississippi river and Great Lakes system gave its farmers access to distant markets. With the exception of the BLACK HAWK WAR (1831–2), relations between settlers and native peoples were relatively peaceful – a factor further stimulating in-migration. Many of the state's

small farmers were inspired by FREE SOIL IDEOLOGY and, subsequently, by the REPUBLICAN party. Although the state contained a number of COPPERHEADS and a sizeable PEACE DEMOCRAT faction, Illinois sent 259,092 men to fight for the Union cause during the CIVIL WAR.

The diversification of the state's economy in the later 19th century was symbolized by Chicago's emergence as a major industrial and transportation center. The tensions accompanying this economic change were visible not only in the HAYMARKET RIOT, the PULLMAN STRIKE and Jane ADDAMS' work among Chicago's immigrants, but also in the support Illinois farmers gave to the GRANGER MOVEMENT and to POPULISM. In 1913 Illinois became the first state east of the Mississippi to grant the vote to women.

In the early 20th century, immigration from Europe – and later the GREAT MIGRATION of African-Americans from the south – further transformed the state. In common with other areas of the midwest, the concerns of communities such as the south-central Illinois town of Peoria grew increasingly detached from those of metropolitan Chicago. The question 'How will it play in Peoria?' – asked by opinion-formers in the 1940s and 50s – helped establish in the national consciousness an image of rural Illinois as an influential bastion of traditional midwestern values. In 1990 Illinois had 11,430,602 residents and was the sixth most populous state in the Union. Former Governors who achieved national prominence include John Peter ALTGELD (1893–7) and Adlai STEVENSON Jr (1949–52).

immigration. In 1790, the year the first federal census was taken, the population of the USA totalled 3,929,214. In 1920 that total stood at 105,710,620. The part played by immigration in this phenomenal increase can be gauged from the fact that the birth rate among the white population already resident in America declined over the course of the 19th century (from 55 live births per 1000 inhabitants in 1800 to 30 live births per 1000 in 1900). Much of the increase in the total population of the 19th-century USA is therefore attributable to immigration. From 1820 to 1920, 30 million immigrants entered the USA, with 15 million arriving in the period 1890–1920 alone. (These immigrants were overwhelmingly white. The Naturalization Act of 1790 precluded non-white persons from taking out citizenship.) Immigration on this scale transformed American society, making it a 'nation of nations'.

Ever since President CLEVELAND dedicated the STATUE OF LIBERTY in New York harbor on October 28 1886, Americans have tended to assume that their immigrant ancestors were pulled to the USA by the promise of American life rather than pushed out of their European and far eastern homelands by economic, political and demographic factors. However, it is important to remember that America was one destination among many chosen by emigrants seeking to escape unemployment or political repression. Structural developments within the shipping trade played a large part in pushing emigrants towards America. By the 1880s German and English steamships were offering a one-way ticket to America for as little as $8, and the journey took just over five days. The journey to Argentina or Australia was longer and more expensive. Cheap fares to America also made possible temporary emigration by young men who sought work in America but intended to return home when conditions suited them. All told, around 25% of all emigrants to the USA eventually returned to their homes or moved to another foreign country. On balance 'push' factors probably outweighed 'pull' factors in explaining 19th-century immigration.

Historians divide immigration to the USA into two phases. In the first phase Germany, Great Britain, Ireland and Scandinavia provided the bulk of emigrants. Just under 5 million Germans emigrated to the USA in the period 1790–1900, representing roughly 25% of all immigration into the USA in the period. Some 4 million Irish Catholics migrated to America in the period 1820–1900. In the decade following the great potato famine of 1846, British officials actively assisted Irish emigration to the USA. Between 1820 and 1900, 2 million Britons and 1 million Scandinavians settled in America. With the exception of the Catholic Irish, these immigrants assimilated relatively easily. They were predominantly Protestant and most were literate. They were used to living under constitutional forms of government and could draw on support and encouragement from descendants of earlier waves of immigrants from their home regions. However, the Catholic Irish were viewed with suspicion by 'old stock' Americans, and were subject to discrimination in employment and housing throughout the 19th century. Early NATIVIST campaigns, such as that launched by the KNOW NOTHING PARTY in 1849, attacked Irish immigrants' religion and supposed fondness for hard liquor.

A nativist backlash also characterized the response of many Americans to a second phase of immigration that began in the 1880s. Between 1885 and 1895 immigration from Russia and from southern and eastern Europe, rose rapidly. Of nearly 18 million immigrants to the USA in the period 1890–1917, only 3.5 million (20% of the total) came from the countries of northwestern Europe that had fueled the first phase of immigration. Between 1882 and 1924, 2.3 million Jewish immigrants entered America, most coming from Poland and Russia; between 1880 and 1914 just over 2 million Catholic Poles emigrated to America; and between 1880 and 1920 over 4 million Italian immigrants entered America. (Concealed within the total figures for Polish and Italian immigration were a large number of economic migrants, perhaps a quarter of the total, who eventually returned to Europe.) Although American employers and the US government encouraged Chinese men to migrate to the USA to take up short-term labor contracts, Chinese immigrants were victimized on the west coast of America precisely because they were 'birds of passage'. In 1882 over 100,000 Chinese men lived and worked in the western USA, and 9% of California's population was of Chinese origin. A vicious nativist campaign organized by such groups as the WORKINGMEN'S PARTY, and supported by Terrence POWDERLY and other labor leaders, induced Congress to pass the CHINESE EXCLUSION ACT in 1882. In the short term, passage of the Chinese Exclusion Act boosted Japanese emigration to Hawaii and mainland America. However, the Japanese government struck a 'gentleman's agreement' with the USA in 1900 that effectively ended Japanese immigration.

The new immigrants found it harder to assimilate than earlier immigrants had done. They did not enjoy that support from 'old stock' families that had helped British, German and Scandinavian settlers to adapt. Few of the new immigrants were Protestant. Most migrated to ethnic neighborhoods in the large industrial cities of the north, fueling nativist critiques of their lifestyles, and hindering their acquisition of the English language. Most new immigrants had previously lived under authoritarian regimes, and the willingness with which they embraced the message of groups such as the SOCIALIST PARTY OF AMERICA or the INDUSTRIAL WORKERS OF THE WORLD troubled American liberals. Although new immigrants played a vital role in the development of America's industrial economy, during the Progressive era of the late 19th and early 20th centuries (*see* PROGRESSIVISM), fears grew that the new immigration was changing the character of the nation.

In 1876 the US Supreme Court ruled that the individual states did not possess the power to regulate immigration. In CHAE CHAN PING VS. US (1889) the Supreme Court ruled that Congress possesses the sole and exclusive authority to admit foreigners to US residence. Pressure on Congress to enact some form of immigration control grew during the first two decades of the 20th century, and during the RED SCARE following US entry in WORLD WAR I and the Russian Revolution, it became unopposable. The EMERGENCY QUOTA ACT (1921) stipulated that no more than 357,000 immigrants from Europe would be admitted to America in a single year. Under the act no European country was permitted to send to the USA more than 3% of the total number of its natives residing in America in 1910. The NATIONAL ORIGINS ACT (1924) lowered the permitted annual total of immigrants to 164,000 (150,000 after 1927), and sharpened the bias against new immigrants by excluding all persons of Asian descent and limiting individual European nations to a quota of no more than 2% of the total number of their natives residing in America in 1890. In 1929 Congress permitted US immigration officials to deny entry visas to persons liable to become a charge on the public. The era of mass European and Asian immigration was over.

The Emergency Quota Act and the National Origins Act set no limit on immigration from Mexico and Central America. Some 5 million BRACEROS (seasonal workers) undertook annual migrations to the USA in the 1940s and 1950s. The Immigration Reform Act of 1965 permits no more than 20,000 Mexican immigrants a year to take up permanent residence in the USA. However, by one estimate over 3 million Mexicans entered the USA between 1971 and 1991, and many stayed after their temporary entry visas had expired.

Occasionally the US government relaxes its immigration policy in response to political pressure. In 1948 President TRUMAN ordered the immigration service to issue entry visas to 42,000 Europeans orphaned or displaced during World War II (a quota later raised to 341,000). Truman's gesture was conditioned in part by growing anger over the refusal of Franklin D. ROOSEVELT's administration to allow more than a handful of Jewish victims of Nazi persecution entry to the USA in the 1930s. Under the National Origins Act no more than 26,000 Germans were permitted to enter the USA annually. As evidence of the Nazi campaign against German Jews began to emerge in the 1930s, Senator Robert Wagner proposed raising that quota to 200,000. Roosevelt let the proposal die in committee, a move supported by organized labor and many congressmen. In May 1939 the steamship *St Louis* left Hamburg carrying 937 mainly Jewish refugees. In what developed into the so-called 'voyage of the damned', these refugees were denied entry to Cuba and the USA and were returned to Europe, where many of them perished in concentration camps. More recently the USA has amended its immigration policy to accommodate refugees fleeing from the communist countries of Southeast Asia and Cuba. Between 1978 and 1984, 443,000 Vietnamese, 137,000 Laotians and 98,000 Cambodians emigrated to the USA. In 1980 Cuban authorities turned a blind eye to attempts by their citizens to cross the Florida straits and seek asylum in America – indeed, Castro added criminals and mental patients to the exodus. President CARTER, hoping to gain votes among Hispanic-Americans, ordered the Immigration Service to grant entry visas to these so-called Marielistas; 125,000 arrived in Florida in the space of three months before Carter amended the policy. But political pressure from the Cuban-America lobby forced a reinterpretation of immigration quotas that permitted 159,000 Cubans to take up permanent residence in the USA between 1981 and 1990.

In 1994, 8.7% of the USA population was foreign-born. This figure represents a decline on the comparable figure for 1920 (13.2%), but suggests the continuing significance of immigration in the shaping of US society.

impeachment, prosecution of a president, vice-president or other 'civil officers' brought by the House of Representatives and tried by the Senate.

Article II Section 4 of the US Constitution stipulates that 'the President, Vice-President and all civil officers of the United States shall be removed from office on impeachment for, and conviction of, treason, bribery, or other high crimes and misdemeanours'. Article I Section 3 specifies that impeachment cases must be tried before the US Senate, that conviction requires a two-thirds majority of the Senators present and that, when a president is impeached, the chief justice of the Supreme Court should preside over his trial. It is the task of the House Judiciary Committee to frame articles of impeachment. The full House of Representatives must approve the articles before an impeachment trial in the Senate can proceed.

Only two presidents, Andrew JOHNSON and Bill CLINTON, have undergone an impeachment trial. Richard NIXON resigned to avoid impeachment proceedings. Andrew Johnson escaped impeachment on any of the eleven charges arising from his alleged violations of the TENURE OF OFFICE ACT by one vote. Seven Republican senators voted against party lines, thus denying their colleagues the two-thirds majority necessary to impeach. Clinton is the only elected president to face, and survive, impeachment proceedings. On February 12 1999 the Senate voted 55–45 against impeaching him for perjury committed during the LEWINSKY SCANDAL. The Senate also voted 50–50 on an impeachment charge that he obstructed justice to suppress the scandal.

implied powers, all powers that the federal government may exercise that are implicit within, and not forbidden by, the Constitution, according to LOOSE CONSTRUCTIONISTS of the Constitution throughout American history. The first example of an 'implied powers' reading of the Constitution was Alexander HAMILTON's defense of his decision to create the BANK OF THE UNITED STATES. LINCOLN made ambitious use of the doctrine when he asserted, in his inaugural address, that SECESSION was unconstitutional because 'Perpetuity is implied if not expressed in the fundamental law of all national governments. It is safe to assert that no government proper ever had a provision in its organic law for its own termination.'

impressment, the Royal Navy's former right to coerce or 'impress' sailors and landsmen into its service. During the 18th and early 19th centuries the Royal Navy stopped American ships, seized deserters from the British service (often on flimsy evidence), and impressed even American-born crewmen. The practice was a major cause of the WAR OF 1812.

inaugural addresses, public speeches to the American people given by US presidents immediately after taking the oath of office. The custom was established by George WASHINGTON, and soon imitated by state governors. Since then inaugural addresses have varied greatly in length and quality.

Washington's second inaugural address (March 4 1793) consisted of just 135 words, and is the shortest on record. On March 4 1841 William Henry HARRISON spoke for 1 hour 40 minutes, mainly in support of freedom of the press. He caught pneumonia and died a month later. Franklin PIERCE delivered his address from memory, but most presidents, striving to strike a statesmanlike note, read from a prepared script.

Presidents often use inaugural addresses to appeal for national unity. Thomas JEFFERSON's first inaugural address (delivered on March 4 1801) urged Americans to put aside party distinctions because 'every difference of opinion is not a difference of principle'. On March 4 1825 John Quincy

ADAMS made a similar and particularly eloquent plea for Americans to put aside party rancor. However, other presidents have used their inaugural addresses to advertise their commitment to controversial policies. On March 4 1829 Martin VAN BUREN announced his determination to oppose the ABOLITION of slavery in the District of Columbia. Grover CLEVELAND's second inaugural address (March 4 1893) fanned the SILVER– GOLD CONTROVERSY with its announcement that 'nothing is more vital to our supremacy as a nation than a sound and stable currency'.

Inaugural addresses often provide examples of wishful thinking. On March 4 1897 William McKINLEY announced 'we want no wars of conquest, we must avoid the temptation of territorial aggression'; by the end of his term, McKinley had fought the SPANISH-AMERICAN WAR, and was presiding over the US occupation of the Philippines and Cuba. Wishful thinking and condescension have been particularly evident in inaugural pronouncements on race relations. On March 4 1881 James GARFIELD told America that 'the elevation of the Negro race from slavery to the full rights of citizenship is the most important political change we have known since the adoption of the Constitution of 1787'. On March 4 1909 William Howard TAFT opined cheerily: 'The progress which the Negro has made in the last fifty years from slavery ... is marvellous, and it furnishes every reason to hope that in the next twenty-five years a still greater improvement in his condition ... may come. The Negroes are now Americans.' Occasionally presidents have difficulty expressing their ideas. On January 20 1989 George BUSH told Americans: 'This is a time when the future seems like a door you can walk right through into a room called tomorrow.'

But on at least three occasions presidents have given inaugural addresses that continue to inspire. On March 4 1865

Abraham LINCOLN asked Americans to begin the work of RECONSTRUCTION 'with malice toward none, with charity for all, with firmness in the right as God gives us to see the right, let us strive on to finish the work we are in, to bind up the nation's wounds'. On March 4 1933 Franklin D. ROOSEVELT, assuming office in the depths of the GREAT DEPRESSION, stated 'my firm belief that the only thing we have to fear is fear itself'. On January 20 1961 John F. KENNEDY challenged Americans to 'Ask not what your country can do for you – ask what you can do for your country.'

income tax. Congress imposed the first US income tax in August 1861 as an emergency measure to raise money to fight the CIVIL WAR. The tax was set at 3% of annual income in excess of $800, and 10% of annual income in excess of $10,000. (The CONFEDERACY also levied an income tax during the war.) The federal income tax was retained after the war, but in 1895 the US Supreme Court, ruling by 5–4 on the case of Pollock vs. Farmers' Loan and Trust Company, found federal income taxes to be unconstitutional; the Court reasoned that Article I Section 9 of the US Constitution prevents Congress from levying a direct tax without reference to the population of the individual states. Both POPULISM and PROGRESSIVISM fueled calls for a constitutional amendment to permit Congress to impose a federal income tax. The SIXTEENTH AMENDMENT, which took effect on February 1913, gave Congress the necessary constitutional authority. The reintroduction of a federal income tax through the Underwood–Simmons Tariff Bill of October 1913 was achieved with relatively little political cost because 95% of the American population was exempt from paying it. However, as more Americans were drawn into the federal tax system, tax became a potent political issue. In the 1980s President REAGAN cut rates of federal income tax in the hope of stimulating the USA's economic development. This proposition proved so popular with the American public that Walter MONDALE suffered a landslide defeat in the presidential election of 1984 for daring to suggest that Federal income tax cuts would be reversed. Since Mondale's defeat, US politicians have sought to lessen the proportion of government expenditure raised by taxes on personal incomes.

Independent Treasury Act (1840, 1846), legislation transferring the management of surplus US funds from the 'pet banks' founded in the individual states following Andrew JACKSON's destruction of the second BANK OF THE UNITED STATES to the US Treasury. The Act also committed the US government to conduct business only in SPECIE. The act was the cornerstone of President VAN BUREN's response to the DEPRESSION OF 1837. It was passed on June 30 1840, repealed in 1841, but reenacted in 1846. WHIGS opposed the transfer because they believed that the distribution of US funds among state banks would help realize Henry CLAY's AMERICAN SYSTEM. Most DEMOCRATS, reluctant to place government money in private institutions, supported the act. The Treasury, and subtreasury depositories in major cities, managed US finances until the creation of the FEDERAL RESERVE SYSTEM (1913).

Indiana, midwestern state bordered to the north by Michigan, to the east by Ohio, to the south by Kentucky and to the west by Illinois. The first permanent European settlement in the territory was founded by French fur traders at Fort Ouiatonon in 1719. Control of Indiana passed to Britain via the first treaty of PARIS (1763) and later to the USA through a military expedition mounted by George Rogers CLARK during the REVOLUTIONARY WAR. Indiana was part of the NORTHWEST TERRITORY whose admission into the Union was laid out in the NORTHWEST ORDINANCE (1787). White settlement of southern Indiana began in earnest following the first treaty of GREENVILLE (1795). Indiana was organized as a US territory on May 7 1800 and entered the Union as the 19th state on December 11 1816.

From 1820 to 1860 the state's population increased by 817%. By the eve of the Civil War Indiana had over a million permanent residents and was the fifth most populous state in the Union. Many in-migrants subscribed to FREE SOIL IDEOLOGY, and Indiana was among a number of midwestern states that barred free blacks from settling within its borders. The state's electorate swung toward the REPUBLICAN party in the 1850s and Indiana eventually supplied 196,363 soldiers for the Union army. Nevertheless during the Civil War many residents supported the PEACE DEMOCRATS and the COPPERHEADS.

Indiana was slower to industrialize than some of its neighbors. In 1900 66% of the state's population lived in rural areas and just 6% were foreign born. European immigrants were drawn to towns in the north of the state by jobs in mines, steel-mills and food-processing plants. Nevertheless Indiana's economic development never produced a metropolis comparable to Chicago, Illinois, Detroit, Michigan or Cleveland, Ohio. In 1990 Indiana had 5,544,159 residents and was the 14th most populous state in the Union. 'Native sons' who have achieved national prominence include the politicians Benjamin HARRISON, Albert BEVERIDGE and Dan QUAYLE.

Indian Claims Commission, commission established on August 13 1946 to investigate and settle grievances caused by US violations of treaties signed with Native American peoples. The creation of the commission reflected the continuing influence of John COLLIER's 'Indian new deal' and gratitude for the contribution made by Native Americans to the US effort in World War II. Between 1946 and 1978 when it was disbanded, the commission heard over 600 cases, settled 400 in Native American plain-

tiffs' favor, and awarded $800 million in compensation.

Indian Removal Act (May 28 1830), legislation by which Congress appropriated $500,000 to remove the FIVE CIVILIZED TRIBES from lands they owned in the southeastern USA. The measure, which had the strong support of President JACKSON, involved relocating the Native Americans affected to RESERVATIONS situated in regions west of the Mississippi known to Americans at the time as the 'great American desert' (present-day Kansas and Oklahoma). Relocation, which was implemented despite the Supreme Court's ruling in WORCESTER VS. GEORGIA, resulted in the loss of at least 3000 lives and the destruction of internal government within the Native American nations. The CHEROKEE dubbed the route of their forced march westwards to the unfamiliar plains the TRAIL OF TEARS. Seminole resistance to relocation was crushed in a second SEMINOLE WAR.

Indian Springs, treaty of (February 12 1825), treaty by which Georgia bought 7300 square miles (18,900 square km) of territory from CREEK leaders. Many Creeks contested their leaders' authority to conclude the sale. President John Quincy ADAMS sympathized, and revised the treaty. Georgia refused to accept his mediation, and threatened to use state militia to enforce the original purchase.

Industrial Relations, Commission on, *see* COMMISSION ON INDUSTRIAL RELATIONS.

industrial unions, trade unions that offered membership to all workers in an industry, regardless of their skill, job description, ethnicity and, to some extent, race. In contrast CRAFT UNIONS offered membership only to men with a particular skill.

Formed in the 1890s, the AMERICAN RAILWAY UNION (ARU) and UNITED MINE WORKERS OF AMERICA (UMWA) were among the first industrial unions. A key figure in the foundation of industrial unionism was Eugene DEBS, the ARU's first president. Mass recruitment gave strikes and boycotts mounted by industrial unions great force. However, the PULLMAN STRIKE (1894) demonstrated that, when faced with an effective industry-wide strike, federal government cited the national interest to cooperate with employers in its suppression.

Legal impediments slowed the organization of industrial workers before World War I. Recruitment languished again following the STEEL STRIKE OF 1919. But the GREAT DEPRESSION and the WAGNER ACT (1935) stimulated efforts to unionize production-line workers, and led to the creation (in 1938) of the CONGRESS OF INDUSTRIAL ORGANIZATIONS (CIO), a breakaway group from the largely craft-based AMERICAN FEDERATION OF LABOR (AFL). At the same time, during the 1930s, production-line workers (particularly in the rabidly anti-union car industry) expressed through SIT-DOWN STRIKES a militancy that leading advocates of industrial unionism, such as CIO president John L. LEWIS of the UMWA, often struggled to contain. Greater prosperity after World War II, and the anti-union TAFT–HARTLEY ACT (1947), witnessed a decline in industrial-union militancy, and in 1955 the AFL and the CIO merged.

Industrial Workers of the World (IWW), anarcho-syndicalist organization founded in June 1905 by William Haywood (1869–1928), Eugene DEBS and Daniel De Leon (1852–1914). The IWW or 'Wobblies' sought to build a political movement capable of overthrowing capitalism from among the ranks of radicalized trade-union members. In keeping with this tactic IWW activists supported strikers abandoned or ignored by the AMERICAN FEDERATION OF LABOR. IWW activists played a particularly important support role in the LAWRENCE TEXTILE STRIKE, and were a strong presence in the Colorado coalfields before and after the LUDLOW MASSACRE. The IWW's leadership advocated forceful but non-violent protest. Nevertheless, IWW activists were frequently beaten up and sometimes lynched by company guards and state authorities. The organization fielded electoral candidates of its own, but also supported Eugene Debs's presidential bids, whether as an independent in 1900 or on behalf of the SOCIALIST PARTY OF AMERICA in 1904, 1908, 1912 and 1920. Membership of the IWW peaked at 100,000 in 1915. Following US entry into WORLD WAR I and during the subsequent RED SCARE, the US government used legislation such as the ESPIONAGE ACT to intimidate and disrupt the Wobblies. By the 1930s the organization had virtually ceased to exist.

In Re Debs (1895), US Supreme Court verdict that upheld a conviction for obstructing the mail against Eugene DEBS, president of the AMERICAN RAILWAY UNION. More importantly, it legitimated the legal tactic by which railroad executives broke the PULLMAN STRIKE (1894). The strike revolved around a union boycott of Pullman coaches. Rail bosses attached mail cars to trains containing Pullman coaches and then argued for court injunctions against the strikers, on the grounds that their protest violated the SHERMAN ANTI-TRUST ACT and interfered with the distribution of mail. By ruling that the Sherman Act could be used to issue injunctions against unions, the Supreme Court confirmed Debs's sentence and made regional strikes all but impossible to mount. Debs spent six months in jail.

Interstate Commerce Act (February 4 1887), legislation that created the Interstate Commerce Commission (ICC), the first federal regulatory body in US history. After the Civil War, railroad companies adopted a number of practices (including rate-fixing, pooling arrangements, and charging more for short-haul than for long-haul freight journeys) that were detrimental to the interests of small farmers in rural areas. In the 1870s a number of midwestern states passed GRANGER LAWS regulating railroad freight charges and business practices. But the US Supreme Court's decision in WABASH,

ST LOUIS AND PACIFIC RAILROAD COMPANY VS. ILLINOIS (1886) stripped states of their regulatory powers.

A Senate investigation of railroad pricing policies heightened demand for federal action. The Interstate Commerce Act stipulated that freight charges on lines passing through more than one state be 'reasonable and just'. The Interstate Commerce Commission was empowered to investigate pricing structures, but it could not set rates. By the 1890s most rail companies had found ways of evading the act's restrictions. Regulation of interstate commerce was tightened up by the HEPBURN ACT (1906).

Interstate Commerce Commission, see INTERSTATE COMMERCE ACT.

Intolerable Acts, collective name given by American colonists during the AMERICAN REVOLUTION to four measures passed by the British Parliament: the ADMINISTRATION OF JUSTICE ACT (May 20 1774), BOSTON PORT BILL (May 31 1774), MASSACHUSETTS GOVERNMENT ACT (May 20 1774) and QUARTERING ACT (June 2 1774).

These measures, passed in the aftermath of the BOSTON TEA PARTY (1773), were deemed intolerable because they stripped Massachusetts of the essentials of democratic self-government and judicial independence. Considering the package in conjunction with the QUEBEC ACT (June 22 1774), Americans throughout the THIRTEEN COLONIES concluded that Britain had a 'settled design' to strip them of liberties that were the birthright of all Englishmen. Hence, although directed against Massachusetts, the measures prompted the first CONTINENTAL CONGRESS to adopt the CONTINENTAL ASSOCIATION to force their repeal.

Iowa, midwestern state bordered to the north by Minnesota, to the east by Wisconsin, Illinois and the Mississippi river, to the south by Missouri, and to the west by Nebraska and South Dakota. The first permanent European settlement in the territory was made near Dubuque by French lead miners in 1788. The USA acquired Iowa from France in the LOUISIANA PURCHASE. Initially under the jurisdiction of Wisconsin, Iowa was organized as a US territory on June 12 1838. It became the 29th state on December 28 1846.

Although native peoples offered little resistance, US settlement of the state proceeded slowly in the period before the Civil War. In 1860 Iowa possessed 674,139 permanent residents. Helped in part by passage of the HOMESTEAD ACT (1862), the state's population soared to 2,231,853 in 1900. Farmers who migrated to Iowa in this period suffered from falling commodity prices and a series of droughts. They supported the GRANGER MOVEMENT and POPULISM. Hard times continued in the 20th century, and between 1920 and 1950 over 400,000 Iowans, most of them farmers, left the state. In the early 20th century Iowans developed a doughty, often left-leaning, political culture that somewhat belies the state's popular image as the quintessential midwestern state. Aspiring presidential candidates, especially Democrats, ignore the views of Iowans at their peril, since caucuses held in the state to apportion delegates to the national parties' conventions occur at the start of the presidential election year. Success or failure in the Iowa caucuses can therefore make or break a campaign for the White House. In 1990 Iowa had 2,776,755 permanent residents and was the 30th most populous state in the Union. The state's famous 'native sons' include BUFFALO BILL and Herbert HOOVER.

Iran–Contra scandal, scandal during REAGAN's presidency involving illegal arms sales to Iran, the proceeds of which were used illegally to fund the Contras, the right-wing guerrillas attempting to seize power from the left-wing government in Nicaragua. Evidence that officials within the Reagan administration had been engaged in this extraordinary subversion of constitutional government began to emerge in 1986. Reagan escaped IMPEACHMENT because, unlike the WATERGATE SCANDAL, the Iran–Contra scandal revolved around events overseas, and because, unlike Nixon, Reagan was a popular president.

Despite the protestations of Reagan loyalists that the scandal was an unplanned aberration, its roots lay in three concerns that were absolutely central to the worldview of the Reagan team. During the presidential election of 1980 Reagan had criticized CARTER's handling of the IRANIAN HOSTAGE CRISIS by suggesting that, unlike Carter, he would take swift action against terrorists. Once in office, Reagan repeated his pledge that he would never negotiate with terrorists. But in the early 1980s terrorist groups supported by Iran carried out a series of attacks on US civilians and military personnel, and took hostage several US citizens resident in Lebanon. Reagan wished to avoid comparisons with the 'impotence' of the Carter administration, while at the same time honoring his pledge to forswear negotiation with terrorists.

A second key ingredient of the scandal was Reagan's commitment to a COLD WAR, anti-communist, foreign-policy agenda. In 1979 left-wing Sandinistas, led by Daniel Ortega, had toppled a US-backed dictatorship in Nicaragua and established a pro-communist regime. Reagan officials eagerly approved a CIA plan to overthrow the Sandinistas by funding and training 'the Contras' (a right-wing Nicaraguan militia with a dubious human-rights record). Reagan officials appealed to the MONROE DOCTRINE, the DOMINO THEORY and the precedent set by Cuba to suggest that the Sandinista regime in Nicaragua posed a threat to vital US strategic interests. But in 1982 Congress passed the Boland Amendment, blocking the use of US funds for any activity designed to 'overthrow the government of Nicaragua'. The wording of the amendment was tightened in 1984.

Passage of the Boland Amendment triggered the third key ingredient of the scandal. Reagan had campaigned as a self-styled 'outsider' who was determined to prevent a bloated Washington establishment from thwarting the will of the people. Key members of the Reagan administration regarded the Boland Amendment as an example of congressional obstruction. Reagan's threefold desires – to take decisive action against terrorism, communism and government inertia – were well known to his staff, and helped to produce the scandal that tarnished his presidency.

From August 1985 to October 1986 agents of the US government made covert arms sales worth $48 million to Iran, which at that time was at war with Iraq. In return Iran promised to use its influence to secure the release of Western hostages held in the Middle East. The cash from the arms sales was to be diverted to the Contras, in violation of the Boland Amendment. The sales and cash transfers were conducted by an amateurish and venal team of intermediaries loosely under the control of National Security Council Adviser John Poindexter and his aide Lieutenant Colonel Oliver North. On January 6 and 17 1986 Reagan signed documents (later destroyed) apparently approving covert arms shipments to Iran. Three hostages were freed (although three more were taken), and some $10 million reached the Contras before the deal became public in November 1986.

The Reagan administration at first attempted a cover-up. Poindexter, North and North's secretary, Fawn Hall, destroyed incriminating documents. Reagan himself denied that he had sought to swap arms for hostages, and claimed to be unaware that proceeds from the arms sales were diverted to the Contras. A congressional committee investigated the matter from May to July 1987. Poindexter told investigators that he had destroyed documents signed by Reagan and withheld from him the existence of cash transfers to the Contras because he wished to provide the president with 'plausible deniability'. North, in full dress uniform, presented himself during the nationally televised hearings as an unswerving patriot whose job it was to interpret the president's wishes and to act on them without waiting for specific orders. His testimony suggested that the Iran–Contra connection was a first step toward the creation of a 'stand-alone' covert action team designed to circumvent congressional oversight.

Congress contented itself with criticizing Reagan's management style, and cited violations of the law so technical that they did not ignite calls for impeachment proceedings. Reagan appointed a special prosecutor, Lawrence Walsh, to investigate criminal charges against the main players. North was charged with conspiracy, but that indictment was dropped when Reagan refused to release classified documents central to the prosecution case. On May 4 1989 North was convicted on the lesser charge of obstructing a congressional investigation, but the conviction was thrown out on appeal. On April 4 1990 Poindexter was convicted of obstructing Congress and making false statements. Reagan survived in office, but his reputation was badly damaged.

Iranian hostage crisis (November 4 1979–January 20 1981), seizure of the staff of the US embassy in Teheran by militant Iranian Shiite Muslims. The episode influenced the outcome of the presidential election of 1980, because US public opinion took the view that President CARTER's handling of it showed him to be ineffectual.

On October 22 1979 Carter allowed the former Shah of Iran to enter the USA for medical treatment. Shiite militants stormed the US embassy in Teheran in protest, seizing its staff. On the orders of Ayatollah Khomeini, the leader of the Islamic Revolution in Iran, all black and female embassy personnel were released, but the remaining 52 hostages faced trial as spies.

Carter froze Iranian assets in the USA, imposed economic sanctions on Iran and expelled all Iranian diplomats. On April 24 1980 he authorized a military rescue mission, which failed when inadequately equipped US helicopters crashed in the desert. Two US aircraft collided as the survivors of the rescue mission were being withdrawn, killing eight servicemen. This debacle seemed to legitimate Ronald REAGAN's call for a massive increase in military expenditure. In a final humiliation for Carter, Iran released the hostages (in return for access to their frozen assets in the USA) on the day Reagan was inaugurated as president.

ironclad oath, proposed oath that would have excluded any former supporters of the CONFEDERACY from participating in RECONSTRUCTION. Under the terms of the WADE–DAVIS BILL of 1864 (subjected to a POCKET VETO by President LINCOLN), the states of the Confederacy would be readmitted to the Union only when a majority of their white inhabitants had sworn an oath of allegiance and when state conventions had drawn up new constitutions repudiating SECESSION and embracing emancipation. To participate in constitutional conventions, whether as a voter or delegate, individuals were required to swear a second, 'ironclad', oath that they had never voluntarily aided the Confederacy. This would have excluded from Reconstruction men who had opposed secession but who had felt compelled to support their state in war. The issue of the oath symbolized the growing disagreement between LINCOLN and RADICAL REPUBLICAN congressmen over Reconstruction policies.

Iroquois Confederacy, alliance of northeastern Native American peoples, reputedly formed by the Onondaga sachem Hiawatha in the 15th century. The alliance brought together the MOHAWK, Oneida, Onondaga, Cayuga, SENECA and ultimately the Tuscarora nations in a confederacy that used diplomacy and trade to limit white expansion in western New York State and lands south of Lake Erie.

Members of the Confederacy renounced war with one another but pursued separate policies in wars involving Europeans and Americans. During the SEVEN YEARS' WAR the Seneca fought with the French against the British, while the remainder of the Confederacy was neutral or pro-British. During the REVOLUTIONARY WAR, the Mohawk, led by Joseph Brant (1742–1807), broke ranks with the Confederacy and fought against the USA. This prompted SULLIVAN'S CAMPAIGN of retaliation and the punitive second treaty of FORT STANWIX (1784) through which the Confederacy was broken. Following the treaty members of the Confederacy were relocated on reservations.

isolationism, the recurrent desire of Americans to avoid involvement in overseas affairs. In his farewell address, published on September 17 1796, George WASHINGTON advised Americans that 'The great rule of conduct for us in regard to foreign nations is to have with them as little political connection as possible.' This fear of what JEFFERSON dubbed 'entangling alliances' with foreign nations, which was perhaps understandable in the light of GENÊT'S MISSION and the QUASI-WAR with France, has informed isolationist sentiment ever since. Another source of isolationist sentiment is the idea that, since the USA is a purer and more principled nation than any other on earth, it cannot gain and will only lose from close involvement with older countries. (By the same token imperialists, such as Senator Albert BEVERIDGE, appealed to the USA's supposed moral superiority to justify the acquisition of overseas territory.) In the period 1914–17, US groups and individuals, among them the WOMEN'S PEACE PARTY and Henry FORD, believed they could broker a settlement to WORLD WAR I which would restore civilization to its senses. The failure of such efforts led many Americans to conclude that their nation's interest was best served by isolation from the conflict. Even some Americans who had supported US intervention in the war concluded from the carnage of the Western front that the USA should in the future have as little to do with the 'old world' as possible. Isolationist sentiment was strongly expressed during the battle over the LEAGUE OF NATIONS. Although the USA did not join the League of Nations, it did not completely isolate itself from world affairs in the aftermath of World War I. Woodrow WILSON ordered US troops to occupy SIBERIA in 1918, Warren HARDING sponsored the WASHINGTON NAVAL CONFERENCE (1921) and the USA signed the KELLOGG–BRIAND PACT in 1928. Nevertheless, Congress passed three Neutrality Acts between 1935 and 1937. The 1937 Act allowed the president to forbid warring nations from purchasing arms and material from the USA. President Franklin D. ROOSEVELT could not afford to ignore the strength of isolationist sentiment the passage of such legislation signified. In the 1940 presidential election campaign Roosevelt challenged the spirit of the Neutrality Acts by offering to provide Britain and France with all aid short of war, but still felt it necessary to pledge that he would not send 'American boys' to fight overseas in WORLD WAR II. It took the Japanese attack on PEARL HARBOR to swing US public opinion unequivocally behind support for US involvement in the war. During the COLD WAR the USA, acting on the precepts of CONTAINMENT and the TRUMAN DOCTRINE, set its face against isolationism by joining the NORTH ATLANTIC TREATY ORGANIZATION.

Iwo Jima, battle of (February 19 1945– March 16 1945), engagement during WORLD WAR II in which US forces captured the tiny Japanese island of Iwo Jima, in the Volcano Islands. Iwo Jima was strategically important because it was only 750 miles (1200 km) south of Tokyo and could be used as a base for US fighters to escort bomber attacks on the home islands. The USA committed three divisions of Marines to the assault: nearly 6000 were killed and 19,000 wounded. The seizure of Iwo Jima represented a great feat of arms and produced one of the most evocative images of the war: a celebrated photograph of four Marines raising the American flag on Mount Suribachi. The USA administered Iwo Jima and the other Volcano Islands until they were returned to Japan in 1968.

IWW, *see* INDUSTRIAL WORKERS OF THE WORLD.

J

Jackson, Andrew (1767–1845), military hero, Democratic statesman and 7th president of the USA (1829–37). Jackson pursued a personal brand of popular nationalism that came to be known be known as JACKSONIAN DEMOCRACY. He extended the powers of the presidency and, with his supporters, transformed the DEMOCRATIC party.

Jackson was born in the backwoods of South Carolina. During the REVOLUTIONARY WAR he was captured and imprisoned by the British. He also lost all but one of his immediate family in the fighting. In 1787 he was admitted to the North Carolina bar and in 1788 he moved to the Tennessee territory. Jackson was elected to the Tennessee state constitutional convention, and went on to represent the state in the US House of Representatives (1796–7) and US Senate (1797–8). During this period, Jackson established a reputation as an impulsive, passionate man. In 1791 he 'married' his beloved Rachel Donelson Robards (1767–1828) without waiting for her divorce from an insanely jealous husband to be finalized. Even after the couple's marriage was put on a regular legal footing in 1794, Jackson defended his wife's honor in several duels. Meanwhile Jackson was also acquiring land and slaves in Tennessee. His plantation, Hermitage, ultimately became one of the more profitable cotton producing concerns in the state.

Jackson acquired regional and then national fame through military service. He commanded Tennessee militia units in the CREEK and SEMINOLE wars. Commissioned into the US army at the conclusion of the WAR OF 1812, he led US troops to victory over the British at the battle of NEW ORLEANS (1815). As military governor of the Florida territory, he presided over the further subjugation of the Seminole nation in 1821. These actions cemented Jackson's reputation as 'Old Hickory': a manly, straight-talking, western democrat. When Jackson was defeated in the presidential election of 1824, his supporters alleged that their man had been done down in a CORRUPT BARGAIN struck by elitist politicians. Although he was a slaveholding plantation owner, small farmers and urban workers saw in Jackson an anti-establishment figure. He won the presidential election of 1828 with a 56% share of the popular vote and a 2 to 1 advantage over incumbent John Quincy ADAMS in the electoral college.

During his two terms as president, Jackson generally pursued a STRICT CONSTRUCTIONIST interpretation of the Constitution. This perspective was demonstrated in the MAYSVILLE ROAD VETO, through which Jackson overrode Henry CLAY's attempt to develop a federally sponsored system of internal improvements, and in Jackson's opposition to the rechartering of the second BANK OF THE UNITED STATES. However, Jackson also justified his battle with the bank by reference to popular anti-capitalism and the argument that a cabal of bankers were enriching themselves with 'the people's money.' Jackson regarded individual and national debt with suspicion. Nevertheless the effect of his SPECIE CIRCULAR was to make credit more easily available to the working man.

Jackson believed that abolitionist agitation might destabilize the Union but he declined to support southern nationalists. During the NULLIFICATION CRISIS he took an uncompromising stance against the extreme STATES' RIGHTS' arguments marshalled by his former vice-president John C. CALHOUN. Jackson was equally unbending in his approach to Indian policy. Believing that he was acting in the national interest, Jackson insisted on full implementation of the INDIAN REMOVAL ACT (1832) and ignored the US Supreme Court's ruling in WORCESTER VS. GEORGIA (1832).

Jackson was the first president to make extensive use of the SPOILS SYSTEM and a KITCHEN CABINET. He quarrelled with former allies, notably Calhoun, in the Peggy EATON affair. The emerging WHIG party sought to make political capital from Jackson's personality and his use of presidential power by dubbing him 'King Andrew.' However, by using his popularity and patronage to define a national power base for the Democratic party, Jackson broke the mold of US politics and in the process redefined the role of both the presidency and political parties.

Jackson, Helen Hunt (1830–85), poet, novelist and author of *A Century of Dishonor* (1881), a scrupulously researched account of US breaches of treaties negotiated with Native American tribes. Her book prompted congressionally sponsored investigations of conditions on the reservations. She served on a commission of investigation whose report led Congress to adopt the DAWES SEVERALTY ACT (1887).

Jacksonian democracy, political philosophy espoused by Andrew JACKSON's faction within the DEMOCRATIC PARTY in the 1820s and 1830s. Like their JEFFERSONIAN forerunners, Jacksonians venerated the common man and excoriated all forms of elitism and privilege except slavery.

On the night of Jackson's inauguration as US president in 1829, thousands of his plebeian supporters gate-crashed the White House celebrations. NATIONAL REPUBLICANS were horrified, but Jackson took the scenes in his stride. From Jackson's populist commitment to egalitarianism flowed commitments to broaden the franchise, to increase the number of government officers elected directly by the people, and to bring more of the 'common folk' into political life through the Democratic Party organization.

Jacksonian Democrats were hostile to institutions that might thwart the will of the common man, especially banks, and offered limited support to the rights of workers. They believed in limited government, and tended to take a STRICT CONSTRUCTIONIST view of the US Constitution. Nevertheless, like their hero, most Jacksonians opposed STATES' RIGHTS and were ardent nationalists. Their main rivals, the WHIG PARTY, believed that Jacksonians corrupted and debased the political process by cynically exploiting the ignorance and vice of the working man. The battle between these two schools of thought lay at the heart of the SECOND PARTY SYSTEM.

Jackson, Jesse (Louis) (1941–), Baptist minister, civil rights campaigner and Democratic politician. In the 1980s Jackson emerged as the first African-American politician to approach the level of support among white voters necessary to secure election to the White House. During the most active period of the CIVIL RIGHTS MOVEMENT Jackson worked within the SOUTHERN CHRISTIAN LEADERSHIP COALITION (SCLC). Although sometimes impatient with its tactics, he was a loyal follower of the SCLC's dominant figure, the Reverend Martin Luther KING. (Jackson was at King's side on the night he was shot dead, and attracted much criticism for rushing to Chicago to give an emotional news conference while still dressed in blood-spattered clothes.) In 1965 King asked Jackson to direct the SCLC's OPERATION BREADBASKET in Chicago. Jackson developed this into a nationwide campaign. In 1971 he founded PUSH (People United to Save Humanity), a programme designed to create jobs for minorities. At the same time he began to build a power base within the DEMOCRATIC PARTY by founding the National Rainbow Coalition, an organization devoted to supporting and mobilizing minority voters. At the 1984 Democratic Party convention Jackson enjoyed the support of 458 delegates. This was far short of Walter MONDALE's total, but a bloc significant enough for Jackson to be allowed to give a prime-time speech to the convention. Jackson ran a determined but populist campaign for the Democrats' nomination in 1988. He was able to generate TV news pictures of large, multiracial crowds chanting 'Run, Jesse, run!', thereby establishing himself as a serious player. He secured 1128 delegates to Michael DUKAKIS's 2876, and expected to be able to influence the party's platform. In the event, Dukakis decided to make few concessions to Jackson's supporters. Swallowing his pride, Jackson eventually campaigned loyally on behalf of Dukakis. For all his achievements in the 1980s, Jackson's political prospects were blighted by the fact that he had never held elective office. Since 1988 Jackson has worked on a variety of community projects, and continues to speak on national affairs on behalf of the Rainbow Coalition.

Jackson, 'Stonewall' (Thomas Jonathan Jackson) (1824–63), Confederate Army general, one of the Confederacy's ablest commanders in the CIVIL WAR. Jackson earned his nickname at the first battle of MANASSAS (Bull Run), where, commanding a brigade of Virginians, he stood his ground on the left flank of the Confederate line 'like a damned stonewall'.

Jackson was educated at West Point Military Academy and served with distinction in the MEXICAN WAR. From 1852 to 1861 he taught at the Virginia Military Institute (VMI). On December 2 1859 he commanded the VMI cadet party that hanged John BROWN following the raid on HARPER'S FERRY. Jackson was a stern, humorless Presbyterian who believed that the Confederate armies were doing the Lord's work. His brilliant conduct of the first SHENANDOAH VALLEY CAMPAIGN in 1862 helped to ensure the defeat of McCLELLAN's ambitious PENINSULAR CAMPAIGN. He fought with distinction at the second battle of MANASSAS, and made a crucial breakthrough at CHANCELLORSVILLE. This proved to be his last battle, as he died after being shot by nervous Confederate sentries.

Japanese-Americans, relocation of, *see* RELOCATION OF JAPANESE-AMERICANS.

Jay, John (1745–1829), FEDERALIST politician, diplomat and jurist. President of the CONTINENTAL CONGRESS in 1778, Jay served subsequently as an envoy to Spain and a US negotiator of the treaty of PARIS (1783). Criticism of the JAY–GARDOQUI NEGOTIATIONS (1785) confirmed in him a federalist outlook later expressed in contributions to the *FEDERALIST PAPERS*. Declining the post of secretary of state in 1789, he was confirmed as first chief justice of the Supreme Court on September 26 1789. Author of CHISHOLM VS. GEORGIA and JAY'S TREATY (1794), he left the Court in 1795, refusing renomination in 1800.

Jay–Gardoqui negotiations (1785–6), negotiations between US Secretary for Foreign Affairs John JAY and Spain's minister to America Don Diego de Gardoqui, conducted in an attempt to end a Spanish blockade of the Mississippi river.

In 1784 Spain had closed the Mississippi to American trade in an attempt to force

America to recognize its interpretation of the northern border of WEST FLORIDA. This action held potentially ruinous consequences for land prices and commercial development in American settlements along the Mississippi and Ohio valleys.

In 1785 CONFEDERATION CONGRESS asked John JAY to negotiate a treaty that would guarantee US access to the Mississippi and RIGHT OF DEPOSIT in New Orleans. Deadlock ensued. On August 29 1786 Congress voted 7–5 to authorize Jay to 'forbear' from demanding the *right* of deposit in return for commercial concessions bearing primarily on the Atlantic trade. The vote in favor of compromise fell short of the majority needed for the ratification of a treaty. The deadlock provoked talk of secession among westerners angered by the eastern states' apparent willingness to compromise on access to the Mississippi. Outstanding issues between the USA and Spain were resolved in the treaty of SAN LORENZO (1795).

jayhawkers, nickname applied to armed opponents of the extension of slavery into BLEEDING KANSAS, and subsequently to Kansas Unionists who raided Missouri during the CIVIL WAR.

Jay's treaty (November 19 1794), resolution of Anglo-American grievances, negotiated by Chief Justice John JAY during Britain's war with revolutionary France.

The agreement bound Britain to withdraw all troops from US soil by 1796, to determine a US–Canadian boundary west of the Great Lakes, to pay damages for the seizure of US shipping, and to allow Americans limited trading access to its Caribbean possessions. The USA undertook to aid the recovery of debts owed by its citizens to British merchants. However, Britain insisted on retaining the right to search US ships for French goods, to forcibly remove 'contraband' in British ports if necessary, and to seize as deserters British-born sailors protected by adopted American citizenship.

The US Senate would not accept limita-

tions on the USA's West Indian trade, but ratified the remainder of the treaty (20–10) on June 24 1795. Nonetheless Jay was reviled by DEMOCRATIC-REPUBLICANS for kowtowing to Britain and injuring the French republic.

jazz, distinctively American musical style. The historical significance of jazz, as opposed to its enduring cultural appeal, lies in the extent to which it reflects the mobility of the American people in general and of African-Americans in particular.

No single individual 'invented' jazz, but pianist Ferdinand Joseph Lamothe 'Jelly Roll' Morton (1890–1941) may be credited with popularizing the polyphonic and syncopated melodies that became hallmarks of the style. Morton grew up in the USA's most cosmopolitan US city, New Orleans. He offset his losses as a gambler by working as a pimp and pianist in the 'sporting houses' or bordellos of New Orleans' Storyville district. Morton's blend of ragtime, string band and gospel styles was captured in a series of 'race records' he recorded in Chicago from 1923 to 1927. In 1926 Morton formed the Red Hot Peppers, a band of skilled New Orleans musicians who became famous for collective and individual improvisation around ensemble playing. In the same year Louis 'Satchmo' Armstrong (1901–71) made the first in a series of recordings in Chicago that popularized 'scat singing' – the use of the voice to improvise musical effects. Armstrong was born in New Orleans and spent his youth in the city's 'home for colored waifs.' Here he took up the cornet and, with the encouragement of Joe 'King' Oliver (1885–1938), found work on riverboats before rejoining Oliver in Chicago. Armstrong's recordings with his 'Hot Five' and 'Hot Seven' took jazz to new heights. Armstrong himself, who later appeared in over 50 HOLLYWOOD movies, became the art form's first crossover star.

Although Morton, Armstrong and Oliver made their own recordings and augmented their earnings by touring with blues stars, jazz gained new admirers primarily through live performances and radio shows by 'big bands' in the late 1920s and 1930s. Two big bands were particularly influential. In 1927, a middle-class native of Washington D.C., Edward Kennedy 'Duke' Ellington (1899–1974), put together a band that began a four-year residence at the Cotton Club in New York's Harlem. Ellington and his collaborator Billy Strayhorn (1915–67) wrote original jazz melodies (like 'Take the A Train') to showcase the individual talents of the band's ever-changing but invariably stellar line-up. Since the Cotton Club was, at least initially, frequented by white audiences, the Ellington band soon received further exposure through word of mouth, radio broadcasts and well-publicized national and international tours. In 1935 a native of Red Bank, New Jersey, William 'Count' Basie (1904–84), put together the Barons of Rhythm in Kansas City. Basie had served a long apprenticeship, first as a vaudeville musician and later as a pianist in a rival Kansas City big band. His band, soon renamed the Count Basie Orchestra and brought to New York, featured a bluesier style and the work of the jazz's first virtuoso saxophonist, Lester Willis 'Prez' Young (1909–59).

Ellington and Basie, together with rival bandleaders Fletcher Henderson (1897–1952) and Cabell 'Cab' Calloway (1907–94), succeeded in creating a diverse but popular jazz form which a mass audience understood as 'swing.' Although Ellington and Basie in particular had ambitions beyond 'jazzing up' popular standards, swing as played by white orchestras – notably those led by Glenn Miller (1904–44) and Tommy Dorsey (1905–56) – dominated the dance halls by emphasizing strict time signatures and by featuring vocalists, notably Frank Sinatra (1915–98), who became bigger draws than the musicians.

During World War II, a younger generation of African-American jazz musicians, often trained in the big bands, created the 'be-bop' style. Its chief progenitor was alto saxophonist Charles Christopher 'Bird' Parker (1920–1955), but other memorable exponents included trumpeter John Burks 'Dizzy' Gillespie (1917–93) and pianist Thelonius Sphere Monk (1917–82). Be-bop was seen at the time as revolutionary and challengingly modern music. With its rise, and the demise of the big bands, jazz went back underground. Be-bop was less radio-friendly than swing and it interested television producers not at all. Most of the leading be-bop players, starting with Parker, were at one time or another self-destructive junkies and hence not suitable candidates for big promotion budgets. White teenagers, who might have been attracted by the air of rebellion associated with be-bop, were drawn instead to the contemporaneous development of rock and roll. The music survived on the strength of legendary club appearances and recordings, especially those made by a second generation of stars that included Miles Dewey Davis (1926–91), Theodore Walter 'Sonny' Rollins (1930–) and John William Coltrane (1926–76).

Although a white audience, not least record company A&R men, appreciated the music, during the 1950s, white participation in be-bop was limited almost exclusively to the composition of preposterously pretentious notes for the sleeves of mono LPs that have since become collectors' classics. White musicians contributed to the development of jazz in other ways. Gerry Mulligan (1927–96) and Dave Brubeck (1920–99) helped create the 'cool jazz' or 'west coast' sound. Other white musicians, many of them British, also popularized an interest in 'traditional' New Orleans jazz. Gunther Schuller (1925–) invented a 'third stream' fusion of jazz and classical music. Stan Getz (1927–91) made a series of popular recordings which drew up the Brazilian bossa nova and samba styles.

Many jazz musicians, especially the great be-bop stars, were baffled and embittered by the money and attention that surrounded rock music in the USA in the 1960s and 70s. Some, notably Miles Davis, attempted a jazz-rock fusion. Others, notably Sonny Rollins and Dizzy Gillespie, stuck to their guns and were rewarded with a modicum of attention in the twilight of their careers. Jazz at present faces a dilemma comparable to that facing classical music – relatively few new players and composers are coming up through the ranks and audiences exhibit a stubborn preference for an established canon.

Jefferson, Thomas (1743–1826), statesman, chief author of the DECLARATION OF INDEPENDENCE (1776), 2nd vice president (1797–1801) and 3rd president of the USA (1801–9).

Jefferson inherited a substantial estate in Virginia, and marriage to Martha Wayles Skelton (1748–82) brought him further lands and slaves. He completed legal training in 1767 but was soon elected to Virginia's assembly, the House of Burgesses, where he served from 1769 to 1775. He was appointed to the second CONTINENTAL CONGRESS and leapt to national prominence as the main author of the Declaration of Independence (1776). Returning to Virginia's House of Delegates (1776–9), he drafted the VIRGINIA STATUTE FOR RELIGIOUS FREEDOM. He was elected governor of Virginia (1779–81) on the eve of a British offensive in the state during the REVOLUTIONARY WAR. Critics charged that he spent more energy on protecting his home at Monticello than on organizing the state's defense. Appointed to CONFEDERATION CONGRESS (1783–4), he drafted the ORDINANCE OF 1784 that organized the western territories. He later served as US minister to France (1785–9). While resident in Paris, he may have conducted affairs with both the British artist Maria Cosway and his household slave Sally Hemings (his former wife's half-sister). It is now thought likely that Jefferson's liason with Hemings produced two sons.

President WASHINGTON appointed Jefferson secretary of state in 1790. Jefferson clashed with Alexander HAMILTON, supported DEMOCRATIC-REPUBLICAN opposition to the FEDERALIST PARTY, and resigned in 1793 in the aftermath of GENÊT'S MISSION. Jefferson was defeated by John ADAMS in the presidential election of 1796. Under the conventions which governed presidential elections at the time Jefferson, the recipient of the second highest tally of votes in the electoral college, was required to serve as Adams' vice president. Jefferson did not share Adams's political outlook and repudiated the ALIEN AND SEDITION ACTS in the KENTUCKY and VIRGINIA RESOLUTIONS.

Following his success in the PRESIDENTIAL ELECTION OF 1800 Jefferson served as president from March 4 1804 until March 4 1809. His main achievement as president was the LOUISIANA PURCHASE. His attempt to use the EMBARGO ACT (1807) to secure US neutrality in the Napoleonic Wars was a failure. In retirement Jefferson helped found the University of Virginia (1819). He died on July 4 1826 (the 50th anniversary of the Declaration of Independence), the same day as his political sparring-partner John Adams.

Jefferson's social and political thought was characterized by contradiction. He argued that white yeoman farmers were the 'chosen people of God', yet he lived off the proceeds of slave labor. He believed that the continued existence of slavery might provoke divine wrath, vengeance from former slaves and a debasement of the slaveholder's character, yet he declined to emancipate his own slaves. Arguing that the 'tree of liberty' should be 'watered with the blood of tyrants', he supported the French Revolution, only to break with it when it entered the Terror. He argued that Washington's NEUTRALITY PROCLAMATION abused presidential authority, yet the LOUISIANA PURCHASE and the trial of Aaron BURR struck Jefferson's opponents as high-handed. In *Notes on the State of Virginia* (1785) Jefferson made explicit, and fretted over, racial prejudices that his contemporaries generally suppressed.

Jeffersonian democracy, a body of political thought rooted in the DEMOCRATIC-REPUBLICAN movement and given focus by Thomas JEFFERSON in the 1790s. Jeffersonian Democrats venerated independent producers (such as farmers and craftsmen), and believed that Andrew HAMILTON's economic program had granted too great an influence to financiers and merchants. Accordingly they sought to establish limits on the power of federal government by advocating a STRICT CONSTRUCTIONIST reading of the US Constitution. Jefferson and Madison developed, through the VIRGINIA and KENTUCKY RESOLUTIONS (1798–9), the doctrine that the individual states retained the right to judge whether federal legislation was constitutional and, if necessary, to interpose their authority to protect their citizens' rights. Jeffersonian Democrats were implacable opponents of the ALIEN AND SEDITION ACTS. They formed the backbone of the DEMOCRATIC PARTY, which began to coalesce during Jefferson's presidency.

Jim Crow, shorthand term for the system of racial segregation and denial of black voting rights that developed in southern states after RECONSTRUCTION. It takes its origins from a blackface minstrel tune, written by Thomas Dartmouth Rice (1808–60), that was popular on Broadway and around the USA in the 1830s.

In the wake of the CIVIL RIGHTS CASES, and especially after the Supreme Court's PLESSY VS. FERGUSON verdict (1896), southern states enacted legislation that denied African-Americans voting rights, confined their children to under-funded school systems and established a pattern of racial segregation in nearly all aspects of daily life. It was

this system that the CIVIL RIGHTS MOVEMENT sought to destroy.

Johnson, Andrew (1808–75), Democratic statesman, vice president (1865) and 17th president of the USA (1865–9) following the assassination of Abraham LINCOLN. Johnson reluctantly oversaw the process of RECONSTRUCTION at the end of the CIVIL WAR, and is one of only two presidents to have undergone an IMPEACHMENT trial.

Johnson was raised in poverty in Tennessee. He taught himself to read and, while working as a tailor, polished oratorical skills that helped him rise – representing the DEMOCRATIC PARTY – through local and state government to the US Senate (1857–62). Johnson was the only US senator from a state that had seceded to support the Union during the Civil War. In 1862 Johnson was made military governor of Tennessee, where he endeared himself to RADICAL REPUBLICANS by declaring that 'treason must be made odious'. Although he had owned five slaves, Johnson detested the planter class's domination of politics in the antebellum south, and was prepared to embrace emancipation in order to break this mould. Lincoln, going to the polls under the NATIONAL UNION banner, adopted Johnson as his running-mate in the PRESIDENTIAL ELECTION OF 1864, despite Johnson's previous service as a Democrat.

Johnson succeeded to the presidency on April 15 1865, and served until March 3 1869. On May 29 1865 President Johnson issued his first PROCLAMATION OF RECONSTRUCTION. This offered former Confederate states prompt readmission to the Union. But, beset by racist visions of miscegenation and black retribution, Johnson refused to safeguard the political and civil rights of former slaves. This put him on a collision course with RADICAL REPUBLICAN congressmen, who overrode his veto of the second FREEDMEN'S BUREAU Bill (1866) and the CIVIL RIGHTS ACT (1866). Johnson implemented congressionally sanctioned military reconstruction reluctantly. His obstruction of this policy was the proximate cause of his impeachment. On February 24 1868 the House of Representatives voted (126–47) to impeach Johnson for violations of the TENURE OF OFFICE ACT (1867). On May 19 and 26 1868 the Senate, sitting as an impeachment court, voted for conviction by 35–19 – one vote short of the necessary two-thirds majority. Johnson completed his term as a 'lame duck'.

Johnson, Hiram Warren (1866–1945), reforming governor of California during the PROGRESSIVE ERA. Johnson was born in Sacramento and trained as lawyer. In 1908, he achieved state-wide prominence by successfully prosecuting the political boss Abe Ruef on charges of corruption. He was elected governor, as a Republican, on a platform which called for regulation of the railroad industry, the creation of a state unemployment insurance system and political reform. He was Theodore ROOSEVELT's running-mate in the PRESIDENTIAL ELECTION OF 1912. Elected to the US Senate in 1916, he represented California until his death. Johnson employed the tenets of ISOLATIONISM to argue against US entry into the LEAGUE OF NATIONS. He declined to serve as Warren HARDING's running mate in 1920 and lost the Republican's presidential nomination to Calvin COOLIDGE in 1924. In later life Johnson broke with mainstream Republicans by supporting the NEW DEAL.

Johnson, Lyndon B(aines) (1908–73), Democratic statesman, vice president (1961–3) and 36th president of the USA (1963–9), following the assassination of President KENNEDY. Johnson's domestic achievements in civil rights reform and in alleviating poverty, summed up in his vision of the GREAT SOCIETY, were overshadowed by his decision to escalate US involvement in the VIETNAM WAR.

Johnson was raised in straitened circumstances in southern Texas. Although he attended college, and later volunteered for service as a naval aviator in World War II, he was a career politician. Johnson represented Texas's Tenth District (as a Democrat) in the US House of Representatives from 1937 until 1949, when he won election to the US Senate. In 1955 he became Senate majority leader, and further honed his already formidable skills of political persuasion. He also began to distance himself from conservative southern Democrats by supporting the CIVIL RIGHTS ACTS of 1957 and 1960.

Although Kennedy's decision to balance the ticket by selecting Johnson as his running-mate helped swing the PRESIDENTIAL ELECTION OF 1960, Johnson, who was a proud and independent man, did not regard himself as a makeweight. As vice president he got on well with Kennedy, but disliked many of Kennedy's younger, liberal advisers. (This mutual antipathy was later played out in the aftermath of Johnson's decision to escalate US involvement in the Vietnam War.)

Johnson succeeded to the presidency when Kennedy was assassinated in Dallas (November 22 1963). Johnson was determined to win the 1964 presidential election without milking the public's posthumous affection for Kennedy. He swept to victory (garnering 61% of the POPULAR VOTE, the highest share achieved in the 20th century) partly because of the apparent extremism of Republican nominee Barry GOLDWATER, but largely through the appeal of his GREAT SOCIETY rhetoric and his sponsorship of the CIVIL RIGHTS ACT OF 1964.

In his second term Johnson secured unprecedented appropriations for domestic welfare programs – chiefly MEDICARE, MEDICAID and the WAR ON POVERTY. In 1960 the USA spent $10 billion on welfare. By 1965 the annual total had reached $25.6 billion. This expenditure changed living standards in the USA, particularly for African-Americans. The proportion of African-Americans living below the poverty line fell from 55% in 1960 to 27% in 1968. Black unemployment fell by 34%, while black family income rose by 53%. Johnson implemented these programs just as the popularity of the slogan BLACK POWER was encapsulating divisions within the CIVIL RIGHTS MOVEMENT, and major riots, such as those in WATTS and DETROIT, were erupting in US cities. Johnson sponsored the VOTING RIGHTS ACT (1965). He committed himself to AFFIRMATIVE ACTION, and made such symbolic gestures as nominating Thurgood MARSHALL to become the first African-American Supreme Court justice and Patricia HARRIS to become the first African-American woman ambassador.

However, for the members of the ANTIWAR MOVEMENT, Johnson's domestic record counted for nothing when set against his escalation of the Vietnam War. Even fellow southern Democrat Senator J. William FULBRIGHT saw a 'kind of madness' in Johnson's 'facile assumption' that he could fund Great Society programs 'while also spending tens of billions to finance an open-ended war in Asia'. Johnson was exempted from the terms of the TWENTY-SECOND AMENDMENT and could, had he wished, have run for president in 1968. However, on March 31 1968 Johnson announced that he would not seek re-election, and on January 20 1969 he retired to his ranch in Texas.

Johnson, Richard M(entor) (1781–1850), JACKSONIAN DEMOCRATIC statesman and vice president of the USA (1837–41). On February 8 1837, for the first and only time in history, the US Senate resolved inconclusive voting in the vice-presidential ELECTORAL COLLEGE: senators voted 33–16 for Johnson, who duly served as President Martin VAN BUREN's deputy.

President Andrew JACKSON had forced the DEMOCRATIC PARTY to accept Johnson, a US senator from Kentucky, as Van Buren's running-mate in the 1836 election. Johnson was known to have taken a slave woman as his common-law wife and to have raised their children as free persons. For this reason, Virginia's electors in the electoral college (who dutifully reported their state's preference for Van Buren) withheld their votes in the vice-presidential electoral college from Johnson. As no vice-presidential candidate gained a majority in the electoral college, the choice reverted to the US Senate.

Johnston, Joseph E(gglestone) (1807–91), Confederate Army general. An able commander, he employed orthodox but essentially defensive tactics in the CIVIL WAR which angered the president of the Confederacy, Jefferson DAVIS.

Johnston, a native of Virginia, was a career soldier. He graduated from West Point Military Academy in 1829, served in the MEXICAN WAR, and had become a brigadier general in the US Army when in May 1861 he resigned to join the Confederate Army. He helped to defeat the Union's 'forward to Richmond' strategy at the first battle of MANASSAS (1861), and blunted McCLELLAN's advance in the PENINSULAR CAMPAIGN (1862). He was severely wounded at the battle of Seven Pines (May 31 1862), and transferred to the Tennessee and Mississippi theater. Davis blamed Johnston for allowing Ulysses S. GRANT to capture VICKSBURG, and in December 1863 Johnston was transferred to command the Confederate armies defending Atlanta. During the battle for ATLANTA Johnston ceded ground while preserving his army. On July 17 1864 Davis, frustrated with Johnston's defensive tactics, relieved him of his command. The Confederate Congress demanded his reinstatement. Restored to command in February 1865, he defied Davis's order to continue the war by surrendering the remaining Confederate armies in the Carolinas to William T. SHERMAN on April 26 1865. After the war he served in the US House of Representatives (1879–81).

Joint Committee on Reconstruction, congressional committee of six senators and nine representatives, established on December 4 1865 to develop a tougher policy on RECONSTRUCTION. Growing criticism of the leniency of President Andrew JOHNSON's PROCLAMATION OF RECONSTRUCTION had led Congress to set up the committee.

The committee's dominant figure was the RADICAL REPUBLICAN Thaddeus STEVENS. The committee formulated the FOURTEENTH AMENDMENT to safeguard the CIVIL RIGHTS ACT OF 1866, and, in a report published on June 20 1866, recommended that the seceding states that had formed the CONFEDERACY be treated as conquered territories, whose readmission to the Union was therefore subject to congressional rather than presidential approval. Acting on this report Congress refused to recognize the provisional governments organized in the states under Johnson's proclamation. The committee oversaw the formulation the RECONSTRUCTION ACTS of 1867. It also gathered evidence on white violence and violations of blacks' civil rights.

Jones, John Paul (1747–92), America's most successful naval commander during the REVOLUTIONARY WAR. Born in Scotland, John Paul emigrated to America in 1773 (adding the surname Jones). In 1778 he took his sloop *Ranger* into the Irish Sea, seizing two prizes, destroying a shore battery at Whitehaven (on April 23), and capturing the Royal Navy sloop *Drake*. In August 1779 Jones, aboard the *Bonhomme Richard*, preyed on Britain's coastal trade. During a fierce battle with HMS *Serapis*, off Flamborough Head on September 23 1779, Jones rejected a call for his ship's surrender with the words 'I have not yet begun to fight.' The audacity and symbolism of Jones's raids made him an American national hero. In 1787 Congress unanimously authorized the presentation of a unique gold medal commemorating his service. Nevertheless, frustrated by cuts in American defense expenditure, Jones joined the Russian navy. He never returned to America.

Jones, 'Mother' (Mary Harris Jones) (1837–1930), trade-union organizer who became a figure of enormous moral authority within labor and reform circles. Born in Ireland and raised in Canada, Jones was the widow of an iron worker. In 1900 she organized a recruitment drive for the UNITED MINE WORKERS OF AMERICA (UMWA) in West Virginia. In 1903 she achieved national prominence by leading impoverished children from Philadelphia on a protest march to Theodore ROOSEVELT's mansion in Oyster Bay, New York. At the age of 84 she helped defuse tensions provoked by the LUDLOW MASSACRE in the Colorado coalfields. An independent radical, Jones criticized both the caution of the UMWA and the ill-discipline of the INDUSTRIAL WORKERS OF THE WORLD.

Joseph, Chief, *see* NEZ PERCÉ.

judicial review, examination of state, congressional or executive action by the US Supreme Court to determine whether the action infringes the US Constitution. The Constitution does not itself explicitly grant the Supreme Court this right, which was asserted by the Court itself, under Chief Justice MARSHALL, in its verdict on MARBURY VS. MADISON (1803). Declaring Section 13 of the Judiciary Act of 1789 unconstitutional, Marshall asserted, 'It is emphatically the province and duty of the judicial department to say what the law is.' Fifty years passed before the Court, in the case of DRED SCOTT VS. SANDFORD, once again declared an act of Congress unconstitutional. Since then the Court has struck down legislation on many occasions, and its right to do so is unquestioned.

K

Kanagawa, treaty of (March 31 1853), treaty with Japan signed by a US mission led by Commodore PERRY. The treaty opened the ports of Shimoda and Hakodate to US trade and made provision for the return of shipwrecked US sailors. Sceptical Japanese officials were persuaded to approve the agreement by the gifts offered by Perry (including a railroad and a Morse telegraph) which were designed to demonstrate US technological achievement. Following the installation of an American consul in Japan (1855), the USA made further trade and residence demands.

Kansas, midwestern state, bordered by Missouri to the east, Oklahoma to the south, Colorado to the west and Nebraska to the north. The USA acquired Kansas through the LOUISIANA PURCHASE. Kansas was organized as a US territory through passage of the KANSAS–NEBRASKA ACT on May 22 1854. Native Americans, relocated to eastern Kansas under the terms of the INDIAN REMOVAL ACT (1830), were driven from the territory to RESERVATIONS in Oklahoma. At the same time, slaveholders and abolitionists rushed to settle in the new territory, triggering the BLEEDING KANSAS interlude. Kansas entered the Union with a constitution outlawing slavery as the 34th state on January 29 1861.

The hatreds aroused during the struggle over the legal status of slavery in Kansas made the state the center of vicious guerilla fighting during the Civil War. In August 1863 QUANTRILL'S RAIDERS (a pro-Confederate militia) destroyed Lawrence, Kansas, in retaliation for raids in Missouri conducted by pro-Union JAYHAWKERS.

The first HOMESTEAD ACT (1862) and the expansion of the nation's rail network sparked substantial in-migration. In 1860 Kansas had 100,000 permanent residents, by 1880 its population numbered 996,000 and by 1900 it had reached 1,400,000. The vast majority of new settlers were white and native-born. However, in 1879 the state received a wave of African-American migrants (the EXODUSTERS) from southern states. Kansas farmers suffered from a series of droughts in the 1890s and enthusiastically endorsed POPULISM. Strong support also existed in the state for PROHIBITION and WOMEN'S SUFFRAGE. (Kansas granted women the right to vote in 1912.)

The state's farmers were hard hit by declining commodity prices in the 1920s and the DUST BOWL of the 1930s. Many gave up the struggle and moved out of the state. The state's economy diversified as its dependence on grain production weakened and new manufacturing and mining industries developed. In 1990 Kansas had 2,477,574 permanent residents and was the 32nd most populous state in the Union. 'Native sons' who have achieved national prominence include Dwight D. EISENHOWER and Bob DOLE.

Kansas–Nebraska Act (May 30 1854), legislation, sponsored by Stephen DOUGLAS, permitting residents of Kansas and Nebraska to decide for themselves whether they would permit slavery in their territories. The act repealed the MISSOURI COMPROMISE under which slavery had been prohibited in both territories. By doing so the Act destroyed one of the foundations of the COMPROMISE OF 1850 and reopened the vexed question of the future status of slavery in the western territories. Douglas justified the measure on the grounds that the residents of future states should adopt constitutions of their choosing. Opponents attributed the act to Douglas's presidential aspirations. Its adoption caused the BLEEDING KANSAS crisis.

Kelley, Florence (1859–1932), social reformer. Kelley was born into a wealthy Quaker family in Philadelphia. She graduated from Cornell in 1882 and during further study at the University of Zürich, translated several works by Karl Marx and Friedrich Engels. In 1886, following the break-up of a disastrous marriage that left her with three children to support, she returned to the USA. In 1891, she joined Jane ADDAMS to work at Hull-House in Chicago. In 1898, she became head of the National Consumers' League (NCL), a position she held until her death. Kelley committed the NCL to campaign for a ten-hour working day for women (achieving a notable victory when the US Supreme Court verdict in MULLER VS. OREGON upheld a landmark state law). She also campaigned for a minimum wage and health benefits for mothers with children.

Kellogg–Briand Pact, agreement signed in Paris on August 27 1928 that committed the USA, France and 13 other nations to renouncing war. The pact originated in discussions between the French foreign minister Aristide Briand and academics from Columbia University. It reflected the widely held sentiment that WORLD WAR I had demonstrated beyond doubt the futility and barbarity of war. In an open letter published in the *New York Times* in June 1928, the president of Columbia University, Nicholas Murray Butler (1862–1947), called on the USA to accept Briand's proposal for the 'outlawry of war'. US Secretary of State Frank Kellogg (1856–1937) acknowledged the letter, and began consultations with Briand that soon produced a draft treaty. The pact was acclaimed by the WOMEN'S PEACE PARTY and by Jane ADDAMS (with whom Nicholas Murray Butler shared the 1931 Nobel Peace Prize). Sixty-two nations ultimately signed the agreement. However, the pact contained no mechanism to coerce or compel nations to obey its terms, and the USA, which had rejected the LEAGUE OF NATIONS, accepted the Kellogg–Briand agreement only on condition that it retained the right to use force in self-defense or to enforce the MONROE DOCTRINE.

Kennedy, Edward ('Ted') M(oore) (1932–), Democratic politician. The younger brother of John F. and Robert F. KENNEDY, Ted Kennedy was first elected to the US Senate from Massachusetts in 1962. He has retained his seat ever since. On July 18 1969 Kennedy drove his car off a narrow bridge on Chappaquiddick Island, Massachusetts. His companion, a young woman named Mary Jo Kopechne, was killed. Kennedy delayed reporting the accident, and was subsequently charged by police with leaving the scene of an accident. He was re-elected to the Senate in 1970 but renounced an anticipated presidential bid in 1972. A well-received speech at the 1976 Democratic Party convention persuaded Kennedy to make a bid for the Democrats' nomination in 1980, but questions concerning his character contributed to his defeat by Jimmy CARTER. Since 1980 Kennedy has sought to establish himself as the keeper of the conscience of the Democratic Party's liberal wing.

Kennedy, John F(itzgerald) (1917–63), Democratic statesman and 35th president of the USA (1961–3). Kennedy was the first Roman Catholic elected to the presidency, and, at the age of 43, the youngest man after Theodore Roosevelt to take up the position. His administration was dominated by the geopolitics of the COLD WAR. At home, it was largely left to his successor, Lyndon B. JOHNSON, to carry through the social reforms that his energetic rhetoric had promised. On November 22 1963 he became the fourth serving president to die at the hands of an assassin.

Kennedy was born into a wealthy family. He was educated at Choate prep school (1931–5), the London School of Economics (1935), Princeton (1935) and Harvard (1936–40). Kennedy's intensely ambitious father Joseph Patrick Kennedy (1888–1969) hired ghost writers to rework his son's Harvard senior thesis, transforming it into a best-selling condemnation of appeasement published as *Why England Slept* (1940). He also used influence to secure his son, who volunteered for Navy service in 1941, a sea command aboard PT 109. Kennedy showed considerable courage when, on August 2 1943, PT 109, on patrol off the Solomon Islands, was sunk by a Japanese destroyer.

Kennedy served as a US representative (1947–53) and senator (1953–61) from Massachusetts before receiving the Democrats' nomination in the PRESIDENTIAL ELECTION OF 1960. Kennedy's campaign slogan was 'Let's get America moving again.' His opponent, Richard NIXON, was Kennedy's near-contemporary in age, but seemed less glamorous and sophisticated. Overcoming voters' suspicion of his Irish Catholic background and relative inexperience, Kennedy won the election by an extremely narrow margin. Kennedy was sworn in as president on January 20 1961. His much-quoted INAUGURAL ADDRESS bound Americans to 'pay any price' to ensure the 'success of liberty.' Kennedy went on to authorize the BAY OF PIGS inva-

sion of Cuba, sent military advisers to South Vietnam in the early stages of the VIETNAM WAR, and took a firm stand during the CUBAN MISSILE CRISIS. He exercised great caution in the one area of domestic affairs, civil rights (*see* CIVIL RIGHTS MOVEMENT), where forceful action on his part might have fulfilled his rhetoric. His charm, and the backing he offered projects such as the APOLLO PROGRAM, lent a credibility to his NEW FRONTIER rhetoric that transcended his administration's modest legislative achievement.

Kennedy's assassination in Dallas, Texas, shocked the world. The WARREN COMMISSION's conclusion that Lee Harvey OSWALD (1949–63) planned and carried out the assassination unaided has since been challenged by any number of conspiracy theories.

Kennedy, Robert F(rancis) (1925–68), Democratic politician. Robert F. Kennedy managed his brother John F. KENNEDY's Senate and presidential elections, served as attorney general in his administration, and ultimately shared the same tragic fate while campaigning for his party's presidential nomination.

'Bobby' Kennedy was educated at Harvard and the University of Virginia Law School. He worked in the Criminal Division of the Department of Justice (1951–2) and as a counsel on the Senate Permanent Subcommittee on Investigations chaired by Senator Joseph McCARTHY. Between 1957 and 1960 he served as the chief counsel on a Senate subcommittee investigating trade-union corruption, and later wrote a book, *The Enemy Within* (1960), assailing crooked union bosses. He collaborated closely with his brother John during the latter's presidency (1961–3), advising him on the CIVIL RIGHTS MOVEMENT and the CUBAN MISSILE CRISIS. In 1964 he resigned from Lyndon B. JOHNSON's administration to seek election to the US Senate from New York State.

Kennedy was one of the first members of the US Senate to criticize Johnson's conduct of the VIETNAM WAR, but he declined to contest the PRESIDENTIAL ELECTION OF 1968 until it became clear that Johnson was vulnerable on the issue. This led some members of the ANTIWAR MOVEMENT to charge Kennedy with opportunism. He might well have won the Democrats' nomination in 1968 had he not been shot dead in Los Angeles on the night of June 6 by a Palestinian refugee named Sirhan Sirhan.

Kent State antiwar protest (May 4 1970), protest against the US invasion of CAMBODIA at the Kent branch of Ohio State University, in which panicked National Guardsmen shot dead four student protesters. On April 30 President NIXON had announced that he had ordered a limited invasion of Cambodia as part of his strategy to end the VIETNAM WAR. ANTIWAR MOVEMENT protests erupted across America. The tragedy at Kent State triggered further protests in which two students at Jackson State, Mississippi, were shot dead by state police (May 14 1970).

Kentucky, BORDER STATE situated to the west of Virginia, the north of Tennessee, the east of Missouri, and to the south of Ohio and Indiana.

The Kentucky country formed part of the original homelands of the CHEROKEE nation, but was claimed by Virginia during the colonial era. In 1775 Richard Henderson purchased substantial tracts of land in Kentucky from the Cherokee through the treaty of SYCAMORE SHOALS. The purchase was made on behalf of the TRANSYLVANIA COMPANY. Daniel BOONE blazed the WILDERNESS ROAD to facilitate white settlement. In 1776, led by George Rogers CLARK, Kentucky settlers dissatisfied with the Transylvania Company petitioned for incorporation within Virginia. Kentucky was administered as a county within Virginia until June 1 1792, when it entered the Union as the 15th state. The state subsequently received an influx of white settlers seeking to establish family farms and slaveholders bent on creating tobacco plantations. Throughout the ANTEBELLUM period, roughly 20% of the state's population (which numbered 1,155,684 in 1860) was enslaved. The CONFEDERACY regarded Kentucky as its 13th member. Despite strong support for the Confederacy within the state, the legislature did not pass an act of SECESSION and over 90,000 residents served in Union forces during the Civil War. Nevertheless, opposition to the THIRTEENTH AMENDMENT within Kentucky led the US government to impose martial law from July 5 1864 to October 12 1865 in a bid to secure the state's loyalty. During RECONSTRUCTION, Confederate sympathizers within the Democratic Party gained control of the state's electoral politics. However, the Kentucky legislature declined to segregate key public facilities, notably the state's school system, and, in comparison to the state's southern neighbors, did relatively little to prevent African-Americans from exercising their civil rights.

By the close of the 19th century, coal mining had emerged as the state's primary industry. In 1900 the state's permanent population numbered 2,147,174. By 1990 this figure had reached 3,685,296 and Kentucky was the 23rd largest state. Over the course of the 20th century, declining demand for coal and the exhaustion of tobacco lands led to the out-migration from the state of over 1,400,000 residents. Abraham LINCOLN was born in Kentucky, and Henry CLAY made his career there, but the state's most famous 'native son' is probably Muhammad ALI.

Kentucky Resolutions, two sets of resolutions (1798 and 1799) passed by the Kentucky legislature regarding STATES' RIGHTS.

(1) On November 16 1798 the Kentucky legislature adopted resolves drafted by Thomas JEFFERSON that asserted that the states were the ultimate guardians of a citizen's liberty, and therefore had the right and duty to judge when the federal government had acted unconstitutionally. Drafted

in response to the ALIEN AND SEDITION ACTS, Kentucky's action inspired the VIRGINIA RESOLUTIONS (December 24 1798).

(2) Northern criticism of Kentucky's action led the speaker of the Kentucky legislature, John Breckinridge, to draft a further set of resolutions clarifying states' rights. Adopted November 22 1799, these suggested that a state had the right to 'nullify' unconstitutional or unjust measures taken by the federal government. This concept was revived and debated during the NULLIFICATION CRISIS of 1832.

Khe Sanh, siege of (1967–8), extended engagement in the VIETNAM WAR in which US forces successfully resisted a North Vietnamese attempt to seize a key airstrip. Extensive US media coverage of this set-piece engagement helped transform American perceptions of the war.

In December 1967, as part of the build-up to the TET OFFENSIVE, two divisions of North Vietnamese soldiers besieged a US Marine garrison guarding Khe Sanh airstrip just south of the demilitarized zone between North and South Vietnam and just west of the Laotian border. The JOHNSON administration, determined to avoid comparisons with the surrender of the French garrison at Dien Bien Phu in 1954, ordered the siege to be broken at all costs. A total of 6000 US reinforcements were helicoptered into the base, and B-52 bombers dropped 100,000 tons of explosives on the surrounding terrain – the heaviest tactical bombardment in history. The siege was lifted on April 5 1968. During the engagement 10,000 North Vietnamese troops were killed, as against 500 US and South Vietnamese deaths. But television pictures of US soldiers cowering under enemy bombardment conveyed the impression of defeat.

King, Martin Luther (1929–68), the dominant figure within the CIVIL RIGHTS MOVEMENT of the 1950s and 1960s. His charismatic oratory and non-violent methods won him a widespread following among whites as well as blacks, and he was awarded the Nobel Peace Prize in 1964. He was assassinated in 1968.

The son of a preacher, King took up the pastorship of the Dexter Street Baptist church in Montgomery, Alabama, in 1954. His speeches on behalf of the MONTGOMERY BUS BOYCOTT (1955–6) established his influence within the community of southern black churches. In 1957 he helped to organize, and became first president of, the SOUTHERN CHRISTIAN LEADERSHIP CONFERENCE (SCLC). Imprisoned during the BIRMINGHAM DESEGREGATION CAMPAIGN (1963), King wrote the *LETTER FROM BIRMINGHAM CITY JAIL*. In this, and in his famous 'I HAVE A DREAM' SPEECH, King reaffirmed his commitment to fight racial discrimination by non-violent protest. The award of the Nobel Peace Prize secured his status as a leader of international renown.

King's celebrity placed him in an awkward position. It gave him unique access to Presidents KENNEDY and JOHNSON. But it led FBI director J. Edgar HOOVER to redouble his efforts to discredit King's character by covert surveillance. It also excited criticism from other campaigners, notably Ella BAKER. During the SELMA FREEDOM MARCH (1965) King's willingness to work with the authorities produced a split between the SCLC and the STUDENT NON-VIOLENT COORDINATING COMMITTEE (SNCC). Inspired by the oratory of MALCOLM X, some African-Americans rejected King's message of racial integration in favor of the assertion of racial pride encapsulated in the slogan BLACK POWER. In the spring of 1967 King began to criticize the VIETNAM WAR publicly. On April 4 1968 he was shot dead by James Earl Ray at the Lorraine Motel, Memphis, while speaking on behalf of striking garbage workers. The assassination triggered riots in 125 US cities and at US Army bases in South Vietnam.

Kiowa, Native American people whose original homelands were probably in Montana, from where they began moving south in the 16th century. The Kiowa were divided into seven bands, including the Kiowa-APACHE, and were resident in Oklahoma and northern Texas when contact with white settlement became inescapable. The Kiowa were particularly susceptible to diseases transmitted by people of European origin. A devastating smallpox epidemic in 1861 contributed to the willingness of the Kiowa to accept confinement to reservation lands agreed in the treaty of MEDICINE LODGE (1867). Some Kiowa warriors participated in the RED RIVER WAR. There are now about 3000 Kiowa in Oklahoma.

Kirkpatrick, Jeane (Duane Jordan) (1926–), academic and diplomat. Born in Oklahoma, Kirkpatrick was educated at Columbia and the Sorbonne. She left a job as an analyst with the State Department to begin an academic career that saw her rise to become professor of government at Georgetown University. During the 1970s Kirkpatrick, a hardline anti-communist, promoted hawkish opposition to DÉTENTE and argued that the focus of US foreign policy should shift towards constructive engagement with the countries of Latin America and the Pacific Rim. In 1981 President REAGAN appointed her as the USA's permanent representative at the UNITED NATIONS, a post she held until 1985. Kirkpatrick's interest in developing closer links between the USA and Latin America led her to oppose the objectives pursued by British prime minister Margaret Thatcher during the Falklands War (1982) between Great Britain and Argentina. Kirkpatrick's stance during UN debates on the Argentinian seizure of the Falkland islands embarrassed Reagan and infuriated Thatcher. On leaving the UN, Kirkpatrick joined the Republican Party and returned to academia.

Kissinger, Henry A(lfred) (1923–), secretary of state under presidents NIXON and FORD (1973–7). A refugee from the Nazis who arrived in the USA in 1938, Kissinger was the first person born outside the USA to hold the post of secretary of state. In 1969 Nixon persuaded Kissinger to leave a professorship at Harvard in order to serve as his special assistant for national security. Kissinger was given the task of realizing Nixon's dream of achieving 'peace with honor' in the VIETNAM WAR. He pursued this through the KISSINGER INITIATIVE, and in 1973 he shared the Nobel Peace Prize with his North Vietnamese counterpart, Le Duc Tho (who refused to accept his award). In the aftermath of the Arab–Israeli war of 1973 Kissinger engaged in 'shuttle diplomacy' in an attempt to bring peace to the Middle East. He was also an architect of the DÉTENTE policy that contributed to the easing of COLD WAR tensions in the 1970s.

Kissinger initiative, series of highly secret diplomatic meetings conducted by Henry KISSINGER that laid the foundations of the peace treaty ending the VIETNAM WAR (January 27 1973).

In January 1969 Richard NIXON had chosen Kissinger as his special assistant for national security and had given him the task of fulfilling his pledge, made prior to the PRESIDENTIAL ELECTION OF 1968, that he had a 'secret plan' to end the war. Kissinger, with Nixon's approval, opened 'backchannel' negotiations with Le Duc Tho of the North Vietnamese politburo. The existence of these discussions was withheld from other participants in the PARIS PEACE TALKS, as well as from the US State Department and the American public, until January 25 1972.

Kissinger and Nixon used these contacts to signal their willingness to abandon pledges made to the USA's client state in South Vietnam – by withdrawing US troops while North Vietnamese forces remained inside South Vietnam – in return for face-saving concessions, chiefly the return of US prisoners of war. Nixon's 'MAD DOG' STRATEGY, a prime example of which was his authorization of the CHRISTMAS BOMBING of Hanoi, was designed to advance Kissinger's backchannel diplomacy. Kissinger and Le Duc Tho shared the 1973 Nobel Peace Prize.

kitchen cabinet, derogatory term for the small group of advisers and confidants whom President JACKSON preferred to consult when making policy. The official cabinet, excluded from Jackson's policy discussions, resented the influence of this group on Jackson's decision-making. Subsequent presidents followed Jackson's example.

Knights of Labor, national labor organization, formed in 1869 as the Noble and Holy Order of the Knights of Labor by nine Philadelphia tailors, led by Uriah Stephens (1821–82). The Knights' philosophy, deeply influenced by Protestant theology, venerated producers of all kinds. Thus farmers, craftsmen, factory workers and even 'honest' employers were eligible to join their ranks. 'Parasites' – liquor dealers, financiers and rack-renting landlords – were demonized.

Under the presidency of Terrence POWDERLY (1879–93), the Knights shed their previous secrecy and pursued an inclusive policy that brought into the labor movement workers spurned by the exclusive CRAFT UNIONS. The Knights accepted Irish-Americans, African-Americans and women, but they excluded Asian workers and campaigned in support of the CHINESE EXCLUSION ACT of 1882. By 1886 the Knights claimed 700,000 members, with 60,000 members in New York City alone. Their lodge halls became self-help centers for working men, and clearing-houses for information on a variety of social-reform campaigns.

The Knights exploited their large membership to organize boycotts in support of better working conditions and an eight-hour day (*see* EIGHT-HOUR MOVEMENT). However, involvement in social protest proved costly. Albert Parsons (1848–87), a member of the Knights, was among the four men the authorities hanged for 'causing' the HAYMARKET RIOT (1886). Although Powderly denounced the riot, the authorities branded the Knights as violent subversives. Skilled workers began defecting to Samuel GOMPERS's AMERICAN FEDERATION OF LABOR and the Knights' membership rapidly declined.

Know Nothing Party, nickname given to the American Party, organized in 1852 to campaign for tougher naturalization laws. The party drew on the support of clandestine groups such as the Order of the Star Spangled Banner, and its members were enjoined to reply 'I know nothing' to strangers' questions. A surge in Irish IMMIGRATION produced an anti-immigrant and anti-Catholic backlash in many northern states that allowed Know Nothing presidential candidate Millard FILLMORE to poll 21.6% of the POPULAR VOTE in the presidential election of 1856. However, after this the party split on the issue of slavery, and by the end of the decade its support had virtually disappeared.

Korean War (1950–3), the first major conflict of the COLD WAR, in which US-led UNITED NATIONS forces fought against the communist North Koreans and Chinese, following the North Korean invasion of South Korea.

At the conclusion of World War II, the Korean peninsula (previously annexed by Japan) was divided at the 38th parallel into two occupation zones. On August 15 1948 the Republic of Korea was formed to the south of the 38th parallel, in the zone formerly occupied by the USA. On September 9 1948 the People's Republic of Korea was established to the north, in the former Soviet zone of occupation. Both republics were pledged to reunify Korea by force.

On June 25 1950 North Korean troops, using Soviet weaponry, invaded South Korea. On June 26 the UN Security Council (then being boycotted by the USSR) condemned the invasion. The same day President TRUMAN authorized air and sea strikes against North Korean forces south of the

38th parallel. On June 27 the UN General Assembly called on member nations to assist South Korea in 'repelling' the North Korean invasion. In response to the UN resolution, Truman ordered ground forces to South Korea and authorized strikes north of the 38th parallel. A US DRAFT was announced on July 7, and General Douglas MACARTHUR was appointed commander in chief of UN forces on July 8. Throughout the war the USA insisted that it was acting on behalf of the UN, and it pulled diplomatic strings to ensure that UN and Nato members sent troops to Korea to lend credence to this position. (Britain and Canada sent tens of thousands of servicemen each.)

North Korean troops narrowly failed to overrun the entire peninsula before the USA/UN could reinforce the South Koreans. Nevertheless, by September 1950, South Korean forces had been driven back to a beachhead around Pusan in the far southeast of the country. On September 15 US troops made an amphibious assault at Inchon half-way up the west of the Korean peninsula. Timed to coincide with a counter-offensive in the Pusan perimeter, this operation did not succeed in trapping the North Korean army south of the 38th parallel (as MacArthur had hoped), but it did result in the recapture of the capital of South Korea, Seoul. US troops pursuing the retreating North Korean army crossed the 38th parallel on October 1 1950. Driving north, advance US units reached the Yalu river, the frontier with China, on October 26 1950. China denounced the UN's pursuit of retreating North Koreans north of the 38th parallel, and warned on October 11 1950 that it would not 'stand idly by' if UN troops occupied North Korea. On October 15 Truman flew to Wake Island, in the middle of the Pacific, to ensure that MacArthur understood the risk of provoking Chinese intervention in the war. Yet on November 24 MacArthur ordered an 'end the war' offensive in the Yalu valley. This provoked an immediate and massive counterattack by Chinese troops. UN troops were forced into a headlong retreat south of the 38th parallel. A modest UN counter-offensive in March 1951 saw the front line stabilize just north of the 38th parallel.

During this campaigning the UN clarified its resolution of June 27 1950 to the effect that it sought a cease-fire and a return to the division of Korea along the 38th parallel. When MacArthur learned that Truman intended to discuss a cease-fire with China, he issued a statement threatening China with an expansion of the war. This scuppered truce talks for three months, and led to a renewed Chinese offensive that was repelled at great cost. Convinced that MacArthur was canvassing support among Republicans for a full-scale, even nuclear, war against China, Truman relieved him of his command on April 11 1951. (On April 19 MacArthur gave a maudlin speech of self-justification to Congress, which included the line 'Old soldiers never die, they simply fade away.')

Truce talks began on July 10 1951. They continued, with interruptions, for two years. During this period costly military operations produced a stalemate. An armistice was eventually signed on July 26 1953. It established a demilitarized zone separating North and South Korea along a frontier slightly to the north of the 38th parallel. On January 19 1954 the US Senate approved a defense pact with South Korea to guarantee the new frontier.

During the fighting 33,629 US servicemen were killed, while 20,617 died from other causes, and 103,284 were wounded. Some REPUBLICANS, notably Richard NIXON, argued that the Truman administration's conduct of the war showed the DEMOCRATS to be 'soft on communism'. Defense spending helped sustain a boom in the US economy, but created the MILITARY-INDUSTRIAL COMPLEX.

Kroc, Ray, *see* McDONALDS.

Ku Klux Klan, white supremacist secret society, first active in the years after the CIVIL WAR, and then revived in the early years of the 20th century. It is known particularly for its acts of terrorism against blacks.

The Klan was originally founded in Pulaski, Tennessee, in May 1866. It used violence and intimidation to achieve the south's REDEMPTION from RECONSTRUCTION by erecting, in partnership with local DEMOCRATIC PARTY leaders, white supremacist regimes. Klan members wore white robes with distinctive masked hoods to disguise their identity, and burned crosses at their night-time meetings. The group took its name from the sound of a rifle bolt being drawn back. Its first leader was former Confederate general Nathan Bedford Forrest (1821–77), and most of its members had served in the Confederate Army. White supremacist terrorism such as the COLFAX MASSACRE, which continued even after the Klan announced its dissolution in 1869, pushed Congress to formulate the FOURTEENTH AMENDMENT (1868), the FIF-TEENTH AMENDMENT (1870), the ENFORCEMENT ACTS (1870–1) and, ultimately, the KU KLUX KLAN ACT (1871). US Attorney General Amos T. Akerman (1821–80) utilized the last-named act in a particularly spirited attempt to break the Klan. However, the Klan withered largely because by 1877 most of its political objectives had been achieved.

In 1915 an Atlanta businessman, Colonel William Joseph Simmons, revived the Klan, adding anti-Semitism, anti-Catholicism and general xenophobia to its anti-black racism. By 1925 it claimed 5 million members. Many of these resided in northern and midwestern states, and some of them held elected office. Scandal and a flirtation with Nazism in the 1930s ended this resurgence. White backlash against the CIVIL RIGHTS MOVEMENT has provided the Klan with a new source of recruits since the 1950s.

Ku Klux Klan Act (April 20 1871), legislation passed during RECONSTRUCTION that protected the FOURTEENTH and FIFTEENTH AMENDMENTS by outlawing secret white supremacist paramilitary organizations. In October 1871 President GRANT used the act to declare nine Klan-controlled counties in South Carolina to be in a 'condition of lawlessness', justifying the suspension of habeas corpus there. The government deployed 2000 federal troops to arrest hundreds of Klansmen, while many more fled. Attorney General Amos T. Akerman (1821–80) prosecuted the ringleaders with vigor, breaking the Klan in that state. The act was unlike other ENFORCEMENT ACTS in that it was aimed at violations of civil and political rights perpetrated by individuals rather than by states.

L

Lafayette (Marie Joseph Gilbert Motier), Marquis de (1757–1834), French general and politician, who fought for the Americans during the REVOLUTIONARY WAR. In 1776, well before ratification of the FRANCO-AMERICAN ALLIANCE, Lafayette volunteered for unpaid service in the Continental Army. Commissioned a major general in 1777, he was wounded at the battle of BRANDYWINE CREEK. Thereafter, his role in the war was largely ornamental. So enduring was the symbolism of his service, however, that US troops in World War I spoke of repaying their country's debt to him.

La Follette, Robert M(arion) (1855–1925), Republican and subsequently Progressive politician. A leading member of the PROGRESSIVE wing of the REPUBLICAN PARTY, La Follette achieved national prominence when, as governor of Wisconsin (1900–6), he pushed through reforms that curbed the power of political bosses, allowed the direct election of state officials and US senators, and delegated selected state regulatory powers to panels of experts. Elected to the US Senate in 1906 he fought for lower TARIFFS, opposed US entry into WORLD WAR I, and led Senate opposition to ratification of the VERSAILLES peace treaty and US entry into the LEAGUE OF NATIONS. As the presidential nominee of the PROGRESSIVE PARTY he received 16% of the votes cast in the presidential election of 1924.

La Huelga, *see* HUELGA, LA.

Lake Champlain, battle of (September 11 1814), US naval victory in New York State during the WAR OF 1812. In the summer of 1814 a British column of some 11,000 troops mounted an invasion of New York State. Their progress depended on control of Lake Champlain. Captain Thomas MacDonough (1783–1825) forced a more powerful British squadron to engage a flotilla of 15 US vessels on his terms. On September 11 the British ships were repulsed in heavy fighting, forcing British soldiers to abandon materiel and retreat northwards.

Lake Erie, battle of (September 10 1813), US naval victory during the WAR OF 1812. A squadron of nine US ships, led by Captain Oliver Perry (1785– 1819), encountered and, after bloody fighting, captured six British vessels. Perry reported, 'We have met the enemy and they are ours.' The victory avenged the loss of the USS *CHESAPEAKE* (Perry named his flagship the *Lawrence* after the commander of the *Chesapeake*, and inscribed 'Don't give up the ship' on his battle flag, echoing Lawrence's dying exhortation to his crew). The victory also allowed US troops to cross Lake Erie, forcing a British evacuation of Detroit (September 18 1813) and leading to US victory at the battle of THAMES RIVER.

Lakota, another name for the Teton-SIOUX.

Landon, Alfred ('Alf') M(ossman) (1887–1987), Republican politician. He was governor of Kansas (1933–7), and ran as the Republicans' nominee in the presidential election of 1936. Despite being endorsed by Al SMITH, the Democratic candidate in the 1928 presidential election, he was defeated in a landslide by Franklin D. ROOSEVELT, gaining only eight votes in the ELECTORAL COLLEGE. He retired from politics in the following year.

Landrum–Griffin Act (September 14 1959), legislation that tightened up the regulation of trade-union activities. The act was passed following revelations that organized crime had infiltrated some US trade unions. Those sections of the act mandating the free election of union officials were drafted by Senator John F. KENNEDY. The act also toughened the law governing secondary picketing in a bid to prevent crooked union locals from running thinly disguised extortion rackets.

Lansing, Robert, see WILSON, WOODROW.

Laos, US operations in. Laos's neutrality in the VIETNAM WAR had been guaranteed by an international agreement signed on July 23 1962, but on February 8 1971 South Vietnamese troops supported by US aircraft invaded Laotian territory in a bid to destroy North Vietnamese bases and supply lines. The USA had been covertly aiding Laotian anti-communists and bombing North Vietnamese 'sanctuaries' in Laos for several years previously. The military performance of South Vietnamese troops during the 1971 invasion was so poor as to cast doubt on the 'Vietnamization' policy announced in the NIXON DOCTRINE. President Nixon, who justified the operation as necessary to establish 'peace with honor' in Vietnam, pressed ahead with US troop withdrawals regardless.

La Raza Unida Party, political party, organized in the large cities of the southwest in the 1970s, that reflected the growing self-assertion of the region's CHICANO (Mexican-American) population. La Raza Unida (which means 'the united people') popularized activist concepts such as AZTLAN, while campaigning to provide working-class Mexican-Americans with an alternative to the Democratic Party. As white male industrial workers deserted the Democrats for the Republicans, the former made greater efforts to retain and build upon their base of support within the Mexican-American community. This drew support away from La Raza Unida. In the presidential election of 1988 the Democratic ticket was headed by two men, Michael DUKAKIS and Lloyd Bentsen, who delivered campaign speeches in the southwest in fluent Spanish.

Lawrence textile strike (1912), industrial action in the Massachusetts town of Lawrence. Events during the strike gripped the attention of the whole country, brought the INDUSTRIAL WORKERS OF THE WORLD (IWW) to national prominence, and helped persuade Theodore ROOSEVELT to contest the PRESIDENTIAL ELECTION OF 1912.

On January 1 1912 a Massachusetts state law limiting women and children to a 54-hour working week took effect. Lawrence's mill owners, who had lobbied against the measure, put all the town's textile workers (without regard to sex or age) on a 54-hour week, but insisted that production levels be maintained. By mid-January 20,000 workers had struck in protest at the resulting pay cut and production speed-up. When the AMERICAN FEDERATION OF LABOR ignored the strikers' appeals for assistance, IWW activists, among them Bill Haywood (1869–1928) and Elizabeth Gurley FLYNN, assumed responsibility for organizing the strike. Following the murder of a female picket, strikers began sending their children out of Lawrence. Reports, some written by Margaret SANGER, describing the poor health and clothing of these children shocked middle-class Americans. Sympathy for the workers deepened when town police, ordered by mill owners to prevent the embarrassing exodus of children, attacked strikers and their families. On March 1, mill owners were forced to meet the strikers' demands. This victory of an organized workforce over vindictive employers prompted talk of a rising tide of socialism, and led Theodore Roosevelt to campaign for the presidency on a platform that urged the timely reform of capitalism to prevent revolution.

League of Nations, international organization established after WORLD WAR I with the aim of preserving world peace. During the period of US neutrality in World War I, the British Foreign Office floated the idea of a League of Nations in an attempt to convince President WILSON that Britain's war aims were principled. Wilson warmed to the idea, and included a call for its creation in his FOURTEEN POINTS.

At the PARIS PEACE CONFERENCE Wilson labored mightily to define the League's aims and remit. Article X of the League's covenant bound member states to respect and preserve the territorial integrity and political independence of every member state. Wilson tried to make this more palatable to US opinion by exempting 'regional understandings' (such as the MONROE DOCTRINE) from the League's jurisdiction, and by providing a mechanism whereby states could withdraw from the League. He also secured undertakings that League agencies would not interfere with US immigration policy, and that the USA would not be required to participate in the administration of former European colonies. Major European powers agreed to establish the League of Nations when they signed the treaty of VERSAILLES (the peace treaty with Germany that included the Covenant of the League) on June 28 1919.

In the USA approval or rejection of the League lay in the hands of the US Senate. Some isolationist senators opposed the League because they opposed any form of 'entangling alliance' with European imperialist powers. However, a majority of objectors in the Senate were so-called 'strong reservationists'. They were led by Republican Senator Henry Cabot Lodge (1850–1924), who on November 6 submitted to the Senate 'Fourteen Reservations' arguing for amendments to the design of the League that would protect US interests. Wilson, who suffered a stroke while touring the country trying to drum up support for the League, insisted that the Senate approve or reject the Versailles peace treaty as it stood. On November 19 1919 the Senate rejected the treaty, and with it US entry into the League, by 53–38.

Lebanon, US intervention in (1958, 1982–4). The USA has intervened twice militarily in this Middle East country to the north of Israel.

(1) On July 15 1958 the USA began landing a force that reached a peak strength of 14,500 in a bid to quell factional fighting fueled by the decision of incumbent president Camille Chamoun to seek re-election in defiance of the Lebanese constitution. The USA claimed that the EISENHOWER DOCTRINE justified their 102-day occupation of the country. Chamoun renounced his candidacy, but the intervention was greeted with anger in the Middle East.

(2) On September 29 1983 Congress approved an escalated military intervention in Lebanon. This grew out of US participation in a multinational UN peacekeeping force sent to Lebanon in November 1982 to maintain a cease-fire in the Lebanese civil war. This US presence angered Muslim fundamentalist terrorist groups. On April 18 1983, 47 people were killed by a bomb planted at the US embassy in Beirut. President REAGAN authorized the use of air and sea strikes to destroy the terrorist bases used to carry out the attack. This increased anti-American attacks to the point where the Reagan administration asked Congress for a full-scale troop deployment. On October 23 1983, 241 US servicemen were killed in a bomb attack on the US barracks in Beirut. Further attacks followed, prompting the

Reagan administration to withdraw all US personnel from Lebanon in February 1984.

Lecompton constitution, proposed constitution for Kansas drawn up by pro-slavery settlers in 1857. President BUCHANAN had asked settlers to resolve the turmoil in BLEEDING KANSAS by drafting a new constitution that would serve as the basis for statehood. In 1857 pro-slavery forces in temporary control of the territorial legislature meeting at Lecompton drafted a constitution permitting slavery. They submitted this constitution for ratification with the stipulation that even if settlers voted not to permit slavery, slaves already imported into Kansas would remain enslaved. This chicanery outraged abolitionists. FREE-SOIL settlers twice rejected the constitution in 1858. In 1859 they secured a constitution prohibiting slavery and emancipating slaves already resident in Kansas.

Lee, Robert E(dward) (1807–70), Confederate general during the CIVIL WAR who eventually became commander in chief of the Confederate Army. He is generally considered one of the most capable military leaders of the war.

Lee was the son of Revolutionary War general 'Light Horse' Harry Lee, and was married to a great-granddaughter of Martha Washington. A career soldier, who saw service in the MEXICAN WAR and on frontier cavalry patrols, Lee was offered command of the Union armies by President Lincoln on April 18 1861. After a night of soul-searching, he decided his first loyalty was to his home state of Virginia. On June 1 1862 he was appointed commander of the Confederate Army of Northern Virginia. Lee relieved pressure on Richmond in the SEVEN DAYS' BATTLES (1862). Following victories at MANASSAS, FREDRICKSBURG and CHANCELLORSVILLE, in 1863 Lee launched a thrust north into Union territory. Defeat at GETTYSBURG (Pennsylvania) proved to be the turning point of the war. In 1864 Lee slowed Ulysses GRANT's advance into Vir-

ginia. But he lacked the forces to exploit his victory in the battle of the WILDERNESS. On April 9 1865, Lee, by now commander in chief of the Confederate Army, surrendered to Grant at APPOMATTOX COURT HOUSE. After the war he became president of Washington College, which was renamed Washington and Lee in his honor.

Legal Tender Acts (1862, 1863), legislation intended to meet the cost of the CIVIL WAR. In February 1862 Congress approved the printing of $150 million worth of paper notes and ordered creditors and debtors to accept them as legal tender. The notes became known as GREENBACKS, and their viability was linked to the enactment of a federal INCOME TAX. In 1863 Congress authorized the Treasury to issue a further $300 million.

legal-tender cases, a number of cases brought before the US Supreme Court regarding the right of the government to issue paper money. In their 1870 ruling on Hepburn vs. Griswold the Supreme Court declared (5–3) that the LEGAL TENDER ACTS of 1862 and 1863 were unconstitutional, in that by forcing creditors to accept paper money (GREENBACKS) they interfered with contracts struck before the passage of the acts. The dissenters argued that such interference was justified in time of war. President GRANT appointed two new justices to the Court, and in 1871 it ruled that the government did have the right to pass legal-tender laws in times of emergency. In an 1884 ruling the Court declared that the US government's right to print paper money, at any time, was implied by Article I Section 8 of the Constitution.

Leisure Class, Theory of the, *see THEORY OF THE LEISURE CLASS.*

Lemke, William, *see* UNION PARTY.

Lend-Lease Act (March 11 1941), legislation that allowed the president to nominate countries that would be eligible to purchase US arms by sale, lease or transfer. The act was the product of a stealthy campaign by

President Franklin D. ROOSEVELT to grant aid to Great Britain without involving the USA in WORLD WAR II. Roosevelt compared the act to lending a neighbor a garden hose to extinguish a house fire. ISOLATIONIST Senator Robert Taft (1889–1953) retorted that lending war materiel was like lending chewing gum – it had no value on return. Through the Act Britain acquired convoy escort vessels that played a crucial role in stemming the shipping losses resulting from German U-boat attacks in the North Atlantic. Lend-Lease aid also played a vital, though largely unacknowledged role, in equipping the Soviet army to repel the German invasion of Russia. All Lend-Lease aid was abruptly canceled following Japan's surrender in August 1945.

Letter from Birmingham City Jail (1963), open letter written by Martin Luther KING during a nine-day period of solitary confinement incurred during the BIRMINGHAM DESEGREGATION CAMPAIGN. King had been imprisoned for breaking a court order banning protest marches. In the letter he sought to defend the CIVIL RIGHTS MOVEMENT from the charge that it created tensions that should be resolved in negotiations with white civic leaders. Published in pamphlet form by American Quakers, King's letter compared injustice to a 'boil' that 'must be exposed, with all the tension exposure creates, to the light of human conscience and the air of national opinion before it can be cured'.

Letters from a Farmer in Pennsylvania, series of twelve essays written by John DICKINSON, which laid out some of the most influential criticisms of British policy made during the AMERICAN REVOLUTION. The essays were published weekly from November 30 1767 in the *Pennsylvania Chronicle*, and then reprinted in pamphlet form throughout the colonies. Dickinson argued that the QUARTERING ACT of 1765 imposed an unconstitutional obligation on colonial assemblies to tax their constituents. He

accepted that the British Parliament might pass laws designed to regulate imperial trade, but argued that the TOWNSHEND ACT (1767) was unjust because it was designed to raise revenue. Dickinson's *Letters* raised the question of how power should be shared between Parliament and the colonies. He sought a negotiated settlement of these issues, urging colonists to petition for repeal of an 'unmerited blow' aimed at 'dutiful children' by a 'beloved parent'. Some of his readers, on both sides of the Atlantic, took a more uncompromising approach.

Levittowns, pioneering postwar suburban housing tracts constructed by the building firm William Levitt and Sons. The first Levittown was built in Hempstead, New York, between 1947 and 1951. It eventually provided over 17,000 private homes. Levitt and Sons drove down the cost of homes in their development by standardizing the design and construction processes, by hiring non-union labor and by utilizing prefabricated components. Modern kitchen appliances were included in the purchase price of a home and the new houses were built around standardized civic amenities. White buyers fleeing ethnic neighborhoods were wooed by the easy credit terms Levitt offered. African-Americans were excluded from the new developments. Although the houses were extremely basic, the privacy they offered was greatly valued and the company subsequently built a second Levittown on the outskirts of Philadelphia and a third in southern New Jersey. By following Levitt and Sons' lead during the BABY BOOM, developers transformed the face of America, creating in the process its distinctive suburban culture.

Lewinsky scandal, scandal involving President CLINTON and a young White House intern. Clinton's sexual encounters with Monica Lewinsky, which came to light in the context of court proceedings arising from a sexual harassment suit brought against him, produced the first IMPEACHMENT trial of an elected president in US history.

In July 1995 Lewinsky joined the White House as an intern. She was, at least initially, smitten with the president. She later testified that on November 15 1995 she had her first sexual encounter with Clinton. In April 1996 she was transferred to the Pentagon after White House staffers complained that she was spending too much time hanging around the presidential quarters. She and Clinton saw less of each other, and as the affair cooled, Lewinsky began confiding in a friend, Linda R. Tripp. From September 1997 Tripp began secretly taping telephone conversations with Lewinsky in which they discussed her affair with Clinton.

Meanwhile, on May 27 1997, the US Supreme Court ruled that Clinton could not use executive privilege to avoid defending a sexual harassment suit brought by Paula Corbin Jones relating to events that occurred when Clinton was governor of Arkansas. In October lawyers representing Jones received a tip-off revealing the existence of Linda Tripp's tapes. The tapes were useful to Jones's lawyers because they held out the possibility of proving a pattern in Clinton's behavior. On November 24 Jones's lawyers subpoenaed Tripp to testify in the harassment case. By this time White House staffers had found Lewinsky a job in New York and removed from her apartment various gifts and notes given to her by the president. On January 7 1998 Lewinsky signed an affadavit for Jones's lawyers in which she denied having had a sexual relationship with Clinton. On January 17 Clinton told Jones's lawyers that he had not had a sexual affair with Lewinsky. This seemed to end matters.

However, on January 12 1998 the tapes made by Linda Tripp were passed to Kenneth Starr, a congressionally appointed independent prosecutor investigating various charges of sexual and financial misconduct leveled against Clinton. Starr reported the substance of the tapes to Congress, and four days later received authorization to investigate the Lewinsky affair. This had serious implications for Clinton. The position of special prosecutor was established after the WATERGATE SCANDAL. Special prosecutors are empowered to establish broad terms of investigation, and are equipped with formidable powers to compel witness testimony.

News media broke the Lewinsky story on January 21 1998. In a televised statement made on January 26 Clinton said: 'I did not have sexual relations with that woman, Miss Lewinsky. I have never told anybody a lie, not a single time – never.' In July Starr issued a subpoena for Clinton to testify before a grand jury investigating the possibility of criminal charges arising from the Lewinsky affair, and at the same time offered Lewinsky immunity from prosecution in return for her testimony. Following his grand-jury testimony on August 17 Clinton told the nation, 'I did have a relationship with Ms Lewinsky that was not appropriate.' Paula Jones's lawyers, who had their harassment case thrown out of court on April 1 1998, now filed to have their suit reinstated, and Clinton faced the possibility of being compelled to testify in that case as well.

Kenneth Starr released his report on September 9 1998. It suggested that there were probable grounds for Clinton's impeachment. The US Constitution charges the House of Representatives with the preparation of articles of impeachment. On October 5 the House Judiciary Committee voted 21–16 to open an investigation of grounds for impeachment, and on October 8 the full House endorsed this decision by 258–176. While a battle raged in the House over whether to impeach the president and, if so, on what charges, on November 13 Clinton reached an out-of-court settlement with Paula Jones in which he paid her $850,000 in return for her agreement to drop her sexual harassment suit. On December 19 the House voted by 228–206 to impeach Clinton for perjuring himself, and by 221–212 to impeach him for obstructing justice. Two other charges, abuse of presidential power and perjury in the Jones case, were dropped.

In accordance with the Constitution the Senate sat in judgment on the impeachment charges. Their deliberations began on January 7 1999. Closing arguments were heard on February 8 1999. Impeachment must be approved by a two-thirds majority of the Senate, in this case 67 votes. On February 12 1999 the Senate voted 55–45 on the impeachment article citing perjury in the Lewinsky case and 50–50 on the article citing obstruction of justice. Since neither article received a two-thirds majority, the case closed and Clinton remained in office.

This outcome seems to have broadly reflected public opinion, with many Americans taking the view that Clinton's behavior was reprehensible, but did not warrant removal from office. Clinton was helped by the health of the US economy, and by the widespread belief that extreme right-wingers were milking the case as a means of discrediting him. Clinton's defense against perjury, that he understood 'sexual relations' to mean full sexual intercourse and that he and Lewinsky had only indulged in oral sex, may also have struck the public as more believable than many commentators assumed. However, his nit-picking and evasive answers to prosecutors (at one point he responded to a question 'It depends what the meaning of "is" is'), as well, of course, as the fact that he had had an affair with a 21-year-old woman, irreparably damaged his standing.

Lewis, John L(lewellyn) (1880–1969), trade-union leader who was a lifelong advocate of INDUSTRIAL UNIONISM, and who struggled throughout his career to bring disciplined 'big labor' into partnership with 'big government'.

The son of a Welsh miner, Lewis himself became a coal-face worker (in Lucas, Iowa) at the age of 16. He joined the UNITED MINE WORKERS OF AMERICA (UMWA), and as its legislative agent in Illinois (1909–11) secured passage of state laws regarding mine safety and workman's compensation. He became president of the UMWA in 1920, a post he held for 40 years. In 1922 he organized a successful strike by workers in bituminous coal fields, but for the rest of the 1920s he followed the policy of the AMERICAN FEDERATION OF LABOR (AFL) of preserving gains made.

In 1934 Lewis was elected vice president of the AFL, and urged that body to exploit the opportunity presented by Franklin D. ROOSEVELT's election by creating a Committee on Industrial Organization to explore ways of unionizing mass-production workers. At the 1935 AFL convention in Atlantic City, New Jersey, the president of the Carpenter's Union questioned the work of this committee and made disparaging remarks about the intelligence and ethnicity of the average factory worker. Lewis mounted the podium, punched him out, resigned from the AFL, and took his UMWA into an alliance with other industrial unions, which, under Lewis's leadership, was formalized (in 1938) as the CONGRESS OF INDUSTRIAL ORGANIZATIONS (CIO).

The CIO was a key member of the NEW DEAL COALITION, but during WORLD WAR II Lewis became alienated from Roosevelt. He pulled the UMWA out of the CIO in 1942. Relations between the CIO and the Democratic Party were furthered strained when, during the UMWA's successful COAL STRIKE OF 1946, Lewis was convicted of contempt of court. Lewis's dress was that of a working-class dandy, his behavior that of a party 'boss', and his abiding loyalty was to the union.

Lewis and Clark expedition (1804–6), expedition to explore the American west led by Captain Meriwether Lewis (1774–1809) and Lieutenant William Clark (1770–1838). The expedition found a way through the Rocky Mountains to the Pacific Ocean.

On January 18 1803, on the eve of the LOUISIANA PURCHASE, President JEFFERSON persuaded Congress to appropriate funds to finance an expedition to explore territory in the Great Plains and Rockies then under French sovereignty. A 27-man 'Corps of Discovery', led by Lewis and Clark, headed northwest from St Louis on May 14 1804. The expedition was accompanied by a SHOSHONI woman called SACAJAWEA who, with her French husband, served as interpreter. Lewis also took his slave. The party wintered near the present site of Bismarck, North Dakota. In the spring of 1805 the party encountered Shoshoni settlements from whom, thanks to Sacajawea's intercession, horses and information about passage through the Rockies were obtained. The expedition reached the Pacific Ocean on November 18 1805. It began its return journey in March 1806, reaching St Louis on September 23. The wealth of information about western lands and peoples brought back by the expedition delighted Jefferson. The US claim to the Pacific northwest, tested in the OREGON BORDER CRISIS, originated in Lewis and Clark's 'discovery' of the region.

Lexington and Concord, battles of (April 19 1775), the first, inconclusive engagements of the REVOLUTIONARY WAR, fought in Massachusetts. The first shots were fired, without command, on Lexington Green, when British troops on a mission to destroy military supplies in Concord panicked and opened fire on a body of retreating MINUTEMEN. The redcoats eventually destroyed targets in Concord, but were harried by a 4000-strong force of minutemen on their march back to Boston. The minutemen had been alerted on the night of April 18 by Paul REVERE, a Boston silversmith who rode through the British lines to warn of the attack.

Liberal Republican Party, a short-lived offshoot of the REPUBLICAN PARTY that coalesced in 1871. Liberal Republicans were alienated by the corruption witnessed during GRANT's presidency, and favored a lenient approach to the RECONSTRUCTION of the south. The party nominated Horace GREELEY to run against the incumbent Grant in the 1872 presidential election, but following Greeley's defeat the party dissolved, with most members joining the DEMOCRATIC PARTY.

Liberator, The, weekly newspaper published by William Lloyd GARRISON that trumpeted the views of the radical wing of the ABOLITION movement in antebellum America. Its first issue, published on January 1 1831, set a tone that would be maintained throughout the paper's existence. In this issue Garrison announced, 'I am in earnest – I will not equivocate – I will not excuse – I will not retreat a single inch; and I will be heard.' The *Liberator* called for the immediate uncompensated abolition of slavery. It was scornful of southern claims that slavery enjoyed protection under the constitution, and it denounced congressmen who 'collaborated' with the slave system. Although the paper had a tiny circulation, perhaps 3000, many southerners assumed that most northerners subscribed to the radical views put forward in the pages of the *Liberator* and agreed with Garrison's inflammatory attacks on the southern way of life. The paper helped to create tensions and misunderstandings that were a major cause of the CIVIL WAR. The paper ceased publication when the THIRTEENTH AMENDMENT (abolishing slavery) was ratified on December 29 1865. *see also* NEWSPAPERS.

Liberty, Sons of, *see* SONS OF LIBERTY.

Liberty Party, political party dedicated to the ABOLITION of slavery by constitutional amendment. It held its first national convention in 1840. In 1844 a strong showing in New York State by its nominee James Birney (1792–1857) hindered the presidential bid of WHIG Henry CLAY, and contributed to the victory of James POLK. But Polk's determination to annex Texas led Liberty Party members to support the FREE SOIL ticket in 1848.

Liberty riot, incident in the early phase of the AMERICAN REVOLUTION. When on June 10 1768 officials appointed under the AMERICAN BOARD OF CUSTOMS ACT attempted to seize John Hancock's ship *Liberty* on suspicion of smuggling, a crowd protected the ship and menaced the officials. The incident prompted the British government to send 2000 troops to Boston.

Lincoln, Abraham (1809–65), Republican statesman and 16th president of the USA (1861–5). He led the Union against the CONFEDERACY in the CIVIL WAR, so bringing about the end of slavery in the USA, but was assassinated at the moment of victory.

Lincoln was born in a log cabin near Hodgenville, Kentucky. The simple integrity contemporaries recognized in him after his death was the product of a youth spent splitting fence rails and traveling a mile for water on the family farm, in what Lincoln described as the 'unpoetical' surroundings of Spencer County, southern Indiana. There was, however, a kind of poetry in the family's hardship there: in 1818, at nine years of age, Lincoln helped bury his mother by whittling the wooden pegs that held together a coffin fashioned for her from logs cut for the family cabin.

Farm life held no attraction for Lincoln, even when the family had moved to the richer lands of the Illinois prairie. In 1828 he built a flatboat and rafted a cargo of produce down the Mississippi river to New Orleans. On his return he ran a store in New Salem, Illinois. In 1832 he volunteered for service in the BLACK HAWK WAR and was elected captain of his militia unit. In 1833 he was made postmaster of New Salem, and in 1834 he entered the state legislature as a WHIG, serving until 1842. Meanwhile, after two years of self-tuition, Lincoln was admit-

ted to the Bar, and he moved to Springfield, Illinois, to open a law practice in 1837. In 1842 he married Mary Todd. She was from a grand, slave-owning Kentucky family, a background that caused Lincoln some political embarrassment during the Civil War. She had made it known that she wished to marry a future president of the USA and, with uncanny judgment, she chose Lincoln, who had just left the state legislature, after rejecting Stephen DOUGLAS, who had just been elected to the US House of Representatives. With Mary's encouragement, Lincoln remained politically active. He was elected to a term in the US House of Representatives (1847–9), but his initial opposition to the MEXICAN WAR dashed any hope of being re-elected. He seemed fated to spend the rest of his life doing what he liked best, practicing criminal law and swapping jokes and tall stories with other lawyers.

The KANSAS–NEBRASKA ACT and BLEEDING KANSAS struggle drove Lincoln to leave the Whigs for the REPUBLICAN PARTY in 1856. On June 17 1858 he announced in the 'HOUSE DIVIDED' SPEECH his intention to challenge Stephen Douglas for election to Illinois's US Senate seat. The LINCOLN–DOUGLAS DEBATES presented fine moral and constitutional reasoning in a carnival atmosphere. They made Lincoln, who lost the election, a national figure.

Lincoln regarded slavery as morally indefensible. He opposed the admission of new slave states into the Union. But he believed that where slavery already existed it enjoyed constitutional protection. Lincoln was, above all else, a constitutionalist. These positions made him a moderate within the Republican Party. In May 1860 he gained (on the fourth ballot) the Republicans' presidential nomination. In the PRESIDENTIAL ELECTION OF 1860 Lincoln received 40% of the POPULAR VOTE, but failed to carry a single southern state. He began his presidency on March 4 1861.

The SECESSION of the southern, slave states began before Lincoln was sworn in. In his inaugural address, Lincoln reiterated that where slavery existed it enjoyed constitutional protection, and that he had neither the right nor the inclination to interfere with its status. But he insisted that secession was unconstitutional as well as impracticable. 'It is safe to assert,' he told an unenthusiastic crowd, 'that no government proper ever had a provision in its organic law for its own termination.' The Union was to be preserved. This was Lincoln's war aim. It was controversial and, in 1861, seemed unachievable. (General George McCLELLAN thought it showed Lincoln to be a 'well-meaning baboon'.) Many northerners thought the Union well rid of the southern slave states. Moderate southerners found it hard to accept that if the Union were preserved on northern terms, southern states would occupy a politically subordinate position within it.

During the war, Lincoln fielded criticism from RADICAL REPUBLICANS who pressed him to destroy slavery. He suspended habeas corpus and used military courts to try COPPERHEADS and PEACE DEMOCRATS, leading even some of his own cabinet to wonder whether Lincoln was in fact destroying the Constitution he sought to preserve. Nonetheless, Lincoln stressed repeatedly that the preservation of the Union was the one true goal of his administration. He justified the EMANCIPATION PROCLAMATION (1863) in these terms and gradually converted public opinion to his view. Even his opponent in the PRESIDENTIAL ELECTION OF 1864, George McClellan, accepted that 'the Union must be preserved at all hazards'. In the GETTYSBURG ADDRESS, Lincoln memorably explained why he believed that Union should be preserved: 'that this nation, under God, shall have a new birth of freedom; and that government of the people, by the people, and for the people, shall not perish from the earth.' Nevertheless, opposition to the draft, concern over restrictions on civil liberties, and racist scare-mongering meant that in 1864 McClellan came within 400,000 of Lincoln's POPULAR VOTE total of 2,216,067.

Lincoln set lenient terms for the reintegration of southern states within the Union. Had he lived he might have found it impossible to harness his own party to the task of binding the nation's wounds 'with malice toward none' and 'with charity for all'. But Lincoln never got the chance to direct RECONSTRUCTION. On April 14 1865 he was shot during the third act of a comedy entitled *Our American Cousin* performed at Ford's Theatre in Washington DC. He died the next day. His assassin was a deranged actor, John Wilkes BOOTH. Lincoln was buried in Springfield, Illinois.

Lincoln Battalion, *see* ABRAHAM LINCOLN BATTALION.

Lincoln–Douglas debates, series of debates between the Republican Abraham LINCOLN and the Democrat Stephen DOUGLAS, rivals in the 1858 Illinois election for the US Senate.

Between August 21 and October 13, Lincoln and Douglas travelled the state holding seven separate debates on slavery and its future status. Each drew large crowds and partisan demonstrations. Transcripts were read by a national audience. Douglas eventually won the seat by formulating the FREEPORT DOCTRINE, which temporized on the question of whether Americans could prevent the spread of slavery in the light of the DRED SCOTT verdict. However, the debates transformed Lincoln into a national figure because he reminded listeners that behind arguments over the KANSAS–NEBRASKA ACT and the Dred Scott case lay the morality of slavery itself. Lincoln asked why southerners ever emancipated faithful slaves unless prompted by uneasy consciences. He insisted that although black slaves might possess inferior moral and intellectual endowments, they had as much right as any white man to eat bread earned by their own labor.

Lindbergh, Charles Augustus (1902–74), pioneering US aviator, fascist sympathizer and the unfortunate subject of one of the great news stories of the 1930s.

Lindbergh was born in Detroit, Michigan, and developed his flying skills carrying airmail from St. Louis to Chicago. His father was a Republican congressman and Lindbergh put his social connections to use to persuade the Ryan Aircraft Corporation of St. Louis to back his bid to become the first man to fly solo across the Atlantic. Flying the *Spirit of St. Louis*, Lindbergh completed a 33-hour transatlantic solo flight on May 21 1927. On his return to the USA, Lindbergh was awarded the Congressional Medal of Honor. He worked subsequently as a consultant to the burgeoning US commercial airline industry and, with his wife Anne Morrow Lindbergh (1906–), undertook further exploratory flights. The Lindberghs were already a glamorous and newsworthy couple when, in 1932, their infant son was kidnapped and murdered in mysterious circumstances. The Lindberghs fled to England in 1935 to escape press attention resulting from the unsolved case.

Lindbergh accepted the tenets of SOCIAL DARWINISM and, during the period 1935–9, became interested in theories of racial purity and the global menace of Soviet communism. He made three visits to Nazi Germany, during which he acted as a test pilot for the Luftwaffe and accepted Nazi awards. Returning to the USA in 1939, he became a strong advocate of ISOLATIONISM and campaigned against Franklin D. ROOSEVELT in the presidential election of 1940. He also urged Congress not to grant LEND-LEASE aid to Britain. During WORLD WAR II Lindbergh volunteered to fly combat missions against the Japanese. In 1954 President EISENHOWER commissioned Lindbergh as a brigadier-general in the US Air Force Reserve and consulted him on the USA's strategic needs.

Lindbergh's last public act was to campaign from the retirement estate he had carved out of Hawaii's rainforest against granting landing rights in the USA to the Anglo-French supersonic plane Concorde.

Little Big Horn, battle of (June 25 1876), engagement in Montana in which a small US Army unit was wiped out by a superior Native American force. It was the defining moment of the third SIOUX WAR, and the Plains Indians' last effective blow against US domination of their lands.

Ordered to surround and observe a massive Native American encampment, General George CUSTER divided his Seventh Cavalry before launching an unwise afternoon attack with just 225 troopers. His entire force was annihilated by 2500 SIOUX and CHEYENNE warriors led by Crazy Horse (Ta-Sunko-Witko, *c*.1842–77) and SITTING BULL. Popular agitation for vengeance ensured that the Teton-Sioux were firmly and finally suppressed. Sitting Bull and his followers fled to Canada, where they were protected by the North-West Mounted Police.

Little Rock school desegregation battle (September 1957), standoff at the Central High School in Little Rock, Arkansas, which illustrated the depth of hostility among southern whites to civil rights reform. The crisis arose from white resistance to the implementation of the US Supreme Court decision in BROWN VS. BOARD OF EDUCATION declaring racial segregation of public schools unconstitutional. Arkansas Governor Orval Faubus (1910–94), who was facing re-election, deployed the state National Guard at the previously all-white high school – ostensibly to prevent violence but effectively blocking enforcement of a federal court order that black pupils be admitted. On September 23, after Faubus had obeyed a federal court order to withdraw the guardsmen, a white mob chased six black pupils from the school premises. On September 24 President EISENHOWER ordered

1000 paratroopers to the school campus, and placed the state National Guard under federal command. On September 25 nine black pupils attended classes. Faubus thwarted further federal intervention by closing the city's entire high-school system for the remainder of the year.

Lochner vs. New York (April 17 1905), US Supreme Court ruling (5–4) that a New York state law preventing bakers from working more than 60 hours a week was unconstitutional. Justice Rufus Wheeler Peckham (1838–1909), from New York State, spoke for the majority when he opined that laws 'limiting the hours grown and intelligent men may labor to earn their living' were 'mere meddlesome interferences' with individual rights. The Court retreated from this position in MULLER VS. OREGON (1908).

Lockean thought, the political philosophy of the English thinker John Locke (1632–1704), which had an important influence on the political principles outlined in the American DECLARATION OF INDEPENDENCE.

In his *Two Treatises on Government* (1690) Locke argued that men created governments by agreement or 'compact' in order to protect and enjoy 'natural rights', especially those of life, liberty and property. Where, for example, a government taxed a people without their consent, it contravened their natural right to enjoy secure possession of property. Since governments derived legitimacy from the consent of the governed, persistent contravention of natural rights released men from their obligation to obey agreements they had entered into, and warranted the creation of a new compact.

These theories were congenial to Americans seeking to justify on principle their opposition to British legislation. They were less useful when applied to problems raised once independence had been secured. How, if at all, could Americans agree on a form of government capable of mediating between legitimate interests (like those of debtor and creditor, or slaveholder and non-slaveholder) without creating either legislative tyranny or perpetual revolt in the name of natural rights? SHAYS'S REBELLION and the KENTUCKY and VIRGINIA RESOLUTIONS turned on this issue.

Loco-focos, nickname given to former members of the WORKINGMEN'S PARTY who joined the reform wing of the Democratic Party in New York in 1834. These radical JACKSONIAN DEMOCRATS sought tighter regulation of banks and corporations, progressive taxation, and support for the working man. The nickname was taken from the brand name of the matches the group used to light candles on a night when mainstream TAMMANY HALL DEMOCRATS plunged a hall in which they had been meeting into darkness. Following the presidential election of 1836 the fledgling party was absorbed once more within the Democratic party.

Lodge, Henry Cabot, *see* LEAGUE OF NATIONS.

Loewe vs. Lawler, *see* DANBURY HATTERS' CASE.

Log Cabin and Hard Cider campaign, nickname for the 1840 presidential election campaign. During the campaign a Democratic newspaper attempted to belittle WHIG nominee William HARRISON by characterising him as a man best suited to sipping cider in a frontier shack. Harrison, of Virginia planter stock, was delighted to be tagged as a rugged frontiersmen. He was toasted in cider at rallies held in log cabins throughout the west. The Whig slogan 'Tippecanoe and Tyler too' reminded voters both of Harrison's victory at the battle of TIPPECANOE CREEK and of the name of his running mate. Harrison won the election.

Long, Huey (Pierce) (1893–1935), charismatic Louisiana politician who in the early 1930s developed the Share-our-Wealth movement, a popular alternative to the NEW DEAL.

Long was elected governor of Louisiana in 1928 on a populist platform that denounced oil corporations. In 1931 he was elected to the US Senate and he resigned the governorship to take up his seat in 1932. He launched the Share-our-Wealth program in 1934. This envisioned fighting the GREAT DEPRESSION by granting every adult American an allowance of $5000 to establish a home, and a guaranteed annual income of $2500. The programme was to be financed by corporate taxes, punitive taxes on personal estates worth more than $1 million, and the expropriation of personal assets in excess of $5 million. Long, and 4.6 million supporters, believed that redistributing wealth would restore purchasing power and end the depression. In March 1935 Long announced he would run against Franklin D. ROOSEVELT in the presidential election of 1936. He was assassinated on September 10 1935. Had he lived he might have drawn enough votes from Roosevelt to allow a Republican victory in 1936.

Long Island, battle of (August 27 1776), engagement during the Revolutionary War in which British forces defeated the Americans defending New York City. Following the battle of BUNKER HILL British forces evacuated Boston and regrouped for an assault on New York City. On July 2 1776, 10,000 redcoats landed on Staten Island. By August, 32,000 troops, including 9000 Hessians, were encamped there. Between August 22 and 25 a British force of 20,000 crossed the bay to Long Island, occupying ground near the present site of John F. Kennedy airport. On August 26–27 the British outflanked American defenses in Flatbush and Brooklyn Heights, inflicting heavy casualties and opening the way for the occupation of the city (*see* NEW YORK CITY, BRITISH OCCUPATION OF).

Lookout Mountain, battle of, *see* CHICKAMAUGA, BATTLE OF.

loose constructionism, reading of the US Constitution that centers on Article I Section 8 (see Appendix 1), which FEDERALISTS and WHIGS interpreted as giving Congress the right to take measures, such as creating a BANK OF THE UNITED STATES, that were both implicit in the powers granted to it by the Constitution and not expressly forbidden. The Supreme Court, in McCULLOCH VS. MARYLAND (1819) gave powerful support to the doctrine. The opposite doctrine, STRICT CONSTRUCTIONISM, argued that the federal government possessed only those powers expressly delegated to it by the Constitution.

Louisiana, southern state, bordered on the east by the Mississippi river and the state of Mississippi, on the south by the Gulf of Mexico, on the west by Texas and on the north by Arkansas. The present state was originally part of the much larger French colony of Louisiana (a vast area that stretched from the Mississippi river west to the Rockies). New Orleans, founded in 1718, and Baton Rouge, founded in 1719, were the principal French settlements. During this period, the economy of southern Louisiana became dependent on trade through New Orleans and the production of cash crops using slave labor. The treaty of PARIS (1763), which concluded the SEVEN YEARS' WAR, transferred Louisiana from French to Spanish jurisdiction. French hegemony within the colony was preserved by the migration of several thousand Acadians (CAJUNS), and France regained control of the colony through the treaty of SAN ILDEFONSO (1800). The USA acquired most of the modern state of Louisiana, as well as the entire French Louisiana territory, through the LOUISIANA PURCHASE (1803). Louisiana became the 18th state on April 30 1812 and its modern boundaries were established through the ADAMS–ONIS treaty of 1819.

By 1860 Louisiana had over 700,000 permanent residents. African-American slaves, employed on cotton and sugar plantations, accounted for nearly half of this total. A distinctive feature of the state's white population was the prominence within it of residents claiming French and Spanish ancestry. The city of New Orleans, home to a thriving free black community, was particularly cosmopolitan. On January 26 1861, Louisiana became the sixth state to join the CONFEDERACY. Union troops seized New Orleans and occupied the state in 1862. Self-government was restored in February 1864, following the adoption of a pro-Union state constitution which outlawed slavery. However, white supremacists seized control of the new state legislature and developed repressive BLACK CODES. The NEW ORLEANS RIOT (1866) was symptomatic of the hostility towards RECONSTRUCTION expressed by much of the state's white population. Congress responded to racial violence and intimidation in Louisiana by imposing a further period of military rule (March 2 1867 to June 25 1868). However, the Democratic party continued its efforts to 'redeem' the state from Republican rule. The COLFAX MASSACRE (1873) exemplified the racial violence which accompanied this struggle. Louisiana was one of four states at the center of the disputed PRESIDENTIAL ELECTION OF 1876. Following the COMPROMISE OF 1877, the Democratic party secured control of Louisiana and set about abridging the civil liberties of the state's African-American population. The legal foundations of a system of racial segregation that eventually dominated the southern United States were laid by US Supreme Court verdicts (notably those in response to the SLAUGHTERHOUSE CASES and PLESSY VS. FERGUSON) upholding the objectives of laws passed by the Louisiana legislature.

In 1900, Louisiana had over 1,300,000 permanent residents, the vast majority of whom were employed in agriculture. Many African-Americans left the state during the GREAT MIGRATION to search for jobs in northern cities. This changed the racial balance of the state's population. In the 1930s, the charismatic politician Huey LONG exploited this change to build a power base within the state. Later, during the CIVIL RIGHTS MOVEMENT, white politicians used a variety of tactics to delay desegregation within the state. In 1990, Louisiana's population numbered 4,219,973, making it the 21st most populous state in the union.

Louisiana Purchase (1803), deal through which the USA acquired the port of New Orleans and all French territory on the west bank of the Mississippi. The deal was struck in Paris, at the behest of President JEFFERSON, on April 11 1803. The USA gained 800,000 square miles (2 million square km) of territory, stretching from New Orleans to the Rockies, for $11,250,000 and the federal government's assumption of responsibility for settling $3,750,000 of claims against France made by US citizens. The purchase, ratified by the US Senate by 26–5 on October 20 1803, doubled the size of the USA. It also secured RIGHT OF DEPOSIT (the right of Americans to transport goods down the Mississippi and deposit them in the port of New Orleans before shipment overseas). Western frontiersmen welcomed the increase in land values and the prospect of future prosperity produced by secure access to the Gulf of Mexico via the Mississippi river system. FEDERALISTS questioned Jefferson's authority to conduct the purchase, but the Supreme Court ruled it legal in American Insurance Company vs. Canter (1828). France formally transferred the territory on December 20 1803.

Lowndes County Freedom Organization (LCFO), black activist group founded in April 1966 to coordinate a voter registration and civil rights campaign in rural Alabama. Its formation marked a turning point in the CIVIL RIGHTS MOVEMENT because LCFO membership was restricted to African-Americans. This policy reflected the frustration accumulated by STUDENT NON-VIOLENT COORDINATING COMMITTEE (SNCC) activists in over two years of local campaigning. Stokeley CARMICHAEL's use of the slogan BLACK POWER in speeches defending the LCFO divided the movement still further. The BLACK PANTHER PARTY appropriated LCFO's logo.

loyalists or **Tories,** those Americans who chose to remain loyal to Britain and the crown during the AMERICAN REVOLUTION and REVOLUTIONARY WAR. At least 20% of America's population was actively loyalist, and many more were only lukewarm supporters of independence. Loyalists could be found among all classes and ethnicities, but they were comparatively rare in New England and Virginia. Veterans of the southern REGULATOR MOVEMENTS sided with Britain during the Revolution in the hopes that royal government might prove more responsive to their needs than government by local American juntas. Elsewhere Americans stayed loyal to Britain from a conviction that America would lose the Revolutionary War or from fear of mob rule. A virtual civil war between loyalists and patriots was fought south of Virginia between 1778 and 1780. Many states enacted legislation permitting the confiscation of loyalist property, and 60,000 loyalists left America in the period 1776–83, a per-capita rate of exile five times greater than that produced by the French Revolution. Many of the exiles, known as United Empire Loyalists, settled in Canada. The treaty of PARIS (1783) bound the American government to restore full property and political rights to loyalists, but CONFEDERATION CONGRESS made little restitution.

Luce, Henry Robinson (1898–1967), journalist and magazine publisher whose most famous title, *Life*, virtually invented the genre of photo-journalism. Luce was born in China to Presbyterian missionaries and educated at Yale and Oxford. While working as reporters on the *Baltimore News* (1920–3), Luce and a former classmate, Britton Hadden, hit on the idea of publishing a weekly news magazine. The pair published the first issue of *Time* on March 3 1923. Following Hadden's death in 1929, Luce built *Time* into an enormously influential publication. Through *Time* magazine Luce pushed a conservative, internationalist and pro-business agenda whose most distinctive feature was implacable opposition to communism, particularly in China and, later, in southeast Asia as a whole. Some of Luce's obsessions – hostility toward the NEW DEAL and support for Wendell Willkie (1892–1944), Franklin D. ROOSEVELT's opponent in the presidential election of 1940 – were unpopular. However Luce's grand vision of the 20th century as the 'American Century' proved enduring. From its founding in 1935 until its liquidation in 1972 *Life* magazine complemented *Time* by celebrating the 'American Century' in pictures. Both publications were shaped by a distinctive house-style which valued immediacy in prose more highly than conformity to grammatical conventions. Among other pioneering magazines launched by Luce were the business weekly *Fortune* (1930) and *Sports Illustrated* (1954).

Ludlow massacre (April 20 1914), incident in which 5 striking coalminers and 13 women and children were killed by state militiamen. The massacre occurred during an attack on a camp that had been set up by striking members of the UNITED MINE WORKERS OF AMERICA (UMWA) outside coal mines in Ludlow, Colorado, owned by John D. Rockefeller Jr (1874–1960). The UMWA issued a call to arms, and INDUSTRIAL WORKERS OF THE WORLD ('Wobbly') activists prepared for imminent revolution. Order in the area was eventually restored by 9000 US Army soldiers.

Ludlow Resolution, resolution that a national referendum be required to confirm any future US declaration of war, put to Congress by Representative Louis Ludlow of Indiana in 1935, 1937 and 1938. The resolution played on ISOLATIONIST concerns and distrust of President Franklin D. ROOSEVELT in the wake of the COURT-PACKING CONTROVERSY. The proposal was finally killed in a tight House vote (209–188) on January 10 1938.

lynching, the hanging of a person without legal sanction or formality by a crowd acting in a frenzy of prejudice and hatred. Probably from 'Lynch's law', named after Charles Lynch (1736–96), Virginia justice of the peace, who headed extralegal trials of TORIES during the American War of Independence. A total of 4753 Americans are believed to have been killed by 'lynch mobs' between 1882 and 1968. US lynch mobs were usually composed of white Americans. Their victims were usually African-American men, but white socialists and trade-union activists were also victimized. Lynching was especially prevalent in the post-RECONSTRUCTION south. Responding to real or imaginary threats to white self-esteem, mobs hanged or tortured 155 African-Americans in 1892 alone. Not a single vigilante was indicted. Lynch mobs often formed following rumors of interracial sexual liaisons within a community, and claimed to be acting in defense of white womanhood. But in fact, as detailed research by the anti-lynching campaigner Ida B. WELLS-BARNETT showed, lynch mobs often targeted upwardly mobile African-Americans without the least regard to 'evidence' of sexual impropriety. African-American soldiers were also singled out by mobs. In 1919, 70 black veterans of World War I were lynched while still wearing their uniforms. Members of the white supremacist KU KLUX KLAN, revived in Georgia in 1915, often organized or concealed such violence. In 1921 the NATIONAL ASSOCIATION FOR THE ADVANCEMENT OF COLORED PEOPLE (NAACP) persuaded the US House of Representatives to pass a federal anti-lynching law, but the bill was defeated in the Senate. Even as late as the 1960s it was difficult if not impossible to secure convictions against southern whites who killed or maimed African-Americans in defense of 'their' community.

M

MacArthur, Douglas (1880–1964), US Army general who played a leading role in the Pacific theater in World War II, and was the controversial commander of UN forces in the first year of the Korean War.

MacArthur graduated from West Point Military Academy in 1903. During World War I he served as a brigade and later divisional commander in the ST MIHIEL and MEUSE–ARGONNE OFFENSIVES. He was twice wounded in action. Between 1930 and 1935 he was chief of staff of the US Army, and he commanded the operation that dispersed the BONUS ARMY from Washington DC in 1932. In 1935 he took up the post of director of the Philippines' national defense forces. He was made field marshal in the Philippines' army in 1936 and resigned from the US army in 1937. He was recalled to the active list of the US army on July 26 1941.

Following PEARL HARBOR, MacArthur was made commander of US forces in the Far East. He was a natural choice since he bore no responsibility for failing to predict the Japanese attack, and had earlier served three stints in the Philippines (1903–4, 1922–30 and 1935–41) and one in Japan (1905–6). He slowed, but could not stop, the Japanese offensive in the Philippines. He was made Supreme Allied Commander of forces in the southwest Pacific on February 22 1942 – shortly before the fall of CORREGIDOR. He left the Philippines vowing, 'I shall return.' On October 20 1944 he did. On August 27 1945 MacArthur presided over the formal ceremony of Japanese surrender aboard the USS *Missouri*. Thereafter he commanded the US occupation of Japan and oversaw the creation of civilian government. MacArthur's titanic ego may have been overstimulated by this period as a proconsul. He expressed his fundamentally conservative world view in an ever more imperial manner.

In 1950 Douglas MacArthur was called to command the UN forces in the KOREAN WAR. He courted Chinese intervention in the war and then, arguing 'there is no substitute for victory,' tried to rally Congressional support for an all-out assault on North Korea and Chinese Manchuria. President TRUMAN relieved him of his command on April 11 1951. On April 19 he bade farewell to Congress and the American people, saying, 'Old soldiers never die, they simply fade away.'

McCarran Act (September 23 1950), legislation, passed over President TRUMAN's veto, that compelled American communists to register with a Subversive Activities Control Board. It barred communists from working in national defense industries and from entering the USA. The act allowed for the internment of 'subversives' in time of national emergency and the withholding of their passports. In 1965 the Supreme Court ruled that compulsory registration violated the FIFTH AMENDMENT.

McCarthy, Eugene J(oseph) (1916–), Democratic politician. One of the earliest opponents of US involvement in the VIETNAM WAR, following the TET OFFENSIVE Democratic Senator McCarthy of Minnesota announced that he would contest the renomination of his party's incumbent president, Lyndon B. JOHNSON, in 1968. McCarthy, whose gentle but principled manner inspired almost fanatical devotion from sections of the ANTIWAR MOVEMENT, very nearly beat Johnson in the New Hampshire PRIMARY ELECTION of March 1968. This moral victory transformed the PRESIDENTIAL ELECTION OF 1968 by prompting Johnson to step aside in favor of Hubert HUMPHREY and encouraging Senator Robert KENNEDY to enter the race. McCarthy did not enjoy enough support within the party to prevent Humphrey's nomination on the first ballot. Many of his supporters were beaten up by police during the CHICAGO CONVENTION RIOTS. McCarthy retired from political office in 1970.

McCarthy, Joseph R(aymond) (1908–1957), Republican politician, notorious for his witch-hunts of alleged communists in the early COLD WAR period. McCarthy was elected to the US Senate from Wisconsin in 1946. He achieved national prominence when, in a speech given in Wheeling, West Virginia, on February 9 1950, he alleged that the State Department harbored 205 communists. McCarthy did not invent RED-BAITING; however, the uncompromising search for alleged subversion he encouraged through the McCARTHY HEARINGS involved a use (or abuse) of senatorial powers characterized by sensationalism, cruelty and a reckless disregard for due process. McCarthyism and 'McCarthyite tactics' eventually became dirty words in US politics.

In the summer of 1953 McCarthy was called before his own creation, the Senate Permanent Investigating Subcommittee of the Government Operations Committee, to answer charges that he had sought to advance the career of a former aide currently serving at the US Army Signal Corps Laboratory, Fort Monmouth, New Jersey. McCarthy in turn alleged that the Army was seeking to discredit him to mask communist infiltration at the installation. His petulance during the televised hearings turned public opinion against him and led the US Senate to vote (67–22) on December 2 1953 to condemn McCarthy's 'contemptuous conduct' and abuse of select-committee privilege. In February 1954 McCarthy used a speaking tour marking Lincoln week to denounce the Democratic Party for 'twenty years of treason'. Such statements united the political establishment against him, and effectively ended his political influence.

McCarthy hearings (1953–4), public and private hearings into alleged communist influence on government and society held by the Senate Permanent Investigating Subcommittee of the Government Operations Committee, under the chairmanship of Senator Joseph McCARTHY.

McCarthy had been alleging communist influence on government, particularly the State Department, since 1950. His Senate hearings attracted great publicity, uncovered little of substance, and blighted many lives. A concurrent investigation by the House Un-American Activities Committee (*see* DIES COMMITTEE) led the entertainment industry to BLACKLIST alleged or avowed communist sympathizers.

Senior political figures from both parties, including President EISENHOWER, condemned the use of innuendo, intimidation and hearsay characteristic of these hearings. They were wound up following a televised 'investigation' of communist influence in the US Army. In response to McCarthy's assault on the integrity of his legal team, counsel for the US Army Joseph Welch asked McCarthy, 'Have you left no sense of decency?'

McClellan, George (Brinton) (1826–85), Union Army general in the CIVIL WAR, and Democratic presidential candidate in 1864.

McClellan graduated second of his West Point Military Academy class in 1846. He served in the MEXICAN WAR, undertook a variety of surveying and engineering tasks, and observed the Crimean War, before resigning in 1857 to pursue a career in railroad management.

In May 1861 McClellan, aged 34, was made a major general in the Union Army. Victory at the battle of RICH MOUNTAIN led to McClellan's promotion to command of the newly formed Army of the Potomac. In the winter of 1861–2 he used his undoubted organizational gifts to drill tens of thousands of raw volunteers into an effective force. He was popular with his troops, who nicknamed him 'little Napoleon'. He also took a keen interest in political feuding within Washington. However, the caution and inflexibility that dominated McClellan's approach to battle-field command – factors that led to stale-mate in the PENINSULAR CAMPAIGN of 1862, and a failure to exploit victory at the battle of ANTIETAM – caused an exasperated LIN-COLN to remove him from command on November 7 1862. McClellan was the Democrats' nominee in the PRESIDENTIAL ELECTION OF 1864. He later served as gover-nor of New Jersey (1878–81).

McCormick, Cyrus Hall (1809–84), inven-tor of a hillside plow and the world's first effective mechanical reaper (1832), both of which helped to transform US agriculture. His use of mass-production techniques at the factory he established in Chicago to produce his reaper proved equally influen-tial within industrial circles. By 1860 McCormick's company was producing 4000 mechanical reapers a year and had built up a worldwide market: a McCormick reaper created a sensation at 1855 International Exposition in Paris by cutting an acre (0.4 ha) of corn in just 21 minutes. McCormick

offered potential purchasers a variety of deferred-payment plans to maintain his market share long after his original patent had expired. He was a tough boss. Job losses caused by the introduction of labor-saving machinery at the McCormick plant in Chicago helped spark the HAYMARKET RIOT (1886).

McCulloch vs. Maryland (March 6 1819), unanimous Supreme Court ruling that by establishing a LOOSE CONSTRUCTIONIST read-ing of the US Constitution paved the way for an expansion in the scope of federal lawmaking. In 1818 Maryland had passed a law requiring all banks not created by its authority to obey state regulations on paper money issue, or pay an annual tax of $15,000. The measure was aimed at the BANK OF THE UNITED STATES, whose cashier in Maryland, James McCulloch, was sued by Maryland when he ignored the law. In announcing the Supreme Court's verdict Chief Justice MARSHALL stated that Congress had acted constitutionally when it estab-lished the bank, and Maryland did not have the right to tax it because the 'power to tax involves the power to destroy'. The ruling used an 'IMPLIED POWERS' reading of Article I Section 8 of the US Constitution to justify broad-ranging federal legislation while at the same time limiting the scope of state legislation.

McDonalds, US corporation that has revo-lutionized eating habits in the USA and the wider world while pioneering influential business practices.

By the time Dick and Maurice McDonald opened their first roadside hamburger stand in the 1940s, American interest in snack foods was over a century old. Hamburgers were first sold commercially by German immigrants in the 1850s. A passion for large sandwiches, nicknamed 'hoagies' by Italians working on Hog Island in the Delaware river or 'subs' by shipbuilders at Groton, Connecticut, swept the USA in the late 19th century. During the PROGRESSIVE ERA, entrepreneurs began to realize the value of associating new foods and drinks with modernity and health. Hot dogs were first sold at Chicago's Columbia Exposition in 1893 and became popular partly because they were considered an 'up-to-date' food. The equally popular ice-cream cone made its debut at the St. Louis Exposition of 1904. COCA-COLA AND PEPSI are the main examples of products that gained national popularity in this period by advertising 'medicinal' benefits.

The drive to serve soft drinks and snack foods as quickly as possible can be traced to rising rates of automobile ownership in the 1920s. As early as 1925, one of California's many roadside hamburger chains was named Snappy Service. The drive-in and drive-through vending formats, which speeded delivery still further, were developed in the 1930s. The McDonald brothers prospered because their stands were the first in California to employ infra-red lamps to keep pre-cooked burgers and fries hot and available to motorists at quick notice. Other chains had their gimmicks – White Castle restaurants, for example, used, and still use, a square hamburger bun. However, the McDonald brothers realized that the expectation of speedy and reliable service is the main draw in the snack-food business.

The McDonald brothers had already begun some half-hearted experiments in franchising their operation when, in 1954, Ray Kroc (1902–84), a representative for a company that manufactured milk-shake machines, visited the McDonalds' stand in San Bernadino, California. Kroc was born in Chicago and never graduated from high school. He played piano in a jazz band, sold real estate and, later, paper cups and plates, before promoting a deluxe milk shake machine. In 1954 Kroc was already comfortably well off. His interest in the McDonalds' operation was prompted by the opportunity he saw in it to act upon a personal business mantra, 'Quality, Service,

Cleanliness and Value,' that was the product of long years of eating on the road.

Kroc persuaded the McDonalds to grant him the exclusive right to license others to use the McDonalds name and methods. He opened his own McDonalds in Des Plaines, Illinois, to demonstrate the profitability of a properly-regulated franchise. Here, and at subsequent stands, cooking and service tasks were closely studied and carefully subdivided. A predominantly part-time and teenage workforce was given careful instruction in the preparation of a standard menu and held to strict standards of honesty and customer service. The restaurants were kept clean and rival vending machines and jukeboxes barred. Families were welcome, loiterers were not. This format proved successful in Des Plaines and Kroc insisted that it be followed without deviation in all other franchises licensed to use the McDonalds name.

Kroc, who bought out the McDonald brothers in 1961, spread the chain by buying land in suitable suburban sites, building standardized restaurants identified by the now famous golden arches and leasing to franchisees. He introduced the character Ronald McDonald to solidify his hold on the children's market in 1963. The Big Mac was first sold in 1968, and the Egg McMuffin in 1971. By 1975 there were over 4000 McDonalds franchises in the USA. In 1995 there were over 8000 franchises in the USA and a further 12,000 around the world. The chain's success has spawned a large number of imitators, most of whom employ the franchised-business format.

McGillivray, Alexander (c.1759–93), activist on behalf of Native American peoples. During the REVOLUTIONARY WAR, McGillivray, of Scottish and CREEK parentage, committed the Creek and SEMINOLE peoples of the southeast to an alliance with Britain, through which he hoped to end US encroachment on Native American lands. He later used his diplomatic skills to play

Spain off against the USA in a bid to protect Native American land rights in Georgia and WEST FLORIDA.

McGovern, George S(tanley) (1922–), Democratic politician. In the PRESIDENTIAL ELECTION OF 1972 McGovern, the Democrats' nominee, campaigned on a platform promising the immediate, unilateral withdrawal of US troops from the VIETNAM WAR, and recorded the lowest share of the POPULAR VOTE ever achieved by a Democratic candidate in a two-way contest. McGovern had served as a bomber pilot in World War II and as a history professor at Dakota Wesleyan University (1949–53) before entering the US House of Representatives in 1956. He represented South Dakota in the US Senate (1963–81) before and after his presidential bid. President NIXON's attempts to spy on the McGovern campaign produced the WATERGATE SCANDAL. In 1984 McGovern launched another campaign for the Democratic nomination, but lost to Walter MONDALE.

McKinley, William (1843–1901), Republican statesman and 25th president of the USA (1897–1901). The SPANISH-AMERICAN WAR took place during his presidency. He died during his second term from wounds received from an assassin.

McKinley was born and raised in Ohio. He entered the Union Army as a private in June 1861. By the close of the Civil War he had been commended for valor at the battle of ANTIETAM and promoted to the rank of brevet major. Returning to Ohio, McKinley opened a law office and began a political career that included stints as a REPUBLICAN US representative (1871–83, 1885–91) and one term as governor of Ohio (1892–6). McKinley lost his seat in Congress for sponsoring the protectionist McKINLEY TARIFF (1890), which was unpopular because it raised consumer prices. Previously he had suppressed his sound-money, GOLD STANDARD instincts to vote for the BLAND–ALLISON ACT (1878) and the SHERMAN SILVER PURCHASE

ACT (1890). This flexibility secured his first-ballot nomination as Republican presidential candidate in 1896.

McKinley was elected president with 51% of the popular vote in 1896, and took up office on March 4 1897. He was re-elected (on the slogan 'Four More Years of the Full Dinner Pail') with 52% in 1900. McKinley's administration put the USA on the gold standard, annexed HAWAII and, to the great delight of Theodore ROOSEVELT (who had charged McKinley with possessing less spine than a chocolate eclair), prosecuted the Spanish-American War with vigor. On September 6 1901, Leon Czolgosz (1873– 1901) fired two point-blank shots at McKinley during a reception in Buffalo, New York. McKinley died on September 14. Czolgosz was electrocuted on October 29 1901 at Auburn State Prison, New York.

McKinley Tariff Act (1890), strongly protectionist legislation sponsored by future President William McKINLEY. Passed on October 1, the act raised import duties on a variety of manufactured goods and raw materials to an average of 49%. Its unpopularity among US exporters and farmers, who feared retaliation from the USA's trading partners, damaged the REPUBLICAN PARTY, and McKinley lost his seat in the House of Representatives. By effectively closing the US market, the tariff devastated the European steel industry. The act exempted Cuban sugar from import duty, prompting a short-lived boom there. However, it imposed unprecedented duties on sugar grown in HAWAII, encouraging US planters on the islands to campaign for US annexation.

McNamara, Robert S(trange) (1916–), secretary of defense (1961–8) under Presidents KENNEDY and Lyndon B. JOHNSON. Described by Johnson as a 'can-do fellow', McNamara's confidence, or hubris, was instrumental in persuading Kennedy and Johnson to escalate US involvement in the VIETNAM WAR. McNamara was just 44 when Kennedy made him secretary of defense in

1961. He had previously worked as a senior manager in the Ford Motor Company. McNamara's trust in managerial systems was reflected in his unshakeable faith in the efficacy of specialist 'counter-insurgency' forces. He persuaded Kennedy to send Green Berets to Vietnam, and announced that the USA would provide counter-insurgency training to nations threatened by communist subversion. He was an influential member of the 'ExCom' committee formed by Kennedy during the CUBAN MISSILE CRISIS, using his authority as secretary of defense to prevent service chiefs from taking provocative action against Soviet ships and planes. McNamara's insistence that US ships had come under attack from North Vietnamese torpedo boats played a crucial role in persuading Congress to pass the TONKIN GULF RESOLUTION (1964), which provided Johnson with the authorization necessary to initiate OPERATION ROLLING THUNDER against North Vietnam. In January 1965 McNamara presented Johnson with a 'fork-in-the-road' memo, which argued for a massive deployment of US ground forces in Vietnam. By 1967 McNamara had begun to doubt whether the USA could win the war in Vietnam, but kept these thoughts to himself, and in February 1968 left government to take up presidency of the World Bank. In 1995 he admitted: 'We were wrong, terribly wrong.'

McNaury–Haugen Bill, proposed measure to support agricultural prices, first introduced into Congress in 1924. The bill sought to create a government agency to buy surplus US crops and withhold them from the market until world commodity prices rose. The measure was popular with US farmers because it did not require them to cut production. In 1928 a heavily revised version of the plan was killed by President Calvin COOLIDGE, who vetoed it on the grounds that it interfered with 'normal exchange relationships.' The worsening depression that afflicted US agriculture in the 1920s contributed significantly to the severity of the GREAT DEPRESSION.

Macon's Bill Number 2 (May 1 1810), legislation governing the conduct of trade with with Britain and France (belligerents in the Napoleonic Wars). Macon's Bill was a contributory cause of the WAR OF 1812. In August 1809 Congress ordered the suspension of trade with Britain and France in protest against both nations' refusal to respect the neutrality of US ships. Macon's Bill permitted the president to reopen trade with both nations. However, it contained the proviso that if either Britain or France pledged to accept US definitions of the neutrality of US shipping, trade with that nation's enemy would cease. In 1810 Napoleon tricked President MADISON into believing that France had complied with these terms. Trade with France resumed. Madison ordered Britain to follow France by accepting US neutrality or face a suspension of trade from February 1811. The British, taking the position that France had not complied with the Bill and that the resumption of US-French trade violated US neutrality by aiding a belligerent, responded by ordering a blockade of New York harbor.

'mad dog' strategy, strategy adopted by President NIXON in relation to the VIETNAM WAR. In a discussion with White House chief of staff H.R. (Bob) Haldeman, Nixon outlined his belief that the application, or threat of, massive force would soon bring a negotiated settlement of the war. The North Vietnamese, Nixon said, would 'believe any threat of force Nixon makes because it's Nixon. We'll just slip the word to them that, "for God's sake, you know Nixon's obsessed about Communism and he has his hand on the nuclear button".' Nixon's decisions to sanction the secret bombing of CAMBODIA from March 1969 and the CHRISTMAS BOMBING of Hanoi (December 1972) were prompted partly by a desire to suggest to the North Vietnamese and others that he just might be a 'mad dog' prepared to go far beyond the military boundaries recognized by KENNEDY and JOHNSON in pursuit of 'peace with honor'. As part of the 'mad dog' strategy, in July 1969 Nixon staffers told US journalists that 'the boss' was considering using nuclear weapons against North Vietnam. Nixon's pose did lend some muscle to the secret peace negotiations with North Vietnam pursued through the KISSINGER INITIATIVE. However, the North Vietnamese concluded, rightly, that the strength of the ANTIWAR MOVEMENT and the realities of presidential politics in a democracy limited Nixon's freedom of maneuver.

Madison, James (1751–1836), Democratic statesman and 4th president of the USA (1809–17). Perhaps more importantly, he exerted an enormous influence on the design and interpretation of the US CONSTITUTION.

Madison was born to affluence in Virginia, but outside the circle of great planters within which Washington and Jefferson moved. He attended Princeton University (1769–71), and by prodigious effort graduated in two years. He took some legal training, but never joined the Bar. He helped draft Virginia's state constitution (1776) and served in the state's House of Delegates (1776–7). A re-election bid failed, because he refused to woo voters with whiskey. He was appointed to Virginia's Council of State (1778–9). During this period he worked closely with Thomas Jefferson and incurred the enmity of Patrick HENRY.

In 1780, at the age of 29, Madison became the youngest member of the CONTINENTAL CONGRESS. Confronted with the weakness of government under the ARTICLES OF CONFEDERATION – its inability to supply the army, establish stable currency or prevent disputes between the states – he developed a nationalist outlook, which eventually informed his contribution to the *FEDERALIST PAPERS*. In 1784 he returned to Virginia's House of Delegates and pushed through Jefferson's VIRGINIA STATUTE FOR RELIGIOUS FREEDOM (1786).

Madison's contribution to the CONSTITUTIONAL CONVENTION (1787) is encapsulated in the first words of the US Constitution, 'We, the People'. Madison sought a strong national government that drew its legitimacy from the people (via the ballot box) and, in turn, operated directly on them. He helped devise, and brilliantly defended, a system of checks and balances that ensured, to his satisfaction, that a government more distant from the people than conventional wisdom thought sensible would not in practice prove authoritarian or tyrannical. Such was his characteristic, and understandable, faith in the wording of the Constitution that he joined HAMILTON in opposing ANTIFEDERALIST demands for a BILL OF RIGHTS and increased influence for the states. However, as a member of the US House of Representatives (1789–97) Madison in fact drafted the Bill of Rights, and, as he grew increasingly alienated from the FEDERALISTS, he developed in the VIRGINIA RESOLUTIONS the notion that a state could interpose its authority in order to protect citizens from unconstitutional federal legislation.

Madison served as Jefferson's secretary of state (1801–9), and on March 4 1809 he began his presidency. His two terms were dominated by tensions with Britain that eventually produced the WAR OF 1812. He served until March 4 1817. In retirement Madison advocated the gradual abolition of slavery and the resettlement of blacks in Africa. During the NULLIFICATION CRISIS he denied that the VIRGINIA and KENTUCKY RESOLUTIONS provided a precedent for nullification or SECESSION.

Mahpiua Luta or **Red Cloud,** *see* SIOUX WARS.

Maine, the most northeasterly state in the Union, bordered by Canada to the north, the Atlantic to the east and New Hampshire to the west.

The first, short-lived, European settlement in the territory was established by

British Puritans in 1607. Massachusetts annexed sparsely-populated territory in 1625 and administered it throughout the colonial and early national periods. The state's permanent population grew rapidly toward the close of the 18th century, but settlers were victimized by the uncertainty surrounding land titles in the territory. On March 15 1820, Maine became the 23rd state as part of the MISSOURI COMPROMISE. Disputes concerning the state's border with Canada were resolved through the WEBSTER-ASHBURTON TREATY (1842). The influence of evangelical Protestantism on the state's population was demonstrated when, in 1851, Maine became the first state to enact a PROHIBITION statute. Many residents also supported the ABOLITION movement. In 1900, the state possessed 694,000 permanent residents. Although this figure increased to surpass 1,200,000 by 1990, in each decade of the 20th century, Maine lost residents through out-migration. These demographic factors gave the state a distinctive, insular identity which has sometimes been lampooned in the mass media. In 1990, Maine was the 38th most populous state in the Union. Its economy is dependent on revenue from manufacturing, mining and tourism. HALF-BREED Republican James G. BLAINE (who was born in Pennsylvania) was tagged as the 'Continental Liar from the state of Maine' at the Republican Party Convention of 1876, thus ending his presidential bid.

Malcolm X, *see* X, Malcolm.

Manassas, battles of (1861, 1862), two engagements fought in Virginia during the CIVIL WAR. They are also referred to as the battles of Bull Run, after a small stream on the battlefield.

(1) On July 21 1861, 32,000 Confederate troops under the overall command of General Pierre G.T. Beauregard (1818–93) routed 30,000 Union troops under General Irwin McDowell (1818–85) 25 miles (40 km) from Washington DC in the first major engage-ment of the war. Poor organization prevented the Confederates from exploiting their victory. Confederate General Thomas Jackson earned his nickname 'Stonewall' in the battle.

(2) Between August 28 and September 1 1862, 48,000 Confederate troops driving northward under the overall command of Robert E. LEE forced 75,000 Union troops under General John Pope (1822–92) to retreat northward. Lee's victory gave the Confederacy command of northern Virginia. But his subsequent advance into Maryland ended in defeat at ANTIETAM.

Manhattan Project, code name given to the US-led scientific mission that produced the atom bombs dropped on HIROSHIMA AND NAGASAKI, which in turn ended WORLD WAR II. On October 2 1939 Albert Einstein wrote to President Franklin D. ROOSEVELT advising him that German scientists might be developing an atomic bomb and that the USA should commit federal funds to atomic research. In June 1942 Dr Vannevar Bush, head of the Office of Scientific Research and Development established to coordinate atomic research, informed Roosevelt that an atom bomb could be built. The Manhattan Project was administered by the US Army Corps of Engineers. Its military director, General Leslie R. Groves, oversaw a $2 billion program to produce raw materials for the bomb at several massive, purpose-built sites dispersed across the USA. Its scientific director, Dr J. Robert Oppenheimer (1904–67), ran the laboratory at Los Alamos, New Mexico, that coordinated research and tested the bomb. Scientists from around the world, many of them refugees from Nazi-occupied European countries, were drawn into the program. Its details were success-fully withheld from German spies, but, despite strict security, Soviet agents soon learned of the project's existence. The world's first nuclear device was successfully detonated at Alamogordo, New Mexico, on July 16 1945. Witnessing the mushroom cloud, Oppenheimer recalled the Hindu scripture: 'I am become death, destroyer of worlds.'

manifest destiny, phrase used in the 19th century to justify US expansion over the North American continent. In the summer of 1845 the journalist John L. O'Sullivan argued that US annexation of TEXAS was justified on the grounds that the USA had a 'manifest destiny to overspread the continent allotted by Providence for the free development of our yearly multiplying millions'. President POLK had used similar arguments in his inaugural address (March 1845). 'Manifest destiny' became the catchphrase of politicians and pundits who supported expansionist policies.

Mann–Elkins Act (June 18 1913), legislation regulating the transport and communications industries. Building on the HEPBURN ACT, the Mann–Elkins Act gave the Interstate Commerce Commission (ICC; established by the INTERSTATE COMMERCE ACT of 1887) greater powers to delay changes in rail freight charges and to investigate their reasonableness. It also extended ICC jurisdiction to the telegraph and telephone industries.

manumission, legal term describing the process by which a slave owner voluntarily freed his slaves. Between 1723 and 1782 private acts of manumission were illegal in Virginia, and other southern states erected similar obstacles to prevent slave owners from discharging former slaves onto the public welfare rolls. Following the AMERICAN REVOLUTION, southern states came under pressure from abolitionists to make it easier for owners to manumit their slaves.

Marbury vs. Madison (February 24 1803), unanimous US Supreme Court ruling that endorsed the principle of JUDICIAL REVIEW. The case arose when, in the last hours of his presidency, John ADAMS appointed FEDERALISTS, among them William Marbury, to a number of vacant judicial posts. Incoming President JEFFERSON ordered the new secretary of state, James MADISON, to withhold Marbury's commission. Marbury sued to demand its delivery. The Supreme Court, John MARSHALL presiding, argued that it lacked jurisdiction and dismissed Marbury's suit. But Marshall also declared Section 13 of the Judiciary Act of 1789 (which Marbury had exploited to bring his suit) unconstitutional. This was the first occasion on which the Court invalidated an act of Congress.

March on Washington (August 28 1963), one of the high points of the CIVIL RIGHTS MOVEMENT, in which 250,000 people from all over the USA converged for a peaceful day-long rally at the Lincoln Memorial in Washington DC. The march was organized by A. Philip RANDOLPH and Bayard Rustin. Its planned emphasis was to protest against racial discrimination in employment, but President KENNEDY skilfully converted public perception of the march into an affirmation of support for the omnibus civil rights bill he sent to Congress on July 1 1963 (*see* CIVIL RIGHTS ACT OF 1964). The leader of the STUDENT NON-VIOLENT COORDINATING COMMITTEE (SNCC), John Lewis (1940–), had actually arrived in Washington with a speech criticizing Kennedy, but he was dissuaded from giving it. Ten speakers, as well as Bob Dylan and Joan Baez, addressed the crowd. But the day was remembered for Martin Luther KING's 'I HAVE A DREAM' SPEECH. The march did not persuade conservative southern congressmen to abandon their opposition to Kennedy's civil rights bill, but it legitimated the aspirations of the Civil Rights Movement around the USA and throughout the world.

March to the Sea (1864), the destructive advance by Union forces through Georgia during the closing phase of the CIVIL WAR. On November 15 1864 Union General William T. SHERMAN (vowing to 'make Georgia howl') ordered his 67,000-strong army on a 285-mile (456-km) march from Atlanta in northwest Georgia to Savannah on the eastern seaboard. Living off the land,

Sherman's army gleefully destroyed railroads, materiel and much civilian property in its path. After a Thanksgiving Day feast in Milledgeville, Georgia, was interrupted by emaciated escapees from ANDERSONVILLE prison camp, the army's 'foraging' took on a vengeful thoroughness that ensured that by the time Savannah was captured (on December 21) a swath of land 60 miles (100 km) wide had been almost completely denuded.

Marshall, George C(atlett) (1880–1959), US Army general, and secretary of state (1947–9). Marshall was a career soldier whose superb organizational skills helped secure Allied victory in WORLD WAR II and the reconstruction of postwar Europe.

Marshall graduated from the Virginia Military Institute in 1901, and was commissioned in the US Army in 1902. As chief of staff of the Eighth Army Corps during World War I, Marshall helped plan the ST MIHIEL and the immense MEUSE–ARGONNE OFFENSIVES. He occupied a variety of staff positions before his appointment as Army chief of staff (1939–45). Marshall's planning ensured the success of Allied landings in North Africa (1942), Sicily (1943), Italy (1943) and Normandy (the D-DAY LANDINGS), and led Churchill to dub him 'the true organizer of victory'. As secretary of state in TRUMAN's postwar administration he created the MARSHALL PLAN to aid European recovery. Marshall was awarded the Nobel Peace Prize in 1953.

Marshall, John (1755–1835), fourth chief justice of the US SUPREME COURT, who was largely responsible for establishing the Court's currently powerful position within the system of checks and balances provided for by the US CONSTITUTION.

Marshall was raised in Virginia, and, although he attended some law lectures at William and Mary College, he was essentially a self-trained lawyer. He saw military service in the Revolutionary War, and sat in the Virginia state legislature (1782–91 and 1795–7). He refused George WASHINGTON's request to serve as attorney general and John ADAMS's request that he serve as US minister to France. He did, however, serve on an extraordinary US mission to France, whose treatment by French agents created the XYZ AFFAIR.

Marshall was serving as secretary of state (1800–1) when Adams nominated him to serve as chief justice of the Supreme Court. During his tenure as chief justice (1801–35), Marshall established the principle that a single justice should be chosen to write an opinion that reflects the views of the majority of the Court. He wrote the Court's opinion in the case of MARBURY VS. MADISON (1803), which established the principle of JUDICIAL REVIEW. Arguing that 'it is emphatically the province and duty of the judicial department to say what the law is', Marshall justified the Court's decision to declare Section 13 of the Judiciary Act of 1789 unconstitutional. This was the first occasion upon which the Supreme Court ruled an act of CONGRESS unconstitutional. Equally significant was Marshall's opinion in the case of McCULLOCH VS. MARYLAND (1819), wherein he utilized an IMPLIED POWERS reading of the Constitution to uphold the constitutionality of the second BANK OF THE UNITED STATES. Marshall also took a broad view of Article I Section 8 of the US Constitution (the 'commerce clause') in his opinion on GIBBONS VS. OGDEN (1824). Marshall's political instincts were FEDERALIST and, enjoying the security of tenure, he espoused them long after the Federalist Party had ceased to be a force in US politics.

Marshall, Thurgood (1908–93), US Supreme Court justice. The great-grandson of a slave, on October 2 1967 Marshall became the first African-American man to be appointed to the Court.

As an undergraduate Marshall worked his way through Lincoln College, Pennsylvania. Denied admission to the University of Maryland because he was black, Marshall studied law at Howard University. After a brief period in private practice, Marshall moved to New York to work with the legal team of the NATIONAL ASSOCIATION FOR THE ADVANCEMENT OF COLORED PEOPLE (NAACP). From 1940 to 1962 he served as head of the NAACP's Legal Defense Fund, and in that capacity presented arguments before the US Supreme Court in the landmark BROWN VS. BOARD OF EDUCATION case. Promoted to the US Court of Appeals by John F. KENNEDY, he was nominated to the Supreme Court by Lyndon B. JOHNSON. Marshall joined a Court that was already liberal and, as a result, authored few opinions of his own. However, until his retirement owing to ill health in 1991, he served as the Supreme Court's conscience.

Marshall Plan, major US program of aid to Europe following WORLD WAR II. In an address given at Harvard on June 5 1947, Secretary of State George C. MARSHALL outlined a plan that would eventually direct $13 billion to Western European economic recovery. His speech defined the twin goals of preserving Europe from 'hunger, poverty, desperation and chaos' and creating 'working economies' capable of providing 'political and social conditions in which free institutions can exist'.

To secure support from the American people, and from Republican congressmen anticipating victory in the PRESIDENTIAL ELECTION OF 1948, Marshall and President TRUMAN presented the plan as a COLD WAR necessity, stressing the role aid might play in averting communist election victories in Western European nations. Yet to soften the plan's implicit anti-communism, Marshall invited the Soviet Union to apply for US economic aid; the Soviets rejected this offer on July 2 1947. On April 2 1948 Congress endorsed the plan by creating the European Recovery Program. This was administered in Paris by Paul Hoffman (1891– 1974), and operated independently of the State Department and with minimal congressional over-

sight. By channeling aid through Hoffman's agency, the plan spared Western European nations much of the humiliation that might have accompanied individual applications for assistance from Washington. Recipient nations used grants and loans of dollars awarded under the program to purchase goods and machinery from the USA. The Marshall Plan therefore strengthened the financial structures established at the BRETTON WOODS CONFERENCE.

Maryland, BORDER STATE sharing boundaries with Pennsylvania to the north, Delaware to the east and Virginia and West Virginia to the south. The DISTRICT OF COLUMBIA, seat of the federal government, lies within Maryland.

One of the THIRTEEN COLONIES, Maryland was originally founded by the second Lord Baltimore, Cecilius Calvert (1605–75), as a refuge for persecuted English Catholics. The first permanent British settlement in the territory was established on June 30 1632. Like Virginia, colonial Maryland's economic development was heavily dependent on the production of tobacco using slave labor. The state's northern border, established through the MASON–DIXON LINE (1768), came to be accepted as the approximate point at which the free labor systems of northern states gave way to the slave societies created in southern states.

Maryland became the 7th state to ratify the US Constitution on April 28 1788. During the 19th century, the state's reliance on slave labour decreased as manufacturing industry, overseas trade, and grain and livestock production provided alternative sources of economic development. In 1800, slaves accounted for 30% of the state's population. By 1860, less than 13% of Maryland's 687,000 permanent residents were enslaved. Nevertheless, significant support for the CONFEDERACY existed within the state and in May 1861, LINCOLN placed Maryland under martial law to prevent its SECESSION. The state was twice invaded by

Confederate forces during the CIVIL WAR.

After the war, Maryland followed other southern states in enacting JIM CROW laws establishing racial segregation. (These were repealed with relatively little opposition in the 1950s). The growth of federal government, and increased defense expenditure during the COLD WAR, contributed to a substantial rise in Maryland's population. In 1900, the state had 1,188,000 permanent residents and was the 26th most populous state in the union. By 1990, Maryland was the 19th most populous state with a population of over 4,700,000. Famous Marylanders include Benjamin BANNEKER, Frederick DOUGLASS and Spiro AGNEW.

Mason–Dixon line, term that identified the cultural boundary in antebellum America between southern slaveholding states and northern free-labor states. It derives from the boundary line between Maryland and Pennsylvania surveyed between 1763 and 1768 by Charles Mason and Jeremiah Dixon. (The term 'Dixie', used to identify the south, is thought to be a corruption of Dixon.) As America expanded westward, the Ohio river and the boundary between Missouri and Arkansas also served to demarcate slave states from free states. Americans still use the term as a shorthand means of contrasting the cultural distinctions between northern and southern states.

Massachusetts, northeastern state (and one of the THIRTEEN COLONIES) bordered by New Hampshire and Vermont to the north, Connecticut and Rhode Island to the south and New York to the west.

Plymouth Colony, the first permanent European settlement in Massachusetts, was established when the *Mayflower* landed 101 'Pilgrim Fathers' on Cape Cod on November 9 1620. (Plymouth remained an independent colony until it was absorbed within Massachusetts on October 17 1691.) The 'Great Migration' of English Puritans to Massachusetts began with the arrival of 700 settlers, led by John Winthrop (1588–1649),

on June 12 1630. Craving autonomy in religious affairs, the first settlers established and defended systems of self-government that were ultimately incompatible with imperial authority. During the AMERICAN REVOLUTION, Massachusetts led resistance to the STAMP ACT and, following the BOSTON TEA PARTY, became the target of the INTOLERABLE ACTS. The REVOLUTIONARY WAR began when armed Massachusetts militiamen confronted British troops at LEXINGTON AND CONCORD and the subsequent battle of BUNKER HILL. Massachusetts' first state constitution actually disenfranchised some residents who had been eligible to vote under British rule. This helped foment SHAYS'S REBELLION, an event which was seized upon by FEDERALISTS seeking to justify RATIFICATION of the US Constitution. On the other hand, in 1783, following the QUOK WALKER case, Massachusetts abolished slavery. Massachusetts became the 6th state to ratify the Constitution on February 6 1788.

In the early years of the 19th century, Massachusetts was the site of rapid industrial expansion. By the 1820s, the majority of its population lived in urban, not rural, areas (Massachusetts was the first state in the union to experience this transformation). Immigration, from mainland Europe and later from Ireland, changed the cultural character of the state's population. The Congregational church, founded by the original Puritan settlers, was finally disestablished in 1833. Nevertheless, acting on the secular precepts of evangelical Protestantism, many residents gave active support to the ABOLITION, TEMPERANCE and WOMEN'S SUFFRAGE movements. In 1860, Massachusetts had over 1,200,000 permanent residents and was the 7th most populous state in the union. During the CIVIL WAR, it sent over 140,000 men to fight against the CONFEDERACY.

By 1900, 30% of Massachusetts' population of 2,805,346 was foreign-born. Although most immigrants settled in the seaport towns of the east coast, immigration and industrialization were divisive issues in Massachusetts and created tensions that were played out in the LAWRENCE TEXTILE STRIKE and the SACCO AND VANZETTI CASE. During the RED SCARE, state governor and future US president Calvin COOLIDGE gained national attention by suppressing a strike by members of the Boston police force. In the 1930s, the state's voters became staunch supporters of the NEW DEAL, and Massachusetts retained for two generations a distinctively liberal political culture. (Massachusetts was the only state carried by George MCGOVERN in the PRESIDENTIAL ELECTION OF 1972).

The state's rate of population increase declined over the course of the 20th century. In 1990, Massachusetts had 6,016,425 residents and was the 13th most populous state in the union. Many prominent statesmen and reformers have been born and raised in Massachusetts, among them three US presidents: John ADAMS, John QUINCY ADAMS and John F. KENNEDY.

Massachusetts Circular Letter, letter sent by the Massachusetts assembly to other colonial legislatures on February 11 1768. The letter, drafted by Samuel ADAMS, denounced the TOWNSHEND REVENUE ACT and urged peaceful protest against it. On April 21 1768 Lord Hillsborough (secretary of state responsible for colonial affairs) denounced the letter, forbade other colonial assemblies from endorsing it, and demanded that Massachusetts issue a retraction. On June 30 1768 the Massachusetts assembly voted (92–17) against retraction. The assembly was immediately dissolved. In protests mounted throughout the colonies against the Townshend Act and the dissolution of the Massachusetts assembly, 92 became a patriotic number.

Massachusetts Government Act (May 20 1774), legislation passed by the British Parliament dictating a 'reorganization' of Massachusetts's local government and judiciary.

It was one of the INTOLERABLE ACTS passed in response to the BOSTON TEA PARTY. Towns were permitted to hold no more than one meeting a year, and their representatives were stripped of the right to choose the colonial legislature's upper house, which was now appointed by the governor instead. Sheriffs, chosen by the appointed upper house, were now charged with selecting jurors. Previously jurors had been chosen by a town or its officials. This act, viewed in conjunction with the QUEBEC ACT, suggested to Americans that the British government had a 'settled design' to strip the colonies of established political rights and judicial procedures.

Maysville Road veto (May 27 1830), veto by President Andrew JACKSON of a bill, sponsored by Henry CLAY, to give federal funding to the construction of a turnpike in Kentucky between Lexington and Maysville. In vetoing the bill Jackson cited STRICT CONSTRUCTIONISM and argued that the proposed road did not benefit interstate commerce.

Meade, George G(ordon) (1815–72), Union Army general. Meade asssumed command of the US Army of the Potomac two days before the turning point of the CIVIL WAR, the battle of GETTYSBURG. He was a career soldier who had graduated from West Point Military Academy in 1835 but spent most of his military life in the Corps of Engineers. Meade's defeat of Robert E. LEE's invasion of Pennsylvania at Gettysburg effectively ended the capacity of the Confederacy to stage major offensives against the Union. However, had Meade pursued the beaten Confederate Army of Northern Virginia with more vigor he might have destroyed it and brought the Civil War to a swift conclusion. He was retained as commander of the Army of the Potomac, but from 1864 operated under the direct supervision of Ulysses S. GRANT.

Medicaid (30 July 1965), program that provides medical benefits for welfare recipients and those just above the poverty line adjudged 'medically indigent.' The legislation that introduced the program was a centerpiece of President Lyndon B. JOHNSON's GREAT SOCIETY initiative. Before the bill was passed, 20% of Americans classified as poor had never seen a doctor. By 1970 that figure had dropped to 8%. The program is administered by the individual states according to criteria established by the federal government. In 1994 the program cost the federal government $120 billion.

Medicare (July 30 1965), program that provides medical benefits for poorer senior citizens and long-term social-security claimants. The enabling act that introduced the program was one of President Lyndon B. Johnson's GREAT SOCIETY initiatives. The act also outlawed racial segregation in US hospitals. The program has contributed to a steady rise in life expectancy and has, therefore, proven enormously expensive.

Medicine Lodge, treaty of (October 28 1867), treaty signed in Kansas that concluded a war of mutual retaliation between the USA and the Native American peoples of the southern plains. The war had three causes. Firstly, during the 1860s, stagecoach and railroad lines had brought ever increasing numbers of US hunters and settlers into the area between the Platte and Arkansas rivers. This area, comprising most of modern Kansas and Colorado, was the traditional hunting ground of the ARAPAHO, CHEYENNE, COMANCHE and KIOWA peoples. The effect on buffalo herds was immediate and devastating. Secondly, during the CIVIL WAR, US Army commanders in the west feared that the Native American nations might aid Confederate raiders unless they were subjugated. Finally, officials of the new state of Kansas (1861) and the new territory of Colorado (1861) did not wish to have organized bands of Native Americans living within their boundaries, and were determined to drive them off or exterminate them. The SAND CREEK MASSACRE (1864) of

Cheyenne and Arapaho by Colorado militiamen prolonged and intensified fighting in the region.

The Medicine Lodge treaty relocated Indian nations living within Kansas and Colorado to reservations in western Oklahoma and eastern New Mexico. In return the US government promised to provide instruction in agricultural techniques and to establish a reservation school system. From the Native American perspective, the treaty compared unfavorably with the second treaty of FORT LARAMIE (1868), which resolved similar disputes between the USA and the SIOUX.

Memphis riot (1866), race riot that took place in Memphis, Tennessee. On May 1 1866 two carts, one driven by a black man, the other by a white, collided on a Memphis street. When police attempted to arrest the black driver, black army veterans who had witnessed the incident intervened to free him. An enraged white mob, comprised chiefly of Irish policemen and firemen, conducted a three-day rampage through south Memphis, home to the families of black soldiers stationed nearby. During the violence, 46 blacks and 2 whites were killed, 5 black women were raped, and 91 homes, 12 schools and 4 churches were burned down, before US troops restored order. This incident, and a similar riot in NEW ORLEANS, shocked the north. REPUBLICAN gains in the subsequent mid-term elections spelt the end of PRESIDENTIAL RECONSTRUCTION and the beginnings of CONGRESSIONAL RECONSTRUCTION.

Meredith, James (Howard) (1933–), African-American whose attempt in 1962 to enroll at the previously all-white University of Mississippi provoked a stand-off whose resolution formed one of the defining moments of the CIVIL RIGHTS MOVEMENT.

Meredith was a mature student who had served nine years in the Air Force and had already completed three years of college course work. He wanted a higher education because 'just to live and breathe that isn't life to me'. The governor of Mississippi, Ross Barnett, vowed to go to jail rather than let Meredith register. He declared himself a registrar of the university, and ordered the arrest of federal officials sent by the KENNEDY administration to enforce a court order to admit Meredith. On September 30 Meredith arrived on campus, surrounded by federal marshals. White students rioted and two were shot dead before the National Guard restored order. Meredith graduated on September 30 1963, and two years later embarked on a 'pilgrimage' to encourage black voter registration in Mississippi. He was shot and wounded by a white supremacist on June 6 1966, but his campaign was taken up by the STUDENT NON-VIOLENT COORDINATING COMMITTEE (SNCC) and the SOUTHERN CHRISTIAN LEADERSHIP CONFERENCE (SCLC). Meredith earned a law degree from Columbia University in 1968.

Meritor Savings Bank vs. Vinson (June 16 1986), US Supreme Court ruling 9–0 that sexual harassment constitutes a form of sexual discrimination outlawed under Title VII of the CIVIL RIGHTS ACT OF 1964. The ruling requires businesses to ensure that employees of one sex do not abuse or intimidate employees of another sex.

Merryman, Ex Parte, *see* EX PARTE MERRYMAN.

Meuse–Argonne offensive (1918), the last major offensive of WORLD WAR I, carried out in northern France and mounted by US troops under the command of General John PERSHING. The objective was to drive northward to Sedan from starting positions in the trench line between Reims and Verdun. Pershing deployed every US division in France in the offensive, bringing 1,200,000 US soldiers into action. The attack began on September 26 and developed into a month-long battle of attrition. However, by November 6 US troops had broken German lines, crossed the Meuse river, and reached the outskirts of Sedan. The offensive was suspended with the armistice on November 11, by which point US forces had suffered 120,000 casualties.

Mexican War (1846–8), war arising from a territorial dispute between the USA and Mexico. In 1845 newly elected President POLK stated that the question of whether TEXAS (independent from Mexico since 1836) should join the Union concerned Texas and the USA alone. Mexico opposed Texan statehood on strategic grounds. It also disputed the US and Texan claim that the southern boundary of the territory ran along the Rio Grande rather than along the more northerly Nueces river.

Polk authorized the SLIDELL MISSION in an attempt to purchase not only disputed Texan territory, but also New Mexico and California. When this failed, Polk ordered troops into the disputed region south of the Nueces and to the west of modern Corpus Christi. A skirmish near the Rio Grande in May 1846 allowed Polk to ask Congress to declare war on the grounds that Mexico had 'shed American blood on American soil'. Some northern WHIGS (among them Abraham LINCOLN) opposed the war, and many more were critical of Polk's role in causing it. Nevertheless the war resolution passed the House by 174–14 on May 11, and the Senate by 40–2 on May 12 1846.

Initial campaigning centered on the lower Rio Grande and northern Mexico. General Zachary TAYLOR, commanding a force of US regulars and short-term volunteers that numbered 6000 at its peak, captured MONTERREY on September 25 1846. Taylor then agreed a temporary armistice, leading Polk to rebuke him. Smarting from criticism, Taylor launched a second campaign in northern Mexico that led to victory at the Battle of BUENA VISTA (February 23 1847). Learning that Polk had appointed General Winfield SCOTT to head a joint Army–Navy expedition against Vera Cruz (and that Scott had stripped him of his regular troops), Taylor asked to be relieved of his command.

In California, US recognition of the pro-US BEAR FLAG REVOLT (June 1846) prompted an uprising by pro-Mexican residents. Resistance to US rule ended when, following the Battle of San Gabriel (January 8–9 1847), US troops under Colonel Stephen Kearney (1794–1848) and Robert Stockton (1795–1866) captured Los Angeles on January 10 1847. The resulting treaty of CAHUENGA safeguarded the rights of Mexican Californians.

In February 1847 General Scott's force began its march southwards along Mexico's Gulf coast. In a novel amphibious operation Scott's troops first encircled and then captured VERA CRUZ (March 27 1847). Scott then marched west towards Mexico City, while a force of Missouri volunteers under Colonel Alexander Doniphan (1808–87) advanced on the capital from the northeast. US forces captured Mexico City on September 14 1847, following the battle of CHAPULTEPEC. The treaty of GUADALUPE-HIDALGO that concluded the war was signed on February 2 1848. Through the treaty the USA gained a vast region of new territory in the west and southwest, comprising all or part of the modern states of California, New Mexico, Arizona, Utah, Nevada, Colorado and Wyoming.

During the war, 1721 US troops were killed in battle, and ten times that number died from disease. Future President Franklin PIERCE and Civil War commanders Robert E. LEE and Ulysses S. GRANT served during the war. The question of whether slavery should be permitted in any, or all, of the vast territory acquired in the war (first raised in debate over the WILMOT PROVISO) was settled in the COMPROMISE OF 1850.

Mexico, US intervention in. During the Mexican revolution and civil war, starting in 1910, the WILSON administration adopted a policy of 'watchful waiting'. In April 1914, when a group of US sailors was detained in the Mexican port of Tampico, Wilson sent Marines to occupy Vera Cruz in retaliation. This crisis passed. But domestic pressure to act on the ROOSEVELT COROLLARY became irresistible when, on March 9 1916, Mexican revolutionaries under Pancho Villa killed 17 US citizens on a raid on Columbus, New Mexico, 400 miles (640 km) north of the border. Wilson appointed General John PERSHING to command of a force of 6000 US regulars, which crossed the Mexican border on March 15 1916 in pursuit of Villa. For the next three years US forces skirmished with Villa's followers and the regular Mexican army. Relations between the USA and Mexico were further strained following publication in 1917 of the ZIMMERMANN TELEGRAM in which Germany offered to aid Mexico in recapturing territory lost to the USA in the MEXICAN WAR of 1846–8.

MIAs, abbreviation used by US bureaucrats to identify servicemen 'missing in action.' At the close of the VIETNAM WAR the USA claimed that there were some 2400 MIAs, the bulk of them pilots shot down over Southeast Asia. Understandably, the relatives of these missing men have demanded of successive US administrations and of the Vietnamese government the fullest possible accounting of the circumstances in which they disappeared. During the 1980s, HOLLYWOOD movies such as the notorious 'Rambo' series and inflammatory political rhetoric fueled a popular perception that some or all of the Vietnam-era MIAs were alive in one or more undisclosed locations in the region. As this belief took hold of the public imagination, pressure from the grass-roots forced sports stadiums, truck dealerships and even some government buildings to display a special flag honoring the MIAs.

Michigan, state in the north midwest, straddling Lake Michigan and bordered by Wisconsin to the west, Indiana and Ohio to the south and Canada to the north and east.

The first European settlement in the territory was established in 1668 at Sault Ste Marie by Fr Jacques Marquette (1637–75). The French subsequently founded Fort

Detroit (1701). Britain acquired Michigan from France through the treaty of PARIS (1763). Native Americans fought PONTIAC'S WAR to prevent further British settlement of the region. Even after the second treaty of Paris (1783), Britain retained a strong military presence in the region. Britain finally agreed to abandon its forts in JAY'S TREATY (1794) although British troops subsequently invaded and occupied Michigan during the WAR OF 1812.

The organization of American government in the region was dictated by the terms of the NORTHWEST ORDINANCE (1787). Michigan became a territory on January 11 1805 and the 26th state on January 26 1837. Substantial in-migration began in the 1830s. In 1840, Michigan had over 200,000 permanent residents; by 1860 its population had reached 749,113. The state supplied over 87,000 troops to the Union during the Civil War. It granted the vote to women in 1918.

Although most migrants to Michigan sought to establish family farms, Michigan's economic development was also shaped by mining, lumber and manufacturing industries. During the PROGRESSIVE ERA, Michigan emerged as a major center of industrial production. As competitors followed Henry FORD's lead, Detroit ('The Motor City' or 'Motown') became the center of the US automobile industry. Between 1910 and 1930, over 1,000,000 Americans migrated to Michigan in search of work in the new industrial plants; among them many African-Americans moving north from southern states as part of the GREAT MIGRATION. During WORLD WAR II, Michigan's production lines helped make the USA the ARSENAL OF DEMOCRACY. During this period, the state was the scene of violence originating in labor militancy (especially during the era of SIT-DOWN STRIKES) and racial bigotry (in June 1943, 25 blacks and 9 whites were killed in rioting in Detroit).

From the 1950s, Michigan's socio-economic structures were transformed by 'white flight' from established cities to new suburbs and by the gradual decline of manufacturing industry. The DETROIT RIOT of 1967 gave early warning of the problems attendant on these developments in Michigan and elsewhere. By the early 1980s, Detroit, and smaller cities such as Flint, Michigan, had become synonymous with the development of a 'rust-belt' of outmoded industries in the northeastern USA. In 1990, Michigan had 9,295,297 permanent residents and was the eighth most populous state in the union. The industrialist Henry Ford was born in Michigan and president Gerald FORD made his career in the state.

Midway, battle of (June 3–6 1942), naval engagement in the central Pacific during WORLD WAR II. The US victory at Midway turned out to be the turning point in the Pacific war and virtually ended Japan's capacity to mount strategic offensives in the Pacific.

Utilizing Allied mastery of Japanese radio codes, two US naval task forces, commanded by Rear Admiral Frank Fletcher and Rear Admiral Raymond Spruance, intercepted an invasion fleet bound for Midway Island, a US base some 1000 miles (1600 km) west of Hawaii. US planes sank all four of the Japanese aircraft carriers in the invasion fleet and shot down 253 Japanese planes. One US carrier was lost and 3500 US servicemen were killed or wounded. The battle prevented Japan from seizing Midway Island as a staging post for an invasion of Hawaii.

military-industrial complex, the combined interests of the military establishment and defense industries in the USA, seen as having an excessive influence on government policy. The phrase was famously used on January 17 1961 by outgoing President EISENHOWER in a farewell address to the American people in which he warned: '[The] conjunction of an immense military establishment and a large arms industry is new in the American experience In the councils of government, we must guard against the acquisition of unwarranted influence, whether sought or unsought, by the military-industrial complex. The potential for the disastrous rise of misplaced power exists and will persist.' The Cuban missile crisis and VIETNAM WAR seemed to confirm Eisenhower's fears.

Milligan, Ex Parte, *see* EX PARTE MILLIGAN.

Minnesota, state in the northern midwest, bordered to the north by Canada, to the east by Lake Superior and Wisconsin, to the south by Iowa and to the west by the Dakotas.

The first permanent European settlement in the territory was established by the French at Fort St. Antoine, Lake Pepin, in 1686. America acquired eastern Minnesota from the French via the treaty of PARIS (1763) and the remainder of the territory through the LOUISIANA PURCHASE (1803). US settlement began to pick up following a cession of land by native peoples in 1837. Minnesota became a US territory on March 3 1849 and the 32nd state on May 11 1858. Between 1850 and 1860, its population jumped from just over 6000 to 172,000.

Many new settlers sought to grow wheat on family farms, but the state was also the site of vibrant mining and lumbering industries. In the late 19th and early 20th centuries, the state attracted a substantial influx of Scandinavian immigrants, helping to produce a distinctive regional culture, celebrated by the humorist Garrison Keillor. For much of the 20th century, Minnesota's electorate has been attracted to candidates offering reform. Liberal Democrats Hubert HUMPHREY and Walter MONDALE made their careers in Minnesota and, more recently, former wrestler Jesse Ventura was elected to the state governorship on a ticket loosely allied with Ross PEROT's Reform Party. Minnesotans also supported a state law on ABORTION (upheld in the US Supreme Court verdict HODGSON VS. MINNESOTA) that

qualified the unrestricted right to choose an abortion implied by the Supreme Court's judgment in ROE VS. WADE. Aside from its two vice presidents, Eugene McCARTHY is the state's most famous 'native son.'

Minor vs. Happersett (March 29 1875), US Supreme Court ruling that the denial of WOMEN'S SUFFRAGE was not unconstitutional. During the 1870s the NATIONAL WOMAN'S SUFFRAGE ASSOCIATION hired lawyers to argue that, since the US Constitution is written in the name of 'We, the people', and since women are people, to deny women the right to vote was an unconstitutional infringement of due process as guaranteed in the FOURTEENTH AMENDMENT. In making its ruling the Supreme Court rejected this argument. Its reasoning was that the Constitution did not confer the right of suffrage on any citizen, and that therefore Fourteenth Amendment guarantees did not apply.

minutemen, units within the colonial militia during the REVOLUTIONARY WAR that could be ready to fight at a minute's notice. The first such units were organized in Massachusetts in September 1774. Connecticut, New Hampshire, Maryland and North Carolina organized similar units following the battles of LEXINGTON AND CONCORD (1775).

Miranda vs. Arizona (June 13 1966), US Supreme Court ruling that policemen must inform suspects of their rights at the time of arrest. Citing the protection of due process written into the FIFTH and FOURTEENTH AMENDMENTS to the US CONSTITUTION, the Court, Chief Justice WARREN presiding, ruled that arresting officers must inform suspects of their right to remain silent, their right to consult a lawyer, and that any statement they make may be used against them in subsequent court proceedings. The perceived impracticability of requiring policemen to inform suspects of their rights prior to the taking of a statement was assailed by the Republican Party.

miscegenation, interbreeding between people of different races. During the PRESIDENTIAL ELECTION OF 1864 Democrats peddled gross racial prejudice in an attempt to discredit LINCOLN. An anonymous pamphlet, *Miscegenation: The Theory of the Blending of the Races*, purported to reveal a secret Republican plan to establish racial equality by encouraging black men to ravish white women.

Missionary Ridge, battle of, *see* CHATTANOOGA, BATTLE OF.

Mississippi, 'deep south' state, bordered on the north by Tennessee, to the east by Alabama, to the south by the Gulf of Mexico, and to the west by the Louisiana, Arkansas and the Mississippi river.

The first permanent European settlement in the territory was established by the French at Fort Rosalie (near Natchez) in 1716. Mississippi was acquired by Britain through the first treaty of PARIS (1763) and by America through the second treaty of Paris in 1783. The USA organized a Mississippi territory (including much of western Alabama) on April 7 1798. Mississippi became a state on December 10 1817. Although its lands were coveted by cotton producers, Mississippi received few US settlers until the CHOCTAW and CHICKASAW nations relocated to RESERVATIONS in Oklahoma in the 1830s. From this point, Mississippi's economy boomed. By 1860, the state had 791,305 permanent residents (55% of whom were enslaved) and grew 25% of the US cotton crop. The state's cotton planters, notably Jefferson DAVIS, were staunch defenders of slavery and, on January 9 1861, Mississippi became the 3rd state to join the CONFEDERACY.

During RECONSTRUCTION, the state enacted draconian BLACK CODES, prevented FREEDMEN from voting, and rejected the THIRTEENTH and FOURTEENTH Amendments (Mississippi has never formally ratified the Thirteenth Amendment). Congress responded by placing Mississippi under

military administration from March 1867 to February 23 1870. In 1870 Mississippi's legislature elected Hiram REVELS to the US Senate. (Revels was the first African-American to serve in the Senate.) Nevertheless, white REDEEMERS stifled the Republican party in the state and ultimately enacted a strict system of racial segregation. Mississippi became synonymous with the JIM CROW south. The state's small farmers, black and white, suffered from the SHARECROPPING and CROP LIEN systems.

Between 1920 and 1970, over 1,300,000 residents, mostly black, left Mississippi for jobs in the north. The state's white political establishment, which commanded a position of influence within the national Democratic Party, was at the forefront of resistance to the CIVIL RIGHTS MOVEMENT. Violence directed against civil rights activists, especially during the MISSISSIPPI FREEDOM SUMMER, made the state the focus of national and international attention. Vestiges of racial segregation within Mississippi's higher education system remain to this day. In 1990, Mississippi had 2,573,216 permanent residents and was the 31st populous state in the union. Elvis PRESLEY, born in Tupelo, is the state's most famous 'native son.'

Mississippi Freedom Democratic Party (MFDP), organization founded in April 1964, at the start of the MISSISSIPPI FREEDOM SUMMER, with the aim of shaming the state and national DEMOCRATIC PARTY by protesting against the exclusion of African-Americans from any role in choosing the Mississippi delegation to the national Democratic convention.

The MFDP organized its own elections, held its own state convention, and sent a multiracial delegation to the Democrats' national convention in Atlantic City. The MFDP demanded that its representatives be seated in the convention, and that the 'official' delegation be withdrawn. Governor John Connally of Texas declared, 'If those baboons walk onto the convention floor we walk out.' President JOHNSON, anxious to prevent white southerners from defecting to GOLDWATER in that year's presidential race, went to extraordinary lengths to railroad the convention into seating the official delegation. Fanny Lou HAMER gave a rousing address to the conference, but Johnson arranged a White House press conference to switch national TV coverage away from her speech. Major figures in the NATIONAL ASSOCIATION FOR THE ADVANCEMENT OF COLORED PEOPLE (NAACP) and SOUTHERN CHRISTIAN LEADERSHIP CONFERENCE (SCLC), including Martin Luther KING, sided with Johnson. The incident created bitterness, and was one cause of the disintegration of the CIVIL RIGHTS MOVEMENT.

Mississippi Freedom Summer (1964), the defining moment of the CIVIL RIGHTS MOVEMENT, during which activists finally broke white resistance to African-American voter registration in the USA's most bigoted state.

The victory was the product of four years' campaigning. In 1960 just 5% of Mississippi's adult blacks were registered voters. A 1961 registration campaign, centering on McComb County, Mississippi, and led by Robert Moses, foundered when FREEDOM RIDERS from the STUDENT NON-VIOLENT COORDINATING COMMITTEE (SNCC) committed to direct action provoked a violent white backlash. In 1962 a more cautious campaign, organized by the SNCC and the SOUTHERN CHRISTIAN LEADERSHIP CONFERENCE (SCLC), galvanized charismatic local figures such as Fanny Lou HAMER, and produced positive results in Sunflower County and Greenwood, Mississippi.

In 1963 movement activists organized a 'freedom vote' among African-Americans excluded by the state's registration process. Allard Lowenstein brought several hundred white college students south to participate in this campaign. The 'freedom vote' was an exercise in political street theater analogous to popular protests organized against

the STAMP ACT during the AMERICAN REVOLUTION. A violent white supremacist backlash against it, which in June 1963 claimed the life of Medgar EVERS – the Mississippi field secretary of the NATIONAL ASSOCIATION FOR THE ADVANCEMENT OF COLORED PEOPLE (NAACP) – only strengthened the determination of the SNCC and the CONGRESS OF RACIAL EQUALITY (CORE) to continue and broaden the campaign in 1964.

During the Freedom Summer of 1964 CORE and the SNCC organized 'freedom schools', staffed by locals and outsiders (among them black and white university students), which offered black Mississippians training in non-violent protest, classes on African-American history, and assistance with voter registration. The campaign produced new martyrs, chiefly Michael Schwerner, Andrew Goodman and black Mississippian John Chaney, whose bodies were discovered outside Philadelphia, Mississippi, 44 days after they were abducted in Neshoba County. It also produced a new heroine in Fanny Lou Hamer, who emerged as the spokeswoman of the MISSISSIPPI FREEDOM DEMOCRATIC PARTY (MFDP), which that year challenged the credentials of the Mississippi delegation at the DEMOCRATIC PARTY's national convention. Overcoming intimidation and violence, Freedom Summer activists increased African-American voter registration and established local organizations that carried forward the fight against discrimination in Mississippi.

The campaign helped persuade Congress to pass the CIVIL RIGHTS ACT OF 1964 and the VOTING RIGHTS ACT of 1965. But beneath the surface resentments flourished between white volunteers and southern black activists, between the SNCC and the SCLC, and between Lyndon B. JOHNSON's administration and the movement's leaders. The refusal of the national Democratic Party to recognize the MFDP convinced many activists of the futility of campaigns that took a narrow view of civil rights. This underlying tension within the movement was later exposed in the furore over the concept of BLACK POWER.

Missouri, central midwestern state, bordered on the north by Iowa, to the east by the Mississippi river, Illinois and Kentucky, to the south by Arkansas and to the west by Kansas and Nebraska.

The first permanent European settlement in the territory was established by French fur traders at St Genevieve in 1735. The city of St. Louis was founded in 1764. The USA acquired Missouri through the LOUISIANA PURCHASE (1803). Missouri became a US territory on June 4 1812 and, following the MISSOURI COMPROMISE, the 24th state on August 10 1821.

Missouri's state constitution permitted slavery but in 1860 only 11% of the state's 1,182,012 residents were enslaved. During the CIVIL WAR Missouri was a BORDER STATE. Its legislature did not pass an act of SECESSION but the CONFEDERACY regarded the state as its 12th member. Missouri was the site of over 1,000 military engagements during the war.

During RECONSTRUCTION, Democrats pledged to enact racial segregation gradually gained control of the state legislature. The state's access to the Mississippi–Missouri river system led to the creation of an economy in which agricultural production was balanced by trade and manufacturing interests centered on Kansas City and St. Louis. In 1900, Missouri was the 5th most populous state in the union and the 7th most valuable producer of manufactured goods. Over the first half of the 20th century, the state experienced substantial out-migration. In 1990, Missouri had 5,117,073 permanent residents and was the 15th most populous state in the union. The state's most famous 'native son' is President Harry S TRUMAN.

Missouri Compromise, agreement reached in Congress in 1820 regarding the issue of slavery in the new territories. On February

13 1819 Representative James Tallmadge of New York introduced an amendment to legislation preparing Missouri for statehood. It proposed that no further slaves should be imported into any territory acquired through the LOUISIANA PURCHASE, and that the children of slaves already resident there should be freed on their 25th birthday. The amendment threatened to make slave states a permanent minority in Congress. Moreover, since Missouri wanted to enter with slavery, it raised the question of whether Congress could, or should, make the renunciation of slavery a precondition for admission into the Union. After heated debate, compromise was reached on March 3 1820. Missouri entered the Union as a slave state, while Maine entered as a free state. Slavery was excluded from the remaining unorganized territories west of the Mississippi and north of 36° 30' acquired through the Louisiana Purchase. This prohibition was ruled unconstitutional in DRED SCOTT VS. SANDFORD (1857). Northern members of the House of Representatives who supported the deal were dubbed DOUGHFACES by colleagues determined to limit the expansion of slavery.

Mobile Bay, battle of (August 5 1864), the largest naval battle of the CIVIL WAR, fought in the Gulf of Mexico, off the Alabama coast, and resulting in the closure of the port of Mobile to Confederate blockade runners. To the warning 'Torpedoes ahead!' the Union commander, Rear Admiral David Glasgow Farragut (1801–70), replied, 'Damn the torpedoes!' and pressed home the attack.

Mohawk, Iroquoian-speaking Native American people. On the eve of the DECLARATION OF INDEPENDENCE just 500 Mohawk survived on homelands west of Schenectady in New York's upper Hudson valley. Pressure from white settlement had forced the Mohawk to sell land and adopt Anglo-American farming techniques. During the REVOLUTIONARY WAR Joseph BRANT persuaded some of the Mohawk's partners in the IROQUOIS CONFED-

ERACY to side with Britain against America. Following America's victory in the war, the Mohawk were stripped of their remaining lands.

Molly Maguires, a radical and clandestine organization of coal miners active in the coal fields of northeastern Pennsylvania in the 1860s and 1870s. The organization originated in 1862 as an offshoot of the Ancient Order of Hibernians, a secret Irish order. Members of the organization, dubbed 'Molly Maguires', were held responsible for a coordinated campaign of attacks on mine and railroad installations. PINKERTON agents hired by the Pennsylvania and Reading Railroad were sent into the coal fields in the 1870s. In 1875, 24 miners alleged to be Molly Maguires were tried in Philadelphia: 10 were hanged and 14 imprisoned.

Mondale, Walter F(ritz) (1928–), Democratic statesman, vice president in Jimmy CARTER's administration (1977–81), and the Democratic Party's candidate in the presidential election of 1984, in which he suffered a landslide defeat by Ronald REAGAN. Mondale was a liberal Democrat who began his political career as an aide to fellow Minnesotan Hubert HUMPHREY. As a US senator (1965–77) he supported civil rights measures, including the controversial BUSSING policy. However, like Humphrey, Mondale also supported president Lyndon B. JOHNSON's position on the VIETNAM WAR longer than most liberals. Mondale got along well with Carter and was regarded as an above-average vice president. However, in 1987 Mondale admitted that within two days of receiving the Democrats' nomination he realized he had no chance of beating Reagan in the 1984 presidential election. In his acceptance speech following his nomination Mondale unwisely announced, 'Mr Reagan will raise taxes, so will I. He won't tell you, I just did.' He was instantly assailed as a 'tax-and-spend' liberal, and meanwhile his running-mate, Geraldine FERRARO, became embroiled in a controversy con-

cerning her husband's finances. The scale of Mondale's defeat was unprecedented. Even with Ferraro on the ticket, a majority of women, Catholics and Italian-Americans voted Republican. Only Minnesota, Mondale's home state, returned a Democratic majority. President CLINTON appointed Mondale ambassador to Japan in 1993.

money trust, any of a small number of banking conglomerates active in the later 19th and early 20th centuries. Those opposed to the activities and corruption of big business, such as the MUCKRAKERS, denounced all TRUSTS, but evidence that a handful of Wall Street financiers, chief among them J.P. MORGAN, effectively controlled the nation's banking and credit institutions was especially troubling. This was because the PROGRESSIVES' preferred solution to monopolizing practices – greater competition – threatened financial insecurity if applied to the big banks. Morgan, the embodiment of the money trust, prevented the PANIC OF 1907 from becoming a depression by summoning leading financiers to the library of his New York townhouse and dictating which banks retained his confidence and which he would allow to collapse. As he told the PUJO HEARINGS, Morgan could do this only because his bank had acquired powerful interests and directorships in virtually every other bank on Wall Street. The creation of the FEDERAL RESERVE SYSTEM in 1913 greatly diminished the extent to which America's financial policy was determined by a handful of private bankers holding interlocking directorships.

Monitor,* USS, vs. CSS *Virginia (March 9 1862), the world's first battle between steam-powered ironclad warships, which took place during the CIVIL WAR at Hampton Roads, Virginia. Designed by John Ericsson,(1803–89) the *Monitor* boasted a revolving armored turret, a shallow draft and relatively high speed. The *Virginia*, whose armored superstructure was built over the hull of the captured USS *Merrimack*, carried more guns than the *Monitor*, but was slower. Nevertheless, on March 8 1862, in the US Navy's worst defeat before Pearl Harbor, the *Virginia* sank two US frigates and captured another, threatening to make the Union blockade of Norfolk, Virginia, and other southern ports untenable. In the ensuing single ship duel, the *Monitor* forced the *Virginia* back to Norfolk for repairs. The *Virginia* never re-emerged.

Monmouth Court House, battle of (June 28 1778), American victory in New Jersey during the REVOLUTIONARY WAR. On June 18 1778, 10,000 British troops evacuated Philadelphia to begin a retreat across New Jersey to New York City. On June 28 advance units of the Continental Army engaged the British but, owing to poor staff work by General Charles Lee (1731–82), were forced to retreat. The main body of WASHINGTON's 13,000-strong army demonstrated the discipline instilled during the winter at VALLEY FORGE as it pressed the British troops pursuing Lee back to their original lines. That night the British army broke camp and continued its retreat, allowing Washington's army to claim victory.

Monroe, James (1758–1831), Democratic statesman and 5th president of the USA (1817–25).

Monroe, a Virginia gentleman, joined the Continental Army at 16 and rose to prominence during the REVOLUTIONARY WAR. He was wounded at the Battle of TRENTON, survived the winter at VALLEY FORGE, and served as adjutant general. He resigned his commission in 1780 to spend three years studying law with JEFFERSON.

A stint in CONFEDERATION CONGRESS (1783–6) was followed by one term in the Senate (1790–4). As minister to France (1794–6) Monroe incurred FEDERALIST displeasure for his opposition to JAY'S TREATY. He served two terms as governor of Virginia (1799–1802, 1811) before being appointed secretary of state by President MADISON. During the WAR OF 1812 Monroe also served as

secretary of war (1814–15). He removed archives, including the original Declaration of Independence, from Washington DC in advance of the British destruction of the city.

On March 4 1817 Monroe became president, serving until March 4 1825. Monroe profited from the collapse of federalism, presiding over an 'Era of Good Feelings' in which partisan rivalry diminished. He considered vetoing the MISSOURI COMPROMISE, but baulked at the risk of civil war. John Quincy ADAMS persuaded him to promulgate what became known as the MONROE DOCTRINE.

Monroe Doctrine, statement of US foreign policy that effectively claimed US hegemony over the whole of the Americas. On December 2 1823, President MONROE used his annual address to Congress to announce that the USA would regard as a threat any attempt by European powers to create new colonial ventures in the western hemisphere. He pledged to respect existing European colonies and to refrain from interfering in the internal affairs of European nations. The announcement, which was drafted by Secretary of State John Quincy ADAMS, had no force in international law, but served as the basis for all future US policy in the western hemisphere.

Montana, state in the upper northwest, bordered to the north by Canada, to the east by the Dakotas, to the south by Wyoming, and to the west by Idaho and Washington.

The USA acquired Montana from France through the LOUISIANA PURCHASE (1803). The first US trading post in the territory, Fort Union, was not established until 1829. In 1862, gold was discovered in southwest Montana. New settlers flooded in, especially after the completion of the BOZEMAN TRAIL, and the USA granted territorial status to Montana on May 26 1864. These developments put US residents on a collision course with the SIOUX and CHEYENNE peoples. The second and third SIOUX WARS were fought in Montana (the latter culminating in the battle of LITTLE BIG HORN). Montana became the 41st state on November 8 1891. In 1900, it had 243,329 residents.

The state's economic development has been dominated by the cattle and mining industries. Some support for PROGRESSIVISM existed within the state – Montana granted women the vote in 1914 and elected Jeanette RANKIN (the first woman to sit in the US House of Representatives).

In recent years, the state has developed a trade in tourism, but in 1990, the state had only 799,065 permanent residents and was the 44th most populous state in the union.

Monterrey, battle of (September 1846), engagement during the MEXICAN WAR, in which US forces captured the Mexican town of Monterrey. General Zachary TAYLOR's force of 6000 US regulars and volunteers drove a larger Mexican force from defensive positions overlooking Monterrey into the town itself. After a four-day siege, the Mexicans surrendered on September 25 1846. Taylor allowed the Mexicans to leave under arms and he agreed to an eight-week armistice. He was criticized for these decisions by President POLK.

Montgomery bus boycott, important early civil rights protest, held in the Alabama city of Montgomery. On December 1 1955 Rosa Parks, a 43-year-old black seamstress, was arrested after she refused to vacate a seat in a section of a Montgomery city bus designated for white use only. In a major protest against JIM CROW that marked the beginning of the modern CIVIL RIGHTS MOVEMENT, black citizens of Montgomery boycotted the city's bus company in a bid to force it to desegregate seating and treat black and white passengers equally. The boycott lasted 381 days. Company revenue dropped by 65%, a factor that helped persuade the operator to meet the protesters' demands. African-Americans throughout the south took inspiration from the organizational flair and communal self-assertion the boycotters demonstrated. The Reverend Martin Luther KING's speeches in support of the protesters captured the mood of the campaign.

Moral Majority, conservative pressure group founded by the Reverend Jerry Falwell in 1979. Its membership was drawn from white fundamentalists who believed that permissive values – in areas such as school prayer, homosexuality and above all ABORTION – were being imposed on the USA by liberal legislators and the judiciary. A bumper sticker popular with liberals at the time read: 'The Moral Majority is neither.'

Morgan, J(ohn) P(ierpont) (1837–1913), financier and industrialist. Born in Hartford, Connecticut, Morgan was educated in Europe. His father owned a London bank, and Morgan returned to the USA in 1857 to run its New York operations. He made a fortune during the CIVIL WAR and began a series of alliances and acquisitions that made J.P. Morgan and Co. the most powerful bank in the world. Morgan formed or controlled dozens of railroad corporations. In 1901 he bought out Andrew CARNEGIE to form US Steel, the world's first billion-dollar corporation.

During the PUJO HEARINGS Morgan told Congress, 'A man I do not trust could not get money [from Wall Street] on all the bonds in Christendom.' Morgan's influence was well-known, and led to his being vilified as the embodiment of a sinister MONEY TRUST. However, before the creation of the FEDERAL RESERVE SYSTEM (1913), Morgan used his power to perform many of the functions of a national central bank. During the DEPRESSION OF 1893, the CLEVELAND administration was forced to rely on a syndicate headed by Morgan to float a crucial government bond issue. By supporting some banks but allowing others to fail, Morgan calmed markets and prevented the PANIC OF 1907 from developing into a full depression. New York's Metropolitan Museum of Art was among the major beneficiaries of bequests made in Morgan's will. His son, J.P.

Morgan Jr, continued his father's banking interests, lending vast sums of money to the Allied nations during World War I.

Mormons, shorthand name given to members of the Church of Jesus Christ of Latter-day Saints. The name derives from texts published in 1830 under the title *The Book of Mormon* by the founder of the church, Joseph Smith (1805–44).

Smith claimed that between 1823 and 1827 angels directed him to recover a series of golden texts buried beneath the ground near Manchester, New York. These revealed an ancient and hitherto unknown Hebrew migration to America, and suggested that Christ had appeared on the North American continent after his resurrection. Smith established the first Mormon church at Fayette, New York, on April 6 1830, and published the texts to aid the conversion of doubters. The tenets of the Mormon church outraged more orthodox Protestants, while their acceptance of polygamy alarmed Americans who were otherwise little interested in religion. Smith and his followers were forced to flee New York State to Kirtland Mills, Ohio, in 1831, and to relocate from Independence, Missouri, where they settled in 1832, to Nauvoo, Illinois, in 1839. Joseph Smith was murdered by locals near Nauvoo in 1844, and in 1846, amid scenes of hysteria, vigilantes destroyed the Nauvoo settlement.

Nevertheless, the Mormons had already proved to be phenomenally successful evangelizers. Following the attack on Nauvoo, Brigham YOUNG led 15,000 survivors to the Salt Lake region of Utah. Young hoped that Congress would admit into the Union a new state based in Utah, organized along distinctively Mormon lines and called Deseret. Congress refused, but made Utah a US territory in 1851. The Mormon settlers who dominated the territory's population insisted on the legality of polygamy, but Congress refused to grant Utah statehood while its constitution permitted men to take more than one wife. In 1857 Congress removed Brigham Young from the territorial governorship, and later charged him with bigamy. In 1882 Congress placed Utah's electoral system under federal supervision, and disenfranchised polygamists. Church leaders capitulated, and in 1896 Utah joined the Union with a constitution that does not safeguard the right of polygamy. However, Mormons still predominate among the population of Utah, and Salt Lake City is the headquarters of what is now a worldwide faith.

Morrill (Higher Education) Act (July 2 1862), legislation that gave to states that had not joined the Confederacy 30,000 acres (12,000 ha) of public land (multiplied by the total of each state's representation in Congress) to be used to establish agricultural and mechanical colleges. The act was sponsored by Justin Morrill (1810–98), Republican senator for Vermont. The measure financed the founding of 69 'land-grant' colleges. Cornell, the University of Wisconsin at Madison and the University of California at Berkeley are among the institutions that owe their existence to the act.

Morristown mutiny (May 25 1780), the most serious of several mutinies during the REVOLUTIONARY WAR staged by troops in the Continental Army over arrears in pay and short rations. The mutiny took place at George WASHINGTON's headquarters at Morristown, New Jersey. Two regiments of Connecticut troops paraded under arms to demand immediate settlement of their pay arrears and a restoration of full rations. The mutineers were surrounded by two regiments of Pennsylvanian troops and an artillery battery and told to give up their ringleaders for execution or face annihilation. This quelled the protest. Pennsylvanian troops staged a mutiny themselves in 1783, during which members of CONFEDERATION CONGRESS were menaced.

Morse, Samuel Finley Breese (1791–1872), artist, founding father of NATIVISM and inventor of the telegraph. Morse was born in Massachusetts and attended Yale before embarking on a career as a painter of historical subjects. On a trip to Rome in 1829, Morse was beaten up for refusing to kneel before a Catholic procession. This incident exacerbated Morse's anti-Catholicism and on his return to the USA, he wrote a series of vitriolic articles calling for curbs on Catholic immigration to prevent the creation of tyranny in the United States. (Morse's fear and loathing of Catholic immigrants was subsequently disseminated by groups such as the KNOW NOTHING PARTY). In the 1830s, Morse abandoned his career as an artist and began studying the feasibility of communication via electrical current. He persuaded Congress to fund a trial telegraph line between Washington and Baltimore. On May 24 1844, Morse sent the world's first telegraph message: 'What hath God wrought.' Within ten years the USA possessed a 23,000 mile network of telegraph lines.

Mott, Lucretia Coffin (1793–1880), pioneer of the WOMEN'S SUFFRAGE movement. She collaborated with Elizabeth Cady STANTON to organize the SENECA FALLS CONVENTION (1848), which marked the beginning of organized feminism in the USA.

Mott, a Quaker preacher, was a member of the AMERICAN ANTISLAVERY SOCIETY, and in 1837 helped found the Antislavery Convention of American Women. The humiliation of being denied accreditation at the London (England) abolition conference in 1840 led her to begin campaigning for women's rights. Like her fellow pioneers Elizabeth Cady Stanton and Susan B. ANTHONY, Mott believed that RADICAL REPUBLICANS ought to have addressed women's rights at the same time as they addressed the concerns of FREEDMEN. She founded the American Equal Rights Association in 1866 to campaign against a broad range of discriminatory practices.

Mount Vernon Conference (March 28 1785), discussion held by delegates from Virginia and Maryland at Mount Vernon, George WASHINGTON's mansion in Virginia. The object of the meeting was to discuss navigation and trade concerns relating to the Potomac river and Chesapeake Bay. Progress made at the meeting convinced delegates to call the ANNAPOLIS CONVENTION, and encouraged talk of radically redrafting the ARTICLES OF CONFEDERATION.

movies, *see* HOLLYWOOD.

muckrakers, name coined by Theodore Roosevelt for investigative journalists and writers of didactic fiction who set out to expose the excesses of predatory capitalism and urban corruption in the late 19th and early 20th centuries.

Henry Demarest Lloyd (1847–1903) was the father of what became a genre, expanding an investigation of TRUSTS originally published in the *Atlantic Monthly* into the influential book *Wealth Against Commonwealth* (1894). Lincoln Steffens's *The SHAME OF OUR CITIES* (1903–5) famously attacked urban corruption. Ida Tarbell (1857–1944), whose father had been put out of business by John D. ROCKEFELLER Sr, published a damning history of Standard Oil in *McClure's Monthly* (1903). The Supreme Court's subsequent verdict in STANDARD OIL OF NEW JERSEY VS. US was hailed as a triumph for muckrakers. Readers of Charles Edward Russell's *The Greatest Trust in the World* (1906) and Upton Sinclair's novel *The Jungle* (1906) applauded the humbling of the Beef Trust in SWIFT AND CO. VS. US. Sinclair's novel shocked Congress into passing the PURE FOOD AND DRUG ACT (1906). Ray Stannard Baker's 'The Railroads on Trial' (*McClure's*, 1906) rallied support for the HEPBURN ACT (1906).

Theodore ROOSEVELT criticized as well as defined the genre when, on April 14 1906, he compared some investigative journalists to the muckraker in *Pilgrim's Progress* who was so fixed on scraping the floor that he never looked upward. As the genre grew in popularity and influence it also became sensationalized, adding force to Roosevelt's call for exposure to give way to constructive reform.

Mugwumps, REPUBLICAN supporters so enraged by STALWART hostility to the PENDLETON ACT and civil-service reform that they supported DEMOCRATIC candidate Grover CLEVELAND in the 1884 presidential election. The term has also been applied more generally to any politically neutral or independent person, and derives from the Algonkian word for 'great chief'.

Muhammad, Elijah, *see* NATION OF ISLAM.

Muller vs. Oregon (February 24 1908), US Supreme Court ruling that unanimously upheld an Oregon state law limiting the hours female laundry workers could be compelled to work. The Court reasoned from quantitative data presented by Louis BRANDEIS that since women's health could be shown to suffer as a result of overly long working days, state laws limiting the hours women might work did not represent an unconstitutional infringement of an employer's FOURTEENTH AMENDMENT right to freely negotiate contracts. The effectiveness of Brandeis's brief can be gauged from the fact that only three years earlier, in LOCHNER VS. NEW YORK, the Court had cited the Fourteenth Amendment to strike down a New York state law limiting the hours of bakery workers. The 1908 decision represented the Supreme Court's first step towards grudging acceptance of progressive labor legislation.

Munn vs. Illinois (March 1 1877), US Supreme Court ruling that upheld the constitutionality of an Illinois state law setting maximum rates for grain storage. The Court held that states could, in the absence of federal legislation, regulate businesses 'affected with a public interest'. Chief Justice Waite (1816–88) added that appeal was 'to the polls, not to the courts'. The decision encouraged the passage of GRANGER LAWS, but the Court reversed its earlier verdict in SANTA CLARA COUNTY VS. SOUTHERN PACIFIC RAILROAD and WABASH, ST LOUIS AND PACIFIC RAILROAD COMPANY VS. ILLINOIS (1888).

My Lai massacre (March 16 1968), massacre of Vietnamese civilians by US troops during the VIETNAM WAR. However unfairly, this isolated incident shaped public perceptions of the behavior of US forces in the war. Doubtless made nervous by the recent TET OFFENSIVE, a company of the US 11th Infantry commanded by Lieutenant William Calley was searching My Lai (a village in Quang Ngai province, South Vietnam) when, on Calley's orders, the soldiers opened fire indiscriminately. They continued until they had killed at least 350 unarmed civilians. The soldiers, backed by the Army, concealed the incident until November 1969. Calley was court-martialed, and in March 1971 convicted of 'at least 22 murders'. He was sentenced to life imprisonment. While the case was still under appeal, President NIXON ordered Calley's release from prison. Calley eventually served three years of jail time.

N

NAACP, *see* NATIONAL ASSOCIATION FOR THE ADVANCEMENT OF COLORED PEOPLE.

NAFTA, *see* NORTH AMERICAN FREE TRADE AGREEMENT.

Nakota, another name for the Yankton-SIOUX.

NASA, *see* NATIONAL AERONAUTICS AND SPACE ADMINISTRATION.

Nashville, battle of (December 15–16 1864), Union victory in Tennessee during the CIVIL WAR. A Union army of 50,000 troops, led by the 'Rock of CHICKAMAUGA', General George Thomas (1816–70), exploited its numerical superiority to rout a force of 24,000 Confederates under General John Bell Hood (1831–79). The defeat left Robert E. LEE's Army of Northern Virginia as the sole remaining military threat to the Union, and prompted southern diarist Mary Chesnut (1823–86) to write, 'the deep waters are closing over us' .

Nation, Carry (Amelia Moore) (1846–1911), campaigner for PROHIBITION. Her own experience (her first husband was an alcoholic doctor) drove her to direct action, and in 1900 she used a hatchet to smash up saloons in Medicine Lodge, Kansas, which were defying a ban on the sale of alcohol. This newsworthy event sparked copy-cat actions across the midwest. Nation edited the *Smasher's Mail*, a journal dedicated to the passage of the EIGHTEENTH AMENDMENT.

National Aeronautics and Space Administration (NASA), agency charged with coordinating the USA's military and civilian space programs. It was created by act of Congress on July 29 1958.

In its early years NASA came under strong pressure, generated by the COLD WAR, to demonstrate that the USA was not falling behind the Soviet Union in the 'space race'; in 1957 the Soviet Union had launched the world's first Earth-orbiting satellite, *Sputnik*, and on April 12 1961 had successfully placed cosmonaut Yuri Gagarin in Earth orbit. On May 25 1961 President KENNEDY announced the APOLLO PROGRAM and set NASA the challenge of landing a man on the Moon within the decade. NASA's manned space-flight program began after Kennedy's announcement with a suborbital flight by Alan Shepherd on July 21 1961. In 1965–6 NASA's Gemini program honed space-flight techniques.

By 1966, 420,000 people were employed by NASA. Despite the escalating cost of the VIETNAM WAR and the GREAT SOCIETY, Congress funded the agency generously. President Lyndon B. JOHNSON, who as Kennedy's vice president had been a keen supporter of NASA, helped rally congressional support by ensuring that crucial headquarters and assembly facilities were built in key southern constituencies.

The Apollo project got off to a bad start

when three astronauts were killed during a simulated launch of the Saturn V rocket conducted on January 27 1967. In December 1968 NASA successfully sent *Apollo 8* into lunar orbit, the necessary prelude for the first manned landing on the Moon on July 20 1969. The final Apollo mission to the Moon was conducted December 7–19 1972.

The cost of space exploration, a sense of anti-climax following the success of the Apollo program, and the lessening of Cold War tensions in the DÉTENTE era, forced NASA to redefine its mission during the 1970s. It developed the Skylab project, a manned space station that was used to conduct a variety of scientific experiments in 1973–4. NASA conducted a symbolic space link-up with Soviet cosmonauts in 1975, and it launched a number of comparatively cheap unmanned exploratory missions. A deep-space probe, *Pioneer 11*, flew within 26,000 miles (41,600 km) of Jupiter in December 1974 and discovered new planetary moons. The *Viking 1* probe, launched on August 20 1975, landed on the surface of Mars on September 3 1976. *Pioneer 2*, launched on August 8 1978, landed on the surface of Venus on December 9 1978. During the same period NASA also began developing the world's first reusable spacecraft, the space shuttle.

The first shuttle flight, by *Columbia*, was successfully completed on April 12 1981. Following this success, congressional funds flowed to NASA once more. In 1975 NASA's budget had shrunk to $3.2 billion, but by 1985 it had increased to $7.3 billion. The increase in NASA funding was partly attributable to the use of the shuttle for secret military missions connected with the STRATEGIC DEFENSE INITIATIVE ('Star Wars'). The shuttle program was suspended for over two years following the CHALLENGER DISASTER (January 28 1986). During an investigation into the in-flight explosion that killed seven astronauts, it emerged that NASA had

been cutting safety corners to retain public funding. The agency rebranded itself under the logo 'Nice and Safe Attitude' in a bid to regain public confidence. Its funding was slashed following the collapse of the Soviet empire in Eastern Europe in 1989. At present NASA has no plans for the further manned exploration of deep space.

National American Woman Suffrage Association (NAWSA), organization created in 1890 as a result of the merger of the NATIONAL WOMAN SUFFRAGE ASSOCIATION (NWSA) and the AMERICAN WOMAN SUFFRAGE ASSOCIATION (AWSA), which had previously been at loggerheads over tactics. Under Susan B. ANTHONY's presidency (1892–1900) the NAWSA continued the NWSA's policy of trying to build bridges with other social-reform campaigners and trade unionists. Between 1900 and 1904, under Carrie Chapman CATT, the NAWSA changed direction and concentrated on encouraging individual states to grant the vote to women (a tactic that had been favored by the AWSA). During WORLD WAR I the NAWSA joined forces with the NATIONAL WOMAN'S PARTY to mount militant action in support of a constitutional amendment to guarantee women's suffrage. It disbanded in 1920. *See also* WOMEN'S SUFFRAGE.

National Association for the Advancement of Colored People (NAACP), moderate integrationist organization that has campaigned for an end to racial discrimination and segregation, and against racism in general.

Founded in 1909, the NAACP was the product of a dialogue between 'fair minded whites and intelligent blacks' initiated in the aftermath of the SPRINGFIELD LYNCH RIOT. Although W.E.B. DU BOIS edited the NAACP's newspaper *The Crisis*, white liberals dominated the leadership in its formative years. James Wheldon Johnson (1871–1938) became the first African-American secretary of the NAACP in 1916. The association pursued an integrationist strategy, funding court cases brought by 'respectable' African-Americans denied rights guaranteed by the FOURTEENTH and FIFTEENTH AMENDMENTS, and lobbying for passage of a federal anti-lynching law. It was highly critical of the black separatist Marcus GARVEY, but, because it largely ignored economic issues, struggled for mass support in black communities. Du Bois, who came around to a philosophy of black economic cooperation not dissimilar to Garvey's, broke with the NAACP in 1934.

Under Walter White, a light-skinned African-American who 'passed' for white on southern fact-finding tours and led the NAACP between 1930 and 1955, the organization grew in strength. A successful lobbying campaign in the PARKER CONFIRMATION HEARINGS (which blocked the appointment of a southern conservative to the Supreme Court) brought the Association new recruits. The NAACP also began to hone its legal strategy, concentrating on challenging segregation in the educational system. Its campaign produced landmark Supreme Court verdicts in the GRADUATE SCHOOL CASES (1950) and BROWN VS. BOARD OF EDUCATION (1954). In the 1950s the NAACP's by now largely black membership took a leading role in the CIVIL RIGHTS MOVEMENT. NAACP moderation was criticized by militant BLACK POWER activists in the 1960s. The Association continues its campaigning work, although in the 1990s some of its members have criticized the NAACP's relatively friendly policy toward the NATION OF ISLAM.

National Defense Education Act (September 2 1958), legislation that initiated a massive expansion in higher education. The act was prompted by COLD WAR fears that the USA was falling behind the USSR in science, following the successful Soviet launch of the first two *Sputnik* satellites in 1957. The act directed $280 million toward science and language training, and established 5500 graduate scholarships. The federal government also appropriated $295 million for low-interest student loans. The resulting expansion in student numbers helped produce the social upheaval of the 1960s.

National Industrial Recovery Act (NIRA) (June 16 1933), NEW DEAL legislation that effectively set out to establish a planned economy in the USA. Passage of this massive legislative measure was the central achievement of President Franklin D. ROOSEVELT's first HUNDRED DAYS.

The act, which built on the BLACK–CONNERY BILL, created a NATIONAL RECOVERY ADMINISTRATION (NRA) charged with bringing together business and labor to draft industry-wide codes setting wages, hours, fair competitive practices, quality standards and production levels. Once written, and approved by the president, these codes were legally binding and exempt from antitrust legislation. Businesses that signed up to the code were permitted to display a blue eagle logo and were required to deal only with other 'blue eagle' companies.

Regulation of this sort had been attempted before, notably by the WAR INDUSTRIES BOARD established during World War I. However, the New Deal's BRAINS TRUST envisioned the NRA's regulatory powers not simply as emergency expedients to counter the GREAT DEPRESSION but as the tools through which a permanent reform of business practice and the creation of a planned economy would be enacted in the USA. Equally unprecedented was NIRA's assumption that a planned economy must include protections for workers. NIRA established a minimum wage of 30 cents per hour, outlawed child labor, banned YELLOW-DOG CONTRACTS, and guaranteed workers' rights to organize unions. Title II of NIRA created the PUBLIC WORKS ADMINISTRATION (PWA), and appropriated $3.3 billion to fund its job-creation programs.

On January 7 1935 the Supreme Court ruled unconstitutional that section of NIRA setting state quotas on oil production. On May 27 1935 the Court ruled (in SCHECTER

POULTRY CORPORATION VS. US) that all NIRA-sanctioned industrial codes were unconstitutional. (This decision was an indirect cause of the COURT-PACKING CONTROVERSY.) Following the Schecter ruling, the Roosevelt administration abandoned the NRA and its commitment to regulate economic behavior directly. Some historians argue that policies pursued after NIRA was struck down constitute a distinct SECOND NEW DEAL.

National Labor Relations Act, the formal name of the WAGNER ACT (1935), which set up the NATIONAL LABOR RELATIONS BOARD.

National Labor Relations Board (NLRB), agency created by the WAGNER ACT (1935) to supervise ballots on the question of whether a workforce wished to be represented by a trade union. The agency was empowered to force employers to recognize and bargain with duly elected union officials. It also had the power to order employers to cease and desist from unfair employment practices. (This aspect of its charter was ruled constitutional in NATIONAL LABOR RELATIONS BOARD VS. JONES AND LAUGHLIN STEEL.) During the NEW DEAL the NLRB was staunchly pro-labor. Even so, only 40% of workplace ballots organized by the NLRB resulted in union recognition. Subsequently the TAFT-HARTLEY ACT (1947) and LANDRUM–GRIFFIN ACT (1959) bound the NLRB to enforce restrictions on union autonomy.

National Labor Relations Board vs. Jones and Laughlin Steel (April 12 1937), US Supreme Court ruling (5–4) that the WAGNER ACT creating the NATIONAL LABOR RELATIONS BOARD was constitutional. The Court's reasoning built on the concept of 'stream of commerce' developed in its judgment on SWIFT AND CO. VS. US. By arguing that legislation compelling employers to bargain with duly elected trade union representatives was protected by Congress's right to regulate interstate commerce, the Court made future constitutional challenges to federal labor-relations legislation less viable.

National Labor Union (NLU), a federation of labour unions set up in 1866 to campaign for an eight-hour working day (*see* EIGHT-HOUR MOVEMENT). The NLU was founded in Baltimore, Maryland, on August 20 1866 by Ira Steward (1831–83) and George McNeill (1837–1906). In 1872 the NLU claimed 640,000 members and formed the National Labor Reform Party. It nominated as its candidate in the 1872 presidential election Supreme Court Justice David DAVIS. Davis withdrew from the race without campaigning for the NLU (but nonetheless received one ELECTORAL COLLEGE vote when Horace GREELEY's votes were redistributed). Following this debacle, the NLU collapsed in confusion and debt.

National Organization for Women (NOW), pressure group founded in Washington DC on June 30 1966. NOW has been at the forefront of campaigns to ratify the EQUAL RIGHTS AMENDMENT (ERA) and to defend liberalized ABORTION law, campaigns that have defined the modern WOMEN'S MOVEMENT in the USA. By demonstrating that it could mobilize women voters in support of candidates who favored its goals, NOW acquired enormous political influence. The decision Congress took in 1972 to send the Equal Rights Amendment to the states for ratification was prompted in part by fear that NOW could defeat the re-election of any congressmen who voted against the measure. NOW lost influence when the ERA failed to achieve ratification in the states. However, it can still rally considerable support for women in high-profile election contests and muster staunch opposition against politicians and justices hostile to women's interests.

National Origins Act (May 26 1924), legislation aimed at restricting European IMMIGRATION. The act was a refinement of the EMERGENCY QUOTA ACT (1921), and further discriminated against eastern and southern Europeans by allowing no country to send more than 2% of the total of its unnaturalized residents in the USA in 1890. (The great upsurge in Russian, Polish and Balkan emigration that troubled PROGRESSIVES and prompted the legislation occurred largely after 1890.) The act also specified that no more than 164,477 European immigrants would be admitted in any year. The law did not go into effect until 1929, and it does not apply to immigration from Canada or Latin America.

national parks. The first area of natural beauty in the USA to be designated a national park was the Yellowstone region of northwestern Wyoming in 1872. Conservation moved up the political agenda following the creation in 1887 of a Division of Forestry within the US Department of Agriculture. Gifford PINCHOT, head of the US Forestry Service (1898–1910), and Scottish-born naturalist and writer John Muir (1838–1914) gradually made the preservation of US areas of outstanding natural beauty one of the hallmark concerns of PROGRESSIVISM. On June 8 1906, Congress passed the Antiquities Act which allows the president to set aside from development, areas of outstanding natural beauty or historical significance. President Theodore ROOSEVELT used the act to preserve Devil's Tower in Wyoming and later to create Yosemite national park in northern California. The US National Park Service was created on August 25 1916 to administer sites set aside under the Antiquities Act. The National Park service currently administers nearly 50 national parks and 112 sites of historical significance (among them the WHITE HOUSE).

National Reclamation (Newlands) Act (June 17 1902), legislation, supported enthusiastically by President Theodore ROOSEVELT, that channelled revenue from land sales in 16 western states into a Reclamation Fund earmarked for irrigation projects. Acting through a Bureau of Reclamation, the federal government has since used the fund to build dams, dykes and reservoirs that have brought hundreds of thousands of acres of western land into cultivation.

National Recovery Administration (NRA), agency created by the NATIONAL INDUSTRIAL RECOVERY ACT (NIRA) (June 16 1933), charged with creating legally binding industry-wide codes regulating wages, prices and competition in US industries. Under the direction of General Hugh Johnson (1882–1942) the NRA drafted 541 codes affecting 22 million US workers and thousands of businesses.

The NEW DEAL'S BRAINS TRUST believed that big business would cooperate with the NRA to create a planned economy in the USA. In fact in 1934 an internal review reported that the NRA's codes were creating monopolies or cartels and driving small businesses to bankruptcy. Moreover the NRA was only partially successful in ensuring that subscribers to its codes upheld the most progressive features of NIRA: minimum wages, abolition of child labor and union recognition. In September 1934 President Franklin D. ROOSEVELT ordered a review of the NRA's industrial codes to ensure that they permitted competition and guaranteed rights of collective bargaining. He let the NRA die in the wake of the Supreme Court's decision in SCHECTER BROTHERS POULTRY CORPORATION VS. US (1935) that industry codes were unconstitutional.

National Republicans, faction within the DEMOCRATIC PARTY that coalesced during the presidency of John Quincy ADAMS, opposed Andrew JACKSON in the presidential elections of 1828 and 1832 and was instrumental in the creation of the WHIG PARTY.

National Republicans supported Henry CLAY'S AMERICAN SYSTEM and the second BANK OF THE UNITED STATES. They used their control of the House of Representatives from 1827 to 1834 to pass legislation, such as the TARIFF OF ABOMINATIONS, which President Jackson opposed and often vetoed (Jackson's frequent recourse to the veto, and his use of the SPOILS SYSTEM, led National

Republicans to dub him 'King Andrew'). Yet despite Jackson's uncompromising position in the emerging NULLIFICATION CRISIS, he won the 1832 presidential election with 55% of the POPULAR VOTE and 219 ELECTORAL VOTES. Clay, representing the National Republicans, won 42% of the popular vote and 49 electoral votes. Following this defeat, most National Republicans joined the Whig Party.

National Security Council (NSC), government body whose role is to provide the president with advice on external threats to the security of the USA. The NSC was established by act of Congress on July 26 1947 at a moment when the USA was committing itself to the COLD WAR doctrine of CONTAINMENT. The secretaries of state and defense sit on the NSC as of right, and the Council also draws on the expertise of a changing, but ever-growing, staff of research analysts. The NSC may choose to submit its advice formally, through numbered 'findings'. The most famous advisory document of this kind was NSC-68, offered to President TRUMAN in April 1950. This urged the USA to begin an immediate and massive defense build-up to counter Soviet expansion. (Truman rejected the advice but US involvement in the KOREAN WAR led to a significant increase in defense expenditure anyway.) Presidents are not obliged to make use of the National Security Council. President NIXON and Henry KISSINGER largely bypassed the apparatus of the NSC in their quest to bring about 'peace with honor' in the VIETNAM WAR. In contrast, during the IRAN–CONTRA SCANDAL members of the NSC acted independently of the president.

National Union Party, banner under which the REPUBLICAN PARTY campaigned during the PRESIDENTIAL ELECTION OF 1864 in an attempt to present themselves as the party of the status quo. (They were also known as Union Republicans.) Incumbent President LINCOLN chose a former Democrat, Andrew JOHNSON, as his running mate

in the election to further demonstrate his commitment to restore the Union of the states that had existed before SECESSION and the CIVIL WAR.

National Urban League, *see* URBAN LEAGUE, NATIONAL.

National War Labor Board (NWLB), agency set up by President WILSON on April 8 1918 to serve as a court of last resort in labor disputes. During WORLD WAR I unions had been taking advantage of labor shortages and the protections afforded by the CLAYTON ANTI-TRUST ACT to mount a wave of strikes that reduced hours and drove up wages. The NWLB prevented lengthy strikes from damaging the war effort, but in the process legitimated many union demands.

National Woman's Party (NWP), party formed in 1916 that re-energized the WOMEN'S SUFFRAGE movement. It was set up under the leadership of Alice PAUL by militants who had left the NATIONAL AMERICAN WOMAN SUFFRAGE ASSOCIATION in 1913. The party organized protests against any politician who did not pledge to support a constitutional amendment securing female suffrage in federal elections. But the party also staged direct actions. In July 1917 Paul led several hundred NWP members in an attempt to storm the White House. When President WILSON pardoned those arrested, the demonstrators refused to accept the pardon. Paul mounted a hunger strike in which she nearly died. However, the party's most crucial achievement was to build alliances at local and state levels with other reform groups. By this tactic women's suffrage became an issue that male trade unionists supported as a means of gaining votes for campaigns of their own. The party disbanded following ratification of the NINTEENTH AMENDMENT (1920) granting the vote to women.

National Woman Suffrage Association (NWSA), organization devoted to securing WOMEN'S SUFFRAGE, founded in 1869 by Elizabeth Cady STANTON and Susan Brownell ANTHONY.

The formulation of the FIFTEENTH AMENDMENT (stipulating that the rights of US citizens could not be abridged on the grounds of race or color) split suffrage activists. Some believed that the amendment should have outlawed discrimination on the basis of gender. One campaigner grumbled that it was intolerable that the amendment gave the vote to 'Patrick, Sambo, Hans and Ung Tung' but withheld it from educated women. Elizabeth Cady Stanton denounced the Fifteenth Amendment and, together with Susan Brownell Anthony, formed the NWSA.

The NWSA accepted no male members, and it took the view that securing votes for women was not an end in itself but part of a larger agenda of women's issues. Its rival, the AMERICAN WOMAN SUFFRAGE ASSOCIATION (AWSA), disputed the NWSA's organization and tactics. The NWSA hired lawyers to argue before the Supreme Court that since the Constitution begins with the words 'We, the People,' and since women are people, withholding votes from women contravened FOURTEENTH AMENDMENT guarantees of due process. The Court dismissed this argument in MINOR VS. HAPPERSETT (1875). Thereafter the NWSA tried to rally congressional support for a constitutional amendment guaranteeing women's right to vote. It also built bridges with labor groups such as the KNIGHTS OF LABOR. The NWSA merged with the AWSA in 1890 to form the NATIONAL AMERICAN WOMAN SUFFRAGE ASSOCIATION.

Nation of Islam, organization that has popularized separatist and Muslim beliefs among African-Americans. It was responsible for the conversion, but not the subsequent actions, of the USA's two most famous black Muslims: Malcolm X and Muhammad ALI.

In 1930 a self-proclaimed prophet named Wallace D. Fard (*c.* 1877–1934) established the Lost-Found Nation of Islam in Detroit. By 1934 Fard claimed 8000 converts. He disappeared in mysterious circumstances, and his position as head of the Nation was claimed by Elijah Poole (1897–1975), a former sharecropper from Georgia known to followers as the Honourable Elijah Muhammad. Under Elijah Muhammad the Nation established branches throughout the USA. Its message, which emphasized the need for African-Americans to lead disciplined personal lives in order to find the strength necessary to supplant the blue-eyed 'white devils' running the USA, proved especially influential among prison inmates — one of whom, Malcolm Little, went on to become the Nation's most famous missionary, taking the name Malcolm X. Elijah Muhammad served a prison sentence himself during World War II for encouraging African-Americans to resist the DRAFT.

But by the late 1950s Muhammad's principles had become harder to define, and the lifestyle enjoyed by his family and close supporters was creating muted criticism within the movement. Nevertheless, charismatic preaching by Malcolm X drew new converts to the movement. By 1960 the Nation claimed 100,000 members and, much to the alarm of Elijah Muhammad, Malcolm X had emerged as the Nation's figurehead. The two men argued following Malcolm X's return to the USA from a pilgrimage to Mecca in 1963. One cause of the schism was the decision made by Cassius Clay, heavyweight boxing champion of the world, to convert to Islam. Malcolm X ignored Elijah Muhammad to engineer Clay's high-profile conversion (which shocked the USA and made the Nation of Islam front-page news in white newspapers). Clay (now Muhammad Ali) sided with Elijah Muhammad in the power struggle that ensued. Nation of Islam loyalists assassinated Malcolm X in 1965.

One of Elijah Muhammad's most fanatical loyalists was a former calypso singer called Louis Farrakhan (1933–). Following Elijah Muhammad's death in 1975, Farrakhan led a breakaway group that appropriated the Nation of Islam's name and much of its organization in protest against the integrationist policies pursued by Warith Deen Muhammad, Elijah Muhammad's son and chosen successor. Under Farrakhan the Nation pursued a separatist agenda. During the 1980s Farrakhan's frequent and unapologetic recourse to anti-Semitism, and the activities of his menacing bodyguard, the Fruit of Islam, excited enormous controversy and alienated the US Jewish community, strong supporters of the CIVIL RIGHTS MOVEMENT, from African-Americans. Organizations such as the NATIONAL ASSOCIATION FOR THE ADVANCEMENT OF COLORED PEOPLE (NAACP) split over how best to respond to Farrakhan. In 1994 Farrakhan claimed the Nation had 100,000 followers. In October 1995 Farrakhan organized the Million Man March on Washington DC. During the march African-American men renewed their commitment to family and community.

nativism, xenophobic prejudice directed against particular immigrant groups, or against IMMIGRATION in general. In 19th-century America, Irish and Chinese immigrants were singled out for abuse in nativist diatribes. Nativist politicians also played on a more general Protestant suspicion of Catholic immigrants. The nativist KNOW NOTHING PARTY, founded in 1852 to campaign for tougher naturalization laws, garnered 21% of the POPULAR VOTE for its nominee Millard FILLMORE in the presidential election of 1856. Although unable to persuade a nation of immigrants to elect an avowedly nativist president, nativists did secure several influential legislative victories. The CHINESE EXCLUSION ACT (1882) barred all Chinese immigration (initially for a period of ten years). In the early 20th century, nativists, abetted by some PROGRESSIVE intellectuals, fomented concern over immi-

gration from Eastern Europe, which encouraged Congress to pass the EMERGENCY QUOTA ACT (1921) and NATIONAL ORIGINS ACT (1924) severely restricting immigration from Russia, Poland, the Balkans and southern Europe. Suspicion of foreigners also helped to fuel the RED SCARE 1919–20 and anticommunist witch-hunts during the COLD WAR.

NATO, see NORTH ATLANTIC TREATY ORGANIZATION.

Nat Turner's Revolt (1831), the largest slave revolt in antebellum America. It prompted a massive backlash in southern states against slave religion and the ABOLITION movement. Nat Turner (1800–31) was a slave on the Travis plantation in Southampton County, southern Virginia. As a Baptist minister Turner was allowed to travel between plantations. He used this freedom to plan an insurrection set to begin when most of the white population of the county would be attending a revival meeting. On August 22 Turner let a small group of armed slaves into the Travis home. They killed the entire family. By the next day some 70 slaves were in armed revolt, and they eventually killed 57 whites in the county. The local militia counterattacked, killing 100 slaves as they restored control. Turner and 19 other slaves were later hanged for their part in the insurrection.

NAWSA, see NATIONAL AMERICAN WOMAN SUFFRAGE ASSOCIATION.

Nebraska, midwestern state bordered by South Dakota to the north, Iowa to the east, Kansas and Colorado the south and Wyoming to the west.

The USA acquired Nebraska from France through the LOUISIANA PURCHASE (1803). The US army established a fort near the modern site of Omaha in 1819 but few Americans settled in the territory until the passage of the KANSAS–NEBRASKA ACT (1854). Under the terms of the act, Nebraskans were free to write a state constitution permitting slavery. Nebraska chose to outlaw slavery and became the 37th state on March 1

1867. At this time the new state had fewer than 50,000 residents.

The HOMESTEAD ACT and the expansion of the nation's RAILROAD network stimulated substantial in-migration to the state. Many new arrivals suffered from a ten-year drought (1887–97) and in the 1890s, over 150,000 residents left Nebraska. Those that remained were staunch supporters of POPU-LISM. The state's most famous resident, William Jennings BRYAN, emerged as the tribune of distressed farmers in the state and in the midwestern region during this period. In 1900, Nebraska had 1,066,300 inhabitants and was the 27th most populous state. Nebraska granted women the vote in 1917. Despite the development of manufacturing, mining and food-proces-sing industries, so many farmers left the state during the 20th century that in 1990 Nebraska had only 1,578,385 residents and was the 36th most populous state in the union. Malcolm X was born in Omaha, Nebraska.

Neutrality Proclamation (April 22 1793), announcement by President Washington in which he 'advised' Americans that Britain and France were at war, but that the USA wished to retain peaceful relations with both. Americans were not to assist either nation. DEMOCRATIC-REPUBLICANS alleged this pronouncement was an unconstitu-tional and partisan response to GENÊT'S MISSION.

Nevada, western state bordered by Oregon and Idaho to the north, Utah and Arizona to the east and California to the south and west.

The USA acquired Nevada from Mexico through the treaty of GUADALUPE-HIDALGO (1848). The first permanent US settlement in the territory was established at Genoa by MORMONS in 1850. In January 1859, James Finney discovered the Comstock Lode (the largest source of silver within the USA) near what became Virginia City, Nevada. Sub-stantial in-migration followed and the USA

granted Nevada territorial status on March 2 1861. Nevada became the 36th state on October 31 1864.

The state's economy was almost entirely dependent on mining, and when silver mines were worked out, miners left the state. In 1900, Nevada had just 42,000 per-manent residents. The state granted women the vote in 1914. In 1931, Nevada legalized gambling. This decision slowly transformed the state's economy and made Las Vegas and Reno major tourist destinations. In 1990, Nevada had 1,201,833 permanent residents and was the 41st most populous state in the union.

Newburgh conspiracy (1783), incident at the close of the REVOLUTIONARY WAR that almost produced a military coup in the USA.

On March 10 1783 officers stationed at the Continental Army's main camp (in Newburgh, New York) circulated two an-onymous remonstrances criticizing Con-gress for not rectifying arrears in pay, for not reimbursing expenditure on food, clothing and horses, and for reneging on a promise to provide lifelong half-pay pen-sions. A handful of officers sought to exploit the contempt that the army felt for Congress by urging officers to refuse to recognize civilian authority.

At an open meeting held in the camp on March 15, WASHINGTON dashed hopes that he might lead an authoritarian junta by denouncing 'immoderate measures'. When, a week later, Congress settled outstanding claims by granting each officer a sum equivalent to five years' full pay, the crisis passed. However, hostility to the extreme autonomy of the states under the ARTICLES OF CONFEDERATION (the underlying cause of the conspiracy) continued to grow.

New Deal, major program of social and eco-nomic reform introduced by President Franklin D. ROOSEVELT in the 1930s with the aim of aiding the USA's recovery from the GREAT DEPRESSION and improving the welfare of the poorer sections of US society.

During the PRESIDENTIAL ELECTION OF 1932, Roosevelt, the Democratic candidate, promised to deliver a 'new deal' for the millions of Americans suffering from the effects of the Depression. Roosevelt made good his pledge, pushing through Congress measures that brought relief to the unemployed, established the basis of a welfare state in the USA, altered forever the relationship between workers and employers, and transformed the role of the federal government. The federal programs Roosevelt initiated were supplemented by the states, and they were so popular with voters that they created a new political alignment, the NEW DEAL COALITION. For these reasons the New Deal era can rank alongside the AMERICAN REVOLUTION, the CIVIL WAR, RECONSTRUCTION and the high days of the CIVIL RIGHTS MOVEMENT as a period during which the essence of the American nation was defined and transformed. Many Americans who lived through the New Deal saw it, for better or worse, as representing a second American Revolution.

The problems confronting Roosevelt on March 4 1933 when he was sworn in as Herbert HOOVER's successor were enormous. In 1933 unemployment reached a record 25% of the workforce. In every major city shantytowns (dubbed HOOVERVILLES) housed workers left destitute and homeless by the Depression. The market price of agricultural commodities was so low that farmers, especially in the south, were forced off the land. In the last days of Hoover's administration depositors began making panic withdrawals from banks, further threatening the stability of the nation's banking system. Thirty-four state governors had ordered banks to close to prevent their complete collapse. International trade was at a near stand-still, largely because at the onset of the Depression the US Congress had ignored the advice of professional economists and passed the protectionist HAWLEY–SMOOT TARIFF, which triggered retaliatory measures from the USA's trading partners.

Conventional wisdom held that the depression, although unusually severe, was part of the normal business cycle, and that the economy would recover more or less of its own accord. Senior congressmen, in both parties, maintained a profound aversion to government programs that interfered with the workings of the market by, for example, limiting the production of agricultural crops, guaranteeing industrial prices or establishing a minimum wage. The corollary of these assumptions was a deep suspicion of government-funded welfare programs. Spending tax revenue on the unemployed was thought likely to encourage the workshy and the inadequate.

By 1933 it was obvious that the scale of the suffering caused by the Great Depression was beyond redress through the traditional American combination of private philanthropy and underfunded state welfare programs. Yet, as the dispersal of the BONUS ARMY protesters demonstrated, conventional political wisdom opposed even indirect federal aid to victims of the Depression. The question of whether the Great Depression would have produced violent social unrest had Roosevelt not acted as he did must remain moot. But one of the greatest challenges facing Roosevelt on assuming office was that effective action to combat the Depression required all Americans, not least himself, to challenge and where necessary abandon the laissez-faire assumptions concerning the nature of the economy and the function of government that had acquired a near sacred status in US political thought.

In his first inaugural address Roosevelt asserted his 'firm belief that the only thing we have to fear is fear itself'. In this speech, and in subsequent FIRESIDE CHATS, Roosevelt established a rapport with the American public that was crucial to the success of the New Deal. By treating the Depression as a massive national emergency, Roosevelt convinced voters that they might expect remedial action to alleviate suffering, but did not give them the impression that he was bent on a fundamental and therefore contentious reform of the US economy.

During his first HUNDRED DAYS, Roosevelt pushed through Congress a series of measures that demonstrated the use of innovation in pursuit of essentially conservative goals – a characteristic of the New Deal as a whole. On assuming office Roosevelt used the powers granted the president by the Trading with the Enemy Act (1917) to order a BANK HOLIDAY. US banks were closed from March 6 to March 13 1933. This halted, temporarily, the run of panic withdrawals that threatened a total collapse of the banking system. During the closure Roosevelt ordered the RECONSTRUCTION FINANCE CORPORATION (an agency established by his predecessor President Hoover) to develop a policy to aid ailing banks, and induced Congress to pass (in one day) an EMERGENCY BANKING RELIEF ACT whose main feature, the FEDERAL DEPOSIT INSURANCE CORPORATION, guaranteed depositors access to their accounts. This bold action had the effect of preserving the nation's banking system. Cautious reform of the system itself was initiated through the BANKING ACT passed in June 1933.

The Roosevelt administration's first attempt to provide relief for the unemployed also helped establish the tone characteristic of the early years of the New Deal. On March 31 1933 Congress created the CIVILIAN CONSERVATION CORPS (CCC). A quarter of a million men aged between 18 and 25 were drafted into the Corps, taken from the cities, housed in camps administered by the War Department, and put to work on forestry projects. In addition to their board and lodging they received a stipend of $30 per month ($25 was deducted at source and sent direct to parents or relatives back home). The design of the CCC reflected the

prevailing assumption that the unemployed should work to receive benefit. It also reflected the lingering suspicion held by middle-class Americans that city life, especially as lived by men from ethnic minorities, bred idleness and vice and militated against the development of 'rugged individualism'. By 1942 over 3 million American men had worked in a CCC-administered camp. Many found the experience enjoyable, and the success of the CCC encouraged the Roosevelt administration to create other workfare programs.

Not content with alleviating unemployment, Roosevelt also pushed the massive NATIONAL INDUSTRIAL RECOVERY ACT (NIRA) (1933) through Congress. This established a NATIONAL RECOVERY ADMINISTRATION (NRA) charged with bringing together business and labor to draft industry-wide codes setting prices, wages, hours, fair competitive practices, quality standards and production levels. Once approved by the president, industry codes were legally binding and exempt from antitrust legislation. Companies that signed up to a relevant code displayed a blue eagle logo, and were required to deal only with other 'blue eagle' firms. Title II of NIRA appropriated $3.3 billion to fund a PUBLIC WORKS ADMINISTRATION (PWA) charged with establishing job-creation programs. The WAR INDUSTRIES BOARD established during World War I provided a precedent for the NRA, whose first director, Hugh Johnson (1882–1942), took the view that the ultimate purpose of industry-wide codes of practice was to get Americans back to work by eliminating wasteful competition between businesses and establishing agreements that would allow US capitalism to function more efficiently. Johnson, and to some extent Roosevelt, did not regard the creation of the NRA as a first step toward root-and-branch reform of US capitalism. However, prominent members of Roosevelt's BRAINS TRUST, notably Raymond Moley (1886–1975) and Adolph Berle

(1895–1971), hoped that the NRA might serve as the means through which some form of national economic planning could be realized in the USA. Believing that business leaders would see the value of cooperating with government and trade unions, progressives wrote into NIRA unprecedented concessions to organized labor. The act established a minimum wage of 30 cents per hour, outlawed child labor, and guaranteed workers the right to organize trade unions. (These features led Henry FORD to denounce the NRA and refuse to cooperate with it.) To the dismay of Roosevelt's progressive advisers, industry codes drawn up under the auspices of the NRA often favored large corporations. The NRA helped to restore corporate profits, but made limited impact on unemployment levels.

Meanwhile the effectiveness of the Public Works Administration established under Title II of NIRA was compromised by the insistence of its director, Harold Ickes (1874–1952), that job-creation programs established through his agency meet stringent financial targets. On November 9 1933 Roosevelt used executive authority to create the CIVIL WORKS ADMINISTRATION (CWA), funding the new agency by diverting money Congress had appropriated for the PWA. Within three months the CWA had set over 4 million Americans to work building roads and schools. No president since LINCOLN had made such breathtaking use of presidential power.

During the Hundred Days, the Roosevelt administration also began to address the problems faced by US farmers. The underlying cause of farmers' woes was overproduction. All farmers realized that limiting production of a particular crop would raise its market value. But no farmer wished to cut his personal income by unilaterally limiting production, and few were willing to be coerced into switching crops. The political power of the nation's farmers was sufficient to force the Hoover administration to pass

an AGRICULTURAL MARKETING ACT (1929), under which the federal government bought surpluses while encouraging farmers to enter into voluntary agreements to limit production or withhold crops from market. This prevented further catastrophic falls in agricultural commodity prices, but did little to limit production. The Agricultural Adjustment Act passed on May 12 1933 provided more extensive and efficient implementation of policies developed during Hoover's administration. The act established an AGRICULTURAL ADJUSTMENT ADMINISTRATION (AAA). This established price supports covering virtually every sector of crop and livestock production. It worked with farmers to create local cooperative agreements to limit production. Crucially it paid a cash subsidy direct to landowners who agreed to take acreage out of cultivation. Just as comparative failure of the National Recovery Administration can be attributed to the leadership given by Hugh Johnson, so the ultimate success of the Agricultural Adjustment Administration reflects the energy and expertise displayed by Roosevelt's secretary of agriculture, Henry A. WALLACE. Wallace combined an extensive knowledge of agriculture with a faith in centralized planning. He appointed like-minded men to head crucial divisions within the AAA. Although in the short term agricultural prices were maintained only by destroying foodstuffs and crops while the unemployed starved and factories lay idle, in the long term New Deal policies wrought a lasting transformation in the USA's rural economy. One side-effect of these policies was that many SHARECROPPERS were forced off land by landlords anxious to receive subsidies for taking land out of production. This contributed to the GREAT MIGRATION of African-Americans from the rural south to the industrialized north.

The lives of those farmers who remained in the rural south were transformed by two further initiatives launched during the early years of the New Deal. Throughout the 1920s Senator George NORRIS had campaigned to make a hydroelectric and munitions complex built during World War I on the Tennessee river at Muscle Shoals, Alabama, the basis of a regional development authority. Roosevelt took Norris's plan and greatly expanded it through the creation (May 18 1933) of the TENNESSEE VALLEY AUTHORITY (TVA) The TVA was an independent public corporation charged with damming and exploiting the Tennessee and Cumberland river systems to generate and distribute electricity, manufacture fertilizer and prevent floods and soil erosion. Its charter bound it to set 'fair and reasonable' rates for the supply of electricity to rural areas. The TVA built dozens of dams, barriers and power stations, and quickly became the largest employer in the south. The RURAL ELECTRIFICATION ADMINISTRATION, established on May 11 1935 by executive order, made low-interest loans to cooperatives formed to extend power lines to inaccessible farms. In 1925 just 4% of US farms had access to electricity. By 1940, 25% of farms were connected to electricity supply, and within a decade virtually all farms were connected to a supply grid.

However, by 1935 the New Deal was encountering criticism. Despite the billions appropriated to fight unemployment, 20% of the workforce remained unemployed. Despite Roosevelt's improvisation and innovation, a number of critics, among them Huey LONG, Charles COUGHLIN and Francis TOWNSEND, demanded that he adopt even more radical policies. Republicans, recovering from the electorate's repudiation of Hoover, began to criticize the scale of federal expenditure and allege that it was subject to waste and mismanagement. A particular target for their attacks was the FEDERAL EMERGENCY RELIEF ADMINISTRATION (FERA), charged with distributing federal funds to state welfare programs. Republicans, joined in some areas by Democrats, alleged that FERA distributed funds with at least one eye on the goal of building political support for Roosevelt's re-election. But the most influential challenge to the New Deal was mounted by the US Supreme Court. In May 1935 the Court, in its judgment on SCHECTER POULTRY CORPORATION VS. US, ruled that industrial codes of practice established under the auspices of the NRA were unconstitutional. In January 1936 the Court, in its verdict on US VS. BUTLER, struck down the main features of the Agricultural Adjustment Act.

The tone of Roosevelt's public pronouncements and the policies pursued by his administration changed in 1935. Roosevelt retreated from earlier attempts to forge a partnership between government, big business, organized labor and the individual states through which a planned recovery and a modicum of economic and financial reform might be achieved. This first phase, prior to 1935, is sometimes referred to by historians as the FIRST NEW DEAL. From 1935, Roosevelt's speeches, and the legislative program sponsored by the White House, began to attack poverty, social injustice and monopolistic corporate business practices. He also redoubled his efforts to force employers to enter into collective bargaining with organized labour. This change in emphasis recognized the near impossibility of a consensual transformation of US capitalism, and it ushered in the most determined effort yet made in the USA to set the limits of permissible business practice and to establish minimum levels of government welfare provision. For these reasons, some historians conclude that the policies championed by Roosevelt from 1935 amount to a SECOND NEW DEAL.

The centerpiece of the legislative program Roosevelt pushed through Congress in a special summer session in 1935 was the SOCIAL SECURITY ACT. This created a federal payroll tax whose proceeds were used to assist states in the creation of programs providing compensation for unemployment. Agricultural workers, domestic servants and small business employees were not protected by this safety net. Nevertheless the act gave 50% of the US workforce some protection against the consequences of unemployment. To put this provision in context it is important to remember that in 1931 only 116,000 workers enjoyed any form of unemployment insurance. In 1933, when 30 million workers were unemployed, 25 states considered establishing proposals for unemployment relief, but all 25 rejected such proposals on the grounds that they would cost too much and encourage idleness. Hence the Social Security Act represented a radical departure from past practice. The act also broke with tradition in the matter of pensions for the elderly. It established a federal program, funded by a tax on employers and employees, which awarded pensions to all citizens over the age of 65. This created the first universal entitlement to social welfare in American history.

The Roosevelt administration responded to the Supreme Court's decision to invalidate the NRA by championing passage of the WAGNER ACT. This restored to trade unions the right to organize, and outlawed anti-union management practices, such as YELLOW-DOG CONTRACTS. The act also established a three-man NATIONAL LABOR RELATIONS BOARD (NLRB) charged with supervising the process by which workforces chose to unionize, and also with the task of preventing companies from adopting anti-union practices. Union leaders took advantage of the act's unprecedentedly friendly attitude towards organized labor to form the CONGRESS OF INDUSTRIAL UNIONS (CIO). The CIO recruited workers into INDUSTRIAL UNIONS, each of which organized a different sector of the economy, such as automobile production, that had previously been hostile to unions.

The EMERGENCY RELIEF APPROPRIATION ACT, passed in May 1935, established the WORKS PROGRESS ADMINISTRATION (WPA). This offered the unemployed temporary jobs on public-works projects. It differed from previous programs in that it paid recipients a relatively generous 'security wage', and created projects for unemployed writers and artists as well as for manual workers. For these reasons Republicans attacked the WPA as an expensive and frivolous 'make-work' scheme.

As the presidential election of 1936 drew nearer, Roosevelt faced an awkward political choice. New Deal programs had alleviated some of the suffering caused by the Great Depression but, as Roosevelt would acknowledge in his second inaugural address, millions of families continued to live on incomes 'so meager that the pall of family disaster hangs over them day by day'. To abandon the commitment to reform risked alienating large sections of the electorate. On the other hand, no attack on the root causes of poverty and social deprivation could be mounted without alienating the middle and upper classes. Moreover Roosevelt's determination to recognize the rights of trade unions encouraged a new wave of labor militancy, including SIT-DOWN STRIKES, which alarmed business leaders. During the 1936 election campaign Republican nominee Alfred LANDON alleged that Roosevelt was bent on destroying the rights of private property and then the American system of government. Landon was defeated in a landslide. But the charge that Roosevelt was bent on a revolutionary and somehow un-American transformation of the American way of life began to stick. Novels and plays sympathetic to the New Deal (some of them produced by WPA-sponsored programs) contributed to a growing conviction among the comfortable middle classes that Roosevelt's policies were left-leaning or even communistic. Many New Dealers, notably Henry Wallace, wore Republican scorn as a badge of honor. But in 1937, as Congress reassembled following Roosevelt's landslide victory, key Democratic politicians were wondering just where Roosevelt's expressed determination to 'paint out' of American life injustice and despair might lead. The nature of the first measure the administration presented to the new Congress, the Judicial Reorganization Bill, confirmed the worst fears of Roosevelt's critics, and led to the COURT-PACKING CONTROVERSY, which derailed the New Deal and tarnished Roosevelt's reputation.

Roosevelt regarded the US Supreme Court verdicts invalidating the NRA and gutting the Agricultural Adjustment Act as forms of willful political sabotage perpetrated by old men out of touch with the mood of the nation. He was determined to use his electoral mandate to prevent the Court from invalidating the Social Security Act or the Wagner Act. The Judicial Reorganization Bill asked Congress to grant Roosevelt the power to appoint one new Supreme Court Justice, up to a maximum of six, for every sitting justice aged 70 or older and every justice who had served more than ten years. While debate over the plan raged, the Supreme Court upheld the constitutionality of the Wagner Act in its verdict on NATIONAL LABOR RELATIONS BOARD VS. JONES AND LAUGHLIN STEEL CORPORATION. This decision seemed to demonstrate that the Supreme Court was prepared to treat New Deal legislation on its merits, and that Roosevelt was seeking to destroy its independence. The reorganization bill was sponsored by the Senate majority leader Joseph Robinson of Arkansas, who had been promised one of the new seats on the Supreme Court. When Robinson died of a heart attack, Roosevelt abandoned the planned reorganization. Ironically, a series of deaths and retirements soon allowed Roosevelt to appoint liberal justices to the Supreme Court without recourse to legislation. However, the 'court-packing' incident damaged Roosevelt's

reputation and encouraged his critics.

In May 1938 the House of Representatives formed the DIES COMMITTEE to investigate charges that communists had infiltrated the WPA and NLRB. The committee found little of substance, but its hearings contributed to the impression that New Deal programs and administrators were bent on imposing alien values on the American system. In the 1938 congressional elections, Republicans gained 8 seats in the Senate and 80 in the House. Although the Democrats retained control of both houses, the combined strength of northern Republicans and conservative southern Democrats was sufficient to block the passage of major new initiatives. During the 1938 elections Roosevelt campaigned against five of his most conservative Democratic critics. All five were re-elected, demonstrating that defying the administration carried few political risks. The new Congress cut funding for relief programs and opposed the extension of job-creation programs. Conservatives lacked the strength to repeal the central features of the New Deal, but Roosevelt's supporters lacked the votes to carry the New Deal forward.

The main cause of growing popular disenchantment with the New Deal was a renewed economic depression. Unemployment fell from a high of 25% in 1933 to 14% in 1937. But by 1938 it had climbed once again to 19%. Manufacturing output surpassed its 1929 level briefly in 1937, but by 1938 was once again slipping back. Congress responded by increasing appropriations for the Public Works Administration and creating America's first food-stamp program. But as Harry Hopkins (1890–1946), former director of the WPA, would later admit, by 1938 Americans were 'bored with the poor, the unemployed, and the insecure'. The will to continue to fight poverty did not exist, and Roosevelt, increasingly preoccupied with the threat to world peace posed by Nazi Germany, had no wish to alienate the electorate in advance of the 1940 presidential election.

The New Deal prevented a complete collapse of the American economy and the outbreak of violent social upheaval. It did not restore economic prosperity to the USA. That function was performed by the massive increase in federal expenditure on rearmament and defense during World War II. Some historians have concluded that the New Deal was a 'holding operation', designed to stave off an even more radical transformation of US political and social life. This judgment tends to obscure the long-term significance of the New Deal. During the 1930s the electorate and the political classes abandoned the assumptions of a laissez-faire political economy. However reluctantly, they became accustomed to the intervention of the federal government in areas of life previously regarded as off limits. They became accustomed to the existence of a large federal bureaucracy and deficits in the federal budget. Finally, as George BUSH would later find, voters and politicians now expected their president to have a vision of where they intended to lead the country. This sea-change in expectations took time to work its way through the system, but it influenced subsequent developments as diverse as the COLD WAR, the CIVIL RIGHTS MOVEMENT and Lyndon B. JOHNSON's vision of the GREAT SOCIETY in the 1960s.

New Deal coalition, collective term used by political scientists for groups within the US electorate who supported the NEW DEAL, gave Franklin D. ROOSEVELT sweeping victories in the 1932, 1936 and 1940 presidential elections, and made the DEMOCRATIC PARTY the dominant force in electoral politics for over 40 years.

Southern whites had long been supporters of the Democratic Party. So too had the working classes in northern cities. In the 1930s African-Americans, especially those who moved north during the GREAT MIGRATION, abandoned the 'party of Lincoln' (the Republicans) and began voting Democrat. Western farmers and organized labor also swung their weight behind the Democrats. The constituent elements of this coalition had previously been divided by ethno-cultural issues. Southern whites, for example, had forced the Democrats into a flirtation with the KU KLUX KLAN during the 1920s, and had been reluctant to vote for Al SMITH in 1928 because he was a Catholic. The urban working class opposed PROHIBITION, but western and midwestern farmers supported it.

Hence it took considerable political skill to manage different interests within the Democratic Party. The electoral power of the alliance Roosevelt forged was such that between 1932 and 1981 the Democrats ceded control of Congress only once (1947–9), and held the presidency for 36 years out of 49. The rekindling of cultural and racial tensions in the 1960s put the coalition under increasing strain, and the defection of the REAGAN DEMOCRATS in 1980 signaled the end of its viability.

New Echota, treaty of (December 29 1835), coerced 'treaty' by which the CHEROKEE nation sold their remaining lands in the southeastern USA in return for a reservation in Oklahoma. The treaty, signed in Georgia, made implementation of the INDIAN REMOVAL ACT (1830) inescapable and rendered Supreme Court decisions in CHEROKEE NATION VS. GEORGIA and WORCESTER VS. GEORGIA pointless. Those Cherokee who attempted to stay in the southeast were forcibly marched west along the TRAIL OF TEARS.

New England, collective term for the northeastern states of Maine, Vermont, New Hampshire, Connecticut, Massachusetts and Rhode Island.

New Freedom, slogan used by Democratic nominee Woodrow WILSON in the PRESIDENTIAL ELECTION OF 1912. Denouncing TRUSTS as 'a great incubus on the productive part of American brains', Wilson pledged to extend a 'New Freedom' to voters. He sought to end monopolistic business practices, restore freedom of competition and extend collective bargaining to trade unions.

New Frontier, the big idea that John F. KENNEDY hoped would inform his presidency, announced in a speech delivered on July 15 1960. His statement that 'We stand on the edge of a New Frontier' encapsulated Kennedy's belief that America had stagnated under EISENHOWER and could be got moving again only by seeking out and surmounting new challenges. Kennedy's support for the APOLLO PROJECT – justified to the American people on the grounds that it would be difficult, not easy, to land a man on the Moon – was entirely in keeping with this rhetoric. But so too was his decision to increase the number of US military advisers in VIETNAM.

New Hampshire, NEW ENGLAND state, bordered by Canada to the north, Maine to the east, Massachusetts to the south and Vermont to the west.

The first permanent European settlement in the territory was established by David Thompson at Rye in 1623. Massachusetts claimed title to New Hampshire's land but the colony's independent status was established by royal charter on September 16 1680. New Hampshire was the most northerly of the THIRTEEN COLONIES, and its economy developed around family farms and the supply of lumber to the Royal Navy. New Hampshire became the 9th state to ratify the US Constitution on June 21 1788.

Textile factories established in the southeast of the state promoted modest economic development in the 19th century. However, New Hampshire attracted few immigrants or in-migrants and by 1900 it had only 410,000 permanent residents. Population growth remained slow in the 20th century. In 1990, New Hampshire had 1,109,252 residents and was the 40th most populous state in the union. Like its neighbor Maine, New Hampshire retains a distinctive and somewhat insular culture.

New Hampshire's voters exert a disproportionate influence on national politics because the state holds the first PRIMARY ELECTION of the presidential cycle. Months in advance of the state's primary election, presidential hopefuls trawl New Hampshire's small towns looking for support among the state's conservative electorate. Defeat in the New Hampshire primary, especially on the Republican side, usually ends a candidate's chances of gaining election to the White House. (Bill CLINTON bucked this trend in the presidential election of 1992.)

The state's most famous native sons are Daniel WEBSTER and Franklin PIERCE.

New Harmony, *see* ONEDIA COMMUNE.

New Jersey, northeastern state, bordered by New York to the north, the Atlantic Ocean to the east and Delaware and Pennsylvania to the south and west.

The first permanent European settlement in the territory was established by Swedish settlers at Fort Nye Elfborg on the Delaware river in 1643. English settlement began in 1664 and New Jersey became a royal colony on April 26 1702.

One of the THIRTEEN COLONIES, New Jersey was the scene of heavy fighting during the REVOLUTIONARY WAR. The state's first constitution allowed women property owners to vote (a privilege withdrawn in 1807). On December 18 1787, New Jersey became the 3rd state to ratify the US Constitution.

Although the state supplied over 75,000 troops to the Union army during the CIVIL WAR, New Jersey contained many COPPERHEADS. The state's electorate voted against LINCOLN in the PRESIDENTIAL ELECTION OF 1864. (George McCLELLAN, Lincoln's opponent in the race, was subsequently elected governor of New Jersey.)

During the 19th century, the contrast between the predominantly rural south of the state and the industrializing and urban north became more pronounced. The northern cities spawned a corrupt Democratic party machine that Woodrow WILSON tried to reform during his tenure as governor of New Jersey (1911–13). The state's population grew rapidly over the course of the 20th century. In 1900, New Jersey had 1,883,669 residents. In 1990, the state had 7,730,188 residents and was the 9th most populous state in the union. This growth in population helped produce sprawling and often ill-planned suburban tracts that have made the state the butt of barbed comments from New Yorkers and comedians. Never at the forefront of the nation's political life, New Jersey has produced one president – Grover CLEVELAND. One of the state's 'native sons' is Paul ROBESON.

New Look defense policy, policy announced in 1953 that committed the USA to build up its nuclear forces while cutting expenditure on conventional forces, in a search for 'more bang for the buck'. The principal architect of the policy was President EISENHOWER's Secretary of State John Foster DULLES. Dulles thought orthodox CONTAINMENT strategy was 'negative, futile, and immoral' because it abandoned 'countless human beings' to life under 'despotic and godless' communism. He hoped the New Look would help bring about ROLLBACK, the 'liberation' of peoples living under communist regimes. The policy ushered in the most dangerous phase of the COLD WAR.

New Mexico, southwestern state, bordered by Colorado to the north, Texas and Oklahoma to the east, Texas and Mexico to the south and Arizona to the west.

The first permanent European settlement in the territory was established by Spanish settlers at San Juan in 1598. When the USA acquired the territory through the treaty of GUADALUPE-HIDALGO (1848), it possessed 70,000 Spanish-speaking inhabitants and virtually no US settlers. Hispanic settlers outnumbered Americans well into the 20th century. New Mexico became the 47th state on January 6 1912. The state remained underpopulated and its economy dependent on mining and cattle ranching. For these reasons, the directors of the MANHATTAN PROJECT chose Alamogordo, New Mexico, to test the world's first atomic bomb. In the second half of the 20th century, the state, along with its neighbors in the southwest, experienced substantial in-migration. Like other 'sun-belt' states, this in-migration was accompanied by increased support for the Republican party within the state. In 1990, New Mexico had 1,515,069 residents and was the 37th most populous state in the Union.

Events in New Mexico have seldom impinged on the national consciousness. On March 9 1916, the town of Columbus became famous when Mexican revolutionaries under the command of Pancho Villa sacked it, killing 17 US citizens. (President WILSON ordered US troops into Mexico in retaliation). The town of Taos became famous as the site of an artistic community whose residents included the painter Georgia O'Keeffe (1887–1986). More recently Roswell, New Mexico, has acquired near sacred status among believers in UFOs. New Mexico resident John COLLIER secured national recognition in the 1930s for his work on behalf of the PUEBLO and other peoples.

New Nationalism, Theodore ROOSEVELT's description of the blend of tougher regulation of big business and comprehensive social-welfare legislation that he offered voters in the PRESIDENTIAL ELECTION OF 1912.

New Orleans, battle of (1814–15), US victory in Louisiana during the WAR OF 1812. In December 1814 crack British troops invaded southern Louisiana seeking to capture New Orleans and control navigation on the Mississippi river. An outnumbered US force led by Andrew JACKSON dug in 5 miles (8 km) from the city. On the morning of January 8 1815 the British mounted a disastrous frontal assault, suffering 2036 casualties while inflicting only 21. The victory forced a

British withdrawal and made Jackson a national hero. It was fought after the treaty of GHENT ending the war had been signed, but before word reached the south.

New Orleans riot (1866), police riot in which 35 blacks and 3 white radicals were killed, and 100 others, including a former governor of Louisiana, were injured. The early stages of RECONSTRUCTION in Louisiana had allowed former Confederates and white supremacists to achieve considerable political power. A small meeting, held in New Orleans on July 30, to discuss enfranchising blacks and weeding former Confederates from government triggered the riot. Northern outrage led to Republican gains in subsequent mid-term elections and the beginning of CONGRESSIONAL RECONSTRUCTION.

Newspapers. America's print media have played an important role in creating and sustaining the nation's democratic culture.

Many of the nation's first newspapers had been established by protégés or partners of Benjamin FRANKLIN. In 1776, each of the THIRTEEN COLONIES possessed at least one newspaper, and major cities like Philadelphia supported several titles. During the AMERICAN REVOLUTION, newspapers helped disseminate REPUBLICAN IDEOLOGY, and later FEDERALISM and ANTIFEDERALISM, to a broad audience. Ninety-two newspapers – eight of them dailies – were published in the USA in 1790. The vitality of the nation's press reflected both the strength of the economy (since advertising revenue was as important as subscription receipts in funding newspaper production) and also a distinctive political culture. In the decade after ratification of the US Constitution, US politics were marked by what has been dubbed a 'paranoid style.' Partisans of both the DEMOCRATIC-REPUBLICAN and FEDERALIST causes, believed that their opponents were disguising their true motives and intentions from voters in order to subvert the Constitution, corrupt public life and even establish tyranny. A free press, through which the public could be kept abreast of the machinations of 'designing men,' was seen as a bulwark of liberty. This worldview had a number of consequences. Americans demanded a constitutional amendment safeguarding the freedom of the press, and the FIRST AMENDMENT offered stronger guarantees in this area than any operating in Europe at the time. Newspaper editors, many of whom were agents of one or other of the main party groupings, felt justified in publishing venomous and highly personal articles purporting to reveal the 'true' nature of political opponents and their schemes. (Thomas JEFFERSON's affair with his slave 'dusky Sally' Hemings was publicised in the press, as was Alexander HAMILTON's affair with a Mrs Reynolds.) Finally, attempts to control the press, such as John ADAMS' use of the ALIEN AND SEDITION ACTS against newspaper editors or Thomas Jefferson's prosecution of the publisher of the *Wasp* – based in Hudson, New York – for criminal libel, carried a negative political cost that dissuaded politicians from subsequent attempts to interfere with press freedom.

The first newspaper to emphasize dispassionate factual reporting in the modern style was probably *Niles' Weekly Register*, published in Baltimore by Hezekiah Niles (1777–1839). Most new titles founded in antebellum America continued to express strong partisan sympathies. The ABOLITION and labor movements spawned hundreds of new titles, many of them short-lived. The industry changed significantly in the 1830s with the advent of the 'penny press.' Newspaper proprietors like James Gordon Bennett Sr (1795–1872), a pioneer in this field, found that by lowering the cover price of their papers, and by actively hawking their product rather than relying on subscriptions, they could turn a profit. Rivalry between mass-circulation papers such as Bennett's *New York Morning Herald* and Horace GREELEY's *New York Tribune* boosted sales still further. In 1860, the *Herald* had a daily circulation of 75,000, the largest in the world. A weekly digest of Greeley's *Tribune*, distributed across the northeast, was read by over 200,000 Americans. Sales figures of this magnitude gave editors like Bennett and Greeley an independent source of political influence. Bennett supported the Democratic party, urged readers to vote for Stephen DOUGLAS over LINCOLN and sympathized with SECESSION. Greeley championed the working man, employed Karl Marx as a European correspondent and was one of the founders of the REPUBLICAN PARTY.

Mass-circulation dailies like the *Herald* or *Tribune* remained rooted in the culture of their home towns and were not national newspapers comparable to the leading British dailies of the time. The farmer in Illinois would not have been interested in, even if he understood, the world as depicted in the pages of a New York daily. At the same time, even within New York and other major metropolises, smaller ethnic newspapers flourished by providing readers with news of life in their particular enclaves of cities whose broader expanses remained foreign. However in the final quarter of the 19th century, the US newspaper industry began to take on a semblance of national organization as Joseph PULITZER and William Randolph HEARST began to assemble newspaper chains. The commercial risks involved in acquiring newspapers in more than one city were huge. (For this reason the Pulitzer and Hearst empires relied heavily on YELLOW JOURNALISM to maintain daily sales and fund new acquisitions.) However, the new magnates like Hearst acquired an enormous and widely-feared political influence. Hearst and Pulitzer were credited with forcing the USA into the SPANISH-AMERICAN WAR and Hearst was also accused of encouraging the assassination of President McKINLEY. During the PROGRESSIVE ERA, the newspaper industry would have made a worthy subject for the MUCKRAKING style of investigative journalism. (However, advertiser-sensitive mass-circulation dailies declined to publish muckrakers and the genre found a public through magazines instead. Hearst's career was retrospectively raked over in the 1941 movie *Citizen Kane*.)

In the 1920s, the 'yellow press' moved slightly upmarket to become populist. The *New York Daily News* pioneered an editorial mix of crime, sport and scandal that continues to influence the tabloid format on both sides of the Atlantic. Under the ownership of Adolph Ochs (1858–1935), the *New York Times* pioneered the achingly respectable format now typical of 'serious' US newspapers and encapsulated in the *Times'* deceptive masthead slogan 'All the news that's fit to print.' (The *Times* was much teased in the 1950s when, in conformity to its house style, it referred to the likes of Elvis Presley as 'Mr Presley'.) During the 1930s Henry LUCE revolutionized the USA's magazine industry through the imaginative use of photo-journalism. At the same time, new ownership chains, notably those founded by Frank Gannett and Samuel Newhouse, had the effect of standardizing the content of local papers.

The *New York Times'* willingness to risk publishing the PENTAGON PAPERS, and the *Washington Post's* role in publicizing the WATERGATE SCANDAL, obscure the influence of a fundamental transformation in the organization of the newspaper industry in the post-war USA. In 1945, 80% of US newspapers were independently owned. In 1990, 80% of the USA's 1600 dailies were owned by corporations and effectively controlled by just 15 corporate chiefs. In 1929, over 500 US cities had competing dailies. In 1990, only 40 cities could offer readers a choice of dailies, and only in 20 of those were readers offered a choice of newspapers under competing ownerships. 98% of the daily newspapers currently published in the USA have no local competition. The *New York Times*, *Wall Street Journal* and *USA Today* use satellite technology to produce national editions but speak to particular sectors of US society rather than to the nation as a whole. The three TV networks and single daily newspaper that typically represent the full spectrum of news sources available to the modern American household, provide good coverage of 'human interest' stories and developments in 'lifestyle' but leave Americans alarmingly ignorant of events in their own nation or especially the wider world.

New York, northeastern state, bordered to the north by Canada and Lake Ontario, to the east by Vermont, Massachusetts and Connecticut, to the south by New Jersey and Pennsylvania and to the west by Lake Erie.

The first permanent European settlement in the territory was established by Dutch settlers at Fort Nassau (near Albany) in 1614. New Amsterdam (modern New York city) was founded on May 4 1626. The British conquered the state from the Dutch on September 7 1664. (New York is unique among the THIRTEEN COLONIES in that it was acquired from a rival European power.) The Dutch reconquered New York in 1673 but returned it to Britain a year later.

During the colonial era, New York developed a distinctive economy and society. On Long Island and in the lower Hudson valley, small towns served as local markets for agricultural goods produced on family farms. In the upper Hudson valley, the mainly Dutch proprietors of quasi-feudal 'patroonships' traded in furs and collected rents from tenant farmers. New York City and its immediate surroundings housed vibrant trading and manufacturing communities. These divergent interests viewed the question of independence from a local perspective. Under pressure from local interests, New York's delegates to CONTINENTAL CONGRESS were initially reluctant to endorse the DECLARATION OF INDEPENDENCE (they at first abstained). During the REVOLUTIONARY WAR, the British occupied New York City, which became the unofficial capital of America's LOYALIST community. The state was also the site of the crucial campaign leading to the British surrender at SARATOGA and of SULLIVAN'S CAMPAIGN against members of the IROQUOIS CONFEDERACY. (New York's strategic importance later made it a key battleground in the WAR OF 1812.)

On July 26 1788, New York became the 11th state to ratify the US Constitution. Powerful interests within the state supported the ANTIFEDERALIST position and opposed RATIFICATION of the Constitution. FEDERALISTS, led in New York by Alexander HAMILTON, published the FEDERALIST PAPERS in a bid to persuade doubters. (They also employed less elevated arm-twisting to ensure that the state joined the union.) New York City was chosen as the seat of the new federal government. A strong DEMOCRATIC-REPUBLICAN movement whose members – later absorbed within TAMMANY HALL – were suspicious of central authority grew up in the city. In 1799, New York passed a law allowing for the abolition of slavery through GRADUAL EMANCIPATION.

New York experienced rapid population growth in the 19th century. By 1820, New York had surpassed Virginia as the most populous state (a position it retained until it was in turn surpassed by California in the 1960s). Consequently, New York became the most valuable prize within the ELECTORAL COLLEGE and the state's voters and politicians exerted a powerful influence on the political life of the nation. During the first half of the 19th century, New York generated such nationally significant social reform and religious movements as the ANTI-MASONIC PARTY, the BARNBURNERS, the KNOW-NOTHINGS, the LOCO-FOCOS, the SENECA FALLS CONVENTION, the WORKINGMEN'S PARTY and the MORMON religion. Many of these movements originated in the tension that existed in the state between an urban, immigrant and increasingly Catholic population and a rural, Protestant, population 'upstate'.

By 1860, New York had 3,880,735 residents and the value of its industrial and agricultural production surpassed that of any other state. Although New York supplied over 448,000 troops to the Union during the Civil War, opposition to the DRAFT coupled with racial prejudice helped produce the NEW YORK CITY DRAFT RIOT – the largest civil insurrection in US history, short of secession itself.

On January 1 1892, the US Immigration service designated Ellis Island in New York harbor the primary processing point for European immigrants. New York City was already cosmopolitan, but it became yet more polyglot and culturally diverse during the Progressive Era. Although the STATUE OF LIBERTY celebrated the opportunities available to immigrants, life in New York's tenements and sweatshops was often hard. Even after the TRIANGLE SHIRTWAIST FACTORY FIRE (1911), many employers flouted occupational safety laws. Even when reformers persuaded the state legislature to enact social reform, their efforts were often defeated by the US Supreme Court. The Court's verdict in the case of LOCHNER VS. NEW YORK, which struck down a state law limiting the working day, was a particularly bitter defeat for reformers. (However, WOMEN'S SUFFRAGE campaigners did score a notable victory when in 1917, New York granted women the right to vote.) Bribery and corruption were almost endemic within local government, despite the national scandal caused by exposure of the TWEED RING and the best efforts of PROGRESSIVE reformers. Local government, particularly in the boroughs of New York, remained in the hands of unscrupulous party bosses until passage of the NEW DEAL. During the 20th century, particular localities within New York City have nurtured cultural movements that have influenced the rest of the nation and the world. The distinctively bohemian Greenwich Village was home to a pioneering feminist circle that included Margaret SANGER and later, following the STONEWALL RIOT, became a center of the GAY RIGHTS MOVEMENT. In Harlem, African-American New Yorkers developed a cultural autonomy that was celebrated in the HARLEM RENAISSANCE and shaped the thought of such activists within the CIVIL RIGHTS MOVEMENT as Ella BAKER.

In 1900, New York state had 7,268,894 residents. In the first three decades of the new century, a further 2.5 million people moved into the state. Population growth slowed from the 1950s onwards. In 1990, New York had 17,990,455 residents. In 1994, the population of Texas exceeded that of New York for the first time and the 'Empire State' became the third most populous in the Union. Such is the prominence of the state that many of its politicians – Aaron BURR, state governor Samuel Tilden (defeated candidate in the PRESIDENTIAL ELECTION OF 1876), 'Al' SMITH, Geraldine FERRARO and state governor Mario Cuomo (1932–) to name but a few – have been the subject of national and international attention. Five US presidents have been born or raised in New York: Martin VAN BUREN, Millard FILLMORE, Chester ARTHUR, Theodore ROOSEVELT and Franklin D. ROOSEVELT.

New York City, British occupation of (1776–83). During the REVOLUTIONARY WAR, following the battle of LONG ISLAND, WASHINGTON withdrew the defeated Continental Army to Manhattan. Defending first the developed southern half of the island and later (from September 16 1776) the sparsely populated Harlem heights in the north, Washington rejected advice from subordinates to burn and then abandon the city (although on September 21 an accidental fire destroyed 300 buildings on Manhattan). Washington's troops blocked an outflanking maneuver at WHITE PLAINS (October 28) but, his position untenable, Washington and the bulk of his army abandoned

New York on December 11 1776. The British occupation lasted for the remainder of the war, and the last British troops left on November 25 1783. During this period New York served as British headquarters and the unofficial LOYALIST capital of America. As in PHILADELPHIA, many residents of the occupied city traded and fraternized with the British.

New York City draft riot (July 13–16 1863), the largest civil insurrection in American history, short of SECESSION itself. The riot began with an attack on the office established to administer the CONSCRIPTION ACT (1863). Mobs of white workers, many of them Irish-American, conducted a racial pogrom in which at least 11 blacks were lynched and hundreds more forced to flee to New Jersey. The city's black orphanage was razed and the homes of prominent REPUBLICANS attacked. Following the arrival of 20,000 troops fresh from the GETTYSBURG campaign order was restored in street skirmishing in which at least 82 rioters were killed or executed. Conscription resumed on August 19, but New York's council paid to hire substitutes for draftees in a bid to avoid renewed violence.

Nez Percé, Native American people of the northwest, who speak a Penutian language. They were known by various names; Nez Percé is French for 'pierced nose'. When first observed by white Americans (during the LEWIS AND CLARK EXPEDITION) some 3000 Nez Percé lived on lands straddling the borders of Idaho, Oregon and Washington. Substantial US encroachment followed the blazing of the OREGON TRAIL in the 1840s, and by the 1860s most Nez Percé had opted to sell their lands to the USA in return for guaranteed reservations. In 1877 the USA attempted to consolidate Nez Percé reservations by forcing a group resident in Oregon's Grande Ronde valley to relocate to Idaho. This prompted a campaign of violent resistance in which 135 Nez Percé warriors ambushed a US cavalry column and killed 35 troopers. Under the leadership of Chief Joseph (1840–1904), the remaining Nez Percé fled east and north towards Canada. The bulk of the party was captured 50 miles (80 km) south of the border on October 3 1877 and forcibly removed to a reservation in Idaho.

Niagara Movement, civil rights organization founded in 1905. Under the leadership of W.E.B. DU BOIS, a convention of African-American leaders and intellectuals met at Niagara Falls, New York, in July 1905. The convention called for a new militancy to be brought to the task of repealing discriminatory JIM CROW laws and securing full civil rights for black Americans. Rejecting the philosophy of moderation and black self-improvement advocated by Booker T. WASHINGTON, and openly criticizing white politicians and black leaders for their failure to condemn and suppress LYNCHING and racial discrimination, members of the movement played a prominent role in the creation in 1909 of the NATIONAL ASSOCIATION FOR THE ADVANCEMENT OF COLORED PEOPLE (NAACP). The Niagara Movement itself disbanded the following year.

Nineteenth Amendment, amendment to the US Constitution that gives US women the right to vote in state and federal elections. It was submitted to the states on June 4 1919, ratified on August 18 1920, and proclaimed on August 26 1920. *See also* WOMAN'S SUFFRAGE.

Ninth Amendment, amendment to the US Constitution that obligates the federal government to honor civil rights not specifically enumerated in the Constitution but currently enjoyed by the people. It was one of the ten amendments making up the BILL OF RIGHTS. For the full text, *see* Appendix 1.

Nixon, Richard M(ilhous) (1913–94), Republican statesman, vice president (1953–61) and 37th president of the USA (1969–74). Although an ardent anti-communist, he brought about DÉTENTE with both China and the USSR, and eventually withdrew US forces from the VIETNAM WAR. He took the unprecedented step of resigning the presidency to avoid impeachment for his role in the WATERGATE SCANDAL.

Nixon was raised, in straitened circumstances, in Yorba Linda and Whittier, California. He attended Whittier College (1930–4) and Duke Law School (1934–7). During World War II Nixon performed unglamorous administrative functions in the US Navy (1942–6). In 1946 Nixon took on a five-term Democratic incumbent for election to the US House of Representatives. He won. Milking COLD WAR fears of communist subversion, Representative Nixon achieved national prominence as the head of a special house subcommittee investigating the Alger HISS affair. In 1950 he was elected to the US Senate from California, his RED-BAITING election campaign having led a California newspaper to dub him 'Tricky Dick'. Although, at 38, Nixon was the youngest man in the Senate, he criticized the TRUMAN administration's conduct of the KOREAN WAR and abetted Joseph McCARTHY's persecution of alleged communists.

EISENHOWER accepted advice to choose Nixon as his running-mate in the 1952 presidential election, but was prepared to dump him when allegations surfaced that Nixon had received secret campaign contributions from Californian businessmen. Nixon's televised 'CHECKERS' SPEECH rebutted the charges, and he served as Eisenhower's vice president from 1953 to 1961. Nixon was the Republican nominee in the PRESIDENTIAL ELECTION OF 1960. He lost to KENNEDY by just 118,000 votes, but behaved with dignity in defeat. The same could not be said of his behavior after losing a subsequent bid to become governor of California in 1962. Lashing out at the press corps he told them they would 'not have Richard Nixon to kick around anymore'. The outburst was widely seen as ending his political career. He moved to New York and practiced law.

As opposition to the Vietnam War mounted, and racial and social tensions of the 1960s increased, Nixon positioned himself for a come-back by campaigning on behalf of selected Republican candidates. He won the Republican nomination for the PRESIDENTIAL ELECTION OF 1968 by appearing more electable than Ronald REAGAN and more palatable to Republicans than the liberal Nelson D. ROCKEFELLER. Nixon told the electorate that he possessed a 'secret plan' to end the Vietnam War, and encouraged them to see in him a reasonable alternative to the supposed liberalism of Democratic nominee Hubert HUMPHREY and the demonstrable extremism of George WALLACE. He was elected, and took office on January 20 1969.

The principles of the NIXON DOCTRINE and the phased withdrawal of US troops, announced on November 3 1969, did little to quell protests against the Vietnam War. Nixon's plan to end the war involved isolating North Vietnam in order to wring concessions from it that would allow him to claim that he had secured 'peace with honor'. Nixon engaged in détente with the USSR and China. But he also authorized the CHRISTMAS BOMBING of Hanoi and, pursuing the 'MAD DOG' STRATEGY, waged war against CAMBODIA and LAOS while ostensibly backing secret peace negotiations with the North Vietnamese pursued through the KISSINGER INITIATIVE.

Nixon took criticism of his presidency personally and, following publication of the PENTAGON PAPERS on July 1 1971, set his vice president, Spiro AGNEW, the task of attacking the 'nattering nabobs of negativism' in the national press. On the domestic front Nixon abrogated the BRETTON WOODS agreement by taking the USA off the GOLD STANDARD. He pushed a tough anti-drugs and crime-prevention agenda and established the Environmental Protection Agency. Having achieved a landslide victory in the PRESIDENTIAL ELECTION OF 1972, Nixon presided over the settlement of the Vietnam

War reached at the PARIS PEACE TALKS (January 27 1973).

Few presidents have possessed a more complicated psyche than Nixon. His morbid fascination with his place in history led him to conflate his remarkable political come-back with a desire, amply demonstrated in the Watergate scandal, to gain pay-back from his supposed enemies. He resigned in shame, on August 9 1974, but was granted an unconditional pardon by President FORD on September 8 1974.

Nixon Doctrine, a policy enunciated by President NIXON concerning the USA's role in resisting communism. On July 25 1969 Nixon announced that the USA would no longer use massive deployments of ground troops to guarantee the territorial integrity of Southeast Asian nations. He reaffirmed America's commitment to supply material aid to nations fighting communism, and its readiness to use nuclear weapons to guarantee the security of Japan. This announcement initiated a policy of 'Vietnamization', under which US troops were withdrawn from the VIETNAM WAR and the burden of the fighting placed on South Vietnamese forces.

NLRB, *see* NATIONAL LABOR RELATIONS BOARD.

NLU, *see* NATIONAL LABOR UNION.

non-importation agreements, the favored form of American protest against unjust British legislation in the earlier stages of the AMERICAN REVOLUTION. By refusing to import British goods Americans forced the British Parliament to choose between repealing offensive legislation or accepting a decrease in trade revenue. The tactic was popular within America because it did not directly harm the interests of the small farmers and artisans who comprised the bulk of the population. Non-importation also allowed Americans to demonstrate their VIRTUE by doing without luxury goods from Europe. In the seaport cities of America, merchants, under coercion from groups such as the SONS OF LIBERTY, organized non-importation agreements to protest against the STAMP ACT and the TOWNSHEND REVENUE ACT. The CONTINENTAL ASSOCIATION of 1774, organized in protest against the INTOLERABLE ACTS, added intercolonial 'non-consumption' and 'non-exportation' to the non-importation tactic.

Nootka Sound crisis (1789), crisis arising from territorial disputes in the Pacific northwest. In 1789 Spain seized four British trading vessels at a British fur-trading post on Nootka Sound, British Columbia, claiming the territory as part of California. The prospect of British troops crossing or impinging upon US soil to strike at Spanish possessions in retaliation threatened US territorial integrity and suggested that the USA might be dragged into war. Spain responded to the British threat by dropping territorial demands in WEST FLORIDA in a bid to achieve better relations with the USA. The treaty of SAN LORENZO (1795) followed.

Norris, George W(illiam) (1861–1944), maverick Republican politician. He was born in Ohio, and practiced law in Indiana before moving to Nebraska, from where he was elected to the US Congress. As a member of the House of Representatives (1903–13), Norris took a leading role in breaking Speaker Joe CANNON's control of the House. He supported Theodore ROOSEVELT in the PRESIDENTIAL ELECTION OF 1912, and in 1913 took up a Senate seat, which he held, first as a Republican and later as an independent, until 1943. Norris opposed entry into World War I and US membership of the LEAGUE OF NATIONS. He sponsored the TWENTIETH AMENDMENT and the NORRIS–LA GUARDIA ACT. His fight for federal ownership of water rights and hydroelectric plants was rewarded with the creation of the TENNESSEE VALLEY AUTHORITY.

Norris–La Guardia Act (March 23 1932), legislation that forbade employers from using injunctions to break strikes and secondary pickets – a favorite tactic since the PULLMAN STRIKE and the Supreme Court judgments IN RE DEBS and LOEWE VS. LAWLER. The act also weakened the legal status of YELLOW-DOG CONTRACTS. The act was sponsored by two maverick Republicans, George NORRIS and Fiorello La Guardia.

North American Free Trade Agreement (NAFTA), trilateral agreement between the USA, Canada and Mexico providing for the gradual phasing-out of TARIFFS levied on trade within the North American continent. Negotiated by the BUSH administration, NAFTA was signed by President CLINTON and ratified by the US Senate on November 20 1993. Proponents of the agreement argued that the US economy would benefit from the creation of the world's largest free-trade zone. Opponents argued that the agreement would lead US multinational corporations to relocate their production plants outside the USA. NAFTA may in time create an economic zone similar to the European Union on the North American continent.

North Atlantic Treaty Organization (NATO), mutual defensive alliance of North American and European countries. It was created by a treaty signed in Washington DC on April 4 1949, and the founder-members were the USA, Belgium, Canada, Denmark, France, Iceland, Italy, Luxembourg, the Netherlands, Norway, Portugal and the UK. Greece and Turkey joined in 1952, West Germany in 1955, and Spain in 1982. Article 5 defined an attack on one member as an attack on all members. The US Senate ratified the treaty on July 21. NATO mirrored the Soviet-dominated Warsaw Pact (created September 1947). By pledging the USA to resist Soviet expansion in Western Europe, the NATO treaty established a balance of power in the region during the COLD WAR. Since the end of the Cold War NATO's role has changed into that of regional peace-keeper and peace-enforcer, notably in the Balkans. Membership has expanded, and now includes Poland, the Czech Republic and Hungary, all previously members of the Warsaw Pact. The USA continues to provide the major military muscle in the alliance.

North Carolina, southern state, bordered to the north by Virginia, to the east by the Atlantic, to the south by South Carolina and Georgia and to the west by Tennessee.

The first, unsuccessful attempt to establish a permanent British settlement in America was made at Roanoake, North Carolina, between 1585 and 1590. Virginians began taking up land on the Albemarle sound in 1657. In 1663, Charles II granted modern North and South Carolina to a group of wealthy Englishmen. The new proprietors failed to attract settlers from the British Isles and their plans were unpopular with Americans. North Carolina received its own legislature in 1665 and became a royal colony on July 25 1725. One of the THIRTEEN COLONIES, North Carolina developed a particularly corrupt and venal system of local government. In the late 1760s, settlers in the territory's western piedmont formed a REGULATOR MOVEMENT to press their grievances against the territory's oligarchs. This insurrection was crushed at the battle of Alamance (1771). As a result, many back-country North Carolinians were LOYALISTS during the REVOLUTIONARY WAR. (The state's CHEROKEE people also sided with the British during the war.)

North Carolina rejected the US Constitution on August 2 1788, but subsequently ratified it (on November 21 1789) to become the 12th state. North Carolina's economy was heavily dependent on the production of tobacco and, later, cotton through slave labor. In 1800, roughly a third of the state's population was enslaved, a percentage which remained unchanged at the outbreak of the Civil War. The state became the 11th member of the CONFEDERACY on May 20 1861. (During the war, North Carolinian soldiers earned the nickname 'tar heels' – because they stood and fought as though they had tar on the heels of their boots).

President Andrew JOHNSON allowed North Carolina to organize a new legislature in May 1865. When the provisional state government passed restrictive BLACK CODES, the US Congress imposed military rule (May 2 1867). Self-government was restored on November 3 1870. Thereafter, white supremacists dominated state government, which, by the close of the 19th century, had disenfranchised most black residents and enacted JIM CROW laws establishing strict racial segregation.

In the early years of the 20th century, North Carolina's economy benefited from the new craze for cigarette smoking and the state became the headquarters of the US cigarette industry. Although over 700,000 residents, most of them black, left the state for jobs elsewhere during the 20th century, North Carolina's population grew through in-migration and natural increase. In 1900, the state had 1,893,818 residents and was the 15th most populous state in the union. In 1990, North Carolina had 6,628,637 residents and was the 10th most populous state. Following the GREENSBORO SIT-IN, North Carolina dismantled its system of racial segregation with relatively little violence. Prominent 'native sons' include future presidents Andrew JACKSON (who was born near North Carolina's border with South Carolina and trained as a lawyer in Salisbury, North Carolina) and James POLK.

North Dakota, north-central state, bordered by Canada to the north, Minnesota to the east, South Dakota to the south and Montana to the west.

The USA acquired the territory from France through the LOUISIANA PURCHASE (1803). The region had fewer than 15,000 white settlers when, in 1861, the US government organized a territory encompassing the modern states of North and South Dakota. The HOMESTEAD ACT and the subjugation of native peoples in a third SIOUX WAR helped promote further settlement.

The territory had 190,000 residents when it became the 39th state on November 2 1889.

By 1920, the state had 646,872 residents. Many of the new arrivals were of German or Scandinavian descent, and they gave the state a distinctive regional culture that it retains to this day. A ten-year drought that began in 1887 ruined many family farmers. Those that survived were staunch supporters of POPULISM. The state later produced a homegrown socialist party and a reforming Non-Partisan League. The state granted women the right to vote in 1917. North Dakota's farmers were hit by a collapse in commodity prices during the 1920s and a further drought in the 1930s. From 1920 to 1950 over 250,000 residents left the state. In 1990, North Dakota had 638,800 residents and was the 47th most populous state in the union.

Even in comparison to its neighbors, North Dakota has occupied a low profile in the national consciousness, a position symbolized in the 1990s when the publishers of a national road atlas omitted the state on the grounds that few readers would be interested in information about North Dakota. During the 1930s, US Senator Gerald Prentice Nye (1892–1971) of North Dakota chaired a congressional investigation into the munitions industry that contributed to the national debate on ISOLATIONISM. The state's best-known 'native son' is probably former US Secretary of State Warren Christopher (1925–).

Northern Securities Company vs. US (March 14 1904), US Supreme Court ruling (5–4) that extended the reach of the SHERMAN ANTI-TRUST ACT (1890) by stating that it was illegal for corporations to merge or exchange stock if such maneuvering had the effect of eliminating competition.

Northwest Ordinance, legislation adopted by CONFEDERATION CONGRESS on July 13 1787 that established the procedures through which settlers on lands north of the Ohio river and east of the Mississippi could organize governments and apply for statehood.

In the first instance, settlers on these lands were to be placed under the jurisdiction of a governor and three judges appointed by Congress. When the population of a territory reached 5000, its inhabitants were permitted to establish a territorial legislature. This legislature, under the supervision of the congressionally appointed governor, was charged with drafting a state constitution. The Northwest Ordinance specified that a minimum of three and a maximum of five states would be formed east of the Mississippi and north of the Ohio. Potential states would be eligible to apply for admission to the union once their population exceeded 60,000 adult males and on condition that their constitutions provided for a republican form of government, supported freedom of religion, and did not allow slavery. In 1803 OHIO became the first state to be admitted to the Union under the terms of the Northwest Ordinance.

In 1790 Congress approved a similar ordinance describing the procedures through which potential states organized in territory south of the Ohio and east of the Mississippi might enter the Union. However, territorial legislatures in this region were permitted to adopt constitutions allowing slavery.

Northwest Territory, former term for land north of the Ohio river and east of the Mississippi river. The region included the present states of Ohio, Indiana, Michigan, Illinois and Wisconsin and was part of the area acquired by the USA at the treaty of PARIS (1783). The future government of the region was outlined in the NORTHWEST ORDINANCE of 1787.

Notes on the State of Virginia, the only full-length book completed by Thomas JEFFERSON. He wrote the *Notes* in response to a questionnaire circulated among members of the CONFEDERATION CONGRESS in 1780 by François Marbois, secretary of the French legation. Marbois sought to gather relatively basic information about the history, manners and wildlife of the American states. Jefferson spent four years working on a vastly more ambitious response. The *Notes* were published privately in a limited edition in Paris in 1785. The first English-language edition was published in London in 1787. The most notorious passages of the *Notes* deal with slavery and religion. Jefferson bluntly asserted the racial inferiority of African-Americans, argued that it would be impossible to emancipate slaves without removing them from America, and contended that the worst feature of the slave system was its effect on the morals of the children of slave owners. In his remarks on religion Jefferson classified most forms of faith as tantamount to dangerous superstition. This was a view wildly out of keeping with the sentiments of most of his countrymen. For this reason Jefferson worried about the effect that publication of the *Notes* might have on his political career, and toyed throughout the remainder of his life with a wholesale revision.

NOW, *see* NATIONAL ORGANIZATION FOR WOMEN.

NRA, *see* NATIONAL RECOVERY ADMINISTRATION.

NSC, *see* NATIONAL SECURITY COUNCIL.

NSC-68, the 68th position paper issued by the NATIONAL SECURITY COUNCIL (NSC), which urged the TRUMAN administration to adopt a more assertive stance in the COLD WAR. Passed to Truman in April 1950, NSC-68 charged that the Kremlin was directing communist expansion around the globe, and recommended that the USA and its allies should undertake 'an immediate and large-scale build-up of our general and military strength' in the hope 'that through means other than all-out war' the USA could 'induce a change in the nature of the Soviet system'. The document assumed that up to 20% of the US gross national product would have to be devoted to this build-up, a measure of the document's deviation from earlier, more modest, theories of CONTAIN-

MENT. Almost immediately after Truman had rejected the document on the grounds of cost, the outbreak of the KOREAN WAR led to a massive US military build-up.

nuclear armament and disarmament, *see* MANHATTAN PROJECT; HIROSHIMA AND NAGASAKI, BOMBING OF; ATOMIC ENERGY COMMISSION; COLD WAR; DÉTENTE.

nullification crisis (1832–3), constitutional crisis that highlighted the differences in economic interests between the northern and southern states, and the tensions between the individual states and the federal government. Secession and civil war were only narrowly avoided.

Nullification, a concept inherent in the KENTUCKY RESOLUTIONS and later refined by John C. CALHOUN, referred to the presumed right of a state to nullify federal legislation it regarded as unconstitutional, oppressive or unjust. It was the application of this doctrine to TARIFF policy during Andrew JACKSON's presidency that precipitated the crisis.

Southern states opposed the levying of import duties on foreign raw materials and manufactured goods, as such duties were seen as ultimately harmful to southern economic interests. The tariffs were intended to protect America's manufacturing and extractive industries – overwhelmingly located in the northern states. Southern opposition arose because such protective tariffs produced retaliatory measures overseas, thereby harming America's export trade in cotton, rice and tobacco – the mainstays of the south's plantation economy.

On December 19 1828 South Carolina's legislature passed eight resolves attacking the TARIFF OF ABOMINATIONS as unjust and unconstitutional. Georgia, Mississippi and Virginia passed similar resolutions. In October 1832, South Carolina, acting on Calhoun's *SOUTH CAROLINA EXPOSITION AND PROTEST*, called a special convention that declared (on November 24) the tariffs of 1828 and 1832 null and void, and threatened secession from the Union unless federal customs officers operating in South Carolina suspended collection of the relevant import duties. President Jackson was willing to discuss tariff revision, but in a presidential proclamation issued on December 10 1832 he dismissed nullification doctrine as unconstitutional and an 'impracticable absurdity'. He warned that secession was treason and threatened to use force against any state declining to implement federal legislation. Calhoun, Jackson's vice president, resigned in protest. Passage of a compromise tariff on March 2 1833 averted armed conflict.

O

OAS, *see* ORGANIZATION OF AMERICAN STATES.

O'Connor, Sandra Day (1930–), US Supreme Court justice. Nominated by President REAGAN, in 1981 she became the first woman to serve on the Court.

A graduate of Stanford Law School, O'Connor served as Arizona's assistant attorney general (1965–8) before being elected (as a Republican) to represent Arizona in the US Senate (1969–75). Between 1972 and 1975 O'Connor was Senate majority leader, the first woman to hold that post. When considering O'Connor's nomination to the Supreme Court, Democrats weighed the political cost of opposing a woman nominee against the likelihood that O'Connor would prove hostile to ABORTION rights guaranteed by ROE VS. WADE. In fact, O'Connor has taken a more nuanced position on abortion than either Republicans or Democrats might have expected.

Office of Strategic Services (OSS), WORLD WAR II intelligence-gathering and covert-action organization, established on June 13 1942 by order of President Franklin ROOSEVELT. During the COLD WAR the OSS was disbanded and its functions assumed by the CENTRAL INTELLIGENCE AGENCY. Hardline anticommunists believed the OSS recruited too many of its agents from within the east-coast and Ivy League elites. The dismissive nickname 'Oh So Social' attached to the OSS by its enemies in Congress helped ensure the organization's demise.

Ohio, midwestern state bordered by Lake Erie and the state of Michigan to the north, by Pennsylvania to the east, the Ohio river, West Virginia and Kentucky to the south and Indiana to the west.

Britain acquired the Ohio territory from France through the first treaty of PARIS (1763). Britain's attempts to block American settlement of the territory in the interests of preserving peace with its native peoples was a source of grievance during the AMERICAN REVOLUTION. The USA acquired Ohio from Britain through the second treaty of PARIS (1783), although Britain retained a substantial military presence in the region until the negotiation of JAY'S TREATY (1794). The organization of government in territory was prescribed by the NORTHWEST ORDINANCE (1787). New permanent US settlements at Marietta and Cincinatti were established in 1788. Following US victory at the battle of FALLEN TIMBERS (1794), Ohio's native peoples were forced to make massive land cessions through the first treaty of GREENVILLE (1795). Substantial US in-migration followed and on March 1 1803, Ohio became the 17th state. During the WAR OF 1812, a coalition of native peoples led by TECUMSEH and PROPHET made an unsuccessful last-ditch bid to halt further TERRITORIAL EXPANSION in the region.

By 1860, Ohio had 2,339,511 inhabitants

and was the third most populous state in the union. Although it attracted foreign-born immigrants, the main source of population increase was the internal migration of white families from other regions of the USA. An equally distinctive feature of the state's development was that, from the 1820s onwards, agricultural production was balanced by industrial development. The state's prominence within the ELECTORAL COLLEGE, its balanced development and the support it gave the Union during the Civil War, helped place Ohio at the center of the nation's political life for much of the late 19th and early 20th centuries. (Future presidents Ulysses S. GRANT, Rutherford B. HAYES, James A. GARFIELD, William McKINLEY, William Howard TAFT and Warren G. HARDING were natives of Ohio).

New industries, notably steelmaking, petroleum refining and rubber production, helped sustain the state's economy during the first half of the 20th century. However, by the 1970s and 80s, the effects of under-investment and out-moded plants had conspired to produce a marked decline in the state's fortunes. In 1990, Ohio had 10,847,115 residents and was the 7th most populous state in the union.

Okies, derogatory term applied by residents of California to the 300,000 workers who left the southern plains states after the DUST BOWL to seek agricultural employment on the Pacific coast. Families abandoning homesteads ruined by soil erosion typically traveled west along ROUTE 66. Many of them took up seasonal and low-paid work in California's commercial orchards while they found their feet. Local residents believed that the newcomers drove down wages and took jobs from native Californians. The California legislature attempted to restrict the entry of indigent persons into the state, but the legislation was ruled unconstitutional by the US Supreme Court in its verdict on Edwards vs. California (1941). The plight of the 'Okies' was described by John Steinbeck (1902–68) in his novel *The Grapes of Wrath*, published in 1939.

Okinawa, battle of (April–June 1945), protracted US campaign in WORLD WAR II to capture the main island in the Ryukyu group to the south and west of the Japanese home islands. The US Tenth Army began its assault on Okinawa on April 1 1945. The Americans committed 183,000 men to the campaign, but it took 82 days to overcome the resistance mounted by a Japanese garrison of 130,000, backed by 2600 kamikaze pilots. At least 100,000 Japanese troops, 70,000 civilians, and 11,000 US servicemen were killed in the fighting. The capture of the island provided a base from which medium-range bombers could join the long-range aerial bombardment of Japan. The scale of Japanese resistance at Okinawa matched that at TARAWA and IWO JIMA, and helped persuade President TRUMAN to authorize the dropping of atomic bombs on HIROSHIMA AND NAGASAKI.

Oklahoma, central state, bordered to the north by Kansas and Colorado, to the east by Missouri and Arkansas, to the south by Texas and to the west by New Mexico.

The USA acquired Oklahoma from France through the LOUISIANA PURCHASE (1803). In 1818, the CHICKASAW nation agreed a treaty with the USA whereby they ceded lands in Tennessee for self-governing RESERVATIONS in Oklahoma. Following the INDIAN REMOVAL ACT (1830), the USA sought to strike similar deals with other members of the FIVE CIVILIZED TRIBES of the southeastern United States. The route to eastern Oklahoma followed by the CHEROKEE nation during their enforced removal became known as the TRAIL OF TEARS. Lands in eastern Oklahoma were also set aside for native peoples displaced by the KANSAS–NEBRASKA ACT (1854). Few Americans wished to settle in Oklahoma until the territory became accessible by train in the 1870s. The OKLAHOMA LAND RUSH (1889) saw some 15,000 Americans attempt to stake claims. A second rush in

1893 proved equally popular. Residents of Oklahoma's reservations sought admission to the union as an independent state (named Sequoyah), but eastern and western Oklahoma entered the Union together on November 16 1907, when Oklahoma became the 46th state. Oklahoma granted women the right to vote in 1918.

Oklahoma was one of the states worst affected by the GREAT DEPRESSION and the DUST BOWL. Over 250,000 OKIES abandoned family farms in the state during this period. The state's oil production, mining and manufacturing industries helped promote economic recovery. In 1990, Oklahoma had 3,145,585 residents and was the 28th most populous state in the Union. Thomas Pryor Gore (1870–1949), who lost his eyesight in a childhood accident and later represented Oklahoma in the US Senate between 1907–21 and 1931–37, achieved a national prominence during the NEW DEAL. The state's most famous 'native son' is probably the athlete Jim THORPE.

Oklahoma land rush, race to stake land claims following President Benjamin HARRISON's decision to permit white settlement on 6 million acres (2.4 million ha) of Oklahoma land formerly reserved for the CHEROKEE nation. The rush began at noon on April 22 1889 when a bugler from the US Fifth Cavalry sounded the 'dinner call'. Some 15,000 potential settlers (nicknamed 'boomers') used horses, buggies and trains in a race to find and occupy the best lands in the newly opened Cherokee strip. The land was free, provided the occupier staked a claim, paid a small registration fee, and undertook to cultivate it for five years. Many of the hopefuls found that infiltrating squatters (nicknamed 'sooners') had already staked a claim to the best lands. This caused an uproar, which led to the government to stage a second great rush on September 6 1893.

Olive-Branch Petition (1775), document proposing reconciliation between the British and the Americans at the beginning of the REVOLUTIONARY WAR. It was written by John DICKINSON, addressed directly to George III, and endorsed by the first CONTINENTAL CONGRESS on July 5 1775. The petition proposed a cease-fire in New England, repeal of the INTOLERABLE ACTS, and future guarantees of American rights and liberties. It arrived in England alongside news of BUNKER HILL. George III rejected the overture and on August 23 1775 declared New England to be in open rebellion.

Omaha beach, one of five Normandy beaches assaulted by Allied troops on D-DAY (June 6 1944). A series of mishaps led to the scattering of the assault force, composed of men from the US Fifth Army Corps. Confronted by unexpectedly stiff German resistance and unfavorable terrain, US forces suffered 2000 casualties before they managed to establish a tenuous beachhead.

Omaha Platform, the platform adopted by the PEOPLE'S PARTY at its national convention in Omaha, Nebraska, on July 4 1892. It incorporated demands generated by two decades of agrarian unrest, and represents the definitive statement of POPULIST values. The party committed itself to FREE SILVER, the nationalization of rail, telephone and telegraph companies, a graduated income tax, and the direct election of US senators. The party's presidential candidate, James B. WEAVER, garnered 9% of the POPULAR VOTE and carried four states in the 1892 election. However, the platform divided Populists and led opponents to tag them as extremists.

Oneida commune, one of the most long-lived, and notorious, of the many utopian communities founded in the USA's early national period. It was established by John Humphrey Noyes (1811–86) in 1848. Forerunners of the Oneida commune included the utopian settlements established by the Shaker sect, the New Harmony commune and Brook Farm. The Shaker sect, established in America in 1776 by 'Mother'

Ann Lee (1736–84), founded a total of 12 utopian settlements in New York State. The Shakers attempted to replicate the lifestyle of early Christians, holding property in common and emphasizing plain living. The New Harmony commune, established in Indiana by Robert Owen (1801–77) in 1826, attempted to demonstrate the virtues of cooperative socialism. Brook Farm, founded in 1841 by George Ripley (1802–80), was based on the transcendentalist values espoused by Ralph Waldo Emerson (1803–82).

The Oneida commune took a commitment to the equality of the sexes often found in utopian societies further than ever before. Noyes believed that Christ had returned to earth in AD 70, but that the long-awaited final millennium had been delayed until sin was eradicated from the earth. Noyes believed that he had achieved a state of sinlessness in 1834, and in 1835 gathered a group of biblical perfectionists about him in Putney, Vermont. At the Oneida commune in New York State, Noyes strove to create a sinless society through 'complex marriage'. This held that every member of the community was married to every other member of the opposite sex. Possessive sexual or emotional relationships, seen as a root cause of sin, were discouraged. Property was held in common. The commune became notorious for 'free love', and Noyes was eventually forced to flee to Canada to escape a bigamy charge. However, the commune flourished, partly through the manufacture of mousetraps and silverware. In 1881 it was wound up and converted into a corporation with a capitalization of $600,000.

'The only good Indian is a dead Indian', remark, attributed to General Philip H. SHERIDAN, that encapsulates the tactics adopted by US troops in the RED RIVER WAR (1874–5). Sheridan's uncompromising approach to warfare had earlier been demonstrated in the Civil War during the SHENANDOAH VALLEY CAMPAIGN.

open-door policy, US policy towards China from 1899, by which the USA pledged support for the preservation of China's territorial integrity and asked all nations to observe free and equal trade policies within China. The policy was formulated by President McKINLEY's secretary of state, John Hay (1838–1905), in response to the Boxer Rebellion in China (1899–1900). Hay feared that Japan and the European nations might exploit the rebellion to seize control of China's markets.

Operation Breadbasket (1965–6), a subsidiary component of a major civil rights campaign organized in Chicago by the SOUTHERN CHRISTIAN LEADERSHIP CONFERENCE (SCLC). Boycotting local stores that did not employ African-Americans, Chicago residents organized alternative stores and co-ops. One of the coordinators of the campaign was Jesse JACKSON.

Operation Cedar Falls (February 1967), major US offensive against a Viet Cong stronghold in the 'Iron Triangle' region just north of Saigon. The operation symbolized the futile ferocity of US tactics in the VIETNAM WAR. While B-52 bombers pounded the area, 30,000 troops surrounded it, and helicopters dropped special forces into the remaining villages. The civilian population was removed. Giant ploughs destroyed the area's field system and all vegetation that might give the Viet Cong cover. The region was then burned and bombed again to destroy underground tunnels. 'It's like building a house with a bulldozer,' one US observer commented.

Operation Chaos, code name for a secret and illegal domestic surveillance programme mounted by the CENTRAL INTELLIGENCE AGENCY (CIA) and directed against the Vietnam-era ANTIWAR MOVEMENT. From 1968 the CIA created 13,000 dossiers on antiwar protesters, and gathered, by covert means, information on some 300,000 US citizens. This violation of the CIA's charter was revealed in a report published on June

10 1975 by a special commission headed by Nelson ROCKEFELLER. The Rockefeller report also revealed that the CIA had been testing mind-altering drugs, including LSD, on individuals without their knowledge. In the aftermath of the report Congress created tougher oversight procedures to regulate the CIA.

Operation Desert Storm, *see* PERSIAN GULF WAR.

Operation Overlord, *see* D-DAY LANDINGS.

Operation Rolling Thunder (1965–8), the overall code name assigned to the bombing campaign against North Vietnam during the VIETNAM WAR. The USA began bombing North Vietnamese targets on March 2 1965, and continued at different levels of intensity (and with a pause between December 24 1965 and January 31 1966) until President JOHNSON completely halted the campaign on October 31 1968.

As the operation progressed its emphasis shifted from the destruction of military bases and supply lines to the destruction of the North Vietnamese economy. The use of B-52 bombers, each one of which carried a 58,000 pound (26,000 kg) payload, helped make this the most intense aerial bombardment in history. The bombing may have actually increased North Vietnam's determination to resist, and it certainly did not cut the flow of arms, troops and supplies south. The campaign was expensive. Each B-52 sortie cost $30,000, and between 1965 and 1968, 950 US planes, costing $6 billion, were shot down. By one estimate the USA spent $9.50 for each dollar of damage it inflicted on North Vietnam.

Although Johnson stopped the bombing in October 1968, in the later stages of the KISSINGER INITIATIVE President NIXON, to universal condemnation, ordered two further bombing offensives against North Vietnam (April 16 –October 23 and December 18–30 1972). The second of these, the CHRISTMAS BOMBING of Hanoi, was the most destructive of the war. During the Vietnam War US planes delivered more than twice the tonnage of bombs they dropped during World War II.

Order of the Patrons of Husbandry, *see* GRANGER MOVEMENT.

Ordinance of 1785, legislation adopted by CONFEDERATION CONGRESS on May 20 1785 that established a standard system for surveying and selling western lands ceded to the USA by Native American nations and the existing 13 states. The ordinance drew on proposals made by Thomas JEFFERSON in 1784. Public land was to be divided by survey into uniform grids. Townships of 6 square miles (15.54 square km) were further subdivided into 36 units of 1 square mile (2.59 square km), quarter sections of which formed the minimum unit of sale. The ordinance reserved for the USA units upon which schools and other public facilities could be built. Under the terms of the ordinance, land in the public domain was offered for sale by auction at a minimum price of $1 per acre (0.4 ha). The subsequent NORTHWEST ORDINANCE (1787) clarified the procedure through which settlers on western lands could apply for admission into the USA.

Oregon, northwestern state, bordered on the north by Washington, on the east by Idaho, on the south by California and Nevada and to the west by the Pacific Ocean.

From the 1790s, the modern state of Oregon was the subject of competing claims by the USA and Britain. In 1818, the USA and Britain resolved their dispute by agreeing jointly to administer the Oregon territory (which included much of the modern state of Washington). The Columbia river demarcated the border between the two jurisdictions. The blazing of the OREGON TRAIL, accomplished in 1842–3, prompted substantial in-migration to British Oregon by US settlers and an American claim, forcefully made by James POLK, to all land on the west coast up to the southern boundary of Alaska. The ensuing OREGON BORDER CRISIS was resolved in 1846 and Congress granted territorial status to Oregon (including the modern state of Washington) on August 14 1848. (Washington became an independent territory in 1853.) Oregon became the 33rd state on February 14 1859. In 1860, Oregon had 52,000 residents.

Further development of the state proceeded slowly until the completion of transcontinental rail links and the final subjugation of the NEZ PERCE nation. Nevertheless the new state had a lively political history. In the PRESIDENTIAL ELECTION OF 1860, pro-slavery southern Democrat John BRECK-INRIDGE chose Oregon's US Senator Joseph Lane (1801–81) as his running-mate in an unsuccessful bid to balance the appeal of the National Democrats' ticket. Later, Republican bosses in the state disputed votes cast for Democrat Samuel Tilden in the PRESIDENTIAL ELECTION OF 1876 and thereby helped elevate Rutherford HAYES to the presidency. During the 1860s and 70s, Chinese workers played a prominent role in developing the mining industry of southwestern Oregon. This brought a NATIVIST backlash into the state's politics. When the state's mines were played out, the lumber industry and the manufacturing concerns it generated became the leading source of non-agricultural employment in Oregon. During the PROGRESSIVE ERA, Oregonians expressed strong support for the TEMPER-ANCE and WOMEN'S SUFFRAGE movements. The state also passed two laws much admired by reformers elsewhere. In 1902, Oregon became the first state to strike at the power of special interests and party bosses by adopting a state-wide initiative and referendum law. (During the 1920s, bigots used the initiative system to force passage of a statute that struck at Catholic schools by requiring children to attend secular institutions in the state system.) In 1908, largely as the result of a campaign led by Florence KELLEY, Oregon mandated a ten-hour working day for women. (This law was subse-

quently upheld by the US Supreme Court in its verdict on MULLER VS. OREGON.) Oregon granted women the right to vote in 1913.

In 1900, Oregon had 413,536 residents but by 1990, its population had grown to 2,842,321, making it the 29th most populous state in the union.

Oregon border crisis, dispute between Britain and the USA over territory in the Pacific northwest, including the present states of Oregon, Washington and Idaho, as well as the southern portion of British Columbia. In the 1844 election campaign, Democrats, encouraged by their candidate, James POLK, alleged that the USA had a right to all land north of California to latitude 54° 40' – the southern limit of Alaska. The Democratic slogan 'Fifty-Four Forty or Fight' angered Britain, discomfited WHIGS, and deflected attention from the question of the statehood of TEXAS. Britain recognized US claims to the modern state of WASHINGTON in 1846, Polk agreeing a boundary on latitude 49°.

Oregon Trail, the principal route by which US settlers migrated to the Pacific northwest from the 1840s. The 2000-mile (3200-km) trail began in Independence, Missouri. Settlers traveled up the Platte river valley, crossed the Rockies at South Pass, Wyoming, and went down the Snake and Columbia river valleys into the Oregon territory. If settlers were driving livestock, the journey took about five months. Discovery of the route in 1842 led to increased US settlement in the northwest, which in turn provoked the OREGON BORDER CRISIS. During the 1850s the SHOSHONE harassed pioneers using the trail.

Oregon vs. Mitchell (December 21 1970), US Supreme Court ruling on a case that challenged the VOTING RIGHTS ACT and the CIVIL RIGHTS ACT OF 1970. The ruling established that Congress could force states to remove literacy requirements from voter registration procedures. The Court also upheld (8–1) Congress's right to establish

30 days as the maximum residency requirement for voting in presidential elections. It struck down (5–4) the section of the 1970 Civil Rights Act establishing 18 as the minimum voting age in state elections. The TWENTY-SIXTH AMENDMENT overturned the latter ruling.

Organization of American States (OAS), regional association established by treaty on May 2 1948, through which the USA attempted to improve relations with its Latin American neighbors during the COLD WAR. The goals of the OAS include the promotion of peace and a cooperative approach to regional problems. The OAS's headquarters are in Washington DC, and its work is aided by a permanent secretariat and several commissions.

Oriskany, battle of (August 6 1777), American victory in New York State during the REVOLUTIONARY WAR. On August 6 1777, 700 US militiamen under General Nicholas Herkimer (1728–77) were ambushed by a force of TORIES and members of the IROQUOIS CONFEDERACY led by Joseph BRANT. Rallying to high ground, US soldiers dispersed their assailants. The action was significant because it helped secure US control of the upper Mohawk valley, preventing the British from reinforcing General John Burgoyne's concurrent thrust southwards down the Hudson valley and contributing to his eventual surrender at SARATOGA. Following the battle, most Iroquois abandoned the British cause. However, American allegations of Iroquois savagery helped prompt SULLIVAN'S CAMPAIGN of retribution, and the perceived treachery of the Iroquois during the war was punished by the second treaty of FORT STANWIX (1784).

Osceola (*c.* 1800–38), Native American leader, of joint British-CREEK ancestry. In 1835 Osceola led the SEMINOLE in a campaign of armed resistance to enforced relocation in Oklahoma. Attacks by his followers on pro-removal Seminole and US officials prompted the second SEMINOLE WAR. In October 1837 Florida militiamen seized Osceola at a parley conducted under a flag of truce. He died the following year in a Charleston prison. He was buried with military honors by regular army officers made uncomfortable by the deceit used to apprehend him.

OSS, *see* OFFICE OF STRATEGIC SERVICES.

Ostend Manifesto (1854), secret memo to President PIERCE from US diplomats urging that a US purchase of Cuba was vital for the protection of slavery, and that war was justified in the event of Spanish resistance. Pierce had authorized the diplomats to explore the purchase of Cuba from Spain. On October 9 1854, following a meeting in Ostend, Belgium, the US envoys to France, Spain and Britain (this last was James BUCHANAN) drafted the memo. When it became public in 1855 abolitionists dubbed it an expansionist manifesto. Pierce lost northern support, but Buchanan gained southern support crucial to his 1856 election victory.

Oswald, Lee Harvey (1939–63), assassin of President John F. KENNEDY. The assassination took place on November 22 1963 in Dallas, Texas. Oswald was an unstable character who joined the US Marine Corps when he was 17. He was dismissed for firing a pistol at bullying platoon mates, and sought political asylum in the Soviet Union. Returning to the USA in June 1962 with a Russian wife, Oswald was harassed by the FBI for his involvement in demonstrations in support of Cuban leader Fidel Castro. In 1963 he purchased by mail order for $19.95 the rifle found in the Texas School Depository Building after the assassination. He was seen fleeing the building immediately after the shooting and was arrested within 45 minutes. He denied shooting the president. While being transferred to the county jail on November 24 1963 Oswald was shot dead by Jack Ruby, a Dallas nightclub owner. This event was captured on live nationwide television. The WARREN COMMISSION established to investigate Kennedy's assassination concluded that Oswald acted alone. Few Americans believe this.

Overlord, Operation, *see* D-DAY LANDINGS.

Owen–Glass Act (1913), *see* FEDERAL RESERVE SYSTEM.

Owens, 'Jesse' (James Cleveland Owens) (1913–80), African-American athlete, whose exploits at the 1936 Olympic Games in Berlin constituted a well-publicized and highly symbolic refutation of Nazi racial theories. Owens, a student at Ohio State University, won gold medals in the 100- and 200-meters sprints, the long jump and the sprint relay, setting two world records in the process. Adolf Hitler, who had hoped the games would demonstrate the superiority of the white Ayran race, left the Olympic stadium rather than suffer the humiliation of having to award gold medals to Owens.

P

Pacific Railroad Act (July 1 1862), legislation that authorized the Union Pacific Railroad to build a line from Omaha, Nebraska, to Utah, where, meeting with the Central Pacific line, the transcontinental rail link would be completed. The Union Pacific was federally subsidized with grants of 6400 acres of public land per mile (1600 ha per km) – a grant that was later doubled – and loans of $16,000 per mile ($9600 per km) and $48,000 per mile ($28,800 per km) in mountainous regions to help meet construction costs. Despite inevitable corruption, which produced the CRÉDIT MOBILIER SCANDAL, the transcontinental link was completed at Promontory Point, Utah, on May 10 1869.

Paine, Thomas (1737–1809), radical pamphleteer who, during the AMERICAN REVOLUTION, played a crucial role in rallying support for a DECLARATION OF INDEPENDENCE and persuading Americans of the viability of a republican form of government.

Paine was 36 when he left England for America in 1774. He had worked as a staymaker, a teacher and an exciseman, failing in all these positions. While living in Lewes, Sussex, Paine wrote a pamphlet petitioning Parliament for an improvement in the pay of excisemen. The repercussions of this protest led to his dismissal from the service in 1774. That year the tobacco shop he ran in addition to his work as an excise officer failed and his second marriage collapsed. He used a cash settlement from his failed marriage to finance a move to America, arriving in Philadelphia in November 1774.

Paine secured work on a local newspaper, the *Pennsylvania Magazine*. He relished the freedom of expression that prevailed among Philadelphia's heterogeneous population of dissenting Protestants. In COMMON SENSE, the wildly successful pamphlet Paine published in January 1776, he argued that America should immediately declare its independence from Britain. He justified this argument by reference to the corruption of the British constitution and the absurdity of all monarchical forms of government. But an important component of Paine's call for independence was the idea that an independent America could serve as an 'asylum' for liberty. Paine's thinking on this was strongly influenced by the virtue and wisdom of the working men he had encountered in Philadelphia. *The Crisis* essays, which were widely reprinted in America's newspapers from December 1776, called on Americans to make sacrifices to ensure that their new and experimental country succeeded in establishing its independence. Paine performed various services for CONTINENTAL CONGRESS and CONFEDERATION CONGRESS. In 1779–80 he served as clerk of the Pennsylvania assembly. During the 1780s he published a steady stream of pamphlets and newspaper essays, many of which, by emphasizing the need for stronger national government and sound financial institutions, anticipated the concerns of the FEDERALISTS.

Between 1788 and 1802 Paine lived in England and France. In *Rights of Man*, published in two volumes in 1791–2, he defended the goals of the French Revolution but in 1793, while resident in France, Paine fell victim to the Terror and was imprisoned. He eventually made his peace with the French government, but remained distrusted in France and reviled in Britain. During the 1790s American DEMOCRATIC-REPUBLICAN societies celebrated Paine's life and work. But following publication of his defense of deism in *The Age of Reason* (1794–6), Paine was anathematized by Federalist polemicists. President JEFFERSON, at considerable political cost, assisted Paine's return to the USA in 1802. Paine's last years were spent in isolation on a farm at New Rochelle, New York. His funeral was attended by just six people. In 1816 Paine's body was exhumed by the English pamphleteer William Cobbett and returned to England for reburial. Unfortunately the body was lost in transit.

Panama, US interventions in (1885, 1901–4, 1989–90). The USA has intervened militarily three times in this Central American country.

(1) In April 1885 US Marines landed in Panama (at that time a province of Colombia) to reopen a railroad line severed during a rebellion.

(2) Between 1901 and 1904 US Marines were deployed in Panama to protect American interests. These forces helped create the independent state of Panama by preventing Colombia from crushing an indigenous Panamanian independence movement in 1903. However, the purpose of the deployment was to guarantee the security of the proposed PANAMA CANAL linking the Atlantic and Pacific oceans. When in 1904 the new Panamanian government allowed the USA to lease from it a zone 20 miles (32 km) wide in which to build the canal, US troops withdrew from Panamanian territory and construction work on the canal began. From 1904 the USA maintained a sizeable garrison within the canal zone.

(3) On December 20 1989, 10,000 US troops mounted an invasion of Panama code-named Operation Just Cause. This was the culmination of a steady breakdown in relations between the USA and the Panamanian dictator General Manuel Noriega. In 1972 the USA had discovered that Noriega was involved in state-sanctioned drug smuggling. The NIXON administration discussed a proposal to assassinate Noriega, but dropped it because Noriega supplied useful intelligence to the USA. In 1987 a Florida grand jury indicted the dictator on drug-smuggling charges, and in 1988 the REAGAN administration imposed economic sanctions on Panama as part of a campaign to ease Noriega from office. In May 1989 Noriega, vowing to maintain an 'iron grip' on Panama, nullified the result of a free election in which he was ousted from the presidency. Angered by the economic sanctions, he ordered his personal militia to harass US servicemen and civilians. A military coup against Noriega launched in October failed for lack of US support. In December 1989 Noriega's militia shot dead a US Marine officer and tortured a US Navy lieutenant in front of his wife. President BUSH, who had refused to assist the earlier coup attempt, now ordered a full-scale invasion. Noriega resisted for four days before taking refuge in the Vatican's embassy in Panama City. He gave himself up on January 3 1990, and April 9 1992 was sentenced by a Florida judge to serve 40 years on drug-trafficking charges. During the invasion 23 US troops died, the majority from 'friendly fire'. Captain Linda Bray of the 988th Military Police Company became the first woman to command US troops in combat

when she led a 30-man unit on a mission to capture the guard-dog kennels used by Noriega's secret police.

Panama Canal, canal that links the Atlantic and Pacific Oceans at the isthmus of Panama, in Central America. Following the SPANISH-AMERICAN WAR, Britain conceded to the USA the exclusive right to build, operate and police an Atlantic–Pacific canal. President Theodore ROOSEVELT instructed Secretary of State John Hay (1838–1905) to purchase from Colombia a canal zone in modern-day Panama. When the Colombian government reneged on the deal in 1903, Roosevelt denounced them as 'a bunch of dagoes', fomented a Panamanian rebellion, sent US Marines to Panama, and swiftly granted diplomatic recognition to the independent state of Panama, from whom he purchased a 10-mile (16-km) wide canal zone. Construction work began in 1904. Roosevelt made a final contribution to the project when he ruled, in 1907, that the canal should not follow a sea-level route, and would therefore need locks. The canal, 40.3 miles (64.5 km) long, cost $365 million. It was completed on August 15 1914. Colonel George Goethals (1858–1928) of the US Army Corps of Engineers, directed the construction effort from 1907, and was the first governor of the Panama Canal Zone. In 1977, in a much criticized treaty, President CARTER's administration returned the canal zone to Panama while retaining the right to operate and defend the canal until 2000.

Panic of 1837, *see* DEPRESSION OF 1837.

Panic of 1857, banking crisis that led to a relatively short-lived economic recession. The Crimean War (1854–6) benefited US grain producers by forcing up world grain prices. Boom conditions were also stimulated by a marked increase in the number of banks and an influx of Californian gold into the economy. But higher interest rates in Britain and France in the aftermath of the Crimean War led European banks to sell

US stocks and bonds. On August 24 1857, an Ohio bank failed following embezzlement in its New York branch. This event, relayed around the country by telegraph, triggered panic withdrawals. The decline in the value of assets held by banks led many to suspend SPECIE payments and to call in loans. Layoffs produced labor unrest in the northeast, and western land values fell sharply. During the recession, which lifted in the winter of 1858–9, the REPUBLICAN PARTY gained electoral support by pledging to protect the working man by raising TARIFFS on imported manufactured goods.

Panic of 1873, panic that triggered a general stock-market slump, low crop prices and widespread unemployment. The panic was set off by the failure of Jay Cooke's (1821–1905) bank, due to a collapse in the value of railroad securities. The GREENBACK PARTY demanded a substantial issue of paper currency to counter the recession. GRANT's administration balanced a modest issue of new currency against the resumption of SPECIE payment (the RESUMPTION ACT).

Panic of 1893, *see* DEPRESSION OF 1893.

Panic of 1907, market panic caused by the failure of several New York finance houses, notably the Knickerbocker Trust Company, in 1907. Prior to the panic, a stock-market boom beginning in 1905 had tempted many investors to make purchases on credit. The panic led to a squeeze on credit, and as loans were called in, businesses failed. In October 1907 the US Treasury deposited substantial funds with New York banks. This preserved liquidity and restored confidence. However, the panic led Congress to appoint a National Monetary Commission which, in 1911, recommended the creation of the FEDERAL RESERVE SYSTEM.

Paoli, battle of (September 21 1777), British victory in Pennsylvania during the REVOLUTIONARY WAR. The battle occurred on the night of September 21 1777, when three regiments of British regulars carried out one of the most daring and notorious exploits of the war. Removing his troops' musket flints to avoid the possibility of a misfire giving the alarm, Major General James Grey led his men into an American encampment. Catching the American soldiers asleep, they bayoneted 300, captured 100, and dispersed the remainder in panic. Americans alleged the slaughter was a war crime.

Paris Peace Conference (January 18 1919–January 16 1920), the conference after WORLD WAR I at which the victorious Allied powers dictated the terms of the peace treaties with the defeated Central Powers. Five treaties emerged from the conference (although the last two were signed after its formal closure): the treaties of VERSAILLES with Germany (1919), Neuilly with Bulgaria (1919), Saint-Germain with Austria (1920), Trianon with Hungary (1920) and Sèvres with Turkey (1920, subsequently revised in 1923 by the treaty of Lausanne).

The US delegation to the conference, headed by President WILSON, was well prepared and staffed by young experts in European history enthused by the task of creating new countries, based on the principles of 'ethnic self-determination', from the ruins of the Austro-Hungarian and Ottoman empires. However, the idealism of Wilson's FOURTEEN POINTS was blunted by the intransigence of the British and French delegations, who wished to impose punitive terms on the defeated powers, especially Germany. Nevertheless, Wilson did manage to moderate some of their more extreme demands, and ensured that the Covenant of the LEAGUE OF NATIONS was incorporated into the Versailles treaty.

Paris peace talks (1968–73), meetings between US and North Vietnamese representatives aimed at reaching a negotiated settlement of the VIETNAM WAR. The principal representatives were Le Duc Tho of North Vietnam and the Americans Averell Harriman (1891–1986) and (from 1969) Henry Cabot Lodge (1902–85).

President Lyndon B. JOHNSON authorized the search for a diplomatic solution in the aftermath of the TET OFFENSIVE, and ordered a halt to the US bombing of North Vietnamese infrastructure (April 7 1968) to show good faith. The first meeting (May 10 1968) established the difficulty of securing a negotiated settlement. The USA insisted that all North Vietnamese troops leave South Vietnam and that the existing government of South Vietnam remain intact. This position gave South Vietnamese communists, who controlled much of the country, no guarantee of political influence, and committed the USA to the support of a corrupt and unpopular regime. Viet Cong and South Vietnamese representatives participated in the talks from January 16 1969. President NIXON authorized the KISSINGER INITIATIVE – a series of bilateral US-North Vietnamese discussions that often undermined the Paris talks – while attempting to use force to extract concessions. The final peace treaty, signed on January 27 1973, allowed North Vietnamese troops to remain in South Vietnam, recognized the Viet Cong's Provisional Revolutionary Government, and included communist representatives in a South Vietnamese Council of National Reconciliation.

Paris, treaties of (1763, 1783 and 1898), treaties that ended the SEVEN YEARS' WAR, the REVOLUTIONARY WAR and the SPANISH-AMERICAN WAR respectively.

(1) The first treaty, which ended the Seven Years' War, was signed on February 10 1763. It was accompanied by the exchange of British, French and Spanish possessions in North America. France traded all mainland territories save the city of New Orleans in order to retain her Caribbean sugar islands. Britain acquired all continental territory east of the Mississippi, gained Canada from France, and EAST and WEST FLORIDA from Spain, in return for Cuba. Spain kept territory west of the Mississippi ceded to it during the war by France.

(2) The second treaty, signed on September 3 1783 and ratified in Congress January 14 1784, formally ended the Revolutionary War. Britain recognized US independence, pledging to cease hostilities and withdraw its troops. The USA recognized debts due to British creditors, and promised to 'earnestly recommend' the restoration of confiscated LOYALIST property. The US-Canadian border as far west as the headwaters of the Mississippi was settled, with Britain renouncing its claims to lands east of the Mississippi. Britain ceded EAST and WEST FLORIDA to Spain (who then disputed the northern boundary of West Florida). Exploiting Britain's European preoccupations, and divisions between France and Spain, the US negotiators – John ADAMS, Benjamin FRANKLIN, John JAY and Henry Laurens (1724–92) – secured a stunning diplomatic victory.

(3) The third treaty, ending the Spanish-American War, was signed on December 10 1898. Spain ceded PUERTO RICO, GUAM and the PHILIPPINES to the USA (the last on payment of $20 million). It also renounced all claim and title to Cuba.

Parker confirmation hearings (1930), US Senate hearings in which, for the first time since 1795, the Senate used its right to reject a presidential nominee for a place on the US Supreme Court (May 7 1930). The nominee was John J. Parker (1885–1958), the choice of President HOOVER. Parker, a North Carolina Republican, was known to be a defender of JIM CROW. The NATIONAL ASSOCIATION FOR THE ADVANCEMENT OF COLORED PEOPLE (NAACP) mounted a huge lobbying campaign to block the nomination. So did the AMERICAN FEDERATION OF LABOR (AFL), concerned by Parker's defense of YELLOW-DOG CONTRACTS. Seventeen Republicans broke party ranks in the 41–39 Senate vote against Parker. The next occasion on which the US Senate used its right to reject nominations to vacancies on the US Supreme Court came in 1969 when it blocked the appointment of Richard NIXON's nominees Clement Haynsworth and G. Harrold Carswell (*see also* BORK CONFIRMATION HEARINGS).

Passing of the Great Race, The, book by Madison Grant (1865–1937), published to acclaim in 1916, that helped generate support for administering literacy tests to immigrants, and for restrictions on immigration from 'undesirable' parts of the world. These restrictions were ultimately established in the EMERGENCY QUOTA ACT (1921) and the NATIONAL ORIGINS ACT (1924). Grant argued that WASP immigrants from northwestern Europe enhanced American society, but immigrants from eastern and southern Europe debased it. Some PROGRESSIVES believed that IQ tests administered under the terms of the SELECTIVE SERVICE ACT (1917) to US Army soldiers proved Grant's thesis. His book influenced attitudes to labor unrest during the RED SCARE.

Patton, George S(mith) (1885–1945), US Army general, the most controversial US commander in WORLD WAR II.

After graduating from West Point Military Academy in 1909 he was commissioned into a cavalry regiment, served with PERSHING in the US invasion of MEXICO in 1916, and commanded a tank brigade in the ST MIHIEL and MEUSE–ARGONNE OFFENSIVES at the close of World War I. In the interwar years he served as chief of cavalry (1928–31) and commander of the Third Cavalry (1932–5). In the latter post he took part in the dispersal of the BONUS ARMY in 1932. Patton retained the affectations of a cavalryman, such as wearing a pair of pearl-handled revolvers, even after he had been promoted to command of a tank corps.

In 1941 Patton trained the Second Armored Division in desert warfare at a base in California. He led the division, and later the Seventh Army, in the Allied invasion of North Africa (1942) and Sicily (1943). Touring a US hospital in Palermo, Sicily, in 1943, Patton slapped a soldier suffering from battle fatigue in the belief that he was malingering. He was reprimanded and denied command of a spearhead army in the D-DAY LANDINGS. However, he went on to command the Third Army in the ST LÔ OFFENSIVE, which broke the stalemate developing around the Normandy beaches, and he later played a crucial role in the battle of the BULGE. Always outspoken, Patton was relieved of command on October 2 1945. The official reason was that he had retained former Nazis within the civilian administration of districts of Germany under Third Army control, but the unofficial reason was that he had predicted, and appeared to relish, war with the Soviet Union. He died soon after from injuries sustained in a car crash.

Paul, Alice (1885–1977), radical campaigner for WOMEN'S SUFFRAGE. Paul brought to the cause the tactics and militancy acquired during three years (1909–12) spent in Britain with radical suffragettes. In 1913 she led militants out of the NATIONAL AMERICAN WOMAN SUFFRAGE ASSOCIATION, founding, in 1916, the NATIONAL WOMAN'S PARTY (NWP) This mounted sensational demonstrations in support of a constitutional amendment to guarantee the right to vote in federal elections. In July 1917, for example, Paul led several hundred women in an attempt to storm the White House. But, behind the scenes, the NWP built crucial alliances with other social reformers at state and local levels. Following passage of the NINETEENTH AMENDMENT, which granted women the vote, Paul began campaigning for an EQUAL RIGHTS AMENDMENT. In 1928 Paul organized the World Party for Equal Rights for Women, known as the World Women's Party. She also successfully lobbied for references to sex equality in the preamble to the United Nations charter and in the 1964 US Civil Rights Act.

Paxton Boys, name given to a group of armed Pennsylvanian frontiersmen who marched on Philadelphia in February 1764 and threatened to occupy the city. During

PONTIAC'S WAR Pennsylvania's Quaker-dominated assembly, citing a mixture of self-interest and pacifist principle, refused to make adequate provision for the protection of western residents from Native American attacks. In 1763 white settlers living in the vicinity of Paxton, Pennsylvania, launched a vendetta against neighboring Native Americans who had been offered protection by the Pennsylvania assembly. The assembly attempted to arrest the ringleaders while removing the Native Americans to the city of Philadelphia for their own safety. The Paxton Boys demanded the release of the white vigilantes and a redress of western grievances. Benjamin FRANKLIN played a crucial role in dissuading the insurgents from their attempted occupation of the city.

Peace Democrats, faction within the Democratic Party, led by Ohio Congressman Clement L. Vallandigham (1820–71) that gained increasing influence among midwestern voters during the spring of 1863. Peace Democrats called for an immediate truce in the CIVIL WAR, a second constitutional convention to develop guarantees of STATES' RIGHTS, and the eventual reintegration of southern states within the Union. Presenting themselves as better Unionists than the Republicans, Peace Democrats opposed conscription and war-time taxes as 'unconstitutional'. They also played on racial fears. On May 1 1863 Vallandigham alleged that the war was being fought for 'the freedom of the blacks and the enslavement [of] whites'. He was arrested under martial law, denied habeas corpus, and deported to Canada. (The Supreme Court subsequently ruled this action unconstitutional in EX PARTE MILLIGAN.) Vallandigham returned to campaign for election to Ohio's governorship in 1864. Although Union victories, coupled with southern insistence that any peace settlement recognize Confederate independence, diminished their appeal, support for the Peace Democrats influenced the timing and scope of the EMANCIPATION PROCLAMATION.

Pearl Harbor, Japanese attack on (December 7 1941), attack on the main US naval base in Hawaii, precipitating America's entry into WORLD WAR II. Japan and the USA were at peace when carrier-based-Japanese warplanes launched a surprise dawr. aid òn the US Navy's Pacific fleet anchored at its main base on the Hawaiian island of Oahu. In the attack 2403 US servicemen and civilians were killed. The raid destroyed eight US battleships. However, the US Navy's aircraft carriers and the base's dockyard installations were spared. On December 8 President Franklin D. ROOSEVELT asked Congress for a declaration of war against Japan. The raid kindled an anti-Japanese hysteria that ultimately led Roosevelt to order the RELOCATION of US citizens of Japanese ancestry.

Peggy Eaton affair, *see* EATON, PEGGY.

Pendleton Act (January 16 1883), legislation reforming the civil service. In the aftermath of the assassination of President GARFIELD, Congress attacked the SPOILS SYSTEM by creating a bipartisan civil-service commission to administer competitive examinations to determine the merit of future applicants for a range of positions within the federal bureaucracy. The act also made it illegal to demand campaign contributions from a federal employee.

Peninsular campaign (March–August 1862), unsuccessful Union campaign during the CIVIL WAR to capture Richmond, Virginia, the Confederate capital.

General George McCLELLAN planned to end the war by transporting a 100,000-strong Union army by sea to the peninsula between Virginia's York and James rivers, prior to an advance westward on Richmond. LINCOLN's suspicion that this would leave Washington DC vulnerable to Confederate attack, later confirmed by the SHENANDOAH VALLEY CAMPAIGN, meant that McClellan's army was stripped of 50,000 troops before it sailed.

McClellan's force landed at Fort Monroe, Virginia, on March 17 1862 but, consistently overestimating the strength and preparedness of Confederate opposition, McClellan delayed his advance at Yorktown and later at Williamsburg. During this time Confederate defenses at Richmond were strengthened. By May, McClellan's army was 6 miles (10 km) from Richmond. But on May 31 Confederate commander Joseph JOHNSTON launched a counterattack against Union forces, during which he was wounded (at Seven Pines, May 31 1862). Responsibility for the defense of Richmond passed to Robert E. LEE who, during what became known as the SEVEN DAYS' BATTLE (June 25–July 1 1862), forced a rattled McClellan into a retreat to the James river. On August 3, over McClellan's protests, Union forces were ordered to evacuate the peninsula. Confederate armies exploited the collapse of the campaign with victory at the second battle of MANASSAS.

Pennsylvania, northeastern state, bordered to the north by New York, to the east by New Jersey, to the south by Delaware, Maryland, Virginia and West Virginia and to the west by Ohio.

The first permanent European settlement in the territory was established by Swedes at Tinicum island, near modern Philadelphia, in 1643. Charles II granted William Penn (1644–1718) title to Pennsylvania and modern Delaware on March 14 1681, creating in the process the largest private estate in the world. Penn sought both to establish a refuge for victims of religious persecution, especially Quakers, and to profit from his grant. The first Quaker settlers arrived in December 1681, and Penn made the first of four trips to his colony in 1682. Although Penn was frustrated by the 'governmentishness' of his colonists, the colony thrived. Features of its development were good relations with local Indians, the rapid establishment of a major city (Philadelphia – 'the city of brotherly love'), the opportunities afforded to immigrants from continental Europe and a climate of unparalleled religious tolerance.

By 1776, Pennsylvania, and the prosperous city of Philadelphia (the largest in America), had established a reputation as the 'best poor man's country' in America. The *Autobiography* of Benjamin FRANKLIN celebrates this period in the state's history, and the apparent VIRTUE of the state's citizenry exerted a powerful influence on statements of REPUBLICAN IDEOLOGY produced by John DICKINSON and Thomas PAINE during the AMERICAN REVOLUTION. In 1776, in a backlash against their Quaker-dominated lower house of assembly, Pennsylvanians created the most radical state constitution in America. In 1780, Pennsylvania became the first of the original THIRTEEN COLONIES to abolish slavery through GRADUAL EMANCIPATION.

The first and second CONTINENTAL CONGRESSES were convened in Philadelphia. The city was occupied briefly by the British during the REVOLUTIONARY WAR, but later served as the site of CONFEDERATION CONGRESS and the CONSTITUTIONAL CONVENTION. On December 12 1788, Pennsylvania became the second state to ratify the federal Constitution. Local ANTIFEDERALISTS complained that the state had been railroaded into ratification and Pennsylvania subsequently produced two major protests against FEDERALIST policies: the WHISKEY REBELLION and FRIES REBELLION. Meanwhile, as the DISTRICT OF COLUMBIA was readied for the reception of the federal government, Philadelphia served as the nation's capital.

In 1800, Pennsylvania had 602,115 residents and was the second most populous state in the union. Throughout the colonial era, and for much of the 19th century, the state contained some of the most productive farmland in America. During the CIVIL WAR Confederate troops invaded Pennsylvania in a campaign to exploit its resources which ended in disaster at the battle of GETTYSBURG. Pennsylvania supplied over 300,000 troops to Union armies during the war. Although the Democratic party retained considerable influence in the state, Pennsylvanians repeatedly elected Thaddeus STEVENS – a RADICAL REPUBLICAN architect of RECONSTRUCTION – to the US House of Representatives.

During the later 19th century, Pennsylvania was a key site of industrial development and labor militancy. The MOLLY MAGUIRES and KNIGHTS OF LABOR were founded in Pennsylvania. The labor leader Terrence POWDERLY made his career in the state. Pennsylvania was an important battleground in the RAIL STRIKE OF 1877. The HOMESTEAD STRIKE (1892) against Andrew CARNEGIE's steel-mills helped define industrial tensions in the PROGRESSIVE ERA.

In 1900, Pennsylvania had 6,302,115 residents and was second only to New York in the size of its population and value of its manufactures. From the 1920s onwards, Pennsylvania and its two chief cities (Philadelphia and Pittsburgh), have experienced a gradual decline. Between 1920 and 1970, over 1,750,000 Pennsylvanians left the state. Its coal and steel communities suffered badly in the GREAT DEPRESSION and in the recession of the late 1970s and early 80s. (A curious feature of the state's response to the Great Depression was that, alone among major industrial states, its voters opposed the NEW DEAL by voting against Franklin D. ROOSEVELT in the PRESIDENTIAL ELECTION OF 1932.) With the decline of manufacturing industry, and the growth of suburbia, the Republican party in the state steadily gained in strength. In the 1980s, Pennsylvania was seen as a key battleground by both sides in the debate over ABORTION law. In 1990, Pennsylvania had 11,881,643 residents and was the fifth most populous state in the Union.

Only one 'native son' – James BUCHANAN – has been elected US President, but the state has produced countless statesmen and social reformers.

Pentagon, term used to identify both the physical location of the US military headquarters and more broadly the upper echelons of the armed forces. President Franklin D. ROOSEVELT ordered the construction of a centralized military headquarters in 1941. The Pentagon building was completed on January 15 1943 at a cost of $83 million. It contains over 17 miles of corridors but its distinctive five-sided design is supposed to ensure that no two offices are separated by more than a 20-minute walk. In 1967 members of the ANTIWAR MOVEMENT, protesting against the Vietnam War, attempted to 'levitate' the Pentagon building – an event celebrated in Norman Mailer's Pulitzer Prize-winning book *The Armies of the Night* (1968).

Pentagon Papers, US Department of Defense study of the USA's involvement in the VIETNAM WAR, commissioned in 1967 by Secretary of Defense Robert McNAMARA. On June 13 1971 the *New York Times* began publishing excerpts from the study, which had been leaked to the press by one of its co-authors, Daniel Ellsberg. Arguing that publication would compromise national security, the NIXON administration sought an injunction against the *Times*. On July 1 the Supreme Court ruled against the government by 6–3; although dissenting Justices Byron White (1917–98) and Potter Stewart (1915–85) opined that Ellsberg might have broken the ESPIONAGE ACT. Nixon was furious. It emerged during investigation of the WATERGATE SCANDAL that Nixon ordered members of his campaign team to steal Ellsberg's psychiatric records in order to discredit him.

People's Party, political party, founded in 1892, that campaigned to establish the values of the POPULIST movement on a national stage. Campaigning on the OMAHA PLATFORM, the party sought a loose fiscal regime, regulation of bank-service and rail-freight charges and a policy of reflation through an issue of silver currency. In the presidential election of 1892 the party received over 1 million votes. In the congressional elections of 1894 seven Populist representatives and six senators were elected. In the west and midwest the party built on previous insurgencies by 'hayseed socialists' (as supporters of the party were derogatorily nicknamed), receiving 40% of the votes cast in some areas. But in the south the DEMOCRATIC PARTY blunted the People's Party's appeal by setting white supporters against blacks, and by disenfranchising Populists in key districts. In 1896, in an attempt to gain support in the northeast and south, the party nominated Democrat William Jennings BRYAN for president and Populist Tom WATSON for vice president. This failed to impress Democrats, while it alienated Populists. The party collapsed following Bryan's defeat.

People vs. Hall (1854), California state supreme court ruling that upheld one of the first statutes passed by the independent state legislature: an 1849 law barring 'blacks', 'mulattos' and 'Indians' from testifying for or against whites. The case arose when in 1853 George Hall and two other white men were found guilty of murdering a Chinese worker named Ling Sing. Hall was sentenced to hang on evidence supplied by Chinese and white witnesses. Hall's lawyer appealed the conviction, citing the 1849 statute. Upholding the appeal against conviction, California's Chief Justice Hugh Murray declared that the 1849 statute clearly and properly barred Chinese residents from testifying in cases involving white defendants.

Perkins, Frances (1880–1965), secretary of labor (1933–45) in President Franklin D. ROOSEVELT's administration. She was the first woman to hold a cabinet post in the USA. As a young woman, Perkins assisted social reformer Jane ADDAMS. During the 1920s she acquired experience of enforcing labor law as a member of New York's state Industrial Commission. In 1929 incoming Governor Roosevelt appointed her to chair the commission, and he persuaded Perkins, who was a good friend of his wife Eleanor, to serve as secretary of labor during his presidency. In 1945 TRUMAN replaced Perkins, who went on to serve as a member of the Civil Service Commission.

Perot, (Henry) Ross (1930–), independent candidate during the presidential elections of 1992 and 1996. Perot, a folksy Texan multimillionaire, emerged from obscurity to become, in 1992, the most successful independent candidate for the presidency since Theodore ROOSEVELT in 1912.

Perot based his candidacy on the idea that government wasn't working and that America's future well-being was threatened by the spiralling federal deficit. He presented himself as a swashbuckling entrepreneur who had graduated from the school of hard knocks characteristic of free-market competition — although in fact he had made his fortune by selling computer equipment to state and federal government. His devoted followers, dubbed 'Perotistas' and organized through a group named 'United We Stand America', placed his name on the ballot in every state in the Union, and as the two main parties held their conventions, Perot enjoyed a substantial lead over both Bill CLINTON and George BUSH in opinion polls. However, on July 16 1992 Perot withdrew from the race, later alleging this was because the Republican Party were planning a smear campaign against his daughter. He re-entered the race in October 1992 and spent a small fortune buying half-hour television slots, during which he explained his economic theories using primitive visual aids. His running-mate, Rear Admiral James Stockdale, achieved celebrity status for his unconventional behavior during a televised vice-presidential debate. A total of 19,741,048 Americans voted for Perot, 19% of those who cast ballots.

Membership in Perot's support group United We Stand America dwindled from a high of over 1 million in 1992 as Perot dithered over whether to run candidates in the 1994 congressional elections. (In the end he did not.) Perot also equivocated before launching a presidential bid in 1996. He did eventually contest the election and received 7,807,588 votes (8.5% of the total cast).

Perry, Matthew C(albraith) (1794–1858), US Navy officer. Commodore Perry achieved national fame as commander of naval forces at the battle of VERA CRUZ (1847). Chosen by President FILLMORE to lead a US mission to Japan, Perry signed the treaty of KANAGAWA (1853) pledging peace, friendship and commerce between Japan and the USA.

Pershing, John J(oseph) (1860–1948), US Army general, commander of the American Expeditionary Force (AEF) sent to France by the USA in WORLD WAR I. Pershing was a cavalryman – his unit rode alongside Theodore ROOSEVELT'S ROUGH RIDERS during the Spanish-American War – who possessed a law degree. Service against the APACHE, in the SPANISH-AMERICAN WAR and in the PHILIPPINES was interspersed with stints as an instructor at the University of Nebraska (1891–5) and at West Point Military Academy (1897–8), and as an official military observer with the Japanese army during the Russo-Japanese War (1905–6). President WILSON appointed Pershing to command the US forces that intervened in MEXICO (1916), before naming him head of the AEF. In France, Pershing directed the massive US offensive in the MEUSE–ARGONNE sector, and successfully prevented US troops from being poached by British and French commanders. He served as army chief of staff from 1921 until 1924.

Persian Gulf War (1991), conflict in which a UN-sanctioned international coalition under US military leadership ended Iraq's seizure of Kuwait.

Even as President BUSH and Soviet Premier Mikhail Gorbachev were signing historic arms-reduction treaties that signalled the end of the COLD WAR, events in the Persian Gulf in 1990 were conspiring to challenge what Bush dubbed the 'new world order'. On August 2 1990 Iraqi troops invaded and captured Kuwait. The UNITED NATIONS Security Council immediately condemned the action. The USA, joined by 27 other nations, sent troops to Saudi Arabia (in an operation dubbed 'Desert Shield') to prevent further Iraqi aggression. On August 8 Bush announced that the USA sought the 'immediate and complete' withdrawal of Iraqi forces from Kuwait and the restoration of Kuwait's independence. He increased the US troop build-up, while at the same time putting in place a UN-sponsored package of sanctions against Iraq. On November 29 1990 the UN Security Council ordered Iraq to withdraw from Kuwait by January 15 1991, and authorized the use of military force if Iraq did not comply. As the deadline approached, Bush sought congressional approval for the use of US troops in the recovery of Kuwait and attacks on Iraq. On January 12 1991 the House of Representatives voted 250–183 and the Senate voted 52–47 to endorse the use of US ground troops against Iraqi forces.

These votes roughly reflected the division of opinion among the American public. Rallying support for his policy, Bush likened Iraqi leader Saddam Hussein to Hitler. He used the DOMINO THEORY to describe the possible consequences of Iraq's invasion of Kuwait. Opponents of war argued that economic sanctions would eventually force an Iraqi withdrawal. They suggested that the USA bore some responsibility for Saddam Hussein's actions, since, in the aftermath of the IRANIAN HOSTAGE CRISIS, the USA had befriended Iraq in its eight-year war with Iran, and had on July 24–25 1990 informed Saddam that the USA had no security commitment to Kuwait and no wish to intervene in inter-Arab disputes. Widely circulated reports suggested that a military reconquest of Kuwait might cost the lives of 10,000 US servicemen. Critics of military action also cited its likely financial cost.

This led Bush to take the extraordinary step of soliciting funding for the war from US allies. Governments friendly to the USA contributed $54 billion to the war chest, while the US Congress chipped in $7 billion.

On January 16 1991 members of the 28-nation coalition, led by the USA and acting on a UN mandate, began bombing targets in Iraq and Kuwait. Iraq retaliated by launching missile attacks on Israel in the hope of provoking a wider confrontation. By late February 600,000 troops, under the overall command of US general Norman Schwarzkopf (1934–), were massed on the Saudi side of the Iraq and Kuwait borders. The ground attack on Iraqi positions in Kuwait and Iraq itself, Operation Desert Storm, began on February 23 1991. The 545,000-strong Iraqi army was swiftly routed, and Schwarzkopf's forces had seized control of much of southern Iraq as well as Kuwait when Bush ordered a cease-fire on February 27. Bush's decision to halt the offensive short of Iraq's capital Baghdad was criticized because it left Saddam Hussein in power. From a military and public-relations perspective the operation was successful. The swift victory cost only 146 US lives (35 of which were caused by 'friendly fire'). In the immediate aftermath of the war Bush's public-approval rating reached 89%, but, to his surprise, he was defeated by Bill CLINTON in the 1992 presidential election.

personal liberty laws, measures enacted by ten northern states designed to frustrate the operation of the FUGITIVE SLAVE ACT (1850). Personal liberty laws generally barred state officials from assisting in the arrest or detention of runaways, and they offered the accused a jury trial in state courts. Accused runaways could testify in their own defense in state proceedings. The US Supreme Court ruled such laws unconstitutional in ABELMAN VS. BOOTH.

Petersburg, battles of (1864–5), series of engagements in Virginia during the CIVIL

WAR, in which Union forces tried to capture the town of Petersburg. Following the battle of COLD HARBOR, the town of Petersburg became the focus of GRANT's attempt to outflank Confederate forces, under LEE, defending Richmond, the Confederate capital. An initial assault on June 9 1864 faltered. On June 15, 16,000 Union troops squandered a chance to overwhelm 5000 Confederate defenders. On June 18, 41,000 Confederates, defending new fortifications, were able to repulse 63,000 Union soldiers. On June 30, Union sappers exploded a huge mine under Confederate lines. But the advantage was lost when Union troops charged into the crater (rather than around it) and were picked off as they attempted to climb out. Grant's exhausted army besieged the town until April 1865. In all, 42,000 Union and 28,000 Confederate casualties were sustained in fighting around Petersburg.

peyote cult, Native American cult that in the 1890s replaced the GHOST DANCE religion as the primary source of cultural revitalization in the reservations of the Great Plains. Native American prophet Quannah Parker developed the cult's blend of hallucinatory peyote ritual and borrowed Christian symbolism. In 1918 the cult was organized as an incorporated church in Oklahoma. In the 1930s John COLLIER, director of the Bureau of Indian Affairs, persuaded the US government to cease seizing supplies of peyote in its attempt to suppress the religion.

Philadelphia, British occupation of. In 1776, at the time of the REVOLUTIONARY WAR, Philadelphia, Pennsylvania, was America's largest city, and the seat of CONTINENTAL CONGRESS. During the summer of 1777 British forces made its capture a priority. On September 26 1777, following the battle of BRANDYWINE CREEK, British troops occupied Philadelphia. Congress was forced to flee to a succession of temporary homes. On October 4 an American counter-attack at the battle of GERMANTOWN failed to dislodge the British occupying force. Washington's army spent an uncomfortable winter at VALLEY FORGE, Pennsylvania. During the occupation, which lasted until June 18 1778, many Philadelphians traded and fraternized with the British.

Philippines, US occupation of. At the conclusion of the SPANISH-AMERICAN WAR (1898) President McKINLEY decided that God intended the USA to administer the Philippines as a colony. The decision sparked an insurrection, led by Emilio Aguinaldo, which sought immediate independence. In 1896 Aguinaldo and Andres Bonifacio had launched a guerilla campaign against Spanish rule that was on the point of securing independence for the islands when the US entered the Spanish-American War. The US campaign against Aguinaldo's nationalists claimed the lives of 200,000 Filipinos and 4,000 US soldiers. Aguinaldo was captured on March 23 1901 and the insurrection declared suppressed on July 4 1902. Between 1901 and 1904 US Governor General William Howard TAFT drew up a constitution for the islands, and purchased, from the Vatican, 390,000 acres (160,000 ha) of church land, which was then distributed to peasants on easy terms. At the same time, the Americans left most of the power in the hands of the Filipino estate-owning elite, eschewing the creation of a large colonial bureaucracy. Taft promised Filipinos independence when stable government was in place, a position that the USA reconfirmed in 1916 and 1934. The islanders achieved independence on July 4 1946.

Pickering, Timothy (1745–1829), FEDERALIST politician who, on May 12 1800, became the first and only US secretary of state to be dismissed from office. The pretext for this extraordinary action was President John ADAMS's conviction that Pickering was plotting against his re-election.

Pickering was a staunch Federalist from Massachusetts. He was brought into the cabinet, first as secretary of war but soon after as secretary of state, by George WASHINGTON in 1795. Washington's successor Adams, who was also a Federalist, kept Pickering in place, but the two men fell out in the aftermath of the XYZ AFFAIR and the ensuing QUASI-WAR with France. Pickering criticized Adams's relatively cautious approach to the international crisis, and advocated a bellicose anti-French policy. After his dismissal, Pickering was elected to the US Senate. He was a leading critic of the JEFFERSON administration, and took part in Federalist plots to establish a separate New England confederacy, culminating in the disastrous HARTFORD CONVENTION.

Pierce, Franklin (1804–69), Democratic statesman and 14th president of the USA (1853–7). Pierce was a native of New Hampshire and a lawyer by training. His rise to power was meteoric. He became speaker of the New Hampshire Assembly at the age of 27, a member of the US House of Representatives at 29 and a US senator at 32. In 1842 he resigned his Senate seat to resume his legal practice. In 1846 he enlisted for service in the MEXICAN WAR as a private, but within a year he was a brigadier general.

A compromise choice as the DEMOCRATIC PARTY's nominee in the 1852 presidential election, Pierce trounced the WHIG candidate, his former commander Winfield SCOTT. Pierce served as president from March 4 1853 to March 3 1857. He believed that slavery enjoyed protection under the Constitution, and that southern fears that northerners might try to force the south to give up its 'peculiar institution' had some justification. However, in his Senate career Pierce had supported the right of abolitionists to make their case against slavery. During his presidency, his role in the OSTEND MANIFESTO affair and his acceptance of the KANSAS–NEBRASKA ACT led disillusioned northern Democrats to dub Pierce a proslavery DOUGHFACE. Following his maladroit handling of the BLEEDING KANSAS turmoil, the Democratic Party refused to consider

him for renomination. In 1863 Pierce was branded a traitor to the Union for criticizing the CIVIL WAR as 'fruitless'.

Pike, Zebulon Montgomery (1779–1813), US Army officer who led two exploratory expeditions through lands acquired in the LOUISIANA PURCHASE. The first (1805–6) traveled to the headwaters of the Mississippi without finding its source. His second expedition (1806–7) explored the Arkansas and Red river systems, before being detained by Spanish authorities in the Rio Grande valley. Pike found, but did not climb, Pikes Peak, Colorado. At the outset of the WAR OF 1812 Pike was commissioned a brigadier general. He led the US force that captured FORT TORONTO, but was killed when the town's powder magazine exploded.

Pinchot, Gifford (1865–1946), government official and conservationist. As head of the US Forestry Service (1898–1910), Pinchot forced the first sustained discussion within federal government of environmental policy. Pinchot, supported by President Theodore ROOSEVELT, sought to prevent wasteful and destructive exploitation of forests, mineral deposits and water sources. In 1908 he founded the National Conservation Commission to make an inventory of what remained of the USA's natural resources; in the same year Roosevelt hosted a White House conference to discuss conservation. In 1910 President TAFT sacked him for suggesting, falsely, that Secretary of the Interior Richard Ballinger (1858–1922) was conspiring with coal companies to plunder Alaskan forests. The furore that surrounded this decision testified to Pinchot's success in raising the political profile of environmental issues.

Pinckney's treaty, *see* SAN LORENZO, TREATY OF.

Pinkerton, Allan (1819–84), founder of a US private detective and security agency. Born in Glasgow, Scotland, Pinkerton emigrated to the USA in 1842. He settled in Kane County, on the outskirts of Chicago, and established a cooper's shop. In 1843 he captured a gang of counterfeiters, and in 1846 was appointed sheriff of Kane County. He established the Pinkerton National Detective Agency in 1850. In February 1861 Pinkerton thwarted an attempt to assassinate Abraham LINCOLN as he traveled to Washington to take up the presidency. During the CIVIL WAR he gathered military information on behalf of the Union. After the war Pinkerton's agency became notorious in radical circles for spying on trade unions and providing protection for strikebreakers. Pinkerton agents were involved in breaking the MOLLY MAGUIRES, helping to smash the RAIL STRIKE OF 1877, and protecting strike breakers during the violent HOMESTEAD STEEL STRIKE. Pinkerton ignored criticism of his anti-union views, arguing that he was protecting the honest working man from duplicitous agitators.

Platt Amendments, series of amendments to Cuba's constitution that made it a US dependency in all but name. At the conclusion of the SPANISH-AMERICAN WAR (1898) Cuba remained under US control. Republican Senator Orville Platt (1827–1905) of Connecticut drafted a series of amendments to Cuba's proposed constitution whose adoption became a condition for US withdrawal. Cuba was prevented from contracting excessive public debt, its capacity to make foreign alliances was limited, and the USA retained the right to intervene in Cuba when it believed good government was threatened. The amendments were incorporated within the Cuban constitution on June 12 1901.

Plessy vs. Ferguson (May 18 1896), US Supreme Court ruling that overturned a challenge to a Louisiana law stipulating that seating in railroad carriages should be racially segregated. The challenge had been brought by a wealthy mulatto, Homer Plessy (1863–1925). With Justice John HARLAN dissenting, the Court affirmed that 'separate but equal' accommodation did not deprive African-Americans of the right to equal protection under the laws guaranteed by the FOURTEENTH AMENDMENT. The justices dismissed Plessy's sensitivity to racial stigmatization as misplaced. This ruling protected the status of racial segregation in almost all areas of southern life. Its most damaging implication was made explicit in a subsequent ruling, Cumming vs. Board of Education (1899), establishing the constitutionality of segregated public school systems. A case arising from the resultant underfunding of black school systems (BROWN VS. BOARD OF EDUCATION) provided the pretext on which, in 1954, the Supreme Court finally overturned the Plessy verdict.

pocket veto, device by which a president puts a congressional bill 'in his pocket' (i.e. delays a decision to sign or veto it) until a congressional term expires, and so renders the legislation inoperative. Presidents find this procedure useful because Congress retains the power to override a formal presidential veto.

Polk, James K(nox) (1795–1849), Democratic statesman, and 11th president of the USA (1845–9), who oversaw a massive expansion in the territory of the USA.

Polk was born in North Carolina, but grew up in Tennessee. He had been a stalwart of the Jacksonian wing of the DEMOCRATIC PARTY in Congress (representative 1825–39, House Speaker 1835–9), but he was a 'dark-horse' candidate for the Democrats' presidential nomination in 1844. WHIGS jibed, 'Who is Polk?'

Polk served as president from March 4 1845 to March 4 1849. He proved to be an unashamed expansionist. Pledging not to seek re-election, he pursued the annexation of TEXAS and the acquisition of CALIFORNIA by purchase (the SLIDELL MISSION) or by force. The outbreak of the MEXICAN WAR allowed Polk to conclude a compromise resolution of the OREGON BORDER CRISIS. Polk meddled in military appointments and in negotiations leading to the treaty of

GUADALUPE-HIDALGO (1848) that ended the Mexican War. His chief domestic initiative was the INDEPENDENT TREASURY ACT (1846). Abraham LINCOLN, an opponent of the Mexican War, suspected Polk was 'deeply conscious of being in the wrong' and believed him to be 'a bewildered, confounded and miserably perplexed man'. But Polk had no regrets about presiding over a 50% expansion of US territory which, in his words, extended 'the dominions of peace' over 'increasing millions'.

Pontiac's War (1763–4), war in which a confederation of Native American nations, led by the Ottawa chief Pontiac (*c.* 1720–69), attacked British posts in lands south of the Great Lakes. Despite the seizure of a number of forts, a strong Anglo-American counterattack destroyed the confederacy. However, the war alerted British ministers to the difficulty of controlling that territory acquired from France in the treaty of PARIS (1763). Concluding that it would cost £10,000 per annum to garrison the NORTHWEST TERRITORY adequately, the British government decided to limit western settlement via the PROCLAMATION OF 1763, and to force the American colonies to contribute revenue for their defense via the SUGAR ACT and the STAMP ACT.

Poole, Elijah, *see* NATION OF ISLAM.

popular vote, term referring to votes cast by US citizens in presidential elections. A majority in the popular vote does not always translate into a majority in the electoral vote (the vote in the ELECTORAL COLLEGE). This is because representation in the electoral college is determined by a state's population. A presidential candidate could, by winning enough large states, gain election despite polling a minority of the total number of votes cast by the electorate nationwide. For example, Benjamin HARRISON became president in the 1888 election on a minority share of the popular vote.

Populism, term that identifies a body of political and economic ideas promulgated with great conviction by western, midwestern, and southern 'hayseed socialists' in the final third of the 19th century. The central tenets of this ideology were shaped by a veneration of manual labor strongly rooted in Protestant theology and by hostility to all forms of capitalism that might bar an independent working man from enjoying the fruits of his endeavors. Populists organized cooperatives and campaigned for the creation of a progressive INCOME TAX, the regulation of rail-freight and warehousing fees, and for a FREE SILVER fiscal policy. Historians have traced the antecedents of this outlook to JEFFERSONIAN DEMOCRACY, Andrew JACKSON's battle against the BANK OF THE UNITED STATES, and the FREE-SOIL IDEOLOGY of the 1840s.

The problems afflicting US farmers in the final third of the 19th century stemmed from the relationship between production and market prices. Farmers were encouraged to expand production during and after the CIVIL WAR. Although farmers boosted output, many of them took on high levels of debt or entered into potentially punitive CROP-LIEN and SHARECROPPING arrangements to do so. From the 1870s onwards the US government enacted deflationary policies designed to retire the GREENBACK dollars printed during the Civil War. As the market value of corn, wheat and cotton fell, farmers were caught in a credit squeeze. A cotton farmer who borrowed $1000 on a 25-year mortgage in 1868 found that by 1888 he had to produce twice as much cotton to maintain his repayments as he did at the start of the loan. He could not afford to hold back his crop from market until prices rose. Meanwhile, thanks to deflation, rail companies, warehousers and the banks made enormous windfall profits from the enhanced value of the dollars they received from farmers. Populists viewed the contrast between the poverty of the agricultural sector and the prosperity of the service sector in moral terms. 'Sockless' Jerry Simpson

(1842–1905) told farmers that the USA was witnessing a struggle between 'the robbers and the robbed'. North Carolina Populist Leonidas Polk argued that there was 'a screw loose' in the US economy. Populists emphatically rejected the laissez-faire values of SOCIAL DARWINISM. For Populists, throwing a hard-working farmer off his land simply for failing to meet an unrealistic burden of debt could never be justified by reference to 'market forces'.

The first organized campaigns to secure redress for hard-pressed farmers were mounted by the GRANGER MOVEMENT of the 1870s. Grangers combined self-help with political activism. Through the movement, farmers attempted to create cooperatives capable of buying the entire output of a particular region and selling it on without recourse to a middleman, thereby boosting the individual farmer's return on his crop. Some Grangers also attempted to establish cooperatively owned grain silos, banks and insurance companies. These efforts at self-help were hampered by the difficulty of organizing individualistic farmers in isolated rural locations, by a shortage of start-up capital and by a lack of expertise. The Granger movement proved more successful as a lobbying organization. In 1871 the state of Illinois established a commission to regulate rail-freight and warehouse fees. Others midwestern states copied the initiative. The constitutionality of these so-called GRANGER LAWS was upheld by the US Supreme Court in MUNN VS. ILLINOIS (1877). However, subsequent Supreme Court rulings, beginning with WABASH, ST LOUIS AND PACIFIC RAILROAD COMPANY VS. ILLINOIS (1886), severely restricted a state's ability to regulate corporations.

The Alliance movement of the 1880s built on foundations established by the Grangers. Three separate farmers' alliances were organized in the period. The Farmers' Alliance and Industrial Union, which originated in Texas, organized the white farmers

of southern states. A separate Colored Alliance organized African-American sharecroppers in the south. A weaker National Farmers' Alliance campaigned on behalf of midwesterners. By 1890 the three alliances claimed a combined membership exceeding 2 million farmers. The main demand of the Alliance movement was the creation of a federal sub-treasury program. This refinement of cooperative ideas espoused by the Grangers asked the federal government to establish warehouses in rural locations. After harvest farmers would deposit their crop in these warehouses and receive in return a treasury note equivalent to 80% of the value of their crop. Farmers could use the note to pay their mortgage. Freed from the necessity to sell their crop as soon as it was harvested, farmers could hold back commodities from the market, thereby raising crop prices and providing them with the means to pay back the treasury advance.

Alliancemen regarded this program as self-evidently just, and explained the failure of federal authorities to enact it by reference to a dark conspiracy to corrupt government organized by bankers, railroad companies and Wall Street. The rhetoric of the PEOPLE'S PARTY – formed in St Louis in 1892 to push the agenda of the Alliance movement – reflected the conviction that the USA was approaching a defining crisis. On July 4 1892 Ignatius Donnelly (1831–1901) read a 'Declaration of Union and Industrial Independence' to delegates attending the first national convention of the People's Party in Omaha, Nebraska. Donnelly told the delegates, 'We meet in the midst of a nation brought to the verge of moral, political, and material ruin.' He pledged that the party would restore government to the hands of the 'plain people' with whom it originated. The OMAHA PLATFORM, on which the party's presidential candidate James B. WEAVER campaigned in 1892, called for the national ownership of railroads and telegraph companies, immediate implementation of the sub-treasury program, a progressive income tax, the SECRET BALLOT and the direct election of US senators. It also contained planks designed to appeal to urban workers, for example a call for federal legislation to establish an eight-hour day. In the south, Populist leader Tom WATSON asked farmers to set aside racial prejudice, telling his audiences, 'You are kept apart that you may be separately fleeced of your earnings.' (Watson later repudiated this egalitarian rhetoric.) Weaver polled over 1 million votes in the presidential election of 1892 and, by carrying the states of Kansas, Colorado, Idaho and Nevada, gained 22 ELECTORAL COLLEGE votes.

These gains were dissipated by a combination of manipulation, miscalculation and intellectual confusion. White southern Populists felt a loyalty to the DEMOCRATIC PARTY that was rooted in memories of RECONSTRUCTION. Since the 1870s they had exerted considerable influence on the southern wing of the Democratic party and, following the failure of Weaver's campaign, many calculated that their grievances would be more likely to be redressed if they worked with local Democratic leaders. At the same time, between 1892 and 1896 southern Democratic leaders made determined efforts to woo the region's white Populists back into the party fold. These efforts included exaggerated descriptions of the realignment of race relations that might follow enactment of the Populist program. When the national Democratic Party chose the Nebraskan William Jennings BRYAN as its nominee in the presidential election of 1896, midwesterners joined southerners in persuading the People's Party to run a 'fusion' ticket. The party endorsed Bryan for president and Tom Watson for vice president. Bryan's CROSS OF GOLD speech brought the SILVER–GOLD CONTROVERSY to boiling point, and the distinctive agenda of the People's Party was drowned out in the ensuing furore. The integrity of the People's Party was compromised by its collaboration with an established party, while Bryan's defeat suggested the impossibility of enacting the Populist agenda through the ballot box. Although the People's Party ran candidates in the presidential elections of 1900, 1904 and 1908, it never regained the strength it had enjoyed in the early 1890s.

Many of the demands of the Populist movement were subsequently met. The HEPBURN ACT of 1906, empowering the Interstate Commerce Commission to regulate rail-freight charges, received a particularly warm welcome from small farmers. The moral urgency of the movement resurfaced during the GREAT DEPRESSION, when it helped to shape the agricultural policies of the NEW DEAL.

Potsdam Conference (July 17–August 2 1945), summit meeting near Berlin involving Allied leaders Harry S TRUMAN, Winston Churchill and Joseph Stalin at the close of WORLD WAR II. During the conference Churchill lost the British general election, and from July 28 his seat at the talks was taken by the new prime minister, Clement Attlee. The Allies agreed to demand the unconditional surrender of Japan, and Truman informed Stalin that the USA was developing a 'new weapon of unusual destructive force' to accomplish this goal. However, the Allies fudged a number of issues relating to the reconstruction of postwar Europe, marking the beginning of the COLD WAR.

Powderly, Terrence V(incent) (1849–1924), trade-union leader who headed the KNIGHTS OF LABOR from 1879 to 1893. Powderly left school at 13 to work on the railroads. He became a machinist in 1866. He joined the Machinists and Blacksmiths National Union, becoming its president in 1872. He was initiated into the Knights of Labor in 1874, and became its Grand Master Workman (or leader) in 1879. Under Powderly the Knights dropped some of their secretive, quasi-Masonic practices. He encouraged the Knights to recruit Irish-American and African-American workers, although he also supported the exclusion of Chinese workers, and was an influential supporter of the CONTRACT LABOR ACT (1885). Although Powderly condemned the HAYMARKET RIOT, discouraged the Knights from mounting strikes, and abandoned POPULISM to support the REPUBLICAN PARTY, during the 1890s the Knights lost ground to the more 'respectable' AMERICAN FEDERATION OF LABOR. Powderly served as mayor of Scranton, Pennsylvania (1880–4), as commissioner general of immigration (1897–1902) and as chief information officer of the Bureau of Immigration (1907–21).

presidential elections. For the outcome of all presidential elections, *see* Appendix 2. Articles on particularly notable presidential elections will be found below.

presidential election of 1800. The peaceful resolution of this disputed election established the viability of the US Constitution, and inaugurated a period in which the DEMOCRATIC PARTY dominated national politics.

In an atmosphere of frenzied partisanship produced by the ALIEN AND SEDITION ACTS, Thomas JEFFERSON and Aaron BURR stood as Democrats and John ADAMS and Charles Cotesworth Pinckney (1746–1825) as FEDERALISTS. Jefferson, and most voters, regarded Burr as the Democrats' vice-presidential candidate. But at this time members of the ELECTORAL COLLEGE cast two votes (supposedly using one to identify a president and the other a vice president), and some electors distributed their votes with the sole intent of preventing Jefferson's election to the presidency. As a result Jefferson and Burr received 73 electoral votes each, with Adams gaining 65. The Constitution dictated that the House of Representatives resolve the impasse created by Jefferson's and Burr's equal showing in the electoral college. Each state's delegation was asked to cast a single vote on behalf of the candidate favored for the presidency by a majority of its members. Although Burr discouraged all attempts to promote him at Jefferson's expense, so evenly were state delegations divided that it took 36 ballots to declare Jefferson president and Burr his deputy. Alexander HAMILTON, a staunch FEDERALIST, was instrumental in persuading New York's delegation to break the deadlock by choosing his former cabinet sparring partner Jefferson over Burr. Congress subsequently formulated the TWELFTH AMENDMENT to clarify procedure in the electoral college.

presidential election of 1860. This election sparked SECESSION and the CIVIL WAR.

By 1860 the US political system was close to breaking point. Outraged southerners held the REPUBLICAN PARTY partly or wholly responsible for John BROWN's attempt to initiate an armed slave rebellion at HARPER'S FERRY. Northerners insisted that the DAVIS RESOLUTIONS (touted by DEMOCRATS as the only terms on which the south would remain within the Union) represented a total surrender to SLAVE POWER. Congressmen, as well as visitors to Congress, routinely carried guns.

Of the nation's major politicians, only the Democrat Stephen DOUGLAS believed that the crisis LINCOLN prophesied in the 'HOUSE DIVIDED' SPEECH could be dodged by a combination of gesture and legislation. But many southerners believed Douglas, author of the FREEPORT DOCTRINE, was a traitor who deserved, as an editorial put it, to 'perish on the gibbet of Democratic condemnation'. Southern delegates arrived at the Democrats' convention in Charleston, South Carolina, determined to block Douglas's nomination unless the party's platform endorsed federal protection for slavery in the territories. Deadlock ensued. A second convention meeting in Baltimore in June nominated Douglas, but only after uncompromising pro-slavery delegates, about a third of the total, had walked out.

These dissidents, adopting the title National Democrats, nominated Buchanan's vice president John C. BRECKINRIDGE on a platform offering cast-iron protection for slavery.

The Republicans relished the Democrats' difficulties, but realized that to exploit them they needed to carry nearly every 'free' state. Their convention, held in Chicago in May, nominated Lincoln, because he had been out of Congress during the 1850s and because he was thought more likely than William SEWARD to carry the midwest.

A fourth party, the Constitutional Unionists, nominated John Bell (1797–1869). Composed chiefly of elderly WHIGS and KNOW-NOTHINGS, this group sought to detach enough moderate support from Lincoln to produce deadlock in the ELECTORAL COLLEGE. It believed that if the election were decided in the House of Representatives some compromise could be cobbled together.

Lincoln grew a beard during the campaign, in deference to advice that it would lend him gravitas. He, Breckenridge and Bell said little. Douglas campaigned throughout the country, including, at great personal risk, the deep south. In New York State, where the electorate was concurrently balloted on a proposal to enfranchise African-Americans, Democrats urged voters to support Lincoln if they wanted to live 'cheek by jowl with a buck nigger'. But even race-baiting failed to place New York, or any other northern state, in Douglas's column. Lincoln won 39.9% of the POPULAR VOTE to Douglas's 29%, while Breckinridge received 18% and Bell 13%. Lincoln gained 180 ELECTORAL VOTES, Breckinridge 72, Bell 39 and Douglas just 12.

presidential election of 1864. Conducted while the CIVIL WAR hung in the balance, this election helped determine its outcome.

In a bid to attract support from WAR DEMOCRATS, the REPUBLICAN PARTY renamed itself the NATIONAL UNION PARTY. At their convention in June 1864, a southerner and former Democrat, Andrew JOHNSON, was brought onto the ticket as LINCOLN's running-mate. Republicans warned voters 'Don't swap horses in the middle of the stream.' But RADICAL REPUBLICAN impatience with Lincoln grew while GRANT's army remained stalled at PETERSBURG. The DEMOCRATIC PARTY, hoping to exploit public shock at the human cost of the war, opposition to the EMANCIPATION PROCLAMATION and unease over Lincoln's use of executive authority, nominated George B. McCLELLAN. The Democratic platform called for a cessation of hostilities. PEACE DEMOCRAT delegates accompanied this demand with a denunciation of 'four years of failure to restore the Union by the experiment of war'. Most northerners blamed the war on the Confederacy and saw an armistice as effectively rewarding southern aggression. Even though McClellan repudiated the Democrats' platform, Lincoln expected McClellan to win. So too did Confederate soldiers, and the prospect stiffened their resolve.

However, SHERMAN's capture of ATLANTA (September 1) changed the political landscape. Republicans rallied behind Lincoln. 'Floating' northern voters were alienated by poisonous Democratic propaganda suggesting that the Emancipation Proclamation's true design was to encourage 'Sambo' to 'nestle in the bosom' of every 'snow white' woman. Nineteen states enacted legislation to allow soldiers to vote from the field. Indiana, under Democratic control, did not, but SHERMAN and GRANT gave leave to soldiers from Indiana to allow them to vote. The military vote split 78%–22% for Lincoln, and was probably crucial to his victory in New York and Connecticut. McClellan came within 400,000 of Lincoln's popular vote total of 2,216,067, but was buried (212–21) in the ELECTORAL COLLEGE. In his second inaugural address Lincoln pledged to 'bind the nation's wounds – with malice toward none, and charity for all'. He was assassinated 41 days later.

presidential election of 1876. This disputed election nearly provoked a second civil war. Its resolution brought an end to RECONSTRUCTION.

The Democratic candidate Samuel J. Tilden (1814–86) outpolled Republican Rutherford B. HAYES by 250,000 in the POPULAR VOTE. Hayes even conceded defeat to Tilden. But Republicans in Florida, Louisiana, Oregon and South Carolina alleged voting irregularities and withheld some or all of their states' votes from the ELECTORAL COLLEGE. Tilden was left one electoral vote short of a majority, while Hayes needed every disputed vote to secure the presidency. Rank and file Democrats denounced Republican attempts to 'steal' the election and their slogan 'Tilden – or Blood' (which Tilden disavowed) suggested a willingness to use force to prevent Hayes from assuming the presidency.

To adjudicate the contested results and decide the election, Congress created a 15-man electoral commission, an equal number of whose members were drawn from the House, the Senate and the Supreme Court. When Associate Justice David DAVIS declined to serve on the commission, Associate Justice Joseph Bradley (1813–92), a GRANT appointee, was brought on instead and cast the vote that broke the partisan deadlock in Hayes's favor (8–7). Irate southern Democrats agreed to accept this outcome only because Hayes, in the COMPROMISE OF 1877, pledged to end RECONSTRUCTION. In 1887 the ELECTORAL COUNT ACT was passed in order to avoid a repetition of such electoral disputes.

presidential election of 1912. This election was unusual in that it was conducted by three candidates, all with strong national support, amid fears of imminent socialist revolution.

The fear of revolution was prompted by the rise of the INDUSTRIAL WORKERS OF THE WORLD (IWW or 'Wobblies') during the LAWRENCE TEXTILE STRIKE. Two of the candidates – Theodore ROOSEVELT for the PROGRESSIVE PARTY, and Democrat Woodrow WILSON – campaigned on anti-corporate, pro-labor platforms. The third candidate, the Republican, was the incumbent President William Howard TAFT.

It was former President Roosevelt's candidacy that gave the election its spice. In 1908 Roosevelt, then heading a Republican administration, had honored a pledge not to seek re-election. He made way for Taft, a hand-picked successor. But in 1910 Roosevelt began making speeches advocating a legislative package – including tougher regulation of big business, and federal social-welfare legislation – which he labeled the NEW NATIONALISM. Although irritated, Taft ignored this implicit criticism. On February 21 1912 Roosevelt announced 'My hat is in the ring' and began to campaign for the Republican nomination, explaining that his earlier pledge bound him only to renounce a third *consecutive* term. At an acrimonious Republican convention in Chicago, marred by fist-fights and walkouts, party bosses, operating from a podium protected by barbed wire, steamrollered delegates into nominating the incumbent President Taft on the first ballot.

The Democrats nominated Wilson on a platform offering voters a NEW FREEDOM – including lower tariffs, federal regulation of rail, telegraph and telephone companies, stricter public-health laws, and constitutional amendments to create a single-term presidency and establish an INCOME TAX. Meanwhile Roosevelt, contradicting reports that he had contracted a fatal illness while on an African safari with the statement 'I feel as strong as a bull moose', secured the nomination of the Progressive Party.

Roosevelt outpolled Taft, attracting 27% of the POPULAR VOTE and 88 votes in the ELECTORAL COLLEGE to Taft's 23% and 8 votes. But by splitting the Republican vote

Roosevelt ensured the election of Wilson. Wilson's share of the popular vote (42%) was lower than that achieved by William Jennings BRYAN in any of his unsuccessful bids in the three previous presidential elections. Yet Wilson won by a landslide in the electoral college, achieving 435 electoral votes.

presidential election of 1932. Held as the GREAT DEPRESSION approached its nadir, this election gave Franklin D. ROOSEVELT the mandate he needed to launch the NEW DEAL program.

On June 14 1932 the REPUBLICAN PARTY, meeting in Chicago, renominated the incumbent President Herbert HOOVER on their first ballot. Despite a last-ditch attempt to 'stop Roosevelt' (which played on his wealthy background and his disability), on June 27 the DEMOCRATIC PARTY convention (also held in Chicago) nominated Roosevelt on the fourth ballot. Roosevelt broke with tradition by accepting the nomination in person. He told delegates, 'I pledge myself to a new deal for the American people.' Other presidential candidates included Jacob S. Coxey, once leader of COXEY'S ARMY, nominated by the Farmer Labor Party; Norman THOMAS, nominated by the Socialist Labor Party; and William Z. Foster (1881–1961), nominated by the COMMUNIST PARTY. James W. Ford (1893–1957) of Alabama became the first African-American candidate in a presidential race when the Communist Party chose him as Foster's running-mate.

However, the election was dominated by Roosevelt and Hoover. Roosevelt chose as his campaign song 'Happy Days Are Here Again'. He promised relief to every constituency in the country, yet pledged to balance the budget. Hoover stressed the virtues of the RECONSTRUCTION FINANCE CORPORATION. He received a hostile reception in many cities, and was deserted by several prominent Republicans, among them Senator Robert La Follette Jr and Senator George NORRIS. In his final campaign speech Hoover predicted that grass would grow in the streets of a thousand towns and cities if Roosevelt won. Nonetheless Roosevelt took 57% of the POPULAR VOTE to Hoover's 40%, and 472 votes in the ELECTORAL COLLEGE to Hoover's 59. The only electorally significant state to buck the national trend was Pennsylvania, where Philadelphia was the only major city to back Hoover. Roosevelt's success in drawing votes from groups previously considered Republican marked the origins of the NEW DEAL COALITION.

presidential election of 1948. This election produced the most unexpected result in modern times, with the incumbent Democratic President Harry TRUMAN being returned to the presidency against all the predictions of the polls.

Truman was unpopular within the DEMOCRATIC PARTY because he allowed northern liberals – among them Hubert HUMPHREY – to write a civil rights plank into the party's platform. Thirty-five southern delegates walked out of the convention during Truman's acceptance speech, and in July these dissidents (dubbed DIXIECRATS) nominated Strom Thurmond (1903–) on a platform pledging a defense of racial segregation. Meanwhile left-wingers – alienated by Truman's failure to seek rapprochement with the Soviet Union, and his perceived use of the MARSHALL PLAN as a weapon in the COLD WAR – deserted the Democrats to join the Communist Party in supporting former Vice President Henry WALLACE, who was running as a Progressive. The REPUBLICAN PARTY nominated Thomas E. Dewey (1902–71) as its candidate.

Confident that in the wake of the NEW DEAL the American people were sick of policy initiatives, Dewey tried to run a 'statesmanlike' campaign, emphasizing his credentials to exercise stewardship and 'good government'. Truman was the more active campaigner. In blunt but folksy language that led a supporter in Seattle to enthuse 'Give 'em Hell, Harry', Truman defended the New Deal, called for a national health-insurance program and attacked the Republicans. Yet most pollsters expected left- and right-wing defections from Truman to secure Dewey's victory.

Thurmond and Wallace each polled over 1 million votes. Wallace drew enough votes from Truman in New York to hand that state to Dewey, and Thurmond gained 39 votes in the ELECTORAL COLLEGE by outpolling Truman in deep-south states. However, Dewey took just 45% of the POPULAR VOTE and 189 votes in the electoral college. Truman's 49% share of the popular vote gave him 303 votes in the electoral college, and the presidency. The day after the election Truman was photographed gleefully holding an early edition of the *Chicago Tribune*, emblazoned with the headline 'Dewey Defeats Truman', which had been printed immediately after Dewey carried New York but before Truman's victories in Ohio and California were known.

presidential election of 1960. This election produced the closest result in recent times, and established television as a major factor in electoral politics.

Despite the misgivings of the outgoing President EISENHOWER, the Republicans, meeting in Chicago, nominated Vice President Richard NIXON on the first ballot. The Democrats nominated John F. KENNEDY, only the second Catholic so honored by a major party. Both candidates pledged to intensify the COLD WAR, and blamed each other's party for communist 'advances' in Cuba and in Quemoy and Matsu (two small islands controlled by the nationalist Chinese that had been the subject of heavy bombardment by the mainland communists). Kennedy's campaign dealt with voter suspicion of his religion and of his comparative youth. Nixon fulfilled a promise to campaign in every state.

The candidates were neck and neck in the polls when, on September 26, they staged the first of four nationally televised debates. Nixon, recalling his 'CHECKERS' SPEECH, believed he understood television techniques and eschewed coaching and make-up. Although he performed creditably, he looked terrible and lost support. In the final stages of the campaign Kennedy won black votes by gesturing towards support for the civil rights campaigner Martin Luther KING. Kennedy's running-mate, Lyndon B. JOHNSON, courted crucial Hispanic voters in the southwest. On November 8, Kennedy took 49.7% of the POPULAR VOTE to Nixon's 49.5%. Kennedy's winning margin of just 118,574 gave him 303 votes in the ELECTORAL COLLEGE to Nixon's 219. *See also* RADIO AND TELEVISION.

presidential election of 1968. This election was notable for producing the highest tally of votes in the ELECTORAL COLLEGE ever gained by a third-party candidate, and for the rioting that accompanied the Democratic Party's nominating convention (August 26–30). The VIETNAM WAR, race relations and law and order were the dominant issues of the election.

The shock caused by the North Vietnamese TET OFFENSIVE and reports of the MY LAI MASSACRE convinced many voters that the USA was betraying its values in a war it could not win. Mainstream political leaders concluded that unequivocal support for war to the bitter end would lose votes. But fearful of being tagged as 'soft on communism', they struggled to define policies that would effect a speedy US withdrawal. On the domestic front, GREAT SOCIETY initiatives had been overshadowed by urban unrest and a white backlash against the CIVIL RIGHTS MOVEMENT.

The Republican Party nominated former Vice President Richard NIXON on the first ballot taken at their convention in Miami. Nixon claimed that he had a secret plan to end the war in Vietnam that would secure 'peace with honor'. The Republican platform promised action to restore law and order and to ease racial tensions, but provided few specifics. Seeking to attract the votes of moderate white southerners, Nixon chose the governor of Maryland, Spiro T. AGNEW, as his running-mate.

Renegade southern Democrat George WALLACE, the former governor of Alabama, ran under the banner of the American Independent Party. Governor Wallace had achieved national notoriety in 1963 when he stood in the doorway of the University of Alabama in an ultimately unsuccessful bid to prevent black students from enrolling. His running-mate was the former Air Force General Curtis LeMay (1906–90), who argued that Vietnam should be 'bombed back to the Stone Age'. The Wallace campaign received strong support from white voters in the deep south. But Wallace's opposition to the policy of BUSSING was also popular among white working-class voters in northern cities.

The search for a Democratic candidate was hindered by the fact that the incumbent President Lyndon B. JOHNSON had presided over the escalation of the Vietnam War. To the consternation of party managers, and the delight of many grass-roots activists, Senator Eugene MCCARTHY, running on an immediate-peace platform, challenged Johnson in the New Hamsphire primary and nearly won. His showing convinced Robert KENNEDY to break with Johnson and seek the nomination as a peace candidate. On March 31 1968 Johnson announced that he would not seek re-election, and his vice president Hubert HUMPHREY entered the race on a platform calling for a phased withdrawal from Vietnam. Robert Kennedy was assassinated on June 6 1968, leaving Humphrey, who possessed strong support in the trade-union movement, as the front-runner for the Democrats' nomination. Humphrey was duly chosen on the first ballot taken at the Democrats' convention in Chicago. Senator Edmund Muskie (1914–) of Maine was his running-mate.

However, a third of the delegates supported McCarthy, and tempers frayed as party managers resisted their attempts to bind Humphrey to an immediate-peace platform. Meanwhile 5000 antiwar demonstrators outside Convention Hall were attacked by police, sparking running battles broadcast on national television (see CHICAGO CONVENTION RIOTS). Although Humphrey and McCarthy eventually effected a reconciliation, and although a week before polling day Johnson announced a halt to the bombing of North Vietnam, the Democratic campaign never recovered from the events in Chicago. Humphrey received 42.7% of the POPULAR VOTE and 191 votes in the ELECTORAL COLLEGE. Nixon received 43.4% of the popular vote, bettering Humphrey's total by 510,000. But he gained 310 votes in the electoral college. Wallace, who carried five states in the deep south, gained 46 electoral votes, and took 13% of the popular vote.

presidential election of 1972. This was the first election held after ratification of the TWENTY-SIXTH AMENDMENT permitted 18-year-olds to vote. It produced a landslide victory for the incumbent President NIXON.

The Republicans renominated Nixon on the first ballot taken at their convention in Miami. The Democrats, still badly divided by their campaign in the PRESIDENTIAL ELECTION OF 1968, nominated Senator George MCGOVERN of South Dakota on their first ballot. McGovern was a long-standing opponent of the VIETNAM WAR, and the Democratic platform called for the 'immediate total withdrawal of all Americans from Southeast Asia'. The Democrats also pledged to enact controls on handguns, and to continue BUSSING. McGovern's first three choices as vice president declined the honor. McGovern eventually chose Senator Thomas Eagleton of Missouri, stood by him '1000%' when it emerged that Eagleton had undergone electric-shock treatment for depression, and then dumped him in favor of Sargent Shriver (1915–). McGovern's campaign never recovered from this debacle. He tried, and failed, to make a campaign issue out of the WATERGATE SCANDAL. His attack on Nixon's failure to end the war allowed Nixon to wrap himself in the American flag by claiming that he, unlike McGovern, would not 'cut and run' until American prisoners of war had been returned. McGovern carried the District of Columbia and just one state – Massachusetts. His total of 17 votes in the ELECTORAL COLLEGE was among the worst ever recorded by a major candidate. Nixon received 520 electoral votes, the third highest total ever.

presidential Reconstruction, term applied to the initial stages of RECONSTRUCTION. LINCOLN and his successor Andrew JOHNSON set lenient terms for the reintegration of former Confederate states into the Union. The MEMPHIS and NEW ORLEANS RIOTS heightened RADICAL REPUBLICAN opposition to this approach. With the creation of the JOINT COMMITTEE ON RECONSTRUCTION, direction of the policy passed to Congress, and the later, more radical phase of Reconstruction is referred to as CONGRESSIONAL RECONSTRUCTION.

Presley, Elvis (Aaron) (1935–77), extraordinary rock-and-roll performer, and a timeless symbol of teen rebellion and American excess. Presley was born in Tupelo, Mississippi, but raised in Memphis, Tennessee. He learnt to sing in a Pentecostal church choir, and in 1953 made a private recording for his mother that led to his 'discovery'. In 1954 Presley had a regional hit; by 1956 he was the bestselling recording artist in the world. Presley's success was rooted in his ability to fuse the white country-and-western style with black rhythm and blues. His stage act, denounced by moralists as sexually suggestive, provoked frenzied reactions from fans, especially young women, and announced the arrival of a distinctively rebellious teenage culture that eventually swept America and the world. For most of his career Elvis was managed by 'Colonel' Tom Parker (1909–97). Parker sought to make Presley into a mainstream figure, talking him into doing national service under the DRAFT and attempting to develop his movie career. Presley abandoned live shows during the 1960s, but in the 1970s developed a second career as a nightclub performer in Las Vegas. He grew increasingly dependent on drugs, and his last years were spent living in a narcotic haze as a virtual recluse in his Memphis mansion, Graceland.

primary elections, system through which voters choose candidates to contest state, federal and some local elections. The introduction of the primary system represented a victory for PROGRESSIVISM. Prior to the introduction of the system, political parties held state-wide conventions to choose candidates for election to state offices. Reformers believed that the convention system allowed party bosses and lobbyists to use bribery to secure undue influence. Democracy suffered, since in many states, receiving the nomination of one or other of the two main parties virtually guaranteed victory in a subsequent general election. Demand for primary elections originated in southern states during the era when a predominantly white electorate provided steadfast support to the Democratic party. In 1896, South Carolina introduced an 'indirect primary' for state-wide elections – namely a poll in which voters choose delegates to a party convention charged with making the final nomination of a candidate. (The numerous state primary elections which are currently a feature of the presidential election cycle are of this indirect type.) In 1903, the state of Wisconsin enacted a 'direct primary' – namely a preliminary election in which some or all of the state's registered voters determine a party's candidate in a subsequent general election. First used in state-wide elections, the system spread to encompass the selection of candidates in local and national races. Individual states determine who may vote in primary elections. In some states, only those voters registered as supporters of a particular party may participate in the selection of that party's candidate. In other states, primaries are 'open' to independents or voters registered under a different party affiliation. The primary system has two disadvantages: it requires voters to undergo an often cumbersome registration process and, by requiring candidates to contest two elections, favors those with the backing of party bosses and special interests.

Princeton, battle of (January 2–3 1777), engagement in New Jersey, one of the wiliest American operations of the REVOLUTIONARY WAR. When British forces reacted to George WASHINGTON's recapture of TRENTON by sending a column of 5200 troops to the town to 'bag the fox', Washington's army broke its camp at Trenton on the night of January 2–3 (leaving campfires burning to deceive the enemy), and marched northeast to attack the British column's rearguard and supply train in and around Princeton. Washington withdrew his army to Morristown, New Jersey, before the main body of British troops could reinforce its beleaguered rearguard.

Proclamation of 1763, proclamation made by George III on October 7 that prohibited settlement west of the Appalachians unless and until treaties with local Native American nations guaranteed settlers' security. The treaty of PARIS (February 1763) had vastly increased Britain's North American empire, and the outbreak of PONTIAC'S WAR brought home the potential cost of garrisoning newly acquired western lands. The 'proclamation line' was revised westward in 1768, but the policy angered those of the THIRTEEN COLONIES who claimed the exclusive right to govern and dispose of lands to their west.

Proclamation of Amnesty and Reconstruction (December 8 1863), announcement by President LINCOLN that inaugurated PRESIDENTIAL RECONSTRUCTION by offering a full pardon to Confederates (excluding high-ranking officers) willing to swear an oath of future loyalty and to pledge to accept the abolition of slavery. Any state in which 10% of those who had voted in 1860 had taken such a loyalty oath was to be permitted to establish a new state government, providing its constitution recognized abolition. RADICAL REPUBLICANS criticized the proclamation's leniency, its failure to enfranchise blacks, and the authorization it gave new state governments to enact temporary laws 'regulating' the 'laboring, landless and homeless class' of FREEDMEN. They sought through the WADE–DAVIS BILL to force former Confederates to sign an IRONCLAD OATH of loyalty to the Union. Nevertheless, the proclamation irrevocably tied reconstruction to abolition. In 1864 new governments were organized in accordance with the proclamation in Arkansas and Louisiana.

Proclamation of Reconstruction (May 29 1865), announcement by President JOHNSON that conferred amnesty and pardon, including a restoration of property rights (except in respect of slavery), on all former Confederates prepared to swear a loyalty oath and accept abolition. Leading Confederates and all owners of taxable property worth more than $20,000 were excluded from this offer. They had to apply for pardons.

Johnson claimed he was continuing LINCOLN's policies of RECONSTRUCTION, and increasing the influence of poorer whites in reconstructed states. However, he issued thousands of pardons to individual applicants. Over the next six weeks he appointed provisional governors to seven unreconstructed states. They were to call conventions to frame new state constitutions recognizing abolition and stipulating that the debt incurred by the secessionist government would not be honored by the 'reconstructed' regime. All those who had been pardoned, and who met antebellum (pre-war) suffrage requirements (which, of course, excluded blacks), could vote for delegates. Lincoln had embraced limited black suffrage, but Johnson believed 'white men alone must manage the South'. By December 1865 RADICAL REPUBLICAN congressmen were opposing Johnson's Reconstruction policies openly. This heralded the end of PRESIDENTIAL RECONSTRUCTION and the beginning of CONGRESSIONAL RECONSTRUCTION.

Progressive Party, political party established in 1912 and revived in 1919. During the PRESIDENTIAL ELECTION OF 1912 Theodore ROOSEVELT drew on his popularity with such groups as the National Progressive Republican League (founded in 1911 by Robert M. LA FOLLETTE) to run on a 'Progressive Party' ticket. The fledgling party collapsed with Roosevelt's defeat, but in 1919 a committee sought to revive it. They persuaded La Follette to accept nomination as the Progressive Party's presidential candidate in the 1924 election. The party's platform called for public ownership of rail lines and water resources, federal action against trusts, relief for farmers, legislation outlawing sex discrimination and child labor, and a relaxation of laws preventing strike action by trade unions. Supported by maverick Republicans and organized labor, La Follette secured 17% of the POPULAR VOTE, but in the ELECTORAL COLLEGE carried only one state – Wisconsin. The party collapsed following La Follette's death in 1925.

Progressivism, loose system of social and political ideas current in the USA between the DEPRESSION OF 1893 and the US entry into WORLD WAR I in 1917. During this period Americans from many walks of life espoused a belief that the social and political problems of the day could be tackled if people would simply embrace change and accept modern advice offered by experts. As the inventor Thomas EDISON put it: 'We've stumbled along for a while trying to run a new civilization in old ways, but we've got to start to make this world over.' So pervasive was the influence of this kind of thinking among middle-class and predominantly Protestant Americans that historians often refer to the period as the Progressive Era.

Two structural developments underpinned the Progressives' cultural ascendancy. The first was the gross inequality of wealth and living standards which were visible in turn-of-the-century America. The second was the expansion of higher education. In 1900 the richest 1% of America's population owned over 80% of America's wealth. Andrew CARNEGIE, by no means the most reviled American capitalist, earned at least $23 million a year, while 80% of the US population worked at subsistence levels. Between 1870 and 1910 the number of colleges and universities in the USA doubled and their enrollment rose from 52,000 in 1870 to 600,000 in 1920. Thousands of American families produced their first-ever college or high-school graduate in this period, reflecting in turn the fact that many young men and women were willing and able to break free from cultural constraints limiting their horizons to embrace new and exciting ideas. The typical Progressive's faith in progress was often strongly reinforced by his or her life experience. WOMEN'S SUFFRAGE and PROHIBITION seemed self-evidently desirable policies to Progressives in part because they attacked the traditional cultural values that so many Progressives had transcended.

Progressives were not opposed to industrial capitalism. However, stirred by the MUCKRAKERS' exposés of corporate collusion and corruption, Progressives supported action against TRUSTS and the industry bosses whom Theodore ROOSEVELT memorably described as 'malefactors of great wealth'. The mindless lifestyles of America's plutocrats also bothered Progressives. Thorstein Veblen's widely read *THEORY OF THE LEISURE CLASS* argued that 'conspicuous consumption' was wrong not so much because it was sinful but because it deflected attention away from the need for a rationally planned system of long-term national economic management. This belief in economic planning gave Progressive thought a passing resemblance to socialism. Both Theodore ROOSEVELT's NEW NATIONALISM and Woodrow WILSON's NEW FREEDOM programs, which were offered to the voters in the PRESIDENTIAL ELECTION OF 1912, called for the nationalization of key industries and resources as well as the tougher regulation of big business. However, Progressives were drawn to such policies not because they wished to redistribute wealth and power but because they believed planning would make capitalism more efficient.

Progressive attitudes towards poverty were equally finely balanced. The Progressive conscience was pricked by works such as Jacob Riis's (1849–1914) *How the Other Half Lives* (1890), which exposed the grim realities of life in US slums. Yet for most Progressives the lifestyles of the urban poor were intolerable because they deprived men and women of access to those blessings of civilization that would allow the working classes to live uplifting and productive lives. Jane ADDAMS, who devoted much of her life to the settlement-house movement, recognized that urban poverty flowed from economic exploitation. However, her work emphasized improving the living conditions and cultural standards of the working poor. Slum tenements troubled Progressives not because they represented an indictment of capitalism but because they demonstrated the failure of city government to manage growth by establishing minimum sanitation provision and sensible building codes. Although Theodore Roosevelt's New Nationalism called for the creation of a comprehensive system of social welfare to assist the poor, most Progressives remained suspicious that government welfare programs would encourage the work-shy and create dependency. Progressives, notably Florence KELLEY, campaigned valiantly for limits to be set on the hours worked by women

and children, but they made their case for such legislation by appealing to the enlightened self-interest of employers rather than to the injustices of the capitalist system.

Progressives were at their most strident and influential in local politics. Their response to the corruption and inefficiency that marred the government of most major US cities was to demand a greater role for non-partisan experts in the administration of city services. Progressives also favored competitive civil-service examinations, PRIMARY ELECTIONS and the SECRET BALLOT as a means of breaking the power of political machines like TAMMANY HALL. Some Progressives made no secret of their belief that democracy would have to give way to expertise if the ills they diagnosed were to be cured. As one Progressive put it: 'Ignorance should be excluded from control. City business should be carried on by trained experts selected on some other principle than popular suffrage.' Progressives could carry the urban poor with them in campaigns against criminally corrupt administrations, but crackdowns on prostitution, Sunday drinking or the distribution of jobs and favors by ward bosses enjoyed only limited support among the foreign-born masses whose morals the Progressives sought to protect and improve. For example, in 1901 the Tammy Hall machine recaptured New York city government from Progressive reformers by running on the slogan 'To Hell with Reform'. Progressive arguments in favor of policies such as Prohibition were often couched in patronizing or chauvinistic terms.

One of the distinguishing characteristics of the Progressive imagination was a desire to organize and associate, which stood in marked contrast to the individualism implicit in theories of SOCIAL DARWINISM. Progressives formed professional bodies such as the American Medical Association (founded in 1901 and claiming 70,000 members by 1910) and myriad civic groups, such as the Boy Scouts of America (1910), the National Housing Association (1910), the Rotary Club (1915) and the National Birth Control League (1915).

Nothing better illustrates the diversity of opinion that existed alongside this desire to organize and lobby than Progressive attitudes toward the changing nature of IMMIGRATION. In the 1890s immigrants from eastern and southern Europe poured into the USA. A member of the American Protective Association (formed in 1887) captured the dark side of the Progressive imagination when, after visiting a ship carrying immigrants, he reported, 'In every face there was something wrong – lips thick, mouth coarse, upper lip too long – or else whole face prognathous.' This wing of the Progressive movement lobbied for health and literacy tests to be applied to immigrants, and for the passage of restrictive legislation such as the EMERGENCY QUOTA ACT (1921) and the NATIONAL ORIGINS ACT (1924). Others trusted that a pluralistic America could achieve the 'orchestration of mankind' and joined the North American League for Immigrants to protect newcomers from 'unscrupulous bankers, steamship captains, and fellow countrymen'.

Perhaps the greatest legacy of the Progressive Era was the preservation of America's sites of natural beauty. The commitment of men such as Theodore Roosevelt and Gifford PINCHOT to the conservation movement was principled and far-sighted. Yet they proceeded knowing that the vast majority of the population would have neither the time nor the money to travel to the inspiring sites they were preserving for the nation. Progressives also successfully cleaned up local politics in dozens of major cities. They were less successful in enacting federal legislation. This was partly because, Louis BRANDEIS notwithstanding, the US Supreme Court was dominated by laissez-faire conservatives and partly because so much of the movement's energy was absorbed by campaigns to secure the EIGHTEENTH and NINETEENTH AMENDMENTS (introducing Prohibition and votes for women respectively).

Prohibition, the constitutional ban on the sale and manufacture of alcohol in the USA that was imposed by the EIGHTEENTH AMENDMENT in 1920, and ended by the TWENTY-FIRST AMENDMENT in 1933.

Support for Prohibition was rooted in three interrelated assumptions of enduring power in American cultural life. Firstly, American Christians held drunkenness to be sinful because it contravened divine teaching that man should strive for moderation in all things. Secondly, many Americans supported Prohibition out of the belief that it was the cause of social deprivation and injustice. For this reason, some activists linked support for Prohibition with support for other reforms, notably WOMEN'S SUFFRAGE, thought likely to aid third-party victims of alcohol abuse. Thirdly, Prohibition was popular as a means both of 'Americanizing' groups resisting the impress of WASP values, and of destroying the power of community figures such as saloonkeepers and ward bosses who might obstruct the passage of PROGRESSIVE reforms. The 'threat' to decency and democracy posed by the defiantly drunken urban worker, usually Irish, was a theme of REPUBLICAN PARTY campaign literature, and loomed large in the Progressive imagination.

Several temperance societies were founded in the USA before the Civil War. The largest was the American Temperance Society, which claimed 1 million members in the 1830s. These societies were primarily concerned with persuading individuals to renounce alcohol. However, after the state of Maine passed a law prohibiting the sale of alcohol in 1851, temperance advocates helped push through Prohibition statutes in 12 other states within four years.

The PROHIBITION PARTY, founded in 1869, campaigned for a constitutional amendment to enact a nationwide ban on the sale of alcohol. The WOMEN'S CHRISTIAN TEMPER-ANCE UNION (founded in 1873) campaigned at state level. During the 1890s Carrie NATION and the ANTI-SALOON LEAGUE OF AMERICA kept up the pressure on state legis-latures. By 1917 only three states allowed the unrestricted sale of liquor. Aside from laws banning Sunday drinking, states also passed measures closing saloons and allow-ing individual counties or towns to prohibit the sale of alcohol. Congress aided cam-paigns to change state and local law by passing the WEBB–KENYON ACT (1913) pro-hibiting the interstate shipment of liquor into 'dry' areas. It sent the Eighteenth Amendment (introducing Prohibition) to the states on December 18 1917. The amend-ment was declared ratified on January 29 1919, and the sale, transportation and com-mercial manufacture of alcohol became ille-gal in the USA on January 16 1920.

Enforcing Prohibition was harder than passing it. The VOLSTEAD ACT (1919) estab-lished a Prohibition Bureau within the Treasury Department. This was never ade-quately funded, and did little to stop boot-leg production or cross-border smuggling. With illicit supplies readily available, en-forcing a ban on the sale of alcohol proved impossible. Prohibition created big crime syndicates and introduced almost endemic corruption into police forces and city governments.

Whereas the Republicans supported Pro-hibition, the Democrats were divided. The 1924 Democratic convention took over 100 roll calls before finally choosing a 'dry' can-didate. The 1928 nominee, Al SMITH, was a 'wet' – an opponent of Prohibition. In 1931 the WICKERSHAM REPORT concluded that Prohibition was all but unenforceable. On February 20 1933 Congress sent the Twenty-first Amendment (repealing the Eighteenth Amendment) to the states. From April 6 1933 Americans could drink legally once more. The Twenty-first Amendment was ratified on December 5 1933, and from

that point responsibility for regulating the sale of liquor was returned to individual states. Many states continue to allow coun-ties and municipalities to ban the sale of alcohol.

Prohibition Party, political party founded in 1869 to campaign for federal legislation to enact PROHIBITION. The party's national focus complemented state campaigns mounted by the WOMEN'S CHRISTIAN TEMPER-ANCE UNION and the ANTI-SALOON LEAGUE OF AMERICA. In the early 1930s the party cam-paigned against repeal of the EIGHTEENTH AMENDMENT (which had introduced Prohi-bition in 1920).

Prophet, the (*c.* 1778–1837), name given to Tenskwatawa, brother of the SHAWNEE chief TECUMSEH, after he had correctly predicted a solar eclipse in 1806. With Tecumseh, Tenskwatawa founded a cultural revival movement among the Shawnee, which also attracted Native American nations further afield. In 1811 a vision in which Native American warriors appeared invulnerable to US settlers' bullets led the Prophet to fight and lose the battle of TIPPECANOE CREEK (1811). He lost credibility, while during THE WAR OF 1812 his brother conducted a last-ditch stand against US expansion.

Public Information, Committee on, *see* COMMITTEE ON PUBLIC INFORMATION.

Public Works Administration (PWA), job-creation agency set up under the NEW DEAL. The NATIONAL INDUSTRIAL RECOVERY ACT (June 16 1933) appropriated $3.3 bil-lion to fund job-creation programs, and the PWA distributed this money among state construction projects and hired jobless workers. However, the director of the PWA, Harold Ickes (1874–1952), insisted that pro-jects meet stringent planning and financ-ing standards. This limited the immediate impact of the PWA on unemployment totals, and prompted President Franklin D. ROOSEVELT to establish the CIVIL WORKS ADMINISTRATION and the WORKS PROGRESS ADMINISTRATION.

Pueblo peoples, collective term for various Native American farming peoples living in urbanized settlements (pueblos) in New Mexico, Arizona and southwestern Colorado. The HOPI and ZUNI are the southwest's chief pueblo dwellers. Although culturally similar, the Pueblo peoples speak a range of unrelated languages.

Puerto Rico, island of the West Indies. It is a self-governing commonwealth 'in association' with the USA. On December 10 1898 the treaty of PARIS, concluding the SPANISH-AMERICAN WAR, transferred Puerto Rico from Spain to the USA. Thereafter the USA attempted to retain control of the island while avoiding the appearance of imperialism.

The Foraker Act (April 12 1900) appointed a US governor, but stipulated that he consult a popularly elected assembly. The US Supreme Court ruled in Downes vs. Bidwell (1901) and Dorr vs. US (1904) that the USA was not obliged to extend citizenship or constitutional guarantees to islanders until Congress saw fit. The Jones Act (March 2 1917) made the island a US territory, gave Puerto Ricans US citizenship, permitted them to elect both houses of their legislature, and incorporated the BILL OF RIGHTS within Puerto Rican law.

In the 1950s Congress opposed calls to grant Puerto Rico independence, largely because these calls were accompanied by acts of terrorism within the USA. Since the 1960s Congress has also opposed calls to grant Puerto Rico statehood, largely due to fears that the island's poverty would drain the federal social-security budget. Puerto Rico is currently a US commonwealth, retaining the right to petition for independence – an option which islanders rejected in a non-binding plebiscite held on November 14 1993.

Pujo hearings, investigation by a subcommittee of the House Committee on Banking and Currency into the so-called 'MONEY TRUSTS' – the USA's banking and financial sectors. The subcommittee, chaired by Louisiana Democrat Arsene Pujo (1861–1939), began its investigation on April 27 1912. Its report, published on February 28 1913, detailed the consolidation of banking interests via interlocking directorates. This led President WILSON to support the creation of the FEDERAL RESERVE SYSTEM.

Pulitzer, Joseph (1847–1911), journalist and pioneering NEWSPAPER publisher. Pulitzer was born in Hungary and emigrated to the USA in 1864. He served briefly in the Union army before settling in St. Louis and working as a reporter on the German language *Westliche Post*. He served briefly in the Missouri legislature (1869) and qualified as a lawyer (1876) before realizing his destiny as a newspaper publisher. In 1878, Pulitzer acquired, and merged, St. Louis' *Post* and *Dispatch* to create the *St. Louis Post-Dispatch*. The new paper mixed gossip and crime with crusading coverage of local corruption stories and responsible coverage of national politics. It became the most influential paper in the midwest. In 1883, Pulitzer moved to New York and purchased the ailing daily *World*. He served one term in Congress as a Representative from New York (1885–6) but abandoned his political career to concentrate on running *World*. Overcoming antisemitism, Pulitzer built *World* into a mass-circulation daily whose only rivals were William Randolph HEARST's *New York Morning Journal* and *New York Evening Journal*. Like Hearst, Pulitzer employed YELLOW JOURNALISM to boost sales and was blamed for creating the hysteria that preceded US entry into the SPANISH-AMERICAN WAR. (The term 'yellow journalism' is thought to derive from a cartoon strip, 'The Yellow Kid,' published in *World*). Pulitzer later took *World* up-market and left bequests in his will to found the Columbia University Graduate School of Journalism and the Pulitzer Prizes.

Pullman strike, industrial action that brought the US rail network to a standstill in June 1894. However, in defeating the strike, employers perfected tactics that prevented nationwide industrial action until passage of the NORRIS–LA GUARDIA ACT in 1932.

During the DEPRESSION OF 1893, George Pullman imposed pay cuts ranging from 25 to 40% on workers at his Pullman Palace Car Company, but left rents and food prices in his company town (Pullman, Illinois) unaltered. In response, the AMERICAN RAILWAY UNION (ARU) imposed a nationwide boycott on any train hauling a Pullman car. When workers were fired for honoring the boycott, the union called a nationwide strike. Owners responded by attaching mail cars to trains containing Pullman coaches, and then appealing to the CLEVELAND administration to use the SHERMAN ANTITRUST ACT to issue injunctions preventing unions from interfering with the free movement of the hybrid 'mail trains'. President CLEVELAND sided with the employers, and authorized the use of federal troops and militiamen to enforce the injunctions. Eugene DEBS (president of the ARU) was arrested for violating an injunction, and, in July 1894, 37 unionists were shot dead in two pitched battles between strikers and troops in Chicago. The US Supreme Court ruling IN RE DEBS upheld the use of such injunctions in industrial disputes.

Pure Food and Drug Act (June 30 1906), legislation that prohibited the interstate shipment of adulterated, unsafe or mislabeled food, drugs or alcoholic beverages. President Theodore ROOSEVELT urged Congress to pass the act in response to the furore created by Upton Sinclair's 'muckraking' novel *The Jungle* (see MUCKRAKERS).

PWA, *see* PUBLIC WORKS ADMINISTRATION.

Q

Quantrill's raiders, pro-Confederate guerrilla band raised by William Clarke Quantrill (1837–65) during the CIVIL WAR. Quantrill himself was brought up in Ohio, owned no slaves, and disliked all blacks. His 'raiders' comprised around 150 men, included Frank and Jesse James. On August 11 1862 this force seized and pillaged Independence, Missouri, an action that secured a Confederate Army commission for Quantrill. In 1863 Union officials arrested 14 western Missouri women suspected of aiding Quantrill, and subsequently 5 of the detainees died when their jail collapsed. This accident drove Quantrill to psychopathic rage. On August 21 1863 his gang occupied and burned Lawrence, Kansas, and murdered 182 civilians. At Baxter Springs, Kansas, Quantrill's raiders turned on pursuing Union cavalry, killing and mutilating 65 soldiers. Driven into hiding, Quantrill undertook a clandestine mission to assassinate LINCOLN, but was shot dead by Kentucky militiamen before he reached Washington.

Quartering Acts (1765, 1774), two legislative measures passed by the British Parliament.

(1) By the terms of the first act (May 15 1765), in the five colonies where troops were garrisoned in settled areas, colonial assemblies were required to make appropriations to provide firewood, some foodstuffs, and bedding for their support. Assemblies, especially New York's, argued that Parliament could not force them to levy taxes on their constituents. New York's assembly made necessary appropriations only on threat of suspension. Parliament let the act expire in 1768.

(2) The second act (June 2 1774) was regarded by Americans as an INTOLERABLE ACT, because it gave colonial governors the power to requisition unoccupied houses, barns and other buildings to shelter troops, even in localities where local government opposed quartering.

Quasi-War (1797–1800), period in which war between the USA and France seemed imminent. The FRANCO-AMERICAN ALLIANCE (1778) had bound the USA to aid France in a war with Britain, but Washington's NEUTRALITY PROCLAMATION (1793) withheld US aid from France during the French Revolutionary Wars. Following JAY'S TREATY (1794) and the XYZ AFFAIR (1797), relations between the USA and France deteriorated to the point where many FEDERALISTS called for war with France. President ADAMS took defensive measures, but refused to make a series of engagements between French and US ships the pretext for war. Negotiations concluded in 1800 ended the Quasi-War.

Quayle, (James) Dan(forth) (1947–), Republican statesman and vice president of the USA (1989–93) under George BUSH.

Bush's decision to select Quayle as his running-mate in the 1988 presidential election astonished political observers. Quayle had been born to affluence, pulled strings to avoid active service during the Vietnam War, and seamlessly created a political career that saw him serve two terms in the US House (1976–80) as the representative of Indiana's Fourth District, and two terms as one of Indiana's US senators (1980–9). He had an impeccably conservative voting record, but a reputation within Congress as a political lightweight. During a debate between the vice-presidential nominees on October 5 1988, Quayle attempted to rebut criticism of his inexperience by comparing himself to John F. KENNEDY. This drew a stinging riposte from Democratic vice-presidential nominee Lloyd Bentsen: 'I knew Jack Kennedy – let me tell you, you're no Jack Kennedy.' Gaffes such as this, and his well-publicized inability to spell 'potato', led Bush to keep Quayle well 'out of the loop' during his presidency. Following Bush's defeat in the presidential election of 1992, Quayle faded into relative obscurity. He sought, unsuccessfully, the Republican Party's nomination for the presidential election of 2000.

Quebec, US campaign to capture (September–December 1775), ambitious invasion of Canada at the outbreak of the REVOLUTIONARY WAR by New Englanders alarmed by the passage of the QUEBEC ACT (1774).

Starting from FORT TICONDEROGA, a column of 1000 US troops, commanded by Brigadier General Richard Montgomery (1738–75), marched on Quebec via Lake Champlain and the St Lawrence. They captured Montreal on November 13 1775. On December 3 Montgomery, with 300 men, linked up with a force of 650 militiamen, commanded by Benedict ARNOLD, which reached the city of Quebec after an arduous trek through the Maine wilderness. At 5 a.m. on December 31, with the bulk of their force bent on returning home at midnight, Montgomery and Arnold launched a hopeless assault on the citadel. In blizzard conditions, Montgomery and 100 militiamen were killed, while 300 were taken prisoner. Arnold, wounded in the assault, ordered a siege, but remaining American troops were driven off in the spring.

Quebec Act (June 22 1774), legislation passed by the British Parliament designed to settle the boundaries and government of Britain's Canadian possessions acquired from France in the treaty of PARIS (1763). Americans regarded this measure as one of the INTOLERABLE ACTS. The new territory of Quebec stretched south and west to the Ohio and Mississippi rivers, thus threatening land claims made by the THIRTEEN COLONIES in the NORTHWEST TERRITORY. Quebec's government had no legislature, and its legal system limited access to trial by jury. Americans feared 'reorganization' along similar lines in their colonies. The act guaranteed the rights of Catholics, provoking a bigoted response in New York and New England.

Quebec Conferences (1943, 1944), two summit meetings during WORLD WAR II between President Franklin D. ROOSEVELT and British prime minister Winston Churchill. During the first (August 11–24 1943) they agreed to launch the D-DAY LANDINGS on May 1 1944, and to supplement these with an invasion of southern France. At their second meeting (September 11–16 1944) they discussed the occupation of postwar Germany and Japan. The two leaders tentatively agreed to a plan suggested by Secretary of the Treasury Henry Morgenthau (1891–1967) that Germany should be permanently stripped of its industry and reduced to a pastoral economy. This idea was subsequently abandoned, although the Soviets dismantled and exported most of the industrial plant in their occupation sector.

Quids, bloc of Democrats led by John Randolph (1773–1833) of Virginia. Fearful of the corrupting effects of power, the Quids employed a STRICT CONSTRUCTIONIST reading of the Constitution during JEFFERSON and MADISON's administrations to oppose measures such as the LOUISIANA PURCHASE. Some observers conferred a third-party status on Randolph's faction by identifying it through the Latin phrase *tertium quid* (literally 'third thing').

Quok Walker case (1781–3), case in which the state Superior Court's verdict established the de facto ABOLITION of slavery in Massachusetts. In April 1781, Quok Walker, a 28-year-old slave, ran away from his master, Worcester County farmer Robert Jennison, and sought refuge with a neighboring farmer, John Caldwell. Ten days later Jennison attempted to remove Walker from Caldwell's farm, beating Walker in the process.

Jennison sued Caldwell for encouraging Walker to run away. Walker sued Jennison for assault. In 1783 the Superior Court dismissed Jennison's suit against Caldwell, and upheld Walker's suit against Jennison. It based its verdict on the state constitution's declaration that 'all men are created free and equal'.

R

RA, *see* RESETTLEMENT ADMINISTRATION.

Radical Republicans, sizeable minority of REPUBLICAN PARTY congressmen who, throughout the CIVIL WAR and RECONSTRUCTION, pushed for tough treatment of the Confederacy and vigorous federal action to extend and safeguard the civil rights of former slaves.

Senator Benjamin Wade (1800–78) of Ohio and Representative Thaddeus STEVENS of Pennsylvania were the Radicals' most influential spokesmen. The WADE–DAVIS BILL, the JOINT COMMITTEE ON RECONSTRUCTION, and the FOURTEENTH AMENDMENT passed Congress as a result of Radical pressure. Radicals also claimed some credit for Lincoln's EMANCIPATION PROCLAMATION (1863) and the THIRTEENTH AMENDMENT. Congressional elections in 1866 produced a Republican majority in both houses of Congress. For the next six years Radicals set the agenda of Reconstruction, forcing impeachment proceedings against President Andrew JOHNSON (who they thought was too lenient toward the south) and shepherding the CIVIL RIGHTS ACT OF 1866, the RECONSTRUCTION ACTS, the FIFTEENTH AMENDMENT and the ENFORCEMENT ACTS through Congress. The domination of Reconstruction policy by the Radicals during this period is often referred to as CONGRESSIONAL RECONSTRUCTION.

Many textbooks continue to portray the Radical Republicans as being motivated by a mixture of hatred for the south and a corrupt desire to assist big business in establishing the economic superiority of the north and west. This view suggests the Radicals were mischief-makers whose cynical appeals to principle were responsible for both the failure of Reconstruction and a legacy of racial hatred in America. It is true that among the arguments that the Radicals employed to justify their commitment to black suffrage in the south, was a desire to punish southern whites. It is also true that the Radicals feared that a resurgence of the DEMOCRATIC PARTY would threaten protection for northern industry inherent in Republican TARIFF policy. Nevertheless, most Radicals genuinely believed that enfranchising African-Americans and protecting their civil rights would be sufficient to bring about an equality between the races that it was America's duty to achieve. Quite simply, at the time no other group of white Americans was prepared even to contemplate racial equality.

radio and television. The history of the 20th century might have been profoundly different had broadcast media not been invented or had they proven unpopular. Of the two media, radio was the most immediately influential.

On Christmas Eve 1906, Reginald Fessenden (1866–1932), the inventor of amplitude modulation (AM), transmitted a

337

program of speech and music from Brant's Rock, Massachusetts, in what was probably the USA's first radio broadcast. From 1907, Lee De Forest (1873–1961), the 'Father of American Radio,' patented a succession of technical innovations and made increasingly sophisticated experimental broadcasts from his home in New York. In 1912, Congress passed a Radio Act, requiring operators to obtain a license from the Department of Commerce and Labor (after 1913 the Department of Commerce) and providing for the orderly assignment of wave lengths. During World War I, the US Navy imposed restrictions on broadcasters in the interests of national security.

Interest in radio assumed the proportions of a mania in post-war America. Newspapers offered regular columns advising Americans on how to construct their own receiving sets (and transmitters). Meanwhile, broadcasters greatly expanded their range of programming. In 1920 WWJ of Detroit and KDKA of Pittsburgh, the nation's first commercial stations, broadcast presidential election returns. In 1921, WJZ of Newark, New Jersey, broadcast commentary on BASEBALL's World Series. In the same year, KYW of Chicago began broadcasting performances of opera and the Rev. Dr Van Etten allowed transmission of services at the Calvary Church, Pittsburgh. The interment of the Unknown Soldier at Arlington National Cemetery in 1921 was carried on radio, so too was the heavyweight title fight between Jack Dempsey and Georges Carpentier. The first news commentary was broadcast in 1921 and the first radio drama in 1922. In 1922, the USA possessed 30 commercial radio stations, by 1923, 556 and by 1927, the year in which Philco marketed the first car radio, 681 radio stations broadcast in the USA and Americans spent $426 million on radio sets. When Calvin COOLIDGE was persuaded to make an eve-of-election address in 1924, he was astonished to learn that over 20 million Americans

throughout the USA heard him. Political campaigning in the USA changed irrevocably from that moment.

Although municipalities and universities founded radio stations, most of the new stations were funded through advertising revenue. Stations side-stepped objections to the intrusive nature of direct advertising by persuading advertisers to sponsor particular shows. Funding through sponsorship encouraged the creation of networks of independent stations because advertisers wanted their sponsored shows to be heard by the largest possible audience. The first networking arrangement was a temporary agreement between WJZ of Newark, New Jersey and WGY of Schenectady, New York, to broadcast the 1922 World Series. The NBC network was formed in 1926 and was soon followed by CBS (1927) and the Mutual Broadcasting System (1934). Amos 'n' Andy, first broadcast in 1928, was the nation's syndicated radio serial. The networks gained even greater audience share, when, following a second Radio Act (1927) the US Congress awarded the best sections of the radio spectrum to those stations with the most powerful transmitters.

Broadcasts made by Franklin D. ROOSEVELT and Fr. Charles COUGHLIN during the 1930s demonstrated the political power of radio. In June 1934, Congress established the Federal Communications Commission to license radio stations and regulate their output. Although the FCC has limited powers of censorship, it is charged with ensuring 'balance' in the treatment of political candidates. (The FCC bars the broadcast media from expressing in their news coverage overtly partisan sympathies of a sort that remain permissible in the case of NEWSPAPER editorials.) The power of radio was further demonstrated by the panic sparked by Orson Welles' dramatization of H.G. Wells' *War of the Worlds* on the CBS network in 1938 and by popular interest in Edward R. Murrow's (1908–65) broadcasts from

Europe in the years preceding US entry into World War II. The US government created its own radio network, the Voice of America, in 1942.

During the second half of the 20th century, television became the USA's dominant broadcast medium. However, radio remained enormously influential in shaping tastes in music. Many Americans gained their first exposure to classical music through radio broadcasts. The fusion of styles brought together in rock and roll, and the sensational careers of stars such as Elvis PRESLEY, are directly attributable to radio's role in shaping tastes. Religious broadcasting also remains an important influence on American life. More recently 'talk radio' moderated by 'shock jocks' has reflected and further promoted a militant mood among many voters.

Television is now the most influential medium, broadcast or printed, in the USA. The first regularly scheduled commercial TV programs were broadcast by NBC from April 1939. By May 1940, 23 stations were operating. In 1961, when 90% of US households owned a TV set, the head of the FCC described the USA's television output as a 'vast wasteland', and the medium was being blamed for the degradation of seemingly every aspect of American life.

The history of television in the USA has been shaped by the fact that it came of age in an era of post-war prosperity and at the height of the COLD WAR. During World War II, the US government restricted both the manufacture of TV sets and the number of broadcasting licenses awarded. In 1952, the FCC announced that it would increase the number of broadcast licenses from 108 to 2051. Without postwar prosperity, which made TV sets affordable for working families, the new licenses would have been of limited worth. However, precisely because disposable income was rising, TV was of immediate interest to advertisers. Without consumerism, television would have been

different, without television, consumerism might never have been denounced as 'mindless.' The content of TV programming was also shaped by the attempt to draw a manichean distinction between 'American' and 'un-American' values that were a feature of domestic politics in Cold War America. Program-makers were well aware that coverage of Richard NIXON'S CHECKERS SPEECH (1952) and the downfall of Joseph McCARTHY during his investigation of the US Army (1954), had established the power of television to shape public perception and they had no wish to alienate politicians or advertisers by risking the promotion of un-American values. Therefore, popular TV shows such as 'Leave to Beaver' and 'Bonanza' celebrated and further promoted the cultural ascendancy of the white middle-class. Moreover, as the scandal over the rigging of TV quiz shows *Twenty-One* and *The $64,000 Question* (1958) made clear, even the makers of programs designed to pander to the lowest common denominator felt the need to engage in cultural engineering by rewarding contestants from deserving cultural backgrounds and defeating or excluding contestants from sectors of US society thought to be less securely integrated within the American system. The fact that the US House of Representatives held an investigation into the rigging of game shows in October 1959 is illustrative of an obsession with the influence of television that was an indirect cause of the vapidity of its content.

During the 1960s, TV coverage of events such as the debate between Richard Nixon and John F. KENNEDY prior to the PRESIDENTIAL ELECTION OF 1960; attacks on protestors during the BIRMINGHAM DESEGREGATION CAMPAIGN; Kennedy's assassination by Lee Harvey OSWALD; Martin Luther KING's 'I HAVE A DREAM' speech; the TET OFFENSIVE; and the culmination of the APOLLO PROGRAM shaped the mood of the times while fracturing the certainties of the Cold War era. During this period, TV networks also established a mutually beneficial relationship with the USA's main SPECTATOR SPORTS.

In 1962, Congress appropriated $32 million to fund educational TV channels. In 1964, Congress ruled that all TV sets sold outside the state in which they were manufactured had to be capable of receiving the UHF band on which most educational channels were located. The Public Broadcasting Act of 1967 appropriated further funding for educational and cultural programming and led to the creation, in 1969, of a non-profit network, the Public Broadcasting System. (A comparable radio network, National Public Radio, was also established in 1969.) Cable television, the development of affordable and standardized video-cassette-recorders and, from the 1980s, satellite broadcast television, have further broadened the options open to US television viewers.

Debate over the cultural influence of television and, to a lesser extent, radio, shows no signs of abating. Indeed, in the mid-1980s, commentators began to detect in the rise of 'tabloid television' and 'talk radio' new and insidious threats to the mental health of the American public.

railroads. The USA's first passenger-carrying railroad company, the Baltimore and Ohio, was incorporated in 1827 and began operation 1830. By 1840, 3328 miles (5325 km) of railroad track had been laid in the USA (more than three times the total in the whole of Europe at that time). By 1850 the USA possessed over 9000 miles (14,400 km) of track, and by 1865 over 35,000 miles (56,000 km). This increase was achieved in the face of vociferous opposition from canal companies and other vested interests, and despite the technological problems, particularly the weakness of iron rails and wooden bridges, that beset the earliest companies.

However, although its mileage was impressive, the USA's early rail system was inefficient. At least eleven different track

gauges were used. Passengers and freight traveling long distances were forced to change trains frequently; at least six times, for example, on a journey from New York to Chicago in the 1860s. The US banking and finance system was ill-equipped to provide the vast capital sums required to establish and maintain rail lines. Desperate to limit financial risk, companies attempted to identify guaranteed markets, and in the process created over-provision that led to financially ruinous competition; for example, 20 companies served the St Louis–Atlanta route in 1860. These factors help to explain why in 1860 the average rail company owned just 100 miles (160 km) of track, and just 40 miles (64 km) in southern states. Many Americans accepted the consolidation of rail lines in the hands of a few ruthless industrial magnates after the Civil War as a price worth paying to bring about a national network.

The USA's railroad industry developed with little regulation but a good deal of government assistance. The first federal subsidy was given to a railroad in 1850. The PACIFIC RAILROAD ACT (1862) committed the federal government to making enormous grants of land and cash to the Union Pacific Company to help it complete the transcontinental rail link. (The first transcontinental rail line was completed when a golden spike was driven home connecting the Union Pacific and Central Pacific lines at Promontory Point, Utah, on May 10 1869.) All told the federal government made subsidies totaling $350 million to rail companies during the period 1862–90. Individual states also made grants of land, cash, or both. Investment on this scale prompted a massive expansion of track mileage. By 1870 there were 53,000 miles (85,000 km) of track in the USA, 164,000 miles (262,000 km) by 1890, and 254,000 miles (406,000 km) when the network reached its maximum size in 1916.

As the rail network expanded, its ownership contracted. The methods used by the likes of Cornelius Vanderbilt (1794–1877) and his rival Daniel Drew (1797–1879) in their battle to consolidate holdings were extraordinarily ruthless, and contributed to national financial turmoil. In 1867 Vanderbilt acquired the New York Central Railroad by the simple expedient of buying two lines connected to it and refusing to allow any train that had touched New York Central track to travel on his rails until the Central's owners sold out. When it was put to Vanderbilt that this represented a form of blackmail he replied 'Can't I do what I want with my own?' Vanderbilt had made his fortune in the Hudson river ferry business. Here he had rubbed up against Daniel Drew. Drew, who followed Vanderbilt into railroads, pioneered the practice of 'watering stock'. (This involved selling more stocks in a company than the value of its assets. The term originated from the trick of feeding cattle salt just before sale to encourage them to drink gallons of water, thereby increasing their weight on market day.) Collaborating with the banker Jay Gould (1836–92), Drew manipulated the value of railroad securities with the intent of taking over Vanderbilt's Erie Railroad. Gould's bank collapsed before the scheme could be completed, sparking the national PANIC OF 1873. Vanderbilt was temporarily bankrupted, but his companies were bailed out by J. P. MORGAN. As the value of railroad stocks fell, companies pushed through wage cuts that led to the national RAIL STRIKE OF 1877.

Between 1865 and 1900 competition and consolidation forced down the average cost of sending a ton of freight by rail from 20 cents per mile to 1.75 cents per mile (12 to 1.05 cents per km). But rail companies used a variety of devices to keep the rates they charged to small farmers high. The POPULIST movement assailed the freight and warehousing fees charged to the small farmer by the big rail companies. However, the US Supreme Court, through its verdicts on

SANTA CLARA COUNTY VS. SOUTHERN PACIFIC RAILROAD (1886) and WABASH, ST LOUIS AND PACIFIC RAILROAD VS. ILLINOIS (1886), made it difficult if not impossible for either federal or state government to regulate rail charges.

The rail industry was also notorious for a poor occupational safety record and the long hours it required employees to work. Unionizing the railroad workforce proved difficult. The AMERICAN RAILWAY UNION (a pioneering example of INDUSTRIAL UNION organization) was all but destroyed in the PULLMAN STRIKE of 1894 when the CLEVELAND administration, conscious of the economic importance of the nation's rail network, permitted employers to take out injunctions against strikers. Ultimately, however, the strategic importance of the rail industry to the nation's economy worked in favor of the workers. In 1916 President WILSON used the threat of a national rail strike to push the landmark ADAMSON ACT (mandating an eight-hour working day) through Congress.

African-Americans may not have been able to travel in the same railroad carriages as whites (the Supreme Court verdict on PLESSY VS. FERGUSON confirmed the legality of such segregation), but the rail industry provided a source of relatively lucrative employment for many African-American men. During the 1920s and 1930s A. Philip RANDOLPH organized African-American railworkers through the Brotherhood of Sleeping Car Porters (BSCP), and eventually gained recognition for the BSCP from both the Pullman company and the AMERICAN FEDERATION OF LABOR.

In 1917 the total mileage of operational rail track in America declined for the first time in US history. The rail network continued to shrink as revenue from passenger and freight services declined in the face of competition from the automobile and eventually the airplane. Representatives of the automobile, aviation and rubber industries replaced agents of the railroad companies as the kings of the congressional lobby. However, during the 1960s and 1970s the federal government, acting largely on environmental grounds, attempted to preserve the USA's rail network. In 1970 Congress created AMTRAK, a semi-public corporation charged with operating a national passenger network. AMTRAK began service on May 1 1971 and successfully wooed passengers back to trains. Its network was cut back in 1979, but it survived an attempt by the REAGAN administration to withdraw its federal subsidy, and continues to operate. The jewel in AMTRAK's crown is the Metroliner service, a high-speed link between New York and Washington. In 1975 Congress established Conrail, a federally subsidized corporation created to prevent major freight carriers from going out of business. Conrail was privatized in 1987. In recent years the US railroad industry has benefited from the growth of the environmental movement. In a sign of the times, Los Angeles opened the first phase of new commuter rail system in 1993.

rail strike of 1877, the first nationwide strike in US history, sparked by a secret decision taken by the presidents of the USA's four largest rail companies to fix fares and cut wages. On July 16 the Baltimore and Ohio company implemented a 10% wage cut. Its workers struck. President HAYES immediately ordered the use of troops to prevent 'insurrection'. In Baltimore, Maryland, state militia fired on strikers, killing 11. The Pennsylvania Railroad implemented its wage cut on July 19. On July 20 militia drafted into Pittsburgh opened fire on strikers, killing 20, and causing rioting in which 20 residents were killed and the Pennsylvania Railroad's yards were destroyed. The strike spread until two-thirds of the US rail network was closed. It lasted two weeks, during which time general strikes were mounted in Chicago and St Louis, and over 100 workers were killed by regular army and militia troops. The significance of the gov-

ernment's decision to use troops to break the strike was not lost on union activists and socialists.

Randolph, A(sa) Philip (1889–1979), labor leader and one of the founding fathers of the modern CIVIL RIGHTS MOVEMENT.

Raised in New York, he worked his way through City College (1912–16). On graduation he joined the SOCIALIST PARTY OF AMERICA and immersed himself in political activism. In 1917 he co-founded *The Messenger*, through which he urged African-American workers to join trade unions and endorse socialist campaigns, preferably those organized by the INDUSTRIAL WORKERS OF THE WORLD (IWW or 'Wobblies'). In 1925 Randolph founded the Brotherhood of Sleeping Car Porters (BSCP). He was elected its president, and in 1929 induced the AMERICAN FEDERATION OF LABOR (AFL) to grant the union affiliate status. During the NEW DEAL, the BSCP grew in strength, and in 1935 won recognition from the Pullman Company. In 1937 the BSCP became the first African-American trade union granted full recognition by the AFL.

Randolph used his trade-union support to wring two landmark concessions from the federal government. In 1941, threatened with a mass march on Washington, President Franklin D. ROOSEVELT established an agency to prevent racial discrimination in new war-production industries. Randolph later used the threat of organized African-American protests, and abstention in the PRESIDENTIAL ELECTION OF 1948, to encourage President TRUMAN to issue Executive Order 9981 desegregating the US armed forces. Randolph sat on the executive of the AFL-CIO from 1955 to 1974. He played a crucial role in the organization of the MARCH ON WASHINGTON (1963).

Rankin, Jeanette (1880–1973), feminist, social reformer and pacifist, who in 1916 became the first woman ever elected to Congress. In 1917 she took her seat in the House of Representatives as a Republican representative from a congressional district in Montana. Rankin was one of 50 representatives to vote against US entry into WORLD WAR I, but was the only member of Congress to vote against US entry into WORLD WAR II. She left Congress in 1943 but continued to work on behalf of pacifist causes. In 1968 she organized the Jeanette Rankin Brigade, a group of 5000 women who marched on Congress in protest against the VIETNAM WAR.

ratification, the process by which a legislative body approves a measure introduced by another body, and so gives it legal force. The US Senate has to ratify any treaty entered into by the president or his administration before the treaty has any force. (In 1919, for example, the Senate refused to ratify the treaty of Versailles, and so blocked the USA's entry into the LEAGUE OF NATIONS.) Similarly, any new constitutional amendment has to be ratified by three-fourths of the states.

In a narrower historical context, the term 'ratification' is applied to the process by which the states gave their approval of the US Constitution between 1787 and 1790. The CONSTITUTIONAL CONVENTION decreed that the US Constitution would take effect when nine states ratified it. Congress agreed to this procedure (September 28 1787) and asked each state to call a convention to consider the Constitution. States ratified in the following order: DELAWARE (December 7 1787), PENNSYLVANIA, NEW JERSEY, GEORGIA, CONNECTICUT, MASSACHUSETTS, MARYLAND, SOUTH CAROLINA and NEW HAMPSHIRE – the ninth state (June 21 1788). During this period Rhode Islanders rejected the Constitution in a referendum (March 24 1788). Massachusetts's approval was conditional on the passage of a BILL OF RIGHTS. VIRGINIA's convention attached similar proposals to its ratification (June 25 1788). News of Virginia's vote, rather than the arguments of the FEDERALIST PAPERS, broke opposition to ratification within NEW YORK's convention

(July 26 1788). NORTH CAROLINA joined on November 21 1789, and RHODE ISLAND bowed to the inevitable on May 29 1790. The combined margin by which ratification was ensured in the three largest states – Massachusetts, Virginia and New York – amounted to a bare 31 votes.

Raza Unida Party, La, see LA RAZA UNIDA PARTY.

REA, see RURAL ELECTRIFICATION ADMINISTRATION.

Reagan, Ronald (Wilson) (1911–), Republican statesman and 40th president of the USA (1981–9). Just short of 70 on entering office, Reagan was the oldest man ever to be elected president. During his presidency US politics moved sharply to the right, and American culture became markedly acquisitive and pro-business. He initially took a hard line in the COLD WAR, although this was virtually ended by the time he left office.

Aside from two troubled terms as governor of California (1967–75), the presidency was the only elected office Reagan held. Between 1932 and 1937 Reagan worked as a radio sportscaster in eastern Iowa. He later revealed that when he was uncertain of a score he would make it up, and like as not it would turn out to be right. Between 1937 and 1965 he worked as a movie actor in HOLLYWOOD. He generally played supporting roles, usually in low-budget productions. He popularized the wearing of a wristwatch with its face on the inside of the wrist. Reagan served as president of the Screen Actors Guild (1947–52, 1959–60). He collaborated with the McCARTHY HEARINGS' investigation of communist subversion in Hollywood. (According to documents obtained through the FREEDOM OF INFORMATION ACT in 1985, Reagan was a secret FBI informant in the 1940s.)

During the EISENHOWER administration Reagan began working as a spokesman for the General Electric corporation, and transformed himself into the acceptable face of the REPUBLICAN PARTY's conservative wing. As governor of California he cut the budget of state agencies by 10% across the board, and cracked down on ANTIWAR MOVEMENT protest. He came within 60 votes of replacing the incumbent President FORD as the Republicans' nominee in the 1976 presidential election, before winning the 1980 nomination on the first ballot. His success in the presidential election owed much to the switch of allegiance of the so-called REAGAN DEMOCRATS.

Reagan became president on January 20 1981. Re-elected in a landslide in 1984, he served until January 20 1989. In his first term Reagan cut federal taxes in accordance with a version of SUPPLY-SIDE ECONOMICS, dubbed 'Reaganomics'. But he ordered massive increases in military expenditure, notably on the STRATEGIC DEFENSE INITIATIVE ('Star Wars'). The budget deficit doubled during his presidency, but, thanks to high interest rates, inflation fell. Reagan ordered an ill-judged intervention in LEBANON (1983) and also in GRENADA (1983). Reagan survived an assassination attempt on March 30 1981. His courage after the attack and his general presentational skills ensured that his personal popularity held up despite the sharp recession his policies produced.

Reagan trounced Democrat Walter MONDALE in the 1984 election, taking 525 votes in the ELECTORAL COLLEGE to Mondale's 13, and 59% of the POPULAR VOTE to Mondale's 41%. During his second term, Reagan moderated his hostility towards the Soviet Union, responding to Gorbachev's attempts to improve relations, and signing the Intermediate Nuclear Forces treaty (1987). It was partly Reagan's massive increase in defense spending that brought the USSR to realize that it could no longer compete in the Cold War. However, it was the IRAN–CONTRA SCANDAL that dominated Reagan's second presidential term. Reagan's claim to be unaware of the policies carried out in his name confirmed in many Americans' minds the impression that their president was an amiable but senile figurehead.

Reagan Democrats, those voters, traditionally Democrats, who switched their allegiance to the Republican Ronald REAGAN in the 1980 presidential election. The decisive switch, which spelt the end of the NEW DEAL COALITION, was most marked among white working-class males, especially in southern and western states. Most were then wooed into the REPUBLICAN PARTY. The primary cause of this migration was hostility to AFFIRMATIVE ACTION and the perceived cost of GREAT SOCIETY welfare programs.

Reconstruction, the period from the end of the CIVIL WAR in 1865 to the withdrawal of federal troops from the former Confederate states in 1877. During this period the federal government brought back the seceded states into the Union, and attempted to restructure southern political institutions and society to various degrees.

The ending of the Civil War posed some difficult questions for the victors. On what terms should the states of the Confederacy be readmitted to the Union? Should these terms be set by the president or by congress? These basic questions were made more complex by the EMANCIPATION PROCLAMATION and the THIRTEENTH AMENDMENT ending slavery. What system of labor should replace slavery? What role, if any, should the US government play in determining the social and political rights of FREEDMEN (and of whites) in southern states? Should northern states expand the civil and political rights of their black populations? All of these questions were canvassed extensively during the period 1865–77, making the Reconstruction era far more than a footnote to the Civil War. During Reconstruction, as in the AMERICAN REVOLUTION and the CIVIL RIGHTS MOVEMENT, northerners and southerners, blacks and whites, rich and poor struggled to define and control America's essence as a nation.

On December 8 1863, long before the

end of the war, LINCOLN initiated PRESIDEN-TIAL RECONSTRUCTION by issuing a PROCLA-MATION OF AMNESTY AND RECONSTRUCTION. Its main feature allowed states that had seceded to form new state governments and rejoin the Union once 10% of those residents who had voted in 1860 had sworn an oath of future loyalty and pledged to accept the EMANCIPATION PROCLAMATION. Lincoln hoped that the proclamation would encourage moderate whites to renounce secession, thereby weakening the Confederacy. Under its terms provisional governments were organized in Tennessee, Arkansas and Louisiana, but Congress refused to seat their delegates while the Civil War continued.

On July 4 1864 Lincoln applied the POCKET VETO to the WADE–DAVIS BILL (1864), which, with its provision for an IRONCLAD OATH, set tough terms for the readmission of southern states. The next two years saw increasing divergence between presidential reconstruction programs – which sought to utilize the experience and goodwill of the antebellum (pre-war) south's white moderates – and CONGRESSIONAL RECONSTRUCTION proposals, which proceeded from the assumption that a generation of southern political leaders was irremediably tainted.

Lincoln's successor, President Andrew JOHNSON, believed that wealthy slave owners had dragged the south into secession. Accordingly, his PROCLAMATION OF RECONSTRUCTION (May 29 1865) stipulated that southerners with taxable property worth $20,000 or more would have to apply for pardons before they could participate in reconstructed government. On the other hand, Johnson (who had worked as a tailor during his youth in Tennessee) assumed that white southern yeoman farmers had been duped by wealthy slave owners, but were essentially decent and could be trusted to reconstruct their states along lines satisfactory to all but the most fanatical RADICAL REPUBLICAN. Hence Johnson's plans for the reconstruction of the southern political sys-

tem allowed poor whites considerable influence. Johnson had no interest in including former slaves in the process of writing new state constitutions; indeed his proclamation specifically precluded black suffrage. Not surprisingly the 'new' governments organized under Johnson's program in the summer of 1865 replicated the power structures of the antebellum south. 'Reconstructed' states enacted BLACK CODES which, by imposing restrictions on their freedom of mobility and employment, kept freedmen in a state little better than slavery. On December 4 1865 Congress formed a JOINT COMMITTEE ON RECONSTRUCTION to develop a more thoroughgoing policy. Two days later Johnson told Congress that Reconstruction was completed. For the rest of Johnson's term Congress and the president battled for control over the pace and scope of Reconstruction.

The nature and tone of the dispute between Congress and Johnson is revealed in the president's explanation of his decision to veto the second FREEDMEN'S BUREAU Bill (1866) and the CIVIL RIGHTS ACT OF 1866. Johnson argued that the USA could not afford the cost of humanitarian relief provided to former slaves and destitute whites through the Freedmen's Bureau. In any case, he went on, Congress had never provided economic relief or rudimentary educational provision 'for our own people'. The bill, he asserted, would convince African-Americans that they did not need to work for a living. Finally he alleged that he had a broader view of the national interest than any congressman. Presumably in keeping with this claim, he vetoed the Civil Rights Act on the grounds that it discriminated against whites. Congress overrode Johnson's veto on both bills and formulated the FOURTEENTH AMENDMENT – safeguarding civil rights – for good measure. With the exception of Tennessee, southern states refused to ratify the amendment and continued to develop black codes. Former Confederate officers and politicians consolidated their power in the 'new' southern governments, abetted by Johnson's generosity in the matter of presidential pardons.

Johnson and southern REDEEMERS hoped that voters in the 1866 congressional elections would repudiate CONGRESSIONAL RECONSTRUCTION. But, in the aftermath of the MEMPHIS and NEW ORLEANS RIOTS, Republicans gained control of both houses of Congress. This marked the beginning of the period which historians describe as RADICAL RECONSTRUCTION. In the spring of 1867 Congress passed a series of RECONSTRUCTION ACTS. These placed all former Confederate states except Tennessee under military government. District commanders were ordered to begin again the process of political reconstruction. They were to identify and register qualified voters (including African-Americans but excluding Confederate officials barred under the FOURTEENTH AMENDMENT) and charged with the supervision of elections to state constitutional conventions. When new state constitutions, which had to include provision for black suffrage, had been ratified by popular vote and approved by Congress, and when each reconstructed state had held elections under federal supervision and accepted the Fourteenth Amendment, their representation in the US Congress was to be restored. By 1868 only four southern states (Virginia, Georgia, Mississippi and Texas) had failed to complete this process. These four delayed in the hopes that the Fourteenth Amendment might not be ratified. It was ratified, however, and Congress was able to insist that the four holdout states accept the FIFTEENTH AMENDMENT, guaranteeing African-American voting rights, as well. By 1870 the political reconstruction of the southern states was complete.

In 1867–8 Congress also considered, and rejected, the notion that the federal government should reform the social structure of southern states in order to effect their complete reconstruction. Radical Republican Thaddeus STEVENS proposed confiscating the lands of some 70,000 'chief rebels' – about 394 million acres (160 million ha); every adult FREEDMAN would be granted 40 acres (16 ha), while the rest would be sold to pay off war debt, provide pensions to Union soldiers, and compensate Unionists for property damage.

For a variety of reasons there was no support within Congress, or without, for including measures of this kind in the Reconstruction Acts that went through Congress in 1867–8. Firstly, most Republicans regarded their duty to former slaves and to the memory of Lincoln as being entirely discharged once freedmen were enfranchised and given access to the legal system. *The Nation* captured this mood when it editorialized that with ratification of the Fifteenth Amendment 'agitation against slavery has reached an appropriate and triumphant conclusion'. Secondly, while most Republicans could support legislation designed to bring equality of access to the ballot box or courthouse, they were reluctant to embrace, and were even hostile toward, any direct federal action designed to impart equality of condition to what they still regarded as two separate races in the south. They tended to assume that blacks and whites would lead separate, but hopefully equal, lives in a reconstructed south. Thirdly, President JOHNSON, by vetoing every Reconstruction Act and sacking military commanders he thought sympathetic to Radical Reconstruction, provoked a fight between Congress and the White House that distracted congressional attention from the plight of landless former slaves, and ended in IMPEACHMENT proceedings being brought against the president. (On May 16 1868 a Senate resolution to impeach Johnson failed by one vote.)

For all these reasons the task of directing the economic reconstruction of the south was ultimately left in the hands of the region's large landowners, merchants and bankers. Large landowners encouraged former slaves and poor white farmers to enter into SHARECROPPING or CROP LIEN agreements. This system of providing the landless and the poor with employment led in turn to a replication of the southern economy's former dependence on cotton production. As cotton prices fell, sharecroppers declined into debt and dependency.

With former Confederate officials barred from voting or holding office, control of the newly reconstructed state governments passed to Republicans. Democratic Party 'redeemers' characterized these governments as corrupt, inefficient and illegitimate. Republican officeholders, especially African-Americans elected to state and national posts, were vilified as CARPETBAGGERS and their supporters as SCALAWAGS. In many regions of the south the KU KLUX KLAN waged a campaign of terror designed to return states to white, Democratic Party, control. On May 22 1872 the GRANT administration pushed a lenient Amnesty Act through an acquiescent Congress. This restored to virtually all former Confederate officials the right to vote and to hold office. It increased greatly the speed with which white rule was reimposed in southern states. Southern congressmen were then able to extract from President HAYES, via the COMPROMISE OF 1877, a commitment to end Reconstruction.

These events left the south's African-Americans in a unique and unenviable position. They were free men, but resided in states that soon found ways to limit their access to the ballot box and the courthouse. The Fourteenth Amendment granted them the rights of US citizens, but successive Supreme Court rulings, culminating in the verdict on PLESSY VS. FERGUSON, confined them to a separate and unequal existence. Southern leaders, among them Booker T. WASHINGTON, urged African-Americans to accept their deliverance from slavery and work to better themselves. Even those who were able to follow Washington's advice found that all too often their reward was intimidation offered by white supremacists beset by fears of 'uppity negroes'. The JIM CROW system (the system of racial segregation and denial of black voting rights) that underpinned the SOLID SOUTH was the most enduring legacy of Reconstruction, and it survived largely intact until it was dismantled in the 1950s and 1960s by the CIVIL RIGHTS MOVEMENT.

Reconstruction Acts (1867–8), four legislative measures that formed the cornerstone of CONGRESSIONAL RECONSTRUCTION. The acts have been described as 'a stunning and unprecedented experiment in interracial democracy'.

(1) Passed over President JOHNSON'S veto, the first act (March 2 1867) required all former Confederate states except Tennessee to recommence the process of readmission to the Union. The ten unreconstructed states were divided into five military districts, whose military governors were to oversee elections for new state constitutional conventions. The act stipulated that blacks should be eligible to elect delegates to the constitutional conventions, and that new state constitutions should enfranchise black voters. It disenfranchised white voters disqualified under the terms of the proposed FOURTEENTH AMENDMENT. When a new constitution had been ratified by a majority of registered voters, and a duly elected state government had ratified the Fourteenth Amendment, a state would be eligible for readmission to the Union.

(2) To prevent state officials from obstructing the first Reconstruction Act, the second act (March 23 1867) authorized military governors to supervise the registration of voters and the conduct of elections. Attorney General Henry Stanbury (1803–81), a Johnson loyalist, questioned the act's legality, and Johnson vetoed it.

(3) After considering objections to the

second Reconstruction Act, Congress passed the third act (July 19 1867). This authorized military commanders to remove state officials appointed before March 2 1867, thus countering the threat that state officials might obstruct the registration of black voters. The act also permitted election officials to disqualify whites suspected of swearing a false loyalty oath. The bill was passed over Johnson's veto. By December 1867 elections had been held in every former Confederate state except Texas.

(4) The fourth act (March 11 1868) stated that a simple majority was sufficient to ratify a new state constitution. The measure was introduced after whites in Alabama tried to thwart the first Reconstruction Act by boycotting a vote on the adoption of a new state constitution – thereby depriving it of the approval of a majority of registered voters. President Johnson refused to sign the act.

The Reconstruction Acts led to the registration of 700,000 black voters, and placed black voters in a majority in five southern states. But they also led to a backlash, in which white supremacists sought the south's REDEMPTION from SCALAWAGS, CARPETBAGGERS and BLACK REPUBLICANS.

Reconstruction Finance Corporation (RFC), federal agency established by President HOOVER on February 2 1932 at the height of the GREAT DEPRESSION. The RFC was authorized by Congress to extend up to $2.5 billion worth of credit to banks, insurance companies and railroads.

Following criticism that the RFC was reluctant to bail out smaller banks or state charities, Congress expanded its remit, and funding, through the EMERGENCY RELIEF AND CONSTRUCTION ACT (July 21 1932). The RFC was the wealthiest federal agency ever created. Under its first director, Jesse H. Jones (1874–1956), the RFC played a crucial role in re-establishing confidence in the banking system during the first HUNDRED DAYS of the NEW DEAL. Jones soon realized that

banks preferred to use RFC credits to secure their own position rather than make loans or investments. He advised President Franklin ROOSEVELT to declare an extraordinary BANK HOLIDAY. While banks remained shut Congress passed the EMERGENCY BANKING RELIEF ACT. In cooperation with the Treasury, Jones used this act to decide which banks should reopen and which were insolvent. The RFC acquired stock in the solvent banks, against which it offered credits to ailing banks and, eventually, funding for New Deal agencies such as the FEDERAL EMERGENCY RELIEF ADMINISTRATION, the FARM CREDIT ADMINISTRATION, the RURAL ELECTRIFICATION ADMINISTRATION, and the RESETTLEMENT ADMINISTRATION.

red-baiting, the use for political ends of allegations that an opponent is now, or was once, a socialist, communist or 'fellow traveler'. Richard NIXON was a particularly adept exponent of this black art.

Red Cloud or **Mahpiua Luta,** *see* SIOUX WARS.

Redeemers, those southerners who, during RECONSTRUCTION, agitated for the REDEMPTION of the south from RADICAL REPUBLICAN state governments. The Redeemers represented a re-creation by southern Democrats of the alliance between leading planters and poor whites that had dominated the ANTEBELLUM south. Redeemers opposed social and political reform, and embraced tacitly white supremacist violence perpetrated by groups such as the KU KLUX KLAN. Following the COMPROMISE OF 1877 (which removed the last remaining federal troops from southern states) some southern Democrat leaders adopted a Progressive agenda. However, most adopted a conservative stance, and were mocked as BOURBONS by southern POPULISTS.

Redemption, term applied by southerners after the CIVIL WAR to their vision of overthrowing RADICAL REPUBLICAN state governments, and of reversing RECONSTRUCTION's attempts at the social and political reform of the south. Southern Democrats – known as REDEEMERS – achieved this goal through the COMPROMISE OF 1877.

Red River War (April 1874–May 1875), conflict in which US troops fought 30 engagements with some 1500 CHEYENNE, COMANCHE and KIOWA warriors in northern Texas and southwestern Kansas. The Native American militants refused to accept confinement on reservations, while the US government sought to prevent them from raiding white settlements and hunting on land taken over by whites. All involved in the war recognized that permanent control of the southern plains rested on the outcome of the fighting. US Major General Philip SHERIDAN coined the expression 'The only good Indian is a dead Indian' during the skirmishing. In fact Sheridan (and his subordinate George CUSTER) rarely caught Native American raiders. It was rather Sheridan's employment of scorched-earth tactics – perfected during the CIVIL WAR in the SHENANDOAH VALLEY CAMPAIGN – that forced the braves to return to their reservations. This outcome, and US victory in the third SIOUX WAR, marked the end of Native American military resistance to US TERRITORIAL EXPANSION.

Red Scare (1919–20), period following the Bolshevik Revolution in Russia in which the US authorities, fearing imminent revolution, employed repressive measures against alleged subversives.

The STEEL STRIKE OF 1919 was the most serious in a rash of labor disputes that saw Boston policemen and even Broadway actors protest against pay and working conditions. Employers were quick to blame the wave of strikes on foreign-born (and especially Eastern European) socialists, anarchists and other 'subversives'. Attorney General A. Mitchell Palmer (1872–1936) fueled and exploited fears of subversion in a bid to gain the Democrats' presidential nomination. Using the Sedition Act (*see* ALIEN AND SEDITION ACTS), and employing a small army of special agents, Palmer detained and deported alleged communists. In January 1920 some 6000 'subversives' were arrested in a nationwide campaign. Palmer believed that the Supreme Court verdicts in SCHENCK VS. US and ABRAMS VS. US gave constitutional cover to these raids. But the Labor Department, which had responsibility for deportations, withdrew its cooperation from Palmer, and mainstream political figures, including Warren HARDING, criticized his excesses. Palmer predicted that revolutionaries would mount an armed insurrection on May 1 1920. When nothing happened, he lost credibility and the scare subsided. However, during it, thousands of Americans were harassed and blacklisted. The trial and subsequent execution of SACCO AND VANZETTI came to symbolize the injustices committed during the period.

Regents of the University of California vs. Baake (June 28 1978), important US Supreme Court ruling on AFFIRMATIVE ACTION in which the Court found by 5–4 that college admissions offices could not prevent white students from competing on merit for college places reserved for minority students. The verdict rested on Title VI of the CIVIL RIGHTS ACT OF 1964, which had been designed to prevent African-Americans from being denied access to federally funded programs. The Court held that colleges might take race and affirmative action into account when admitting students, but that they could not operate rigid quotas.

Regulator movements, political groups organized during the 1760s among frontiersmen and yeomen farmers in North and South Carolina. Regulators sought fairer, more efficient local government and the disestablishment of the Anglican church. They seized on criticism of 'taxation without representation' made during protests against the STAMP ACT and the TOWNSHEND ACT to demand more seats in colonial assemblies for western regions.

In North Carolina, Regulators campaigned

against unjust court fees, speculative litigation and corruption in governmental circles. Local oligarchs in the colony, backed by the royal governor, used the colonial militia to disperse an armed Regulator insurrection at the battle of Alamance (1771). As a result many back-country North Carolinians were only lukewarm supporters of American independence. In South Carolina the planter elite considered using force to suppress local Regulators, but ultimately agreed to meet many of their demands. During the REVOLUTIONARY WAR British commanders developed a southern strategy to build upon disaffection in the Carolina back-country. Regulator movements illustrate the manner in which REPUBLICAN IDEOLOGY was used to justify a fundamental reform of domestic as well as imperial governance.

relocation of Japanese-Americans. On February 19 1942 President Franklin D. ROOSEVELT, bowing to public fears triggered by the Japanese attack on PEARL HARBOR, authorized the secretary of war to define restricted military areas on the Pacific seaboard, and to deport from them Japanese-American residents. Some 110,000 first-, second and third-generation Japanese-Americans were ordered from their homes on the west coast and 'relocated' in camps in the interior. A handful remained in their homes. Families were separated and businesses ruined. The policy was rescinded on January 2 1945. On August 10 1988 Congress created a trust fund to compensate survivors and their families.

Report on Manufactures, report written by Treasury Secretary Alexander HAMILTON, and submitted to Congress on December 5 1791, that bound the USA to erect TARIFFS to protect domestic manufacturing industries, to offer bounties to encourage agricultural improvements, and to fund a model manufacturing corporation located in New Jersey. The report was strongly opposed in the slave states, whose planters were

angered by the implication that production organized around slavery was inefficient, and who would be hurt by retaliatory European tariffs on tobacco, cotton and rice. This opposition ensured that the report's main recommendations were ignored. The corrupt misuse of federal funds diverted to the Society for Establishing Useful Manufactures in New Jersey was exploited in partisan attacks on Hamilton.

Report on the Public Credit, report written by Treasury Secretary Alexander HAMILTON, and submitted to Congress on January 14 1790, that proposed that the US government should assume responsibility for the repayment of all debts incurred either by the central government or by the states during the REVOLUTIONARY WAR. The controversy surrounding the report marks the beginning of party politics in the USA, and found unlikely resolution in a congressional decision to make DISTRICT OF COLUMBIA the nation's capital.

The USA had borrowed $40 million from its own citizens to fight the Revolutionary War. It owed foreign, primarily Dutch, creditors $11 million. In addition the individual states had debts totalling $25 million. Hamilton called for repayment to be at par, i.e. the US government would not take into account the depreciation suffered by government bonds during the war. Further, repayment would be made to the current owners of bonds and certificates, bringing massive profits to speculators who had bought up apparently worthless securities in advance of the report.

Hamilton's design was threefold. Firstly, he wished to signal that the USA was wedded to sound financial practice. Secondly, he believed that the measure would create a capitalist class in the USA, one with a direct interest in the future prosperity and well-being of the country, and which would use its stake in the domestic debt to fund measures of internal improvement. Lastly, he believed that if states were left with the responsibility for paying off their war debt, they would obstruct or contest federal economic policy.

States that had paid off their war debt, chief among them Virginia, bitterly opposed Hamilton's call for the federal government to assume responsibility for the repayment of debt that laggard states had left outstanding. Most DEMOCRATIC-REPUBLICANS also objected to the profit that speculators would make. (James MADISON tried, unsuccessfully, to rally support for a plan that would compensate former soldiers who had been forced to sell at a discount government securities given in lieu of pay.)

On April 12 1790 the House of Representatives defeated a motion for the federal assumption of state debts. Pennsylvanian and Virginian congressmen extracted a promise that the national capital would be moved southward from New York, first to Philadelphia, then to Washington, as the price of their eventual acceptance of assumption (July 26). The need to provide a revenue stream capable of meeting repayment led Congress to adopt Hamilton's proposal for an excise tax on whiskey (March 3 1791). This decision sparked the WHISKEY REBELLION.

republican ideology, term employed by historians to describe the body of political ideas used by Americans during the AMERICAN REVOLUTION to justify independence and to conceptualize the creation of a nation state.

Political theory suggested to 18th-century Americans that while republics were preferable to monarchies, they were also vulnerable to subversion by designing tyrants. Republican ideology suggested that the tendency of republics to degenerate into tyrannies could best be combated by identifying and inculcating VIRTUE within the citizenry. The need to nurture and protect a virtuous (i.e. disinterested and public-spirited) citizenry led Americans who subscribed to republican ideology to venerate small pro-

ducers, craftsmen and independent farmers. This gave republican ideology a radical tinge. In a polity that lacked a monarch the people would be sovereign, aristocracy would be insupportable, and privileges would have to be earned.

The preamble to the US CONSTITUTION, 'We the people of the United States, in order to form a more perfect union...', frankly embraces popular sovereignty. It followed from the fact of popular sovereignty that the broad mass of the people needed to be enfranchised, that they should be encouraged to seek elective office, and that their property be protected from predatory financiers. Although not fundamentally anti-commercial, republican ideology viewed with suspicion the activities of international merchants, financiers and owners of large plantations. It tended to assume that their interests conflicted with those of the community as whole.

Thomas PAINE's pamphlet *COMMON SENSE* made a powerful contribution to the development of republican ideology in America by arguing that a viable republic, continental in scale, could be established in an independent United States of America. Previously Americans had tended to accept the theories of the French thinker Charles de Secondat Montesquieu (1689–1755), who argued that republics thrived only in relatively small communities, possessed of a homogeneity of interests, such as the city states of Renaissance Italy. (Indeed, after 1776 politicians seeking to retain the political power of the individual states continued to invoke Montesquieu.) Paine argued that America's size presented no obstacle to the creation of a successful republic, because the vast majority of its population was made up of those men (small farmers) most likely to possess the virtue necessary to create a republic that could serve as an asylum for liberty.

However, during the REVOLUTIONARY WAR Paine, and a number of more conservative thinkers, came to the conviction that republican ideology encapsulated overly optimistic assumptions about the behavior of the American people. Small farmers proved reluctant to volunteer for service in the Continental Army, putting the needs of their farm above the needs of their country. Their tribunes in the state legislatures contributed to the financial woes of the CONFEDERATION CONGRESS by withholding subsidies from it. During SHAYS'S REBELLION (1786–7) small farmers in Massachusetts closed the court system to prevent the enforcement of laws distraining debtors' property. In their various ways these developments contributed to a recognition that republican government could produce what James MADISON termed the 'tyranny of the majority'. In the *FEDERALIST PAPERS* Madison sought to define a 'republican solution' to this problem. Madison's solution contained two features that presaged the growth of liberalism in the 19th century: first, the recognition that minority interests (for example those of creditors) were no less deserving of the protection of government than individuals; and second, the assertion that the checks and balances built into the US Constitution allowed individuals to pursue their self-interest without harming the community as a whole.

Even in its most cautious formulations, republican ideology called for the creation of governmental forms more democratic than any currently in existence in Europe, and encouraged the development of a robustly populist political culture in America. During the 19th century the ideas of republican ideology were revived and reworked in JEFFERSONIAN DEMOCRACY, FREE-SOIL IDEOLOGY, and the POPULIST movement.

Republican Party, political party formed in February 1854 with the aim of achieving 'the re-establishment of liberty and the overthrow of SLAVE POWER'. After the Civil War RADICAL REPUBLICANS attempted a major social and political reform of the south, including the establishment of equal rights for African-Americans. But later in the 19th century the party changed its complexion, becoming the party of big business, and moving to the right of the Democratic Party. It now represents a range of conservative values.

To begin with the Republican Party was not explicitly abolitionist, but strongly opposed the KANSAS–NEBRASKA ACT and was outraged by BLEEDING KANSAS. Drawing on support from former KNOW NOTHINGS, WHIGS and FREE SOILERS, the party gained 108 seats in the House and 15 in the Senate in congressional elections held in the fall of 1854. John C. FRÉMONT, the party's first presidential nominee, gained 33% of the popular vote in 1856. Abraham LINCOLN, the party's nominee in 1860, won a convincing victory on a platform that denounced all plans of SECESSION as treason. During the Civil War, the party controlled both houses of Congress. Radical Republicans demanded immediate abolition and a punitive policy towards the south. Following Union victory and Lincoln's death, the party enjoyed the support of virtually all FREEDMEN and most northerners, except the urban working classes. Radical Republicans alienated white southerners during RECONSTRUCTION, and for roughly a century after the COMPROMISE OF 1877 the party had little influence in the SOLID SOUTH.

Nonetheless, the Republicans dominated presidential politics. Between 1860 and 1928 only two presidents (CLEVELAND and WILSON) were elected on the Democratic ticket. During this period, despite support for its HALF-BREED and MUGWUMP factions, the party set its face against reform and defended business interests and 'hard' money. During the GREAT DEPRESSION black voters deserted the Republican Party and helped to create the Democrats' NEW DEAL COALITION. Since the 1970s the party has gained increasing support among white southern males (REAGAN DEMOCRATS) and opponents of the ROE VS. WADE decision on abortion. The party remains an effective force in presidential politics, but since 1931 the Republicans have controlled both houses of Congress only in the periods 1947–9, 1953–5 and since 1995.

reservations, areas set aside for Native American peoples. In 1830, acting on the assumption that Native American settlements east of the Mississippi were impeding the TERRITORIAL EXPANSION of the USA, Congress, with the strong support of President JACKSON, passed the INDIAN REMOVAL ACT. This created reservations for native peoples west of the Mississippi in the future states of Oklahoma and Kansas. The FIVE CIVILIZED TRIBES of the southeast resisted forced relocation to these reservations. The CHEROKEE were forcibly marched west along the TRAIL OF TEARS. After the Civil War the US government attempted to confine native peoples living on the Great Plains west of the Mississippi to specific 'reserved' lands. The treaties of MEDICINE LODGE and FORT LARAMIE represented important steps in this process. The DAWES SEVERALTY ACT (1887) attempted to convert native peoples living on reservations into yeomen farmers by breaking up reservation lands into private allotments. The hunger of white settlers for 'unoccupied' Native American lands, epitomized by the OKLAHOMA LAND RUSH (1889), posed another threat to the integrity of the reservation system. John COLLIER, an activist on behalf of Native American peoples, won repeal of the Dawes Act through the WHEELER–HOWARD ACT (1934), which allowed Native American tribes to purchase additional lands from the US government, and began to protect the governmental autonomy of Native American reservations. The USA currently possesses over 250 federal reservations. However, less than half of those persons identifying themselves as Native Americans reside on reservations.

Resettlement Administration (RA), NEW DEAL agency created on May 1 1935 by executive order of President Franklin D. ROOSEVELT, using the EMERGENCY RELIEF APPROPRIATION ACT (1935). The RA's director was Rexford Tugwell (1891–1979). The agency complemented the work of the AGRICULTURAL ADJUSTMENT ADMINISTRATION by helping families farming poor, exhausted or deforested land to move to other farms or to cities. It also granted loans to families seeking to buy tools or equipment to upgrade the quality of their land. The suburban towns of Greenbelt (near Washington DC), Greenhills (near Cincinnati) and Greendale (near Milwaukee) were built by the RA to provide low-income housing for city workers.

Resumption Act (1875), legislation that permitted holders of GREENBACKS (paper money) to exchange their notes for SPECIE (hard currency) from January 1 1879. The act was signed by President GRANT on January 10 1875. Since the USA no longer minted silver dollars, the act tied US monetary policy to gold, exacerbating the SILVER–GOLD CONTROVERSY. The GREENBACK PARTY opposed the act because they believed holders of paper money would exchange their currency for gold, making money worth more while reducing the amount of paper money in circulation. There was no rush to redeem greenbacks in 1879 because the USA had accumulated a gold reserve large enough to ensure that the notes in circulation held creditors' confidence.

Revels, Hiram R(hoades) (1827–1901), clergyman and Republican politician, the first African-American to be elected to the US Senate. Born in North Carolina to free black parents, Revels was an ordained minister in the AFRICAN METHODIST EPISCOPAL CHURCH. During the CIVIL WAR he served as chaplain to black troops stationed in Mississippi. He represented Mississippi in the US Senate from 1870 to 1871.

Revere, Paul (1735–1818), prosperous Boston silversmith who carried messages for the city's COMMITTEES OF CORRESPONDENCE during the AMERICAN REVOLUTION. On the night of April 18 1775 Revere and a colleague, William Dawes (1745–99), broke the British cordon surrounding Boston and rode to Lexington to warn John ADAMS and John Hancock (1737–93) that British troops had been sent to arrest them. Revere was himself arrested as he rode on to Concord to warn the MINUTEMEN of the approaching British column. By raising the alarm Revere and Dawes helped spark the battles of LEXINGTON AND CONCORD. Revere later engraved the plates from which the first US currency was printed.

Revolutionary War (1775–83), the war by which the American colonies achieved their independence from Britain. The war is sometimes referred to by British historians as the American War of Independence.

Popular mythology treats the Revolutionary War as an uncomplicated and heroic war of national liberation. In fact, as many as 20% of America's population sided with Britain, and suffered confiscation of property and exile as a result. The majority of Americans who served as private soldiers in the Continental Army did so because they could not avoid service. Throughout the war Americans sought to protect and enlarge local interests. The war allowed VERMONT to assert and defend independent statehood. South Carolina cited 'military necessity' in a bid to annex Georgia. Georgia, in turn, sought to capture the British colony of EAST FLORIDA. Further north the New England states, abetted by New York, sought to acquire Canada and settle scores with Native American neighbors (notably the IROQUOIS CONFDERACY and the SHAWNEE).

America's eventual success owed at least as much to military and financial aid provided (for reasons of their own) by France, Spain and the Netherlands as it did to the valor or effectiveness of its fighting forces. (For example, 90% of the gunpowder used by American troops was supplied by France.) For all the patriotism engendered during it,

the war revealed the weakness and suggested the inadequacy of America's national institutions. The Continental Army was undermanned and often poorly supplied. Continental currency became so inflated as to be valueless. The CONFEDERATION CONGRESS lacked power and was often inquorate. Thus the war not only secured independence, but also fostered debate over the design of the American nation state.

The first shots in the war were fired at LEXINGTON AND CONCORD on April 19 1775. After this initial skirmish, New England militiamen confined British troops in Boston. On June 17 1775 they thwarted a British attempt to break the siege of Boston at the battle of BUNKER HILL. On June 16 the CONTINENTAL CONGRESS appointed George WASHINGTON commander in chief of the Continental Army, and authorized the issue of $2 million in bills of credit to fund military preparations. In October 1775 Congress created a Navy and Marine Corps. Fighting spread even as delegates within Congress, led by John DICKINSON, argued against a formal declaration of independence. In November, Virginia state militia defeated a regiment of former slaves raised following DUNMORE'S PROCLAMATION. Exploiting the capture of FORT TICONDEROGA on Lake Champlain, a force of New Englanders, led by Richard Montgomery (1738–75) and Benedict ARNOLD, invaded Canada in the winter of 1775–6. They occupied Montreal briefly, but were routed following an unsuccessful assault on QUEBEC.

On May 2 1776 France authorized covert aid to America. Yet despite the British evacuation of Boston (March 4–5 1776) and the adoption of the DECLARATION OF INDEPENDENCE, the balance of the military campaigning favored Britain. US defeats at the battles of LONG ISLAND and WHITE PLAINS led to the British occupation of NEW YORK CITY (September 15 1776). Thereafter, Washington's army, losing men through desertion and disease, retreated through New Jersey.

Tactical victories at TRENTON and PRINCETON allowed Washington time to stabilize his force and defend Philadelphia.

In the spring and summer of 1777 British forces, now under the overall command of Sir William HOWE, sought two objectives: firstly to establish control of the Mohawk and Hudson valleys in New York State, thereby isolating New England, and secondly to occupy PHILADELPHIA, which was the seat of the Continental Congress. US victories at ORISKANY, FORT STANWIX, BENNINGTON and BEMIS HEIGHTS disrupted coordination of the British campaign in New York, and led to the greatest British humiliation of the war – the surrender of 5700 troops at SARATOGA on October 13 1777. This had a huge effect on American morale, and convinced France to recognize American independence (February 6 1778) and to propose a FRANCO-AMERICAN ALLIANCE. However, further south, victories at BRANDYWINE CREEK, PAOLI and GERMANTOWN allowed British troops to occupy Philadelphia (September 26 1777), forcing Washington's army into winter quarters at VALLEY FORGE. There, despite privations, Washington's army was drilled into an effective fighting force by Baron von STEUBEN. In 1778, the mettle of the newly disciplined force was demonstrated at the battle of MONMOUTH COURT HOUSE.

In 1778 John Paul JONES staged the first of several audacious raids on British shipping. In the north, George Rogers CLARK and John SULLIVAN began campaigns of retribution against SHAWNEE and IROQUOIS fighting against the Americans. In August 1778 an unsuccessful attempt to recapture Newport, Rhode Island, inaugurated Franco-American military cooperation. But in what proved to be the war's turning point, British forces, now under the command of Major General Henry CLINTON, attempted to capitalize on the strength of LOYALIST sentiment in southern colonies by shifting the focus of their operations to Georgia and the Carolinas. They established a tenuous military control of the region by the capture of SAVANNAH and CHARLESTON, and by victory at the battle of CAMDEN, South Carolina. However, Loyalist leaders, to whom British forces ceded political control of captured territory, strengthened and even created American resistance by engaging in acts of expropriation and retribution. A civil war, conducted via guerrilla tactics, consumed much of the south. In the summer of 1781 British General Charles CORNWALLIS invaded Virginia in a bid to isolate southern partisans from their main source of supply. He expected, but did not receive, support from Clinton. Exploiting British divisions, Washington isolated Cornwallis's force, besieged it at YORKTOWN, and forced its surrender (October 18 1781). On March 5 1782 the British Parliament authorized peace negotiations, whose eventual outcome was the treaty of PARIS (1783). The last British troops on the eastern seaboard left New York City on November 25 1783.

During the war 240,000 American men bore arms (21,000 as Loyalists). Nearly 5000 free blacks enlisted in American forces, service that some northern states recognized when considering ABOLITION and GRADUAL EMANCIPATION. A total of 26,000 American soldiers died, a per-capita death rate 40 times greater than that experienced during the VIETNAM WAR. Some 60,000 American Loyalists left America, a per-capita rate of self-exile about six times that witnessed in the French Revolution. The shabby treatment and unsatisfactory payment of soldiers by state and national government during the war prompted mutinies (the most serious of which occurred at MORRISTOWN, New Jersey) and even talk of a military coup (the NEWBURGH CONSPIRACY). The war left state and national government with a combined debt of $85 million (valued in gold) or $360 million (valued in inflated Continental currency). The size of this debt, and the likelihood that government under the ARTICLES OF CONFEDERATION would struggle to repay it, prompted many Americans to support FEDERALIST calls for a CONSTITUTIONAL CONVENTION.

Reykjavik Conference (October 1986), summit meeting in the Icelandic capital between President REAGAN and Soviet leader Mikhail Gorbachev. Contrary to all expectations, the conference came close to ending the COLD WAR arms race, and almost brought about immediate and complete nuclear disarmament. The proposal foundered because Gorbachev insisted that work on the US STRATEGIC DEFENSE INITIATIVE, a project dear to Reagan, should be confined to the laboratory. Reagan's willingness to contemplate abandoning nuclear deterrence enraged other leaders of the NORTH ATLANTIC TREATY ORGANIZATION, notably British prime minister Margaret Thatcher, who had spent the previous six years persuading the British public to accept the stationing of US-controlled nuclear-tipped cruise missiles in Britain and elsewhere in Europe.

RFC, *see* RECONSTRUCTION FINANCE CORPORATION.

Rhode Island, small northeastern state, bordered on the north and east by Massachusetts, to the south by Long Island Sound and to the west by Connecticut.

The first permanent American settlement in the territory was established at Warwick by Roger Williams (*c.*1603–83) in 1634. Williams, his followers, and many subsequent settlers fled to Rhode Island to avoid persecution by Puritan authorities in neighboring Massachusetts. On July 18 1663, Williams secured a royal charter confirming Rhode Island's independence as a colony.

Rhode Island was the smallest of the THIRTEEN COLONIES and, during the AMERICAN REVOLUTION, the state came to be regarded by theorists of REPUBLICAN IDEOLOGY as providing an object lesson on the shortcomings of popular sovereignty. During the REVOLUTIONARY WAR its chief port, Newport,

was occupied by the British (1776–9). Partly as a result, small farmers, who formed the largest interest group in the state, gained control of the legislature. Although the legislature passed a law abolishing slavery through GRADUAL EMANCIPATION in 1784, its members, bowing to local interests, also issued a flood of paper money with which they attempted to pay debts owed to CONFEDERATION CONGRESS and foreign creditors. Rhode Island did not send delegates to the CONSTITUTIONAL CONVENTION. The irresponsibility of the state's legislature was criticized in the FEDERALIST PAPERS and formed the immediate inspiration for James MADISON's warning that the 'tyranny of the majority' was as injurious as the tyranny of an individual. Rhode Islanders voted to reject the federal constitution in 1789. On May 29 1790, Rhode Island became the last of the original colonies to join the union.

From 1791, when the English immigrant Samuel Slater (1768–1835) established America's first cotton mill at Pawtucket, the state experienced rapid industrial growth. In 1860, Rhode Island had 174,620 residents and was the 29th most populous state in the union. Although the state sent over 23,000 men to fight for the Union during the Civil War, such was Rhode Island's dependence on the textile trade that the loyalties of its mill-owners and workers were severely tested by the US blockade of southern ports. After the war immigration, principally from southern Europe, boosted Rhode Island's population to 595,986 by 1915. (During this period, Rhode Island became the only state in the union where Catholic residents outnumbered Protestants.) In the late 19th century Newport, Rhode Island, emerged as a summer resort favored by the beneficiaries of America's GILDED AGE. Rhode Island granted women the right to vote in 1917.

In 1990 Rhode Island had 1,003,464 residents and was the 43rd most populous state in the union.

Rich Mountain, battle of (July 11 1861), engagement in West Virginia during the CIVIL WAR in which a force of 4000 Union soldiers dislodged 1250 Confederates from the town of Beverley, capturing their commanders. Major General George McCLELLAN exploited this victory to establish Union control over northern West Virginia. This success launched McClellan's career as the 'young Napoleon' in whom Union hopes of a prompt and crushing defeat of Confederate resistance were briefly invested.

right of deposit, the right of Americans to transport goods down the Mississippi and deposit them in the port of New Orleans before shipment overseas. The USA claimed this right was granted by the treaty of PARIS (1783), but Spain did not recognize the treaty, and in 1784 closed the Mississippi to American commerce in an attempt to force concessions on the northern boundary of WEST FLORIDA from America. American attempts to secure access to New Orleans informed the JAY–GARDOQUI NEGOTIATIONS (1785) and the treaty of SAN LORENZO (1795). Following the treaty of SAN ILDEFONSO (1800), by which France regained the Louisiana territory from Spain, France rescinded the right of deposit (October 16 1802), encouraging JEFFERSON to authorize the LOUISIANA PURCHASE.

***River Queen* peace talks,** unsuccessful peace talks towards the end of the CIVIL WAR; also referred to as the Hampton Roads Conference. On February 3 1865, President LINCOLN, accompanied by Secretary of State William H. SEWARD, met three Confederate commissioners aboard a steamer anchored off Hampton Roads, Virginia, to discuss terms for ending the war. Lincoln offered generous treatment to former Confederates, going so far as to float the idea of compensating slave owners for the loss of 'property' caused by the THIRTEENTH AMENDMENT. However, he insisted that unconditional Confederate surrender precede the reintegration of southern states into the Union. When the Confederate commissioners reminded Lincoln that King Charles I had negotiated with rebels in arms, Lincoln replied that his only recollection of Charles was that he lost his head. As the Confederate commissioners were only authorized to negotiate for independence, the talks quickly broke down.

Robeson, Paul (Bustill) (1898–1976), singer, actor and radical. Robeson was born in Princetown, New Jersey and was an outstanding scholar and athlete at the state's Rutgers University. He began a law degree at Columbia before embarking on a career as an actor and singer. During the 1930s, Robeson made repeated visits to England, where he met leading black intellectuals such as C.L.R. James (1901–89) and Jomo Kenyatta (1898–1978). He also visited the Soviet Union. During WORLD WAR II, the US government recruited Robeson to boost the morale of troops and munitions workers. During this period he gave a memorable performance in a Broadway production of *Othello* and recorded a best-selling album. When Robeson criticized the COLD WAR policies of the TRUMAN administration, the State Department – branding Robeson 'one of the most dangerous men in the world' – confiscated his passport. He was placed on a BLACKLIST and denied work. His passport was restored in 1958 and he spent much of his later life in Europe.

Robinson, Jackie (Jack Roosevelt Robinson) (1919–72), the Brooklyn Dodgers' second-baseman, who in 1947 became the first African-American to play in BASEBALL's major leagues. Robinson's calm demeanor and exceptional ability helped still the furore that greeted the desegregation of America's national pastime. Robinson left baseball in 1957. He became a vice president of the Chock Full o'Nuts Coffee Corporation and a prominent backer of liberal Republican Nelson D. ROCKEFELLER.

Rockefeller, John D(avison), Sr (1839–1937), industrial magnate. Demonized by MUCKRAKERS as the organizer of the ultimate industrial TRUST (Standard Oil), Rockefeller was the world's first billionaire. His father sold snake oil through traveling medicine shows, and Rockefeller's critics charged that he used similar practices to build up Standard Oil from a single refinery into a series of interlocking corporations controlling 85% of US oil production. He retired in 1897, and over the next 40 years gave away over $530 million to educational charities and the University of Chicago. His son, John Davison Rockefeller Jr (1874–1960), expanded the family's holdings in the mining industry. He was an implacable enemy of trade unions and showed no remorse when miners striking against his Colorado Fuel and Iron Company were gunned down by militiamen in the LUDLOW MASSACRE (1914). Later in life he established the Rockefeller Center in New York City.

Rockefeller, Nelson (Aldrich) (1908–79), Republican statesman and vice president of the USA (1974–7). Rockefeller was appointed to the vice-presidency by president Gerald FORD under the terms of the TWENTY-FIFTH AMENDMENT. Nelson Rockefeller was the grandson of the founder of Standard Oil, John Davison ROCKEFELLER. During Senate confirmation hearings it emerged that he possessed a personal fortune worth in excess of $200 million. Nelson Rockefeller was a liberal Republican. He had served as assistant secretary of state under Franklin D. ROOSEVELT and as an adviser on international development in the TRUMAN administration. This association harmed his repeated attempts to gain the Republican presidential nomination; he was booed by hard-line GOLDWATER supporters at the Republicans' 1964 convention. He was elected to four terms as governor of New York State, resigning in December 1973 to head the Commission on Critical Choices for America. Deeply distrusted by conservatives, Rockefeller announced in 1975 that he would not seek the Republican presidential or vice-presidential nomination in 1976.

Rodham Clinton, Hillary (1947–), the most politically influential first lady since Eleanor ROOSEVELT, and possibly the most long-suffering ever. Hillary Rodham married Bill CLINTON in 1975. By the time the pair met at Yale University Law School, Hillary Rodham had already renounced her youthful enthusiasm for Barry GOLDWATER's brand of Republicanism, and had gained a reputation for activism on behalf of liberal Democratic causes. On graduation in 1973 she worked for the Children's Defense Fund, before accepting a post teaching law at the University of Arkansas-Fayetteville. In 1977 she resigned to join the Rose law firm in Little Rock, and she continued to serve as a litigator even while her husband was governor of Arkansas. As first lady Hillary Rodham Clinton assisted in the selection of her husband's cabinet and, as chair of a task force on health-care reform, headed an unsuccessful attempt to persuade Congress to adopt a root-and-branch reform of the US system of medical insurance designed to provide universal health care. She was also forced to make a number of public appearances with her husband in a bid to limit the political damage caused by sex scandals such as the LEWINSKY SCANDAL. In 1999 the Clintons purchased a home in New York and Hillary Rodham Clinton susbequently announced that she would seek election to one of the state's seats in the US Senate in 2000.

Roe vs. Wade (January 22 1973), US Supreme Court ruling by 7–2 that states may not prevent women from choosing to abort a foetus during the first trimester of pregnancy. The ruling ignited a conflict over ABORTION that shapes the cultural and political landscape of the USA to this day.

The case arose when a single woman, identified by the pseudonym 'Jane Roe', sued Dallas District Attorney Henry Wade in an attempt to overturn Texan law prohibiting abortion. The Supreme Court based its judgment in favor of Roe on the argument that the FOURTEENTH AMENDMENT establishes a definition of due process that guarantees personal liberty, and that a right to privacy is an integral component of personal liberty. The Roe verdict also invalidated all state laws restricting access to abortion in the second trimester of pregnancy where such laws could not be shown to bear 'a reasonable relation' to the 'protection of maternal health'. The Court found that states could prevent women from undergoing abortion in the third trimester of pregnancy.

Women's-rights activists were delighted by the Court's unequivocal affirmation of a woman's right to choose an abortion. The Court reinforced its expansive reading of the Fourteenth Amendment in Planned Parenthood of Central Missouri vs. Danforth (July 2 1976), when it ruled that states could not require women to obtain the consent of a husband or parent before obtaining an abortion in the first trimester of pregnancy.

rollback, policy propounded in 1953, at the height of the COLD WAR, by US Secretary of State John Foster DULLES, when he announced the USA's determination to 'liberate' peoples living under communist regimes. Dulles sought to move beyond the CONTAINMENT of communism to its 'rollback'. Dulles believed that rollback might be achieved through the massive build-up of US nuclear forces announced in the NEW LOOK DEFENSE POLICY. Many of the concepts associated with Dulles's strategic thinking, such as 'massive retaliation' and 'brinksmanship', scared the USA and its allies as much as, if not more than, they scared Soviet and Chinese leaders. In October 1956 Hungarian nationalists rose in revolt against Soviet domination. Dulles and EISENHOWER declined this opportunity to 'roll back' communism by sending military assistance to the Hungarian rebels. However, the concept did inform US policy towards Southeast Asia and Cuba.

Rolling Thunder, Operation, *see* OPERATION ROLLING THUNDER.

Roosevelt, (Anna) Eleanor (1884–1962), influential first lady, social reformer and diplomat. She was a niece of Theodore Roosevelt, and married her fifth cousin Franklin D. ROOSEVELT on March 17 1905. As a young woman, Roosevelt was active in the social-reform movements of the PROGRESSIVE era. During her husband's presidency she achieved a political influence that no first lady except Hillary RODHAM CLINTON has matched. Eleanor Roosevelt campaigned vigorously for her husband in the New York gubernatorial and US presidential election campaigns of 1928, 1930 and 1932. She wrote a syndicated newspaper column ('My Day') while first lady, and kept her own schedule of speaking engagements and press conferences. After Franklin D. Roosevelt's death, she served as US delegate to the United Nations General Assembly (1945, 1949–52, 1961–2) and chaired the UN Commission on Human Rights (1946). She was a founder member of AMERICANS FOR DEMOCRATIC ACTION, and a staunch supporter of liberal Democrat Adlai STEVENSON. Just before her death, she prodded President KENNEDY into creating a presidential commission on the status of women (1961).

Roosevelt, Franklin D(elano) (1882–1945), Democratic statesman, and 32nd president of the USA (1933–45). A fifth cousin to Theodore ROOSEVELT, he was and will remain, following passage of the TWENTY-SECOND AMENDMENT (1951), the longest-serving president in US history: he took up office on March 4 1933, and served until his death on April 12 1945, shortly after the start of his fourth term. During the 1930s his administration's NEW DEAL policies not only helped to pull the USA out of the GREAT DEPRESSION, but also initiated widespread social and economic reforms. In the first two years of WORLD WAR II, while the USA remained nominally neutral, Roosevelt actively aided the Allied cause. He also embarked on a mobilization of the USA's industrial, economic and military might that, once it entered the war, helped to ensure Allied victory.

Roosevelt was born to wealth and influence. Educated at Groton Academy and Harvard, he was admitted to the New York Bar in 1907. In 1911 he was elected to the New York state senate on an anti-TAMMANY Democratic ticket. In 1913 Woodrow WILSON made him assistant secretary of the Navy. He served in this post until 1920, when he resigned to contest the presidential election as the running-mate of the Democratic nominee James M. Cox (1870–1957). In 1921 Roosevelt contracted polio. Through prodigious exercise he regained the ability to stand unaided, but he never walked again. With the encouragement of his formidable wife, Eleanor ROOSEVELT, he remained active in politics. At the 1924 and 1928 Democratic conventions he gave keynote speeches on behalf of the man he dubbed 'the Happy Warrior': Al SMITH. (Smith repaid him by leading a 'stop Roosevelt' movement at the 1932 convention, and campaigned against him during the 1936 presidential election.)

In 1928 Roosevelt was elected governor of New York State. He tackled the Great Depression in his state by directing aid to New York's farmers and to the unemployed. He cut working hours for women and children. Perhaps more importantly, through radio broadcasts dubbed FIRESIDE CHATS he demonstrated concern for the plight of the common man. Although some Democrats opposed Roosevelt's nomination, he won a massive victory in the PRESIDENTIAL ELECTION OF 1932 and, by pulling together the NEW DEAL COALITION among disparate electoral groups, helped ensure two generations of Democratic ascendancy in Congress.

Relying heavily on able advisers (dubbed the BRAINS TRUST) and superb political skills, Roosevelt restored economic prosperity while forcing through measures (notably the SOCIAL SECURITY ACT and the WAGNER ACT) that made good his promise of a 'New Deal' for the American people. His GOOD-NEIGHBOR POLICY toward Latin American nations represented something of a new diplomatic deal. During his second term the US economy faltered and Roosevelt dissipated much of his popularity in the COURT-PACKING CONTROVERSY. His re-election owed much to the growing crisis in world affairs.

In 1940 Roosevelt broke with convention to seek a third term as president. He believed that US neutrality in World War II would aid the Axis powers and injure the USA's long-term interests. Such was the strength of the American public's opposition to involvement in the war, of which ISOLATIONISM was but one source, that during the 1940 campaign Roosevelt was forced to pledge that he would keep America out of the war. However, even before PEARL HARBOR Roosevelt, following a policy of 'preparedness', made a number of decisions that would affect the outcome of the war. On July 20 1940 he authorized the creation of a two-ocean navy. On December 20 1940 he created the Office of Production Management to coordinate defense build-up. Having prepared public opinion with the 'ARSENAL OF DEMOCRACY' SPEECH, he pushed through Congress the LEND-LEASE ACT, which allowed substantial aid to Britain and other anti-Axis powers. His FOUR FREEDOMS speech clarified US aims in the event of war and led to the promulgation of the ATLANTIC CHARTER.

Roosevelt was shocked by the Japanese attack on Pearl Harbor and dubbed it 'a day that will live in infamy.' He brought considerable tact to his diplomatic dealings with the main Allied leaders, Churchill and Stalin – although he irritated Churchill by pushing Britain to renounce its empire, and Stalin by insisting at the YALTA CONFERENCE on free elections in postwar Europe. Although he was successful in the 1944 presidential election, Roosevelt's percentage of the popular vote (53%) was smaller than that in 1936 or 1940. Roosevelt died, of a cerebral haemorrhage, on April 12 1945.

Roosevelt, Theodore ('Teddy') (1858–1919), PROGRESSIVE Republican statesman, vice president (1901) and 26th president of the USA (1901–9). Roosevelt succeeded to the presidency as a Republican following the assassination of President William McKINLEY. At 42 he was the youngest president America had so far seen. At home he pursued social reform, attacked the power of TRUSTS, and intervened on behalf of the public interest in disputes between business and labour. In foreign affairs his aggressively imperialistic policy was to 'talk softly and carry a big stick'. He ran again for the presidency in 1912, as the nominee of the PROGRESSIVE PARTY, but was defeated.

Two generations of US presidents, taking LINCOLN as their model, had sought to present themselves to the public as men of quiet and humble integrity. Roosevelt was loud, cocky and ambitious. Born into a wealthy family, he attended Harvard and, briefly, Columbia Law School. During his childhood, in an attempt to overcome various illnesses, Roosevelt established a lifelong devotion to the pursuits of a 'strenuous life', including boxing, judo and body-building. He later took up big-game hunting, and was also a keen conservationist and supporter of the US NATIONAL PARKS and forestry service.

In 1882, at the age of 23, Roosevelt was elected as a Republican assemblyman in New York State. He denounced party-machine politics, and crossed party lines to aid Governor Grover CLEVELAND's attempt to reform the state's civil service. Yet in the 1884 presidential election Roosevelt ditched Cleveland, shunned the Republicans' MUGWUMP faction, and supported a STALWART liable to oppose civil-service reform. Maneuvering of this kind, a constant feature of his political life, ensured that Roosevelt was loathed by the political establishment. He lost his seat and his first wife in 1884, and

spent two years ranching in South Dakota. In 1886 he ran for mayor of New York City, and was trounced. He was appointed to the US Civil Service Commission in 1889, and in 1895 began two years' service as president of the New York City Police Board. In this capacity he took part in a celebrated campaign to ensure that saloons stayed closed on Sundays. Belated support for McKinley's presidential bid was rewarded with the post of assistant secretary to the Navy (1897–8).

At the outbreak of the SPANISH-AMERICAN WAR (1898) Roosevelt resigned from government to join a volunteer cavalry unit known as the ROUGH RIDERS. He returned from service in Cuba a national hero. Doing a deal with Republican Party bosses (which he subsequently broke), he was elected governor of New York State (1898–1900). When McKinley's vice president, Garret Hobart (1844–9), died in office, New York Republicans, desperate to get Roosevelt out of their state, lobbied McKinley to appoint Roosevelt as Hobart's successor. Roosevelt duly became McKinley's running mate in the 1900 presidential election, and, following McKinley's assassination, succeeded to the presidency on September 14 1901. Easily re-elected in 1904, he served until March 3 1909.

Roosevelt used the presidency – which he described as a 'bully pulpit' – to denounce trusts. His administration made vigorous and effective use of the SHERMAN ANTI-TRUST ACT (1890), scoring victories in NORTHERN SECURITIES COMPANY VS. US and SWIFT AND COMPANY VS. US. He pushed for passage of the ELKINS ACT and the HEPBURN ACT, regulating rail companies. During the COAL STRIKE OF 1902 he threatened to take over mines unless owners negotiated in good faith. Roosevelt's administration pushed through the Meat Inspection Act (1906) and the PURE FOOD AND DRUG ACT, as well as the NATIONAL RECLAMATION ACT. Roosevelt described this blend of antitrust, mildly pro-labor, and Progressive policies as the 'Square Deal'. The fact that trust magnates J. P. MORGAN and Edward Harriman were major contributors to his 1904 election campaign bothered critics, but not Roosevelt. Roosevelt decided the route of the PANAMA CANAL, creating the state of Panama in the process. He expanded the scope of the MONROE DOCTRINE with his formulation of the ROOSEVELT COROLLARY, in which he effectively declared US hegemony in the Americas. In 1906 this bellicose man was awarded the Nobel Peace Prize, for mediating a negotiated settlement of the Russo-Japanese War of 1905.

During the 1904 election campaign Roosevelt pledged that, since he had already served a near full term, he would not, if elected, seek re-election for a third term. He groomed William TAFT as his successor and took credit for his victory in 1908. But President Taft angered Roosevelt by raising TARIFFS and firing the conservationist Gifford PINCHOT from the US Forestry Service. Amid fears of imminent socialist revolution sparked by the LAWRENCE TEXTILE STRIKE, Roosevelt entered the PRESIDENTIAL ELECTION OF 1912. Denied the Republican nomination, he ran as the PROGRESSIVE PARTY candidate, attracting 27% of the POPULAR VOTE and 88 votes in the ELECTORAL COLLEGE. This was a better return than Taft's, but Roosevelt was nonetheless denounced by loyal Republicans for splitting their vote and ensuring the election of Democratic nominee Woodrow WILSON. During WORLD WAR I Roosevelt sought to escape retirement by offering to lead a corps of volunteer soldiers to France. Wilson rejected the idea. Roosevelt was a fifth cousin of the future president Franklin ROOSEVELT, and the uncle of Eleanor ROOSEVELT.

Roosevelt corollary, corollary to the MONROE DOCTRINE issued on December 6 1904 by President Theodore ROOSEVELT. The Monroe Doctrine asserted that the Caribbean, Central America and South America were closed to further European colonization. Roosevelt's corollary stated that only the USA might act as an 'international police power' in the region. His pronouncement was prompted by rumors that Germany and Britain were contemplating armed intervention in Venezuela to recover debts owed to their citizens. Presidents Roosevelt, TAFT and WILSON used the corollary to justify a number of US interventions in the region. Franklin D. ROOSEVELT's GOOD-NEIGHBOR POLICY softened the hegemonic implications of his namesake's words.

Rosenberg trial, sensational espionage case conducted amid the wave of COLD WAR paranoia that followed the announcement that the USSR had acquired atomic weapons. Several of the hundreds of scientists who worked on the MANHATTAN PROJECT during World War II passed atomic secrets to the Soviet Union. Some did so out of loyalty to the Communist Party, others in the belief that no nation should possess a nuclear monopoly. In 1951 Ethel Rosenberg (1915–53), her husband Julius (1918–53) and Morton Sobell were accused of passing details of the atom bomb to the Soviet Union. Testimony against them came from convicted spies and from Ethel Rosenberg's brother David Greenglass, who was under indictment for espionage but had been promised leniency if he cooperated with the prosecution. The Rosenbergs admitted to being supporters of the COMMUNIST PARTY OF THE USA but, dismissing the character of the evidence against them, refused to cooperate with the prosecution. Judge Irving Kaufman sentenced all three defendants to death for perpetrating 'a diabolical conspiracy to destroy a god-fearing nation'. Demonstrations for and against the verdict were mounted throughout the USA. The Rosenbergs, who had two young sons, were executed on June 19 1953. Morton Sobell was sentenced to a 30-year prison term.

Ross, Betsy (1752–1836), Philadelphia seamstress who is reputed to have manufactured the first American flag at the request of George WASHINGTON. CONTINENTAL CONGRESS approved the stars-and-stripes design of the American flag on June 14 1777.

Ross, John (1790–1866), influential CHEROKEE leader (known to the Cherokee as Kooweskoowee) who opposed President JACKSON's policy of INDIAN REMOVAL. The son of a Scottish trader and a one-quarter Cherokee woman, Ross served alongside Jackson during the first CREEK WAR. In 1827 he wrote a Constitution for the Cherokee nation that he hoped would serve as the basis for their admission into the union as an independent state. From 1839 until his death, Ross, serving as chief of the United Cherokee Nation, used his considerable diplomatic skills to preserve Cherokee autonomy on western reservations.

Ross, Nellie Tayloe, *see* WYOMING.

Rough Riders, nickname for the First US Volunteer Cavalry Regiment, which fought in Cuba during the SPANISH-AMERICAN WAR. The creation of the regiment was authorized by Congress on April 22 1898, on the eve of the war. The commander of the Rough Riders was Colonel Leonard Wood (1860–1927), and their most famous volunteer was Theodore ROOSEVELT. The regiment's nickname derived from the horsemanship and courage displayed during the Cuban campaign. On July 1 1898, Rough Riders, among them Roosevelt, captured Kettle Hill after repeated charges through heavy fire. This action contributed to the collapse of Spanish resistance in Cuba.

Route 66. The first arterial highway to link the midwest with California opened in 1926. In 1946, Bobby Troup immortalized Route 66 in a song that states accurately: 'It winds from Chicago to L.A./ More than 2000 miles all the way.' The highway's winding route was deliberately chosen to help isolated farmers market their crops. Many of the obscure towns along the route whose euphony is celebrated in the song – for example Winona, Arizona – sprouted brothels, fast food stands and even amusement parks on the strength of the road. However, the first users of Route 66 were not teenagers searching for kicks but OKIES fleeing the DUSTBOWL for a new life in California. In John Steinbeck's *Grapes of Wrath* (1939), the highway is referred to as the 'mother road.' Route 66 became synonymous with the pleasures of driving while listening to the radio in the 1940s and 50s. The Federal Highway Act of 1956 appropriated funding for a network of four-lane interstate highways and, as these came into operation, US Route 66 was downgraded to a minor road and, in many sections, built over. A preservation trust is currently reviving use of the surviving sections of original road. The town of Springfield, Illinois, recently voted to boost a tourist trade previously dominated by its association with Abraham LINCOLN, by upgrading for classic-car enthusiasts and lovers of Americana that section of Route 66 that passes through the center of town.

Rural Electrification Administration (REA), agency established to issue low-interest loans to cooperatives seeking to generate or distribute electricity in areas not served by utility companies. The REA was created by President Franklin D. ROOSEVELT by executive order on May 11 1935. By 1939, 417 cooperatives had been formed. Just 4% of America's farms had access to electricity in 1925; by 1940 25% were served by power lines.

Rusk, (David) Dean (1909–94), foreign-policy specialist and secretary of state (1961–9) under Presidents KENNEDY and JOHNSON. Born in Georgia, Rusk was educated at Davidson College, North Carolina, and the University of Oxford. He served in the US Army during World War II, and between 1946 and 1951 held a variety of posts in the Department of War and the State Department. From 1951 to 1961 he was president of the Rockefeller Foundation. Rusk was a firm supporter of the USA's COLD WAR policy of 'containing' Soviet expansion. He urged Kennedy to take forceful action during the CUBAN MISSILE CRISIS of 1962, and fully supported Johnson's decision to escalate the USA's involvement in the VIETNAM WAR.

Ruth, 'Babe' (George Herman Ruth) (1895–1948), BASEBALL's first superstar, known as the 'Sultan of Swat' or simply 'the Bambino'. In 22 seasons as a professional he hit 714 home runs and compiled a batting average of .342. Ruth was a difficult, larger-than-life character. He loved kids but hated management. He did little physical training, often preparing for a game by eating hot dogs and drinking beer.

He began his career in 1914 as a pitcher with the Boston Red Sox. He was sold to the New York Yankees in the close season of 1919, and it was as a Yankee that he established his reputation as a batter. He hit 60 home runs in the 1927 season and altogether played in ten World Series. In a 1932 World Series game against the Chicago Cubs at Wrigley Field, Chicago, Ruth pointed to an area of the bleachers prior to a pitch, then smashed the subsequent delivery to that spot for a game-winning home run. Heroics of this sort ensured that he drew crowds even when playing for the Boston Braves in the twilight of his career. In 1936 Ruth was among the first five members inducted into baseball's Hall of Fame. He ended his baseball career as a coach for the Brooklyn Dodgers.

S

Sacajawea (*c*.1790–1812), young SHOSHONI woman who helped ensure the success of LEWIS AND CLARK's expedition to explore western lands acquired in the LOUISIANA PURCHASE. In 1800 Sacajawea was captured by the Hidatsa SIOUX and sold into marriage with Toussaint Charbonneau, a French trader. In 1804 husband and wife were hired as expedition guides and interpreters by Captain Meriwether Lewis. In the spring of 1805 Sacajawea directed the expedition to Shoshoni homelands in western Wyoming where the explorers acquired the horses that enabled them to become the first US citizens to cross the Rockies.

Sacco and Vanzetti case, case involving two Italian-born anarchists, Nicolo Sacco (1891–1927) and Bartolomeo Vanzetti (1888–1927), who were sentenced to death on July 14 1921 for the murder of a clerk and guard during the course of a robbery at a shoe factory in Braintree, Massachusetts. The evidence against them was circumstantial, and the prosecution played on their political beliefs and the fact that they had refused to register for military service under the terms of the SELECTIVE SERVICE ACT (1917). The convictions were reviewed and appealed, but the pair were executed on August 23 1927. The case came to symbolize the excesses of the RED SCARE.

St Lô offensive (July–August 1944), campaign during WORLD WAR II in which US troops broke the developing stalemate around the Normandy beachhead established following the D-DAY LANDINGS (June 6 1944).

Six weeks after the initial landings the Allied advance was faltering. Resupply operations had been disrupted by bad weather in the English Channel, and experienced German reinforcements had reached the front. In the east, British and Canadian forces had been badly mauled while attempting to break out of the beachhead. Further west, the US First Army had taken longer than expected to cut the Cotentin peninsula and complete the capture of the crucial port of Cherbourg.

On July 25 1944 units of the US Seventh Army Corps began an advance (dubbed 'Operation Cobra') south and west from the Utah and OMAHA beachheads through St Lô. By July 30 they had reached Avranches, at the base of the Cotentin peninsula, and were in position to isolate Brittany. On August 1 the US Third Army under General George PATTON was released to drive west toward Brest, south and east towards Paris, and north towards the 'Falaise pocket', in which the remaining German armies were isolated and all but destroyed. Nearly 100,000 Allied soldiers died in the offensive and its associated operations.

St Mihiel offensive (September 12–16 1918), major engagement in France, the first independent offensive mounted by American troops in WORLD WAR I. It was directed against a German salient in the line of trenches between Verdun and St Mihiel. General John PERSHING committed 14 US divisions (about 550,000 men) and supporting French troops to an operation that forced German forces to retreat to the northeast. US forces suffered 6000 casualties.

SALT (Strategic Arms Limitation Talks), *see* DÉTENTE.

Sand Creek massacre (November 29 1864), premeditated attack on 500 CHEYENNE and ARAPAHO who had surrendered to US authorities at Fort Lyon, Colorado. The massacre was carried out by 700 Colorado militiamen under Colonel John Chivington, and at least 200 Native Americans were killed. Chivington planned the massacre in a bid to become territorial governor of Colorado.

San Francisco Conference, *see* UNITED NATIONS.

Sanger, Margaret Louise (née Higgins, 1883–1966), social reformer who spent her adult life campaigning to make birth control (a term she coined) available to working-class women. After training as a nurse in White Plains, New York, in her thirties Sanger lived in Greenwich Village, New York, and moved in socialist circles that included Bill Haywood (leader of the INDUSTRIAL WORKERS OF THE WORLD) and the anarchist Emma GOLDMAN. She began writing articles on birth control for the socialist newspaper *Call*. In 1914 she was prosecuted under the 'Comstock laws' (preventing the mailing of obscene material) for distributing copies of her pamphlet *What Every Girl Should Know*, but on February 18 1916 won a famous victory when the US government declined to use the same statutes to prosecute her for distributing a pamphlet entitled *Family Limitation*. In October 1916 she opened her first birth-control clinic, in Brownsville, New York. To the annoyance of veterans of the WOMEN'S SUFFRAGE move-

ment, Sanger argued in her book *Woman and the New Race* (1920) that women benefited more from access to birth control than they did from legal and political enfranchisement.

San Ildefonso, treaty of (October 1 1800), treaty by which Spain secretly transferred its Louisiana colony to France, which had lost it to Spain in the treaty of PARIS (1763). Spain continued to administer New Orleans. Napoleon Bonaparte then threatened to rescind America's RIGHT OF DEPOSIT (access to the port of New Orleans), spurring President Jefferson to authorize the LOUISIANA PURCHASE.

San Jacinto, battle of (April 21 1836), engagement in TEXAS during the struggle for independence from Mexico. Texans led by Samuel Houston ambushed a larger Mexican force; crying 'Remember the Alamo' they killed 600 Mexicans and captured 700. The action forced Mexican recognition of Texan independence.

San Lorenzo, treaty of (October 27 1795), treaty negotiated by Thomas Pinckney (1750–1828), the US minister to Great Britain, that resolved disputes between Spain and the USA that had proved insoluble during the JAY–GARDOQUI NEGOTIATIONS (1785). Spain, preoccupied by the NOOTKA SOUND CRISIS, accepted that the northern boundary of WEST FLORIDA ran along the 31st parallel. It granted the USA free navigation of the Mississippi and RIGHT OF DEPOSIT in New Orleans. These US gains were threatened by the treaty of SAN ILDEFONSO (1800).

Santa Clara County vs. Southern Pacific Railroad (1886), US Supreme Court ruling that unanimously accepted a claim first made by ex-senator and corporate lawyer Roscoe Conkling (1829–88) that Congress had intended the FOURTEENTH AMENDMENT's due process clause to apply to legal 'persons', i.e. corporations. The decision allowed corporations to argue that where state laws regulating trade limited their future profits, a violation of the corporation's civil right to due process had occurred. The decision reversed the logic of MUNN VS. ILLINOIS (1877). Its application made state laws regulating public carriers and monopolies virtually unworkable.

Saratoga, British surrender at (October 17 1777), surrender in New York State of 5700 British, German and loyalist troops under the command of Major General John Burgoyne to American forces commanded by Major General Horatio GATES. The surrender proved to be the turning point of the REVOLUTIONARY WAR. It followed an unsuccessful British attempt to dislodge American troops from BEMIS HEIGHTS, and marked the final failure of a campaign to seize control of New York State via an invasion launched southwards from the Adirondacks. Denied reinforcement, unable (following the battle of BENNINGTON) to forage in the surrounding countryside, and confined to densely wooded terrain, Burgoyne's exhausted column surrendered on the understanding that it would be allowed to return to England. In fact, the force spent the rest of the war under guard in Virginia.

Savannah, British capture of (December 29 1778). The capture of Savannah, Georgia, inaugurated a British campaign to win the REVOLUTIONARY WAR by capitalizing on the strength of LOYALISM in the south. Advised by runaway slaves of the weak points in Savannah's defenses, a British task force of 3500 men under the command of Lieutenant-Colonel Archibald Campbell seized Georgia's major seaport town from Major General Robert Howe's defending force of 850 men on December 29 1778. Much of Georgia now fell under British control, making the recapture of the state's main city a political priority for Congress. On September 3 1779 a joint US-French force besieged the city. But a premature assault on October 9 was repulsed at the cost of 800 casualties. British troops held the town until July 11 1782.

savings-and-loans crisis, economic/financial crisis that developed in the 1980s as a result of the 'deregulation' policy pursued by President REAGAN. Prior to 1982, US 'thrifts' (mortgage-granting institutions also known as savings-and-loan companies) had been restricted to providing home-purchase loans from savings held on deposit. In 1982 Congress changed the law governing thrifts to allow them to invest their capital in real estate, stock and currency options, and even foreign loans. In the late 1980s the real-estate market collapsed, dragging up to 740 thrifts into bankruptcy, and overwhelming the resources of the Federal Savings and Loan Insurance Corporation, which was charged with guaranteeing depositors' savings. On August 9 1989 President BUSH signed into law a federal bail-out package, whose main feature was the creation of the Resolution Trust Corporation (RTC), which administered and sold the assets of insolvent thrifts to guarantee the viability of those remaining. Even after the creation of the RTC, it has been estimated that US taxpayers will have to find $500 billion over the next 40 years to bail out the industry.

'Say it ain't so Joe', plaintive challenge issued to the White Sox player 'Shoeless' Joe Jackson by a boy in Chicago troubled by rumors that Jackson and his teammates had taken a bribe to lose BASEBALL's 1919 World Series.

Scalawags, pejorative term applied by white southerners, especially REDEEMERS, to those of their white southern neighbors who collaborated with RADICAL REPUBLICANS to implement the RECONSTRUCTION ACTS. The term may derive from Scalloway, a district in the Shetland Islands known for runty cattle and sheep.

Schecter Poultry Corporation vs. US (May 27 1935), unanimous US Supreme Court ruling (in what was dubbed the 'sick chicken case') that gutted the NATIONAL INDUSTRIAL RECOVERY ACT (NIRA) and, with it, the central policy assumptions of President

Franklin D. Roosevelt's first NEW DEAL administration. The NIRA had established a NATIONAL RECOVERY ADMINISTRATION (NRA), which wrote detailed and legally binding codes prescribing wages, prices and business procedures for hundreds of industries. Small businesses found it difficult, and costly, to comply with NRA codes. The Schecter Poultry Corporation, a small business supplying kosher chickens in New York City, appealed a conviction for violating NRA codes by paying low wages, butchering birds in kosher fashion and selling ailing chickens. The Supreme Court found the original conviction unjust, arguing that the NIRA sanctioned an unconstitutional regulation of intrastate commerce and an unacceptable delegation of power to the executive branch of government.

Schenck vs. US (March 3 1919), unanimous US Supreme Court ruling that FIRST AMENDMENT guarantees of free speech do not apply in wartime, or when the exercise of free speech poses 'a clear and present danger' to the community. The case was brought by a man imprisoned under the ESPIONAGE ACT (1917) for circulating a pamphlet criticizing SELECTIVE SERVICE.

Schwarzkopf, Norman, *see* PERSIAN GULF WAR.

SCLC, *see* SOUTHERN CHRISTIAN LEADERSHIP CONFERENCE.

Scopes trial (July 10–21 1925), trial that tested a law passed in Tennessee in 1924 making it illegal for teachers to instruct students that 'man has descended from a lower order of animals'. With the backing of the AMERICAN CIVIL LIBERTIES UNION (ACLU), John Thomas Scopes created the test case by instructing schoolchildren on Darwin's theory of evolution. Clarence Darrow (1857–1938) defended Scopes, while William Jennings BRYAN acted for the prosecution. Bryan's arguments showed that he knew little and cared less about science. He justified the law by reference to Protestant fundamentalism. Bryan and the law's supporters were derided by urban sophisticates, but Scopes was convicted and fined. The law, and similar statutes in other states, remained on the books.

Scott, Winfield (1786–1866), US Army general and WHIG politician. A career soldier, Scott was appointed commander in chief of the US Army in 1841 following service in the WAR OF 1812, SEMINOLE WARS and BLACK HAWK WAR. Scott's victories during the MEXICAN WAR made him a national hero (although his methodical style also earned him the nickname 'Old Fuss and Feathers'). In 1852 Scott was the Whig presidential nominee. He was defeated in the election by a former subordinate, Franklin PIERCE. By the time he retired from the Army on November 1 1861 he was so fat he could not mount a horse.

Scottsboro boys case, case that exemplified the distinctly unequal justice meted out to African-Americans in the JIM CROW south. In 1931 nine black men, one of them just 12 years old, were accused of raping two white women aboard a freight train near Scottsboro, Alabama. Following a trial riddled with hearsay evidence and procedural error, an all-white jury convicted all nine defendants. Eight were sentenced to death. The COMMUNIST PARTY OF THE USA and later the NATIONAL ASSOCIATION FOR THE ADVANCEMENT OF COLORED PEOPLE (NAACP) took up the defendants' case. As the inadequacy of the legal representation afforded the defendants, together with the weakness of the prosecution's evidence against them, became known, the case attracted international attention. Eventually the death sentences were quashed and the alleged victims amended their testimony. But five of the defendants served long prison terms.

search and destroy, strategy adopted in the VIETNAM WAR by General William WESTMORELAND, who ordered US troops to identify organized enemy units, isolate them and destroy them. The favored approach of the US armed forces in the war was aggression, and search-and-destroy missions were carried out in defiance of local terrain and the guerrilla tactics of their Vietnamese opponents. The strategy assumed that US forces could 'attrit' the enemy to such a point that the military threat to the independence of South Vietnam would be removed. US commanders accordingly relied on the BODY-COUNT to measure the success of their campaign. Enemy forces frustrated the strategy by ambushing US columns and then preventing them from calling in air support by 'sticking to their belts' in close-quarter fighting.

SEATO, see SOUTHEAST ASIAN TREATY ORGANIZATION.

secession, the process by which eleven southern states broke away from the Union in 1860–1 to form the Confederate States of America (the CONFEDERACY). New England states had threatened secession at the HARTFORD CONVENTION and South Carolina had threatened to secede during the NULLIFICATION CRISIS. Since Abraham LINCOLN and the REPUBLICAN PARTY unequivocally denied the right of a state to leave the Union, the secession of southern states that followed Lincoln's victory in the PRESIDENTIAL ELECTION OF 1860 provided the immediate cause of the CIVIL WAR.

On December 20 1860 a special convention approved (169–0) an ordinance dissolving 'the union now subsisting between South Carolina and other states.' South Carolina's lead was followed by Mississippi, Florida, Alabama, Georgia, Louisiana and Texas (February 1 1861). Thus the seven states of the 'lower south' left the Union before LINCOLN's inauguration as president. Following the bombardment of FORT SUMTER at the start of the Civil War, Virginia, Arkansas, Tennessee and North Carolina seceded (May 20 1861). Secession was popular, partly because many southerners doubted that it would lead to a prolonged war. Ironically, the constitution adopted by the Confederacy prohibited any member

state from seceding. Following the war, the Supreme Court ruled secession unconstitutional in TEXAS VS. WHITE (1869).

Second Amendment, amendment to the US Constitution protecting the right of citizens to keep and bear arms in order to allow state militias to mobilize speedily. It was one of the ten amendments making up the BILL OF RIGHTS. For the full text, see Appendix 1.

Second Great Awakening, terms applied to a widespread religious revival, stressing Calvinistic principles, that swept much of the midwest and northeast during the first four decades of the 19th century. TEMPERANCE, ABOLITION and other social reform campaigns drew upon the energies unleashed in this revival.

Historians have argued that a first 'Great Awakening' (characterized by an enthusiastic response to charismatic preachers and schisms within established denominations) featured in the histories of most of the THIRTEEN COLONIES in the 35 years preceding independence. This first revival did not touch those areas, chiefly the Ohio valley, that witnessed the most rapid population growth in the years after the conclusion of the REVOLUTIONARY WAR. Many of the new residents were culturally Protestant but not organized within established congregations. Itinerant preachers therefore found an eager audience in these western districts. The Cane Ridge camp meeting, held in Bourbon county, Kentucky, in August 1801, marked the start of the USA's second great revival. Over 10,000 people attended the meeting. Ministers preached in relays, urging their audience to realize its innate depravity, renounce sin and prepare for salvation through immediate conversion to a godly life. At this, and at subsequent 'camp meetings,' men and women wept, writhed and spoke in tongues in response to charismatic preaching. Converts established new congregations and spread the gospel in yet more remote areas.

In contrast, rural New England (and especially the 'burned-over district' of upstate New York) had been deeply affected by the colonial revival. In its aftermath, many residents had 'lapsed' into what orthodox theologians regarded as an overly comfortable deism. From the 1820s, charismatic preachers, notably Charles Grandison Finney (1792–1875), held western-style revival meetings across the northeast. A major revival held in the winter of 1830–1 at Rochester, New York, produced thousands of new converts.

Revival meetings featured lay preaching and the testimony of the converted. They thereby accustomed 'ordinary' men and, especially, women, to self-assertion and public speaking. Revival ministry emphasized the individual's moral agency but warned that association with sin jeopardised salvation. As a result, converts felt obliged not only to renounce sinful behavior, such as drinking, but also to campaign against sinful institutions, for example slavery. Hence the moral urgency that infused many of the great social reform movements of the 19th century can be traced to the Second Great Awakening.

Second New Deal, term used by some historians to suggest a change in emphasis in the NEW DEAL from the summer of 1935 onwards. President Franklin D. ROOSEVELT's first inaugural address (1933) had asked Americans to collaborate with big business and government to work through the national emergency of the GREAT DEPRESSION. In May 1935, the US Supreme Court ruled the legislative embodiment of this approach, the NATIONAL INDUSTRIAL RECOVERY ACT, unconstitutional. Calling Congress into a special summer session, Roosevelt abandoned previous attempts at the detailed regulation of big business through the NATIONAL RECOVERY ADMINISTRATION and instead put forward legislation delineating corporate practices that would not be tolerated. At the same time, Roosevelt urged further expenditure on job creation programs and the creation of a national social-security system. Roosevelt's second inaugural address (1937), which contained a denunciation of social injustice and called for the eradication of poverty, reflected a change in priorities and presentation that has lead some historians to distinguish the policies pursued between 1933–5 from those pursued subsequently.

second party system, term used by historians to refer to the period from 1834 to 1852, when the two main political parties struggling for control of Congress and the presidency were the DEMOCRATIC PARTY and the WHIG PARTY.

In 1828 congressional opponents of Andrew JACKSON adopted the label NATIONAL REPUBLICANS, and in 1834 left the Democratic Party to join former members of the ANTI-MASONIC PARTY and LOOSE CONSTRUCTIONIST southerners in the newly formed Whig Party. The Whigs' program was not inherently populist, but, as the LOG CABIN AND HARD CIDER CAMPAIGN of 1840 demonstrated, they proved adept electioneers. The Whig Party was the first political casualty of the crisis over slavery that dominated politics from 1850. It ran its final presidential candidate in 1852. Thereafter most Whigs joined the new REPUBLICAN PARTY, signaling the collapse of the second party system.

secret ballot, voting system which prevents the bribery or intimidation of a voter. In 1888 Louisville, Kentucky, became the first US municipality to issue voters with a ballot paper printed at the expense of the local authority and listing the names of all candidates. Since the voter no longer had to obtain a ballot paper from one or other of the parties contesting an election, his preference remained secret. Pressure from PROGESSIVE reformers ensured that the system was widely copied.

segregation, racial, see JIM CROW; CIVIL RIGHTS MOVEMENT.

Selective Service Acts (1917, 1940), legislative measures that set up draft boards for recruiting men into the US armed forces.

(1) The first act (May 18 1917) established local draft boards to register and classify for military service all American men between the ages of 21 and 30. Conscious of opposition to US involvement in WORLD WAR I, and mindful of resistance to the CONSCRIPTION ACT passed during the Civil War, President WILSON emphasized the 'voluntary' nature of a measure that ultimately registered 24,234,021 men. The process threw up some startling data: 25% of registrants were found to be illiterate, and 33% were physically unfit, while IQ tests administered to the 2 million registrants actually inducted into the armed forces revealed, at least to the satisfaction of the tests' PROGRESSIVE designers, that the average soldier had a mental age of 13, and that half could be classified as 'morons'.

(2) The system of local boards was revived through the Selective Service and Training Act (September 16 1940) as President Franklin D. ROOSEVELT prepared America for possible involvement in WORLD WAR II. This was the first peacetime draft in US history, and through it 10 million men were inducted into the armed forces. The act expired on March 31 1947, but re-established in a bill passed on June 24 1948. Modified and renewed, the system remained in place until June 30 1973. During the COLD WAR some 5 million men were drafted into the US armed forces. 1.5 million conscripts served in the KOREAN WAR and 2 million men were drafted during the VIETNAM WAR. Elvis PRESLEY was the most famous draftee of the period. Muhammad ALI was the most notable of the 136,000 drafted men who refused to serve in Vietnam. *See also* DRAFT.

Selma Freedom March (1965), civil rights protest that produced one of the CIVIL RIGHTS MOVEMENT's greatest victories (a commitment from President Lyndon B. JOHNSON to push what became the VOTING RIGHTS ACT of 1965), but it also marked the moment when the movement's momentum began to dissipate under the pressure of disputes over strategy and objectives.

In 1964 the SOUTHERN CHRISTIAN LEADERSHIP CONFERENCE (SCLC) began a voter-registration drive in Selma, Alabama, later joined by members of the STUDENT NONVIOLENT COORDINATING COMMITTEE (SNCC). As in the earlier BIRMINGHAM DESEGREGATION CAMPAIGN, organizers could count on divisions within the white community and the likelihood that violent resistance from the local police would produce television pictures that would in turn force federal action. On March 7 1965, 600 demonstrators, led by John Lewis and Hosea Williams, were attacked by police after crossing Selma's Edmund Pettus Bridge at the beginning of a march on Alabama's state capital, Montgomery. Martin Luther KING called for a second march two days later, but, unbeknownst to SNCC, did a deal with federal authorities that saw the second demonstration turn back after a symbolic crossing of the Pettus Bridge. President Johnson announced his intention to send a voting-rights bill to Congress on March 14. King led a court-sanctioned march on Montgomery on March 21. King's willingness to negotiate with the federal government, often in secret, alienated SNCC members who had suffered white supremacist violence during campaigns such as the MISSISSIPPI FREEDOM SUMMER.

Seminole, Native American people of CREEK ancestry, who speak a Muskogean language. They were regarded by the USA as one of the FIVE CIVILIZED TRIBES. The Seminole migrated from Georgia to Florida in the later 18th century. Their willingness to accept runaway slaves as tribal members, and their raids into Georgia and Alabama, provoked the first SEMINOLE WAR with the USA in 1817. Most Seminole resisted the forced relocation to western reservations mandated by the INDIAN REMOVAL ACT

(1830). This prompted a second SEMINOLE WAR, after which most Seminoles were moved to Oklahoma.

Seminole Wars (1817–18, 1835–42), two wars fought between the SEMINOLE people and US forces.

(1) On November 21 1817 Andrew JACK-SON led a force of US regulars, militiamen, and CREEK warriors into Spanish WEST FLORIDA in retaliation for Seminole raids on US settlements. In the course of a campaign that lasted until October 31 1818, Jackson's force pursued Seminole war parties, burned Seminole towns, and executed two Britons, captured in the Spanish fort of St Marks, whom Jackson suspected of abetting the insurgents. The campaign enhanced Jackson's fame and prompted the ADAMS–ONIS TREATY.

(2) In December 1835, under the charismatic leadership of OSCEOLA, some Seminole tribesmen began armed resistance to relocation. It took 10,000 US regulars (led by Zachary TAYLOR), thousands of militiamen, the capture of Osceola by trickery, and the use of scorched-earth tactics to remove 3824 rebel Seminole to Oklahoma. The USA concluded the campaign on May 10 1842, leaving small bands of Seminole at large, some of whom skirmished with US soldiers in the spring of 1858.

Senate, *see* CONGRESS.

Seneca, Native American people, the largest and most westerly member of the IROQUOIS CONFEDERACY. The Seneca's homelands lay in western New York State, although tributary peoples settled on the Allegheny and Ohio rivers. During the SEVEN YEARS' WAR the Seneca fought with France against Britain and the USA. During the REVOLUTIONARY WAR most Seneca fought with Britain against the USA. As a result, they were penalized and dispersed following SULLIVAN'S CAMPAIGN.

Seneca Falls Convention (1848), conference held in New York State to discuss the condition and rights of women. Under the leadership of Lucretia MOTT and Elizabeth Cady STANTON the conference issued (on July 19 1848) a Declaration of Sentiments, whose ninth article called for women 'to secure to themselves their sacred right to the elective franchise'. This marked the beginning of the WOMEN'S SUFFRAGE movement in the USA.

separation of powers, the doctrine that the power to make the law, enforce the law and interpret the law must be distributed among separate government agencies. The separation of the powers of the legislature, the executive and the judiciary forms a system of checks and balances in democratic government, and is one of the central concepts which is enshrined in the US CONSTITUTION. Accordingly, in the USA CONGRESS proposes and passes legislation, which the presidency then enforces, and the SUPREME COURT interprets. Each branch of the US government is independent of the others, is selected by a different procedure, and enjoys different terms of office. By this means the concentration of excessive power in the hands of a particular individual or body is avoided.

Seton, Saint Elizabeth Ann (née Bayley) (1774–1821), the first native-born American to be canonized, and the founder (in 1810) of the USA's first order of nuns, the Sisters of Charity of St Joseph. Seton converted to Catholicism in 1805, following a trip to Italy on which her husband died. She returned to the USA, and in 1809 opened, in Baltimore, Maryland, the USA's first Catholic elementary school. Seton and the Sisters of Charity also founded and ran St Joseph's College for Women, in Emmitsburg, Maryland. She was beatified in 1963, and canonized in 1975.

Seven Days' battles (June 26–July 2 1862), Confederate counteroffensive during the CIVIL WAR that marked the final frustration of George McCLELLAN'S PENINSULAR CAMPAIGN. Union troops had reached positions 6 miles (10 km) from Richmond when they were driven back at the battle of Seven Pines (May 31–June 1). During that battle Confederate commander Joseph E. JOHNSTON was severely wounded and replaced as commander of the Army of Northern Virginia by Robert E. LEE. Lee attempted to destroy McClellan's Union army in a fast-paced counteroffensive. The Seven Days' battle began with an attack at Mechanicsville on the right flank of the Union line (June 26–27). Lee then developed his counteroffensive with a series of assaults on the center of the Union lines at Gaine's Mill (June 27), Savage's Station (June 29) and Frayser's Farm (June 30). This drove McClellan's army back across the Chickahominy river to the James river. On July 1 Lee's army made a desperate attempt to break Union defenses around Malvern Hill. The Union lines held and Lee's army retreated towards Richmond. McClellan was ordered to evacuate the peninsula on August 3 1862.

Seventeenth Amendment, amendment to the US Constitution, submitted to the states on May 13 1912 and officially proclaimed on May 31 1913, that allows the voters of each state to select US senators. US senators had previously been chosen by state legislatures. The direct election of senators was a major goal of POPULIST and PROGRESSIVE campaigners.

Seventh Amendment, amendment to the US Constitution establishing the right to trial by jury in most common-law (civil) suits. It was one of the ten amendments making up the BILL OF RIGHTS. For the full text, *see* Appendix 1.

Seven Years' War (1756–63), war between Britain, Prussia and Hanover on one side, and France, Spain, Austria and Russia on the other. Fighting took place in Europe, India and North America. Outside of the European theater, the war was principally a struggle between Britain and France for colonial possessions. The fighting in North America is sometimes referred to as the French and Indian War. Britain declared war against France on May 17 1756, and against Spain on January 2 1762. The treaty of PARIS (February 10 1763) concluded hostilities.

The war in North America originated in disputes between Britain and France over ownership of lands in the Ohio valley. It resulted in significant territorial gains for the British. Britain acquired EAST and WEST FLORIDA from Spain and all remaining lands east of the Mississippi plus Canada from France. These gains led Britain to adopt revenue-raising measures that would be-come a bone of contention in the AMERICAN REVOLUTION. During the war 60,000 American militiamen fought for the British, and 11,000 enlisted in the British Army. George WASHINGTON achieved military fame in the war.

Seward, William H(enry) (1801–72), Whig and subsequently Republican politician, and secretary of state (1861–9). Born and raised in New York State, Seward's original political allegiance was to the ANTI-MASONIC PARTY. He became a WHIG in 1834. He served two terms as governor of New York (1838–42) before resuming a successful legal practice. Elected to the US Senate in 1848, Seward attracted notice for a speech that denounced the COMPROMISE OF 1850 on the grounds that a 'higher law' than the Constitution bound him to oppose any concession to slaveholders' interests. He joined the REPUBLICAN PARTY and sought, unsuccessfully, its presidential nomination in 1856 and 1860. LINCOLN appointed Seward secretary of state, a post he held until 1869. During the CIVIL WAR Seward purged the State Department of Confederate sympathizers, skilfully resolved the TRENT and ALABAMA AFFAIRS and blocked European diplomatic recognition of the Confederacy. In 1865 Seward suffered knife wounds in an assassination attempt linked to that which claimed Lincoln's life. In 1867, to much ridicule, he engineered the purchase from Russia of ALASKA, which became known as 'Seward's Folly'.

Shame of Our Cities, The, series of MUCK-RAKER essays by Lincoln Steffens (1866–1936) that investigated urban corruption and party-machine politics. The essays were first published in *McClure's Monthly* (1903–5), and struck a chord with PROGRESSIVES. Steffens argued that prevailing patterns of city government displayed 'moral weakness', and were symptomatic of 'a freed people who had lost the will to be free'. Although corruption undoubtedly existed, recent studies show that big cities were run efficiently. The burden of Steffens's argument, and its appeal to Progressives, was that the influence of upper-middle-class Protestants on city government ought to be increased, while that of working-class Catholics (especially the Irish) should be decreased.

sharecropping, labor system that dominated southern plantation lands in the period after RECONSTRUCTION. Landless families, usually African-American, rented small plots from white landowners. They paid their rent and met the cost of seed, tools and supplies by pledging a portion of the crop they raised to the landowner. As cotton prices tumbled, working families found it harder to earn a living from the system and fell into debt. Many landowners inflated the cost of essential supplies, adding to the indebtedness and dependency of the sharecropper. *See also* CROP LIEN.

Shaw, Anna Howard (1847–1919), redoubtable campaigner for WOMEN'S SUFFRAGE and TEMPERANCE, and the first American woman to be ordained as a Methodist minister (1880). She went on to obtain an MD from Boston University in 1886. Shaw served as president of the NATIONAL AMERICAN WOMAN SUFFRAGE ASSOCIATION between 1904 and 1915.

Shawnee, Algonkian-speaking Native American people who in the late 18th century mostly lived in southwestern Pennsylvania and southeastern Ohio. Although few in number, the Shawnee were implacable opponents of white expansion. They fought against encroachment in PONTIAC'S WAR and the REVOLUTIONARY WAR, but were forced to cede land to the USA through the treaty of GREENVILLE (1795). In the early 19th century Shawnee leader TECUMSEH set about forging a wide-based alliance of various Native American nations to resist further US expansion. This movement was broken when Tecumseh's brother the PROPHET led Shawnee braves to defeat at the battle of TIPPECANOE CREEK (1811). The Shawnee fought with Britain against the USA in the WAR OF 1812. Their spirit broken, the Shawnee were ultimately relocated on reservations in Oklahoma, where today some 2000 Shawnee still live.

Shays's Rebellion (1786), rebellion in Massachusetts led by the Revolutionary War veteran Daniel Shays, in protest against high taxes and the role of the courts in issuing foreclosure notices for the non-payment of debt. In late August 1786 inhabitants of western Massachusetts began using force to prevent local courts from meeting to enforce foreclosure notices. On September 26 500 armed men, led by Shays, prevented the Massachusetts Supreme Court from meeting in Springfield. The state governor mobilized 4000 militia and, in January 1787, successfully prevented 1200 Shaysites from seizing the US arsenal at Springfield. Shays was captured on February 4 1788. Sentenced to death, he was pardoned on June 13 1788. A newly elected state assembly placated western protesters. Alexander HAMILTON was among many FEDERALISTS who saw the rebellion as portending the 'tyranny of the majority', and hence justifying a radical revision of the ARTICLES OF CONFEDERATION.

Shenandoah Valley campaigns (1862, 1864–5), two important campaigns in northwest Virginia during the CIVIL WAR.

(1) In the spring of 1862 Confederate General Thomas 'Stonewall' JACKSON commanding a force of 17,000, prevented a

36,000-strong Union army from joining the PENINSULAR CAMPAIGN, and kept alive the possibility of a Confederate advance northward and eastward against Washington DC. Utilizing a series of feints and rapid marches – which demonstrated Jackson's strategic doctrine: 'Always mystify, mislead, and surprise the enemy' – the Confederate force won victories at McDowell (May 13), Front Royal (May 23), Winchester (May 25), Cross Keys (June 8) and Port Republic (June 9). These actions contributed to the failure of Union General George McCLELLAN's thrust against Richmond (the Confederate capital), and stymied Union plans to use the valley as a springboard for the invasion of eastern Tennessee.

(2) In the summer of 1864 Major General Jubal Early (1816–94) led a Confederate raiding force of 20,000 men northward through the Shenandoah Valley and east across the Potomac. By July 11 Early was 5 miles (8 km) from Washington, but declined to assault its impressive defenses. Union forces under Major General Philip SHERIDAN hounded Early's column, forced it to retreat into the valley, and between September 1864 and March 1865 systematically destroyed it. Sheridan authorized a scorched-earth policy to destroy the valley's capacity to supply the Confederacy.

Sheridan, Philip H(enry) (1831–88), Union Army general. A career soldier, during the CIVIL WAR Sheridan emerged as one of the Union's most effective and uncompromising commanders. Following the capture of CHATTANOOGA by Union troops in September 1863, Sheridan steadied Union lines during the Confederate victory at CHICKAMAUGA, and led a charge up 'Missionary Ridge' that relieved pressure on the town. In 1864 Sheridan's scorched-earth tactics in the second SHENANDOAH VALLEY CAMPAIGN denied Confederate forces defending Richmond a vital source of supply. He stayed in the US Army after the war and became famous for pronouncing, during the RED RIVER WAR (1874–5), that 'The ONLY GOOD INDIAN IS A DEAD INDIAN.'

Sherman, William Tecumseh (1820–91), Union Army general, who, as commander of western forces from March 1864, made a major contribution to the Union's victory in the CIVIL WAR.

Sherman was a career soldier, graduating from West Point Military Academy in 1840 and seeing service in the MEXICAN WAR. Like his friend Ulysses GRANT, Sherman resigned his commission (1855) to pursue unsuccessful civilian ventures. Sherman failed as a banker and dabbled in law before accepting a post as superintendent of a military academy in Alexandria, Louisiana (1859–61).

Rejoining the US Army shortly after the outbreak of hostilities, Sherman commanded a brigade at the first battle of MANASSAS, was promoted to major general after SHILOH, and helped secure the capture of VICKSBURG. In March 1864 he took over a Union army in eastern Tennessee still recovering from its drubbing at the battle of CHICKAMAUGA and led them on a campaign that captured the Confederate stronghold of ATLANTA. He began his famous MARCH TO THE SEA on September 1 1864. On April 26 1865 Sherman accepted the surrender of Confederate forces in North Carolina, bringing fighting in the Civil War to a close. He stayed in the Army, succeeding Grant as its commander in 1869. He held this post until his retirement in 1884.

Sherman Anti-Trust Act (July 2 1890), legislation that made a pioneering attempt to regulate TRUSTS (monopolies, cartels, and other corporate structures that stifled competition). In the act, Congress drew upon its power to regulate interstate commerce to declare illegal 'every contract, combination in the form of a trust – or conspiracy – in restraint of trade or commerce among the several states'. However, the Senate Judiciary Committee, largely responsible for the bill, failed to define sufficiently terms like 'trust' or 'restraint'. As interpreted by the

Supreme Court, the act applied to trade unions (IN RE DEBS), but did not apply to manufacturers (US VS. E.C. KNIGHT COMPANY). Theodore ROOSEVELT's administration used the act vigorously, and restored something of its intent.

Sherman Silver Purchase Act (July 14 1890), legislation that forced the Treasury to purchase, but not necessarily to coin, 4.5 million ounces of silver per month (an amount equivalent to the entirety of US production). The purchases were to be made by legal-tender Treasury notes, redeemable in gold or silver. The act increased the money supply, but did not satisfy demands for FREE SILVER. Hard-money advocates of the GOLD STANDARD feared, rightly, that Treasury notes would be redeemed in gold, depleting federal reserves. The act was repealed during the DEPRESSION OF 1893 (October 30 1893). Both passage and repeal heightened the SILVER–GOLD CONTROVERSY.

Shiloh, battle of (April 6–7 1862), Union victory in Tennessee during the CIVIL WAR. Following the capture of FORT DONNELSON, Union forces under GRANT launched a major offensive southward through central Tennessee. By April, advance divisions had crossed the Tennessee river and threatened Corinth, Mississippi, a railroad junction crucial to the Confederate cause. Poor planning by Grant allowed retreating Confederate forces to launch a successful counterattack at Shiloh, Tennessee, on April 6. In hard fighting each side lost over 1700 dead. That evening Grant rejected calls for a retreat: 'I propose to attack at daylight and whip them.' A further 17,000 men were killed or wounded on April 7 as Union troops pushed back the Confederates. The scale and ferocity of the fighting was unprecedented. After Shiloh the Civil War became a 'total war'.

Shoshoni, Native American people who lived and hunted in western Wyoming, eastern Idaho, northeastern Utah and southwestern Montana. Their language belongs to the Uto-Aztecan family.

In the spring of 1804 Shoshoni gave the LEWIS AND CLARK EXPEDITION horses, and, by identifying the South Pass through the Rockies, enabled the expedition to reach the Pacific. Unfortunately for the Shoshoni, by the 1840s a steady stream of US settlers was following in the expedition's footsteps, crossing their land via the OREGON TRAIL. In a treaty negotiated at FORT LARAMIE in 1851, Shoshoni bands in Wyoming and Montana who had been harassing US pioneers were assigned reservation lands on the headwaters of the Big Wind river, Wyoming. (The USA later occupied portions of this reservation following the discovery that it sat atop oil reserves. The Shoshoni sued for compensation and in 1935 won a $30 million settlement.)

Militant Shoshoni in northern Utah, threatened by depletion of game, harassed travelers and Mormon settlers. On January 29 1863 Californian militiamen massacred a Shoshoni war party on the Bear river, southeastern Idaho. This led to the creation of a second Shoshoni reservation, near Fort Smith, Idaho. Its residents agreed to allow US travelers access to western trails, and accepted the building of a railroad. In return the US government promised payment of annuities and food subsidies. Today about 9000 Shoshoni still live on the reservations. The COMANCHE are an offshoot of the Shoshoni.

Siberia, US intervention in (1918–20). In August 1918 President WILSON ordered the deployment of 10,000 US troops in and around the Russian city of Vladivostok, on the Pacific coast of Siberia. The deployment was part of a joint operation, together with Britain, to protect foreign investments from expropriation by the Bolsheviks, and also to prevent Japan from using the Russian Revolution as the pretext for the seizure of Siberian mineral deposits. US troops were involved in several skirmishes with Bolshevik

Red Army soldiers before their withdrawal in April 1920.

silver–gold controversy, long-running controversy in the later 19th century between supporters of a 'hard-money' approach to US fiscal policy (based on gold) and supporters of an inflationary 'soft money' policy (based on silver).

Financial and monetary policy are political issues in all nations – but rarely have they aroused such passions as they did in the USA at the height of the silver–gold controversy. Slogans such as 'Free coinage of silver at 16–1 with gold' may sound dry, but for many they encapsulated fervently held beliefs. For example, to the mayor of Cleveland, speaking in 1896, the slogan heralded 'the first great protest of the American people against monopoly and the privileged classes'.

The controversy had its roots in three facets of the American experience. Firstly, the USA possessed near universal white male suffrage. Secondly, there was a cultural fixation with the worth of money and labor that could be traced as far back as the Puritans. Lastly, there was a clear conflict between the soft-money interests (and raw political power) of the nation's farmers, and the hard-money interests (and high-level political influence) of the nation's bankers.

Before the Civil War America's currency was composed of paper money issued by state and local banks and by SPECIE (gold and silver coins) struck by the US Mint. During the Civil War gold and silver coinage became scarce. US Treasury Secretary Salmon P. CHASE ordered millions of dollars' worth of GREENBACKS to be printed. This paper currency could not be redeemed in gold (its viability rested on an INCOME TAX), but creditors were required to accept it for repayment of debt. Such an expansion in the money supply was of great benefit to farmers and other debtors. As the US government began retiring greenbacks, so the money supply contracted. During the PANIC OF 1873, GRANT's administration agreed to allow an increase in the number of paper dollars in circulation. But it balanced this concession to debtors by removing from circulation all silver dollars (the 'CRIME OF '73') and (through the RESUMPTION ACT of 1875) allowing paper dollars to be exchanged for gold from January 1 1879. Farmers who rushed to join the newly formed GREENBACK PARTY in 1873–4 alleged that speculators greedy for gold would hoard paper dollars and severely contract the money supply. Greenbackers' rhetoric suggested avaricious Wall Street speculators were bent on corrupting the government and crippling the hard-working farmer. (In the event, an economic upturn meant that holders of dollars did not immediately convert them into gold on January 1 1879.)

Advocates of soft money believed that the discovery of substantial deposits of silver in Colorado, Nevada and Utah had provided the USA with a unique opportunity to create a money supply that was plentiful, intrinsically valuable and detached from world market forces. They believed the US government should adopt 'bimetalism': coining a circulating currency from silver while allowing existing notes to be exchanged for gold. In a bid to ensure that a silver dollar coin remained in equal in value to both a gold dollar coin and to a paper dollar backed by gold, 'silverites' fell back on an exchange rate established during Andrew JACKSON's presidency: the 16–1 ratio. This specified that there should be 16 times as much silver in a silver dollar (371.25 grains) as gold in a gold dollar (23.22 grains). In theory this ratio took account of the fact that silver was less valuable than gold because it was more plentiful. In fact, as more silver mines began production in the west, the value of silver dropped. By the mid-1870s the silver content of a silver dollar was worth 90 cents. Wall Street interests argued that a potentially ruinous inflation would be the inevitable outcome of the silverites' demand that the US Treasury reauthorize the minting of a silver coinage. (Advocates of a silver currency feared the potential effects of inflation less than the consequences of monetary deflation then observable).

The BLAND–ALLISON ACT (1878) authorized the US Treasury to purchase, and coin at its discretion, between 2 and 4 million dollars' worth of silver a month. The Treasury duly made purchases (at the minimum level), but chose to exercise its right not to coin silver. With crop prices rising as part of a general economic upturn, pressure on farmers and other debtors eased.

The rural depression that began in 1885, and which spawned POPULISM, revived the silver issue. With the support of senators from newly admitted western states and members of the House of Representatives elected by farmers' alliances (see POPULISM), Congress passed the SHERMAN SILVER PURCHASE ACT (1890). This compromise measure required the US Treasury to buy at prevailing market prices 4.5 million ounces of silver per month – virtually the entirety of US production, and a massive sop to western mining interests. The Treasury was directed to issue not coins but paper notes (redeemable in gold or silver as the Treasury saw fit) to a value equivalent to its silver reserve. This measure did increase the money supply, but not by as much (or as directly) as advocates of the free and unlimited coinage of silver demanded. It was opposed by the Republican Party, and some eastern Democrats, who supported hard money and the GOLD STANDARD. They charged that the Silver Purchase Act would inflate the value of silver and lead the Treasury to issue notes that would command confidence only if redeemable in gold. As the DEPRESSSION OF 1893 gathered pace and a run on US gold reserves began, 'goldbugs' argued that the USA was heading for the worst of all possible financial worlds. In order to support a silver currency whose value would, they were sure, inflate to the point of worthlessness, the USA would be forced to acquire, at insupportable cost, ever larger reserves of gold. President CLEVELAND sided with the goldbugs. Announcing that the USA was 'entitled to a sound and stable currency and to money recognized as such on every exchange and in every market in the world', Cleveland called Congress into special session. After a bitter fight, in which the Democrats were split, the Sherman Silver Purchase Act was repealed on October 30 1893.

Western and southern Democrats found repeal insupportable. For them it was the very fact that the value of gold was set by shadowy and self-interested money-market men that made it an indefensible and un-American basis for the nation's finances. Silver Democrats were quick to point out that the US Treasury's pursuit of gold contracted the money supply while allowing bankers such as J.P. MORGAN to make huge profits. A popular newspaper, *Coin's Financial School*, purported to reveal the secret financial cabals that were preventing the honest US farmer from enjoying the benefits of free silver. William Jennings BRYAN emerged as the political leader of the free-silver movement. His 'CROSS OF GOLD' SPEECH to the 1896 Democratic convention, in which he pictured 'mankind' being crucified on a 'cross of gold', captured the passions associated with the issue. Bryan was nominated by a divided Democratic Party, and endorsed by the PEOPLE'S PARTY, on a platform that called for the unlimited coinage of silver at a ratio of 16–1 to gold. (The 16–1 ratio was by this time wildly out of line with the respective market values of silver and gold.) Bryan lost the 1896 presidential election to Republican William McKINLEY. In 1900 the USA went on the GOLD STANDARD. Although 'free silver' theories surfaced again in the GREAT DEPRESSION, since the creation of the FEDERAL RESERVE SYSTEM (1913) taxes, tariffs, and the federal budget, rather than the money supply itself, have been the central themes of economic debate in Congress.

Sioux, name applied by Europeans and white Americans to a number of Native American peoples, speaking at least ten distinct languages, living principally in Minnesota, the Dakotas, Wyoming and Montana. The name derived from the Objiwa word for 'enemy'. They are also collectively known as the Dakota ('allies'), a term also applied to one of the main groups of Sioux.

In 1800 there were approximately 25,000 Sioux living and hunting on the northern Great Plains. Their numbers increased during the first half of the 19th century, creating demands on the region's stock of buffalo that became unsustainable once white settlement began in earnest in the 1860s. By the mid-19th century, most Sioux peoples belonged to bands organized within one of three loose confederations: the Santee-Sioux (or Dakota), the Yankton-Sioux (or Nakota) and the Teton-Sioux (or Lakota).

The Santee-Sioux lived on lands straddling the Nebraska–South Dakota and Minnesota–South Dakota state boundaries. In a treaty agreed at FORT LARAMIE in 1851 they accepted restrictive reservation agreements, but when these were broken by the USA in 1862 they embarked on the first SIOUX WAR. The Yankton-Sioux lived on lands within South Dakota, and most accepted reservation status peacefully.

The Teton-Sioux were heavily dependent on buffalo, and many moved north and west into North Dakota and Montana during the 19th century in order to maintain their hunting patterns. During the 1860s SITTING BULL encouraged Teton bands to accept centralized authority. The Teton, under Sitting Bull's leadership, were the main protagonists of the second and third Sioux Wars against US encroachment. They defeated General CUSTER at the battle of LITTLE BIG HORN (1876). The GHOST DANCE religious revival proved particularly influential among Teton-Sioux, and was an indirect cause of the massacre at WOUNDED KNEE (1890), which marked the final demoralization of the Sioux. Today there are some 40,000 Sioux, mostly living on reservations in North and South Dakota, Montana and Nebraska.

Sioux Wars (1862–4, 1865–7, 1876–7), three bloody wars between the SIOUX and US forces. The wars were caused by a series of US blunders and insults, the size and pride of the Sioux nation, and the dependence of many of its members on buffalo hunting.

(1) During the Civil War the US government delayed payment of subsidies upon which the Santee-Sioux had come to depend. Santee-Sioux hunters broke treaty restrictions on their activities and, as US troops were withdrawn from the Dakotas, settlers and militant warriors clashed. In August 1862 Santee-Sioux, led by Little Crow, raided the Minnesota valley, killing nearly 400 settlers and seizing 370 captives. On November 1 most of the raiders surrendered to US authorities: 38 were hanged on December 26. President LINCOLN rejected advice to mount a war of extermination against the Sioux nation, but he did send experienced US troops to North Dakota. For the next two years this force hunted down defiant Sioux militants.

(2) In 1865 the discovery of gold in Montana led the US government to break treaty agreements with the Teton-Sioux by attempting to fortify the BOZEMAN TRAIL. Two thousand Sioux and CHEYENNE, led by Red Cloud (Mahpiua Luta, 1822–1909), waged a two-year campaign against US soldiers and migrants in northern Wyoming and south-central Montana. On December 21 1866 Red Cloud's warriors annihilated a detachment of US soldiers in the FETTERMAN MASSACRE. Over the next year Red Cloud's warriors attacked forts along the Bozeman trail. A treaty signed at FORT LARAMIE, Wyoming, in November 1868 pledged the USA to abandon its forts on the trail.

(3) In 1876, 2400 US troops were sent to Montana to force Teton-Sioux and Cheyenne militants onto reservations. At Rosebud, Montana, on June 17 1876 and at LITTLE BIG HORN (June 25), warriors led by Crazy Horse (Ta-Sunko-Witko, 1842–77) and SITTING BULL slaughtered US troops and forced their retreat. In the summer of 1877 most of the warriors were hunted down and captured. Sitting Bull led a band of Hunkpapa Teton-Sioux to Canada. He returned to the USA to surrender on July 19 1881.

sit-down strikes, tactic used in industrial disputes, in which strikers occupied factories to prevent employers from bringing in non-union workers, and to avoid the beatings often inflicted on pickets outside plants. In the winter of 1936–7 members of the UNITED AUTOMOBILE WORKERS (UAW) employed this tactic in Flint, Michigan, against the rabidly anti-union General Motors (GM). Withstanding assaults from the police, and also the company's attempt to freeze them out by turning off the heating, strikers brought GM production to a standstill. On February 3 1937 the company agreed to negotiate with UAW representatives. Despite the misgivings of the CONGRESS OF INDUSTRIAL ORGANIZATIONS (CIO) and warnings from President Franklin D. ROOSEVELT, the GM workers' victory sparked copy-cat occupations elsewhere.

Sitting Bull or **Tatanka Iyotake** (c.1831–90), Native American leader, born into the Hunkpapa section of the Teton-SIOUX, who orchestrated the final armed resistance of the Plains Indians to US expansion. His subsequent world-wide fame was mainly thanks to an appearance in 'BUFFALO BILL' Cody's (1846–1917) Wild West Show.

Sitting Bull established his valor fighting the Crow people on the Great Plains, and, later, US soldiers in the first SIOUX WAR. During the 1860s and 1870s he created and led a confederacy among the Teton-Sioux whose disciplined mode of warfare played a crucial role in the defeat of General CUSTER at the battle of LITTLE BIG HORN (1876) during the third SIOUX WAR. Sitting Bull led Sioux survivors to Canada in order to escape retaliation for Little Big Horn, but returned to surrender to US authorities at Fort Buford, North Dakota, on July 19 1881. Confined to a reservation in South Dakota, Sitting Bull was hunted by photographers and autograph-seekers (and actually began to charge his pursuers). In 1883 his captors took him on a tour of eastern cities, and in 1885 he toured with Cody. He was shot dead on December 15 1890 by reservation police made skittish by the GHOST DANCE religious revival.

Sixteenth Amendment, amendment to the US Constitution that establishes Congress's right to levy a federal INCOME TAX. The amendment was submitted to the states on July 12 1909, and officially proclaimed on February 25 1913. It negated the US Supreme Court's ruling, in the case of Pollock vs. Farmers' Loan and Trust Company (1895), that such taxes were unconstitutional.

Sixth Amendment, amendment to the US Constitution establishing the right of an accused person to a speedy and public trial before an impartial jury. It was one of the ten amendments making up the BILL OF RIGHTS. For the full text, *see* Appendix 1.

Skinner vs. Oklahoma (June 1 1942), unanimous US Supreme Court ruling that declared state laws mandating the sterilization of convicted rapists and other felons unconstitutional. The Court's reasoning, based on the FOURTEENTH AMENDMENT, was similar to that used in the landmark ROE VS. WADE verdict of 1973.

slaughterhouse cases, cases brought in 1873 before the US Supreme Court, whose ruling made a significant restriction on the scope of the FOURTEENTH AMENDMENT, and, by its implications, allowed southern states to keep blacks from enjoying full social and political rights and protection under the law.

In 1869 the Louisiana assembly permitted a company to monopolize the slaughterhouse trade in New Orleans. Disaffected rivals sued on the grounds that the assembly's action had deprived them of access to a livelihood in contravention of the Fourteenth Amendment. On April 14 1873 the Supreme Court ruled 5–4 against the plaintiffs's suits. The majority argued that the Fourteenth Amendment covered the narrow purpose of enlarging the federal citizenship rights of former slaves. The distinction the majority drew between federal and state citizenship rights placed most political and economic rights within the realm of state citizenship, and thus beyond the amendment's scope.

slave power, pejorative term employed by northerners and some southern Democrats (among them Andrew JOHNSON) to describe the national political influence of southern planters who owned large numbers of slaves. Northern business blamed slave power for opposition to protective TARIFFS. Midwesterners infused with FREE-SOIL IDEOLOGY blamed passage of the KANSAS–NEBRASKA ACT (1854) on slave power. Abolitionists argued that the FUGITIVE SLAVE ACT (1854) represented the intrusion of slave power into northern states. The principal objective of the REPUBLICAN PARTY was the destruction of the political influence of the great plantation owners, a group dubbed by Michigan Republicans as an 'aristocracy the most revolting and oppressive with which the earth was ever cursed'.

slavery, system of involuntary servitude established in the colonial era, and finally outlawed in the USA by the THIRTEENTH AMENDMENT. The first enslaved Africans sold in the THIRTEEN COLONIES were brought to Virginia by Dutch traders in 1619. In the 1630s merchants in Massachusetts and Rhode Island entered the slave trade. Although enslaved African-Americans were imported into all regions of America, from the late 17th century Virginian tobacco

planters and South Carolinian rice producers became the most avid purchasers of slave labor in colonial America. Roughly 275,000 slaves were imported into Britain's American colonies before 1776.

The unique legal status of slavery was also established in the colonial era. Slaves were 'chattel', that is the property of their owner. They could be sold or bequeathed as their owner saw fit. The children of slave parents, and those of a slave woman and a free man, were deemed to be slaves from birth. Slaves could not bring suit against abusive masters or local whites, who were equipped with draconian powers to 'discipline' their workforce. Slavery was justified by reference to a racial ideology, made explicit in Thomas JEFFERSON's *NOTES ON THE STATE OF VIRGINIA*, which held that African-Americans were less than fully human.

Agitation in favor of the ABOLITION of slavery began to surface during the AMERICAN REVOLUTION. The future state of Vermont outlawed slavery in 1777. Pennsylvania passed a GRADUAL EMANCIPATION law in 1780. The QUOK WALKER case (1783) produced the de facto abolition of slavery in Massachusetts. Nevertheless delegates to the CONSTITUTIONAL CONVENTION (1787) made a number of concessions to the interests of slaveowners. Chief among these was the CONNECTICUT COMPROMISE which, by including three-fifths of a state's slave population in calculations designed to apportion seats in Congress and the ELECTORAL COLLEGE, granted slaveowners an effective veto on federal action against slavery.

A northerner, ELI WHITNEY, granted slavery a new lease of life south of the MASON–DIXON line through the invention of the cotton gin. This machine, patented in 1793, greatly increased the efficiency with which seeds could be separated from cotton fibre. As it became both feasible and profitable to increase the acreage of cotton under production, southern planters, often abetted by northern investors, bought slaves to work as field hands on plantations in Georgia, Alabama and the Mississippi delta. Around 60,000 enslaved Africans were imported into the USA between 1776 and 1808 (when the USA renounced the overseas slave trade). However, even after 1808 the USA's internal market was capable of meeting southern planters' demand for slaves.

Historians hotly contest the effects of the slave labor system upon the slaves themselves. There is a general agreement that African-American slaves were not completely dehumanized. Some historians argue that during the last quarter of the 18th and the first half of the 19th century a quasi-autonomous African-American slave culture began to take shape. This argument rests on the fact that, after the Revolution, as northerners and small farmers in the south abandoned slavery, so an increasing percentage of the enslaved African-American population was held by a decreasing percentage of the white population. It became more common for slaves to live on plantations in which the African-American population outnumbered the white population. (By the eve of the CIVIL WAR only 25% of white southerners held slaves, but over 50% of all slaves resided on plantations containing 20 or more bondsmen.) To pacify their workforce, and to profit from natural increase, white plantation owners were prepared, when it suited them, to recognize slave marriages. In addition, some planters, hoping to encourage slaves to accept their lot, allowed or encouraged Christian worship among their enslaved workforce. Family ties and religious belief afforded some slaves a tenuous means of cultural resistance to the racial hegemony of the slave labor system. The savage repression that followed revolts led by DENMARK VESEY and NAT TURNER helps explain why outright rebellion was comparatively rare. Nonetheless several studies have shown that plantation slaves were able to exert some control over the conditions and pace of their working lives. Slaves hired out as day laborers, or those who worked in occupations such as the maritime trades, had even greater opportunity for self-assertion.

On the eve of the Civil War there were nearly 4 million African-American slaves in the USA. The vast majority of these unfree workers lived within the eleven states that would eventually form the CONFEDERACY. Historians and economists debate the extent to which the production of such crops as cotton and sugar by means of slave labor retarded the growth of the southern economy. Slavery was not unprofitable. However, it seems clear that the south's financial and emotional investment in slavery hindered the diversification of the region's economy. During the 1840s, when cotton prices were low, southern financiers invested in railroads, ironworks and factories. However, the south's banking and credit networks were ultimately dependent on the value of slaves and land. Planters and financiers entertained a willingness to invest in alternative forms of economic activity only insofar as these would complement and safeguard their much larger investment in the production of cash crops using slave labor. When cotton prices rose during the 1850s southerners lost interest in economic diversification. Indeed by seeking to protect and expand their investment in the slave labor system, southern politicians helped cause a political crisis that triggered the Civil War and the demise of the south's 'peculiar institution.'

Slidell mission (1845), unsuccessful diplomatic mission to Mexico on the eve of the MEXICAN WAR. Hoping to avoid war with Mexico over the issue of the annexation of TEXAS, President James POLK authorized John Slidell (1793–1871), a Spanish-speaking Louisianan, to offer $30,000,000 for New Mexico and California and Mexican recognition of the Rio Grande border. Hostilities in the Mexican War began when Slidell returned empty-handed.

Smith Act (June 28 1940), legislation reflecting fear of communist subversion. The Act required aliens to register annually and strengthened the US government's powers of deportation. It made it a criminal offense to teach, advocate or organize in pursuit of the violent overthrow of the US government.

Smith, Al (Alfred Emmanuel Smith) (1873–1944), Democratic politician who unsuccessfully stood for the presidency in 1928. Smith was born in New York's Lower East Side and worked as a boy in the Fulton Street fish market. He held a number of posts in New York City government before being elected to two terms as state governor (1919–20, 1923–8). In 1928 Smith was chosen to head the Democrats' ticket, becoming the first Catholic to be nominated for the presidency by a major political party. Smith was joined on the ticket by Senator Joseph Robinson (1872–1937) of Arkansas, the first southern resident to be nominated by a major party since the Civil War. Smith's presidential bid was torpedoed by his opposition to PROHIBITION, his identification with the urban working class, and by anti-Catholic prejudice. His Republican opponent Herbert HOOVER won a landslide victory. Smith opposed the NEW DEAL, and in 1936 endorsed the Republican candidate Alf LANDON in preference to Franklin D. ROOSEVELT.

smoke-filled room, phrase that became synonymous with political deal-making following the rancorous Republican convention in Chicago in June 1920. Delegates could not agree on a presidential nominee. A decision was eventually made at 2:00 a.m. on June 11 by Republican senators meeting in Suite 404–406 on the 13th floor of the Blackstone Hotel – the original smoke-filled room. As his campaign manager Harry Daugherty (1860–1941) had predicted, Warren HARDING, everybody's second choice, emerged as the nominee.

SNCC, *see* STUDENT NON-VIOLENT COORDINATING COMMITTEE.

social Darwinism, body of social and political thought that argued that civilization was best advanced through unfettered individual competition. Social Darwinism was popularized in the USA in the last quarter of the 19th century through the writings of Herbert Spencer (1820–1903) and William Graham Sumner (1840–1910). Spencer asserted that a process of natural selection akin to that outlined in Charles Darwin's *Origin of the Species* (1859) governed society as well as nature. He elevated 'survival of the fittest' to the status of an iron law, and explained wealth and poverty by reference to it. Sumner, a Yale professor, argued in works such as *The Absurd Effort to Make the World Over* (1895) that all forms of business regulation injured the health of civilization by interfering with the competition among individuals from which only the fittest would survive. Horatio ALGER's fiction introduced young boys to the competitive forces of nature. Wealthy industrialists who had made their fortunes from collusive TRUST arrangements and the manipulation of stock found these theories particularly congenial. PROGRESSIVISM and POPULISM hotly contested the claims made by social Darwinists. *See also* SOCIAL GOSPEL.

social gospel, belief among many American Protestants at the beginning of the 20th century that Christians had a duty to combat the causes and effects of poverty. This conviction was powerfully outlined by Walter Rauschenbusch (1861–1918) in his widely read *Christianity and the Social Crisis* (1907). Rauschenbusch was a Baptist minister whose experiences running a settlement house in New York's 'Hell's Kitchen' convinced him that the laissez-faire values of SOCIAL DARWINISM had injured the moral health of America's great cities. The ideas of the social-gospel movement exerted a powerful influence on PROGRESSIVISM.

Socialist Party of America, political party formed in Indianapolis in July 1901. By 1912 the party had 112,000 members, and in that year 79 cities in 24 states elected Socialist mayors.

The labor leader Eugene DEBS helped found the party, and stood as its nominee in the presidential elections of 1904, 1908, 1912 and 1920. In 1912 Debs gained 6% of the POPULAR VOTE. His 1920 campaign was remarkable in that it was conducted from Atlanta penitentiary, where he was serving a ten-year sentence for violating the ESPIONAGE ACT of 1917: he gained 900,000 votes. The Socialists opposed US entry into WORLD WAR I, and later suffered official harassment during the RED SCARE. During the 1930s the party lost ground to the COMMUNIST PARTY OF THE USA.

Social Security Act (August 14 1935), NEW DEAL legislation that made provision for unemployment benefit, pensions and help to other needy members of society. President Franklin D. ROOSEVELT liked to claim that his act introduced the world's first system of 'cradle-to-grave' social security. It did not. But the programs established by the act, although they barely met the minimum requirements of human decency, were revolutionary in a country where government had hitherto resisted any Federal alleviation of poverty, on the grounds both of the Protestant work ethic and of cost. In 1931 only 116,000 US workers enjoyed any form of insurance against unemployment. Yet in 1933, at the nadir of the GREAT DEPRESSION, 30 million Americans were out of work. In that year 25 states considered unemployment compensation bills. Every single one was rejected as too costly, and liable to create a 'work-shy' workforce.

The 1935 Social Security Act created a federal payroll tax on businesses that employed more than eight workers. States that developed unemployment compensation programs could apply to have up to 90% of the cost of their provision met through the payroll tax. Federal government also supplied assistance in the administration of unemployment relief to states, like Mississippi and South Carolina, that had no competent welfare agencies. Agricultural workers, domestic servants and small business employees were left out of the program, and there were wide variations in compensation between states. Nevertheless, the act made half the US workforce eligible for some form of unemployment compensation.

Thanks largely to efforts of Dr Francis TOWNSEND, senior citizens were far better organized than the unemployed. As a result, that section of the Social Security Act treating pensions was entirely federal in administration, and included most Americans. Employers and employees contributed through taxes to a fund that awarded pensions ranging from $10 to $85 a month (depending on the number of years in which an individual paid into the plan) to all Americans over the age of 65. The act also authorized the federal government to bail out existing state programs aiding needy senior citizens.

Finally, the act authorized matching funds from the federal government to be spent in support of state programs aiding the disabled, the indigent and single-parent families. Unfortunately the act set no minimum standard of coverage in these areas, and, by prescribing a ceiling on federal contributions, gave states an incentive to be less generous than they might wish.

Employer and employee contributions to these plans were raised over time, but the basic structure of provision remained substantially unaltered until the GREAT SOCIETY initiative of the 1960s.

solid south, term derived from the voting behavior of white inhabitants of the eleven former states of the CONFEDERACY, together with their white neighbours in Kentucky and Missouri, who, from RECONSTRUCTION to the EISENHOWER era, could be counted upon to support the DEMOCRATIC PARTY candidate in a presidential election. The only exceptions to this trend came in 1928, when white voters in Texas, Virginia, Florida and North Carolina balked at voting for Al SMITH (a Catholic opponent of PROHIBITION), and 1948, when DIXIECRATS abandoned the party in protest at TRUMAN's determination to include a civil rights plank in the party's platform. In the 1960s white southerners rebelled against the Democratic Party's willingness to embrace the CIVIL RIGHTS MOVEMENT by voting for Barry GOLD-WATER, George WALLACE or Richard NIXON. Since the 1980s white southern males (the so-called REAGAN DEMOCRATS) have voted overwhelmingly for Republican candidates.

Sons of Liberty, name adopted by clandestine groups formed in American cities in the summer of 1765 to organize resistance to the implementation of the STAMP ACT. The Sons of Liberty were among the first to mount active opposition to British policy in the early years of the AMERICAN REVOLUTION. In Boston, New York and Charleston, the Sons of Liberty – usually artisans, prosperous tradesmen, lesser merchants or radical lawyers – intimidated officials appointed to collect Stamp Act duties, and ensured that the act was never enforced. They took their name from a speech made during a House of Commons debate on the Stamp Act in which the MP Isaac Barré described Americans as 'sons of liberty'. Boston's Sons of Liberty were accused of organizing and condoning a riot in which the house of Thomas Hutchinson (1711– 80), governor of Massachusetts, was destroyed. For this reason, although the Sons of Liberty could claim credit for the repeal of the Stamp Act in March 1766, established American political leaders distrusted them, and feared they might unleash an uncontrollable social revolution.

South Carolina, southern state, bordered on the north by North Carolina, to the east by the Atlantic, and to the south and west by Georgia.

The first permanent European settlement in the territory was established by English settlers at Charles Town (now Charleston) in 1670. Originally part of the proprietary colony of Carolina, South Carolina gained its own assembly in 1670 and became a royal colony on May 29 1721. The colony's economy was dominated by the production of indigo and rice using slave labor. From 1710, the majority of the state's population was enslaved. The great plantation owners, most of whom lived as absentee landlords in Charleston, dominated colonial politics. (This provoked a REGULATOR MOVEMENT among backcountry settlers in the late 1760s.) South Carolina's political elite, conscious of the value of their export trade, played an assertive role in the AMERICAN REVOLUTION. During debate over the non-exportation provisions of the CONTINENTAL ASSOCIATION of 1774 and later during discussion on the future of slavery at the CONSTITUTIONAL CONVENTION, South Carolina's delegates defended their special interests. Nevertheless, many residents of the state were LOYALIST and, during the REVOLUTIONARY WAR, the British sought to build a 'southern strategy' around disaffection in the state. The British occupied Charleston in 1780 and at the battle of CAMDEN (1780) inflicted the heaviest defeat of the war on the American army. On May 23 1788, South Carolina became the eighth state to ratify the US Constitution.

From 1793, the state's economy was transformed by a boom in cotton production that revived demand for slave labor and prompted a substantial out-migration of family farmers. South Carolina's economy was so closely tied to cotton that the state's political establishment gave whole-hearted support to the uncompromising STATES' RIGHTS doctrine laid out by John C.

CALHOUN in the *SOUTH CAROLINA EXPOSITION AND PROTEST*. South Carolina's threat to suspend operation of TARIFF laws that it deemed unacceptable brought the NULLIFICATION CRISIS to boiling point in 1832.

In 1860, South Carolina had 703,708 residents, 57% of whom were enslaved. On December 20 1860, a state convention passed an ordinance of SECESSION, the first step in the creation of the CONFEDERACY. The bombardment of FORT SUMTER in Charleston harbor marked the beginning of the CIVIL WAR. In 1865, the state was devastated in the later stages of Union general William T. SHERMAN'S MARCH TO THE SEA.

In June 1865, President Andrew JOHNSON authorized the creation of a provisional government in South Carolina. This abolished slavery but enacted draconian BLACK CODES. Congress placed the state under military administration in March 1867 before restoring self-government and congressional representation on June 25 1868. South Carolina was one of the states at the center of the disputed PRESIDENTIAL ELECTION OF 1876 and, following the COMPROMISE OF 1877, the Democratic party gained control of the state and made it a leading member of the SOLID SOUTH. By 1895, South Carolina had disenfranchised all but a handful of black voters and enacted numerous JIM CROW laws establishing racial segregation.

In 1900, South Carolina had 1,340,316 inhabitants, 58% of whom were African-Americans. Nearly a million residents left the state in the 20th century, the majority of them blacks taking part in the GREAT MIGRATION to seek work in northern cities. (This transformed the state's racial demographics to the point where in 1990, African-Americans accounted for just 30% of South Carolina's population.) The state's white establishment was united in its opposition to the CIVIL RIGHTS MOVEMENT. South Carolina's US Senator, Strom Thurmond (1902–), became nationally famous for mounting the longest FILIBUSTER on record in an unsuccessful bid to block passage of the CIVIL RIGHTS ACT (1957). White South Carolinians, alienated by the Civil Rights Movement, delivered the state to Barry GOLDWATER in the presidential election of 1964 and since then the Republican party has grown in strength in the state.

In 1990, South Carolina had 3,486,207 residents and was the 25th most populous state in the union. John C. Calhoun remains the state's most famous 'native son'.

South Carolina Exposition and Protest, pamphlet written in 1828 by US Vice President John C. CALHOUN, which furnished the constitutional justification for the southern STATES' RIGHTS position during the NULLIFICATION CRISIS. Reacting to passage of the TARIFF OF ABOMINATIONS, Calhoun argued that states retained under the Constitution the right to interpose their authority to protect their citizens from injurious federal legislation. In practice this meant that where a special state convention found a federal law to be unconstitutional, it might declare the law null and void, and suspend its operation within a state until an amendment to the Constitution overturning the action of the state convention was passed. President Andrew JACKSON dismissed this argument as an 'impracticable absurdity.'

South Dakota, north-central state, bordered to the north by North Dakota, to the east by Minnesota and Iowa, to the south by Nebraska and to the west by Montana and Wyoming.

The USA acquired the territory from France through the LOUISIANA PURCHASE (1803). A fur-trading post was established at Fort Pierre in 1817 but US settlement began in earnest following passage of the KANSAS–NEBRASKA ACT (1854). When Congress created the Dakota territory in 1861, there were just under 5000 white residents in the region. Potential settlers were deterred by the lack of rail links and the strength of the SIOUX nation. The discovery of gold in the Black Hills and the US victory in the third SIOUX WAR stimulated in-migration by settlers seeking to establish family farms. On November 2 1889, South Dakota became the 40th state in the union. In 1890, US troops massacred Sioux followers of the GHOST DANCE revival at WOUNDED KNEE, South Dakota.

The state's farmers were strong supporters of POPULISM. They suffered greatly from a ten-year drought 1887–97 and, later, from low commodity prices. In 1900, South Dakota had 401,570 inhabitants but its economy was stagnant and the state witnessed substantial out-migration during the 20th century. In 1918, South Dakota granted women the right to vote. Economic diversification since 1945 has helped revive the state's fortunes but in 1990, South Dakota had just 696,004 residents and was the 45th most populous state in the union. The WOUNDED KNEE PROTEST mounted by members of the AMERICAN INDIAN MOVEMENT in 1973 made South Dakota the brief focus of international attention. Famous South Dakotans include Sioux leader SITTING BULL and George McGOVERN.

Southeast Asian Treaty Organization (SEATO), COLD WAR mutual defense pact created by a treaty signed in Manila on September 8 1954. It bound the USA, Britain, France, Australia, New Zealand, the Philippines, Thailand and Pakistan to treat an attack on any one member as an attack on all members. Although modeled on the NORTH ATLANTIC TREATY ORGANIZATION, SEATO did not possess a unified military command structure and did little to implement the goals of US CONTAINMENT doctrine in the region. It was dissolved during the DÉTENTE era on June 30 1977.

Southern Christian Leadership Conference (SCLC), organization that eclipsed the NATIONAL ASSOCIATION FOR THE ADVANCEMENT OF COLORED PEOPLE (NAACP) as the leader of the CIVIL RIGHTS MOVEMENT in southern states. It was founded in Montgomery, Alabama, in January 1957 by the Reverend Martin Luther KING and the Reverend Ralph ABERNATHY.

King and Abernathy had witnessed the efficacy of nonviolent protest during the MONTGOMERY BUS BOYCOTT. Eschewing the NAACP's emphasis on legal challenges to JIM CROW, they sought to bring black churchgoers into carefully selected campaigns of direct action. The SCLC was obstructed by some church elders, reluctant to become involved in civil rights protests. It also faced criticism, particularly from the STUDENT NON-VIOLENT COORDINATING COMMITTEE (SNCC) and the CONGRESS OF RACIAL EQUALITY (CORE), for its relatively autocratic organization and the overwhelming influence that King exerted on its decision-making processes.

Yet the SCLC was largely responsible for the BIRMINGHAM DESEGREGATION CAMPAIGN and the SELMA FREEDOM MARCH. It rallied support for the MARCH ON WASHINGTON, the CIVIL RIGHTS ACT OF 1964 and the VOTING RIGHTS ACT of 1965. In 1965–6 the SCLC mounted a major campaign in Chicago to protest against segregation in public housing. Some spin-offs from this, notably OPERATION BREADBASKET, made headway. But the force of the campaign was blunted when Mayor Richard J. Daley and SCLC leaders agreed on a package of compromises. Such deal-making was unpopular with radicalized African-Americans, and led to a decline in the SCLC's membership and influence. The SCLC was brought close to collapse by King's assassination on April 4 1968.

Spanish-American War (1898), war that resulted in the US occupation of the former Spanish colonies of Cuba, PUERTO RICO, GUAM and the PHILIPPINES. John Hay (1838–1905), secretary of state in President McKINLEY's cabinet, dubbed the conflict a 'splendid little war.'

Historians fiercely debate the question of whether the war was fought with the intent or effect of establishing the USA as an imperial power. Certainly at the time many

Americans thought their nation had an imperial destiny. Militant Protestants believed that God had favored the USA with his blessing in order that it might serve the divinely ordained purpose of civilizing the peoples of the Caribbean, Central America and Asia. Other contemporary commentators concluded that the social unrest and economic dislocation unleashed by the DEPRESSION OF 1893 could be cured only by the acquisition of foreign territories. There was broad agreement that the Spanish empire was decadent, and that Cubans and Filipinos were representatives of lesser, child-like, races. Republican Senator Albert J. BEVERIDGE encapsulated imperialist sentiment when he thundered: 'God has not been preparing the English-speaking and Teutonic people for a thousand years for nothing but vain and idle self-admiration. He has made us the master organizers of the world to establish system where chaos reigns that we may administer government among savages and senile peoples.' Yet for all this, in 1897 President McKinley used his inaugural address to denounce 'wars of conquest' and 'territorial aggression', and promised there would be 'no jingo nonsense' in his administration. Events in Cuba forced him to think again.

The McKINLEY TARIFF (1890) made Cuban sugar competitive in US markets, and prompted a boom on the island. This boom was brought to an abrupt halt by the passage of the WILSON–GORMAN TARIFF (1894). During the ensuing depression, Cuban nationalists launched a rebellion against Spanish rule. In February 1896 Spanish officials began confining supporters of independence in squalid concentration camps, a policy that was sensationalized and denounced by YELLOW JOURNALISM. On February 9 1898, William Randolph HEARST's New York *Journal* published a purloined letter, written by the Spanish ambassador to the USA, Dupuy de Lôme, which contained derogatory remarks about President McKin-

ley. On February 15 1898 the USS *Maine*, which had been sent to Cuba to protect US citizens and property, blew up and sank at anchor in Havana harbor, resulting in the deaths of 260 US sailors. 'Remember the *Maine* – to hell with Spain' became a popular slogan. Despite Spanish apologies and concessions, on April 11 1898 McKinley asked Congress to authorize 'forcible intervention' in Cuba. On April 20 Congress recognized Cuban independence, and empowered the president to use force to remove Spanish troops from the island. It also approved an amendment disclaiming any US interest in exercising sovereignty over the island. Spain reacted by declaring war on the USA on April 24. The following day, Congress approved (by 310–6 in the House, 42–35 in the Senate) a formal declaration of war against Spain.

On the outbreak of war, Commodore George Dewey (1837–1917) led the US Asiatic Squadron to the Spanish colony of the Philippines, where on May 1 he destroyed eight Spanish warships in the battle of Manila Bay. Subsequently, US soldiers, assisted by Filipino nationalist guerrillas under Emilio Aguinaldo, occupied Manila (August 13 1898). Meanwhile the US Navy blockaded Cuba. On June 20 17,000 US regulars and ROUGH RIDER volunteers landed at Daiquiri, Cuba. On a march westward to Santiago, Theodore ROOSEVELT made his reputation in an assault that captured Kettle Hill near San Juan on July 1 1898. US troops occupied Santiago on July 17 1898, taking 24,000 Spanish troops prisoner and effectively ending Spanish resistance. In the treaty of PARIS (signed December 10 1898), Spain ceded Puerto Rico, Guam and the Philippines to the USA (the Philippines on payment of $20 million). Spain also ceded all claim and title to Cuba. During the war the USA, citing its need for a naval base in the Pacific, annexed HAWAII.

President McKinley claimed that a night of prayer convinced him that the USA should retain the Philippines as a colony. This decision led Filipino patriots, under Aguinaldo, to wage a campaign for independence. After three years of fighting and the deployment of 65,000 US troops, the US governor of the Philippines, future president William Howard TAFT (who rose to national prominence during this period), granted the islanders independence on terms. Cuba was placed under US military administration. Although US troops left the island on May 20 1902, the insertion of the PLATT AMENDMENT into the Cuban constitution left the island a colony in all but name. 379 US servicemen died in combat in the war. A further 5000 died from tropical diseases and from food poisoning contracted from the consumption of tainted meat supplied by corrupt US contractors.

specie, hard currency (gold or silver coins) as distinct from paper money (private or US government bank notes). The Mint Act of 1792 specified the gold content of a dollar coin at 24.75 grains (1.6038 g), and set the value of an ounce (28.3495 g) of gold and an ounce of silver at 15:1 (i.e. declaring gold fifteen times more valuable than silver). The Coinage Act of 1832 specified that there should be sixteen times the weight of silver in a silver dollar coin (371.25 grains) as gold in a gold dollar coin (23.22 grains) – establishing a ratio of 16:1 that later became an article of faith for advocates of FREE SILVER.

During the Civil War the US government began printing large quantities of paper notes dubbed GREENBACKS. Yet from December 31 1861 holders of this paper currency were forbidden from exchanging notes for gold or silver coins. The USA continued to mint a small number of gold and silver coins, but the nation's money supply was effectively composed of paper notes. The potentially inflationary consequences of this shift from specie to paper money alarmed financial interests. In 1875 advocates of 'sound money' persuaded Congress to pass the RESUMPTION ACT permitting once

more the exchange of paper dollars for gold coin. This decision helped ignite the SILVER–GOLD CONTROVERSY.

Specie Circular, edict issued by President JACKSON on July 11 1836 announcing that from August 15 the US government would accept only gold or silver (SPECIE) in payment for public lands. The measure was aimed at controlling western land speculation, which was being fueled by paper money issued by banks whose liquidity depended on yet more sales. Sales of tracts under 320 acres were exempted until December 15 in an attempt to protect homesteaders. The measure made specie scarce, contributing to the DEPRESSION OF 1837. In March 1837 Jackson vetoed a congressional attempt to repeal the measure. It was eventually repealed by joint resolution on May 21 1838.

spectator sports, like BASEBALL, the USA's other main spectator sports – basketball and football – have been shaped by, and in their turn have influenced, the cultural history of America. Unlike baseball, both basketball and football developed as college sports and, however unwisely, both continue to be regarded as potential vehicles of moral instruction. A distinctive feature of the USA's most popular spectator sports is that star players share prominence with coaches.

The first intercollegiate football game was played on November 6 1869 between Rutgers and Princeton. The modern game evolved with the introduction of the scrimmage (1880), downs and measured yardage (1882) and the forward pass. During the 1890s, the coaches of Yale's triumphant teams tirelessly celebrated the 'character forming' aspects of the game in a bid to deflect criticism from the university faculty. The injuries and even fatalities associated with the game, as well as the willingness of colleges to recruit essentially professional players for their teams, prompted the formation in 1906 of the National Collegiate Athletic Association (NCAA). The NCAA introduced rule changes that made the game safer and supervised the creation of regional leagues. During the PROGRESSIVE ERA, the triumphs of teams from Harvard and the CARLISLE INDIAN SCHOOL engaged fans with no connection to either college. Other college teams, notably the Notre Dame 'Fightin' Irish' football team, became talismans for particular ethnic and cultural groups. Locker-room rhetoric such as Notre Dame coach Knute Rockne's 'WIN ONE FOR THE GIPPER' speech passed into popular folklore.

The current popularity of professional football is of comparatively recent origin. The National Football League (NFL) was founded in 1920 and rooted in the industrial cities of the northeast. Popular with the urban working classes, the game's breakthrough to a national audience was partly dependent on innovation within the television industry (*see* RADIO AND TELEVISION). In 1963, soon after the first use of a slow-motion videotape replay in a television broadcast, the CBS network signed a contract to televise NFL games. In 1966, the NFL merged with its rival the American Football League. The first Superbowl was staged in 1967 and proved a huge hit with TV audiences. The ABC network's broadcasts of 'Monday Night Football' further cemented the game's place in sports fans' affections. The apparent distinction between 'corinthian' college amateurs and hardened pros, which worked to the detriment of professional football's popularity, was steadily eroded in the late 20th century. In 1984, the leading college teams won the right to negotiate television contracts independent of the NCAA. Partly as a consequence of the revenue generated by independent deals, the top flight of college football became a professional sport in all but name.

The rules of basketball were first codified at a college that trained YMCA gym instructors in Springfield, Massachusetts, by James Naismith (1861–1939) in 1891. Naismith, a muscular Christian who had been born in Canada and once played professional lacrosse, set out to invent an indoor game that was simple, interesting and wholesome to fill the months between the close of the football season and the start of the baseball season. Naismith's 'New Game' featured a round ball, to encourage passing, and an elevated target, to reward skill over power. He originally intended to use boxes for goals, but the gym's janitor, who had nothing suitable, suggested a couple of empty peach baskets. Basketball was immediately popular with both men and women. It was promoted across the USA with missionary zeal by members of the YMCA and by settlement house workers, among them Jane ADDAMS. (Within a year of the game's invention, for example, a Springfield graduate had organized a basketball league among the Sioux nation in South Dakota.)

As played under Naismith's rules, the game was usually low-scoring. Few courts had backboards, so the bank shot and the lay-up were almost unknown. It took time for players to learn to evade the prohibition on running with the ball by developing the offensive dribble. (These new techniques were popularized in Philadelphia, a city whose role in the development of basketball is comparable to New York's role in the development of baseball.) Despite the prohibition on physical contact, many games revolved around groups of players attempting to wrestle the ball from one another's hands. The first women's leagues interpreted the rules in such a way as to prevent some players from shooting, thus giving their game a resemblance to the British women's sport netball.

In the game's early years, a shortage of gyms with ceilings sufficiently high to accommodate the game led to pro and amateur teams sharing rented facilities like dance halls and playing one-off games against each other. Attempts by the American Athletic Union to prevent amateur players and clubs from any fraternization with professionals, foundered on this issue. On the other hand, campaigners were able to exploit the supposed threat to young men's morals implicit in a lack of facilities, to persuade municipal authorities and school districts to build courts. During the NEW DEAL, thousands of municipal auditoriums and gyms were built by the WORKS PROGRESS ADMINISTRATION. Many of these featured the longer courts and sophisticated scoreboards that are today regulation.

In 1905, the leading college teams formed an independent league and approved rules more akin to today's games. This league was originally run by students but control gradually passed to the NCAA. The first national NCAA tournament, forerunner of today's 'March Madness,' was staged in 1939. State high school competitions, the most celebrated of which is Indiana's, also grew in popularity during the 1930s. During World War II, the US armed forces promoted basketball as a means of maintaining fitness levels. During the build-up to D-DAY, 20,000 US servicemen based in the British Isles took part in a tournament that culminated in a grand final at the Royal Albert Hall.

The first significant professional basketball league – the American League – was launched in 1926. It adopted college rules in order to encourage graduating college stars to join professional ranks. The National Basketball Association (NBA) was founded in 1950. It became racially integrated in 1951. The NBA adopted the 24 second shot clock in 1954, an innovation that helped transform the pro game into a distinctively high-paced spectacle. The NBA signed its first TV contract in 1955. In recent years basketball, in both its pro and college variants, has proved particularly popular with an affluent BABY BOOM generation. Unlike baseball and football, sports in which crucial positions such as pitcher and quarterback tend to be occupied by white players, African-Americans have dominated the skilled positions in basketball. The growing popularity of the NBA has been credited in some circles with breaking long-held racial stereotypes. Certainly the peerless Michael Jordan (1963–) has earned a place within American popular culture that few African-American athletes have ever matched and he enjoys a name recognition around the world approaching that of Paul ROBESON and Muhammad ALI.

Basketball is a distinctive sport in two other respects: many women play the game and their main leagues enjoy uncommon levels of resourcing and respect. Title IX of the Federal Education Act of 1972 prohibits colleges that operate sexually discriminatory policies or programs from the receipt of federal funds. To avoid breaching the act, colleges and universities had to increase the money they spent on women's athletic programs. The chief beneficiary was women's basketball. In 1974, only 242 colleges fielded women's basketball teams; by 1980, over 1500 colleges funded women's teams. The women's version of the national NCAA college tournament grows in prestige each year and has recently gained its own TV exposure. Greater strength in the college game also led to the creation in 1977 of a professional women's basketball league.

Like baseball, football and basketball developed in the context of urbanization. The application of hard-headed business management to each sport has resulted in teams being moved from their original cities or in cities suffering the humiliation of being denied a major league franchise. More recently, team owners have built stadia outside downtown areas in suburban locations which are often inaccessible by public transport. Spectator sports grew up in cities but increasingly, their home is in the suburbs.

spoils system, the practice of rewarding supporters with positions in federal or state government. The spoils system was popularized by President JACKSON, who replaced over one-fifth of the federal bureaucracy following his victory in the 1828 presidential election. New York politician William Marcy (1786–1857) defended the system, arguing 'to the victor belong the spoils'.

Spotsylvania Court House, battle of (May 1864), inconclusive but bloody engagement in Virginia during the CIVIL WAR. Developing a campaign initiated with the battle of the WILDERNESS, Union General Ulysses S. GRANT tried to turn the southern flank of General Robert E. LEE's Confederate army defending Richmond, Virginia (the Confederate capital). In a series of frontal assaults against entrenched Confederate positions on May 9–12 and May 18 1864, Union forces suffered 11,000 casualties. Although they inflicted comparable losses on the Confederates, Lee's lines held. Grant's army moved south in an attempt to capture COLD HARBOR.

Springfield lynch riot (1908), race riot in Springfield, Illinois. On August 14 1908 rumors that a black man had raped a white woman sparked three days of anti-black violence in the town. The rioting engulfed a PROHIBITION PARTY campaign meeting and led to at least one black man being lynched by a mob. Order was restored by the intervention of state militia, and by a belated denial of rape by its alleged victim. The symbolism of these events moved white liberals to join African-American NIAGARA MOVEMENT activists in the creation of the NATIONAL ASSOCIATION FOR THE ADVANCEMENT OF COLORED PEOPLE (NAACP).

Square Deal, slogan encapsulating the blend of trust-busting and mildly pro-labor policies that President Theodore ROOSEVELT offered the electorate in 1904.

Stalwarts, nickname applied to corrupt REPUBLICAN PARTY bosses and their followers in the late 19th century. In the aftermath of RECONSTRUCTION, the Republican Party had lost much of its radicalism, but retained solid support among northern voters. This allowed state political machines, controlled by Republican Party bosses, to flourish. The power of the bosses rested on their ability to deliver patronage to claimants. Reformers within the party (dubbed MUGWUMPS and HALF-BREEDS) seized on a remark made by Charles GUITEAU after his assassination of President GARFIELD (1881) – that as a stalwart Republican he deserved a government post – to discredit the influence of the bosses and to attack corruption.

Stamp Act (March 22 1765), legislation passed by the British Parliament that helped to provoke the AMERICAN REVOLUTION.

Parliament passed the act in the aftermath of the SEVEN YEARS' WAR with the intent of raising £100,000 to defray the costs of maintaining a military garrison in North America. The act required Americans to print legal documents, newspapers, property titles, pamphlets and even college degrees on specially watermarked or 'stamped' paper. Enforcement of the act was to be entrusted to local officials paid a percentage of the revenue they collected.

American objections to the act, summarized in a 'Declaration of Rights and Grievances' drawn up by the STAMP ACT CONGRESS, cut to the heart of the colonies' constitutional relationship with Britain. American protesters argued that it was an 'undoubted right' of all Englishmen wherever they lived 'that no taxes should be imposed on them' unless their own consent had been given personally or by their representatives. Since the colonies were not, and could not feasibly be, represented in the British Parliament, the act was unconstitutional. American pamphleteers also made the point that the act would drain the colonies of SPECIE (hard currency in gold and silver), thereby depressing the economy and with it America's already sizeable indirect contribution to Britain's wealth. Offenses against the act were to be heard in VICE-ADMIRALTY COURTS, which did not allow jury trials, thereby depriving Americans of another cherished right.

Americans never complied with the act. Officials appointed to collect stamp duty were intimidated into resignation, and in the seaport towns NON-IMPORTATION AGREEMENTS brought trade with Britain to a standstill. Parliament repealed the act on March 18 1766, but on the same day passed the DECLARATORY ACT asserting its right to tax the colonies.

Stamp Act Congress (October 7–25 1765), meeting of representatives from nine of the THIRTEEN COLONIES, held in New York City, which drew up a 'Declaration of Rights and Grievances' to protest at the STAMP ACT and 'other late acts for the restriction of American commerce'. The 27 delegates who attended the Congress rehearsed arguments that would become familiar during the AMERICAN REVOLUTION. They pledged allegiance to the British crown and Parliament, but insisted that it was their right as Englishmen that no tax be levied on them except by their freely given consent. Since the colonies could not be represented in Parliament, this meant in practice that colonial legislatures should possess the exclusive power of taxation. The Congress was the first occasion on which delegates from all the colonies met collectively. No comparable meeting was held until the first CONTINENTAL CONGRESS convened in September 1774.

Standard Oil Company of New Jersey et al. vs. US (May 15 1911), US Supreme Court ruling that ordered the break-up of the Standard Oil Company.

The Standard Oil TRUST had been organized in 1879 by John D. ROCKEFELLER Sr. In a secret agreement, Rockefeller-owned companies coordinated extraction, refinement and transportation operations through the Standard Oil Company of Ohio. Rockefeller bullied railroad companies, banks and state legislatures into granting his companies concessions. His actions lowered the price of oil for consumers, but attracted the attention of PROGRESSIVES and MUCKRAKERS because, by the turn of the century, Rockefeller controlled 85% of the US oil production market, and 90% of America's exports of domestic oil. When the Ohio state Supreme Court ordered the trust broken up (1892), Rockefeller reorganized his operations through the Standard Oil Company of New Jersey. Despite munificent philanthropic bequests, Rockefeller was denounced as a 'malefactor of great wealth'.

In 1911 the US Supreme Court ordered (8–1) the Standard Oil Company broken up. However, the Court's reasoning departed from the SHERMAN ANTI-TRUST ACT (1890) – which forbade combinations in restraint of trade – and argued instead that the 'rule of reason' permitted companies to cooperate among themselves if, unlike Standard Oil, they did not unduly stifle competition. This ruling prompted passage of the CLAYTON ANTI-TRUST ACT (1914).

Stanton, Edwin M(cMasters) (1814–69), secretary of war (1862–8) in the administrations of Abraham LINCOLN and Andrew JOHNSON. Stanton's organizational flair played a major role in securing Union victory in the CIVIL WAR. Stanton was raised in Ohio. Although nominally a Democrat, he was a staunch opponent of slavery. James BUCHANAN appointed Stanton US attorney general in 1860. Lincoln confirmed this appointment before moving him to replace the corrupt Simon Cameron (1799–1889) at the war department. Stanton argued with Andrew Johnson over RECONSTRUCTION, and in February 1868 Johnson fired him. Citing the TENURE OF OFFICE ACT (1867), Stanton refused to leave and barricaded himself inside the war department to await the outcome of Johnson's IMPEACHMENT trial. When Johnson was acquitted, Stanton retired and accepted an appointment to the US Supreme Court. He died before he could be sworn in.

Stanton, Elizabeth Cady (1815–1902), campaigner for women's rights, who with Susan B. ANTHONY helped to found the US WOMEN'S SUFFRAGE movement.

In 1840 Stanton, Lucretia MOTT and a number of other American women traveled to an anti-slavery convention in London. They were refused accreditation because of their gender. This incident led Stanton and Mott to plan the SENECA FALLS CONVENTION (1848) to discuss women's rights. The convention's call for the right to vote for women marked the beginning of the women's suffrage movement.

Like her close collaborator Susan B. Anthony, Stanton greeted the FIFTEENTH AMENDMENT with dismay. She was irritated that uneducated and unappreciative men could vote when women could not. In 1878 Stanton headed a delegation from the NATIONAL WOMAN SUFFRAGE ASSOCIATION (NWSA) that addressed a congressional committee on the justice of women's suffrage. She was patronized and ignored by congressmen: Senator Wadleigh of New Hampshire, for example, read a newspaper, cut his nails, yawned and sharpened a pencil during her presentation.

For Stanton, suffrage was always but one part of a larger campaign to secure women's rights. From 1869 Stanton edited *Revolution*, a feminist journal. In one of its earliest editions she thundered 'Society as organized today under the power of man is one grand rape of womanhood.' She served as president of NWSA and the NATIONAL AMERICAN WOMAN SUFFRAGE ASSOCIATION, but did not live to see passage of the NINETEENTH AMENDMENT, which gave women the vote.

Star Wars, *see* STRATEGIC DEFENSE INITIATIVE.

states' rights, the rights and powers reserved by individual states, as opposed to those exercised by the federal government. The extent of these rights and powers depends on differing interpretations of the US Constitution.

Prior to the CIVIL WAR the term 'states' rights' encapsulated a body of political and constitutional concepts that were developed with exceptional vigour by opponents of centralized authority. States'-rights phi-losophy held that individual states were the ultimate guarantors of a citizen's personal liberties. This was because state government was closer to the people than distant federal authority, and therefore provided a better reflection of the people's wishes. Advocates of states' rights also made the point that state government predated federal government. As developed in the VIRGINIA and KENTUCKY RESOLUTIONS of 1798–9, these arguments were used to justify the right of the states to review federal legislation, to nullify any federal legislation that the states adjudged unconstitutional, and to interpose their authority to prevent the federal government from enforcing legislation that might abridge the liberties of a state's citizens.

On November 24 1832 a special convention in South Carolina drew on states'-rights arguments to declare the TARIFFS of 1828 and 1832 'null and void', thereby provoking the NULLIFICATION CRISIS. In the aftermath of this crisis the leading theorist of states' rights, John C. CALHOUN, propounded a modified version of the doctrine in which the concept of a CONCURRENT MAJORITY was used to justify opposition to federal action against slavery. The constitution of the Confederate States of America (the CONFEDERACY) was suffused with the language of states' rights. Following the USA's victory over the Confederacy in the Civil War, states' rights doctrine became associated with treason.

Statue of Liberty, dedicated on October 28 1886, 'Liberty Enlightening the World' dominates New York harbor and symbolizes an international perception of America as a land of freedom and opportunity.

In 1865, French journalist and republican Édouard René Lefevre de Laboulaye (1811–83) hit upon the idea of erecting a giant statue in the USA to celebrate Franco-American commitment to republican government. The statue, which is 151 feet high, was designed by Frédéric Auguste Batholdi

(1834–1904). A public subscription in France raised $400,000 to meet construction costs. The USA provided the site, Liberty Island (formerly Bledsoe's Island), and an 89-foot pedestal purchased by public subscription that raised $270,000. The statue was completed in Paris in 1884. It was shipped across the Atlantic in over 200 crates and reassembled on its pedestal. President CLEVELAND presided over the dedication ceremony.

In 1892, the US Immigration Service designated nearby Ellis Island in New York harbor as its primary processing center for European immigrants. This decision meant that for an increasing number of future Americans the statue was the first landmark they saw in their adopted country, and it made 'Lady Liberty' an object of veneration and fascination. The New York poet Emma Lazarus (1849–87) composed the inscription that graces the pedestal. Its allusion to 'poor … huddled masses, yearning to breathe free' became celebrated. (Lazarus' references to 'the wretched refuse' of Europe's 'teeming shore' have been quietly forgotten.) In 1982, President REAGAN launched a public appeal to repair and restore both the Statue and Ellis Island. The Statue was rededicated, with great celebrations, in its centenary year.

steel strike of 1919, unsuccessful industrial action in the Pittsburgh region. By characterizing the strike as part of an attempted revolutionary insurrection, rather than a dispute over union recognition, employers helped create the RED SCARE.

The defeat of the HOMESTEAD STRIKE (1892) had brought a temporary end to attempts to unionize US steel mills. But in 1918 the AMERICAN FEDERATION OF LABOR (AFL) authorized a massive drive to unionize steelworkers. This succeeded because the AFL recruited organizers fluent in Eastern European languages and did not encroach upon existing CRAFT UNIONS. Steel companies in the Pittsburgh region refused to

negotiate on union recognition, and, despite pleas from President Woodrow WILSON, fired union activists. On September 22 1919 their workers struck. Local police forces, state militia and private guards were employed to keep the mills open and break the strike. In January 1920 workers returned to the mills.

Steuben, Frederick William (Augustus), Baron von (originally Friedrich Wilhelm Ludolf Gerhard Augustin, Freiherr von Steuben) (1730–94), Prussian officer who helped to turn the Continental Army into a disciplined fighting force during the REVOLUTIONARY WAR.

Steuben was a penniless soldier of fortune. By claiming to be a lieutenant general, securing testimonials from prominent Americans (among them Benjamin FRANKLIN), and by offering to serve without pay, he wangled a position as drillmaster to the Continental Army. During the winter of 1777–8, at VALLEY FORGE, Pennsylvania, Steuben imparted an approximation of Prussian close-order drill to American troops. (He spoke little English, and relied on other officers to translate his explanatory comments spoken in French.) Steuben's efforts gave the Continental Army greater tactical cohesion, preventing a repeat of the confusion witnessed at the battle of GERMANTOWN, and contributing to success at the battle of MONMOUTH COURT HOUSE. Ironically in the light of the 1990s controversy about gays in the US armed forces, Steuben was a homosexual. He spent his retirement in the USA, living with two young men on a farm in Ohio granted to him by a grateful nation.

Stevens, Thaddeus (1792–1868), RADICAL REPUBLICAN politician and campaigner for the rights of African-Americans. Born in Vermont, Stevens settled in Pennsylvania and practiced law. He sat as a WHIG in the US House of Representatives (1848–53), and became a leading opponent of slavery. Defeated in a re-election bid, Stevens provided free legal services to fugitive slaves. He was an early convert to the REPUBLICAN PARTY, and, from 1859 until his death, represented the party's radical wing in Congress. During the CIVIL WAR Stevens urged LINCOLN's administration to 'free every slave, slay every traitor, burn every rebel mansion, if these things be necessary to preserve this temple of freedom'. One of the architects of CONGRESSIONAL RECONSTRUCTION, Stevens helped to coordinate impeachment proceedings against President JOHNSON (1868). His will stipulated that he be buried in a negro cemetery, in protest against the segregation of burial plots.

Stevenson, Adlai (Ewing), Jr (1900–65), the Democratic nominee in the presidential elections of 1952 and 1956. A humane, witty and literate man, Stevenson was seen by many Democrats as embodying values of decency that were being driven from public life by the likes of Richard NIXON and Joseph McCARTHY. Stevenson was the son of Grover CLEVELAND's vice president, Adlai Stevenson Sr (1835–1914). He was educated at Princeton, University and Harvard Law School. He worked in the AGRICULTURAL ADJUSTMENT ADMINISTRATION, helped to create the UNITED NATIONS, and served as governor of Illinois (1948–52) before gaining the Democrats' presidential nomination in 1952. Democrats warmed to the theme of Stevenson's acceptance speech, 'Let's talk sense to the American people', but voters preferred Dwight D. EISENHOWER's more complacent style.

Stimson, Henry L(ewis) (1867–1950), government official. In the course of a career in government service that brought him into contact with an unusually broad range of politicians and policies, Stimson served as secretary of war (1911–13) under TAFT, secretary of state (1929–33) under HOOVER and secretary of war (1940–5) under Franklin D. ROOSEVELT. He was trained as a lawyer, and his work on Wall Street cases brought him to the attention of Theodore ROOSEVELT, who appointed him a US district attorney in 1909. During World War I Stimson saw active service in an artillery unit. In 1927 President COOLIDGE sent Stimson to broker a peace settlement in the Nicaraguan civil war. Almost immediately afterwards he began a two-year stint as governor general of the Philippines. On January 7 1932, in response to the Japanese invasion of Manchuria, he issued the so-called 'Stimson Doctrine', which stated that the USA would not recognize territorial acquisitions taken by force. The LEAGUE OF NATIONS adopted this policy in March 1932. As secretary of war during WORLD WAR II, Stimson presided over the USA's massive arms build-up. Often presented as an unwavering supporter of the bombing of HIROSHIMA AND NAGASAKI, Stimson in fact explored alternatives to the use of the atomic bomb

Stone, Lucy (1818–93), co-founder of the AMERICAN WOMAN SUFFRAGE ASSOCIATION (AWSA) in 1869, who played an important role in developing support for WOMEN'S SUFFRAGE among campaigners for the ABOLITION of slavery. In the 1850s, following the SENECA FALLS CONVENTION, Stone organized annual conventions in Worcester, Massachusetts, to discuss women's rights. In 1858, while resident in New Jersey, she allowed officials to distrain her goods for non-payment of state taxes, in order to dramatize her point that women were taxed without being granted representation. From 1872 to 1893 she co-edited, together with her husband Henry Blackwell, a campaigning magazine entitled the *Woman's Journal.*

Stonewall riot, *see* GAY RIGHTS MOVEMENT.

Strategic Arms Limitation Talks (SALT), *see* DÉTENTE.

Strategic Arms Reduction Talks (START), *see* DÉTENTE.

Strategic Defense Initiative (SDI), defense program, announced by President REAGAN in March 1983. Reagan and Secretary of Defense Casper Weinberger (1917–)

urged Congress to provide funding to build a shield of laser and particle-beam weapons in outer space that would destroy intercontinental nuclear missiles before they could reach US targets. The initiative threatened one of the central assumptions of nuclear deterrence in the COLD WAR, that of 'mutually assured destruction' (MAD). SDI was derided in the USA as 'Star Wars'. The USSR took the proposal seriously because it would allow the USA to launch a nuclear attack without risking reprisal. The feasibility and morality of the project were hotly contested, although defense contractors and university laboratories, in the USA and Great Britain, eagerly sought a share of the program's massive research funding. Reagan's attachment to the program, which some commentators thought demonstrated a senile confusion between strategic thought and 1950s B-movies, led to the collapse of the REYKJAVIK CONFERENCE, and proved a stumbling block in successive Strategic Arms Reduction Talks. The USA spent $30 billion on the project before President CLINTON announced its cancellation in 1993.

strict constructionism, reading of the US Constitution that insists that federal government only possesses those powers expressly delegated to it in the Constitution. This argument was first put forward during the 1790s by many DEMOCRATIC-REPUBLICANS, who were fearful of the corrupting effects of power on the new federal government. The TENTH AMENDMENT supported this reading of the Constitution, while Alexander HAMILTON's argument that the power to create a BANK OF THE UNITED STATES was implied within the Constitution contravened it (this alternative reading of the Constitution is known as LOOSE CONSTRUCTIONISM). John Randolph's QUID faction applied strict constructionism to the policies of JEFFERSON's and MADISON's administrations. In 1830 President JACKSON vetoed the MAYSVILLE ROAD VETO on strict constructionist grounds.

Student Non-Violent Coordinating Committee (SNCC), organization, informally known as 'Snick', that played a key role in the CIVIL RIGHTS MOVEMENT. The SNCC was formed in October 1960 in the wake of the GREENSBORO SIT-IN. SNCC members brought to the Civil Rights Movement a youthful fervor that was often at odds with the caution advocated by the NATIONAL ASSOCIATION FOR THE ADVANCEMENT OF COLORED PEOPLE (NAACP) and the SOUTHERN CHRISTIAN LEADERSHIP CONFERENCE (SCLC). SNCC members played a major role in the successful FREEDOM RIDER campaign, and worked tirelessly on voter registration during the MISSISSIPPI FREEDOM SUMMER. Prominent SNCC activists included Ella BAKER, John Lewis (1940–), Jesse JACKSON and Stokeley CARMICHAEL. Under Carmichael's leadership the SNCC endorsed BLACK POWER and expelled its white members. In 1968 it merged with the BLACK PANTHER Party.

Subversive Activities Control Board, see McCARRAN ACT.

Suffolk Resolves, resolutions adopted on September 9 1774 by representatives of Massachusetts towns meeting in Suffolk County to protest against the INTOLERABLE ACTS. The Suffolk Resolves declared the acts unconstitutional, pledged disobedience, and called for a provincial congress to receive taxes until the repeal of the MASSACHUSETTS GOVERNMENT ACT. Delegates also demanded military preparedness and resistance to the seizure of any patriot leader. The CONTINENTAL ASSOCIATION adopted by the first CONTINENTAL CONGRESS matched the militancy of these resolutions.

Sugar Act (April 5 1764), the British Parliament's first attempt to raise revenue from the colonies. The act created grievances that helped to produce the AMERICAN REVOLUTION. The main feature of the act halved the duty levied on molasses imported into the mainland American colonies from the West Indies. This cut in duty was thought likely to persuade American rum distillers to use

West Indian molasses, thereby producing a secure source of revenue that could be used to offset the cost of maintaining a British military garrison in America. To prevent American drinkers from boycotting rum, a new levy was charged on wine imported from Portugal's Atlantic islands. The act also disturbed New England's trade by requiring certain goods, including potash, iron, lumber and whale fins, to be shipped to Britain, and to pass through British customs, before trans-shipment elsewhere. Finally, the Sugar Act created a VICE-ADMIRALTY COURT, located in Halifax, Nova Scotia, to hear smuggling cases. Americans protested against the creation of this court because it did not provide for trial by jury and required a defendant to prove his innocence.

Sullivan's campaign (1778–9), military campaign against the IROQUOIS CONFEDERACY. During the REVOLUTIONARY WAR Mohawk chieftain Joseph BRANT emerged as the leader of an Iroquois force that sided with the British on the grounds that they had at least tried, through the PROCLAMATION OF 1763, to limit TERRITORIAL EXPANSION by white settlers in North America. In 1778 Brant's warriors conducted a series of raids and massacres on settlements in central New York State and in Pennsylvania's Wyoming Valley. George WASHINGTON commissioned John Sullivan (1740–95) to 'lay waste' and 'destroy' Iroquois settlements. By December 1779 most of Brant's supporters had fled to Canada. The weakened Iroquois eventually signed the second treaty of FORT STANWIX (1784).

supply-side economics, the dominant intellectual influence on Ronald REAGAN's presidency. Supply-siders held that cuts in federal income tax would stimulate personal savings and investment. This in turn would provide capital that could be used to modernize factories, stimulating the economy and ultimately increasing government revenues.

Reagan eagerly endorsed this theory, which George BUSH had famously described as 'voodoo economics'. In keeping with supply-side thinking the FEDERAL RESERVE BOARD ('the Fed') raised interest rates to reduce inflation. Inflation rates fell, largely because of a collapse in oil prices. But the Fed's tight-money policies triggered a recession. By November 1982 10.8% of the workforce was unemployed, the highest figure since the Great Depression. Reagan proved unable to cut federal government expenditure, which grew even as receipts fell. Democrats demanded that the welfare budget remain untouched as the price of their support for Reagan's defense build-up. Meanwhile Americans spent, rather than saved, their tax cuts. Those with money bought foreign 'designer' goods, especially cars. This created a trade deficit, which Treasury Secretary James A. Baker (1930–) attempted to reverse by engineering a slide in the value of the dollar.

In 1980 the USA was the world's largest creditor nation; in 1988 it was the world's largest debtor. The fall-out from the supply-side experiment was a structural transformation of the US economy in which service industries replaced manufacturing and agriculture as the prime generators of jobs.

Supreme Court, US, the highest court in the federal system. Its jurisdiction is described in Article III Sections 1 and 2 of the US CONSTITUTION (*see also* Appendix 1). The Constitution grants CONGRESS the power to organize and staff the Supreme Court but, in its unamended form, the Constitution left open several issues regarding the Court's function. Congress specified through the Judiciary Act of 1789 that the Supreme Court be composed of a chief justice and five associate justices. Congress has since amended this arrangement, legislating for a five-member court in 1801, a seven-member court in 1807, a nine-member court in 1833, a ten-member court in 1864, an eight-member court in 1866 and a nine-member court in 1869. Members of the Supreme Court are nominated by the president, but must be approved by the US Senate. Since justices may serve for life, a president can, by nominating justices who share his views, continue to influence US politics even after he has left office.

The Senate used its power of approval for the first time in 1795, when it rejected John Rutledge (1739–1800), George WASHINGTON's nominee for the post of chief justice. In the early 19th century, under Chief Justice John MARSHALL, the Court established itself as equal in power to Congress and the presidency. In its 1803 verdict on MARBURY VS. MADISON the Court claimed the right of JUDICIAL REVIEW; that is the right to invalidate state and federal laws it regards as unconstitutional. Although the Court has used this power sparingly, verdicts invalidating acts of Congress – such as those in DRED SCOTT VS. SANDFORD (1857) and SCHECTER POULTRY CORPORATION VS. UNITED STATES (1935) – have altered the course of American history. Verdicts upholding acts objectionable to many Americans – such as PLESSY VS. FERGUSON (1896) legitimating JIM CROW segregation laws in southern states – have proved equally influential.

Until 1891 Supreme Court justices were required to 'ride circuit', hearing appeals in distant parts of the USA. This created an enormous workload and a backlog of cases for the justices, and this militated against the nomination of legal intellectuals to the Court. From RECONSTRUCTION to the NEW DEAL the court was dominated by conservatives who took an unimaginative and even reactionary view of legislation regulating businesses, and of the protections afforded to civil rights by the FOURTEENTH and FIFTEENTH AMENDMENTS. Able justices who joined the bench during this period – such as John Marshall HARLAN, Oliver Wendell HOLMES and Louis BRANDEIS – struggled to influence their colleagues. In 1937 Franklin D. ROOSEVELT proposed a reorganization of the Court, the express purpose of which

was to protect New Deal legislation by appointing justices sympathetic to its aims. This proposal provoked the COURT-PACKING CONTROVERSY.

A series of deaths, retirements and imaginative nominations by Roosevelt, TRUMAN, and EISENHOWER created a more liberal court. Chief Justice Earl WARREN, nominated by Eisenhower in a move he later regretted, signaled the changed mood of the Court in his opinion on BROWN VS. BOARD OF EDUCATION (1954). This verdict invalidated state laws establishing racially segregated school systems and, as elaborated from the bench in 1955, required local government to desegregate their school systems with 'all deliberate speed'. Never quite as liberal as conservative critics charged, the 'Warren court' nonetheless contributed to the successes of the CIVIL RIGHTS MOVEMENT and to the social upheavals of the 1960s. Following the verdict on ROE VS. WADE (1973), which had the effect of liberalizing ABORTION law, the balance of the Court began to change as more conservative justices nominated by presidents NIXON, FORD, REAGAN and BUSH joined the bench. The current Supreme Court, under chief justice William Rehnquist, is generally seen as sharing a conservative complexion.

For a full list of Supreme Court justices, their sponsors and their period of service see Appendix 3.

Swann vs. Charlotte-Mecklenberg Board of Education (April 20 1971), unanimous US Supreme Court ruling that upheld 'bus transportation as means of school desegregation'. BUSSING pupils from one ethnic group into schools dominated by another group achieved the goal of desegregating school systems, but was deeply unpopular with white parents.

Swift and Co. vs. US (January 30 1905), unanimous US Supreme Court ruling against the Swift Company (the so-called 'Beef Trust'). The ruling reversed the Court's earlier ruling in US VS. E.C. KNIGHT (1895), which had gutted the intent of the SHERMAN ANTI-TRUST ACT (1890) by exempting manufacturing corporations from federal anti-trust legislation. In its 1905 decision, hailed by MUCKRAKERS and PROGRESSIVES, the Court coined the notion of a 'stream of commerce' to argue that although meat-packing took place within state boundaries it was essential to the interstate marketing of beef products, and therefore subject to federal regulations governing interstate trade.

Sycamore Shoals, treaty of (March 17 1775), treaty by which Richard Henderson's TRANSYLVANIA COMPANY purchased 26,500 square miles (68,600 square km) of land between the Ohio and Cumberland rivers from the CHEROKEE for £10,000. Daniel BOONE blazed the WILDERNESS ROAD to facilitate settlement of this area. Existing states feared the precedent established by a treaty between a private company and a Native American nation.

T

Taft, William Howard (1857–1930), jurist, Republican statesman, 27th president of the USA (1909–13) and chief justice of the US Supreme Court (1921–30) – the only man to have served in both capacities.

As a boy growing up in Ohio, Taft preferred to umpire baseball games rather than participate as a player. A law career beckoned. He practiced law in Cincinnati and served as a public prosecutor before his appointment as a federal judge (1892–1900) on the 6th US Circuit Court. During this period he also served as dean of the University of Cincinnati's law school. President McKINLEY appointed Taft, a staunch Republican, to preside over the US occupation of the PHILIPPINES (1900–4). His administration of the islands was so even-handed that in the winter of 1902–3 McKinley's successor, Theodore ROOSEVELT, twice offered Taft a place on the US Supreme Court so that he could bring in a tougher governor. Taft refused the position he coveted. However, he did serve as Roosevelt's secretary of war (1904–8).

When in 1908 Roosevelt renounced a second election campaign, Taft was an obvious and popular choice as Republican presidential nominee. Following his successful campaign, he became president on March 4 1909, and served until March 3 1913. President Taft invented the concept of DOLLAR DIPLOMACY. His administration contin-ued Roosevelt's attack on TRUSTS, scoring a notable victory in STANDARD OIL COMPANY OF NEW JERSEY VS. US. Nonetheless Roosevelt criticized Taft's administration, opposed his renomination, and, by running against him in the PRESIDENTIAL ELECTION OF 1912, ensured Taft's defeat.

Taft was professor of law at Yale between 1913 and 1921. He was a prominent supporter of PROHIBITION and the LEAGUE OF NATIONS. President Harding appointed Taft chief justice on June 30 1921. In this capacity his opinions on cases such as BAILEY VS. DREXEL FURNITURE COMPANY displayed his deep hostility to labor unions. His jurisprudence was also informed by an unflinching commitment to the free market.

Taft–Hartley Act (June 23 1947), legislation, passed over President TRUMAN's veto, that rescinded some rights granted to unions by the WAGNER ACT (1935). It outlawed closed shops, prohibited strikes not sanctioned by a majority of a workforce, and allowed the president to apply for an injunction creating a 'cooling off' period in disputes deemed likely to damage the national interest. The act also prohibited trade unions from contributing to political campaigns, and barred members of the Communist Party from serving as union officials.

Tammany Hall, political organization that dominated the New York state legislature and the national DEMOCRATIC PARTY for over 100 years.

The Society of St Tammany (named after the Delaware chief Tamenend) was founded in New York City in 1786. Its original purpose was to collect and distribute aid to veterans of the Revolutionary War and their families. Aaron BURR mobilized Tammany in support of Thomas JEFFERSON in the PRESIDENTIAL ELECTION OF 1800, and from then on the organization's interests were as much political as charitable.

Tammany bosses (or 'sachems') distributed aid and favors to working-class New Yorkers in return for votes. Candidates in city and state elections who lacked the support of Tammany became all but unelectable. Given New York's importance within the ELECTORAL COLLEGE, Tammany bosses could influence the selection of Democratic presidential candidates and even the outcome of presidential elections. During the Civil War, Tammany leaders succumbed to corruption. In 1868 the organization completed a lavish 'Hall' just off Union Square, from which the notorious TWEED RING despoiled the city's coffers. Tammany maintained its hold over working-class Democrats until the provision of basic welfare services in the NEW DEAL rendered the machine's distribution of aid and favors redundant.

Taney, Roger Brooke (1777–1864), fifth chief justice of the US Supreme Court, and the first Catholic to be appointed to it. Taney will be forever remembered as a man who helped to cause the CIVIL WAR by authoring the Court's opinion on DRED SCOTT VS. SANDFORD (1857).

Prior to his appointment to the Supreme Court, Taney had served as Maryland's attorney general (1827–31), as US attorney general (1831–3), as acting secretary of war (1831) and acting secretary of the Treasury (1833–4). He was an unflinching supporter of President Andrew JACKSON during the battle over the recharter of the second BANK OF THE UNITED STATES. Jackson nominated Taney to serve as chief justice, and he was confirmed on March 15 1836. In 1837 Taney cast the deciding vote in the case of CHARLES RIVER BRIDGE VS. WARREN BRIDGE. Speaking for the majority, he concurred in a verdict that curbed the growth of monopolies, arguing that 'we must not forget that the community also has rights'. Twenty years later, in the Dred Scott case, Taney argued that the MISSOURI COMPROMISE and the COMPROMISE OF 1850 established an unconstitutional infringement of slaveholders' rights. During the Civil War, Taney's verdict on EX PARTE MERRYMAN upheld the rights of civilians.

Tarawa Atoll, battle of (November 1943), one of the bloodiest battles fought between US and Japanese troops in WORLD WAR II. The US 2nd Marine Division launched an amphibious assault on Tarawa, an island in the Gilbert archipelago (now part of the Republic of Kiribati), on November 21 1943. The 5000-strong Japanese garrison fought until only 17 of its number remained alive and unwounded. Although the US Marines eventually captured the island, 913 of them were killed and 2000 wounded in the assault. The battle played a relatively minor role in the US 'island-hopping' strategy. However, the scale and nature of Japanese resistance in battles such as Tarawa helped convince US military planners that an assault on the Japanese home islands might cost 1 million US casualties. This calculation influenced the decision to drop atomic bombs on HIROSHIMA AND NAGASAKI in 1945.

Tariff of Abominations (1828), the nickname applied to a proposal made by JACKSONIAN DEMOCRATS on the House Committee on Manufactures to levy unprecedentedly high duties on raw materials being imported into the USA. Democratic supporters of Andrew JACKSON (drawn chiefly from southern constituencies exporting staples such as cotton) proposed the tariff knowing that it would trigger retaliatory measures abroad. They did so in the hope that the incumbent president John Quincy ADAMS (a New Englander) would be forced to veto the measure (and thereby lose his remaining support in the south), or approve it and alienate his support among northerners whose livelihoods depended on international trade. When Congress unexpectedly approved the duties (May 13 1828), southern protests, led by South Carolina, produced the NULLIFICATION CRISIS.

tariffs, duties levied on imported goods. Such duties may be levied with the primary purpose of raising revenue, or with the intent of protecting domestic industry or agriculture. Throughout its history, Congress has squabbled over whether and how to raise tariff revenue from imports. Tariffs have been set at a flat rate, applying a fixed cost to the importation of named goods and commodities, and also levied in *ad valorem,* which takes into account the commercial value of the items assessed. Low tariffs, broadly applied, provide governments with a relatively painless way of raising revenue. High tariffs, selectively applied, raise consumer prices and provoke retaliation from foreign nations.

Generations of US congressmen have proven unable to resist the temptation to propose punishing and highly selective tariffs in a bid to protect their constituents' interests. Some schemes devised by Congress caused political instability in foreign nations – for example the McKINLEY TARIFF (1890) and the WILSON–GORMAN TARIFF (1894). Others, notably the HAWLEY–SMOOT TARIFF (1930), have contributed to worldwide economic depression. The domestic consequences of measures such as the TARIFF OF ABOMINATIONS (1828) have provoked crises within the US political system. Millions of dollars in campaign contributions and armies of lobbyists have been deployed by special interests to convince Congress to propose, amend or repeal tariff policies.

Ta-Sunko-Witko or **Crazy Horse,** *see* LITTLE BIG HORN, BATTLE OF; SIOUX WARS.

Tatanka Iyotake, *see* SITTING BULL.

Taylor, Zachary (1784–1850), US Army general, WHIG statesman and 12th president of the USA (1849–50). Taylor, who died in office, was the last US president to be born before the adoption of the Constitution.

Taylor's long military career included service in the WAR OF 1812, the BLACK HAWK WAR and the second SEMINOLE WAR. 'Old Rough and Ready' achieved national prominence during the MEXICAN WAR, capturing MONTERREY (1846) and defeating a superior force at the battle of BUENA VISTA (1847).

Born in Virginia but raised in Kentucky, Taylor was reluctant to enter politics. He once told a Whig trying to persuade him to stand to 'shut up and drink your whiskey.' The presidency was the first (and only) elected office Taylor held. The Whigs nominated him in 1848 because, as a war hero and the owner of 100 slaves, it was thought that he would oppose the WILMOT PROVISO's prohibition on the extension of slavery into territory acquired during the Mexican War. In fact, after becoming president on March 5 1849, Taylor supported measures to curb the spread of slavery. Shortly before his death he intimated that he would veto the 'Omnibus Bill' enacting the COMPROMISE OF 1850, and use force to prevent pro-slavery southern states from seceding. He died on July 9 1850.

Tea Act (May 10 1773), legislation passed by the British Parliament to boost the East India Company's sales of tea in America. The act increased the resentment of the American colonists, and was one of several British laws that contributed to the AMERICAN REVOLUTION.

Facing bankruptcy, the East India Company had extracted parliamentary agreement to the act, by which Company tea bound for America was exempted from paying import duty when it passed through Britain. The Company was also permitted to sell direct to the colonies. Even with TOWNSHEND ACT duty paid, Company tea would be cheaper than any competing supply. Several features of the act irritated Americans. Parliament's willingness to accommodate the East India Company stood in stark contrast to its reluctance to recognise the rights of colonial legislatures. Americans believed the act had little do with the regulation of imperial trade and viewed it as an internal tax in all but name. They were angered by what they took to be Parliament's assumption that American consumers were so wedded to tea drinking that they would stomach the payment of an indirect subsidy to the East India Company. For these reasons the arrival of the first shipment of East India Company tea in America prompted the BOSTON TEA PARTY.

Teapot Dome scandal, corruption scandal of the early 1920s involving President HARDING's secretary of the interior, Albert B. Fall (1861–1944). In order to ensure that the US Navy had a secure source of fuel, the federal government had acquired a number of US oil fields. In 1921 Fall persuaded Harding's cabinet to transfer administration of these fields to his department. Fall then gave the Mammoth Oil Company secret and illegal permission to drill on a federal oil field in Teapot Dome, Wyoming. Mammoth gave Fall $308,000 and a herd of cattle. In 1929 Fall told a disbelieving court that these transactions were loans, not bribes.

Tecumseh (1768–1813), SHAWNEE leader who, together with his brother the PROPHET, founded a widespread Native American cultural revival in the early 19th century. Tecumseh called on Native American nations to return to traditional values, and to resist the expansion of white settlement, especially in the NORTHWEST TERRITORY. Tecumseh was promoting this message among the Cherokee when his brother provoked the disastrous battle of TIPPECANOE CREEK (1811). Tecumseh returned to lead a last-ditch war against US expansion, but

was killed at the battle of THAMES RIVER (1813). William HARRISON, governor of the Indiana territory and commander of the US forces that defeated Tecumseh, believed the Shawnee leader would have founded an empire to rival that of the Aztecs had he not lived in the shadow of the USA.

Teheran Conference (November 28– December 1 1943), summit meeting in Iran during WORLD WAR II involving Allied leaders Franklin D. ROOSEVELT, Winston Churchill and Joseph Stalin. Stalin agreed to coordinate the timing of a Soviet counter-offensive against Germany with the launch of the Anglo-American D-DAY LANDINGS planned for 1944. He also agreed to declare war on Japan. This was the first occasion on which Roosevelt and Stalin met, and it quickly became clear that Stalin did not share the world view encapsulated in Roosevelt's FOUR FREEDOMS rhetoric.

television, *see* RADIO AND TELEVISION.

Tennessee, southern state, bordered to the north by Kentucky and Virginia, to the east by the Appalachians and North Carolina, to the south by Georgia, Alabama and Mississippi, and to the west by the Mississippi river, Arkansas and Missouri.

The first US settlements in the territory were established in the Watauga river valley in 1769. The town of Nashville was founded in 1779. US settlers clashed with CHEROKEE raiders during the REVOLUTIONARY WAR. Alienated from military support, residents organized the state of FRANKLIN and in August 1784 sought admission into the Union as the 14th state. (The plan was blocked by North Carolina.) Tennessee was organized as a US territory on August 7 1789 and became the 16th state on June 1 1796. At that time it had 77,000 residents, 14% of whom were enslaved.

As the state grew, its economy developed along distinct regional lines. Subsistence farming dominated the mountainous east; further west tobacco and cotton were cultivated using slave labor. Andrew JACKSON's plantation, Hermitage, (near Nashville), was among the largest in the state. In 1860 Tennessee had 1,109,801 residents, 25% of whom were slaves. The state's slaveowners exercised a disproportionate influence within Tennessee politics. On May 7 1860 Tennessee became the tenth state to secede from the union and join the CONFEDERACY. Only Virginia was the site of more military engagements than Tennessee during the CIVIL WAR. Key battles fought in the state include SHILOH and CHATTANOOGA. Tennessee resident Andrew JOHNSON, a political opponent of the state's slaveowners, organized a pro-Union military government in the state in March 1862. As US president, Andrew Johnson restored Tennessee's congressional representation on July 24 1866. On October 4 1869 REDEEMERS gained control of the state legislature. Over the next 30 years the state, now dominated by Democrats, disenfranchised blacks and imposed racial segregation.

In 1900 Tennessee had 2,020,016 residents, many of them extremely poor. From the 1920s some 600,000 residents, most them black, took part in the GREAT MIGRATION, by leaving Tennessee for jobs in the north. The creation of the TENNESSEE VALLEY AUTHORITY (1933) greatly stimulated and diversified the state's economy. In 1990 Tennessee had 4,877,185 residents and was the 16th most populous state in the union. The state's most famous 'native son' is Davy CROCKETT. Residents who have made history include US presidents Andrew JACKSON and Andrew JOHNSON – and a boy from Memphis named Elvis PRESLEY.

Tennessee Valley Authority (TVA), major regional development agency, whose creation on May 18 1933 was one of the landmarks of the NEW DEAL. Like many agencies established in the period, the TVA built on previous government initiatives, and sought to integrate publicly owned assets within the US economy.

During World War I, President WILSON's administration had built a hydroelectric and munitions manufacturing complex at Muscle Shoals (Alabama) on the Tennessee river. In the 1920s the COOLIDGE and HOOVER administrations attempted to sell this into private ownership. A group of congressmen, led by Senator George NORRIS, opposed the sale and urged the government to use the complex as the basis for a regional development authority. Franklin D. ROOSEVELT, and members of his BRAINS TRUST, visited Muscle Shoals in January 1933. Once in power Roosevelt presented Congress with an expanded version of Norris's plan.

The TVA was an independent public corporation charged with controlling and utilizing the Tennessee and Cumberland rivers (and their tributaries) to generate and distribute electric power, manufacture fertilizer and prevent floods and soil erosion. The authority's charter bound it to set 'fair and reasonable' rates for the supply of electricity to rural areas (a yardstick later applied to private utility companies). The TVA built dozens of dams, barriers and power plants, making it the largest employer in the south. Working in cooperation with the RURAL ELECTRIFICATION ADMINISTRATION, the Authority contributed to a permanent improvement in living conditions for millions of southerners.

Tenskwatawa, *see* PROPHET, THE.

Tenth Amendment, amendment to the US Constitution reserving to the states and their citizens all powers neither delegated to the federal government nor denied them explicitly. This amendment (part of the BILL OF RIGHTS) reflected ANTIFEDERALIST fears that the federal government would consolidate its power at the expense of the states and the people. It was often cited by STATES' RIGHTS theorists. For the full text, *see* Appendix 1 .

Tenure of Office Act (March 2 1867), legislation, passed over President JOHNSON's veto, that protected CONGRESSIONAL RECON-

STRUCTION by barring the president from dismissing any officeholder whose appointment required Senate advice or approval. Johnson tested the law by dismissing, reinstating, and dismissing again (February 21 1868) Secretary of War Edwin STANTON. (Stanton supported the creation by the RECONSTRUCTION ACTS of military districts in southern states. Johnson opposed this policy.) Eight of the eleven charges in Johnson's IMPEACHMENT trial revolved around violations of this act. It was repealed on March 5 1887.

territorial expansion. The process by which the territorial boundaries of the USA came to include a broad swathe of the North American continent, stretching from 'sea to shining sea' and beyond to GUAM, HAWAII and other Pacific islands, lies at the heart of America's conception of itself as a nation, and has been identified by some historians as the key factor in the nation's history. Even before the 1840s, when John O'Sullivan popularized the idea that America had a MANIFEST DESTINY to expand westward across the continent, America's Founding Fathers sought ways of acquiring land beyond the boundaries of the original THIRTEEN COLONIES. Long before Frederick Jackson Turner developed the FRONTIER THESIS to explain the historical significance of westward expansion, Benjamin FRANKLIN, Thomas JEFFERSON and legions of foreign visitors to the USA had identified America's western lands as the crucible in which the nation's identity and its future were being forged. However, the growth of the USA was incremental and never inevitable. In all periods of America's history there was opposition, domestic and foreign, to further expansion.

At the close of the SEVEN YEARS' WAR, Britain sought (through the PROCLAMATION OF 1763) to define the western boundaries of the thirteen colonies, and to confine further settlement to the east of the 'proclamation line'. This policy contradicted colonial charters: Virginia, for example, claimed that the crown had previously established its western boundary as the Pacific Ocean. The policy infuriated westerners who had fought against hostile Native American nations in the Seven Years' War and in PONTIAC'S WAR, and who now regarded lands in the NORTHWEST TERRITORY as theirs by right of conquest. It also threw into question the legality of cessions and purchases currently being negotiated between colonial legislatures and Native American nations. Developments such as the treaty of FORT STANWIX (through which, in 1768, the IROQUOIS CONFEDERACY ceded to Americans most of western New York and the modern state of Kentucky) forced the British authorities to redraw the proclamation line. However, Britain remained hostile to the activities of corporate bodies, such as the TRANSYLVANIA COMPANY, which acquired land from colonial legislatures or direct from Native American nations. Officials in London, and on America's eastern seaboard, were also troubled by the 'scum' and 'banditti' who squatted on western lands in complete defiance of the Proclamation.

A sense that Britain was blocking territorial expansion was one cause of the AMERICAN REVOLUTION. The DECLARATION OF INDEPENDENCE charged George III with attempting 'to prevent the population of these states' through the Proclamation of 1763, and with inciting 'merciless Indian savages' to attack residents of 'our frontiers'. During the REVOLUTIONARY WAR, American offensives against Native American nations allied with the British, such as SULLIVAN'S CAMPAIGN, had the twin aims of securing existing settlements and seizing lands currently controlled by hostile tribes. However, both the CONTINENTAL CONGRESS and the CONFEDERATION CONGRESS also sought to secure the northern and southern borders of the USA.

American statesmen believed, with some justification, that Britain sought to use its presence in Canada to isolate or even recapture the USA. The QUEBEC ACT passed by the British Parliament in 1774 was regarded by Americans as an INTOLERABLE ACT because it created a huge new British province, within which toleration was afforded to French Catholics, stretching south and west from eastern Canada to the Ohio river. Throughout the revolutionary and early national periods American statesmen dreamt of incorporating Canada within the USA. Benedict ARNOLD was among the leaders of an American expedition that attempted this mission in 1775. The ARTICLES OF CONFEDERATION (1781) made provision for Canada to join the USA if it chose. During the WAR OF 1812 and after, Americans toyed with the idea of incorporating Canada by conquest or by exhortation. Further south, Americans cast covetous eyes towards Florida. During the Revolutionary War, American forces made repeated attempts to seize the Floridian peninsula. Not only were these unsuccessful, but, by the treaty of PARIS (1783), EAST and WEST FLORIDA were awarded to Spain. On the other hand, the treaty, which concluded the Revolutionary War, doubled the size of the USA. US territory now stretched west from the Atlantic to the Mississippi river, and south from the Great Lakes to the 31st parallel (the northern border of Spanish West Florida).

The breakdown of restrictions on westward expansion during the American Revolution posed a number of problems for the USA. The most delicate of these was how to incorporate newly settled territories within the federal Union without disturbing the balance of existing states. Following the treaty of SYCAMORE SHOALS in 1775, settlers using the WILDERNESS TRAIL blazed by Daniel BOONE poured into the Kentucky and Tennessee country. In 1784 settlers in eastern Tennessee led by John Sevier (1745–1815) organized a putative state named FRANKLIN, and petitioned Congress for admission to the USA. Their efforts were blocked by

North Carolina and Virginia, which disputed the settlers' land titles. The political outlook of settlers such as those in eastern Tennessee was complicated. They sought the independence of statehood, but also supported the creation of a central government strong enough to protect them from Native American attack and from interference from existing states. Many western frontiersmen adopted a FEDERALIST outlook during the RATIFICATION of the US Constitution. There existed an implicit threat that areas of the west settled by white Americans might organize governments independent of the USA, or even ally themselves with a European power. This threat was made credible by the fact that the economic viability of the west depended on access to the port of New Orleans (via the Ohio–Mississippi river system) and, until 1803, New Orleans was under European control. The potential for these western issues to produce conflict among existing members of the USA was realized during the congressional discussion of the JAY–GARDOQUI NEGOTIATIONS on Mississippi trade issues during 1786.

Through the ORDINANCE OF 1785 and the NORTHWEST ORDINANCE (1787), which applied initially to land north of the Ohio river and east of the Mississippi, Congress established a system for surveying new territories and organizing governments within them. The Ordinance of 1785 bound the USA to survey and sell western lands in standard rectangular subdivisions. Within each surveyed township acreage was reserved for schools and other public buildings. The Northwest Ordinance laid out the process through which settlers who purchased land in western territories could apply for admission to the USA. It required the US government to oversee the creation of republican forms of government in western territories, and barred the introduction of slavery into the region north of the Ohio river. A similar ordinance was adopted in 1790 to govern the organization of states south of the Ohio. In this region however, settlers were permitted to organize governments recognizing the legality of slavery.

Several issues retarded the settlement of western lands. The Native American nations of the northwest, although defeated at the battle of FALLEN TIMBERS (1794) and forced to sign the punitive first treaty of GREENVILLE (1795), continued to resist US settlement of the Ohio and Indiana country. In 1811, under the leadership of the brothers PROPHET and TECUMSEH, a coalition of nations dominated by the SHAWNEE attempted a last-ditch stand against further US expansion. Defeated at the battle of TIPPECANOE (1811) and abandoned by the British following the battle of THAMES RIVER (1813), the nations of the northwest were forced into further cessions through a second treaty of Greenville. Native resistance to westward expansion was equally pronounced in the southeast. The powerful CREEK and CHEROKEE nations used a combination of war and diplomacy to slow the settlement of western Georgia, Alabama and Mississippi. As in the north, the War of 1812 provided the pretext for US forces to assert control over lands claimed by native peoples. Creek military resistance to US expansion into the Alabama country was largely overcome following Andrew JACKSON's victory at the battle of HORSEHOE BEND (1814), which ended the first CREEK WAR. Jackson followed up this action by subjugating the Floridian peninsula in the first SEMINOLE WAR. However, a 'final solution' to the continued native presence in the southeastern USA was not reached until Jackson, by now president of the USA, enthusiastically enforced the INDIAN REMOVAL ACT of 1830. On Jackson's orders the FIVE CIVILIZED TRIBES of the southeast were forcibly deported from their homelands to RESERVATIONS west of the Mississippi. (The route of the Cherokee nation's enforced march became known as the TRAIL OF TEARS.)

Britain and Spain also resisted US expansion. During the War of 1812, US troops and settlers occupied most of Spanish East and West Florida. (Spain finally ceded these territories to the USA in 1819 through the ADAMS–ONIS TREATY.) At the same time Britain withdrew its military presence from the Great Lakes region. However, Britain's desire to continue to exert influence on the North American continent led it to attempt to seize the mouth of the Mississippi, a move defeated by Andrew Jackson's victory at the battle of NEW ORLEANS (1815). Even after the War of 1812, Britain drove a hard bargain in the negotiations over the US–Canadian border that produced the WEBSTER–ASHBURTON TREATY of 1842, and it was prepared to risk conflict with the USA during the OREGON BORDER CRISIS of 1845–6.

There is some irony in the fact that it was a European nation, France, that made the most significant contribution to US expansion. France sold its vast Louisiana territory west of the Mississippi to the USA in 1803. The LOUISIANA PURCHASE, negotiated at the behest of Napoleon Bonaparte and Thomas JEFFERSON, more than doubled the size of the USA and made it, at a stroke, the dominant power west of the Mississippi. After the purchase, the western boundary of the USA stretched south and east from a point in the Pacific northwest disputed by Britain to a point on the Gulf of Mexico that was disputed by Spain. The southern and central boundaries of the purchase (which were disputed by Spain) were defined in the Adams–Onis treaty of 1819. The British continued to dispute the northern boundary of the purchase until 1846.

This vast acquisition raised once again the question of how new states might be admitted into the Union without disturbing the balance of existing states. Congress believed it had solved this problem when, in 1820, it adopted the MISSOURI COMPROMISE. This barred the residents of territories north of the 36th degree of latitude (with the exception of Missouri) from entering the Union with constitutions that permitted slavery. Maine (a free state) joined in 1820, Missouri (a slave state) joined in 1821. Arkansas (a slave state) joined in 1836, Michigan (a free state) in 1837.

Ironically, the perceived political stability of the USA was one reason why residents of TEXAS, who had declared their independence from Mexico in 1836, sought admission to the Union in 1845. The Texas question threatened the stability of the Union both because its admission would cause war with Mexico and because Texans wanted to join the USA with a constitution which permitted slavery. Expansionists, president James POLK chief among them, welcomed the MEXICAN WAR (1846–8). They saw it as providing the means to finally establish the USA as the pre-eminent power on the continent. The WILMOT PROVISO, a congressional resolution demanding that slavery be outlawed from any territory acquired in the Mexican War, gave fair warning that some northern congressmen, fearful of SLAVE POWER, sought to separate the expansion of slavery from the territorial expansion of the USA. US victory in the Mexican War produced the advantageous treaty of GUADALUPE-HIDALGO (1848), which moved the boundary between the USA and Mexico closer to the position it now occupies today: the USA acquired from Mexico all or part of the future states of California, New Mexico, Arizona, Utah, Nevada, Colorado and Wyoming. The continental expansion of the USA was completed through the GADSDEN PURCHASE (1853) of lands south of New Mexico and Arizona, and the purchase of ALASKA in 1867.

To what use should newly acquired territories be put? Southern slave owners wished to ensure that slavery could expand into those areas of the west where it was economically viable. The REPUBLICAN PARTY, many of whose members espoused the principles of FREE-SOIL IDEOLOGY, sought to reserve the west for family farmers. Congress believed that, through the COMPROMISE OF 1850, it had defused the tensions arising from the question of whether slavery should be permitted in newly acquired western lands. However, despite the vast size of the USA, Americans believed that there was not enough land to satisfy both slave owners and small- farmers. The Great Plains were commonly referred to as the 'great American desert'. Slave owners had no desire to settle there, and family farmers were deterred by the difficulty of breaking the plains sod and by the region's distance from markets. One reason why the BLEEDING KANSAS episode, which followed passage of the KANSAS–NEBRASKA ACT (1854), proved so bitter was that slave owners and small farmers alike regarded Kansas as a plum within an otherwise relatively worthless portfolio of territories.

Even before the CIVIL WAR, mining companies, cattle barons and RAILROAD companies valued at least portions of the trans-Mississippi west. Small farmers were more sceptical. During the Civil War Congress passed the HOMESTEAD ACT (1862) granting 160 acres (65 ha) of western land free of charge to anybody who undertook to farm it for five years. The Timber Culture Act (1873) gave 160 acres (65 ha) to anybody who would plant trees, a scarce commodity on the western plains. The Desert Land Act (1877) allowed potential settlers to purchase up to 640 acres (259 ha) of land at $1.25 per acre ($3.09 per ha), provided they undertook to irrigate it. The railroad companies, themselves the recipients of substantial land grants through legislation such as the PACIFIC RAILROAD ACT (1862), joined the federal government in promoting the settlement of the west.

However, even if a western homesteader acquired his land free of charge, he still faced a struggle for survival. The modern plough, invented by John Deere (1804–86), sometimes proved unable to handle the thick sod of the great plains. Crops, once planted, might be eaten by cattle herds. BARBED WIRE provided a technological solution to this problem, but barbed wire was expensive. (Arable farmers took the position that the onus to build barbed-wire fences fell on cattlemen, not on themselves.) Once a crop was in, it had to be transported to market. The fees charged by rail companies and grain-silo operators cut into the western farmer's profit margin. As the market value of crops fell, many farmers borrowed money to increase production, and many were led into a ruinous cycle of indebtedness. By the close of the 19th century, an entire political philosophy (POPULISM) had evolved to explain the grievances of the western farmer. American popular culture suggests that the pioneering homesteader stuck to the task of creating a viable family farm come hell or high water. However, two-thirds of the homesteaders who settled Kansas after 1862 failed. The interplay of opportunity and constraint in the life of the small farmer on the western plains produced high levels of internal migration. In 1910 less than half of western farmers had lived for more than five years on the land they were cultivating. Territorial expansion did not leave in its wake a more rooted population. The frenzy of the OKLAHOMA LAND RUSH (1889) suggests the extent to which Americans clung to the belief that somewhere in their vast country they might finally find a patch of land that would provide a good living on easy terms.

At the close of the 19th century, in a coda to the territorial expansion of the USA witnessed during the century, a number of US politicians came to the conviction that America had a MANIFEST DESTINY to acquire an empire. As Senator Albert BEVERIDGE put it, God had made Americans the 'master organizers of the world' and given them a duty to rule over the 'savage and senile' peoples of the earth. The SPANISH-AMERICAN WAR (1898) produced a debate over whether America should take possession of con-quered territory similar in tone to that which accompanied the earlier Mexican War. An unusual coalition, acting on a variety of impulses, opposed the acquisition of an empire. Anti-imperialists numbered among their ranks Grover CLEVELAND and William Jennings BRYAN, Andrew CARNEGIE and Samuel GOMPERS (president of the AMERICAN FEDERATION OF LABOR), as well as exponents of both PROGRESSIVISM and SOCIAL DARWINISM. Although the USA occupied Cuba and the Philippines (and administered Guam and Puerto Rico) after the Spanish-American War, it did not follow the British example and organize a formal empire. It has instead expanded its influence beyond its borders by informal imperial arrangements – although these have often proved no less constraining to their subjects than formal imperial ties.

Tet offensive (January–February 1968), coordinated North Vietnamese–Viet Cong assault on major towns and cities of South Vietnam, launched on January 30 1968. The offensive was eventually repulsed by US and South Vietnamese troops, but proved the turning point of the VIETNAM WAR. The offensive's timing (it began on the Vietnamese new-year holiday) and coordination took the USA by surprise. Communist forces gained temporary control of highly symbolic targets in Saigon: the airport, the presidential palace and the courtyard of the US embassy. American public opinion, led by media figures such as CBS newscaster Walter Cronkite (who had been prepared to accept General WESTMORELAND's claim that the USA was winning the war), began to shift in favor of finding a way out of it. President Lyndon B. JOHNSON told aides, 'If I've lost Cronkite's support, I've lost the war.' US and South Vietnamese troops re-established control of most towns within a month, killing 45,000 North Vietnamese and Viet Cong troops in their counteroffensive. But a 'credibility gap' had been opened that supporters of the war could not close.

Texas, central southern state, bordered to the north by Oklahoma and Arkansas, to the east by Louisiana, to the south by Mexico and the Gulf of Mexico and to the west by New Mexico.

The first permanent European settlement in the territory was established by Spanish missionaries at San Francisco de los Tejas in 1716. The territory was originally part of the Spanish Empire. The USA argued that some or all of Texas was included in the LOUISIANA PURCHASE but renounced claims to Texas in the ADAMS–ONIS TREATY (1819). Following the collapse of the Spanish Empire, Texas became a Mexican province. The Mexican government encouraged US immigration in a bid to garrison its northern borders against COMANCHE raids. In the 1820s Stephen Austin (1793–1836) encouraged some 8000 settlers to take up land on the Brazos river. Mexico outlawed slavery in Texas in 1829, forbade further US immigration in 1830 and curbed provincial autonomy in 1835.

In June 1835, US settlers abetted by 'Texican' residents began an armed rebellion against Mexico, and on March 1 1836 declared Texas independent. Despite their defeat at the ALAMO (March 6 1836), the Texans went on to victory at the battle of SAN JACINTO (April 21 1836), after which Mexico recognized Texan independence. The republic of Texas received diplomatic recognition from Britain, France and the USA.

Most Texans and Americans believed that independence would give way to US statehood. However, opposition to the addition of a slave state, the likelihood of war with Mexico if Texas were admitted to the Union and the larger context of TERRITORIAL EXPANSION all stalled US annexation. Eventually, on March 1 1845 the House and the Senate, prompted by John TYLER, approved a joint resolution in favor of annexation. This sparked the MEXICAN WAR. Texas became the 28th state on December 29 1845. Mexico recognized Texan statehood in the treaty of GUADELUPE-HIDALGO (1848).

The state of Texas quickly became a leading producer of cotton. In 1860 it had 604,215 residents of whom 30% were slaves. On February 1 1861 Texas became the seventh state to secede from the Union and join the CONFEDERACY. In June 1865 President Andrew JOHNSON recognized a provisional government in the state. The new legislature abolished slavery but refused to let African-Americans vote or to ratify the FOURTEENTH AMENDMENT. Congress imposed military rule on March 2 1867. Full self-government and congressional representation were restored on March 30 1870. Over the next 30 years the Texas legislature disenfranchised black voters and imposed racial segregation.

Following the Civil War Texas became the largest US producer of cotton. At the same time the state's booming cattle industry ushered in the golden age of the COWBOY. Following the conclusion of the RED RIVER WAR of 1874–5 family farmers settled the Texas 'panhandle' in increasing numbers. The state's oil reserves were first identified in 1901.

In 1900 Texas had 3,048,710 residents and was the sixth most populous state in the Union. It granted women the vote in 1918. By 1990 the state's population numbered 16,986,510 and Texas was the third most populous state. (Its population surpassed New York's in 1994.) This growth reflected the strength of the state's economy. During the COLD WAR Texas became a major center of the oil and aerospace industries. Its numerous military bases brought billions of dollars into the state's economy. President Lyndon B. JOHNSON also channeled spending associated with the APOLLO PROGRAM Texas's way. During this period Houston and Dallas-Fort Worth became major US cities and the state developed a brash reputation. Dallas became the unfortunate subject of global attention when on

November 22 1963 Lee Harvey OSWALD assassinated President KENNEDY in the city. Lyndon B. JOHNSON, Texan to the core, is the state's most famous politician.

Texas vs. White (1869), US Supreme Court ruling (6–3), in an important test of the legality of RECONSTRUCTION legislation, that SECESSION was illegal and that therefore the states of the CONFEDERACY had never enjoyed any legal existence. The Court decided that, nevertheless, Congress had a constitutional duty to provide every state with a republican form of government in the aftermath of a rebellion. This judgment affirmed the Republican Party's view of secession, first outlined by LINCOLN; it also implied that the RECONSTRUCTION ACTS (1867–8) were constitutional.

Thames River, battle of (October 5 1813), US victory in southwestern Ontario during the WAR OF 1812. Evacuating Detroit on September 18 1813, British regulars and SHAWNEE warriors led by TECUMSEH retreated northeast into Ontario. On October 5, US troops, led by William HARRISON, met and defeated this force, killing Tecumseh. The defeat ended Native American hopes of exploiting the war to halt US expansion in the NORTHWEST TERRITORY. Demoralized by the death of Tecumseh, the Native American nations made concessions in the second treaty of GREENVILLE (1814).

Theory of the Leisure Class, The (1899), analysis of the cultural values of the affluent by the social scientist Thorstein Veblen (1857–1929). The book became an influential text in the PROGRESSIVE era. Veblen argued that expenditure on ostentatious displays of wealth in an attempt to secure social prestige produced social unrest and threatened economic competitiveness. He saw the existence of a leisure class as evidence of the American economy's orientation towards short-term exploitation rather than long-term development. He argued that professional social scientists should play a much greater role in the planning and controlling of social and economic development.

Third Amendment, amendment to the US Constitution prohibiting the illegal quartering of troops. It was one of the ten amendments making up the BILL OF RIGHTS. For the full text, *see* Appendix 1.

third party system, term which is used by historians to denote the period, beginning in the last quarter of the 19th century and extending up to the present, in which state, congressional and presidential politics in the USA have been dominated by the struggle between the REPUBLICAN PARTY and the DEMOCRATIC PARTY.

During RECONSTRUCTION the Republicans briefly established a national political hegemony. This was shaken by the scandals which rocked President GRANT's administration and, following the disputed PRESIDENTIAL ELECTION OF 1876 and the COMPROMISE OF 1877, the Democratic Party began to re-establish itself as a national political force. This process took time. Between 1876 and 1928 only two Democrats (Grover CLEVELAND and Woodrow WILSON) were elected to the White House and the Republicans dominated Congress. The Republicans' grip on Congress and the presidency was eventually broken during the GREAT DEPRESSION. Franklin ROOSEVELT's victory in the PRESIDENTIAL ELECTION OF 1932 signaled the emergence of the NEW DEAL COALITION that ushered in a period during which the Democratic Party dominated national and congressional politics. Dwight D. EISENHOWER was the only Republican elected to the presidency between 1932 and 1968. In the 1970s disaffected Democrats (later dubbed REAGAN DEMOCRATS) began switching party allegiance in protest against inflation, high taxation and social policies such as AFFIRMATIVE ACTION. Ronald REAGAN's victory in the presidential election of 1980 demonstrated the increased significance of the so-called 'sun-belt' states of the southwest within the ELECTORAL COLLEGE, as well as the growing influence of religious groups such as the MORAL MAJORITY on voting behavior. In 1994 the Republican Party, running on the CONTRACT WITH AMERICA platform devised by Newt Gingrich (1943–), gained control of both houses of Congress for the first time since 1954. In the immediate aftermath of the Republican Party's triumph in the 1994 congressional elections, some pundits predicted that the GOP was about to enter a new period of hegemony. In the event, Republican intransigence during negotiations to reduce the federal budget deficit produced a government shutdown which allowed the Democratic Party to recover lost ground in the 1996 congressional elections.

thirteen colonies, term given to those British colonies in North America that declared their independence from Britain in 1776, sent delegates to both the second CONTINENTAL CONGRESS and the CONFEDERATION CONGRESS, and ratified the CONSTITUTION. The thirteen colonies were CONNECTICUT, DELAWARE, GEORGIA, MARYLAND, MASSACHUSETTS, NEW HAMPSHIRE, NEW JERSEY, NEW YORK, NORTH CAROLINA, PENNSYLVANIA, RHODE ISLAND, SOUTH CAROLINA and VIRGINIA.

Thirteenth Amendment, amendment to the US Constitution that abolished slavery. It followed the EMANCIPATION PROCLAMATION (1863) and the conclusion of the CIVIL WAR. Sent to the states for ratification on February 1 1865, it took effect on December 18 1865. By that time fewer than 67,000 persons remained legally enslaved. Mississippi has never ratified this amendment.

Thomas, Norman (Mattoon) (1884–1968), Socialist politician. An ordained Presbyterian minister, Thomas was the SOCIALIST PARTY OF AMERICA's nominee in the five presidential elections held between 1928 and 1948. His best showing came in the PRESIDENTIAL ELECTION OF 1932, when he won 884,649 votes. During the COLD WAR Thomas was a critic of CONTAINMENT doctrine, and in later life participated in the Vietnam-era ANTIWAR MOVEMENT.

Thornburgh vs. American College of Obstetricians (June 11 1986), US Supreme Court ruling that struck down, by 5–4, the main features of a Pennsylvania law that restricted access to ABORTION. The law restricted access by making it difficult for women to show that they had given their 'informed consent' to the procedure. The Court found that it was unconstitutional to demand that women seeking an abortion prove they had read materials on alternatives, or that a second physician be present during abortion surgery.

Thorpe, Jim (1888–1953), Native American athlete, born on a Fox nation RESERVATION in Oklahoma. Thorpe was one of the USA's first national sports celebrities and the unhappy focus of international controversy.

Thorpe, whose given name was Wa-tho-huck (Bright Path) was sent to the CARLISLE INDIAN SCHOOL in Pennsylvania in 1904. In 1907 he became a member of the school's athletic and football teams. In 1909 he took two years out to play minor league baseball as a professional. Returning to Carlisle, he played on the school's football team and helped it compile an 11–1 record in 1911 season. Thorpe was named an All-American. Switching to track and field, Thorpe won gold medals in the decathlon and pentathlon at the 1912 Olympic Games in Stockhom, Sweden. On his return to the USA, Thorpe enjoyed another outstanding season on the football field and was once more named an All-American. However, in January 1913 a journalist revealed that Thorpe had played professional baseball. Following a huge furore in which Thorpe was accused of an unAmerican 'betrayal' of the amateur ideal, the US Amateur Athletic Union stripped him of his Olympic medals. Thorpe's supporters saw racial bigotry lurking behind the controversy. Thorpe played professional baseball from 1913 to 1919 and professional football from 1915 until

1928. In 1920 he became the first commissioner of the newly formed National Football League. His Olympic medals were restored to his descendants in 1982.

three-fifths clause, see CONNECTICUT COMPROMISE.

time zones. A meeting of railroad companies in Chicago on November 18 1883 divided the USA into four standard time zones. The division carried the force of law when Congress passed the Standard Time Act (March 19 1918).

Tippecanoe Creek, battle of (November 7–8 1811), engagement in Indiana in which the SHAWNEE were defeated by US forces. Fearful that the Shawnee chief TECUMSEH was creating an alliance among the Native American nations of the NORTHWEST TERRITORY, US settlers in the Indiana territory demanded a pre-emptive strike against a Shawnee town at the confluence of the Wabash and Tippecanoe rivers. US troops under Governor William HARRISON reached the town on November 6 1811, but were attacked at dawn next day by Shawnee under the leadership of Tecumseh's brother the PROPHET. Rallying, the US forces destroyed the town on November 8. This action abrogated the first treaty of GREENVILLE, and forced the Shawnee to wage a last-ditch war against the USA without secure backing from other Native American nations or the British. This war ended with the defeat of the Shawnee and the death of Tecumseh at the battle of THAMES RIVER (1813).

Tonkin Gulf Resolution (August 7 1964), congressional resolution that authorized President Lyndon B. JOHNSON to escalate the VIETNAM WAR. It was later described as the 'functional equivalent of a declaration of war'.

The Johnson administration began mounting covert and unauthorized operations against North Vietnam in the spring of 1964. On August 4 two US destroyers (the *Maddox* and the *Turner Joy*), which had been engaged in this campaign, radioed reports that they had been attacked by North Vietnamese patrol boats in the Gulf of Tonkin. Declining to verify the reports, or to admit to the pre-existence of a US campaign against North Vietnam, Johnson presented the incident to congressional leaders as evidence of unprovoked North Vietnamese aggression.

On August 7 the House voted 414–0 and the Senate 88–2 to allow the president to take 'all necessary measures to repel any armed attack against forces of the United States and to prevent further aggression'. The two Democratic Senators who voted against the resolution were Ernest Gruening (1887–1974) of Alaska and Wayne Morse (1900–74) of Oregon. The resolution was repealed by Congress on December 31 1970. President NIXON continued offensive operations anyway.

Tories, see LOYALISTS.

Townsend, Francis E(verett) (1867–1960), retired doctor from Long Beach, California, who developed an imaginative plan to end the GREAT DEPRESSION. In 1934 he suggested that every American over 60 be given a pension of $200 per month but be required to spend it within 30 days. The cost of the pensions was to be met by a 2% tax on commercial transactions. Half a million Americans joined 3000 Townsend clubs to lobby for the plan. Congress, despite receiving a petition of support signed by 20 million people, was unimpressed. Nevertheless, the popularity of the Townsend movement spurred Franklin D. ROOSEVELT's administration to push through one of the great achievements of the NEW DEAL – the SOCIAL SECURITY ACT (1935). Most of Townsend's support evaporated following the Social Security Act's creation of a modest federal pension. Some of his followers joined opponents of the New Deal in Charles COUGHLIN's National Union for Social Justice.

Townshend Revenue Act (June 29 1767), legislation passed by the British Parliament that placed duties on tea, glass, lead, paper and paint imported into the American colonies. The act provided a revenue stream that would contribute to, but not meet, the salary costs of crown administration in the colonies. Charles Townshend, the chancellor of the exchequer, characterized the duties as uncontroversial overseas trade regulations, quite distinct from any attempt to levy internal taxes on American colonies lacking representation in Parliament (*see also* TEA ACT). This argument was demolished by John DICKINSON, and contested by colonial assemblies, who recognized the act's threat to their exclusive right to levy taxes. A fresh NON-IMPORTATION AGREEMENT forced the repeal of all duties, except that on tea, on April 12 1770. However, this did little to slow down the momentum of the AMERICAN REVOLUTION.

Trail of Tears (1838), forced march of the CHEROKEE from their homelands to a western reservation. About 15,000 Cherokee defied the treaty of NEW ECHOTA (1835) by remaining in their traditional settlements in the southeastern USA. In 1838 the US army forced these resisters to march westward to a reservation in Oklahoma, at the cost of 3000 lives.

transcendentalism, 19th-century philosophical movement, inspired by Immanuel Kant's (1724–1804) *Critique of Pure Reason* (1781) and enthralled by the possibility that man could seek truth and fulfilment through spiritual intuition and obedience to the dictates of individual conscience. The USA's 'Transcendentalists' were a group of writers and reformers who kept in touch with one another through their writing and through meetings of a 'Transcendental Club' in Boston during the 1830s and 1840s. The central figure in US transcendentalism was Ralph Waldo Emerson (1803–82).

Emerson attended Harvard University before training as a Unitarian minister. He was ordained in 1829, but in 1831 resigned his pastorate at Boston's Second Street church in reaction against what he took to be the formalism of UNITARIANISM. Emerson traveled to England, where he met Wordsworth, Coleridge and Carlyle and read widely in neo-Platonist philosophy and Eastern spiritualism. On his return to the USA in 1835, Emerson settled in Concord, Massachusetts, and formed a circle that included Margaret Fuller (1810–50), David Thoreau (1817–62) and Nathaniel Hawthorne (1804–64). Emerson published his most enduring work, *Nature*, in 1836. Over the next ten years he and his circle elaborated their critique of organized religion and their vision of philosophical fulfilment.

Transcendentalists argued that truth transcends time and place and needs no external support. They argued, for example, that humans intuitively recognize the truth and value of the Ten Commandments and obey them, or ought to obey them, from choice rather than from habit or obligation. More controversially, Transcendentalists argued that truth as defined by the received wisdom of the age might actually obscure understanding. Most American Protestants did not believe in the literal truth of the miracles described in the Bible. Transcendentalists in contrast argued that miracles happen all the time, but pass unnoticed in a material age where people accept as true only that which can be quantified or explained by science. The group argued that in order to appreciate the transcendent truths that ought to guide human action, Americans had to be ready to challenge received wisdom and think for themselves. Critics charged that this philosophical stance was a recipe for anarchy and licentiousness. In 1840, a group of Transcendentalists, led by George Ripley (1802–80), began an experiment in communal living at Brook Farm, West Roxbury, Massachusetts. The Brook Farm experiment lasted for six years and was important in the dissemination within the USA of the socialist ideas of Charles Fourier (1772–1837).

The Transcendentalists published numerous tracts and essays and founded several short-lived but influential newspapers. The movement's major works are Emerson's *Nature* and Thoreau's *Walden* (1854). Margaret Fuller's *Woman in the Nineteenth Century* (1855) was a pioneering exploration of feminism and Thoreau's *Civil Disobedience* (1849), written in reaction to the MEXICAN WAR, was rediscovered by a youthful audience in the 1960s.

Transylvania Company, company formed by Richard Henderson in January 1775 with the intention of buying KENTUCKY from the CHEROKEE and establishing an independent colony. The company collapsed when VIRGINIA contested land purchases made following the treaty of SYCAMORE SHOALS (1775) and extended county government to Kentucky settlers.

Trent affair (1861), international crisis in the first year of the CIVIL WAR. On November 8 1861 a Union Navy ship stopped the British steamer *Trent* and removed two Confederate commissioners en route for Britain. The seizure turned British opinion against the Union side, and led to a crisis only resolved by the release of the men on December 26 1861.

Trenton, battle of (December 26 1776), American victory in New Jersey during the REVOLUTIONARY WAR. Following the British occupation of NEW YORK CITY (December 1776), WASHINGTON's army retreated through New Jersey and into Pennsylvania. On December 13 British commanders sent the bulk of their troops back to New York for the winter, leaving small garrisons of HESSIANS in New Jersey's major towns. On December 26 1776 Washington led 2500 troops across the ice-strewn Delaware river and successfully recaptured Trenton. The Americans took 900 prisoners for the loss of 5 lives, providing a much needed boost to flagging morale.

Triangle Shirtwaist Factory fire (March 25 1911), one of the worst industrial accidents in US history, in which a fire in a sweatshop on New York's Lower East Side claimed the lives of 146 Jewish and Italian women workers. Investigators found that the factory's fire exits had been sealed shut. The proprietors were tried for manslaughter but were acquitted. Al SMITH was among the city and state politicians who pushed tough occupational health-and-safety laws through the state legislature in the wake of the fire.

Truman, Harry S (1884–1972), Democratic statesman, vice president (1944–5) and 33rd president of the USA (1945–53), following the death in office of President Franklin D. ROOSEVELT. His presidency witnessed the beginnings of the COLD WAR, while at home he attempted to continue the NEW DEAL policies of his predecessor under the FAIR DEAL slogan.

In his youth Truman held a variety of jobs in his native Missouri, and saw service in World War I, before being elected judge of Jackson County, Missouri, in 1922. He owed his advancement to the Democratic Party machine in Kansas City, but by the time he was elected to the US Senate in 1934 Truman had established a reputation as an honest and incorruptible administrator. These qualities were displayed during his chairmanship of a Senate committee overseeing defense expenditure during WORLD WAR II. Between 1941 and 1944 Truman's committee discovered wastage totaling $15 billion.

Roosevelt, pressured to drop Vice President Henry WALLACE from the ticket, chose Truman as his running-mate in the 1944 presidential election. Truman succeeded to the presidency on April 12 1945, won a surprise victory in the PRESIDENTIAL ELECTION OF 1948, and served until January 20 1953.

Truman assumed office on the eve of the POTSDAM CONFERENCE, which decided the fate of postwar Europe. The conference also called for Japan's unconditional surrender, an outcome achieved on August 10 1945 after Truman had authorized the dropping of atomic bombs on HIROSHIMA AND NAGASAKI (August 6 and 9). Truman's support for the UNITED NATIONS and, later, the MARSHALL PLAN ensured that the postwar US did not revert to an ISOLATIONIST foreign policy. Indeed the TRUMAN DOCTRINE, by committing the USA to aiding governments fighting communist influence, helped to initiate the Cold War, and led the USA to enter the KOREAN WAR in 1950. In the same year he authorized development of the hydrogen bomb.

In 1949 Truman proposed his FAIR DEAL program of social reforms, extending social security and improving working conditions. Nearly all the measures were rejected by Congress. In 1952 Truman ordered a federal seizure of US steel mills to prevent a strike, although the Supreme Court ruled in YOUNGSTOWN VS. SAWYER that this action exceeded presidential authority. However, Truman vetoed the TAFT–HARTLEY ACT curbing trade-union rights. As a senator, Truman had sponsored federal legislation against lynching, and as president he established a commission on civil rights, and ended racial segregation in the US armed forces. He is famous for saying, 'If you can't stand the heat, get out of the kitchen.'

Truman Doctrine, COLD WAR policy that expanded the strategy of CONTAINMENT by binding the USA to support, economically and financially, all 'free peoples who are resisting attempted subjugation by armed minorities or outside pressures'. The doctrine was defined by President TRUMAN in a speech which was given to a joint session of Congress on March 12 1947. The immediate inspiration for this proposition was the possibility of communists gaining control of the Greek and Turkish governments. Despite its open-ended commitment to fighting communism, the doctrine was endorsed by the Senate (67–23) on April 23 1947. Some $400 million was channeled to Greece and Turkey in a new escalation of the Cold War.

trusts, generic term applied to a variety of anti-competitive corporate structures, including monopolies, cartels (price-fixing agreements among nominally independent corporations) and holding companies (created following the purchase of a controlling interest in rival corporations).

The DEPRESSION OF 1893 provided a great stimulus to the creation of trusts. Between 1897 and 1904, 4227 companies that survived the depression merged into 257 corporations. Among those corporations, 318 trusts formed, which laid claim to 40% of US manufacturing capacity. In his first State of the Union address (1901) Theodore ROOSEVELT encapsulated the USA's ambivalent attitudes to trusts. He told congressmen, many of whom were virtual puppets of corporate magnates, that trusts had 'on the whole' done 'great good'. Nevertheless, people were worried the trusts might hurt the 'general welfare'. Accordingly, 'combination and concentration should be, not prohibited, but supervised and within reasonable limits controlled'. The first federal legislation attempting to 'supervise' trusts (the SHERMAN ANTI-TRUST ACT of 1890), was rendered all but but irrelevant by the US Supreme Court's verdict in UNITED STATES VS. E.C. KNIGHT (1895). The Supreme Court took a more expansive view of the Sherman Act in its verdict on SWIFT AND CO. VS. US (1905). Legislation such as the HEPBURN ACT (1906) targeted 'control within reasonable limits'. Supreme Court judgments in SWIFT AND CO. VS. US (1905) and STANDARD OIL COMPANY OF NEW JERSEY VS. US (1911) – utilizing the concepts of 'stream of commerce' and 'rule of reason' – provide classic expressions of judicial control.

Truth, Sojourner (c.1797–1883), popular and influential speaker on behalf of ABOLITION and civil rights. She was born into slavery in New York but in 1827 ran away from her master (who had refused to obey

New York's emancipation law) and adopted the name Isabella Van Wagener. Settling in New York City, she became an ardent evangelical and, following a profound religious experience in 1843, changed her name to Sojourner Truth. She traveled the country preaching against slavery and in favor of women's suffrage. In 1850 she published *The Narrative of Sojourner Truth* and in 1852 gave her most celebrated address, 'Ain't I a Woman?' During RECONSTRUCTION, Truth campaigned for FREEDMEN to be given access to land and education.

Tubman, Harriet (*c*. 1821–1913), former slave who became a leading activist on behalf of ABOLITION. In 1849 Tubman escaped from slavery in Maryland to freedom in New York. She joined the UNDERGROUND RAILROAD and became known as 'Moses' for her success in leading fugitives north. Her 19 trips to Maryland brought freedom to 300 slaves, including her parents and a sister. Slave owners posted a bounty of $40,000 for her capture. During the Civil War she served with Union forces as a nurse, laundress and spy. In 1865 she founded the Harriet Tubman Home for Indigent and Aged Negroes. She did not receive a pension for her services during the Civil War until 30 years after it had ended and spent her last years in poverty.

Ture, Kwame, *see* CARMICHAEL, STOKELEY.

Turner, Nat, *see* NAT TURNER'S REVOLT.

Turner thesis, *see* FRONTIER THESIS.

Tuskegee syphilis scandal, secret medical research carried out on African-Americans without their knowledge. In 1932 Tuskegee, Tennessee, a town in which 26% of black males were infected with syphilis, was chosen as the site of a secret US Public Health Service investigation into the effectiveness of antibiotic treatments of the disease. Experimental antibiotics were used on 201 infected black males, while 399 were 'treated' with placebos. The secret trial continued until 1972, when the *Washington Post* brought its existence to light. By then over 100 sufferers had died from the disease or related ailments. In December 1974 the US government awarded $7 million to survivors, their heirs, and to persons infected by carriers. President CLINTON issued a formal apology on May 18 1997.

TVA, *see* TENNESSEE VALLEY AUTHORITY.

Tweed Ring, corrupt circle of New York City politicians centered on William Marcy Tweed (1823–78). Tweed first entered New York city politics an alderman (1852–3). After one term in the US House of Representatives (1853–5), Tweed returned to New York and with the help of TAMMANY HALL was elected to New York City's Board of Supervisors. In 1870 Tweed, who was by now Tammany's 'boss', became commissioner of public works in New York City: a post which offered unrivaled opportunities for corruption. Tweed and his associates manipulated the city's Board of Audit to siphon $75 million from city coffers. In November 1872 Tweed was convicted of forgery and larceny. He escaped from prison in 1875 and took up exile in Cuba and Spain. He was extradited from Spain to New York in 1876, where he died in jail awaiting trial on a civil suit.

Twelfth Amendment, amendment to the US Constitution regarding voting procedures in presidential elections. Inspired by the PRESIDENTIAL ELECTION OF 1800, the amendment modified Article II Section 1 of the Constitution by stipulating that the ELECTORAL COLLEGE should cast separate ballots to elect the president and vice president. The amendment also established the 4th of March in the year following a presidential election as the day on which an old presidential term expired and a new one began. (This latter provision was modified by the TWENTIETH AMENDMENT.) The Twelfth Amendment took effect on September 25 1804.

Twentieth Amendment, amendment to the US Constitution that stipulates that annual sessions of Congress begin on January 3 of the year following an election rather than on the first Monday in December as previously. The amendment also modifies the TWELFTH AMENDMENT by moving the date of presidential inaugurations forward from March 4 to January 20. These two changes reduced the time in which an outgoing 'lame duck' Congress or president holds office without power. The amendment was devised by Senator George NORRIS, whose almost single-handed lobbying led to the amendment's official adoption on February 6 1933.

Twenty-fifth Amendment, amendment to the US Constitution that clarifies procedures governing presidential succession. The amendment was inspired by the assassination of John F. KENNEDY. It was submitted to the states on July 6 1965, and ratified on February 10 1967. The amendment guarantees that the office of vice president will remain filled by allowing a sitting president to nominate a deputy, subject to congressional approval. (This provision was first used when President NIXON nominated Gerald FORD to succeed the disgraced Spiro T. AGNEW.) It also allows a vice president to assume the presidency when the incumbent is incapacitated, and permits a president to resume office upon recovery.

Twenty-first Amendment, amendment to the US Constitution that repealed the EIGHTEENTH AMENDMENT (the constitutional basis upon which PROHIBITION rested). It was ratified and proclaimed on December 5 1933.

Twenty-fourth Amendment, amendment to the US Constitution that prohibits a state from using a poll tax to bar citizens from voting in federal elections. (Many southern states had previously used such taxes as a means of preventing African-American citizens from voting.) The amendment was submitted to the states on August 27 1962 and ratified on January 23 1964. The VOTING RIGHTS ACT of 1965 strengthened the protections contained within the Amendment.

Twenty-second Amendment, amendment to the US Constitution that bars anyone from being elected president more than twice, or from being re-elected president more than once if he has served over two years of another president's term (i.e. if a vice president takes over the presidency after less than two years; TRUMAN was exempted from the latter provision). The amendment, which reflected concern that future presidents might seek to emulate ROOSEVELT's unprecedented four terms in office, was submitted to the states on March 21 1947, and took effect on March 1 1951.

Twenty-seventh Amendment, amendment to the US Constitution that stipulates that if members of the US House of Representatives or US Senate vote to raise their salaries, the increase will take effect only after the election of a new House of Representatives. The amendment guarantees that congressmen who vote themselves arbitrary or excessive pay increases run the risk of being removed from office before they can enjoy the fruits of their labor. First sent to the states on September 25 1789, this amendment languished until the 1980s, when revelations of congressional 'sleaze' generated renewed support for its passage. On May 7 1992 Michigan became the 33rd state to ratify the amendment, and it took effect on May 19 1992.

Twenty-sixth Amendment, amendment to the US Constitution that stipulates that all citizens of 18 or over are eligible to vote in state and federal elections. The amendment was sent to the states on March 23 1971 and ratified on June 30 1971.

Twenty-third Amendment, amendment to the US Constitution that allows the residents of the DISTRICT OF COLUMBIA (DC) to vote in presidential elections by apportioning to DC as many representatives in the ELECTORAL COLLEGE as its population warrants, but no more than the representation of the smallest state. The amendment was ratified on April 29 1961.

Tyler, John (1790–1862), statesman, vice president (1841) and 10th president of the USA (1841–5), following the death in office of President HARRISON. He was initially a JACKSONIAN DEMOCRAT, then a WHIG. While in office he pursued an independent line, although he generally favored STATES' RIGHTS and southern interests.

Prior to his election as president, Tyler served several stints in the Virginia House of Delegates (1811–16, 1823–5, 1838–40) and a term as governor of Virginia (1825–7). While serving as a US senator (1827–36) he broke with Andrew JACKSON and joined the emerging Whig Party (Tyler cast the only vote opposing a bill authorizing Jackson to use force to resolve the NULLIFICATION CRISIS).

Tyler helped balance a Whig ticket, headed by Harrison, which won a convincing victory in the 1840 LOG CABIN AND HARD CIDER presidential campaign of 1840, employing the memorable slogan 'Tippecanoe and Tyler too'. Tyler succeeded to the presidency on April 6 1841, and served until March 1845. As president, Tyler twice vetoed a bill to charter a third Bank of the United States sponsored by Whig leader Henry CLAY. Furious Whig congressmen dubbed Tyler 'the accident of an accident'. On September 11 1841 all of Tyler's cabinet save Daniel WEBSTER resigned. This ended Tyler's political career. However, his administration made several notable achievements, including the reorganization of the US Navy and the ending of the Second SEMINOLE WAR.

Tyler was the first vice president to confront the death of an incumbent president. He established the vice president's pre-eminent right of succession to all presidential powers (and returned all mail addressed to 'Acting President Tyler'). He was the first president to marry during his term.

U

U-2 incident (1960), incident that increased tensions during the COLD WAR. On May 1 1960, on the eve of a US–Soviet summit, an American U-2 spy plane was shot down over the USSR and its pilot (Gary Powers) captured. After accepting advice to deny that a program of overflights by U-2 planes existed, President EISENHOWER was confounded when the Soviets produced Powers at a press conference. Eisenhower's lie shocked Americans and set back US–Soviet relations.

UMWA, *see* UNITED MINE WORKERS OF AMERICA.

Un-American Activities, House Committee, *see* DIES COMMITTEE.

Uncle Sam, nickname applied to the US government and, personified as an elderly New Englander, a recurrent motif in cartoons and popular prints. The first use of 'Uncle Sam' as slang for the federal government appears to have been noted in a New York State newspaper. According to the *Troy Post* of September 7 1813 a meat inspector named Samuel Wilson – whose job it was to certify barreled beef as fit for the US army – marked barrels packed in his nephew's slaughterhouse with 'U.S.' for 'Uncle Sam'. The habit of referring to the US government as 'Uncle Sam' apparently then spread across the nation from upstate New York. The first pictorial representation of Uncle Sam was made in political cartoons drawn during the presidential election of 1832. In time Uncle Sam became a national icon analogous to the British figure John Bull. During World War I recruiting posters depicted a stern Uncle Sam and the legend 'I want you for the U.S. Army.' The figure declined in popularity during the 1960s, although ironically many members of the Vietnam ANTIWAR MOVEMENT paid homage to common depictions of Uncle Sam by fashioning articles of clothing from the American flag.

Uncle Tom's Cabin, novel by Harriet Beecher Stowe (1811–96), famous for its impassioned attack on slavery. First published serially in the abolitionist newspaper the *National Era* in 1851–2, the novel became a huge bestseller in the USA and in Britain. Stowe was the daughter of a Congregational minister, and gave the slave Tom, hero of her tale, a Christ-like humility. In response to southern claims that she had exaggerated the cruelties of slavery, Stowe published a key providing documentary evidence for the plausibility of her story. In 1862 LINCOLN borrowed this key from the Library of Congress and, later that year, greeted Stowe at the White House with the words, 'So you're the little woman who wrote the book that made this great war.' 'Uncle Tom' later became a pejorative term for any black thought to display an overly servile demeanor towards whites.

underground railroad, network of clandestine safe-houses and discrete routes used by free blacks and abolitionists in the decades before the CIVIL WAR to assist fugitive slaves to safety in northern states or Canada. In many northern communities black leaders and sympathetic whites formed vigilance committees to resist attempts by bounty-hunters and, later, federal officials to seize and return suspected runaway slaves to their owners. These committees supplied 'conductors' to the railroad; men and women such as John BROWN and Harriet TUBMAN, who guided fugitives from one area to the next. The network could only assist fugitives from the upper south, and aided at most 500 runaways in a year. The railroad's existence infuriated southern slave owners, who demanded that the FUGITIVE SLAVE ACT (1850) include federal aid for the recapture of runaway slaves. The activities of the railroad continued until Union victory in the Civil War brought slavery to an end. *See also* ABOLITION.

UNIA, *see* GARVEY, MARCUS.

Union, the, the union or federation of the states that makes up the United States of America. The term is also applied collectively to those states that did not secede from the USA in 1860–1 and that fought against the seceded states of the CONFEDERACY in the CIVIL WAR.

Union Party, political party formed by followers of Father Charles COUGHLIN, Dr Francis TOWNSEND and Senator Huey LONG to contest the presidential election of 1936. The party proposed radical alternatives to the NEW DEAL. Its platform called for federal assistance to refinance home and farm mortgages, a massive increase in old-age pensions, protective TARIFFS, punitive taxes on the wealthy, and the tougher regulation of big business. The party's presidential nominee was William Lemke (1878–1950), a Republican senator from North Dakota. Lemke garnered just 1.6% of the POPULAR VOTE and the party was disbanded in 1939.

Union Republicans, *see* NATIONAL UNION PARTY.

unitarianism, intellectual movement within American Protestantism in the early national period.

Although British theologians contributed to the doctrine, Unitarianism was developed most fully, and gained its greatest influence, in the USA. Unitarians rejected concepts central to Calvinism, notably man's innate depravity and the doctrine of predestination, in favor of a theology which emphasized the perfectibility of man. Unitarians' rejection of a triune God (Father, Son and Holy Ghost) and their affirmation of a unitary deity (whence the denomination derived its name) symbolized the self-consciously rational or 'liberal' tone of their theology. The creed was formalized by William Ellery Channing (1780–1842) in 1819 and the American Unitarian Association was founded in 1825.

Critics charged that Unitarians were little better than deists and that Unitarianism provided a form of Christianity for rationalists who did not really believe in God. However, Channing accepted the existence of the supernatural and attempted to prevent Unitarianism from developing into a sect set apart from the mainstream Protestant tradition. Unitarians provided staunch support to the ABOLITION movement and the WHIG party. Unitarianism was criticized during the SECOND GREAT AWAKENING for pandering to its adherents' spiritual vanity. TRANSCENDENTALISM charged the doctrine with complacency.

United Empire Loyalists, those LOYALISTS who left America to settle in Canada during and after the REVOLUTIONARY WAR.

United Mine Workers of America (UMWA), a prototypical INDUSTRIAL UNION, founded in 1890, which organized underground and surface workers without regard to race or ethnicity. In the 1890s Richard DAVIS conducted membership drives among African-American miners that added to the union's strength and made it the largest multiracial organization in the USA.

Recruitment soared after the successful COAL STRIKE OF 1902, and by 1910 nearly one-third of all mine workers were unionized (at a time when less than 10% of the general workforce held union membership). UMWA lobbying, organized by John L. LEWIS, persuaded the Illinois legislature to pass safety and compensation laws that became industry standards. The UMWA was most militant in western 'hard rock' fields. In 1914, following the LUDLOW MASSACRE, UMWA officials called on miners to arm themselves. However, the UMWA was affiliated with the AMERICAN FEDERATION OF LABOR (AFL), and in the 1920s, now led by Lewis, the union followed AFL policy by preserving gains made and striking only when success seemed likely. In 1935 Lewis took the UMWA into the Committee of Industrial Organizations (the precursor of the CONGRESS OF INDUSTRIAL ORGANIZATIONS), a move that led to suspension from the AFL. The UMWA's greatest victory was achieved in the COAL STRIKE OF 1946.

United Nations (UN), international organization set up in 1945 to prevent future conflict, and to encourage international cooperation in the resolution of economic, political, social, and humanitarian problems.

President Franklin D. ROOSEVELT was determined that Allied victory in WORLD WAR II would be accompanied by a US commitment to create a stable world order. Thinking himself a more realistic statesman than Woodrow WILSON (who had conceived the unsuccessful LEAGUE OF NATIONS at the end of World War I), Roosevelt believed the world's four great powers – the USA, Britain, the USSR and a non-communist China – should police new global arrangements. Yet the language of Roosevelt's first sketch of a postwar security agreement (the ATLANTIC CHARTER) resembled that of Wilson's FOUR-TEEN POINTS. On January 1 1942, 26 nations signed a United Nations Declaration, affirming the principles of the Atlantic Char-

ter. Hard thinking on the shape of the new international body was done at the DUM-BARTON OAKS CONFERENCE in 1944. This resulted in the presentation of a draft charter of the United Nations Organization to a second conference, held in San Francisco between April 25 and June 26 1945. The charter called for the creation of a General Assembly, in which all nations were represented, and a Security Council drawn from eleven nations. The Security Council was charged with resolving international disputes, and the USA, USSR, China, Britain and France were given permanent seats on it. The Security Council possesses the power to requisition military force to ensure compliance with its judgments. Despite the US Senate's long-standing reluctance to enter into any security agreement which might impinge on its right to decide where and when US troops would be deployed overseas, on July 28 1945 the Senate approved the UN Charter by 89–2.

The first session of the UN General Assembly convened in London on January 10 1946. The UN's effectiveness was soon compromised by emerging COLD WAR tensions. In the KOREAN WAR and PERSIAN GULF WAR, the USA acted on its interests under a UN mandate. The USA was less willing to accept the jurisdiction of the UN's International Court of Justice and in the 1980s Republicans were deeply critical of the activities of UNESCO, the UN's educational and cultural wing. In recent years the USA has brought the UN to the brink of collapse by withholding its membership dues.

United States vs. Butler (January 6 1936), US Supreme Court judgment which ruled that the Agricultural Adjustment Act of 1933 (which set up the AGRICULTURAL ADJUSTMENT ADMINISTRATION) was unconstitutional. The act was a centerpiece of the FIRST NEW DEAL. It paid subsidies to farmers who agreed to take land out of production, thereby raising prices as foodstuffs became comparatively scarcer. The subsidies were funded, in part, by a tax on food-processing plants. In its ruling the Supreme Court declared (6–3) that this tax was unconstitutional, and struck down the act.

United States vs. Cruikshank (1876), US Supreme Court ruling that eroded the effectiveness of some of the civil rights legislation brought in under RECONSTRUCTION.

The case concerned was an appeal against murder convictions lodged by three of the ringleaders of the COLFAX MASSACRE (in which over 50 blacks had been murdered). The convictions had been obtained by reference to the ENFORCEMENT ACT (1870). The Court quashed the convictions, arguing that race had not been specified as the assailants' motivation for conspiring to deprive the victims of their civil rights. The Court, under Morrison Remick Waite (1816–88), also asserted that the FOURTEENTH AMENDMENT could be used only to prosecute states (rather than individuals) for civil rights violations. This undermined the Enforcement Act, and placed the punishment of an individual's violation of civil rights legislation in the hands of state and local authorities, which were often unwilling or unable to protect blacks.

United States vs. E.C. Knight (1895), US Supreme Court ruling that gutted the SHERMAN ANTI-TRUST ACT (1890) by declaring unconstitutional those sections of it that applied to manufacturing. The US government had used the act to attack the E.C. Knight Company's near monopoly of domestic sugar-refining. However, in its 1895 verdict the Supreme Court ruled by 8–1 that action against monopolies in manufacturing industry could not be justified by reference to the government's right to regulate interstate commerce. The Court eventually reversed itself in SWIFT AND COMPANY VS. US (1905).

United States vs. Reese (1876), US Supreme Court ruling that had the effect of depriving many blacks in southern states of the right to vote. The first ENFORCEMENT ACT (1870) had made it illegal to interfere with any citizen's right to vote. In its 1876 verdict the Supreme Court ruled by 8–1 that the act exceeded the authority of the FIFTEENTH AMENDMENT by improperly abridging a state's right to restrict access to the vote for reasons other than race. In the wake of the verdict, southern states used a number of devices (such as literacy tests and poll taxes) to restrict black voting rights.

United Steel Workers of America vs. Weber (June 27 1979), US Supreme Court ruling that established the legality of voluntary programs of AFFIRMATIVE ACTION. The Court ruled by 5–2 that numerical targets for minority representation in particular job grades, if established in an attempt to correct past under-representation, do not contravene Title VII of the CIVIL RIGHTS ACT OF 1964, even when the effect of such targets is to deny white workers the employment or promotion they would have enjoyed if the program did not exist.

Universal Negro Improvement Association (UNIA), *see* GARVEY, MARCUS.

Urban League, National, organization founded in 1911 by the amalgamation of two groups offering assistance to African-Americans joining the GREAT MIGRATION from rural areas to northern cities. The Urban League has historically concentrated on offering economic assistance to migrants, while the NATIONAL ASSOCIATION FOR THE ADVANCEMENT OF COLORED PEOPLE (NAACP) has tackled discrimination and civil rights issues. Membership and funding declined when NEW DEAL programs extended social security. However, under Whitney Young (executive director 1961–71) the League attracted corporate sponsorship by undertaking to combat the influence of BLACK POWER militants.

US vs., *see* UNITED STATES VS.

Utah, western state, bordered by the states of Wyoming and Idaho to the north, Nevada to the west, Arizona to the south and Colorado to the east.

The first permanent US settlements in the territory were made by MORMON settlers, led by Brigham YOUNG, in the Salt Lake Valley in 1847. The USA acquired title to the territory from Mexico via the treaty of GUADELUPE-HIDALGO (1848) which ended the MEXICAN WAR. Brigham Young's followers set about organizing a distinctively Mormon state (which they called Deseret) and lobbied Congress for admission into the Union. Congress rejected the plan and, in 1851 organized the US territory of Utah. The Mormon practice of polygamy caused a breach between the federal government and Utah's settlers. In 1857 President BUCHANAN ordered the removal of Brigham Young, the territorial governor, for his failure to enforce US law. Buchanan sent cavalry to the territory, sparking a panic in which Mormons massacred 120 non-Mormon emigrants at Mountain Meadows, Utah, in August 1857. (Young was pardoned in June 1858 and remaining US troops were withdrawn from the territory during the Civil War.) In 1882 Congress disenfranchised Utah's polygamists and instituted the federal supervision of state elections. These actions were upheld by the US Supreme Court in 1890. Utah's territorial government granted women the vote in 1870. This privilege was rescinded in 1887. Utah entered the Union as the 45th state on January 4 1896 with a constitution that did not permit polygamy. One of the new state legislature's first acts was to grant women the right to vote.

Following completion of the transcontinental railroad the state's mining industry boomed. In 1900 Utah had 276,749 residents. Its farmers and miners suffered badly during the GREAT DEPRESSION and many left the state. Thanks partly to the high fertility rate of the state's Mormon population, Utah had 1,722,850 residents in 1990 and was the 35th most populous state in the Union. Brigham Young is the state's most famous citizen.

V

Vallandigham, Clement L., *see* PEACE DEMOCRATS.

Valley Forge, site in Pennsylvania where, between December 19 1777 and June 18 1778, WASHINGTON's 10,000-strong Continental Army camped in primitive shelters among rolling hills, some 18 miles (29 km) northwest of Philadelphia. The army, suffering from desertion, disease and poor diet, lost 25% of its strength. However, during the winter the able-bodied were drilled by Baron von STEUBEN. The newly disciplined troops performed well at the battle of MONMOUTH COURT HOUSE.

Van Buren, Martin (1782–1862), Democratic statesman, vice president (1833–7) and 8th president of the USA (1837–41).

As a New York state senator Van Buren helped create the Democratic political machine known as the ALBANY REGENCY. Elected to the US Senate in 1821, he became secretary of state in JACKSON's administration in 1829, and served as vice president in Jackson's second administration (1833–7). In the presidential election of 1836 he won 170 votes in the ELECTORAL COLLEGE to William Henry HARRISON's 73.

Van Buren served as president from March 4 1837 to March 4 1841. He was measured and managerial where Jackson had been passionate. His response to hardship caused by the DEPRESSION OF 1837 was to support the highly technical INDEPENDENT TREASURY ACT. The economic depression contributed to his defeat by Harrison in the LOG CABIN AND HARD CIDER presidential campaign of 1840. Van Buren's attempts to reform the Albany Regency (for which he was labeled a BARNBURNER), together with his opposition to TEXAS statehood, secured him the presidential nomination of the FREE SOIL PARTY in 1848. His strong showing in New York swung the election in favor of WHIG nominee Zachary TAYLOR.

Vera Cruz, battle of (March 1847), US capture of the city of Vera Cruz, Mexico, during the MEXICAN WAR. In the US Army's first amphibious operation, Commodore Matthew PERRY landed 13,000 soldiers commanded by General Winfield SCOTT on beaches to the south of the fortress of Vera Cruz on Mexico's Gulf coast. This unopposed operation allowed US forces to encircle, besiege and capture (March 27 1847) the city. Scott's force then began the march on Mexico City that would bring the war to its conclusion.

Vermont, New England state, bordered to the north by Canada, to the east by New Hampshire, to the south by Massachusetts and to the west by New York.

The first US settlement in the territory was founded at Fort Dunmer (near modern Brattleboro) in 1724. Both New York and New Hampshire claimed the right to grant land in the territory. During the AMERICAN

REVOLUTION Vermont residents, led by Ethan ALLEN, seized the opportunity to organize an independent state. Vermont's first constitution, written in 1777, outlawed slavery and provided for universal male suffrage. Congress made statehood conditional on approval from New York. After agreeing to settle claims against it made by New York, Vermont became the 14th state on March 4 1791.

Throughout its history the state has been sparsely populated and the majority of its residents have lived in isolated rural communities. Vermont had 154,465 residents in 1800, and 343,641 in 1900. Relatively few immigrants chose to settle in the state and it retained traditional New England characteristics well into the 19th century. Vermont's population decreased during the first half of the 20th century. More recently it has developed a tourism industry and the character of some of its small towns has been altered by an in-migration of urbanites fleeing the 'rat-race.' In 1990 it had 562,758 residents and was the 48th most populous state in the union. Stephen DOUGLAS, Chester ARTHUR and Calvin COOLIDGE were born in Vermont, although all three made their careers outside the state.

Versailles, treaty of (June 28 1919), peace treaty between Germany and the victorious Allied powers following the end of WORLD WAR I. The discussions leading up to the treaty were part of the PARIS PEACE CONFERENCE (commencing January 18 1919), and the treaty was signed in the palace of Versailles on the outskirts of Paris.

The US delegation was led by President Woodrow WILSON. During the conference Wilson retreated from the idealism of the FOURTEEN POINTS – giving way on Anglo-French demands that the final treaty attribute blame for the war to Germany and, consequently, that it establish provision for the payment of reparations – in return for the incorporation within it of the covenant of the LEAGUE OF NATIONS. On July 10 1919 Wilson presented the treaty to Congress. On November 19 1919 the US Senate refused to sign the treaty or to join the League.

Vesey, Denmark (c.1767–1822), former slave accused of planning a slave revolt. In May 1822 Vesey, who had purchased his own freedom, was identified by a black informer as the ringleader behind a plot to stage a large-scale slave revolt in Charleston, South Carolina, and nearby plantations. The authorities moved to prevent the revolt, arresting 139 blacks and 4 whites. In court cases held between June 18 and August 9 47 blacks were sentenced to death. Ten sentences were commuted, but Vesey was among those who were hanged.

vice-admiralty courts, courts in the colonial period that heard criminal and civil cases concerning trade and shipping. They had no jury, and were presided over by a judge appointed by the crown. The SUGAR ACT (1764) and the AMERICAN BOARD OF CUSTOMS ACT (1767) extended vice-admiralty jurisdiction to cases arising from smuggling or impressment, which had previously been heard before a jury in local, American, courts.

Vicksburg, siege of (1863), successful Union siege of Vicksburg, Mississippi, during the CIVIL WAR. In the spring of 1863 GRANT brilliantly deployed a Union force (which reached 71,000 at its peak) to first isolate and then surround the strategic town on the Mississippi river. After a six-week siege the Confederate garrison of 29,000 surrendered on July 4. Following the surrender, Union forces quickly established control of the Mississippi, and opened it to northern commerce. The Confederacy was split and its generals and politicians wrangled over whether Vicksburg could, or should, have been saved.

Vietnam War (1945–75), conflict in Vietnam and neighboring countries of Southeast Asia in which the USA became heavily involved. The war developed in two phases.

The first phase (1946–54) involved the successful struggle by communist-led nationalists (the Viet Minh) to free Vietnam from French colonial rule. This ended in 1954 when two independent states were created, communist North Vietnam and non-communist South Vietnam. The second phase (1959–75) involved the successful struggle by North Vietnam and South Vietnamese communist guerrillas (the Viet Cong) to take over the government of South Vietnam and reunite the country. It was in this second phase that the USA, from the early 1960s to 1973, committed its armed forces on a massive scale to prevent communist victory, both in Vietnam and in the neighboring countries of Laos and Cambodia.

The USA's decision to wage war to prevent the creation of independent communist governments in these countries was the bloodiest and costliest consequence of the assumptions that dominated US foreign policy during the COLD WAR. The Vietnam War not only visited appalling devastation on Southeast Asia, it also produced deep divisions within the USA. Successive administrations, driven ultimately by nothing more than the pursuit of a spurious 'credibility', flirted with covert and even unconstitutional action and generated opposition that tested American society almost to breaking point.

The USA first became interested in Vietnam, then part of French Indochina, during WORLD WAR II. When the Japanese occupied the region (at the invitation of its Vichy French administrators), the US OFFICE OF STRATEGIC SERVICES (OSS) supplied aid and advice to the Viet Minh, an umbrella group of Vietnamese nationalists who were waging a guerrilla war against the Japanese. The most powerful group within the Viet Minh was the Indochinese Communist Party, formed in 1941 by Ho Chi Minh. On September 2 1945 Ho seized the opportunity created by Japan's retreat to proclaim Vietnam independent of France in a speech which drew upon the US DECLARATION OF INDEPENDENCE. Ho established a republic whose capital was Hanoi.

When France sent troops to Vietnam to re-establish colonial rule, Ho, quoting the ATLANTIC CHARTER, appealed to the USA and the UN for aid to preserve Vietnam's independence. But, by the logic of the Cold War, TRUMAN's administration had to support the French-backed pro-Western regime based in Saigon. Truman reasoned that the loss of Vietnam would weaken France, whose 'help we need to balance Soviet power in Europe'. By 1954 the USA had supplied aid totaling $2.6 billion to the Saigon government. But even with financial and French military assistance, the South Vietnamese government could not defeat the Viet Minh. Indeed, on May 7 1954 Ho Chi Minh's forces won a stunning victory when, after a lengthy siege, the 12,000-strong French garrison at Dien Bien Phu surrendered to them. During the siege President EISENHOWER endorsed the DOMINO THEORY (that if Vietnam fell under communists control, other countries in the region would 'topple' after it), but declined all French requests for US military assistance.

The first phase of the war was concluded with the signing of the Geneva Agreements on July 20 1954. These established a cease-fire in the region, recognized the partition of Vietnam along the 17th parallel, and created a 3-mile (5-km) demilitarized zone (the DMZ) either side of the frontier. Under the agreements Vietnamese citizens were free to choose on which side of the border they would live, and were promised an election to determine whether they wished the country to be reunified. The USA did not sign the Geneva Agreements, but on August 20 1954 Eisenhower committed the USA to defend the territorial integrity of South Vietnam, and on February 23 1955 dispatched US military advisers to train the South Vietnamese army. By 1960 there were 900 US advisers 'in country.'

The USA had tied itself to defending the regime in South Vietnam established by Ngo Dinh Diem in June 1954. Diem was a Catholic who had spent some time in an American seminary. Most of his subjects were Buddhists. Diem was unpopular, paranoid, and used corruption to purchase such support as he had. But, as Lyndon B. JOHNSON put it, Diem was 'the only boy we got out there'. The USA accepted Diem's decision to create an independent republic of South Vietnam (October 26 1955); it accepted his refusal to hold the promised plebiscite on reunification; and it said little when an alternative 'election' gave him the backing of 98.2% of the electorate. South Vietnamese communist guerrillas, the Viet Cong, began a campaign against Diem's regime. On July 8 1959 the Viet Cong defeated a South Vietnamese army force near Bien Hoa. Two American advisers were killed, the first US casualties of the war. On October 1 1960 the Viet Cong organized the National Liberation Front to coordinate political and guerrilla warfare against Diem's regime, with the ultimate goal of placing all Vietnam under the control of Ho Chi Minh's Hanoi government.

On May 11 1961, in one of his first acts as president, KENNEDY sent 400 Special Forces troops to mount covert actions north of the DMZ and in Laos and Cambodia. He also dramatically increased the number of 'advisers' supporting the South Vietnamese army. By 1963 there were 16,300 in Vietnam. The inadequacy of the South Vietnamese army was demonstrated when, under US guidance, it bungled a campaign staged around Ap Bac in January 1963. By 1963 opposition to Diem, graphically expressed by a Buddhist monk who burned himself alive in front of US television cameras, had grown to the point where Washington connived in a military coup against its former client (November 1 1963). Nonetheless, Kennedy stated in a television interview conducted on September 2 1963 that the war was 'theirs' for the South Vietnamese to win or lose.

In the spring of 1964 President JOHNSON approved an increase in the scale of covert action against North Vietnamese targets. He maneuvered Congress into passing the TONKIN GULF RESOLUTION (August 7 1964), which gave him authorization to use any force necessary to prevent North Vietnamese attacks on US military personnel. In February 1965 Johnson ordered limited retaliatory air attacks against North Vietnamese targets after the Viet Cong had attacked US servicemen at Pleiku and Qui Nhon. This was soon followed by a covert decision to launch a massive air offensive against North Vietnam, and to commit US ground forces to independent action against the Viet Cong–North Vietnamese army. (OPERATION ROLLING THUNDER, which began on March 2 1965 and continued, with pauses, throughout the war, was the largest aerial bombardment in history. US planes eventually flew 526,000 sorties over North Vietnam, and dropped 6 million tons of explosives, more than twice the total dropped during World War II.) Both the scale of the bombing offensive and the decision to use newly deployed US troops on independent SEARCH AND DESTROY missions were concealed from the American public until June 8. Johnson had hoped that his offensive would convince the North Vietnamese that he meant business and that they, in turn, would order the Viet Cong to cease guerrilla activities. It was therefore as much in anger as in sorrow that on July 28 Johnson announced publicly his decision to build up US forces. By the end of 1965 there were 184,300 US troops in Vietnam. By the end of 1969 the total had reached 536,000. Some 2 million US servicemen eventually saw combat in Vietnam. The financial cost of the war escalated accordingly. By 1967 the USA was spending $2 billion a month on Vietnam. The total cost has been put at $106.8 billion.

The USA brought a massive superiority in firepower to the ground war in Vietnam. Where they could deploy this advantage in set-piece counteroffensive campaigns (such as the battle of the IA DRANG VALLEY, the relief of KHE SANH, or the ultimate defeat of the TET OFFENSIVE), US troops inflicted massive casualties on the enemy. Although 47,000 US servicemen died in combat in Vietnam, US armed forces killed nearly 1 million Viet Cong and North Vietnamese soldiers. Employing the logic of the BODY-COUNT, US commanders argued that the more US troops were deployed, the more enemy soldiers would be killed – and the quicker the war would be over. In December 1967, for example, US commander William WESTMORELAND assured Americans that he could see 'light at the end of the tunnel', and asked for yet more troops to secure final victory. Although the ANTIWAR MOVEMENT was growing in strength, until 1968 the most vociferous critics of Johnson's policy were the 'hawks', who argued that his prosecution of the war was insufficiently vigorous. In a congressional debate on the war held in 1967 the House minority leader, Republican Representative Gerald FORD, called on Johnson to unleash the full might of the US armed forces or get out of Vietnam.

The Tet offensive – a coordinated Viet Cong and North Vietnamese assault on all major towns and cities in South Vietnam beginning on January 30 1968 – made a mockery of Westmoreland's claims, and exposed the limitations of US military strategy. Heavy bombing and repeated search-and-destroy missions had self-evidently not destroyed the ability of the North Vietnamese and Viet Cong to move freely throughout the countryside. Although they had suffered terrible losses, the North Vietnamese and Viet Cong demonstrated that they had maintained their combat effectiveness by picking and choosing where and when they would engage US forces. US

strategy called upon its armed forces to fight an aggressive war against an elusive enemy employing guerrilla tactics. The US Army and Marine Corps were not trained for such a war, and the main burden of the fighting fell on poor white and African-American conscripts whose morale was affected by their almost unlimited access to drugs and prostitution in Vietnam, and by reports of upheavals back home. The fact that the US officer corps was almost exclusively white, and largely southern, created racial tensions within the armed forces. Many enlisted men in Vietnam – especially after the NIXON DOCTRINE (announced in 1969) committed America to a policy of 'Vietnamization' and US troop withdrawals – were uncertain as to why they were fighting. Discipline suffered, with the Army admitting 2000 incidents of FRAGGING (officers being injured by their own men) in 1970 alone. Mounted with a ferocity born of frustration, military initiatives such as OPERATION CEDAR FALLS (1967) threatened to destroy the country the USA sought to save. During the war 6.5 million people fled South Vietnam, 450,000 South Vietnamese civilians were killed, and large tracts of the country were left uninhabitable by the use of land mines, napalm and the defoliant AGENT ORANGE.

On April 7 1968 President JOHNSON, under strong pressure from the antiwar movement, announced a partial cessation of the bombing of North Vietnam. The PARIS PEACE TALKS began on May 10, and a general cessation of the bombardment of North Vietnam was announced on October 31 1968. However, Richard NIXON, victor of the rancorous PRESIDENTIAL ELECTION OF 1968, continued and extended the war in pursuit of 'peace with honor'. Although Nixon began withdrawing US troops and training South Vietnamese soldiers to assume the burden of fighting the Viet Cong, he also authorized a secret bombing campaign against CAMBODIA (March 1 1969) and a ground invasion of Viet Cong 'sanctuaries' on Cambodian soil (April 30 1970). These actions prompted massive antiwar demonstrations throughout the USA. Reports of the MY LAI MASSACRE and the publication of the PENTAGON PAPERS created further disillusionment. On December 31 1970 Congress repealed the Tonkin Gulf Resolution in a bid to deny Nixon the authority to widen the war. But Nixon did not regard the repeal as binding, and in February 1971 authorized a joint US–South Vietnamese incursion into LAOS.

The existence of the KISSINGER INITIATIVE – a series of secret bilateral discussions between the USA and North Vietnam conducted outside the framework of the Paris peace talks – was made public in January 1972. In the later stages of these discussions, following a North Vietnamese offensive across the DMZ in March 1972, Nixon adopted the 'MAD DOG' STRATEGY. The last US combat troops left Vietnam on August 13 1972, but Nixon, determined to present himself as the man who had saved the US prisoners of war, authorized the CHRISTMAS BOMBING of Hanoi (December 1972). The USA, and a reluctant South Vietnam, signed peace agreements with North Vietnam and the Viet Cong on January 27 1973. The fact that the peace treaty permitted North Vietnamese troops to remain in South Vietnam and gave partial recognition to South Vietnam's communists left the 'honor' of the peace in some doubt. Thereafter the USA provided massive financial assistance to the government of South Vietnam. It refused to send troops to repel a renewed Viet Cong–North Vietnamese offensive that began in January 1975 and led to the final collapse of America's client regime. Television pictures of Vietnamese men and women fighting to board US helicopters prior to the fall of Saigon (April 29 1975) symbolized the final failure of US policy in the region.

Virginia, southern state, bordered to the north by Maryland and West Virginia, to the east by the Chesapeake bay and Atlantic Ocean, to the south by North Carolina and Tennessee and to the west by Kentucky.

The first permanent European settlement in the territory was established at Jamestown in 1607 by Britons sponsored by the Virginia Company of London. Virginia became a royal colony on May 13 1625. The colony's viability was established through the cultivation of tobacco for export. The first slaves arrived in Virginia in 1619 but it was not until the 1680s that tobacco planters switched en masse to slave labor. In the 18th century the colony developed a secondary economy based on a trade in grain and livestock produced on family farms. Virginians, among them George WASHINGTON, also took an active role in the development of plans to settle the Kentucky and Ohio country.

Virginia was the largest and most populous of the THIRTEEN COLONIES. Its great planters, although politically cautious, were proud men who identified with the world view of the English gentry and felt affronted by the PROCLAMATION OF 1763, the STAMP ACT and subsequent imperial measures enacted by the British Parliament. Virginia's great statesmen played a crucial role in the AMERICAN REVOLUTION and the state was the site of the YORKTOWN campaign, the decisive engagement in the REVOLUTIONARY WAR. Virginia became the tenth state when it ratified the Constitution on June 25 1788.

Three Virginians were particularly influential in the development of American nationhood. Thomas JEFFERSON, main author of the DECLARATION OF INDEPENDENCE, helped develop the policies which governed the TERRITORIAL EXPANSION of the United States and also drafted the landmark VIRGINIA STATUTE FOR RELIGIOUS FREEDOM. James MADISON, an influential figure at the CONSTITUTIONAL CONVENTION, defended the US Constitution in the FEDERALIST PAPERS and later drafted the federal BILL OF RIGHTS. George Washington, former commander in chief of the Continental Army, presided over the Constitutional Convention and was unanimously elected as the nation's first president. During the 1790s Jefferson and Madison broke with Washington by supporting America's first opposition party, the DEMOCRATIC-REPUBLICAN movement and by drafting the VIRGINIA RESOLUTIONS.

In 1800 Virginia had 886,149 residents and was the most populous state in the union (a position it retained until it was surpassed by New York in the 1820s). Tobacco remained the state's main source of revenue and, despite the hopes of some planters, slavery remained central to the state's economy. In 1860 Virginia had 1,219,630 residents, of whom 39% were enslaved. On April 17 1861 Virginia became the eighth state to secede and join the CONFEDERACY. (On June 11 1861 WEST VIRGINIA seceded from Virginia and was recognized by Congress as the 35th state on June 20 1863.) Richmond, Virginia, became the capital of the Confederacy and a Virginian, Robert E. LEE, became the principal Confederate general. Virginia was the site of more military engagements during the CIVIL WAR than any other state.

The first state government established during RECONSTRUCTION passed BLACK CODES and refused to ratify the FOURTEENTH AMENDMENT. In March 1867 Congress organized a military government in the state but restored self-government and congressional representation on January 26 1870. The Democratic party gained control of Virginia and at the close of the 19th century disenfranchised black voters and imposed racial segregation.

From the NEW DEAL onwards Virginia's economy has benefited from the explosive growth of the suburbs that house federal government workers and from the expansion of military bases located within its borders. In 1990 Virginia had 6,187,358 residents and was the twelfth most populous state in the union.

A very high proportion of the south's most prominent politicians and social reformers have been born or raised in Virginia. Four of the first five US presidents (Washington, Jefferson, Madison and James MONROE) were Virginians. Presidents William Henry HARRISON, John TYLER, Zachary TAYLOR and Woodrow WILSON were born in Virginia but made their names elsewhere.

Virginia Resolutions, resolutions which were drafted by James MADISON and adopted by the Virginia legislature on December 24 1798. Like the KENTUCKY RESOLUTIONS, the Virginia Resolutions asserted that the states retained the right to judge the constitutionality of federal legislation. They denounced the ALIEN AND SEDITION ACTS as unconstitutional, and asserted the state's right to interpose its authority to protect citizens from violations of rights by the federal government.

Virginia Statute for Religious Freedom (January 16 1786), act passed by the Virginia legislature that outlawed any state interference with private religious opinions, and prevented any religious denomination from enlisting the support of the state. Thomas JEFFERSON listed the passage of this act as one of the three greatest achievements of his life. The novelty of this complete separation of church from state, and the eloquence of the language with which it was justified, ensured the statute's fame in both America and Europe. As the controversy over whether prayers should be allowed at school assemblies demonstrates, the rationalist assumptions inherent in the separation of church and state continue to trouble Americans. The Virginia Statute served as a model for the FIRST AMENDMENT; however, several New England states retained an established church until well into the 19th century.

virtue, one of the central concepts of the REPUBLICAN IDEOLOGY utilized by Americans during the AMERICAN REVOLUTION. The concept was derived from civic humanist thought, and defined the duties and privileges of citizenship in a republic, implying that men had duty to act in a disinterested manner, placing the good of the republic above their own narrow self-interest.

Cincinnatus, a Roman farmer who in 458 BC was appointed dictator, defeated Rome's enemies, and returned to his farm within the space of 16 days, was often held up as exemplifying that virtue to which Americans should aspire. America's Protestant denominations strongly reinforced the theme of self-denial bound up with theories of virtue. The influence of virtue on America's political imagination was at its strongest in the period preceding independence, and the CONTINENTAL ASSOCIATION provides a good illustration of its use.

Volstead Act (October 28 1919), enabling legislation, passed after the EIGHTEENTH AMENDMENT was ratified, that introduced PROHIBITION to the USA. It banned, as of January 16 1920, the sale, transportation and commercial manufacturing of beverages containing over 0.5% alcohol. Prohibition was repealed with ratification of the TWENTY-FIRST AMENDMENT on December 5 1933.

Voting Rights Act (August 6 1965), legislation outlawing the discriminatory registration procedures that had effectively disenfranchised southern blacks. The bill was pushed through Congress by President Lyndon B. JOHNSON, in response to the SELMA MARCH organized by Martin Luther KING. The act suspended, for five years, the use of literacy tests in all states or electoral districts where less than 50% of adults had voted in 1964. It empowered federal examiners to take over registration procedures in these areas, and it provided stiff penalties for intimidating potential voters. Mississippi had just 22,000 black registered voters in 1960. By the end of 1965 it had 175,000. The CIVIL RIGHTS ACT OF 1970 extended these provisions.

W

Wabash, St Louis and Pacific Railroad vs. Illinois (1886), US Supreme Court ruling (6–3) that an Illinois law preventing railroad companies from demanding higher freight fees for short trips than for longer trips infringed the US Constitution's stipulation that exclusive control over interstate commerce rested with Congress. The ruling invalidated GRANGER LAWS, and prompted renewed demands, by POPULISTS especially, for Congressional action to regulate corporate business activity.

Wade–Davis Bill (1864), proposed legislation that signaled the determination of RADICAL REPUBLICAN congressmen to enact RECONSTRUCTION measures more punitive than those put forward by President LINCOLN. The bill, which was largely the work of Senator Benjamin Wade (1800–78), assumed that the states of the CONFEDERACY had left the Union. It decreed that they could not be readmitted until all military resistance had ceased and a majority of the white inhabitants had sworn an oath of allegiance to the Union. It demanded that the Senate confirm the appointment of provisional governors for former rebel states and that, under gubernatorial supervision, these states adopt constitutions renouncing secession, ending slavery and disenfranchising former Confederate officeholders. Finally it stipulated that the US government would be responsible for repaying debts incurred by the Confederacy. Lincoln used the POCKET VETO to kill the bill on July 4 1864. This enraged Radical Republicans and prompted publication of the WADE–DAVIS MANIFESTO, which advised Lincoln to leave Reconstruction policy to Congress.

Wade–Davis Manifesto, attack on President LINCOLN published on August 5 1864 in the New York *Tribune*. Lincoln was attacked for appeasing the south, usurping congressional authority by using executive orders to promote RECONSTRUCTION, and for vetoing the WADE–DAVIS BILL. The manifesto was the prelude to a RADICAL REPUBLICAN attempt to replace Lincoln as the party's nominee in the 1864 presidential election.

Wagner Act (July 5 1935), pro-labor legislation that formed a landmark of the NEW DEAL. The act was formally known as the National Labor Relations Act, but was popularly identified with its chief sponsor, Senator Robert F. Wagner (1877–1953) Democrat, New York. The Supreme Court verdict in SCHECTER POULTRY CORPORATION VS. US (1935) invalidating the NATIONAL INDUSTRIAL RECOVERY ACT had removed legal protection for workers' rights to organize trade unions and to engage in collective bargaining with employers. The Wagner Act restored these rights, and outlawed anti-union management practices such as YELLOW-DOG CONTRACTS. The act also established a three-man NATIONAL LABOR RELA-

TIONS BOARD (NLRB) charged with supervising the procedure by which a workforce decided to unionize, certifying trade unions, and hearing complaints against employers. The NLRB had the power to compel employers to bargain with duly elected union officials, and could use cease-and-desist orders to prevent companies from adopting anti-union tactics. The constitutionality of these powers was upheld by the Supreme Court in NATIONAL LABOR RELATIONS BOARD VS. JONES AND LAUGHLIN STEEL CORPORATION (1937). Passage of the Wagner Act encouraged the AMERICAN FEDERATION OF LABOR to create a Committee for Industrial Organization (forerunner of the CONGRESS OF INDUSTRIAL ORGANIZATIONS), which began the task of unionizing semiskilled and unskilled workforces in mass-production industrial corporations.

Walker, Quok, see QUOK WALKER CASE.

Wallace, George C(orley) (1919–98), Democratic politician. Wallace achieved national notoriety on June 11 1963 when, while serving as governor of Alabama, he stood in the doorway of the admissions office of the University of Alabama to prevent two African-American students (the first ever admitted to the university) from registering. His resistance was largely symbolic – National Guardsmen protecting the students soon forced Wallace to step aside – but the event made him a hero to many white southerners. Wallace, who was a lifelong Democrat, had contested the 1958 Alabama gubernatorial election as a modernizing moderate. He was defeated. In 1962, running as an opponent of court-ordered racial integration and a defender of the JIM CROW system, he was elected in a landslide. Wallace contested the PRESIDENTIAL ELECTION OF 1968 on behalf of the American Independent Party. The party's platform expressed deep hostility towards the CIVIL RIGHTS MOVEMENT, BUSSING and all forms of AFFIRMATIVE ACTION. Wallace's running-mate was former Air Force General Curtis LeMay (1906–90), who was famous for arguing that Vietnam should be 'bombed back to the Stone Age'. The Wallace campaign received strong support among white voters in the deep south. He carried five southern states and won 13% of the POPULAR VOTE. However, the main beneficiary of Wallace's campaign was Richard NIXON, who, by comparison to Wallace, appeared moderate. On May 15 1972 Wallace was left paralyzed by an assassination attempt. He served two more terms as governor of Alabama, his last election campaign in 1982 being noteworthy for his conversion to the cause of racial toleration and harmony.

Wallace, Henry A(gard) (1888–1965), Democratic statesman, secretary of agriculture in Franklin D. ROOSEVELT'S NEW DEAL administrations, then Roosevelt's vice president (1941–5).

Wallace was a member of a distinguished family of midwestern agriculturalists. His grandfather founded *Wallace's Farmer*, an agricultural journal, which Wallace edited from 1921 to 1933. His father served as secretary of agriculture in HARDING and COOLIDGE's cabinets. Wallace himself crossbred a variety of hybrid corn that was used by most midwestern farmers. President HOOVER's timid response to the growing agricultural crisis of the 1920s drove Wallace to abandon the Republican Party for the Democrats. As a member of Roosevelt's cabinet, Wallace's instincts and expertise (both demonstrated in the Agricultural Adjustment Act that created the AGRICULTURAL ADJUSTMENT ADMINISTRATION) led him to continue to favor central planning and government intervention in agricultural markets. His populist political style was demonstrated in the creation of a food-stamp program in 1939.

Roosevelt selected Wallace as his running mate in the 1940 presidential election. The vice presidency was the only elected office Wallace ever held. In this capacity, during

WORLD WAR II, Wallace advocated closer ties with the Soviet Union. This led to his being placed under FBI surveillance, and caused Roosevelt to demote him to the post of secretary of commerce in response to demands from southern Democrats that he be dropped from the 1944 ticket. TRUMAN fired Wallace in 1946 for opposing the COLD WAR. Running as a Progressive, with the endorsement of the COMMUNIST PARTY OF THE USA, Wallace polled over a million votes in the PRESIDENTIAL ELECTION OF 1948.

Wall Street Crash (October 1929), massive fall in the value of shares traded on the New York Stock Exchange. It was the Wall Street Crash that triggered the GREAT DEPRESSION. Share prices had been rising steadily for more than a year as small investors, making purchases on 'margins' (a form of credit), drove values upward. The first tremor in the stock market came on 'black Thursday' (October 24 1929). On that day nearly 13 million shares were traded, but heavy buying by the J.P. MORGAN bank prevented a price collapse. Following further heavy trading on Friday, the market lurched downward on 'black Monday' (October 28), when an average of 13% was wiped off the value of industrial stock. The following day, 'black Tuesday', 16 million shares were sold, and the market went into a free fall from which it did not begin to recover until July 1932. In early October 1929 the Dow Jones Index stood at 381, whereas at its lowest point (March 1932) it stood at 41, representing an 85% decline in value, which wiped out $75 billion in industrial capital.

war hawks, term coined by John Randolph (1773–1833) to describe mainly southern and western congressmen, among them Henry CLAY and John C. CALHOUN, who supported the WAR OF 1812 because they regarded British depredations against US shipping as an affront to national honor.

War Industries Board, agency established on July 28 1917 to coordinate and increase production during WORLD WAR I. The board was endowed with unprecedented powers of intervention in US industry. It could order the conversion of existing production lines to wartime supplies, or order the creation of new lines. It could set prices and award contracts. The NATIONAL RECOVERY ADMINISTRATION (NRA) of the NEW DEAL era was heavily influenced by this largely successful experiment in government control.

War of 1812 (1812–15), conflict between the USA and Britain. The cause of the war was the failure of the British to respect US neutrality during the Napoleonic Wars. In the end the Americans achieved a limited victory, but the outcome of the war, which helped to strengthen the USA as a nation state, bore little relation to the reasons the Americans had gone to war in the first place.

Neither Britain nor France respected the neutrality of US shipping during the Napoleonic Wars. The Royal Navy's practice of IMPRESSMENT (stopping US vessels and abducting from them British-born sailors) particularly angered Americans. Congress enacted the EMBARGO ACT (1807) and MACON'S BILL NUMBER 2 (1810) in an attempt to use trade boycotts to coerce recognition of US neutrality. France responded to Macon's Bill by feigning an interest in negotiation. Britain responded to it by blockading New York harbor and conducting an aggressive seizure of US ships and sailors. WAR HAWK congressmen, many from western constituencies with little direct interest in the Atlantic trade, alleged that Britain's actions were an intolerable affront to national honor. Opposition to war came from New England FEDERALISTS, who believed that the USA should support Britain in its war with France, and the QUID faction of the DEMOCRATIC-REPUBLICANS, who sought to maintain a strict neutrality in dealings with both Britain and France.

President MADISON asked Congress for a declaration of war against Britain on June 1 1812. The House approved 79–49 on June

4. Senate approval by 19–13 followed on June 18. War was proclaimed the following day. The proclamation was condemned in New England town meetings and by the Massachusetts and Connecticut assemblies. Britain sought to exploit this disaffection by initially excluding New England's ports from its naval blockade of the coastline of the USA.

Most of the land engagements fought during the war occurred on the US–Canadian border. In the summer of 1812, US troops, mainly militiamen, crossed the Detroit river into Ontario, but were driven back by a combined force of British troops and Native American warriors led by TECUMSEH. The US garrison at Fort Dearborn was massacred on August 15 , and the US garrison at Fort Detroit surrendered the following day. Further east the inadequacy of US forces was underlined when a campaign against Montreal had to be abandoned because New York militiamen refused to cross the Canadian border. In the south, Creek warriors massacred the garrison of Fort Mims, Alabama, thereby drawing the USA into the CREEK WAR. In April 1813 US troops captured FORT TORONTO, but were soon forced to abandon it. Ill-disciplined troops set the town of York (present-day Toronto) ablaze before retreating, providing a pretext for the subsequent destruction of WASHINGTON DC by the British. The loss of the USS CHESAPEAKE in an engagement with HMS Shannon on June 1 1813 marked the low point of the USA's fortunes in the war, although 'Don't give up the ship' – the last words of the Chesapeake's captain James Lawrence (1781–1813) – became a rallying cry. Two crucial victories in the west began to restore the balance of power. In September 1813 US vessels defeated a British flotilla in the battle of LAKE ERIE. This allowed US troops under William Henry HARRISON to cross the lake to pursue and defeat (at the battle of THAMES RIVER) British troops and their Native American allies under

Tecumseh. However, the USA proved unable to exploit these victories in a combined northerly and easterly advance on Montreal. A British counterattack in December 1813 resulted in the burning of Buffalo, New York. US troops later gained some revenge by defeating an equal number of British regulars at the battle of CHIPPEWA.

In the spring of 1814 the Royal Navy established a total blockade of US ports, and British army commanders, strengthened by the arrival of troops from Europe, planned a three-pronged invasion of the USA. The first element, a thrust south from Montreal, was halted by US victory at the battle of LAKE CHAMPLAIN. In a supporting operation, British troops landed at Benedict, Maryland, on August 19 1814. Marching north they captured and burned Washington DC on August 24–25. An attack on Baltimore was thwarted when, despite intense bombardment, US troops held Fort McHenry. (This incident inspired Francis Scott Key to write the words of the US national anthem, 'The Star Spangled Banner'.) The British force re-embarked and was deployed in a campaign directed against the USA's Mississippi river trade. This campaign was defeated by US victory at the battle of NEW ORLEANS.

The peace treaty of GHENT (1815) barely touched on the issues that had caused the war, but it did recognize US territorial claims in the NORTHWEST TERRITORY and WEST FLORIDA. More generally, the war established, at home and abroad, the viability of the US nation state. The war had disastrous consequences for Native American confederacies in the northwest and southeast. Crushed militarily and abandoned by their allies, they were forced to cede land and were left powerless to resist US TERRITORIAL EXPANSION east of the Mississippi. Both Federalists and old-style Democratic-Republicans lost all remaining political influence as a result of the war. (Indeed Federalist opposition to the war, which culminated in the HARTFORD CONVENTION, was presented as treasonous by jubilant Democrats.) The war enhanced the reputations of future presidents Andrew JACKSON and William Henry HARRISON.

War on Poverty, a massive attack on the causes of poverty, announced by President Lyndon B. JOHNSON in his State of the Union address on January 8 1964, in which he also hinted at new measures for the relief of the poorest members of society. The program was initially presented as a fulfill-ment of John F. KENNEDY's vision, but John-son later made it an integral part of his GREAT SOCIETY rhetoric.

On March 16 1964 Johnson's managers presented Congress with an omnibus Economic Opportunity Act costed at $947 million. Enacted on August 30 1964,this created such programs as VISTA (through which volunteers performed community service work in deprived areas) and the Job Corps (which set up camps in which men and women learned vocational skills while performing conservation work). Underpriv-ileged children were offered 'Head Start' summer programs to prepare them for ele-mentary school, while the Older Americans Act created public-service jobs for retirees. The most significant relief measure created was the federal food-stamp program, which continues to provide the unemployed and the poor with access to basic nutrition.

Johnson's programs significantly reduced the percentage of Americans, particularly African-Americans, living in poverty. How-ever, 49 days after trialing the initiative Johnson announced he would cut personal and corporate taxes, and in 1965 he esca-lated the VIETNAM WAR, while creating the MEDICARE and MEDICAID programs. As a result, by 1970 the US budget deficit stood at $382 billion, and Congress began look-ing for ways to cut Johnson's programs.

War Powers Act (November 7 1973), legis-lation, passed over President NIXON's veto, that reversed the cavalier delegation of mil-itary authority from Congress to the presi-dency that was an inherent feature of the EISENHOWER DOCTRINE and the TONKIN GULF RESOLUTION. The act, prompted by Nixon's actions against CAMBODIA, requires presi-dents to notify Congress within 48 hours if they despatch troops to a foreign conflict or increase US troop deployments overseas. Troop deployments not endorsed by Con-gress within 60 days must be rescinded unless the president certifies that an addi-tional 30 days are required to effect safe withdrawal. The act allows Congress to order an immediate withdrawal of troops by concurrent resolutions from House and Senate.

Warren, Earl (1891–1974), 14th chief jus-tice of the US Supreme Court. Between 1953 and 1969 Warren presided over the most liberally inclined Supreme Court in American history, and helped to cement the achievements of the CIVIL RIGHTS MOVEMENT.

Warren was born in Los Angeles, and trained as a lawyer at the University of Cal-ifornia. He served as California's attorney general from 1939 to 1943 before being elected to the first of three terms as state governor (1943–53). It was a mark of his popularity that in his first re-election bid he was endorsed by both the Democratic and the Republican parties. Warren was Repub-lican nominee Thomas Dewey's running-mate in the PRESIDENTIAL ELECTION OF 1948. He contested for the Republican nomina-tion in 1952, but soon gave his support to EISENHOWER.

In 1953 Eisenhower nominated Warren to serve as chief justice. In virtually his first act as chief justice Warren wrote the ver-dict of the Supreme Court in BROWN VS. BOARD OF EDUCATION. This overturned the precedent established by the Court in PLESSY VS. FERGUSON by ruling racially segregated school systems unconstitutional. The ver-dict on the Brown case was bitterly opposed in southern states, and helped to provoke the LITTLE ROCK SCHOOL DESEGREGATION

BATTLE of 1957. Undaunted, Warren prodded the Court into a series of rulings that dismantled the JIM CROW system and promoted further congressional action on civil rights. In 1963–4 Warren presided over the presidential commission established to investigate the assassination of John F. KENNEDY. This experience may have given Warren an inflated sense of his own importance. By the end of his tenure as chief justice Warren's colleagues had grown uncomfortable with his domineering style, and even liberals questioned the wisdom of verdicts such as that in MIRANDA VS. ARIZONA (1966), which provide a suspected criminal with an exhaustive description of his rights.

Warren Commission, seven-member commission, headed by US Chief Justice Earl WARREN, appointed by President Lyndon B. JOHNSON to investigate the assassination of President KENNEDY (November 22 1963). Lee Harvey OSWALD was arrested after the shooting and was soon shown to have purchased the rifle discovered in the building from which the shots were fired. Oswald denied the crime but was himself shot dead by an assassin, Jack Ruby, before further questioning could proceed. The Warren Commission report, issued on September 27 1964, concluded that Oswald acted alone. Critics charge that ballistic evidence and acoustical analysis of film of the assassination suggest gunfire from a secondary source, and therefore the existence of a conspiracy.

Washington, northwestern state, bordered on the north by Canada, to the east by Idaho, on the south by Oregon and to the west by the Pacific ocean.

Washington was originally part of the Oregon territory and the subject of competing British and US ownership claims. In 1818 the USA and Britain resolved their dispute by agreeing to a joint administration of the Oregon territory. The modern state of Washington fell under British jurisdiction. US settlement north of the Columbia river provoked the OREGON BORDER CRISIS, (resolved in favour of the USA in 1846). Congress granted territorial status to Oregon, including Washington, on August 14 1848. Washington became a territory in its own right on May 2 1853. In 1860 it had just 11,000 residents.

The development of rail links with the rest of the USA spurred the state's development. This was also accompanied by a vicious NATIVIST campaign. In 1885 four months of anti-Chinese rioting in Seattle forced President CLEVELAND to place the city under martial law. Washington became the 42nd state on November 11 1889 and by 1900 had 518,103 residents. In the early years of the 20th century, the INDUSTRIAL WORKERS OF THE WORLD (IWW) gained many recruits in Washington, and suffered violent reprisals as a consequence. In 1926 Seattle, scene of an anti-IWW riot in 1913, became the first major US city to elect a woman mayor when Bertha Knight Landes (1868–1943) stood successfully on a reform ticket. Over the course of the 20th century, Washington's economy has diversified away from family-run farming and lumbering enterprises to include such high-tech businesses as airplane manufacturing and internet shopping. In 1990 Washington had 4,866,692 residents and was the 18th most populous state in the union.

Between 1989 and 1995 Tom Foley, a native of the city of Spokane, Washington, achieved national political influence when he served as Speaker of the US House of Representatives.

Washington, Booker T(aliaferro) (1856–1915), educationist, reformer and advocate of African-American self-help. Washington achieved national prominence as the founder and head of the Tuskegee Normal and Industrial Institute in Alabama. The institute, established in 1881, provided vocational training for African-Americans. Its ethos reflected Washington's conviction that many descendants of slaves were ill-prepared for freedom, that African-Americans had to take sole responsibility for their advancement, and that for them to demand full political and civil rights was premature. The autobiographical basis of these beliefs was made clear in Washington's widely read *Up From Slavery* (1901). Lacking the funds to receive a vocational education at the Hampton Institute, Virginia, Washington worked his way through the school as a janitor (1872–5). He taught at an elementary school in Washington DC, before returning to Hampton in 1879 to run its night school. At Tuskegee, Washington was given the opportunity to put his self-help creed into operation on a large scale. At its peak the school had an enrollment of 1500, a faculty of 200, and an annual budget of $300,000. Graduates learned trades, but they also learned not to question discrimination. Washington's accommodationist stance on race relations, encapsulated in his ATLANTA EXPOSITION SPEECH, comforted whites but angered more radical African-Americans such as W.E.B. DU BOIS and other members of the NIAGARA MOVEMENT.

Washington DC, *see* DISTRICT OF COLUMBIA.

Washington DC, British destruction of (August 24–25 1814), the most dramatic incident in the WAR OF 1812, although it played a relatively minor role in the war's outcome. In the summer of 1814 the British army planned an invasion of the USA from Canada. To support this thrust they planned a diversionary raid on the upper Chesapeake and Washington. The invasion from Canada was thwarted by the US victory at the battle of LAKE CHAMPLAIN, but on August 19 1814 British troops landed at Benedict, Maryland, and proceeded with the diversionary plan. They captured the city of Washington on August 24, forcing President MADISON to abandon the city and seek refuge in the countryside. Lacking the force to occupy the city, British troops set it ablaze in retaliation for the US destruction of York, Ontario, following the battle of

FORT TORONTO. Secretary of State James MONROE had the foresight to remove official archives, including the DECLARATION OF INDEPENDENCE, from the city before the British gained control. A subsequent attack on Baltimore was thwarted when, despite intense bombardment, US troops held Fort McHenry. (This incident inspired Francis Scott Key to write the words of America's national anthem, 'The Star Spangled Banner'.)

Washington, George (1732–99), soldier and statesman who led the Continental Army to victory in the REVOLUTIONARY WAR, and served as 1st president of the USA (1789–97). In both presidential elections in which he stood, Washington received every vote cast in the ELECTORAL COLLEGE, an achievement no president will ever match.

Washington was born into a comfortable Virginian family. He inherited the Mount Vernon estate in 1752, and in 1759 augmented his fortune by marriage to Martha Custis (1732–1802), a wealthy widow. Washington had been appointed surveyor for Culpepper County, Virginia, in 1749. This initiated a lifelong interest in western land settlement. In 1754 he was commissioned to lead Virginian militiamen on a mission to clear French settlers from land claimed by Virginia in the vicinity of present-day Pittsburgh, Pennsylvania. His force was defeated. In 1755 he joined an unsuccessful campaign which was conducted by British regulars in the region. This period of military service gave Washington, who had been denied a commission in the British army, a lifelong hatred of both military politics and the arrogance of the British officer class. From 1759 to 1774 Washington represented Frederick County in Virginia's House of Burgesses. He was a member of Virginia's delegation to the first and second CONTINENTAL CONGRESS, and was appointed to command of the Continental Army on June 15 1775. Washington's appointment bound Virginia to the common cause, but encouraged backbiting criticism among disappointed officers, culminating in the CONWAY CABAL, which the hot-tempered Washington found exceedingly irritating.

During the Revolutionary War, Washington's main concern was to preserve the Continental Army both from conclusive defeat by the British and from destructive neglect by Congress. At the battles of TRENTON and PRINCETON Washington displayed dashing generalship. However, he was more usually cautious and, at the battles of LONG ISLAND, BRANDYWINE and GERMANTOWN, demonstrated a potentially disastrous inflexibility. The discipline imparted to the army by Baron von STEUBEN during the winter at VALLEY FORGE compensated for some of Washington's shortcomings, and, ironically, his stolid style helped him make effective use of the FRANCO-AMERICAN ALLIANCE. His genuine hatred of political posturing within the army led him to quash the NEWBURGH CONSPIRACY. Washington resigned his command on November 3 1783. He interrupted his retirement from public life to host the MOUNT VERNON CONFERENCE (1785), and to accept appointment as president of the CONSTITUTIONAL CONVENTION. He was an obvious and generally popular choice to serve as the nation's first president. He took up office on March 4 1789, was re-elected in 1792, and served until March 3 1797.

President Washington was a conservative. He instinctively sided with his administration's FEDERALIST cabinet members (especially HAMILTON). He took the role of chief executive very seriously, and found it difficult to believe that opposition to his NEUTRALITY PROCLAMATION, to the suppression of the WHISKEY REBELLION or to JAY'S TREATY could be loyal or principled. DEMOCRATIC-REPUBLICANS, encouraged by JEFFERSON, charged Washington's administration with monarchical tendencies, and opened the factional divisions that underpinned the FIRST PARTY SYSTEM. In 1795 the US Senate rejected Washington's bid to make John Rutledge (1739–1800) chief justice of the Supreme Court. Washington's presidency established three crucial precedents: that a president should choose his own cabinet, that he should serve no more than two terms (this was eventually incorporated within the US constitution via the TWENTY-SECOND AMENDMENT), and that seniority within the Supreme Court should not determine the choice of chief justice. In his farewell address on September 17 1796, Washington warned of the dangers of political parties and of permanent foreign alliances (this latter point was a source of later US ISOLATIONISM). In 1798, during the QUASI-WAR, he agreed to serve as commander in chief of the US Army in the event of French invasion. His last words were "Tis well.'

Washington Naval Conference (November 12 1921–February 6 1922), international gathering to discuss disarmament and outstanding territorial grievances. Acting in response to a Senate resolution adopted on December 14 1920, President Warren HARDING invited representatives of the principal powers to attend the conference, which was presided over by US Secretary of State Charles Evans HUGHES. Delegates agreed to scrap some of their largest battleships, to build no more for ten years, and to freeze the relative size of their navies. The conference also produced an agreement to outlaw the use of poison gas and to restrict submarine warfare. To these undertakings the delegates also appended a variety of agreements resolving competing claims to Pacific islands and the northern provinces of China. The US Senate narrowly approved these treaties, but with provisos that reflected the continuing strength of ISOLATIONIST sentiment.

WASP, acronym for 'White Anglo-Saxon Protestant,' coined in the 1950s by University of Pennsylvania sociologist Professor E. Digby Baltzell. Another acronym, PIGS (Poles, Italians, Greeks and Slavs), describes, but does not flatter, the immigrant groups who so troubled WASPs at the end of the 19th and beginning of the 20th centuries.

Watergate scandal (1972–4), scandal that arose from President NIXON's role in commissioning and concealing illegal actions against political opponents. It led to the preparation of impeachment proceedings against him and, ultimately, to his resignation from office.

On July 17 1972 five men were apprehended during a burglary of the headquarters of the Democratic National Committee in the Watergate building, Washington DC. The burglars were found to possess the phone number of White House consultant E. Howard Hunt and bank notes traceable to the Committee to Re-elect the President (CREEP). On August 29 Nixon stated that no one in his administration was involved in the break-in. The trial of the burglars was delayed until after the PRESIDENTIAL ELECTION OF 1972. By that time Bob Woodward and Carl Bernstein, investigative reporters for the *Washington Post*, had published compelling evidence that CREEP had engaged in an illegal 'dirty tricks' campaign against not only the Democratic Party but also private citizens. Woodward and Bernstein's conclusion that Nixon aides had offered to pay the Watergate burglars for their silence was seemingly confirmed by a letter written by former CREEP staffer James McCord that was produced at the burglars' sentencing hearing (March 23 1973).

Meanwhile, it emerged that John Dean, the president's personal lawyer, had been receiving copies of all FBI files relating to the break-in and the investigation of dirty tricks undertaken by Nixon operatives nicknamed 'plumbers'. This seemed to substantiate allegations that Nixon, or his aides, had tried to obstruct justice. Nixon sacked Dean on April 30 1973, at the same time accepting the resignations of Attorney General Richard Kleindienst, White House Chief of Staff H.R. Haldeman (1925–99), and domestic adviser John Ehrlichman.

On May 17 1973 the US Senate established a seven-member select committee (under the chairmanship of Senator Sam Ervin) to investigate the activities of CREEP, and on May 18 Congress appointed a special prosecutor, Archibald Cox, to prepare charges where evidence of illegal surveillance or obstruction of justice was discovered. On May 22 Nixon admitted that he had concealed evidence of wrongdoing, but denied that he had known about, still less ordered, the activities attributed to his former subordinates. John Dean flatly contradicted Nixon's claim in testimony to the Ervin Committee on June 25–29.

On July 16 a former White House aide, Alexander Butterfield, revealed that all conversations in the White House and Executive Office Building were recorded by an automated taping system installed at Nixon's request. The tapes offered a means of establishing the president's role, but Nixon, citing executive privilege, refused to release them. In October 1973 Nixon offered to provide special prosecutor Cox with authenticated summaries of nine tape-recordings on condition that Cox make no further attempt to subpoena White House documents. When Cox refused the deal, Nixon ordered Cox's removal. On October 20 Attorney General Elliott Richardson and his deputy William Ruckelshaus resigned rather than enforce Nixon's request to fire Cox. Solicitor General Robert H. Bork, (*see* BORK CONFIRMATION HEARINGS) hastily promoted to attorney general, complied. This 'Saturday Night Massacre' triggered the introduction of 16 impeachment resolutions in the House of Representatives. Nixon sought to deflect criticism by releasing the nine tapes Cox had demanded. One was found to contain an 18-minute gap produced by deliberate erasure.

Preliminary impeachment hearings began on October 30 1973. By now the enormity of the Nixon administration's vendetta against political enemies, and the scale of its covert operations, were daily rehearsed in Congress and the media. On July 27 1974 the House Judiciary Committee voted to recommend that Nixon be impeached for obstructing the investigation of the Watergate break-in. On July 29 it approved an impeachment article citing Nixon's role in ordering the 'violation of the constitutional rights' of US citizens. On July 30 1974 it approved an article citing Nixon's refusal to comply with subpoenas demanding the release of evidence. However, on the same day, the committee voted down (26–12) articles citing Nixon for exceeding his military authority in the case of CAMBODIA and for demeaning the office of the president.

On August 5 1974 Nixon released transcripts of three tapes, recording conversations held on June 23 1972, which seemed to show that he was party to the planning of the Watergate burglary and already considering concealment strategies. On production of this 'smoking gun', Nixon's remaining support among Republicans evaporated. On August 8 1974, left with no doubt that an impeachment hearing would be staged in the Senate, Nixon announced his resignation. On September 8 Nixon's successor, President Gerald FORD, issued Nixon with an unconditional pardon for all federal crimes he had committed, planned or was alleged to have committed. Among the Nixon aides subsequently convicted on various counts of perjury and obstruction of justice were H.R. Haldeman, John Ehrlichman and the former attorney general and head of CREEP, John Mitchell. Nixon maintained a position of qualified innocence until his death in 1994.

Watson, Tom (Thomas Edward Watson) (1856–1922), POPULIST politician who during the 1890s emerged as a standard-bearer of the PEOPLE'S PARTY. Born and raised in Georgia, he established a successful criminal-law practice before entering the Georgia state assembly (1882–3). During the 1880s he left the Democratic Party and embraced the tenets of Populism. Although he opposed the decision of the People's Party to contest the presidential election of 1896 on a fusion ticket with the Democrats, Watson agreed to serve as William Jennings BRYAN's running-mate. He contested the presidential elections of 1904 and 1908 as the nominee of the People's Party, but fared poorly. During this period Watson became increasingly anti-Semitic and published a virulent anti-Catholic tract. He opposed US entry into WORLD WAR I. In 1920 he was elected to the US Senate, with backing from the KU KLUX KLAN, and was a prominent opponent of the LEAGUE OF NATIONS.

Watts riot (August 11–16 1965), major riot in a black district of Los Angeles. Coming just five days after President Lyndon B. JOHNSON signed the VOTING RIGHTS ACT, the Watts riot suggested to a shocked middle America that the moderate integrationist rhetoric they associated with Martin Luther KING and the CIVIL RIGHTS MOVEMENT could not claim universal approval among African-Americans.

Watts was a run-down district near Los Angeles International Airport. Its residents suffered routine harassment and beatings from the Los Angeles police. The riot began when a white policeman pulled over a black driver on suspicion of drunken driving. Police responded to taunting and scuffling by sealing off Watts. Gangs armed with Molotov cocktails looted stores and attacked police, and 34 rioters and policemen were shot dead. Some 3900 arrests were made, and property valued at $200 million was destroyed before National Guard units restored order.

WCTU, *see* WOMEN'S CHRISTIAN TEMPERANCE UNION.

Weaver, James B(aird) (1833–1912), POPULIST politician who represented the PEOPLE'S PARTY in the presidential election of

1892. He polled over a million votes and carried four states. Weaver was raised in Iowa and served in the Union Army during the Civil War, achieving the brevet rank of brigadier general. He represented the GREENBACK PARTY in the US House of Representatives (1879–81, 1885–9) and in the presidential election of 1880.

Webb–Kenyon Interstate Liquor Act (March 1 1913), legislation that greatly increased the effectiveness of state PROHIBITION laws by forbidding the transportation of liquor from 'wet' states into 'dry' states.

Webster, Daniel (1782–1852), WHIG politician who twice served as secretary of state (1841–3, 1850–2). Webster was a leading member of that political generation (whose other luminaries were John C. CALHOUN and Henry CLAY) that shaped and maintained the SECOND PARTY SYSTEM, but lived to see it torn apart by conflict between the slave states of the south and the 'free' states of the north.

Webster attended Dartmouth College before studying law in Salisbury, New Hampshire, and Boston. Elected to represent a New Hampshire district in the US House of Representatives (1812–20), Webster opposed the WAR OF 1812 and protective tariffs. He moved to Boston in 1816 and established a legal practice so prestigious that, while serving in Congress, Webster argued landmark cases (including DARTMOUTH COLLEGE VS. WOODWARD and McCULLOCH VS. MARYLAND) before the US Supreme Court. As a US senator representing Massachusetts (1827–1841, 1844–50), Webster advocated a nationalist perspective, now supporting a tariff to protect US manufactures and expressing hostility to the expansion of slavery.

During the WEBSTER–HAYNE DEBATE (1830), at the height of the NULLIFICATION CRISIS, Webster dismissed STATES' RIGHTS arguments against the TARIFF OF ABOMINATIONS with a ringing declaration: 'Liberty *and* Union, now and forever, one and inseparable!' This made him the darling of northern Whigs. Webster served as secretary of state under presidents HARRISON and TYLER (1841–3). However, when Tyler betrayed Whig principles by vetoing the recharter of the BANK OF THE UNITED STATES, Webster declined to join the rest of the cabinet in a protest resignation – ostensibly because he wished to conclude negotiation of the WEBSTER–ASHBURTON TREATY (1842).

Webster's support within the Whig Party was further damaged during debate over the WILMOT PROVISO barring slavery from territory acquired during the MEXICAN WAR. Webster supported the proviso, but later rallied northern support for the COMPROMISE OF 1850 (permitting slavery in some new territories) on the grounds that it was the only means of preserving the Union. This position helped to avert civil war, but earned Webster the enmity of northern abolitionists and the suspicion of pro-slavery southerners. Webster was serving as secretary of state in President FILLMORE's cabinet at the time of his death.

Webster, Noah (1758–1843), lexicographer. Webster was trained as a lawyer at Yale, but while working as a teacher in Goshen, New York, turned his attention to standardizing American English. His *Grammatical Institute of the English Language* (1783) distinguished American spelling and grammar from British forms. Webster was an active FEDERALIST, and from 1793 to 1803 worked as a political pamphleteer and journalist. Turning his attention to lexicography in the 1800s, Webster began work on *An American Dictionary of the English Language*, which, when published in two volumes in 1828, secured him an international reputation.

Webster–Ashburton Treaty (August 9 1842), treaty between the USA and Britain that settled the boundary between Canada and Maine, and that also clarified the northern boundaries of Vermont, New York and US territory west of the Great Lakes and east of the Rockies. The USA and Britain further agreed basic extradition procedures, and action to suppress the West African slave trade. Secretary of State Daniel WEBSTER remained in President TYLER's cabinet in order to conclude the treaty negotiations. Alexander Baring, 1st Baron Ashburton, headed the British delegation. The treaty was ratified by the Senate on August 20 1842.

Webster–Hayne debate (January 19–27 1830), memorable US Senate debate – between Daniel WEBSTER of Massachusetts and Robert Hayne (1791–1839) of South Carolina – that helped to define the NULLIFICATION CRISIS. Hayne denounced as an 'evil' the consolidation of national government at the expense of STATES' RIGHTS. Webster, celebrating 'Liberty *and* Union, now and forever, one and inseparable!', argued that states had no constitutional right to nullify federal legislation, because the constitution provided adequate mechanisms to resolve disputes between the states and the federal government.

Webster vs. Reproductive Health Services (July 3 1989), US Supreme Court ruling (5–4) on a major ABORTION case. The ruling was hailed as a victory by 'pro-life' anti-abortion activists. The Court upheld the constitutionality of a Missouri law that barred the use of public facilities or public employees in any abortion not necessitated by a threat to the life of the mother. The Court accepted arguments that life begins with conception and that unborn children have protectable interests.

Wells-Barnett, Ida Bell (1862–1931), prominent African-American journalist and civil rights campaigner who conducted a crusade against LYNCHING in the JIM CROW south. Born in Mississippi, from 1884 she taught at a school near Memphis, Tennessee, and attended classes at Fisk University in Nashville. She was a staunch Baptist. In 1887, Wells mounted a court challenge to a Tennessee law forcing African-American rail passengers to sit in segregated carriages. (Her suit was upheld by a lower court but thrown out by the state supreme court.) From 1891, she edited and published *Free Speech*, a Memphis journal denouncing discrimination. One of her first editorial decisions was to investigate the lynching of three black businessmen accused of molesting a white woman on a Memphis trolley car. She also organized an African-American boycott of the city's trolley cars. Her press was smashed by rioters and she received numerous death threats. After a period in exile in the north, and a lecture tour of England, she settled in Chicago and married local publisher Frederick Lee Barnett. Here she wrote *A Red Record* (1895), the first statistical survey of lynching in the USA. Wells was a founding member of the NIAGARA MOVEMENT and harried the NATIONAL ASSOCIATION FOR THE ADVANCEMENT OF COLORED PEOPLE to take a stand against lynching. She also tried, with little success, to persuade the NATIONAL AMERICAN WOMAN SUFFRAGE ASSOCIATION to condemn lynchings carried out by mobs claiming to be defending white womanhood.

West Florida, former territory on the Gulf of Mexico incorporating the northwest part of the present-day state of FLORIDA, and areas in the south of the modern states of Mississippi and Alabama. The rest of present-day Florida comprises the former territory of EAST FLORIDA.

By the treaty of PARIS (1783) Britain ceded West Florida to Spain. The territory was defined as the area bounded on the north by the 31st parallel, and stretching west from the Apalachicola and Chattahoochee rivers (the eastern boundary of modern Alabama) to the Mississippi river. (Spain sought a more northerly boundary in the JAY–GARDOQUI NEGOTIATIONS of 1785.)

Southern expansionists, including Jefferson, believed that the LOUISIANA PURCHASE included West Florida. On October 27 1810 President James MADISON authorized US seizure of West Florida from the Mississippi to the Perdido rivers. This region was incorporated with the newly formed Mississippi territory on May 14 1812. Following the capture of the Spanish fort at Mobile, Alabama, on April 15 1813, Spanish influence in the region dwindled. Spain renounced all remaining claims to Floridian territory in the ADAMS–ONIS TREATY (1819).

Westmoreland, William C(hilds) (1914–), US Army general who served as commander in chief of US and South Vietnamese forces engaged in the VIETNAM WAR from 1964 to 1968. Westmoreland was a career soldier who fought as a paratrooper in World War II and held combat commands in the Korean War. He inclined to aggressive tactics, and in Vietnam developed the concept of SEARCH AND DESTROY missions. He argued that the BODYCOUNT showed that the USA was winning a war of attrition against the Viet Cong and North Vietnamese. The communist TET OFFENSIVE (1968) shattered US confidence in Westmoreland's strategy. In February 1968 President Lyndon B. JOHNSON refused Westmoreland's request for a further 206,000 troops, and removed him from command by appointing him Army chief of staff. Westmoreland retired in 1974. He has argued that defeatist US media coverage of the war snatched defeat from the jaws of victory.

West Virginia, eastern state in the Alleghany mountains bordered by Ohio and Pennsylvania to the north, Maryland to the east, Virginia to the south and Kentucky to the west. The state was formed during the CIVIL WAR from territory originally administered by VIRGINIA.

The first permanent European settlements in the territory were established on the eastern slopes of the Alleghanys in 1726. Wheeling, founded in 1772, was the first settlement on the west slope. In 1860 residents of the Virginia counties that eventually formed the state of West Virginia numbered 376,688 (roughly 25% of Virginia's total population). On April 17 1861 Virginia seceded from the union to join the CONFEDERACY. On June 11 1861 residents of Virginia's northwestern counties, who had few ties to slavery and many grievances against the state's planter-dominated government, convened at Wheeling and organized a pro-Union provisional government. Union troops gained control of northwest Virginia following the battle of RICH MOUNTAIN (1861). On June 20 1863 West Virginia entered the union as the 35th state. It abolished slavery in February 1865.

In 1900 West Virginia had 958,800 residents. The mainstays of the state's economy were subsistence farming and coal mining. Workers in both sectors faced great hardship in the 20th century. As many as 1,347,600 residents left the state between 1940 and 1970. In 1990 the state had 1,793,477 residents and was the 34th most populous state in the union. The test pilot 'Chuck' Yeager (1923–), a pioneer of the US space program, is one of West Virginia's most famous 'native sons.'

Wheeler–Howard Act (June 18 1934), legislation that halted the attempt to break up Native American tribes and turn their members into private land-owners, an approach that had formed the basis of US policy since the passage of the DAWES SEVERALTY ACT (1887). The act, actually drafted by John COLLIER, was formally titled the Indian Reorganization Act. Tribes were now encouraged to create constitutional governments, purchase additional lands, and apply for federal loans to start businesses. The act also gave preferential treatment to Native Americans seeking jobs in the federal civil service.

Whig Party, political party that coalesced during Andrew JACKSON's presidency. The Whig Party's battle with the DEMOCRATIC PARTY for national political supremacy between 1834 and 1852 lay at the heart of the SECOND PARTY SYSTEM.

On April 14 1834 Henry CLAY first characterized Jackson's opponents as 'Whigs'. Clay himself, along with John Quincy

ADAMS, was a leader of the Democratic Party's anti-Jackson NATIONAL REPUBLICAN faction. Clay's allusion to the 'Glorious Revolution' against Stuart absolutism that occurred in Britain in 1688–9 captured one unifying theme of the emerging Whig Party – a detestation of 'King Andrew's' use of the veto, the SPOILS SYSTEM and presidential power. Whigs supported the second BANK OF THE UNITED STATES and believed Jackson's efforts to destroy it abused presidential authority.

Support for the bank was consistent with another unifying theme within the Whig Party, the belief that a LOOSE CONSTRUCTION of the US Constitution justified the federal government in taking action to stimulate the economic development of the country. This outlook was developed in Henry Clay's AMERICAN SYSTEM, which called for high TARIFFS and a government-funded program of internal improvements. While JACKSONIAN DEMOCRATS often assailed capitalists as financial aristocrats, Whig politicians, notably Daniel WEBSTER, argued that there was no inherent conflict of interest between labor and capital in the USA, and suggested that 'the path to wealth' was open to all industrious and talented Americans regardless of their backgrounds.

One wing of the party – the 'Conscience Whigs' – matched their veneration of meritocracy and the 'self-made man' with opposition to slavery and the INDIAN REMOVAL ACT. The remnants of the ANTI-MASONIC PARTY also venerated meritocracy, but joined the Whig Party for the rather less noble reason that they believed that American values were threatened by sinister forces within the Jacksonian Democratic Party. The Whig Party drew its support from British and German Protestant immigrants, farmers producing for commercial markets, free blacks, aspiring laborers, the professional middle classes, businessmen, and active members of the Presbyterian, Congregational and UNITARIAN churches. The Whigs

also received tactical support in Congress from John CALHOUN's southern STATES' RIGHTS faction.

In 1836 the Whig Party ran three presidential candidates in an unsuccessful attempt to have the election decided in the House of Representatives. In the 1840 LOG CABIN AND HARD CIDER CAMPAIGN they nominated as their candidate a popular military leader, William Henry HARRISON, but were then denied the fruits of victory when Harrison died after less than a month in office, after which his vice president and successor John TYLER repudiated Whig policies. In 1848 the party again won the presidency with the MEXICAN WAR hero Zachary TAYLOR, but he died 15 months into his term. Whigs controlled the Senate in 1841–4 and the House of Representatives in 1841–2 and 1847–8. The party was torn apart following passage of the KANSAS-NEBRASKA ACT (1854), with most of its members joining the new REPUBLICAN PARTY.

Whiskey Rebellion (1794), revolt in western Pennsylvania against a federal tax on whiskey. On July 26 1790 Congress had enacted the main provision of Alexander HAMILTON's *REPORT ON THE PUBLIC CREDIT* – that the federal government should assume all responsibility for the repayment of REVOLUTIONARY WAR debt. On March 3 1791 Congress, on Hamilton's recommendation, levied a tax on US whiskey distillers as part of a package of measures designed to fund debt repayment. Western small farmers, who routinely distilled surplus corn into whiskey to augment their income, refused to pay the new duties. In 1794 violent resistance to collection of the tax in western Pennsylvania, and the apparent acquiescence of state authorities, led Hamilton to prevail upon President WASHINGTON to call out 15,000 troops to enforce collection. This expedition, which Hamilton accompanied, arrested 150 suspected evaders. Two were later sentenced to death but reprieved by Washington. DEMOCRATIC-REPUBLICANS assailed Hamilton and, quietly, questioned Washington's judgment.

Whiskey Ring, collusion between whiskey distillers and federal tax officials to pocket a substantial portion of the excise on whiskey due to the government. The ring's activities were uncovered in May 1875. The size of the ring (238 indictments were eventually issued) and the sums involved (an estimated $2 million in the city of St Louis alone) shocked the public. Among those indicted was President GRANT's personal secretary Orville Babcock. Grant's intercession ensured that Babcock was not among the 110 conspirators convicted.

White House, name given to the official residence in Washington DC of the president of the USA. Situated on the south side of Pennsylvania Avenue, a site chosen by George WASHINGTON, the 'Executive Mansion' (as it was then known) was built between 1792 and 1799 to the design of an Irish-born architect, James Hoban (1762–1831). The building was restored, and its smoke-damaged exterior painted white, following the British destruction of Washington DC during the WAR OF 1812. The building was restored again between 1948 and 1955 after a survey found the structure to be unsound. The interior layout and decoration of the building have been changed by a succession of first ladies. The building's most notable feature is the distinctive oval office used as the presidential study.

The White House, and a second building in its grounds, house the presidential secretariat as well as the president and his family.

White Plains, battle of (October 1776), engagement in New York State during the REVOLUTIONARY WAR. On October 12, 15,000 British troops landed at Pell's Point, New York. They sought to cross the Hudson river and move south, cutting off American forces in northern Manhattan from sources of supply in New Jersey. In a confrontation on October 28 WASHINGTON's army slowed, but could not stop, the encircling British

column. This action made the British occupation of NEW YORK CITY inevitable.

Whitewater affair, financial controversy that dogged the presidency of Bill CLINTON and has tarnished the reputation of Hillary RODHAM CLINTON. In the late 1970s the Clintons became part-owners of the Whitewater Land Development Corporation. This was a real-estate company that hoped to build a residential and leisure complex in rural Arkansas. In 1993 allegations surfaced that the Morgan Guaranty SAVINGS-AND-LOAN company, based in Arkansas, had during the 1980s funneled unaccounted funds into the Whitewater project, and that these had been diverted to the Clintons. The Whitewater corporation collapsed, as did the Morgan Guaranty company. In a further twist to the scandal, Roger Altman, a former director of the Resolution Trust Corporation (RTC) appointed to the Treasury Department by President Clinton in 1993, resigned in 1994 after it was alleged that he had bent RTC disclosure rules to conceal Morgan Guaranty's payments and to allow the Clintons to recoup their initial investment.

Whitney, Eli (1765–1825), inventor of the cotton gin, a machine capable of separating the seeds from cotton fibers. The cotton gin made large-scale cotton production both feasible and profitable, thereby giving slavery a new lease of life in Georgia, Alabama and Mississippi. Whitney was born in Massachusetts and educated at Yale. The problems associated with cleaning cotton captured his imagination on a tour of the southern states made after his graduation in 1792. When perfected, Whitney's machine allowed a single operator to clean up to 50 pounds (23 kg) of cotton in a day. Whitney patented the design in 1794, but by that time several rival models were on the market. He spent most of the profit gained from his invention fighting court cases for patent infringement. In 1798 Whitney won a government contract to produce 10,000 muskets. To complete the contract on time he pioneered the use of machine-tooled interchangeable parts, which allowed the muskets to be assembled by relatively unskilled workers.

Wickersham Report, investigation of organized crime and compliance with PROHIBITION. President HOOVER appointed the Commission on Law Observance and Enforcement in 1929 to carry out this investigation, under the chairmanship of the former attorney general George Wickersham (1858–1936). Wickersham's Report, which Hoover passed to Congress on January 20 1931, did not recommend repeal of the EIGHTEENTH AMENDMENT (which enshrined Prohibition in the Constitution). However, the Report all but admitted that Prohibition was unenforceable. In the 1932 presidential election both major parties endorsed repeal of the Eighteenth Amendment.

Wilderness, battle of the (May 1864), inconclusive engagement in Virginia during the CIVIL WAR. In the spring of 1864 a Union army of 100,000, under the overall command of GRANT, mounted the strongest strike against the Confederate capital (Richmond, Virginia) yet attempted. Waiting until this Union force had entered the dense forest and scrub south of the Rapidan river and west of Fredricksburg, LEE, commanding 61,000 Confederate troops, counterattacked. In fierce fighting on May 5–6 Grant's troops suffered 17,000 casualties to Lee's 7000. Many wounded were burnt alive in forest fires. At this point Grant reminded his army of his promise to Lincoln, 'whatever happens, there will be no turning back', and ordered a flanking maneuver that culminated in the battle of SPOTSYLVANIA COURT HOUSE.

Wilderness Road, route through the Cumberland Gap in the Appalachians northwest into Kentucky. The trail was blazed in 1775 by Daniel BOONE on behalf of the TRANSYLVANIA COMPANY, and opened Kentucky and Tennessee to US settlers.

Wilmot Proviso, proposed amendment to a bill funding the MEXICAN WAR (1846–8) that would have banned slavery from all territory acquired from Mexico during the war. The proviso was proposed by David Wilmot (1814–68), a Democratic Representative from Pennsylvania, on August 8 1846. Twice successful in the House of Representatives, Wilmot's measure was defeated in the Senate. Senator John CALHOUN, arguing against the proviso in debates held during February 1847, demanded that Congress organize new territories in such a way as to provide equal access to all citizens, including those who sought to bring slaves with them. Calhoun also cited the NORTHWEST ORDINANCE in support of the argument that the people of a state could form or adapt any government they chose so long as it was republican. Although Wilmot's amendment was defeated, it reopened debate over the future of slavery; helping to spark the creation of the FREE SOIL PARTY (1848) and making the COMPROMISE OF 1850 necessary.

Wilson, (Thomas) Woodrow (1856–1924), Democratic statesman and 28th president of the USA (1913–21). Wilson initiated a number of progressive reforms at home, but his presidency was overshadowed by WORLD WAR I, into which he led the USA in 1917 against strong ISOLATIONIST opposition. In his FOURTEEN POINTS he formulated the basis of a just peace, but he was obliged to give way on several of the points at the PARIS PEACE CONFERENCE in return for British and French support for his idea of a LEAGUE OF NATIONS.

Raised in Georgia, Wilson studied for a year at Davidson College, Tennessee, before completing his undergraduate education at Princeton. He began a legal career, but in 1883 dropped it to study for a PhD in political science at Johns Hopkins. Professor Wilson taught political science at Bryn Mawr, Wesleyan, Johns Hopkins and, from 1890, Princeton. In 1902 he became the first lay president of Princeton. He introduced the preceptorial system (in which small groups of students are guided through weekly reading by an instructor), but failed to rid the campus of dining clubs or create graduate schools in the mould of Johns Hopkins.

In 1910 Wilson was elected governor of New Jersey, with the support of Democratic Party bosses. During his governorship (1911–13) he waged war on TRUSTS and political corruption. Wilson was a technocratic PROGRESSIVE. Although he was a good public speaker, he had few political friends and limited support in the country at large. His victory in the PRESIDENTIAL ELECTION OF 1912 was caused by the split in Republican ranks provoked by Theodore ROOSEVELT. Wilson began his presidency on March 4 1913, and served until March 3 1921. In his 1916 re-election bid, Wilson polled 49% of the POPULAR VOTE and carried the ELECTORAL COLLEGE by just 23 votes in a tough fight with the Republican candidate, Charles Evans HUGHES.

Wilson entered office determined to pursue progressive reform. He established the COMMISSION ON INDUSTRIAL RELATIONS and supported the creation of the FEDERAL RESERVE SYSTEM and the FEDERAL TRADE COMMISSION. He gave his backing to the CLAYTON ANTI-TRUST ACT, the ADAMSON ACT and the FEDERAL FARM LOAN ACT. But events abroad, which led Wilson order US intervention in MEXICO and entry into World War I, dominated his presidency. When Wilson attended the Paris Peace Conference in person, he became the first serving US president to leave the country.

On September 25 1919, during a long speaking tour in which he tried to rally support for the League of Nations, Wilson suffered the first of three strokes that left him incapacitated for the remainder of his presidency. His doctor and his wife, Edith Bolling Galt Wilson (1872–1961), concealed the extent of his ill-health. Mrs Wilson took over many of her husband's executive duties. Wilson's vice president, Thomas Riley Marshall (1854–1925) – famous only for saying that what the country needed was 'a really good five-cent cigar' – dodged the issue of whether a sitting president could be removed from office on the grounds of incapacity. When Wilson's secretary of state, Robert Lansing (1864–1928), convened cabinet meetings on his own authority, Wilson demanded, and obtained, Lansing's resignation. Clinging to power, Wilson hoped to turn the 1920 presidential election into a referendum on the League. The nation, whole-heartedly endorsing Warren HARDING's call for a return to 'normalcy', repudiated him.

Wilson–Gorman (Tariff) Act (August 28 1894), legislation that reduced tariffs on a variety of imported goods and raw materials but raised duties on others. The strongly protectionist McKINLEY TARIFF (1890) had raised the cost of living and led to voter unrest, and this, coupled with the onset of the DEPRESSION OF 1893, led Congressional Democrats to push through the Wilson–Gorman Act. President CLEVELAND denounced, but did not veto, the act, because its drafters protected favored interests by raising import tariffs on selected commodities. The most significant of these was sugar, and this had the effect of bringing Cuba's four-year sugar boom to a sudden halt. This in turn contributed to unrest on the island, a contributory factor in the outbreak of the SPANISH-AMERICAN WAR (1898). The act also established a federal INCOME TAX, a provision ruled unconstitutional by the Supreme Court in the case of Pollock vs. Farmers' Loan and Trust Company (1895).

Winnebago War (1827), war between US forces and the Winnebago peoples of the Santee-SIOUX confederacy. The discovery of lead in southeastern Wisconsin had increased friction between US settlers and the Winnebago. In June 1827 Winnebago leader Red Bird killed four whites and scalped a young girl, in revenge for what he believed, mistakenly, had been the execution of two Winnebagos by US soldiers. Red Bird later surrendered to prevent a retaliatory US pogrom against the Winnebago.

'Win one for the Gipper', catchphrase (meaning 'give it everything you've got') reputedly paraphrasing the peroration of a pep talk given to the Notre Dame football team by coach Knute Rockne (1888–1931). The original 'Gipper' was George Gipp (1895–1920), a member of the team's famed 'Four Horsemen of the Apocalypse' offensive unit, whose untimely death captured the nation's attention. In the 1940 movie *Knute Rockne – All American*, the future president Ronald REAGAN, playing the dying Gipp, asks Rockne to tell his team mates to 'Win one for the Gipper.' (Reagan, who beat John Wayne to play Gipp in the movie, enjoyed being called 'Gipper'.) Coach Rockne's motivational powers were so celebrated that his name became synonymous with stirring oratory.

Wisconsin, northern midwestern state, bordered to the north and east by Lake Superior, the state of Michigan and Lake Michigan, to the south by Illinois, and to the west by Minnesota and Iowa.

The first permanent European settlements in the territory were established by French missionaries in 1670. Britain acquired Wisconsin from France via the first treaty of PARIS (1763). The USA acquired the territory from Britain at the conclusion of the REVOLUTIONARY WAR, but Britain refused to evacuate its remaining forts in the area until the ratification of JAY'S TREATY (1794). Meanwhile Wisconsin's passage to statehood was laid out in the NORTHWEST ORDINANCE (1787).

US settlement began in earnest in the 1820s. Following the WINNEBAGO and BLACK HAWK wars, the territory's remaining native Americans sold their lands. Wisconsin became a US territory in 1836 and entered the union as the 30th US state on May 29 1848. In 1860 the state had 775,881 inhabitants and during the Civil War it supplied the armies of the Union with nearly 100,000 men.

Manufacturing, brewing and lumbering boosted the state's development after the war and brought foreign-born immigrants (chiefly German, Scandinavian and Irish) into the state. In 1900 the state had 2,069,042 residents. Milwaukee, a mid-sized industrial metropolis, was the state's chief city. Wisconsin's farmers were supporters of POPULISM and many of its industrial workers were attracted by socialism. Reformers dominated state politics in the early years of the 20th century. In 1903 Wisconsin struck against the power of party bosses by enacting the nation's first system of direct PRIMARY ELECTION. Robert LA FOLLETTE, one of the architects of PROGRESSIVISM in the USA, served as state governor (1901–06) and US Senator (1906–25) during this period. Joseph McCARTHY, a native of Wisconsin and architect of a rather different political agenda, defeated La Follette's son to gain election to the US Senate in 1946. In the 1980s Wisconsin's experiments with state 'workfare' programs attracted much national attention. In 1990 the state had 4,891,769 residents and was the 16th most populous state in the union.

Wobblies, *see* INDUSTRIAL WORKERS OF THE WORLD.

Women's Christian Temperance Union (WCTU), organization founded in 1874 with the aim of persuading people to stop drinking rather than to prohibit them from so doing. The WCTU motto was 'Do Everything'. One tactic adopted by WCTU activists was to enter saloons to conduct prayers and sing hymns in an attempt to awaken drinkers' consciences. Under the presidency of Frances Willard (1839–98) the WCTU built bridges with the KNIGHTS OF LABOR and the WOMEN'S SUFFRAGE movement, treating heavy drinking as symptomatic of wider problems within industrial society. Gradually most WCTU members, including Willard herself, transferred their energies to the single issue of PROHIBITION. In the 1890s the WCTU lost members to the ANTI-SALOON LEAGUE OF AMERICA.

Women's Movement, an informal coalition of lobbying groups and feminist theorists that, since the 1950s, has pursued the overall objective of improving the status of women within American society.

During WORLD WAR II many women had been recruited into the workforce, but after the war they were encouraged to resume the role of 'homemakers'. This cultural pressure, allied with postwar prosperity, helped produce the BABY BOOM and a distinctive but arid suburban lifestyle, whose negative effects on women were celebrated, when not ignored, within American culture. Betty Friedan's best-selling *The Feminine Mystique* (published in 1963) presented a comprehensive critique of the ways in which American prosperity had stifled women's creativity and opportunities for personal growth. The enormous debate provoked by Friedan's book is often identified as the moment when a Women's Movement began to take to shape. Other sources of inspiration included anger at the patronizing treatment many women received from male members of the CIVIL RIGHTS MOVEMENT. In this, and later during the Vietnam ANTIWAR MOVEMENT, women often found themselves being asked to stuff envelopes, make coffee or serve as the girlfriends of male campaigners. (For example, when asked what position women should adopt in the struggle for BLACK POWER, Stokeley CARMICHAEL replied, 'Prone.')

In 1966 the NATIONAL ORGANIZATION OF WOMEN (NOW) was founded and began campaigning for passage of an EQUAL RIGHTS AMENDMENT (ERA) modeled on the FOURTEENTH and FIFTEENTH AMENDMENTS to the US Constitution. It hoped that the ERA would serve to outlaw sexual discrimination. At the same time women began campaigning for liberalized ABORTION laws. It proved difficult to meld these legal, political and social demands into a single coherent campaign. A Women's Strike for Equality held on August 26 1970 in support of the ERA and abortion on demand drew limited support. Public understanding of the movement's goals was easily influenced (often negatively) by symbolic issues such as feminist opposition to beauty pageants or the employment of gender-specific language. Nevertheless, by mobilizing women voters, NOW was able to ensure that the ERA passed Congress and was sent to the states for ratification. Ironically it was a body of elderly men, the US SUPREME COURT, that gave the Women's Movement its greatest victory, the 1973 ROE VS. WADE verdict liberalizing abortion law.

Women's Peace Party, political party formed in 1915 by Jane ADDAMS and Carrie Chapman CATT with the aim of preventing US entry into WORLD WAR I.

women's suffrage, the right of women to vote in federal, state and local elections. The origins of organized campaigning to secure women the right to vote can be traced to the SENECA FALLS CONVENTION called by Elizabeth Cady STANTON and Lucretia MOTT. On July 19 1848 the convention issued a declaration pledging to secure the vote for women. Lucy STONE called annual conventions to discuss tactics, and, together with Stanton and Mott, kept the campaign alive in the 1850s. The first generation of suffrage activists were middle-class Protestant women, usually resident in New England states, who were also deeply involved in campaigning for the ABOLITION of slavery.

Many women felt a sense of betrayal after the Civil War as RADICAL REPUBLICAN congressmen pushed through the FOURTEENTH and FIFTEENTH AMENDMENTS safeguarding the voting and citizenship rights of often poorly educated African-American men, while ignoring the claims of educated white women. Their disappointment sometimes had a bitter edge. Susan Brownell ANTHONY criticized Congress for giving the vote to 'Patrick, Sambo, Hans and Ung Tung' but withholding it from women. Elizabeth Cady STANTON reflected on the Constitution's opening words – 'We, the people' – and wondered why Congressmen thought women were not people. Lucy Stone, together with abolitionist figures such as Julia Ward HOWE (author of the 'Battle Hymn of the Republic') and many male supporters, shrugged off their disappointment to form the AMERICAN WOMAN SUFFRAGE ASSOCIATION (AWSA) in 1869. Other activists, led by Anthony and Stanton, refused to join the AWSA, forming instead the NATIONAL WOMAN SUFFRAGE ASSOCIATION (NWSA) to campaign for a constitutional amendment securing women's right to vote. The NWSA accepted no male members. It saw voting as one among many rights that women needed to secure, and many of its members, led by Stanton, took an active interest in other social-reform campaigns. Its rival, the AWSA, regarded securing the vote as an end in itself, and avoided involvement in other campaigns.

In 1875 the NWSA forced the US Supreme Court to consider its claim that, since women were US citizens, to deny them the vote was an unconstitutional infringement of the Fourteenth Amendment. The Court dismissed the argument (in its ruling on MINOR VS. HAPPERSETT). In 1878 the NWSA sent a delegation, led by Stanton, to argue its case before a congressional committee. Stanton was patronized and humiliated by scornful congressmen.

In 1882 select committees of the House and Senate recommended women's suffrage, but no bill was drawn up. In 1887 a bill to establish women's suffrage was debated in the Senate and rejected 34–16. Meanwhile the AWSA concentrated its efforts on persuading individual states to grant women the vote. During this period the AWSA persuaded several states to hold referendums on the question of women's

suffrage. None was successful, although the number of states and territories permitting women to vote grew gradually. Wyoming's territorial legislature enfranchised women in 1869. The territory of Utah followed suit in 1870, although its legislature later reversed this decision. In 1893 Colorado became the first state to grant women the vote. Pressure to pass a constitutional amendment granting the vote to women grew in intensity from 1911 when, following a successful referendum campaign managed by Carrie Chapman CATT, California enfranchised women.

Brewers and distillers were staunch opponents of women's suffrage, because they feared (correctly) that enfranchised women would vote in favor of a constitutional amendment to establish PROHIBITION. Progress was also slowed by divisions over tactics, which persisted even after the AWSA and NWSA merged in 1890 to form the NATIONAL AMERICAN WOMAN SUFFRAGE ASSOCIATION (NAWSA). Under Susan B. Anthony's presidency (1892–1900) the NAWSA forged links with trade unionists and social reformers, exploiting the argument that women voters would add to the pool of electoral support for progressive programs. This policy ultimately gave the NAWSA a membership of 2 million in 1917, and allowed it to campaign at both state and federal level. But despite the suffragists' victory in the California state referendum, by 1917 only 15 states had granted women full suffrage rights.

In 1913 Alice PAUL led militant suffragists out of the NAWSA. Organizing themselves as the NATIONAL WOMEN'S PARTY, and exploiting the heightened value attached to women's work during WORLD WAR I, militants mounted demonstrations against politicians who would not pledge to support a constitutional amendment to establish women's suffrage. The most notorious of these was an attempt by several hundred women to storm the White House in July

1917. President WILSON, who had brought the USA into the war in order to make the world 'safe for democracy', made women's suffrage an administration priority. Congress passed legislation sending the NINE-TEENTH AMENDMENT (granting women the vote) to the states on June 4 1919. The amendment took effect on August 26 1920.

Woodhull, Victoria Claflin (1838–1927), spiritualist, feminist and publisher. In 1872, Woodhull became the first woman to seek election as President of the United States.

Victoria Claflin was born and raised in the state of Ohio. During her childhood, she and her sister, Tennessee Celeste, staged spiritual seances for paying customers and peddled an 'elixir of life' in traveling medicine shows. Victoria married Dr. Canning Woodhull in 1853 but divorced him in 1866. Moving to New York, she gained the confidence of the financier Cornelius Vanderbilt (1794–1877) and, with her sister, opened a successful brokerage firm. The sisters founded *Woodhull and Claflin's Weekly* in 1870. (This journal 'broke' one of the great scandals of the 19th century, the alleged affair between the distinguished Congregational minister Henry Ward Beecher (1813–87) and a parishioner.) Victoria Woodhull (who married three times and divorced twice) advocated free love and equal rights (including suffrage) for women. She campaigned against prostitution, abortion and sexual hypocrisy. Her bid for the presidency was supported by the NATIONAL WOMAN SUFFRAGE ASSOCIATION but attracted few votes.

Worcester vs. Georgia (March 3 1832), US Supreme Court ruling (5–1) that overturned the convictions of two missionaries deemed in violation of a Georgia statute forbidding residence in Cherokee territory without license from that state. Chief Justice John MARSHALL found that the USA had always regarded Native American nations as 'independent political communities' whose territory was completely separated from that of the states. Moreover, federal government was alone charged with the regulation of Native American affairs. Georgia's convictions of the two missionaries thus had no force. This robust defense of the autonomy of Native American nations – a defense that built upon the Court's decision in CHEROKEE NATION VS. GEORGIA – prompted Justice Story to write: 'The Court can [now] wash their hands clean of the iniquity of oppressing the Indians and disregarding their rights.' Georgia ignored the ruling. President Andrew JACKSON, despite his opposition to NULLIFICATION, made no attempt act on the ruling, arguing that 'John Marshall has made his decision, now let him enforce it.' The federal government continued to implement the INDIAN REMOVAL ACT (1830).

Workingmen's Party, (1) the first labor-oriented political organization in the USA. Established in Philadelphia in 1828 and relaunched in New York in 1829, the party represented the radical wing of JACKSONIAN DEMOCRACY. Drawing its support from the ranks of skilled craftsmen and tradesmen, the party called for universal male suffrage, protection from imprisonment for debt, and legislation to create a ten-hour working day. The party's commitment to the creation of a society in which the working man could advance himself led it to call for the creation of a publicly funded educational system and for the abolition of elitist institutions such as the second BANK OF THE UNITED STATES. These views were aired in a newspaper, *The Working Man's Advocate* edited by George Henry Evans. Rapid gains in membership were offset by factional fighting and disputes over tactics. In 1831 the party split, with some members forming a new organization, the Equal Rights Party, but most joining the reform or LOCO-FOCOS wing of the Democratic Party.

(2) NATIVIST organization founded in California in 1877 to campaign for restrictions on the immigration of Chinese workers. The party's leader, Dennis Kearney (the son

of an Irish immigrant), denounced Chinese immigrants for driving down wages. Although the party collapsed after modest electoral gains in 1879, it helped to create support for the CHINESE EXCLUSION ACT passed by Congress in 1882.

Works Progress Administration (WPA), federal agency established in May 1935, following passage of the EMERGENCY RELIEF APPROPRIATION ACT, with the aim of offering temporary employment on public-works projects to millions of Americans. Unlike previous make-work programs, the WPA paid workers a relatively generous 'security wage' (although the hours a WPA employee could work were capped). Another novel feature of the WPA was that it created, through initiatives such as the Federal Art Project and the Federal Writers' Project, work for artists and writers as well as for manual workers. The WPA also sponsored a massive oral history of African-American life, which remains an invaluable historical source. In 1938 the reputation of the WPA's director, Harry L. Hopkins (1890–1946), was tarnished by allegations that WPA workers were being pressured to vote Democratic (allegations that led to passage of the HATCH ACT). The WPA was wound up on June 30 1943, by which time there was hardly a town or city in the USA which did not possess a road, bridge, school, hospital or post office built by the agency.

World War I (1914–18), global conflict between the Central Powers (principally Germany, Austria-Hungary and Turkey) and the Allied Powers (principally Britain, France, Russia and, from 1915, Italy). The USA remained neutral until eventually joining in on the Allied side in 1917 as an 'associated power'. Hostilities were mostly concentrated in Europe, but there was also fighting in Africa, the Middle East and the Atlantic Ocean. US military involvement was principally on the Western Front in Europe, and helped to bring about the eventual Allied victory.

On August 4 1914 – the day that Britain declared war on Germany – President WILSON announced that the USA would observe neutrality in the conflict. Two weeks later Wilson asked the USA to observe impartiality in thought and deed. Neutrality was popular with German-Americans, Irish-Americans, socialists, pacifists, the WOMEN'S PEACE PARTY and many Democrats. ISOLATIONISTS viewed the slaughter on the Western Front as vindicating their view that the USA should at all costs avoid entangling itself in the affairs of the corrupt 'old world'.

However, US neutrality harmed Germany while indirectly aiding Britain and France. Germany was prevented from purchasing food and materiel from the USA by Britain's naval blockade. By contrast Britain and France, acting through the US financier J.P. Morgan Jr, purchased $3 billion worth of supplies from the USA. Germany resorted to ever more aggressive submarine warfare in an effort to cut Allied trade with America. On May 7 1915 a German submarine sank the liner *Lusitania* without warning: 1198 passengers, among them 128 Americans, were drowned. Although this incident strengthened Wilson's conviction that German militarism represented a greater evil than British imperialism, his response was to demand assurances that Germany would abandon unrestricted submarine warfare. (Even this was too much for Secretary of State William J. BRYAN, who resigned on June 7 1915 alleging that Wilson's demands ran the risk of involving the USA in the war.) On May 4 1916, in what was hailed as a diplomatic victory for the USA, Germany reimposed restrictions on its submarine commanders.

In the 1916 presidential election Wilson campaigned on the slogan 'He kept us out of the war', and won a narrow victory. Stalemate on the Western Front during the winter of 1916–17 led Wilson to call on the belligerents to accept 'peace without victory'. But Germany sought to break the deadlock by resuming unrestricted submarine warfare (February 1 1917). Diplomatic relations between the USA and Germany were severed on February 3 1917. On March 1 the ZIMMERMANN TELEGRAM, in which Germany pledged to help MEXICO recapture territory from the USA in the event of war, was made public. On March 12 Wilson ordered that US merchant ships be armed to deter attack. Calling Congress back into special session, Wilson asked for a declaration of war 'to make the world safe for democracy'. The Senate approved the declaration by 82–6 on April 4 , and the House by 373–50 on April 6.

On May 17 1917 Congress passed the SELECTIVE SERVICE ACT, through which 1,600,400 men, among them 400,000 African-Americans, were drafted into the Army or National Guard. Millions more volunteered, so that by the end of the war 4,791,172 men had served in the armed forces. The Wilson administration took an interventionist approach to the task of regulating the wartime economy. It took over the running of the nation's rail system, it established the WAR INDUSTRIES BOARD to direct production of military supplies, and it established the NATIONAL WAR LABOR BOARD to settle strikes and labour disputes. (Agencies established under the NEW DEAL built on experience acquired during this experiment in federal planning and control.) Wilson and Congress were also able to whip up war hysteria in the USA with alarming ease. The creation of the COMMITTEE ON PUBLIC INFORMATION (which disseminated anti-German propaganda) and the passage of the ESPIONAGE ACT and the Sedition Act (*see* ALIEN AND SEDITION ACTS) encouraged bigoted 'patriots' to mount witch-hunts against socialists, pacifists, trade unionists and other 'undesirables'. The RED SCARE and COLD WAR anti- communism built on standards of intolerance established during the war.

The USA entered the war as an 'associated power'. It did not endorse Franco-British war aims, and Wilson's formula of 'peace without victory' held out to Germany the prospect of a less punitive peace settlement. (However, the FOURTEEN POINTS that Wilson outlined in January 1918 – in a desperate bid to persuade Russia to continue fighting – were only marginally more palatable to Germany than Allied peace proposals.) Wilson resisted demands that US troops be fed into existing British and French units. He ordered the creation of a separate US army, the American Expeditionary Force (AEF) under the command of General John PERSHING. AEF troops began arriving in France in August 1917 and immediately replaced battered and demoralized French troops near Verdun. On March 28 1918 Pershing temporarily permitted US troops to serve under French command in order to counter the great German offensive on the Western Front made possible by Germany's peace treaty with Russia. On August 10 1918 the AEF First Army was organized, and in September 1918 it conducted two major independent operations in the ST MIHIEL and MEUSE–ARGONNE sectors. Over 1.2 million US troops were deployed in the latter offensive. In total 53,000 US servicemen died in combat, a further 63,000 from disease. The scale, human cost and decisive influence of US involvement gave US diplomats leverage at the VERSAILLES and PARIS PEACE CONFERENCES. Immediately prior to the armistice of November 11 1918 (which ended fighting in World War I), Wilson agreed to a series of British and French amendments to his Fourteen Points. These called for the dismemberment of Prussia via the creation of the 'Polish Corridor', and payment by Germany of massive reparations in atonement for its war guilt. Wilson hoped to balance this concession to Britain and France by securing their support for the creation of a LEAGUE OF NATIONS. He was advised by Secretary of State Robert Lansing (1864–1928) that a preliminary negotiating document agreed among the Allies and containing proposals for a League would constitute a treaty under the US Constitution and would require Senate approval. For Wilson this opened a nightmare scenario in which the Allies, Congress and Germany would delay and amend first the negotiating document and then the treaty, dashing the prospects of a 'lasting peace'. He decided to use the Paris conference to write a final peace treaty (including the League) which would then be presented to Congress and Germany as a fait accompli. Wilson traveled to Europe to oversee negotiations. All the major Allied Powers except the USA signed the the treaty of VERSAILLES (ending the war with Germany and establishing the League of Nations) on June 28 1919.

Wilson returned to the USA to present the treaty to the Senate on July 10. In September, in advance of the crucial Senate vote, Wilson embarked on a tour of the USA to rally public support for the treaty. During this tour he suffered the first of three strokes that left him incapacitated. He instructed his supporters to reject any compromise on the treaty, and on November 19 1919 and March 19 1920, Senate rejected it. On March 20 1920 Wilson vetoed a joint resolution of Congress declaring the war concluded. Wilson hoped that the presidential election of 1920 would provide a solemn referendum on the question of US entry into the League of Nations. The Democratic party platform pledged that the USA would join the League as soon as possible. The election was won by a Republican candidate, Warren HARDING, who soon decided that the League 'is not for us'. On July 2 1921, Congress passed a joint resolution ending the state of war existing between the USA and the Central Powers. The Senate ratified previously negotiated peace treaties with Germany, Austria-Hungary, Bulgaria and Turkey on October 18 1921.

World War II (1939–45), global conflict that began with the German invasion of Poland on September 1 1939. The USA entered the war on December 8 1941 (the day after the surprise Japanese attack on PEARL HARBOR), when Congress approved President Franklin D. ROOSEVELT's request for a declaration of war against Japan. Germany and Italy declared war on the USA on December 11. The economic and industrial might of the USA ultimately ensured Allied victory in the war, both in Europe and in the Pacific. Fully conscious of the contribution the USA was making to the war effort, Roosevelt forced his main war-time allies, Britain and the USSR, to accept the USA as first among equals. Decisions made during the war on the basis of US self-interest, (notably to delay opening a 'second front' in Europe until US forces could be brought to a state of maximum preparedness, and to use atomic weapons against Japan to avoid the loss of American lives attendant on an invasion of the Japanese home islands), changed both the course of the war and shape of the post-war world.

In a FIRESIDE CHAT broadcast on September 3 1939 (the day that Britain and France declared war on Germany) Roosevelt committed the USA to a policy of neutrality in the war, but added that he could not ask Americans to remain neutral in thought as well as deed. Although Roosevelt pledged during the 1940 presidential election campaign that he would not commit American troops to the conflict, he himself was not neutral in thought, and used executive authority to check Japanese expansionism and aid Britain in its fight against Germany. In June 1940 Roosevelt ordered the transfer to Great Britain of obsolete and surplus military equipment. In September he ordered an embargo on the export of iron and steel to Japan, the first of a series of measures designed to deprive Japan of the capacity to wage war. At the same time Congress approved massive increases in defense expenditure and passed the Selective Training and Service Act (September 16 1940), which created the first peacetime draft in American history. Once re-elected Roosevelt created the Office of Production Management to coordinate the USA's defense build-up, outlined the FOUR FREEDOMS the USA sought to protect, positioned the USA as the ARSENAL OF DEMOCRACY, and pushed the LEND-LEASE ACT through Congress. Even while the USA remained formally neutral, Roosevelt and Churchill collaborated on the drafting of the ATLANTIC CHARTER, and US destroyers took part in convoy duties in the North Atlantic.

The Japanese attack on Pearl Harbor was unexpected but, because it failed to destroy the US Navy's carrier fleet or the base's dockyard facilities, did not land the knock-out blow its planners had hoped to deliver. Nevertheless, in the first six months of the war Japanese troops consolidated control over French Indochina and captured Singapore, Hong Kong, the Dutch East Indies, Guam, Wake Island, the Philippines and most of New Guinea. Often outnumbered, US forces resisted these advances unsuccessfully at BATAAN and CORREGIDOR in the Philippines and successfully at the battle of the CORAL SEA. A decisive US naval victory at the battle of MIDWAY (June 3–6 1942) ended the threat of a Japanese invasion of Hawaii, and proved to be the turning point in the Pacific war. In August 1942 US troops mounted their first counterattack of the war at GUADALCANAL.

US forces pursued three main objectives for the remainder of the war in the Pacific. In the western region of the theater they sought to use air superiority to re-establish Allied control of Burma, end the threat of an invasion of India, and secure supply routes to the USA's Chinese allies. In the south US strategy focused on preventing the capture of New Guinea and the isolation of Australia. In these two regions, US forces fought in conjunction with British, Australian and other Commonwealth forces. In the east and center, US troops pursued an 'island-hopping' strategy designed to secure bases from which punitive air raids on the Japanese home islands could be mounted. The third of these objectives, the 'island-hopping' strategy, was carried forward by US troops, usually Marines, acting with little support from other Allied forces. Fighting in this campaign produced heavy casualties, as at TARAWA, and images, such as the raising of the American flag on Mount Suribachi, IWO JIMA, which continue to define the Pacific war in the American imagination. Although US troops did not defeat Japan single-handedly, the capture of islands from which heavy bomber attacks could be mounted on Japan was a vital pre-condition of the eventual Allied victory.

In the spring of 1941 US and British military planners had drafted the secret ABC-1 AGREEMENT stipulating that, if the USA were drawn into war with both Japan and Germany, American forces would pursue a 'Germany first' strategy. Roosevelt stuck to this agreement, although it took three years for US ground troops to be brought into decisive action against the main German armies. From August 17 1942 the US Eighth Air Force, operating from bases in Great Britain, began daylight raids of ever-increasing intensity on European targets. In November 1942, in Operation Torch, British and US troops landed in Morocco and Algeria. Coordinating their advance with a renewed British Eighth Army offensive in the Western Desert, the Allies forced the surrender of 250,000 Axis troops at Cape Bon, Tunisia, on May 12 1943. The Allies followed up their success in North Africa with the invasion of Sicily (July 10 1943) and landings on the Italian mainland (September 3 and 9 1943). American General Dwight D. EISENHOWER took overall command of these operations, and from December 31 1943 assumed supreme command of Allied forces in Western Europe.

At the CASABLANCA CONFERENCE held in January 1943, Churchill and Roosevelt had decided that it would be impossible to meet Stalin's demand that a 'second front' be opened in northern Europe that year, and had approved operations against Sicily and Italy instead. This decision may have made military sense but it strained relations with Stalin, who believed the USSR was being left to fight Germany alone (20 million Russian servicemen and civilians were killed during World War II). US–Soviet relations were further tested by events in Italy. On July 25 1943 Mussolini resigned as Italy's head of state, and a new government, led by former fascist Marshall Pietro Badoglio, was installed. Following the Allied invasion of Italy, on September 8 1943, Badoglio ordered the unconditional surrender of Italian troops. German troops occupied those areas of Italy not under Allied control, and on September 15 Mussolini established a fascist government in German-controlled Italy. To Stalin's amazement, Churchill and Roosevelt recognized the authority of Badoglio's government in areas of Italy occupied by the Allies and permitted it to change sides and declare war on Germany (albeit as a 'co-belligerent' rather than an 'ally'). Furthermore the two Western leaders refused to permit Soviet participation in the Allied occupation of Italy. This led Stalin to believe that former fascists, hostile to the Soviet Union, would be permitted to form governments in other liberated areas of Europe, and that Britain and the USA would actively prevent communists from forming governments in liberated countries. The rift between Churchill and Roosevelt on the one hand and Stalin on the other caused by the delayed opening of the second front and divisions over the reconstruction of postwar Europe became glaringly apparent at the TEHERAN CONFERENCE in November 1943, and was a contributory cause of the COLD WAR.

By the close of 1943 the strength of the US industrial economy was beginning to make a decisive impact on the war. For example, in 1940 the USA produced 6000 warplanes, but in 1943 it produced 86,000. Finally snapping out of a recession that Roosevelt's NEW DEAL program had been unable to cure, the US economy proved abundantly capable of supplying the 'arsenal of democracy'. Leading US Corporations dictated the terms of conversion to wartime production. The cost of retooling production lines and establishing new factories was met by the federal government. Manufacturers insisted that profit margins on defense contracts be safeguarded from cost overruns. Defense contracts were not subject to competitive bidding and, on Roosevelt's orders, the arrangements large corporations made to share contracts among themselves were exempt from antitrust legislation. During the war Harry S TRUMAN chaired a Senate subcommittee that uncovered fraud and waste in defense contracts totaling $15 billion. Yet Secretary of War Henry STIMSON defended the huge wartime profits made by major manufacturing corporations with the argument that 'in a capitalist country, you have to let business make money out of the process or business won't work'. Regardless of the manner in which it was achieved, the conversion of US industry to defense production had the effect of making the US armed forces the best equipped and supplied military force in the history of warfare. It also made possible the successful completion of the MANHATTAN PROJECT, which produced the world's first atomic bombs.

The military potential of the USA's vast resources of manpower and materiel was decisively realized in the D-DAY LANDINGS of June 6 1944, which opened the long-awaited 'second front' in Europe. By the spring of 1944, 3 million US servicemen were massed in Great Britain waiting to take part in the assault on the Normandy beaches code-named Operation Overlord.

Eisenhower exercised overall command of this operation, the largest airborne and amphibious assault in the history of warfare. US Army Chief of Staff George C. MARSHALL played a crucial role in planning the attack and organizing supply lines for the invasion. Thanks largely to American logistical support the Allies were able to land 176,000 front-line combat troops on five different beaches within 48 hours. Within three weeks, 1 million troops, 171,000 vehicles and 566,648 tons of supplies (including ten mobile COCA-COLA bottling plants) had passed through the beachheads. German resistance, especially at OMAHA BEACH, threatened to blunt the invasion, but the courage of the Allied troops, complemented by the superiority of the reinforcements at their disposal, carried the day.

As in the Pacific theater, US troops did not win the war in Western Europe single-handedly, but they did make an especially valuable contribution to Allied victory. As the second front developed, it confronted stiffening German resistance. In July 1944 the US Third Army under General George PATTON broke a developing stalemate around the Normandy beachhead with the ST LO OFFENSIVE. In December 1944 the US First, Ninth and Third Armies withstood and then repulsed a last-ditch German counter-offensive at the battle of the BULGE on the Belgium–Luxembourg border. On March 7 1945 US troops established a crucial bridgehead on the east bank of the Rhine at Remagen. Each of these actions played a crucial role in speeding the collapse of Nazi Germany and the unconditional surrender of German troops formally announced on 'Victory in Europe' Day, May 8 1945. In accordance with agreements among the Allies reached at the YALTA and POTSDAM CONFERENCES, Germany was divided into four occupation zones, and on August 8 1945 the USSR entered the war against Japan.

At the Potsdam Conference Roosevelt's successor President TRUMAN had informed Stalin that the USA was developing a 'new weapon of unusual destructive force' for use against Japan. Some historians have claimed that Truman's decision to use atomic weapons to bomb the Japanese cities of HIROSHIMA AND NAGASAKI was motivated by a desire to issue an implied threat to the USSR. However, Allied policy, agreed at Potsdam, called for Japan's unconditional surrender. On July 29 1945 Japan rejected an ultimatum to surrender, despite the fact that from March 1945 US aircraft had been mounting incendiary attacks on 66 Japanese cities, resulting, according to Japanese sources, in 260,000 deaths and 9 million people left homeless. Such intransigence on the part of the Japanese convinced Truman, his main advisers, and every member of the 750,000-strong Allied force being assembled for the final assault, that Japanese forces would mount a suicidal defense of their home islands. US military planners estimated that an invasion of Japan would produce 1 million Allied casualties and an equal number of civilian deaths. Truman, whose unenviable decision it was to make, seems to have believed that using atomic bombs represented the lesser of two evils. Following the dropping of the bombs, Japan announced its unconditional surrender on August 14 1945, and on September 2 General Douglas MACARTHUR presided over a formal surrender ceremony aboard the USS *Missouri* anchored in Tokyo Bay, bringing World War II to a close. During the war, 12.5 million Americans had been drafted into the armed forces, 321,000 were killed, and 800,000 were wounded or captured.

The effect of the war on America's home front were as momentous as its effect on the world order. The war brought full employment, and Conservative Democrats and Republicans used this as the pretext to kill NEW DEAL agencies such as the CIVILIAN CONSERVATION CORPS and the WORKS PROGRESS ADMINISTRATION. Annual per-capita income rose from $373 to $1074 between 1940 and 1945. To combat inflation the Office of Price Administration, created in January 1942, rationed staple foodstuffs and gas, and set maximum retail prices on dozens of commodities.

During the war 6.3 million American women entered the workforce, often taking jobs in areas, such as manufacturing industry, traditionally closed to them. Despite the value of their work, independent women workers were often accused of undermining family values. Although women who joined military units enjoyed the same pay and benefits as male recruits, women who worked on production lines were often paid less than a male worker performing the same task.

The war also highlighted racially discriminatory practices. In the spring of 1941 the trade unionist A. Philip RANDOLPH threatened the Roosevelt administration with a mass march on Washington to protest at the exclusion of African-Americans from new, high-paying jobs in defense plants. The administration created the Fair Employment Practices Commission to combat discrimination in the defense industry, but this had little effect. Racial discrimination was also pronounced in the armed forces. The Marine Corps refused to admit African-Americans except as servants, and the US Army organized black recruits into segregated units, usually commanded by white officers. African-American soldiers from northern cities were shocked by the discrimination they experienced in and around military training camps in southern states. The US Army even persuaded the British government to create local JIM CROW laws segregating pubs and other facilities near bases in Britain housing troops assembling for the D-Day invasion. Other ethnic groups also suffered. The attack on Pearl Harbor created a wave of anti-Japanese hysteria that led Roosevelt to order the RELOCATION of 100,000 Japanese-Americans

living on the west coast. Mexican BRACEROS, recruited to work on west-coast farms, also suffered discrimination, which produced the ZOOT SUIT RIOTS.

On a more positive note, the scale of US mobilization generated united political support for passage of the GI BILL, which offered millions of veterans the chance to attend college or receive vocational training.

Fueled by domestic and international demand, the American economy did not suffer a significant post-war depression. Postwar prosperity created a standard of living for ordinary Americans that was the envy of the world. In recognition of the wartime service performed by African-Americans, political leaders took their first faltering steps towards dismantling the Jim Crow system of racial segregation in the USA. President TRUMAN used executive powers to integrate the US armed forces and Hubert HUMPHREY was instrumental in writing a modest civil rights plank into the Democratic platform in the PRESIDENTIAL ELECTION OF 1948. Finally, by bringing Americans into contact with countrymen they would otherwise never have met, the war helped foster a national consciousness that began to supplant regional identities.

Wounded Knee, massacre at (1890), massacre of Teton-SIOUX in South Dakota, marking the final suppression of Native Americans by US forces. To combat militancy among the Teton-Sioux inspired by the GHOST DANCE religious revival, the US Army pursued a policy of disarming Sioux bands and resettling them near reservation trading posts. On December 29 1890 a Teton Ghost Dancer, probably angered by mistreatment of women and children and news that soldiers had shot SITTING BULL, shot a Seventh Cavalry trooper during a tense disarmament session at Wounded Knee, South Dakota. The cavalrymen, supported by artillery, began firing indiscriminately. At least 150 Sioux men, women and children, together with 25 US soldiers, were killed. BUFFALO SOLDIERS from the Ninth Cavalry helped suppress Sioux reprisals sparked by the massacre.

Wounded Knee protest (1973), protest by the AMERICAN INDIAN MOVEMENT (AIM), which began on February 7 1973 when 200 armed members of the group occupied the Oglala Sioux tribal reservation at Wounded Knee, South Dakota. A reservation faction alienated by the corruption and passivity of tribal elders had solicited intervention from AIM in support of their grievances. However, the occupation of this highly symbolic site, scene of the massacre of the same name, swiftly became the focus of national and international attention. Several thousand US marshals and local vigilantes surrounded the reservation to prevent Native Americans and their sympathizers from joining the protest. After a 70-day siege, in which shots were exchanged and two protesters killed, a negotiated settlement of the local issues prompting the protest was reached. The passions aroused by the reservation seizure made a settlement of outstanding national grievances harder to achieve.

WPA, *see* WORKS PROGRESS ADMINISTRATION.

Wright, Wilbur (1867–1912) and **Orville** (1871–1948), pioneer aviators who designed, built and, in 1903, flew the first powered airplane. The Wright brothers had little formal education. They were selling and making bicycles from a shop in Dayton, Ohio, when they were bitten by the aviation bug. Their attempt to build a powered aircraft was successful in part because they approached the task from first principles. They made painstaking experiments with gliders, and built a wind tunnel to test the aerodynamic qualities of various wing shapes, before beginning the construction of their first powered aircraft in October 1902. It weighed 750 pounds (341 kg), 170 pounds (77 kg) of which was accounted for by a 12 horsepower (8952 watt) gas-driven engine. The brothers shipped their aeroplane to Kitty Hawk, North Carolina, for final assembly prior to testing. Orville made the first flight on December 17 1903. It lasted 12 seconds. Later that day Wilbur stayed aloft for 59 seconds. By 1905 a much modified Wright machine could stay aloft for over 30 minutes and cover a distance of 24 miles (38 km). The brothers took out a patent on their design in 1906, and in 1909 founded the Wright Company to produce airplanes for the US Army.

Wyoming, western state, bordered on the north by Montana, on the east by Nebraska and South Dakota, on the south by Utah and Colorado and on the west by Idaho.

The USA acquired most of the modern state of Wyoming from France through the LOUISIANA PURCHASE. The first permanent US settlement was established at Fort Laramie in 1834. Remaining boundary issues were resolved, and US title confirmed, through the treaty of GUADELUPE-HIDALGO (1848) that ended the MEXICAN WAR.

US settlement began in earnest following the subjugation of the SIOUX and CHEYENNE people in the second SIOUX WAR and the completion of the transcontinental RAILROAD. Wyoming became a US territory on July 25 1868. The state's plains were utilized by cattle ranchers and later by sheep farmers. Wyoming entered the union as the 44th state on July 10 1890. In 1900 it had 92,531 residents. Mining and oil industries diversified the state's economy in the early years of the 20th century. (The TEAPOT DOME scandal centered on oil reserves in the state.)

In 1869 Wyoming became the first US territory to allow women to vote and hold office. These rights were safeguarded in the state constitution. In 1925 Wyoming native Nellie Tayloe Ross (1876–1977) became the first woman to serve as a state governor when her husband William Bradford Ross (1873–1925) died in office. (In 1926 she stood for reelection and was defeated.) In 1990 Wyoming had 453,588 inhabitants and was the least populous state in the union.

X Y Z

X, Malcolm (1925–65), militant African-American activist. A fiery orator and critic of the CIVIL RIGHTS MOVEMENT, Malcolm X was the son of a devotee of black separatist Marcus GARVEY. While serving a prison sentence for burglary, he experienced a religious conversion, dropped his 'slave name' (Malcolm Little), and joined the black Muslim organization, the NATION OF ISLAM. (He broke with the Nation of Islam in the winter of 1963–64.) Malcolm X criticized the Civil Rights Movement's emphasis on integration, which he described as a form of African-American cultural suicide. He also criticized non-violent protest, because it stripped African-Americans of their legitimate right to self-defense. This argument was frequently interpreted as sanctioning black violence against whites. By 1964 his criticisms of the personality cult he saw developing around Martin Luther KING, and of the VIETNAM WAR, were striking a chord with growing numbers of disillusioned activists belonging to the STUDENT NON-VIOLENT COORDINATING COMMITTEE (SNCC) and the CONGRESS OF RACIAL EQUALITY (CORE). On February 21 1965 he was shot dead at the Audubon Ballroom, New York City, by Nation of Islam loyalists.

XYZ affair (1797), diplomatic incident that led to a serious deterioration in relations between the USA and France. JAY'S TREATY (1794) had already damaged Franco-American relations. In the summer of 1797 President John ADAMS sent three commissioners to France to secure a treaty of commerce and amity. On arrival they were treated disrespectfully, and told by secret agents (identified as X, Y and Z) that a treaty could be obtained only by payment of bribes. When Adams informed Congress of this approach, FEDERALISTS demanded war with France, and attacked the patriotism of DEMOCRATIC-REPUBLICANS. Between 1797 and 1800 a QUASI-WAR with France existed.

Yalta Conference (February 4–11 1945), summit meeting in the Crimea towards the end of WORLD WAR II which involved the Allied leaders Franklin D. ROOSEVELT, Winston Churchill and Joseph Stalin. With victory over Germany in sight, the leaders discussed arrangements for the reconstruction of postwar Europe. Roosevelt secured Stalin's agreement to the Declaration of Liberated Europe. This bound the Allies to recognize freely elected governments in liberated states. Churchill, Stalin and, to some extent, Roosevelt undermined this public declaration by secretly dividing occupied Europe into 'spheres of influence'. Roosevelt and Churchill also sought to encourage the Soviet Union to declare war against Japan by agreeing to allow Russia to occupy such areas of Asia as its military forces might overrun. The secret agreements reached at Yalta reflected the current military situation. Britain and the USA were not able, even had they been willing, to force the Soviet Union to allow free elections in those areas of eastern Europe, notably Hungary, Romania and Bulgaria, that were firmly under the control of the Red Army. The creation of communist regimes in these countries, in apparent defiance of the Declaration of Liberated Europe, confused and alarmed public opinion in the West and encouraged the belief that the Soviet Union was bent on expansion. The Western powers, particularly Britain, insisted that Poland (although under the control of the Red Army), should be offered free elections. Stalin believed that this demand masked a desire to strip the Soviet Union of the protection afforded by a buffer state on its western border. Designed to reduce postwar tensions, the Yalta Conference actually helped create the COLD WAR.

Yarborough, Ex Parte, *see* EX PARTE YARBOROUGH.

Yazoo land fraud, scandal beginning on January 7 1795, when four land companies, whose shareholders included state legislators, purchased from Georgia 35 million acres (14 million ha) of land in Mississippi and Alabama (including the Yazoo river basin) at the bargain price of $500,000. In 1796 a new legislature, critical of the corruption surrounding the transaction, invalidated the sale. In 1802 Georgia ceded its claims to western lands to the USA. JEFFERSON's administration suggested compensating holders of land warrants issued by the four companies by distributing among them 5 million acres (2 million ha) of the US government's holdings. QUIDS, led by John Randolph, blocked the deal. The Supreme Court ruled on the affair in FLETCHER VS. PECK (1810). It declared unanimously that the original grant by sale was a contract, and that the subsequent rescinding law was unconstitutional. In 1814 claimants against the companies were awarded $4 million.

yellow-dog contract, type of employment contract stipulating that a worker was employed on condition that he did not seek to join a trade union. The popularity of yellow-dog contracts, with employers, grew after an early attempt to outlaw their use was ruled unconstitutional in ADAIR VS. US (1908). The NORRIS–LA GUARDIA ACT (1932) made yellow-dog contracts unenforceable, and the WAGNER ACT (1935) made them illegal.

yellow journalism, term applied to sensational or lurid 'news' reporting. Many Americans in the late 19th century had little interest in the details of issues such as the SILVER–GOLD CONTROVERSY or POPULISM. Although millions read uplifiting literature of the sort peddled by Horatio ALGER, or investigative material produced by MUCKRAKERS, Americans retained an appetite for stories about murder, rape and Native American atrocities. William Randolph HEARST built a newspaper empire by catering to this taste. The political influence of yellow journalism became an issue during the SPANISH-AMERICAN WAR. Sensational reports of Spanish atrocities created a war hysteria, and when the illustrator Frederic Remington (1861–1909) complained to Hearst that nothing seemed to be happening in Cuba, Hearst cabled back, 'You supply the pictures and I'll supply the war.' Hearst's papers were also held to have incited the assassination of President McKINLEY. Sensational journalism fueled the anti-German hysteria that preceded US entry into WORLD WAR I and the RED SCARE that followed. Although the style persists (as in the *New York Post* headline 'Headless Body Found in Topless Bar', and in the weekly *National Enquirer*), the creation of degree programs in journalism has tended to make the profession more respectable.

Yippies, nickname given to members of the Youth International Party (YIP), founded in February 1968 by Jerry Rubin, Abbie Hoffman, Paul Krassner and Ed Saunders.

Yippies denounced the VIETNAM WAR and American capitalism, while embracing a non-materialistic, cooperative, 'hippie' lifestyle. The Yippie credo was laid out in Abbie Hoffman's widely read *Steal This Book* (1971).

Yorktown, British surrender at (1782), the final episode in the REVOLUTIONARY WAR, involving the surrender of the British army at Yorktown, Virginia, to American and French forces.

The climactic campaign of the war began in the summer of 1781 when 7500 British troops under the command of Lieutenant General Charles CORNWALLIS conducted a series of raids in Virginia designed to deprive American troops in the Carolinas of their main source of supply. On June 4 British cavalrymen very nearly captured Governor JEFFERSON and the Virginia legislature during a raid on Charlottesville. As American reinforcements reached the area, Cornwallis retreated to the coast. On August 1 British forces began fortifying a base at Yorktown, on the York river leading into Chesapeake Bay, and awaited the arrival of reinforcements from New York.

On August 14 WASHINGTON learned that a French fleet accompanied by 3000 troops intended to sail from the West Indies to Chesapeake Bay. Abandoning plans for an assault on New York City, Washington ordered the bulk of the Continental Army to march to Virginia. The French fleet, under Admiral de Grasse, began blockading Yorktown on August 31. It defeated a smaller British squadron at the battle of CHESAPEAKE CAPES (September 5), and helped 9000 American and 7800 French soldiers join the siege of Yorktown. Alexander HAMILTON distinguished himself in an action that captured a key British redoubt (October 14). On October 19 Cornwallis's 7500 troops surrendered. The 7000 reinforcements Cornwallis had been awaiting arrived off Chesapeake Bay on October 24, but immediately sailed back to New York.

When it learnt of the surrender, the British Parliament voted to cease further prosecution of the war (March 5 1783). Peace talks, which led to the treaty of PARIS, began on April 12 1783.

Young, Brigham (1801–77), MORMON leader. Young led the first party of what became a great wave of Mormon settlers into the Salt Lake region of UTAH in July 1847. He had converted to the Mormon faith in 1832 and quickly gained a place on the Quorum of the Twelve Apostles, the church's governing body. Following the murder of the church's founder, Joseph Smith, in 1844, Young assumed overall leadership. In December 1847 he was named president and prophet of the church. Young played a crucial role in organizing the migration of Mormon settlers to Utah. He hoped that sheer weight of numbers would force Congress to accept a distinctively Mormon state, Deseret, into the Union. This plan foundered due to congressional opposition to polygamy. Young, who was a polygamist, was stripped of the territorial governorship in 1857 for refusing to uphold US law regarding this matter. However, in 1871, despite the fact that he had 20 wives and had fathered 57 children, he was acquitted of bigamy.

Youngstown Sheet and Tube Co. vs. Sawyer (June 2 1952), US Supreme Court ruling (6–3) that President TRUMAN had exceeded his authority by ordering a federal takeover of US steel mills in order to prevent a threatened strike from damaging the KOREAN WAR effort.

Zangara incident (February 15 1933), attempted assassination of Franklin D. ROOSEVELT, in which Giuseppe Zangara, a bricklayer, fired five shots at the president as he toured Miami. Roosevelt was unharmed, but the mayor of Chicago, traveling with Roosevelt, was killed. Zangara shouted 'Too many people are starving to death' before opening fire. He was executed on March 20 1933.

Zimmermann telegram, a decoded, or possibly fabricated, telegram sent by Germany's foreign minister to the German ambassador in Mexico, passed to the USA on February 24 1917 by British intelligence. The telegram suggested terms for a German alliance with Mexico in the event that the USA declared war on Germany; in particular that Germany would offer Mexico financial assistance to recapture the massive territory ceded to the USA by the treaty of GUADALUPE-HIDALGO (1848). Made public on March 1, the telegram provoked a storm of anti-German rhetoric, and helped push the USA into WORLD WAR I.

Zoot suit riots, race riots during WORLD WAR II targeting Mexicans and Mexican-Americans. During the war demand for labor in southern California skyrocketed. Local Mexican-Americans found employment in occupations from which they had previously been excluded, and many Mexicans migrated north to work on wartime assembly lines. Wages were high and 'zoot suits' (flashy, loose-fitting, broad-lapeled garments) became a symbol of the new-found prosperity enjoyed by Mexican and Mexican-American workers.

In June 1943, following rumors that a Mexican gang had beaten up a party of US soldiers, resentful whites in Los Angeles began attacking any Mexican 'punk' caught wearing a zoot suit in their neighborhood. Los Angeles police took no action until the Roosevelt administration, worried by the negative publicity the unrest was generating, ordered the suppression of the race-baiting.

Zuni, Native American PUEBLO PEOPLE who have lived in settlements straddling the modern boundary of New Mexico and Arizona since the pre-Columbian era. Although they suffered from APACHE raids in the late 18th and 19th centuries, the Zunis' sedentary lifestyle and remote homelands protected them from harassment by US settlers. Some 8000 Zunis now live on reservations in New Mexico.

MAPS AND APPENDICES

Maps   471

APPENDIX 1
Constitutional documents   475

APPENDIX 2
The Presidents of the United States   495

APPENDIX 3
Membership of the United States
Supreme Court   519

APPENDIX 4
Subject index   523

APPENDIX 5
Further reading   537

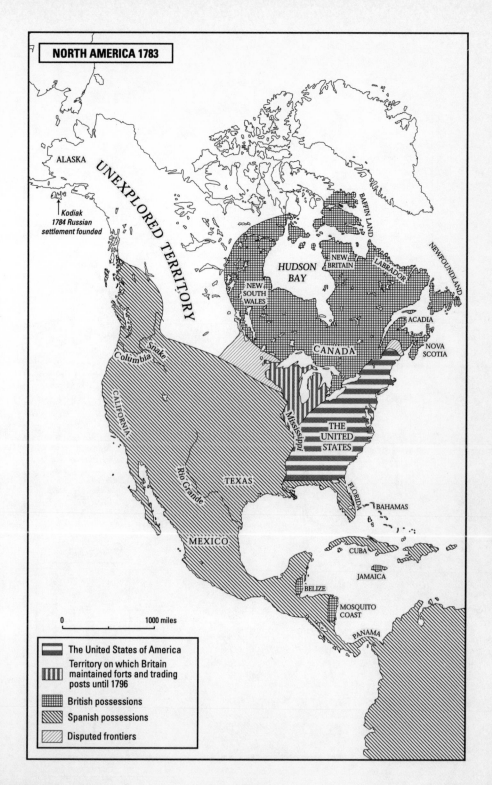

NORTH AMERICA 1783

ALASKA

↑ Kodiak
1784 Russian
settlement founded

UNEXPLORED TERRITORY

HUDSON BAY

BAFFIN LAND

NEW SOUTH WALES

NEW BRITAIN

LABRADOR

NEWFOUNDLAND

ACADIA

CANADA

NOVA SCOTIA

Columbia

Snake

CALIFORNIA

Mississippi

THE UNITED STATES

FLORIDA

BAHAMAS

Rio Grande

TEXAS

MEXICO

CUBA

JAMAICA

BELIZE

MOSQUITO COAST

PANAMA

0   1000 miles

The United States of America

Territory on which Britain maintained forts and trading posts until 1796

British possessions

Spanish possessions

Disputed frontiers

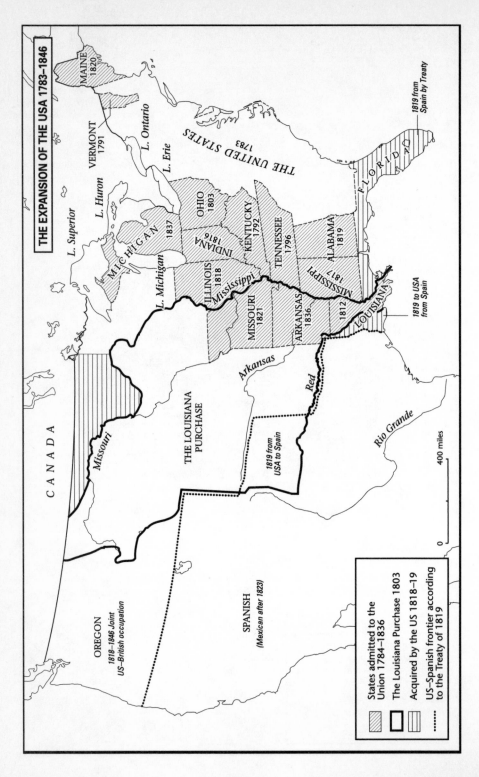

THE EXPANSION OF THE USA 1783–1846

CANADA

L. Superior

L. Huron

L. Michigan

L. Ontario

L. Erie

MAINE 1820

VERMONT 1791

THE UNITED STATES 1783

MICHIGAN 1837

OHIO 1803

INDIANA 1816

ILLINOIS 1818

KENTUCKY 1792

TENNESSEE 1796

Mississippi

MISSOURI 1821

ARKANSAS 1836

MISSISSIPPI 1817

ALABAMA 1819

LOUISIANA 1812

FLORIDA

1819 from Spain by Treaty

1819 to USA from Spain

Arkansas

Red

Rio Grande

Missouri

THE LOUISIANA PURCHASE

1819 from USA to Spain

OREGON
1818–1846 Joint
US–British occupation

SPANISH
(Mexican after 1823)

0   400 miles

States admitted to the
Union 1784–1836

The Louisiana Purchase 1803

Acquired by the US 1818–19

US–Spanish frontier according
to the Treaty of 1819

472

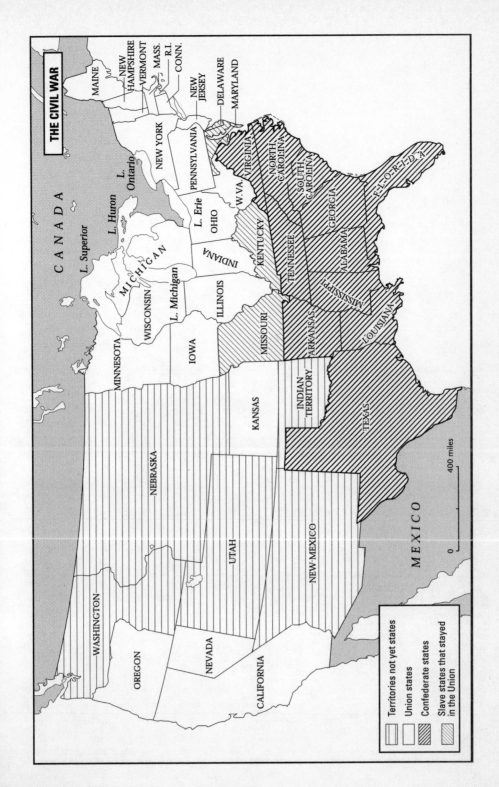

THE CIVIL WAR

CANADA

L. Superior
L. Huron
L. Ontario
L. Erie
L. Michigan

MAINE
NEW HAMPSHIRE
VERMONT
MASS.
R.I.
CONN.
NEW YORK
NEW JERSEY
DELAWARE
MARYLAND
PENNSYLVANIA
W.VA.
VIRGINIA
NORTH CAROLINA
SOUTH CAROLINA
GEORGIA
FLORIDA
OHIO
INDIANA
KENTUCKY
TENNESSEE
ALABAMA
MISSISSIPPI
MICHIGAN
WISCONSIN
ILLINOIS
IOWA
MINNESOTA
MISSOURI
ARKANSAS
LOUISIANA
INDIAN TERRITORY
KANSAS
NEBRASKA
TEXAS
UTAH
NEW-MEXICO
WASHINGTON
OREGON
NEVADA
CALIFORNIA

MEXICO

0   400 miles

Territories not yet states
Union states
Confederate states
Slave states that stayed in the Union

473

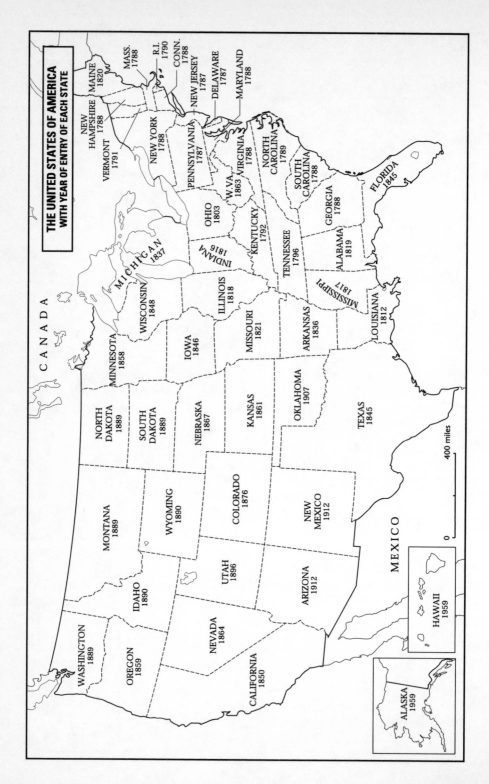

THE UNITED STATES OF AMERICA
WITH YEAR OF ENTRY OF EACH STATE

CANADA

MEXICO

MAINE 1820

MASS. 1788

R.I. 1790

CONN. 1788

NEW HAMPSHIRE 1788

VERMONT 1791

NEW YORK 1788

NEW JERSEY 1787

DELAWARE 1787

MARYLAND 1788

PENNSYLVANIA 1787

W.VA. 1863

VIRGINIA 1788

NORTH CAROLINA 1789

SOUTH CAROLINA 1788

GEORGIA 1788

FLORIDA 1845

OHIO 1803

KENTUCKY 1792

TENNESSEE 1796

ALABAMA 1819

MISSISSIPPI 1817

MICHIGAN 1837

INDIANA 1816

ILLINOIS 1818

WISCONSIN 1848

MINNESOTA 1858

IOWA 1846

MISSOURI 1821

ARKANSAS 1836

LOUISIANA 1812

NORTH DAKOTA 1889

SOUTH DAKOTA 1889

NEBRASKA 1867

KANSAS 1861

OKLAHOMA 1907

TEXAS 1845

MONTANA 1889

WYOMING 1890

COLORADO 1876

NEW MEXICO 1912

WASHINGTON 1889

IDAHO 1890

OREGON 1859

UTAH 1896

NEVADA 1864

CALIFORNIA 1850

ARIZONA 1912

400 miles

0

HAWAII 1959

ALASKA 1959

474

CONSTITUTIONAL DOCUMENTS

THE DECLARATION OF INDEPENDENCE

July 4 1776

When, in the course of human events, it becomes necessary for one people to dissolve the political bonds which have connected them with another, and to assume, among the powers of the earth, the separate and equal station to which the laws of nature and of nature's God entitle them, a decent respect to the opinions of mankind requires that they should declare the causes which impel them to the separation.

We hold these truths to be self-evident: that all men are created equal; that they are endowed by their Creator with certain unalienable rights; that among these are life, liberty, and the pursuit of happiness; that to secure these rights, governments are instituted among men, deriving their just powers from the consent of the governed; that whenever any form of government becomes destructive of these ends, it is the right of the people to alter or to abolish it, and to institute new government, laying its foundation on such principles, and organizing its powers in such form, as to them shall seem most likely to effect their safety and happiness. Prudence, indeed, will dictate that governments long established should not be changed for light and transient causes; and accordingly all experience hath shewn that mankind are more disposed to suffer, while evils are sufferable, than to right themselves by abolishing the forms to which they are accustomed. But when a long train of abuses and usurpations, pursuing invariably the same object, evinces a design to reduce them under absolute despotism, it is their right, it is their duty, to throw off such government, and to provide new guards for their future security. Such has been the patient sufferance of these colonies; and such is now the necessity which constrains them to alter their former systems of government. The history of the present King of Great Britain is a history of repeated injuries and usurpations, all having in direct object the establishment of an absolute tyranny over these states. To prove this, let these facts be submitted to a candid world.

He has refused his assent to laws, the most wholesome and necessary for the public good.

He has forbidden his governors to pass laws of immediate and pressing importance, unless suspended in their operation till his assent should be obtained; and when so suspended, he has utterly neglected to attend to them.

He has refused to pass other laws for the accommodation of large districts of people, unless those people would relinquish the right of representation in the legislature, a right inestimable to them, and for-midable to tyrants only.

He has called together legislative bodies at places unusual, uncomfort-able, and distant from the depository of their public records, for the sole purpose of fatiguing them into compliance with his measures.

He has dissolved representative houses repeatedly, for opposing, with manly firmness, his invasions on the rights of the people.

He has refused for a long time, after such dissolutions, to cause others to be elected; whereby the legislative powers, incapable of annihilation, have returned to the people at large for their exercise; the state remain-ing in the mean time exposed to all the dangers of invasion from with-out, and convulsions within.

He has endeavored to prevent the population of these states; for that purpose obstructing the laws for naturalization of foreigners; refusing to pass others to encourage their migration hither, and raising the condi-tions of new appropriations of lands.

He has obstructed the administration of justice, by refusing his assent to laws for establishing judiciary powers.

He has made judges dependent on his will alone, for the tenure of their offices, and the amount and payment of their salaries.

He has erected a multitude of new offices, and sent hither swarms of officers to harass our people and eat out their substance.

He has kept among us, in times of peace, standing armies, without the consent of our legislatures.

He has affected to render the military independent of, and superior to, the civil power.

He has combined with others to subject us to a jurisdiction foreign to our constitution, and unacknowledged by our laws, giving his assent to their acts of pretended legislation:

For quartering large bodies of armed troops among us;

For protecting them, by a mock trial, from punishment for any murders which they should commit on the inhabitants of these states;

For cutting off our trade with all parts of the world;

For imposing taxes on us without our consent;

For depriving us, in many cases, of the benefits of trial by jury;

For transporting us beyond seas to be tried for pretended offenses;

For abolishing the free system of English laws in a neighboring province, establishing therein an arbitrary government, and enlarging its boundaries, so as to render it at once an example and fit instrument for introducing the same absolute rule into these colonies;

For taking away our charters, abolishing our most valuable laws, and altering fundamentally the forms of our governments;

For suspending our own legislatures, and declaring themselves invested with power to legislate for us in all cases whatsoever.

He has abdicated government here, by declaring us out of his protection and waging war against us.

He has plundered our seas, ravaged our coasts, burnt our towns, and destroyed the lives of our people.

He is, at this time, transporting large armies of foreign mercenaries to complete the works of death, desolation, and tyranny, already begun with circumstances of cruelty and perfidy scarcely paralleled in the most barbarous ages, and totally unworthy of the head of a civilized nation.

He has constrained our fellow-citizens, taken captive on the high seas, to bear arms against their country, to become the executioners of their friends and brethren, or to fall themselves by their hands.

He has excited domestic insurrections amongst us, and has endeavored to bring on the inhabitants of our frontiers, the merciless Indian savages, whose only known rule of warfare is an undistinguished destruction of all ages, sexes, and conditions.

In every stage of these oppressions we have petitioned for redress in the most humble terms; our repeated petitions have been answered only by repeated injury. A prince, whose character is thus marked by every act which may define a tyrant, is unfit to be the ruler of a free people.

Nor have we been wanting in our attentions to our British brethren. We have warned them, from time to time, of attempts by their legislature to extend an unwarrantable jurisdiction over us. We have reminded them of the circumstances of our emigration and settlement here. We have appealed to their native justice and magnanimity, and we have conjured them, by the ties of our common kindred, to disavow these usurpations which, would inevitably interrupt our connections and correspondence. They, too, have been deaf to the voice of justice and of consanguinity. We must, therefore, acquiesce in the necessity which denounces our separation, and hold them, as we hold the rest of mankind, enemies in war, in peace, friends.

We, therefore, the representatives of the United States of America, in General Congress, assembled, appealing to the Supreme Judge of the world for the rectitude of our intentions, do, in the name, and by the authority of the good people of these colonies, solemnly publish and declare, that these United Colonies are, and of right ought to be, FREE AND INDEPENDENT STATES; that they are absolved from all allegiance to the British crown, and that all political connection between them and the state of Great Britain is, and ought to be, totally dissolved; and that, as free and independent states, they have full power to levy war, conclude peace, contract alliances, establish commerce, and do all other acts and things which independent states may of right do. And for the support of this declaration, with a firm reliance on the protection of Divine Providence, we mutually pledge to each other our lives, our fortunes, and our sacred honor.

John Hancock	Benjamin Harrison	Lewis Morris
Button Gwinnett	Thomas Nelson Jr	Richard Stockton
Lyman Hall	Francis Lightfoot Lee	John Witherspoon
George Walton	Carter Braxton	Francis Hopkinson
William Hooper	Robert Morris	John Hart
Joseph Hewes	Benjamin Rush	Abraham Clark
John Penn	Benjamin Franklin	Josiah Bartlett
Edward Rutledge	John Morton	William Whipple
Thomas Heyward Jr	George Clymer	Samuel Adams
Thomas Lynch Jr	James Smith	John Adams
Arthur Middleton	George Taylor	Robert Treat Paine
Samuel Chase	James Wilson	Elbridge Gerry
William Paca	George Ross	Stephen Hopkins
Thomas Stone	Caesar Rodney	William Ellery
Charles Carroll of Carrollton	George Read	Roger Sherman
	Thomas McKean	Samuel Huntington
George Wythe	William Floyd	William Williams
Richard Henry Lee	Philip Livingston	Oliver Wolcott
Thomas Jefferson	Francis Lewis	Matthew Thornton

THE CONSTITUTION OF
THE UNITED STATES OF AMERICA

Preamble

We the people of the United States, in order to form a more perfect union; establish justice, insure domestic tranquility, provide for the common defense, promote the general welfare, and secure the blessings of liberty to ourselves and our posterity, do ordain and establish this Constitution for the United States of America.

Article I

Section 1

All legislative powers herein granted shall be vested in a Congress of the United States, which shall consist of a Senate and House of Representatives.

Section 2

The House of Representatives shall be composed of members chosen every second year by the people of the several states, and the electors in each state shall have the same qualifications requisite for electors of the most numerous branch of the state legislature.

No person shall be a representative who shall not have attained to the age of twenty five years, and been seven years a Citizen of the United States, and who shall not, when elected, be an inhabitant of that state in which he shall be chosen.

Representatives and direct taxes shall be apportioned among the several states which may be included within this Union according to their respective numbers, which shall be determined by adding to the whole number of free persons, including those bound to service for a term of years, and excluding Indians not taxed, three fifths of all other persons.[1] The actual enumeration shall be made within three years after the first meeting of the Congress of the United States, and within every subsequent term of ten years, in such manner as they shall by law direct. The number of representatives shall not exceed one for every thirty thousand, but each state shall have at least one representative; and until such enumeration shall be made, the state of New Hampshire shall be entitled to choose three, Massachusetts eight, Rhode-Island and Providence Plantations one, Connecticut five, New York six, New Jersey four, Pennsylvania eight, Delaware one, Maryland six, Virginia ten, North Carolina five, South Carolina five, and Georgia three.

[1] This provision was suspended by passage of the FOURTEENTH AMENDMENT.

When vacancies happen in the representation from any state, the executive authority thereof shall issue writs of election to fill such vacancies.

The House of Representatives shall choose their Speaker and other Officers; and shall have the sole power of impeachment.

Section 3
The Senate of the United States shall be composed of two senators from each state, chosen by the legislature thereof,[1] for six years; and each senator shall have one vote.

Immediately after they shall be assembled in consequence of the first election, they shall be divided as equally as may be into three classes. The seats of the senators of the first class shall be vacated at the expiration of the second year, of the second class at the expiration of the fourth year, and of the third class at the expiration of the sixth year, so that one third may be chosen every second year; and if vacancies happen by resignation, or otherwise, during the recess of the legislature of any state, the executive thereof may make temporary appointments until the next meeting of the legislature, which shall then fill such vacancies.[2]

No person shall be a senator who shall not have attained to the age of thirty years, and been nine years a citizen of the United States, and who shall not, when elected, be an inhabitant of that state for which he shall be chosen.

The vice president of the United States shall be president of the Senate, but shall have no vote, unless they be equally divided.

The Senate shall choose their other officers, and also a president pro tempore, in the absence of the vice president, or when he shall exercise the office of president of the United States.

The Senate shall have the sole power to try all impeachments. When sitting for that purpose, they shall be on oath or affirmation. When the president of the United States is tried, the Chief Justice shall preside; and no person shall be convicted without the concurrence of two thirds of the members present.

Judgment in cases of impeachment shall not extend further than to removal from office, and disqualification to hold or enjoy any office of honor, trust or profit under the United States: but the party convicted shall nevertheless be liable and subject to indictment, trial, judgment and punishment, according to law.

[1] This provision was superseded by passage of the SEVENTEENTH AMENDMENT.
[2] This provision was modified by passage of the SEVENTEENTH AMENDMENT.

Section 4

The times, places and manner of holding elections for senators and representatives, shall be prescribed in each state by the legislature thereof; but the Congress may at any time by law make or alter such regulations, except as to the places of choosing senators.

The Congress shall assemble at least once in every year, and such meeting shall be on the first Monday in December, unless they shall by law appoint a different day.[1]

Section 5

Each house shall be the judge of the elections, returns and qualifications of its own members, and a majority of each shall constitute a quorum to do business; but a smaller number may adjourn from day to day, and may be authorized to compel the attendance of absent members, in such manner, and under such penalties as each house may provide.

Each house may determine the rules of its proceedings, punish its members for disorderly behavior, and, with the concurrence of two thirds, expel a member.

Each house shall keep a journal of its proceedings, and from time to time publish the same, excepting such parts as may in their judgment require secrecy; and the yeas and nays of the members of either house on any question shall, at the desire of one fifth of those present, be entered on the journal.

Neither house, during the session of Congress, shall, without the consent of the other, adjourn for more than three days, nor to any other place than that in which the two houses shall be sitting.

Section 6

The senators and representatives shall receive a compensation for their services, to be ascertained by law, and paid out of the treasury of the United States. They shall in all cases, except treason, felony and breach of the peace, be privileged from arrest during their attendance at the session of their respective houses, and in going to and returning from the same; and for any speech or debate in either house, they shall not be questioned in any other place.

No senator or representative shall, during the time for which he was elected, be appointed to any civil office under the authority of the United States, which shall have been created, or the emoluments whereof shall have been increased during such time; and no person

[1] This provision was modified by the TWENTIETH AMENDMENT.

holding any office under the United States, shall be a member of either house during his continuance in office.

Section 7

All bills for raising revenue shall originate in the House of Representatives; but the Senate may propose or concur with amendments as on other bills.

Every bill which shall have passed the House of Representatives and the Senate, shall, before it become a law, be presented to the president of the United States; if he approve he shall sign it, but if not he shall return it, with his objections to that House in which it shall have originated, who shall enter the objections at large on their journal, and proceed to reconsider it. If after such reconsideration two thirds of that house shall agree to pass the bill, it shall be sent, together with the objections, to the other house, by which it shall likewise be reconsidered, and if approved by two thirds of that house, it shall become a law. But in all such cases the votes of both houses shall be determined by yeas and nays, and the names of the persons voting for and against the bill shall be entered on the journal of each house respectively. If any bill shall not be returned by the president within ten days (Sundays excepted) after it shall have been presented to him, the same shall be a law, in like manner as if he had signed it, unless the Congress by their adjournment prevent its return, in which case it shall not be a law.

Every order, resolution, or vote to which the concurrence of the Senate and House of Representatives may be necessary (except on a question of adjournment) shall be presented to the president of the United States; and before the same shall take effect, shall be approved by him, or being disapproved by him, shall be repassed by two thirds of the Senate and House of Representatives, according to the rules and limitations prescribed in the case of a bill.

Section 8

The Congress shall have power to lay and collect taxes, duties, imposts and excises, to pay the debts and provide for the common defense and general welfare of the United States; but all duties, imposts and excises shall be uniform throughout the United States;

To borrow money on the credit of the United States;

To regulate commerce with foreign nations, and among the several states, and with the Indian tribes;

To establish a uniform rule of naturalization, and uniform laws on the subject of bankruptcies throughout the United States;

To coin money, regulate the value thereof, and of foreign coin, and fix the standard of weights and measures;

To provide for the punishment of counterfeiting the securities and current coin of the United States;

To establish post offices and post roads;

To promote the progress of science and useful arts, by securing for limited times to authors and inventors the exclusive right to their respective writings and discoveries;

To constitute tribunals inferior to the Supreme Court;

To define and punish piracies and felonies committed on the high seas, and offenses against the law of nations;

To declare war, grant letters of marque and reprisal, and make rules concerning captures on land and water;

To raise and support armies, but no appropriation of money to that use shall be for a longer term than two years;

To provide and maintain a Navy;

To make rules for the government and regulation of the land and naval forces;

To provide for calling forth the militia to execute the laws of the Union, suppress insurrections and repel invasions;

To provide for organizing, arming, and disciplining, the militia, and for governing such part of them as may be employed in the service of the United States, reserving to the states respectively, the appointment of the officers, and the authority of training the militia according to the discipline prescribed by Congress;

To exercise exclusive legislation in all cases whatsoever, over such District (not exceeding ten miles square) as may, by cession of particular states, and the acceptance of Congress, become the seat of the government of the United States, and to exercise like authority over all places purchased by the consent of the legislature of the state in which the same shall be, for the erection of forts, magazines, arsenals, dock-yards, and other needful buildings; – and

To make all laws which shall be necessary and proper for carrying into execution the foregoing powers, and all other powers vested by this Constitution in the government of the United States, or in any department or officer thereof.

Section 9

The migration or importation of such persons as any of the states now existing shall think proper to admit, shall not be prohibited by the Congress prior to the year one thousand eight hundred and eight, but a tax or duty may be imposed on such importation, not exceeding ten dollars for each person.

The privilege of the writ of habeas corpus shall not be suspended, unless when in cases of rebellion or invasion the public safety may require it.

No bill of attainder or ex post facto law shall be passed.

No capitation, or other direct, tax shall be laid, unless in proportion to the census or enumeration herein before directed to be taken.[1]

No tax or duty shall be laid on articles exported from any state.

No preference shall be given by any regulation of commerce or revenue to the ports of one state over those of another; nor shall vessels bound to, or from, one state, be obliged to enter, clear, or pay duties in another.

No money shall be drawn from the Treasury, but in consequence of appropriations made by law; and a regular statement and account of the receipts and expenditures of all public money shall be published from time to time.

No title of nobility shall be granted by the United States: and no person holding any office of profit or trust under them, shall, without the consent of the Congress, accept of any present, emolument, office, or title, of any kind whatever, from any King, prince, or foreign state.

Section 10

No state shall enter into any treaty, alliance, or confederation; grant letters of marque and reprisal; coin money; emit bills of credit; make any thing but gold or silver coin a tender in payment of debts, pass any bill of attainder, ex post facto law, or law impairing the obligation of contracts, or grant any title of nobility.

No state shall, without the consent of the Congress, lay any imposts or duties on imports or exports, except what may be absolutely necessary for executing its inspection laws: and the net produce of all duties and imposts, laid by any state on imports or exports, shall be for the use of the Treasury of the United States; and all such laws shall be subject to the revision and control of the Congress.

No state shall, without the consent of the Congress, lay any duty of tonnage, keep troops, or ships of war in time of peace, enter into any

[1] This provision was superseded by passage of the SIXTEENTH AMENDMENT.

agreement or compact with another state, or with a foreign power, or engage in war, unless actually invaded, or in such imminent danger as will not admit of delay.

Article II

Section 1

The executive power shall be vested in a president of the United States of America. He shall hold his office during the term of four years, and, together with the vice president, chosen for the same term, be elected, as follows.

Each state shall appoint, in such manner as the legislature thereof may direct, a number of Electors, equal to the whole number of senators and representatives to which the state may be entitled in the Congress: but no senator or representative, or person holding an office of trust or profit under the United States, shall be appointed an Elector.

The Electors shall meet in their respective states, and vote by ballot for two persons, of whom one at least shall not be an inhabitant of the same state with themselves. And they shall make a list of all the persons voted for, and the number of votes for each; which list they shall sign and certify, and transmit sealed to the seat of the government of the United States, directed to the president of the Senate. The president of the Senate shall, in the presence of the Senate and House of Representatives, open all the certificates, and the votes shall then be counted. The person having the greatest number of votes shall be the president, if such number be a majority of the whole number of Electors appointed; and if there be more than one who have such majority, and have an equal number of votes, then the House of Representatives shall immediately choose by ballot one of them for president; and if no person have a majority, then from the five highest on the list the said House shall in like manner choose the president. But in choosing the president, the votes shall be taken by States, the representation from each state having one vote; a quorum for this purpose shall consist of a Member or Members from two thirds of the states, and a majority of all states shall be necessary to a choice. In every case, after the choice of the president, the person having the greatest number of votes of the Electors shall be the vice president. But if there should remain two or more who have equal votes, the Senate choose from them by ballot the vice president.[1]

The Congress may determine the time of choosing the Electors, and the day on which they shall give their votes; which day shall be the same throughout the United States.

[1] This procedure was modified by the TWELFTH AMENDMENT.

No person except a natural born citizen, or a citizen of the United States, at the time of the adoption of this Constitution, shall be eligible to the office of president; neither shall any person be eligible to that office who shall not have attained to the age of thirty five years, and been fourteen years a resident within the United States.

In the case of removal of the president from office, or of his death, resignation, or inability to discharge the powers and duties of the said office,[1] the same shall devolve on the vice president, and the Congress may by law provide for the case of removal, death, resignation or inability, both of the president and the vice president, declaring what officer shall then act as president, and such officer shall act accordingly, until the disability be removed, or a president shall be elected.

The president shall, at stated times, receive for his services, a compensation, which shall neither be increased nor diminished during the period for which he shall have been elected, and he shall not receive within that period any other emolument from the United States, or any of them.

Before he enter on the execution of his office, he shall take the following Oath or Affirmation: – 'I do solemnly swear (or affirm) that I will faithfully execute the Office of president of the United States, and will to the best of my ability, preserve, protect and defend the Constitution of the United States.'

Section 2
The president shall be commander in chief of the Army and Navy of the United States, and of the militia of the several states, when called into the actual service of the United States; he may require the opinion, in writing, of the principal officer in each of the executive departments, upon any subject relating to the duties of their respective offices, and he shall have power to grant reprieves and pardons for offenses against the United States, except in cases of impeachment.

He shall have power, by and with the advice and consent of the Senate, to make treaties, provided two thirds of the senators present concur; and he shall nominate, and by and with the advice and consent of the Senate, shall appoint ambassadors, other public ministers and consuls, judges of the Supreme Court, and all other officers of the United States, whose appointments are not herein otherwise provided for, and which shall be established by law: but the Congress may by law vest the appointment of such inferior officers, as they think proper, in the president alone, in the courts of law, or in the heads of departments.

[1] This was modified by the TWENTY-FIFTH AMENDMENT.

The president shall have power to fill up all vacancies that may happen during the recess of the Senate, by granting commissions which shall expire at the end of their next session.

Section 3

He shall from time to time give to the Congress information of the state of the Union, and recommend to their consideration such measures as he shall judge necessary and expedient; he may, on extraordinary occasions, convene both houses, or either of them, and in case of disagreement between them, with respect to the time of adjournment, he may adjourn them to such time as he shall think proper; he shall receive ambassadors and other public ministers; he shall take care that the laws be faithfully executed, and shall commission all the officers of the United States.

The president, vice president and all civil officers of the United States, shall be removed from office on impeachment for, and conviction of, treason, bribery or other high crimes and misdemeanors.

Article III

Section 1

The judicial power of the United States, shall be vested in one Supreme Court, and in such inferior courts as the Congress may from time to time ordain and establish. The judges, both of the supreme and inferior courts, shall hold their offices during good behavior, and shall, at stated times, receive for their services, a compensation, which shall not be diminished during their continuance in office.

Section 2

The judicial power shall extend to all cases, in law and equity, arising under this Constitution, the laws of the United States, and treaties made, or which shall be made, under their authority; – to all cases affecting Ambassadors, other public ministers and Consuls; – to all cases of admiralty and maritime jurisdiction; – to controversies to which the United States shall be a party; – to controversies between two or more states; – between a state and citizens of another state;[1] – between citizens of different states; – between citizens of the same state claiming lands under grants of different states, and between a state, or the citizens thereof, and foreign states, citizens or subjects.

In all cases affecting ambassadors, other public ministers and consuls, and those in which a state shall be party, the supreme court shall have original jurisdiction. In all the other cases before mentioned, the

[1] This was modified by the ELEVENTH AMENDMENT.

Supreme Court shall have appellate jurisdiction, both as to law and fact, with such exceptions, and under such regulations as the Congress shall make.

The trial of all crimes, except in cases of impeachment, shall be by jury; and such trial shall be held in the state where the said crimes shall have been committed; but when not committed within any state, the trial shall be at such place or places as the Congress may by law have directed.

Section 3

Treason against the United States, shall consist only in levying war against them, or in adhering to their enemies, giving them aid and comfort. No person shall be convicted of treason unless on the testimony of two witnesses to the same overt act, or on confession in open court.

The Congress shall have power to declare the punishment of treason, but no attainder of treason shall work corruption of blood, or forfeiture except during the life of the person attainted.

Article IV

Section 1

Full faith and credit shall be given in each state to the public acts, records, and judicial proceedings of every other state. And the Congress may by general laws prescribe the manner in which such acts, records and proceedings shall be proved, and the effect thereof.

Section 2

The citizens of each state shall be entitled to all privileges and immunities of citizens in the several states.

A person charged in any state with treason, felony, or any other crime, who shall flee from justice, and be found in another state, shall on demand of the executive authority of the state from which he fled, be delivered up, to be removed to the state having jurisdiction of the crime.

No person held to service or labor in one state, under the laws thereof, escaping into another, shall, in consequence of any law or regulation therein, be discharged from such service or labor, but shall be delivered up on claim of the party to whom such service or labor may be due.[1]

Section 3

New states may be admitted by the Congress into this Union; but no

---

[1] This clause was superseded by the THIRTEENTH AMENDMENT.

new state shall be formed or erected within the jurisdiction of any other state; nor any state be formed by the junction of two or more states, or parts of states, without the consent of the legislatures of the states concerned as well as of the Congress.

The Congress shall have power to dispose of and make all needful rules and regulations respecting the territory or other property belonging to the United States; and nothing in this Constitution shall be so construed as to prejudice any claims of the United States, or of any particular state.

Section 4
The United States shall guarantee to every state in this Union a republican form of government, and shall protect each of them against invasion; and on application of the legislature, or of the executive (when the legislature cannot be convened) against domestic violence.

Article V

The Congress, whenever two thirds of both houses shall deem it necessary, shall propose amendments to this Constitution, or, on the application of the legislatures of two thirds of the several states, shall call a convention for proposing amendments, which, in either case, shall be valid to all intents and purposes, as part of this Constitution, when ratified by the legislatures of three fourths of the several states, or by conventions in three fourths thereof, as the one or the other mode of ratification may be proposed by the Congress; provided that no amendment which may be made prior to the year one thousand eight hundred and eight shall in any manner affect the first and fourth clauses in the ninth section of the first article;[1] and that no state, without its consent, shall be deprived of its equal suffrage in the Senate.

Article VI

All debts contracted and engagements entered into, before the adoption of this constitution, shall be as valid against the United States under this Constitution, as under the Confederation.

This Constitution and the laws of the United States which shall be made in pursuance thereof; and all treaties made, or which shall be made, under the authority of the United States, shall be the supreme law of the land; and the judges in every state shall be bound thereby, any thing in the Constitution or laws of any state to the contrary notwithstanding.

1 This clause was made redundant by passage of the THIRTEENTH AMENDMENT.

The senators and representatives before mentioned, and the members of the several state legislatures, and all executive and judicial officers, both of the United States and of the several states, shall be bound by oath or affirmation, to support this Constitution; but no religious test shall ever be required as a qualification to any office or public trust under the United States.

Article VII

The ratification of the conventions of nine states, shall be sufficient for the establishment of this Constitution between the states so ratifying the same.

Done in convention by the unanimous consent of the States present, the seventeenth day of September in the year of our Lord one thousand seven hundred and eighty-seven and of the Independence of the United States of America the twelfth. In witness whereof we have hereunto subscribed our names.

George Washington	Robert Morris	Daniel Carroll
John Langdon	George Clymer	John Blair
Nicholas Gilman	Thomas Fitzsimmons	James Madison
Nathaniel Gorham	Jared Ingersoll	William Blount
Rufus King	James Wilson	Richard Dobbs
William S. Johnson	Gouvernor Morris	Spraight
Roger Sherman	George Read	Hu Williamson
Alexander Hamilton	Gunning Bedford Jr	John Rutledge
William Livingston	John Dickinson	Charles Cotesworth
David Brearley	Richard Bassett	Pinckney
William Paterson	Jacob Broom	Pierce Butler
Jonathan Dayton	James McHenry	William Few
Benjamin Franklin	Daniel of St Thomas	Abraham Baldwin
Thomas Mifflin	Jenifer	

THE BILL OF RIGHTS

First Amendment

Congress shall make no law respecting an establishment of religion, or prohibiting the free exercise thereof; or abridging the freedom of speech, or of the press; or of the right of the people peaceably to assemble, and to petition the government for a redress of grievances.

Second Amendment

A well regulated militia, being necessary to the security of a free state, the right of the people to keep and bear arms shall not be infringed.

Third Amendment

No soldier shall, in time of peace, be quartered in any house without the consent of the owner, nor in time of war, but in a manner to be prescribed by law.

Fourth Amendment

The right of the people to be secure in their persons, houses, papers, and effects, against unreasonable searches and seizures, shall not be violated, and no warrants shall issue but upon probable cause, supported by oath or affirmation, and particularly describing the place to be searched, and the persons or things to be seized.

Fifth Amendment

No person shall be held to answer for a capital, or otherwise infamous crime, unless on a presentment or indictment of a grand jury, except in cases arising in the land or naval forces, or in the militia, when in actual service in time of war or public danger; nor shall any person be subject for the same offense to be twice put in jeopardy of life or limb; nor shall be compelled in any criminal case to be a witness against himself, nor be deprived of life, liberty, or property, without due process of law; nor shall private property be taken for public use, without just compensation.

Sixth Amendment

In all criminal prosecutions, the accused shall enjoy the right to a speedy and public trial, by an impartial jury of the state and district wherein the crime shall have been committed, which district shall have been previously ascertained by law, and to be informed of the nature and cause of the accusation; to be confronted with the witnesses against him; to have compulsory process for obtaining witnesses in his favor, and to have the assistance of counsel for his defense.

Seventh Amendment

In suits at common law, where the value in controversy shall exceed twenty dollars, the right of trial by jury shall be preserved, and no fact tried by a jury, shall be otherwise re-examined in any court of the United States, than according to the rules of common law.

Eighth Amendment

Excessive bail shall not be required, nor excessive fines imposed, nor cruel and unusual punishments inflicted.

Ninth Amendment

The enumeration in the Constitution, of certain rights, shall not be construed to deny or disparage others retained by the people.

Tenth Amendment

The powers not delegated to the United States by the Constitution, nor prohibited by it to the states, are reserved to the states respectively, or to the people.

OTHER AMENDMENTS

The following three amendments to the US Constitution abolished slavery, established the civil rights of former slaves and governed the process by which the states that had seceded to form the Confederacy were reintegrated within the United States.

Thirteenth Amendment

Section 1
Neither slavery nor involuntary servitude, except as a punishment for crime whereof the party shall have been duly convicted, shall exist within the United States, or any place subject to their jurisdiction.

Section 2
Congress shall have power to enforce this article by appropriate legislation.

Fourteenth Amendment

Section 1
All persons born or naturalized in the United States, and subject to the

jurisdiction thereof, are citizens of the United States and of the state wherein they reside. No state shall make or enforce any law which shall abridge the privileges or immunities of citizens of the United States; nor shall any state deprive any person of life, liberty, or property, without due process of law; nor deny to any person within its jurisdiction the equal protection of the laws.

Section 2

Representatives shall be apportioned among the several states according to their respective numbers, counting the whole number of persons in each State, excluding Indians not taxed. But when the right to vote at any election for the choice of electors for president and vice president of the United States, representatives in Congress, the executive and judicial officers of a State, or the members of the legislature thereof, is denied to any of the male inhabitants of such state, being twenty-one years of age and citizens of the United States, or in any way abridged, except for participation in rebellion, or other crime, the basis of representation therein shall be reduced in the proportion which the number of such male citizens shall bear to the whole number of male citizens twenty-one years of age in such state.

Section 3

No person shall be a senator or representative in Congress, or elector of president and vice president, or hold any office, civil or military, under the United States, or under any State, who, having previously taken an oath, as a member of Congress, or as an officer of tl   United States, or as a member of any State legislature, or as an executive or judicial officer of any State, to support the Constitution of the United States, shall have engaged in insurrection or rebellion against the same, or given aid or comfort to the enemies thereof. But Congress may, by a vote of two thirds of each house, remove such disability.

Section 4

The validity of the public debt of the United States, authorized by law, including debts incurred for payment of pensions and bounties for services in suppressing insurrection or rebellion, shall not be questioned. But neither the United States nor any State shall assume or pay any debt or obligation incurred in aid of insurrection or rebellion against the United States, or any claim for the loss of emancipation of any slave; but all such debts, obligations and claims shall be held illegal and void.

Section 5

The Congress shall have power to enforce, by appropriate legislation, the provisions of this article.

Fifteenth Amendment

Section 1

The right of citizens of the United States to vote shall not be denied or abridged by the United States or by any State on account of race, color, or previous condition of servitude.

Section 2

The Congress shall have power to enforce this article by appropriate legislation.

THE PRESIDENTS OF THE UNITED STATES

Results of presidential elections, and selected cabinet officials

Cross-references to the main text are indicated in SMALL CAPITALS.

For full explanations of the ELECTORAL COLLEGE and POPULAR VOTE, see the relevant entries in the main text of the dictionary.

George WASHINGTON

independent-Federalist 1st president, *served* April 30 1789–March 4 1797 (two terms)

Washington's administrations were dominated by the emergence of factional disputes between DEMOCRATIC-REPUBLICANS and Federalists which were exacerbated by his handling of GENÊT'S MISSION, the NEUTRALITY PROCLAMATION, the WHISKEY REBELLION and JAY'S TREATY.

result of the presidential election of 1789
Washington was the unanimous first choice of all 69 members of the electoral college; 34 members nominated John ADAMS as their second preference.

result of the presidential election of 1792
George Washington, independent–Federalist, 132 votes in the electoral college.

Washington was the unanimous first choice of an electoral college whose membership had been increased by the admission of new states and the conclusion of the first federal census; 77 members of the elec-toral college nominated John ADAMS as their second preference; 50 chose George Clinton (1739– 1812).

vice president
John ADAMS, *served* 1789–97

secretary of state
(1) Thomas JEFFERSON, *served* 1790–3
(2) Edmund Jennings Randolph (1753–1813), *served* 1794–5
(3) Timothy PICKERING, *served* 1795–7

secretary of the treasury
(1) Alexander HAMILTON, *served* 1789–95
(2) Oliver Wolcott (1760–1833), *served* 1795–7

secretary of war
(1) Henry Knox (1750–1806), *served* 1789–94
(2) Timothy PICKERING, *served* January–December 1795
(3) James McHenry (1753–1826), *served* 1796–7

John ADAMS

Federalist 2nd president, *served* March 4 1797–March 4 1801

Adams's administration was dominated by the QUASI-WAR with France and by a furore over the ALIEN AND SEDITION ACTS.

result of the presidential election of 1796
John Adams, Federalist, 71 electoral college

votes; Thomas Jefferson, Democratic-Republican, 68 votes.

vice president
Thomas JEFFERSON, *served* 1797–1801

secretary of state
(1) Timothy PICKERING, *served* 1797–1800
(2) John MARSHALL, *served* 1800–1

secretary of the treasury
(1) Oliver Wolcott (1760–1833), *served* 1797–1800
(2) Samuel Dexter (1761–1816), *served* January–May 1801

scecretary of war
(1) James McHenry (1753–1816), *served* 1797–1800
(2) Samuel Dexter (1761–1816), *served* 1800–1

Thomas JEFFERSON

Democratic-Republican 3rd president, *served* March 4 1801–March 4 1809 (two terms)

Jefferson's administrations were dominated by international affairs and continued partisan wrangling. Jefferson concluded the LOUISIANA PURCHASE.

result of the PRESIDENTIAL ELECTION OF 1800
Thomas Jefferson, 73 electoral college votes; Aaron BURR, also Democratic-Republican, 73 votes; John ADAMS, Federalist, 65 votes, Charles Cotesworth Pinckney (1746–1825), Federalist, 64 votes, John JAY, Federalist, 1 vote. Since Jefferson and Burr received an equal number of electoral votes, the election was decided in the House of Representatives.

result of the presidential election of 1804
Thomas Jefferson, Democratic-Republican, 162 electoral college votes; Charles Cotesworth Pinckney, Federalist, 14 votes. This was the first presidential election held after ratification of the TWELFTH AMENDMENT

clarifying procedures in the electoral college.

vice president
(1) Aaron BURR, *served* 1801–5
(2) George Clinton (1793–1812), *served* 1805–9

secretary of state
James MADISON, *served* 1801–9

secretary of the treasury
(1) Samuel Dexter (1761–1816), *served* 1801
(2) Albert Gallatin (1761–1849), *served* 1801–9

secretary of war
Henry Dearborn (1751–1829), *served* 1801–9

James MADISON

Democratic-Republican 4th president, *served* March 4 1809–March 4 1817 (two terms)

Madison's administrations were dominated by international affairs and the WAR OF 1812.

result of the presidential election of 1808
James Madison, 122 electoral college votes; Charles Cotesworth Pinckney (1746–1825), Federalist, 47 votes; George Clinton (1739–1812), Democratic-Republican, 6 votes.

result of the presidential election of 1812
James Madison, Democratic–Republican, 128 electoral college votes; De Witt Clinton (1769–1828), Federalist, 89 votes.

vice president
(1) George Clinton (1739–1812), *served* 1805–12
(2) Elbridge Gerry (1744–1814), *served* 1813–14
Both Clinton and Gerry died in office.

secretary of state
(1) Robert Smith (1757–1842), *served* 1809–11
(2) James MONROE, *served* 1811–17

secretary of the treasury
(1) Albert Gallatin (1761–1849), *served* 1809–14
(2) George W. Campbell (1769–1848), served February–October 1814
(3) Alexander Dallas (1759–1817), *served* 1814–16
(4) William H. Crawford (1772–1834), *served* 1816–17

secretary of war
(1) William Eustis (1753–1825), *served* 1809–12
(2) John Armstrong (1758–1843), *served* 1813–14
(3) James MONROE, *served* 1814–15
(4) William H. Crawford (1772–1834), served 1815–16

secretary of the navy
(1) Paul Hamilton (1762–1816), *served* 1809–12
(2) William Jones (1760–1831), *served* 1813–14
(3) Benjamin Crowninshield (1772–1851), *served* 1815–17
   Hamilton was an alcoholic ill-equipped to deal with the challenges of the WAR OF 1812. Jones performed ably.

James MONROE
Democratic 5th president,
served March 4 1817–March 4 1825 (two terms)

Monroe presided over a period of reduced partisan tension dubbed the 'era of good feelings'.

result of the presidential election of 1816
James Monroe, 183 electoral college votes; Rufus King (1755–1827), Federalist, 34 votes.

result of the presidential election of 1820
James Monroe, Democratic, 231 electoral college votes; John Quincy ADAMS, independent– Democratic, 1 vote.

vice president
Daniel D. Tompkins (1774–1825), *served* 1817–25
   Crushed by debt, Tompkins turned to the bottle and sometimes presided over the Senate while drunk.

secretary of state
John Quincy ADAMS, *served* 1817–25

secretary of the treasury
William H. Crawford (1772–1834), *served* 1817–25

secretary of war
John C. CALHOUN, *served* 1817–25

John Quincy ADAMS
independent-Democratic 6th president,
served March 4 1825–March 4 1829

Adams's administration was dominated by the fall-out from the 'CORRUPT BARGAIN' OF 1824.

result of the presidential election of 1824
John Quincy Adams, independent–Democratic, 108,740 votes (30.5% of the total cast), 84 electoral college votes; Andrew JACKSON, Democratic, 153,544 votes (43.1% of the total), 99 electoral votes; Henry CLAY, Democratic, 47,136 votes (13.2% of the total), 37 electoral votes; William H. Crawford (1772–1834), Democratic, 46,618 votes (13.1% of the total), 41 electoral votes.
   No candidate achieved a majority in the electoral college, so the election was decided in the House of Representatives.

vice president
John C. CALHOUN, *served* 1825–9

secretary of state
Henry CLAY, *served* 1825–9

secretary of the treasury
Richard Rush (1790–1859), *served* 1825–9

secretary of war
(1) James Barbour (1775–1842), *served* 1825–8

(2) Peter B. Porter (1773–1844), *served* 1828–9

Andrew JACKSON

Democratic 7th president, *served* March 4 1829–March 4 1837 (two terms)

Jackson's administrations were dominated by battles of the recharter of the second BANK OF THE UNITED STATES, the NULLIFICATION CRISIS, the Peggy EATON affair and the INDIAN REMOVAL ACT.

result of the presidential election of 1828
Andrew Jackson, Democratic, 647,502 votes (56% of the total cast), 178 electoral college votes; John Quincy ADAMS, National Republican, 530,189 votes (44% of the total), 83 electoral college votes.

result of the presidential election of 1832
Andrew Jackson, Democratic, 687,502 votes (55% of the total cast), 219 electoral college votes; Henry CLAY, National Republican, 530,189 votes (42.4% of the total), 49 electoral college votes; others, 18 electoral college votes.

vice president
(1) John C. CALHOUN, *served* 1829–32
(2) Martin VAN BUREN, *served* 1833–7
In December 1832 Calhoun became the first serving vice president in US history to resign.

secretary of state
(1) Martin VAN BUREN, *served* 1829–31
(2) Edward Livingston (1764–1836), *served* 1831–3
(3) Louis McLane (1786–1857), *served* 1833–4
(4) John Forsyth (1780–1841), *served* 1834–7

secretary of the treasury
(1) Samuel D. Ingham (1779–1860), *served* 1829–31
(2) Louis McLane (1786–1857), *served* 1831–3

(3) William J. Duane (1780–1865), *served* June–September 1833
(4) Levi Woodbury (1789–1851), *served* 1834–7
McLane and Duane were reassigned for refusing Jackson's demand that they withdraw federal deposits from the second BANK OF THE UNITED STATES.

secretary of war
(1) John Eaton (1790–1856), *served* 1829–31
(2) Lewis Cass (1782–1866), *served* 1831–6

Martin VAN BUREN

Democratic 8th president, *served* March 4 1837–March 4 1841

Van Buren's administration was dominated by the DEPRESSION OF 1837.

result of the presidential election of 1836
Martin Van Buren, Democratic, 765,483 votes (51% of the total cast), 170 electoral college votes; William Henry HARRISON, Whig, 548,007 votes (36% of the total), 73 electoral college votes; Hugh Lawson White (1773–1840), Whig, 145,396 votes (10% of the total), 26 electoral college votes; Daniel WEBSTER, Whig, 42,247 votes (3% of the total), 14 electoral college votes.

vice president
Richard Mentor JOHNSON, *served* 1837–41
Johnson is the only US vice president to have been elected by the US Senate.

Secretary of state
John Forsyth (1780–1841), *served* 1837–41

secretary of the treasury
Levi Woodbury (1789–1851), *served* 1837–41

secretary of war
Joel R. Poinsett (1779–1851), *served* 1837–41
An accomplished botanist, Poinsett introduced the poinsettia to the USA.

William Henry HARRISON

Whig 9th president,
served March 4–April 4 1841

Harrison was the first president to die in office.

result of the presidential election of 1840
William Henry Harrison, Whig, 1,274,624 votes (53% of the total cast), 234 electoral college votes; Martin VAN BUREN, Democratic, 1,127,781 votes (47% of the total cast), 60 electoral college votes.

vice president
John TYLER

secretary of state
Daniel WEBSTER

secretary of the treasury
Thomas Ewing (1789–1871)

secretary of war
John Bell (1797–1869)

John TYLER,

Whig 10th president,
served April 6 1841–March 4 1845

Tyler was the first vice president to accede to the presidency on the death of an incumbent. By returning all mail addressed to the 'acting president', Tyler established the principle that a promoted vice president enjoys the full power and status of the presidency. Tyler's administration was blighted by the mass resignation of his cabinet in September 1841, in protest at his abandonment of WHIG policies.

vice president
Tyler served without a vice president

secretary of state
(1) Daniel WEBSTER, *served* 1841–3
(2) Abel P. Upshur (1790–1884), *served* 1843–4
(3) John C. CALHOUN, *served* 1844–5

secretary of the treasury
(1) Thomas Ewing (1789–1871), *served* April–September 1841
(2) Walter Forward (1786–1852), *served* 1841–3
(3) John C. Spencer (1788–1855), *served* 1843–4
(4) George M. Bibb (1776–1859), *served* 1844–5

secretary of war
(1) John Bell (1797–1869), *served* April–September 1841
(2) John C. Spencer (1788–1855), *served* 1841–3
(3) William Wilkins (1779–1865), *served* 1844–5

James POLK

Democratic 11th president,
served March 4 1845–March 4 1849

Polk's administration was dominated by the MEXICAN WAR.

result of the presidential election of 1844
James Polk, Democratic, 1,338,464 votes (50% of the total cast), 170 electoral college votes; Henry CLAY, Whig, 1,300,097 votes (48% of the total), 105 electoral college votes; James Birney (1792–1857), Liberty Party, 62,300 votes (2% of the total), no electoral college votes.

vice president
George Mifflin Dallas (1792–1864), *served* 1845–9

secretary of state
James BUCHANAN, *served* 1845–9

secretary of the treasury
Robert J. Walker (1801–69), *served* 1845–9

secretary of war
William L. Marcy (1786–1857), *served* 1845–9

secretary of the navy
(1) George BANCROFT, *served* 1845–6
(2) John Y. Mason (1799–1859), *served* 1846–9

Zachary TAYLOR

Whig 12th president,
served March 5 1849–July 9 1850

During his brief administration Taylor held out against passage of the COMPROMISE OF 1850.

result of the presidential election of 1848
Zachary Taylor, Whig, 1,360,967 votes (47% of the total cast), 163 electoral college votes; Lewis Cass (1782–1866), Democratic, 1,222,342 votes (42.5% of the total), 127 electoral college votes; Martin VAN BUREN, Free Soil Party, 291,263 (10% of the total), no electoral college votes.

This was the first presidential election in which voting took place nationwide on the same day.

vice president
Millard FILLMORE, *served* 1849–50

secretary of state
John M. Clayton (1796–1856), *served* 1849–50

secretary of the treasury
William M. Meredith (1799–1873), *served* 1849–50

secretary of war
George W. Crawford (1798–1872), *served* 1849–50

secretary of the interior
Thomas Ewing (1789–1871), *served* 1849–50
The department of the Interior was created by act of Congress on March 3 1849.

Millard FILLMORE

Whig 13th president,
served July 10 1850–March 4 1853

Fillmore was the second man to accede to the presidency on the death of an incumbent. His administration was dominated by the growing crisis over slavery.

vice president
Fillmore served without a vice president

secretary of state
(1) Daniel WEBSTER, *served* 1850–2
(2) Edward Everett (1794–1865), *served* 1852–3

secretary of the treasury
Thomas Corwin (1794–1865), *served* 1850–3

secretary of war
Charles M. Conrad (1804–78), *served* 1850–3

secretary of the interior
(1) Thomas M. T. McKennan (1794–1852), *served* August 1850
(2) Alexander H. H. Stuart (1807–91), *served* 1850–3

Franklin PIERCE

Democratic 14th president,
served March 4 1853–March 4 1857

Pierce's administration was dominated by the KANSAS–NEBRASKA ACT and a furore over the OSTEND MANIFESTO.

result of the presidential election of 1852
Franklin Pierce, Democratic, 1,601,117 votes (51% of the total cast), 254 electoral college votes; Winfield SCOTT, Whig, 1,385,453 votes (44% of the total), 42 electoral college votes; John P. Hale (1806–73), Free Soil Party, 155,825 votes (5% of the total), no electoral college votes.

vice president
William Rufus DeVane King (1786–1853), served March–April 1853
The oath of office was administered to King in Cuba, where the vice president elect was seeking relief from tuberculosis. He

returned to the USA but died before assuming his duties.

secretary of state
William L. Marcy (1786–1857), *served* 1853–7

secretary of the treasury
James Guthrie (1792–1869), *served* 1853–7

secretary of war
Jefferson DAVIS, *served* 1853–7

secretary of the interior
Robert McClelland (1807–80), *served* 1853–7

James BUCHANAN
Democratic 15th president,
served March 4 1857–March 4 1861

Buchanan's administration was dominated by the growing crisis over slavery. Buchanan is the only life-long bachelor to have occupied the White House.

result of the presidential election of 1856
James Buchanan, Democratic, 1,832,955 votes (45% of the total cast), 174 electoral college votes; John C. FREMONT, Republican, 1,339,932 votes (33% of the total), 114 electoral college votes; Millard FILLMORE, Know Nothing and Whig, 871,731 votes (22% of the total), 8 electoral college votes.

vice president
John Cabell BRECKINRIDGE, *served* 1857–61

secretary of state
(1) Lewis Cass (1782–1866), *served* 1857–60
(2) Jeremiah S. Black (1810–83), *served* 1860–1

secretary of the treasury
(1) Howell Cobb (1815–68), *served* 1857–60
(2) Philip F. Thomas (1810–90), *served* 1860–1
(3) John A. Dix (1798–1879), *served* January–March 1861

secretary of war
(1) John B. Floyd (1807–63), *served* 1857–60

(2) Joseph Holt (1807–94), *served* January–March 1861

secretary of the interior
Jacob Thompson (1810–85), *served* 1857–61

Abraham LINCOLN
Republican 16th president,
served March 4 1861–April 15 1865

Lincoln is commonly adjudged the greatest of US presidents. He was the first president to die at the hands of an assassin.

result of the PRESIDENTIAL ELECTION OF 1860
Abraham Lincoln, Republican, 1,865,593 votes (40% of the total cast), 180 electoral college votes; Stephen DOUGLAS, Democratic, 1,382,713 votes (30% of the total), 12 electoral college votes; John C. BRECKINRIDGE, Democratic, 848,356 votes (18% of the total), 72 electoral college votes; John Bell (1797–1869), Constitutional Union Party, 592,906 votes (12% of the total), 39 electoral college votes.

result of the PRESIDENTIAL ELECTION OF 1864
Abraham Lincoln, Republican, 2,206,938 votes (55% of the total cast), 212 electoral college votes; George B. McCLELLAN, Democratic, 1,803,787 votes (45% of the total), 21 electoral college votes.

vice president
(1) Hannibal Hamlin (1809–91), *served* 1861–5
(2) Andrew JOHNSON, *served* March 4–April 15 1865

secretary of state
William Henry SEWARD, *served* 1861–5

secretary of the treasury
(1) Salmon P. CHASE, *served* 1861–4
(2) William P. Fessenden (1806–69), *served* 1864–5
(3) Hugh McCulloch (1808–95), *served* 1865

secretary of war
(1) Simon Cameron (1799–1889), *served* 1861–2
(2) Edwin M. STANTON, *served* 1862–5

secretary of the navy
Gideon Welles (1802–78), *served* 1861–5

secretary of the interior
(1) Caleb B. Smith (1808–64), *served* 1861–2
(2) John P. Usher (1816–89), *served* 1863–5

Andrew JOHNSON
independent–Democratic 17th president, *served* April 15 1865–March 3 1869

Johnson acceded to the presidency following the assassination of Abraham LINCOLN. Johnson's administration was dominated by RECONSTRUCTION. He was the first president to be the subject of an IMPEACHMENT trial.

vice president
Johnson served without a vice president

secretary of state
William H. SEWARD, *served* 1865–9

secretary of the treasury
Hugh McCulloch (1808–95), *served* 1865–9

secretary of war
(1) Edwin M. STANTON, *served* 1865–8
(2) John M. Schofield (1831–1906), *served* 1868–9

secretary of the interior
(1) John P. Usher (1816–89), *served* 1865
(2) James Harlan (1820–99), *served* 1865–6
(3) Orville H. Browning (1806–81), *served* 1866–9

Ulysses S. GRANT
Republican 18th president, *served* March 4 1869–March 4 1877 (two terms)

Grant's administrations were dominated by RECONSTRUCTION and corruption.

result of the presidential election of 1868
Ulysses S. Grant, Republican, 3,013,421 votes (52% of the total cast), 214 electoral college votes; Horatio Seymour (1810–86), Democratic, 2,703,249 (47% of the total), 80 electoral college votes.

result of the presidential election of 1872
Ulysses S. Grant, Republican, 3,597,070 votes (56% of the total cast), 286 electoral college votes; Horace GREELEY, Liberal Republican and Democratic, 2,834,079 votes (44% of the total), 66 electoral college votes.
   Greeley died after the general election but before the electoral votes were cast. The electoral college distributed Greeley's electoral votes among minority candidates.

vice president
(1) Schuyler Colfax (1823–1885), *served* 1869–73
(2) Harry Wilson (1812–75), *served* 1873–5
   Colfax was heavily implicated in the CRÉDIT MOBILIER SCANDAL. Wilson died in office.

secretary of state
(1) Elihu B. Washburne (1816–87), *served* March 5–March 16 1869
(2) Hamilton Fish (1808–93), *served* 1869–77

secretary of the treasury
(1) George S. Boutwell (1818–1905), *served* 1869–73
(2) William A. Richardson (1821–96), *served* 1873–4
(3) Benjamin H. Bristow (1832–96), *served* 1874–6
(4) Lot M. Morrill (1812–83), *served* 1876–7

secretary of war
(1) John A. Rawlins (1831–69), *served* March–September 1869
(2) William T. SHERMAN, *served* September–October 1869

(3) William W. Belknap (1829–1890), *served* 1869–76

(4) Alphonso Taft (1810–91), *served* March–May 1876

(5) James D. Cameron (1833–1918), *served* 1876–7

Belknap was impeached by the US Senate on bribery charges.

secretary of the interior
(1) Jacob D. Cox (1828–1900), *served* 1869–70
(2) Columbus Delano (1809–96), *served* 1870–5
(3) Zachariah Chandler (1813–79), *served* 1875–7

Rutherford HAYES

Republican 19th president,
served March 4 1877–March 4 1881

Hayes's administration was dominated by the developing SILVER–GOLD CONTROVERSY.

result of the PRESIDENTIAL ELECTION OF 1876
Rutherford B. Hayes, Republican, 4,036,572 votes (48% of the total cast), 185 electoral college votes; Samuel J. Tilden (1814–86), Democratic, 4,284,020 votes (51% of the total), 184 electoral college votes.

Hayes was awarded the presidency by a 15-man electoral commission appointed by Congress.

vice president
William Almon Wheeler (1819–87), *served* 1877–81

secretary of state
William M. Evarts (1818–1901), *served* 1877–81

secretary of the treasury
John Sherman (1823–1900), *served* 1877–81

secretary of war
(1) George W. McCrary (1835–90), *served* 1877–9

(2) Alexander Ramsey (1815–1903), *served* 1879–81

secretary of the interior
Carl Schurz (1829–1906), *served* 1877–81

James A. GARFIELD

Republican 20th president,
served March 4 1881–September 19 1881

Garfield was the second president to die at the hands of an assassin.

result of the presidential election of 1880
James A. Garfield, Republican, 4,453,295 votes (48.5% of the total cast), 214 electoral college votes; Winfield S. Hancock (1824–1886), Democratic, 4,414,082 votes (48.1% of the total), 155 electoral college votes; James B. WEAVER, Greenback–Labor, 308,578 votes, no electoral college votes

vice president
Chester A. ARTHUR, *served* March 4 1881–September 20 1881

secretary of state
James G. BLAINE, *served* 1881

secretary of the treasury
William Windom (1827–1891), *served* 1881

secretary of war
Robert T. Lincoln (1843–1926), *served* 1881
The son of Abraham LINCOLN.

secretary of the interior
Samuel J. Kirkwood (1813–94), *served* 1881

Chester A. ARTHUR

Republican 21st president,
served September 20 1881–March 4 1885

Arthur acceded to the presidency following the assassination of James A. GARFIELD. Arthur's administration was marked by battles over civil-service reform and TARIFFS.

vice president
Arthur served without a vice president

secretary of state
(1) James G. BLAINE, *served* September–
December 1881
(2) Frederick T. Freylinghuysen (1817–85),
served 1881–5

secretary of the treasury
(1) William Windom (1827–91), *served*
September–November 1881
(2) Charles J. Folger (1818–84), *served* 1881–4
(3) Walter Q. Gresham (1832–95), *served*
September–October 1884
(4) Hugh McCulloch (1808–95), *served*
1884–5

secretary of war
Robert T. Lincoln (1843–1926), *served* 1881–5
The son of Abraham LINCOLN.

secretary of the interior
(1) Samuel J. Kirkwood (1813–94), *served*
1881–2
(2) Henry M. Teller (1830–1914), *served*
1882–5

Grover CLEVELAND

Democratic 22nd president,
served March 4 1885–March 4 1889

Cleveland interrupted a long sequence of
Republican administrations.

result of the presidential election of 1884
Grover Cleveland, Democratic, 4,879,507
votes (48.5% of the total cast), 219 electoral
college votes; James G. BLAINE, Republican,
4,851,981 votes (48.2% of the total), 182
electoral college votes; Benjamin F. Butler
(1818–93), Greenback–Labor, 175,370 votes,
no electoral college votes.
    During the election campaign Cleveland
admitted fathering a child out of wedlock.

vice president
Thomas Andrews Hendricks (1819–85),
served March–December 1885

secretary of state
Thomas F. Bayard (1828–98), *served* 1885–9

secretary of the treasury
(1) Daniel Manning (1831–87), *served*
1885–7
(2) Charles S. Fairchild (1842–1924), *served*
1887–9

secretary of war
William C. Endicott (1826–1900), *served*
1885–9

secretary of the interior
(1) Lucius Q. C. Lamar (1825–93), *served*
1885–8
(2) William F. Vilas (1840–1908), *served*
1888–9

secretary of agriculture
Norman J. Colman (1827–1911), *served*
1889
    The department of Agriculture was
created in 1862 and raised to cabinet status
on February 11 1889.

Benjamin HARRISON

Republican 23rd president,
served March 4 1889–March 3 1893

Harrison's administration was dominated
by TRUSTS, TARIFFS and the SILVER–GOLD
CONTROVERSY.

result of the presidential election of 1888
Benjamin Harrison, Republican, 5,447,129
votes (48% of the total cast), 233 electoral
college votes; Grover CLEVELAND,
Democratic, 5,537,857 (48.6% of the total),
168 electoral college votes.

vice president
Levi Parsons Morton (1825–1920), *served*
1889–93

secretary of state
(1) James G. BLAINE, *served* 1889–92
(2) John W. Foster (1836–1917), *served*
1892–3

secretary of the treasury
(1) William Windom (1827–91), *served*
1889–91
(2) Charles Foster (1828–1904), *served* 1891–3

secretary of war
(1) Redfield Proctor (1831–1908), *served*
1889–91
(2) Stephen B. Elkins (1841–1911), *served*
1891–3

secretary of the interior
John W. Noble (1831–1912), *served* 1889–93

secretary of agriculture
Jeremiah M. Rusk (1830–93), *served* 1889–93

Grover CLEVELAND

Democratic 24th president,
served March 4 1893–March 4 1897

Cleveland was the first president to serve
two non-consecutive terms

result of the presidential election of 1892
Grover Cleveland, Democrat, 5,555,425
votes (46% of the total cast), 277 electoral
college votes; Benjamin HARRISON, Republican,
5,182,690 votes (43% of the total), 145
electoral college votes; James B. WEAVER,
People's Party, 1,029,846 votes (8.5% of the
total), 22 electoral college votes.

vice president
Adlai Ewing Stevenson (1835–1914), *served*
1893–7

secretary of state
(1) Walter Q. Gresham (1832–95), *served*
1893–5
(2) Richard Olney (1835–1917), *served* 1895–7

secretary of the treasury
John G. Carlisle (1835–1910), *served* 1893–7
Became known as the 'Judas of Kentucky'
for his position in the SILVER–GOLD
CONTROVERSY.

secretary of war
Daniel S. Lamont (1851–1905), *served* 1893–7

secretary of the interior
(1) Hoke Smith (1855–1931), *served* 1893–6
(2) David R. Francis (1850–1927), *served*
1896–7

secretary of agriculture
J. Sterling Morton (1832–1902), *served*
1893–7

William McKINLEY

Republican 25th president,
served March 4 1897–September 14 1901

McKinley's administrations were dominated
by the SPANISH-AMERICAN WAR and the
SILVER–GOLD CONTROVERSY. He was the third
US president to be assassinated.

result of the presidential election of 1896
William McKinley, Republican, 7,102,246
votes (51% of the total cast), 271 electoral
college votes; William Jennings BRYAN,
Democratic, 6,492,559 votes (47.7% of the
total), 176 electoral college votes.

result of the presidential election of 1900
William McKinley, Republican, 7,218,491
votes (51% of the total cast), 292 electoral
college votes; William Jennings BRYAN,
Democratic, 6,356,734 votes (45% of the
total), 155 electoral college votes.

vice president
(1) Garret Augustus Hobart (1844–99), *served*
1897–9
(2) Theodore ROOSEVELT, *served* March–
September 1901
Hobart died in office.

secretary of state
(1) John Sherman (1823–1900), *served* 1897–8
(2) William R. Day (1849–1923), *served* April–September 1898
(3) John M. Hay (1838–1905), *served* 1898–1901

secretary of the treasury
Lyman J. Gage (1836–1927), *served* 1897–1901

secretary of war
(1) Russell A. Alger (1836–1907), *served* 1897–9
(2) Elihu Root (1845–1937), *served* 1899–1901

secretary of the interior
(1) Cornelius N. Bliss (1833–1911), *served* 1897–8
(2) Ethan A. Hitchcock (1835–1909), *served* 1898–1901

secretary of agriculture
James Wilson (1835–1920), *served* 1897–1901

Theodore ROOSEVELT
Republican 26th president,
served September 14 1901–March 4 1909

Roosevelt acceded to the presidency following the assassination of William MCKINLEY. Roosevelt's administrations were dominated by foreign affairs and a battle against TRUSTS.

result of the presidential election of 1904
Theodore Roosevelt, Republican, 7,628,461 votes (58% of the total cast), 336 electoral college votes; Alton B. Parker (1852–1926), Democratic, 5,084,223 votes (37.6% of the total), 140 electoral college votes; Eugene V. DEBS, Socialist, 402,283 votes (3% of the total), no electoral college votes.

vice president
Charles Warren Fairbanks (1852–1918), *served* 1905–9

secretary of state
(1) John M. Hay (1838–1905), *served* 1901–5
(2) Elihu Root (1845–1937), *served* 1905–9

secretary of the treasury
(1) Lyman J. Gage (1836–1927), *served* 1901–2
(2) Leslie M. Shaw (1848–1932), *served* 1902–7
(3) George B. Cortelyou (1862–1940), *served* 1907–9

secretary of war
(1) Elihu Root (1845–1937), *served* 1901–4
(2) William Howard TAFT, *served* 1904–8
(3) Luke E. Wright (1846–1922), *served* 1908–9

secretary of the interior
(1) Ethan A. Hitchcock (1835–1909), *served* 1901–7
(2) James R. Garfield (1865–1950), *served* 1907–9

secretary of agriculture
James Wilson (1835–1920), *served* 1901–9

secretary of commerce and labor
(1) George B. Cortelyou (1862–1940), *served* 1903–4
(2) Victor H. Metcalf (1853–1936), *served* 1904–6
(3) Oscar S. Straus (1850–1926), *served* 1906–9

The department of Commerce and Labor was established by act of Congress on February 14 1903. Oscar S. Straus was the first Jewish man to serve in the cabinet.

William H. TAFT
Republican 27th president,
served March 4 1909–March 4 1913

Taft is the only man to have served as president of the USA and chief justice of the Supreme Court (*see* Appendix 3).

result of the presidential election of 1908
William H. Taft, Republican, 7,675,320
votes (52% of the total cast), 321 electoral
college votes; William Jennings BRYAN,
Democratic, 6,412,294 votes (43% of the
total), 162 electoral college votes; Eugene
DEBS, Socialist, 420,793 votes (3% of the
total), no electoral college votes.

vice president
James Schoolcraft Sherman (1855–1912),
served 1909–12

secretary of state
Philander C. Knox (1853–1921), *served*
1909–13

secretary of the treasury
Franklin MacVeagh (1837–1934), *served*
1909–13

secretary of war
(1) Jacob M. Dickinson (1851–1928), *served*
1909–11
(2) Henry L. STIMSON, *served* 1911–13

secretary of the interior
(1) Richard A. Ballinger (1858–1922), *served*
1909–11
(2) Walter L. Fisher (1862–1935), *served*
1911–13

secretary of agriculture
James Wilson (1835–1920), *served* 1909–13

secretary of commerce and labor
Charles Nagel (1849–1940), *served* 1909–13

Woodrow WILSON
Democratic 28th president,
served March 4 1913–March 3 1921 (two
terms)

Wilson's administrations were dominated
by WORLD WAR I and his battle to persuade
Congress to accept the LEAGUE OF NATIONS.

result of the PRESIDENTIAL ELECTION OF 1912
Woodrow Wilson, Democratic, 6,296,547
votes (42% of the total cast), 435 electoral
college votes; Theodore ROOSEVELT,
Progressive, 4,118,571 votes (27.4% of the
total), 88 electoral college votes; William H.
TAFT, Republican, 3,436,720 votes (23% of
the total), 8 electoral college votes; Eugene
DEBS, Socialist, 900,672 votes (6% of the
total), no electoral college votes.

result of the presidential election of 1916
Woodrow Wilson, Democratic, 9,127,695
votes (50% of the total cast), 277 electoral
college votes; Charles Evans HUGHES,
Republican, 8,533,507 votes (46% of the
total), 254 electoral college votes.

vice president
Thomas Riley Marshall (1854–1925), *served*
1913–21
   Marshall became famous for suggesting,
'What this country needs is a really good
five-cent cigar.'

secretary of state
(1) William Jennings BRYAN, *served* 1913–15
(2) Robert Lansing (1864–1928), *served*
1915–20
(3) Bainbridge Colby (1869–1950), *served*
1920–1

secretary of the treasury
(1) William G. McAdoo (1863–1941), *served*
1913–18
(2) Carter Glass (1858–1946), *served* 1918–20
(3) David Houston (1866–1940), *served*
1920–1

secretary of war
(1) Lindley M. Garrison (1864–1932), *served*
1913–16
(2) Newton D. Baker (1871–1937), *served*
1916–21

secretary of the navy
Josephus Daniels (1862–1948), *served*
1913–21

secretary of the interior
(1) Franklin K. Lane (1864–1921), *served* 1913–20
(2) John B. Payne (1855–1935), *served* 1920–1

secretary of agriculture
(1) David F. Houston (1866–1940), *served* 1913–20
(2) Edwin T. Meredith (1876–1928), *served* 1920–1

Meredith later founded the magazine *Better Homes and Gardens*.

secretary of commerce
(1) William C. Redfield (1858–1932), *served* 1913–19
(2) Joshua W. Alexander (1852–1936), *served* 1919–21

secretary of labor
William B. Wilson (1862–1934), *served* 1913–21

The department of Labor was established as an agency independent of the department of Commerce by act of Congress on March 4 1913.

Warren G. HARDING

Republican 29th president,
served March 4 1921–August 2 1923

Harding's administration was wracked by corruption. He died in office.

result of the presidential election of 1920
Warren G. Harding, Republican, 16,143,407 votes (60.4% of the total cast), 404 electoral college votes; James M. Cox (1870–1957), Democratic, 9,130,328 votes (34.2 % of the total), 127 electoral college votes; Eugene DEBS, Socialist, 919,799 votes (3.4% of the total), no electoral college votes.

vice president
Calvin COOLIDGE, *served* 1921–3

secretary of state
Charles Evans HUGHES, *served* 1921–3

secretary of the treasury
Andrew Mellon (1855–1937), *served* 1921–3

secretary of war
John W. Weeks (1860–1926), *served* 1921–3

secretary of the interior
Albert B. Fall (1861–1944), *served* 1921–3
Fall was heavily implicated in the TEAPOT DOME SCANDAL.

secretary of agriculture
Henry C. Wallace (1866–1924), *served* 1921–3

secretary of commerce
Herbert HOOVER, *served* 1921–3

secretary of labor
James J. Davis (1873–1947), *served* 1921–3

Calvin COOLIDGE

Republican 30th president,
served August 3 1923–March 3 1929

Coolidge acceded to the presidency following the death of Warren G. HARDING. His administrations were unremarkable.

result of the presidential election of 1924
Calvin Coolidge, Republican, 15,718,211 votes (54% of the total cast), 382 electoral college votes; John W. Davis (1873–1955), Democratic, 8,385,283 votes (28% of the total), 136 electoral college votes; Robert M. LAFOLLETTE, Progressive, 4,831,289 votes (16.6% of the total), 13 electoral college votes.

vice president
Charles Gates Dawes (1865–1951), *served* 1925–9

secretary of state
(1) Charles Evans HUGHES, *served* 1923–5
(2) Frank B. Kellogg (1856–1937), *served* 1925–9

secretary of the treasury
Andrew W. Mellon (1855–1937), served
1923–9

secretary of war
(1) John W. Weeks (1860–1926), served 1923–5
(2) Dwight F. Davis (1879–1945), served
1925–9
   A keen tennis player, Davis donated the
cup to the international tennis tournament
that commemorates his name.

secretary of the interior
(1) Hubert Work (1860–1942), served 1923–8
(2) Roy O. West (1868–1958), served 1928–9

secretary of agriculture
(1) Henry C. Wallace (1866–1924), served
1923–4
(2) Howard M. Gore (1877–1947), served
1924–5
(3) William M. Jardine (1879–1955), served
1925–9

secretary of commerce
(1) Herbert HOOVER, served 1923–8
(2) William Whiting (1864–1936), served
1928–9

secretary of labor
James J. Davis (1873–1947), served 1923–9

Herbert HOOVER
Republican 31st president,
served March 4 1929–March 4 1933

Hoover's administration was overshadowed
by the WALL STREET CRASH and the GREAT
DEPRESSION.

result of the presidential election of 1928
Herbert Hoover, Republican, 21,391,993
votes (58% of the total cast), 444 electoral
college votes; Al SMITH, Democratic,
15,016,169 votes (41% of the total), 87
electoral college votes; Norman THOMAS,
Socialist, 267,835 votes (0.7% of the total),
no electoral college votes.

vice president
Charles Curtis (1860–1936), served 1929–33

secretary of state
Henry L. STIMSON, served 1929–33

secretary of the treasury
(1) Andrew W. Mellon (1855–1937), served
1921–32
(2) Ogden L. Mills (1884–1937), served
1932–3

secretary of war
(1) James W. Good (1866–1929), served
March–November 1929
(2) Patrick J. Hurley (1883–1963), served
1929–33

secretary of the interior
Ray Lyman Wilbur (1875–1949), served
1929–33

secretary of agriculture
Arthur M. Hyde (1877–1947), served 1929–33

secretary of commerce
(1) Robert P. Lamont (1867–1948), served
1929–32
(2) Roy D. Chapin (1880–1936), served
1932–3

secretary of labor
(1) James J. Davis (1873–1947), served
1929–32
(2) William N. Doak (1882–1933), served
1930–3

Franklin D. ROOSEVELT
Democratic 32nd president,
served March 4 1933–April 12 1945 (three
full terms)

Roosevelt enacted the NEW DEAL and led the
USA in WORLD WAR II. He is the longest-
serving president in US history. He died in
office before completing an unprecedented
fourth term.

result of the PRESIDENTIAL ELECTION OF 1932
Franklin D. Roosevelt, Democratic,
22,829,501 votes (57% of the total cast), 472
electoral college votes; Herbert HOOVER,
Republican, 15,760,684 votes (40% of the
total), 59   electoral college votes; Norman
THOMAS, Socialist, 881,951 votes (2.2% of
the total), no electoral college votes.

result of the presidential election of 1936
Franklin D. Roosevelt, Democratic,
27,757,333 votes (60.8% of the total cast),
523 electoral college votes; Alfred M. LANDON,
Republican, 16,684,231 votes (36.5% of the
total), 8 electoral college votes; William Lemke
(1878–1950), Union Party, 892,267 votes
(2% of the total), no electoral college votes.

result of the presidential election of 1940
Franklin D. Roosevelt, Democratic,
27,313,041 votes (54% of the total cast), 449
electoral college votes; Wendell L. Willkie
(1892– 1944), Republican, 22,348,480 votes
(44% of the total), 82 electoral college votes.

result of the presidential election of 1944
Franklin D. Roosevelt, Democratic,
25,612,610 votes (53.5% of the total cast),
432 electoral college votes; Thomas E.
Dewey (1902–71), Republican, 22,017,617
votes (46% of the total), 99 electoral college
votes.

vice president
(1) John Nance Garner (1868–1967), *served*
1933–41
(2) Henry A. WALLACE, *served* 1941–5
(3) Harry S TRUMAN, *served* January–April
1945
   Garner is remembered for saying: 'The
vice-presidency isn't worth a bucket of
warm spit.'

secretary of state
(1) Cordell HULL, *served* 1933–44
(2) Edward R. Stettinius (1900–49), *served*
1944–5

secretary of the treasury
(1) William H. Woodin (1868–1934), *served*
March–December 1933
(2) Henry Morgenthau (1891–1967), *served*
1934–45

secretary of war
(1) George H. Dern (1872–1936), *served*
1933–6
(2) Harry H. Woodring (1890–1967), *served*
1936–40
(3) Henry L. STIMSON, *served* 1940–5

secretary of the navy
(1) Claude A. Swanson (1862–1939), *served*
1933–9
(2) Charles Edison (1890–1969), *served*
January–June 1940
(3) Frank Knox (1874–1944), *served* 1940–4
(4) James V. Forrestal (1892–1949), *served*
1944–5

secretary of the interior
Harold L. Ickes (1874–1952), *served* 1933–46

secretary of agriculture
(1) Henry A. WALLACE, *served* 1933–40
(2) Claude R. Wickard (1893–1967), *served*
1940–5

secretary of commerce
(1) Daniel C. Roper (1867–1943), *served*
1933–8
(2) Harry L. Hopkins (1890–46), *served*
1938–40
(3) Jesse H. Jones (1874–1956), *served*
1940–5
(4) Henry A. WALLACE, *served* 1945–6

secretary of labor
Frances PERKINS, *served* 1933–45
Perkins was the first woman to serve in the
cabinet.

Harry S TRUMAN
Democratic 33rd president,
served April 12 1945–January 20 1953

Vice president Truman acceded to the presidency following the death of the incumbent Franklin D. ROOSEVELT. Truman's administrations were dominated by the COLD WAR and the KOREAN WAR.

result of the PRESIDENTIAL ELECTION OF 1948
Harry Truman, Democratic, 24,179,345 votes (49.5% of the total cast), 303 electoral college votes; Thomas Dewey (1902–71), Republican, 21,991,291 votes (45% of the total), 189 electoral college votes; Strom Thurmond (1903–), States' Rights–Democratic, 1,176,125 votes (2.4% of the total), 39 electoral college votes; Henry A. WALLACE, Progressive, 1,157,326 votes (2.4% of the total), no electoral college votes; Norman THOMAS, Socialist, 139,572 votes.

vice president
Alben William Barkley (1877–1956), *served* 1949–53

During his first term Truman served without a vice president.

secretary of state
(1) Edward R. Stettinius (1900–49), *served* 1944–5
(2) James F. Byrnes (1879–1972), *served* 1945–7
(3) George C. MARSHALL, *served* 1947–9
(4) Dean ACHESON, *served* 1949–53

secretary of the treasury
(1) Henry Morgenthau (1891–1967), *served* 1945
(2) Frederick M. Vinson (1890–1953), *served* 1945–6
(3) John W. Snyder (1896–1985), *served* 1946–53

Vinson resigned to become chief justice of the US Supreme Court.

secretary of war
(1) Henry STIMSON, *served* 1945
(2) Robert P. Patterson (1891–1952), *served* 1945–7

(3) Kenneth C. Royall (1894–1995), *served* July–September 1947

Patterson urged the creation of a new integrated department of Defense which superseded the departments of War and the Navy.

secretary of defense
(1) James V. Forrestal (1892–1949), *served* 1947–9
(2) Louis A. Johnson (1891–1966), *served* 1949–50
(3) George C. MARSHALL, *served* 1950–51
(4) Robert A. Lovett (1895–1986), *served* 1951–3

The department of Defense was created by act of Congress on August 10 1949. Between 1947 and 1949 the secretary of defense held cabinet rank while the reorganization of the Navy and War departments proceeded.

secretary of the interior
(1) Harold L. Ickes (1874–1952), *served* 1933–1946
(2) J. A. Krug (1907–70), *served* 1946–9
(3) Oscar L. Chapman (1896–1978), *served* 1949–53

secretary of agriculture
(1) Claude R. Wickard (1893–1967), *served* 1940–5
(2) Clinton P. Anderson (1895–1975), *served* 1945–8
(3) Charles F. Brannan (1903–92), *served* 1948–53

secretary of commerce
(1) Henry A. WALLACE, *served* 1945–6
(2) W. Averell Harriman (1891–1986), *served* 1946–8
(3) Charles Sawyer (1887–1979), *served* 1948–53

secretary of labor
(1) Frances PERKINS, *served* 1945
(2) Louis B. Schwellenbach (1894–1948), *served* 1945–8
(3) Maurice J. Tobin (1901–1953), *served* 1948–53

Dwight D. EISENHOWER

Republican 34th president,
served January 20 1953–January 20 1961
(two terms)

Eisenhower's administrations were dominated by the COLD WAR.

result of the presidential election of 1952
Dwight D. Eisenhower, Republican, 33,936,234 votes (55.1% of the total cast), 442 electoral college votes; Adlai STEVENSON, Democratic, 27,314,992 votes (44.4% of the total), 89 electoral college votes.

result of the presidential election of 1956
Dwight D. Eisenhower, Republican, 35,590,472 votes (57.6% of the total cast), 457 electoral college votes; Adlai STEVENSON, Democratic, 26,022,752 votes (42.1% of the total), 73 electoral college votes.

vice president
Richard M. NIXON, *served* 1953–61

secretary of state
(1) John Foster DULLES *served* 1953–9
(2) Christian A. Herter (1895–1967), *served* 1959–61

secretary of the treasury
(1) George M. Humphrey (1890–1970), *served* 1953–7
(2) Robert B. Anderson (1910–1989), *served* 1957–61

secretary of defense
(1) Charles E. Wilson (1890–1961), *served* 1953–7
(2) Neil H. McElroy (1904–72), *served* 1957–9
(3) Thomas S. Gates (1906–83), *served* 1959–61

Wilson is remembered for declaring at his confirmation hearing: 'For years I thought what was good for our country was good for General Motors and vice versa'.

secretary of the interior
(1) Douglas McKay (1893–1959), *served* 1953–6
(2) Frederick A. Seaton (1909–74), *served* 1956–61

secretary of agriculture
Ezra Taft Benson (1899–94), *served* 1953–61

secretary of commerce
(1) Sinclair Weeks (1893–1972), *served* 1953–8
(2) Lewis Strauss (1896–1914) *served* 1958–9
(3) Frederick H. Mueller (1893–1976), *served* 1959–61

secretary of labor
(1) Martin P. Durkin (1894–1955), *served* January–September 1953
(2) James P. Mitchell (1900–64), *served* 1953–61

secretary of health, education and welfare
(1) Oveta Culp Hobby (1905–95), *served* 1953–5
(2) Marion B. Fulsom (1893–1976), *served* 1955–8
(3) Arthur S. Flemming (1905–96), *served* 1958–61

The department of Health, Education and Welfare was created by act of Congress on April 1 1953.

John F. KENNEDY

Democratic 35th president,
served January 20 1961–November 22 1963

Kennedy faced the CUBAN MISSILE CRISIS. His assassination shocked the world.

result of the PRESIDENTIAL ELECTION OF 1960
John F. Kennedy, Democratic, 34,226,721 votes (49.9% of the total cast), 303 electoral college votes; Richard NIXON, Republican, 34,108,157 votes (49.9% of the total), 219 electoral college votes. Although not a declared candidate, Senator Harry Byrd of Virginia was awarded 15 electoral college votes.

vice president
Lyndon JOHNSON, *served* 1961–3

secretary of state
Dean Rusk (1909–94), *served* 1961–3

secretary of the treasury
C. Douglas Dillon (1909–), *served* 1961–3

secretary of defense
Robert McNAMARA, *served* 1961–3

secretary of the interior
Stewart L. Udall (1920–), *served* 1961–9

secretary of agriculture
Orville L. Freeman (1918–), *served* 1961–3

secretary of commerce
Luther H. Hodges (1898–1974), *served* 1961–3

secretary of labor
(1) Arthur J. Goldberg (1908–90), *served* 1961–2
(2) W. Williard Wirtz (1912–), *served* 1962–3

secretary of health, education and welfare
(1) Abraham Ribicoff (1910–98), *served* 1961–2
(2) Anthony J. Celebrezze (1910–98), *served* 1962–3

Lyndon B. JOHNSON

Democratic 36th president,
served November 22 1963–January 20 1969

Johnson acceded to the presidency following the assassination of John F. KENNEDY. He pushed the CIVIL RIGHTS ACT OF 1964 and the GREAT SOCIETY programme through Congress but escalated the VIETNAM WAR.

result of the presidential election of 1964
Lyndon Johnson, Democratic, 43,129,484 votes (61% of the total cast), 486 electoral college votes; Barry GOLDWATER, Republican, 27,178,188 votes (38% of the total), 52 electoral college votes.

vice president
Hubert HUMPHREY, *served* 1965–9
    During his first term Johnson served without a vice president.

secretary of state
Dean Rusk (1909–94), *served* 1963–9

secretary of the treasury
(1) C. Douglas Dillon (1909–), *served* 1963–5
(2) Henry H. Fowler (1908–), *served* 1965–8
(3) Joseph W. Barr (1918–96), *served* December 1968–January 1969

secretary of defense
(1) Robert McNAMARA, *served* 1961–8
(2) Clark M. Clifford (1906–98), *served* 1968–9

secretary of the interior
Stewart L. Udall (1920–), *served* 1963–9

secretary of agriculture
Orville L. Freeman (1918–), *served* 1963–9

secretary of commerce
(1) Luther H. Hodges (1898–1974), *served* 1963–5
(2) John T. Connor (1914–), *served* 1965–7
(3) Alexander B. Trowbridge (1929–), *served* 1967–8
(4) Cyrus R. Smith (1899–1990), *served* 1968–9

secretary of labor
W. Willard Wirtz (1912–), *served* 1963–9

secretary of health, education and welfare
(1) Anthony J. Celebrezze (1910–98), *served* 1963–5
(2) John W. Gardner (1912–), *served* 1965–8
(3) Wilbur J. Cohen (1913–87), *served* 1968–9

secretary of housing and urban development
(1) Robert C. Weaver (1907–97), *served* 1966–9
    Weaver was the first African-American to serve in the cabinet. The department of Housing and Urban Development was created by act of Congress on September 9 1965.

Richard M. NIXON

Republican 37th president,
served January 20 1969–August 9 1974

Nixon's administrations were dominated by the VIETNAM WAR and the WATERGATE SCANDAL. He resigned the presidency to escape IMPEACHMENT.

result of the PRESIDENTIAL ELECTION OF 1968
Richard M. Nixon, Republican, 31,785,480 votes (43.5% of the total cast), 301 electoral college votes; Hubert HUMPHREY, Democratic, 31,270, 533 votes (42.7% of the total), 191 electoral college votes; George WALLACE, American Independent, 9,906,141 votes (13.5% of the total), 46 electoral college votes.

result of the PRESIDENTIAL ELECTION OF 1972
Richard M. Nixon, Republican, 47,169,911 votes (60.7% of the total cast), 520 electoral college votes; George McGOVERN, Democratic, 29,170,383 votes (37.5% of the total), 17 electoral college votes.

vice president
(1) Spiro T. AGNEW, *served* 1969–73
(2) Gerald FORD, *served* December 6 1973–August 9 1974
   Agnew resigned in 1973, the first vice president since John C. CALHOUN to do so. Ford was the first vice president appointed under the terms of the TWENTY-FIFTH AMENDMENT.

secretary of state
(1) William P. Rogers (1913–), *served* 1969–73
(2) Henry KISSINGER, *served* 1973–4

secretary of the treasury
(1) David M. Kennedy (1905–96), *served* 1969–71
(2) John B. Connally (1917–93), *served* 1971–2
(3) George P. Schultz (1920–), *served* 1972–4
(4) William E. Simon (1927– 2000), *served* 1974

secretary of defense
(1) Melvin Laird (1922–), *served* 1969–73

(2) Elliot L. Richardson (1920–99), *served* January–May 1973
(3) James R. Schlesinger (1929–), *served* 1973–4

secretary of the interior
(1) Walter J. Hickel (1919–), *served* 1969–70
(2) Rogers C. B. Morton (1914–79), *served* 1971–4

secretary of agriculture
(1) Clifford M. Hardin (1915–), *served* 1969–71
(2) Earl L. Butz (1909–), *served* 1971–4

secretary of commerce
(1) Maurice H. Stans (1908–98), *served* 1969–72
(2) Peter G. Peterson (1926–), *served* 1972–3
(3) Frederick B. Dent (1922–), *served* 1973–4

secretary of labor
(1) George P. Schultz (1920–), *served* 1969–70
(2) James D. Hodgson (1915–), *served* 1970–3
(3) Peter J. Brennan (1918–), *served* 1973–4

secretary of health, education and welfare
(1) Robert H. Finch (1925–), *served* 1969–70
(2) Elliot L. Richardson (1920–99), *served* 1970–73
(3) Caspar W. Weinberger (1917–), *served* 1973–5

secretary of housing and urban development
(1) George Romney (1907–95), *served* 1969–73
(2) James T. Lynn (1927–), *served* 1974–5

Gerald FORD

Republican 38th president,
served August 9 1974–January 20 1977

Ford acceded to the presidency following the resignation of Richard M. NIXON, thus becoming the first man to occupy the positions of vice president and president without winning an election. Ford's administration was dominated by inflation and the fall-out from the VIETNAM WAR and WATERGATE.

vice president
Nelson A. ROCKEFELLER, *served* 1974–7. Rockefeller was appointed under the terms of the TWENTY-FIFTH AMENDMENT.

secretary of state
Henry KISSINGER, *served* 1974–7

secretary of the treasury
William E. Simon (1927–2000), *served* 1974–7

secretary of defense
(1) James R. Schlesinger (1929–), *served* 1974
(2) Donald S. Rumsfeld (1932–), *served* 1975–7

secretary of the interior
(1) Rogers C. B. Morton (1914–79), *served* 1971–5
(2) Stanley K. Hathaway (1924–), *served* June–July 1975
(3) Thomas S. Kleppe (1919–), *served* 1976–7

secretary of agriculture
(1) Earl S. Butz (1909–), *served* 1974–6
(2) John A. Knebel (1936–), *served* 1976–7

secretary of commerce
(1) Frederick B. Dent (1922–), *served* 1974–5
(2) Rogers C. B. Morton (1914–79), *served* April–December 1975
(3) Elliot L. Richardson (1920–99), *served* 1975–7

secretary of labor
(1) Peter J. Brennan (1918–), *served* 1973–5
(2) John T. Dunlop (1914–), *served* 1975–6
(3) W. J. Usery (1923–), *served* 1976–7

secretary of health, education and welfare
(1) Caspar W. Weinberger (1917–), *served* 1973–5
(2) F. David Matthews (1935–), *served* 1975–7

secretary of housing and urban development
(1) James T. Lynn (1927–), *served* 1974–5
(2) Carla A. Hills (1934–), *served* 1975–7

Jimmy CARTER

Democratic 39th president,
served January 20 1977–January 20 1981

Carter's administration was dominated by the poor performance of the domestic economy and the IRANIAN HOSTAGE CRISIS.

result of the presidential election of 1976
Jimmy Carter, Democratic, 40,830,763 votes (50% of the total cast), 297 electoral college votes; Gerald FORD, Republican, 39,147,973 votes (48% of the total), 241 electoral college votes.

vice president
Walter MONDALE, *served* 1977–81

secretary of state
(1) Cyrus R. Vance (1917–), *served* 1977–80
(2) Edmund Muskie (1914–96), *served* 1980–1

secretary of the treasury
(1) W. Michael Blumenthal (1926–), *served* 1977–9
(2) G. William Miller (1925–), *served* 1979–81

secretary of defense
Harold Brown (1927–), *served* 1977–81

secretary of the interior
Cecil D. Andrus (1931–), served 1977–81

secretary of agriculture
Robert S. Bergland (1928–), *served* 1977–81

secretary of commerce
(1) Juanita M. Kreps (1921–), *served* 1977–9
(2) Philip M. Klutznick (1907–99), *served* 1980–1
Kreps had previously been the first woman to head the New York Stock Exchange. She resigned for personal reasons.

secretary of labor
F. Ray Marshall (1928–), *served* 1977–81

secretary of health, education and welfare
(1) Joseph A. Califano (1931–), *served* 1977–9

On October 17 1979 the department of Health, Education and Welfare was reorganized by an act of Congress which created the department of Health and Human Services and a separate department of Education. Patricia Roberts HARRIS served as secretary of health and human services 1979–81.

secretary of housing and urban development
(1) Patricia Roberts HARRIS, *served* 1977–9
(2) Moon Landrieu (1930–), *served* 1979–81

secretary of education
Shirley M. Hufstedler (1925–), *served* 1979–81

The department of Education was created from the old department of Health, Education and Welfare by act of Congress on October 17 1979.

Ronald REAGAN

Republican 40th president.
served January 20 1981–January 20 1989 (two terms)

Reagan was the oldest man ever elected president and the first divorced man to gain the presidency. His administrations were dominated by a structural transformation of the US economy, a defense build-up and the IRAN–CONTRA SCANDAL.

result of the presidential election of 1980
Ronald Reagan, Republican, 43,899,248 votes (50.7% of the total cast), 489 electoral college votes; Jimmy CARTER, Democratic, 36,481,435 votes (41% of the total), 49 electoral college votes; John B. Anderson (1922–), independent, 5,719,437 votes (6.6% of the total), no electoral college votes.

Result of the presidential election of 1984
Ronald Reagan, Republican, 54,455,075 votes (59% of the total cast), 525 electoral college votes; Walter MONDALE, Democratic, 37,577,185 votes (41% of the total), 13 electoral college votes.

vice president
George BUSH, *served* 1981–9

secretary of state
(1) Alexander M. Haig (1924–), *served* 1981–2
(2) George P. Schultz (1920–), *served* 1982–9

secretary of the treasury
(1) Donald T. Regan (1918–), *served* 1981–5
(2) James A. Baker (1930–), *served* 1985–8
(3) Nicholas A. Brady (1930–), *served* 1988–9

secretary of defense
(1) Caspar A. Weinberger (1917–), *served* 1981–7
(2) Frank C. Carlucci (1930–), *served* 1987–9

secretary of the interior
(1) James G. Watt (1938–), *served* 1981–3
(2) William P. Clark (1930–), *served* 1983–5
(3) Donald P. Hodel (1935–), *served* 1985–9

Watt attempted to open national parks to business development and argued that trees caused pollution.

secretary of agriculture
(1) John R. Block (1935–), *served* 1981–6
(2) Richard E. Lyng (1918–), *served* 1986–9

secretary of commerce
(1) Malcolm Baldridge (1922–87), *served* 1981–7
(2) C. William Verity (1917–), *served* 1987–9

secretary of labor
(1) Raymond J. Donovan (1930–), *served* 1981–5
(2) William E. Brock (1930–), *served* 1985–7
(3) Anne Dore McLoughlin (1941–), *served* 1987–9

In 1985 Donovan became the first cabinet member ever indicted on criminal charges while in office. He was charged with fraud and larceny relating to a construction project completed before he took office. He resigned following his indictment and was later acquitted.

secretary of health and human services
(1) Richard S. Schweiker (1926–), *served* 1981–3
(2) Margaret M. Heckler (1931–), *served* 1983–5
(3) Otis M. Bowen (1918–), *served* 1985–9

secretary of housing and urban development
Samuel R. Pierce (1922–), *served* 1981–9
   Reagan bumped into 'Silent Sam' Pierce, an African-American, five months after his appointment and failed to recognize him.

secretary of education
(1) Terrel H. Bell (1922–96), *served* 1981–5
(2) William J. Bennet (1943–), *served* 1985–8
(3) Lauro F. Cavazos (1927–), *served* 1988–9

George BUSH

Republican 41st president,
served January 20 1989–January 20 1993

Bush was the first serving vice president to be elected to the White House since Martin VAN BUREN. His administration was dominated by foreign affairs, particularly the PERSIAN GULF WAR.

result of the presidential election of 1988
George Bush, Republican, 48,886,097 votes (54% of the total cast), 426 electoral college votes; Michael DUKAKIS, Democratic, 41,809,074 votes (46% of the total), 111 electoral college votes.

vice president
Dan QUAYLE, *served* 1989–93

secretary of state
(1) James A. Baker (1930–), *served* 1989–92
(2) Lawrence S. Eagleburger (1930–), *served* 1992–3

secretary of the treasury
Nicholas S. Brady (1930–), *served* 1989–93

secretary of defense
Richard Cheney (1941–), *served* 1989–93

secretary of the interior
Manuel Lujan (1928–), *served* 1989–93

secretary of agriculture
(1) Clayton Yuetter (1930–), *served* 1989–91
(2) Edward Madigan (1936–), *served* 1991–3

secretary of commerce
(1) Robert Mossbacher (1927–), *served* 1989–92
(2) Barbara H. Franklin (1940–), *served* 1992–3

secretary of labor
(1) Elizabeth Dole (1936–), *served* 1989–90
(2) Lynn Martin (1939–93), *served* 1990–3

secretary of health and human services
Louis Sullivan (1933–), *served* 1989–93

secretary of housing and urban development
Jack Kemp (1935–), *served* 1989–93

secretary of education
(1) Lauro F. Cavazos (1927–), *served* 1989–90
(2) Lamar Alexander (1940–), *served* 1991–3

Bill CLINTON

Democratic 42nd president,
served January 20 1993–

Clinton is the only elected president to have faced an IMPEACHMENT trial.

result of the presidential election of 1992
Bill Clinton, Democratic, 44,908,254 votes (43% of the total cast), 370 electoral college votes; George BUSH, Republican, 38,102,343 votes (37% of the total), 168 electoral college votes; H. Ross PEROT, United We Stand America, 19,742,165 votes (19% of the total), no electoral college votes.

Perot's showing was the best by any third-party candidate since the PRESIDENTIAL ELECTION OF 1912.

result of the presidential election of 1996
Bill Clinton, Democratic, 45,238,951 votes, (50% of the total cast), 379 electoral college votes; Bob DOLE, Republican, 37,607,011 votes (41% of the total), 159 electoral college votes; H. Ross PEROT, Independent, 7,807,588 votes (8.5% of the total), no electoral college votes.

vice president
Al GORE, *served* 1993–

secretary of state
(1) Warren M. Christopher (1925–), *served* 1993–7
(2) Madeleine ALBRIGHT, *served* 1997–

secretary of the treasury
(1) Lloyd Bentsen (1921–), *served* 1993–5
(2) Robert E. Rubin (1938–), *served* 1995–9
(3) Lawrence H. Summers (1954–), *served* 1999–

secretary of defense
(1) Les Aspin (1938–95), *served* 1993–4
(2) William J. Perry (1927–) *served* 1994–7
(3) William S. Cohen (1940–), *served* 1997–

secretary of the interior
Bruce Babbit (1938–), *served* 1993–

secretary of agriculture
(1) Mike Espy (1953–), *served* 1993–5
(2) Dan Glickman (1944–), *served* 1995–

secretary of commerce
(1) Ronald H. Brown (1941–96), *served* 1993–6
(2) Mickey Kantor (1939–), *served* 1996–7
(3) William H. Daley (1948–), *served* 1997–

secretary of labor
(1) Robert B. Reich (1946–), *served* 1993–7
(2) Alexis M. Herman (1948–), *served* 1997–
Alexis Herman is the first African-American to head the department of Labor.

secretary of health and human services
Donna E. Shalala (1941–), *served* 1993–

secretary of housing and urban development
(1) Henry G. Cisneros (1947–), *served* 1993–7
(2) Andrew Cuomo (1957–), *served* 1997–

MEMBERSHIP OF THE UNITED STATES SUPREME COURT

Cross-references to articles in the main text are indicated in SMALL CAPITALS. Chief justices are highlighted in *italics*.

John JAY, nominated by George WASHINGTON, served 1789–95, *chief justice* 1789–95.

James Wilson (1742–98), nominated by George Washington, served 1789–98.

John Rutledge (1739–1800), nominated by George Washington, served 1790–1 (acting *chief justice* 1795, confirmation rejected by US Senate).

William Cushing (1732–1810), nominated by George Washington, served 1790–1810.

John Blair (1732–1800), nominated by George Washington, served 1790–6.

James Iredell (1751–99), nominated by George Washington, served 1790–9. Iredell's lone dissenting opinion in CHISHOLM VS. GEORGIA formed the basis of the ELEVENTH AMENDMENT.

Thomas Johnson (1732–1819), nominated by George Washington, served 1791–3.

William Paterson (1745–1806), nominated by George Washington, served 1793–1806.

Samuel Chase (1741–1811), nominated by George Washington, served 1796–1811.

Oliver Ellsworth (1745–1807), nominated by George Washington, served 1796–1800, *chief justice* 1796–1800.

Bushrod Washington (1762–1829), nominated by John ADAMS, served 1799–1829 (the nephew of George Washington).

Alfred Moore (1755–1810), nominated by John Adams, served 1799–1804.

John MARSHALL, nominated by John Adams, served 1801–35, *chief justice* 1801–35.

William Johnson (1771–1834), nominated by Thomas JEFFERSON, served 1804–34.

Brockholst Livingston (1757–1823), nominated by Thomas Jefferson, served 1806–23.

Thomas Todd (1765–1826), nominated by Thomas Jefferson, served 1807–26.

Joseph Story (1779–1845), nominated by James MADISON, served 1811–45.

Gabriel Duval (1752–1844), nominated by James Madison, served 1812–1835.

Smith Thompson (1768–1843), nominated by James MONROE, served 1823–43.

Robert Trimble (1776–1828), nominated by John Quincy ADAMS, served 1826–8.

John McLean (1785–1861), nominated by Andrew JACKSON, served 1829–61. McLean's dissenting opinion in DRED SCOTT VS. SANDFORD was hailed by supporters of ABOLITION.

Henry Baldwin (1780–1844), nominated by Andrew Jackson, served 1830–44.

James Wayne (1790–1867), nominated by Andrew Jackson, served 1835–67.

Philip P. Barbour (1783–1841), nominated by Andrew Jackson, served 1836–41.

Roger B. TANEY, nominated by Andrew Jackson, *chief justice* 1836–64.

John Catron (1786–1865), nominated by Andrew Jackson, served 1837–65.

John McKinley (1780–1852), nominated by Martin VAN BUREN, served 1837–52.

Peter V. Daniel (1784–1860), nominated by Martin Van Buren, served 1841–60.

Samuel Nelson (1792–1873), nominated by John TYLER, served 1845–72.

Levi Woodbury (1789–1851), nominated by James POLK, served 1845–51.

Robert C. Grier (1794–1870), nominated by James Polk, served 1846–70.

Benjamin R. Curtis (1809–74), nominated by Millard FILLMORE, served 1851–7.

John A. Campbell (1811–89), nominated by Franklin PIERCE, served 1853–61.

Nathan Clifford (1803–81), nominated by James BUCHANAN, served 1858–81.

Noah H. Swayne (1804–84), nominated by Abraham LINCOLN, served 1862–81.

Samuel F. Miller (1816–90), nominated by Abraham Lincoln, served 1862–90.

David DAVIS, nominated by Abraham Lincoln, served 1862–77.

Stephen J. Field (1816–99), nominated by Abraham Lincoln, served 1863–97.

Salmon P. Chase (1808–73), nominated by Abraham Lincoln, *chief justice* 1864–73. Chase presided over the IMPEACHMENT trial of Andrew JOHNSON.

William Strong (1808–95), nominated by Ulysses S. GRANT, served 1870–80.

Joseph P. Bradley (1813–92), nominated by Ulysses S. Grant, served 1870–92.

Ward Hunt (1810–86), nominated by Ulysses S. Grant, served 1873–82.

Morrison R. Waite (1816–88), nominated by Ulysses S. Grant, *chief justice* 1874–88.

John Marshall HARLAN, nominated by Rutherford B. HAYES, served 1877–1911.

William B. Woods (1824–87), nominated by Rutherford B. Hayes, served 1881–7.

Stanley Matthews (1824–89), nominated by James A. GARFIELD, served 1881–9.

Horace Gray (1828–1902), nominated by Chester A. ARTHUR, served 1882–1902.

Samuel Blatchford (1820–93), nominated by Chester A. Arthur, served 1882–93.

Lucius Q.C. Lamar (1825–93), nominated by Grover CLEVELAND, served 1888–93.

Melville W. Fuller (1833–1910), nominated by Grover Cleveland, *chief justice* 1888–1910. In 1895, Fuller delivered the majority opinion that struck down the federal INCOME TAX in the case of Pollock vs. Farmers' Loan and Trust Company.

David J. Brewer (1837–1910), nominated by Benjamin HARRISON, served 1889–1910.

Henry B. Brown (1836–1913), nominated by Benjamin Harrison, served 1891–1906.

George Shiras (1832–1924), nominated by Benjamin Harrison, served 1892–1903.

Howell E. Jackson (1832–95), nominated by Benjamin Harrison, served 1893–95.

Edward D. White (1845–1921), nominated by Grover CLEVELAND, served 1894–1921, *chief justice* 1910–21. White was the first chief justice to be appointed from within the Court.

Rufus W. Peckham (1838–1909), nominated by Grover Cleveland, served 1896–1909. Peckham delivered the majority opinion in LOCHNER VS. NEW YORK.

Joseph McKenna (1843–1926), nominated by William McKINLEY, served 1898–1925.

Oliver Wendell HOLMES, nominated by Theodore ROOSEVELT, served 1902–32.

William R. Day (1849–1923), nominated by Theodore Roosevelt, served 1903–22.

William H. Moody (1853–1917), nominated by Theodore Roosevelt, served 1906–10.

Horace H. Lurton (1844–1914), nominated by William Howard TAFT, served 1910–14.

Charles Evans HUGHES, nominated by William Howard Taft, served 1910–16, *chief justice* 1930–41.

Willis Van Devanter (1859–1941), nominated by William Howard Taft, served 1911–37.

Joseph R. Lamar (1857–1916), nominated by Wiliam Howard Taft, served 1911–16.

Mahlon Pitney (1858–1924), nominated by William Howard Taft, served 1912–22. Pitney delivered the majority opinion in DUPLEX PRINTING PRESS CO. VS. DEERING.

James C. McReynolds (1862–1946), nominated by Woodrow WILSON, served 1914–41.

Louis D. BRANDEIS, nominated by Woodrow Wilson, served 1916–39.

John H. Clarke (1857–1945), nominated by Woodrow Wilson, served 1916–22.

George Sutherland (1862–1942), nominated by Warren HARDING, served 1922–38.

Pierce Butler (1866–1939), nominated by Warren Harding, served 1922–39.

Edward T. Sanford (1865–1930), nominated by Warren Harding, served 1923–30.

Harlan Fiske Stone (1872–1946), nominated by Calvin COOLIDGE, served 1925–46, *chief justice* 1941–6.

Owen J. Roberts (1875–1955), nominated by Herbert HOOVER, served 1930–45.

Benjamin N. Cardozo (1870–1938), nominated by Herbert Hoover, served 1932–8.

Hugo Black (1886–1971), nominated by Franklin D. ROOSEVELT, served 1937–71.

Stanley F. Reed (1884–1980), nominated by Franklin D. Roosevelt, served 1938–57.

Felix Frankfurter (1882–1965), nominated by Franklin D. Roosevelt, served 1939–62.

William O. Douglas (1898–1980), nominated by Franklin D. Roosevelt, served 1939–75.

Frank Murphy (1890–1949), nominated by Franklin D. Roosevelt, served 1940–9.

James F. Byrnes (1879–1972), nominated by Franklin D. Roosevelt, served 1941–2.

Robert H. Jackson (1892–1954), nominated by Franklin D. Roosevelt, served 1941–54. Jackson took a sabbatical from the Court to serve as chief prosecutor in the Nuremberg trials of Nazi war criminals 1945–6.

Wiley B. Rutledge (1894–49), nominated by Franklin D. Roosevelt, served 1943–9.

Harold H. Burton (1888–1964), nominated by Harry TRUMAN, served 1945–58.

Frederick M. Vinson (1890–1953), nominated by Harry Truman, *chief justice* 1946–53.

Thomas C. Clark (1899–1977), nominated by Harry Truman, served 1949–67.

Sherman Minton (1890–1965), nominated by Harry Truman, served 1949–56.

Earl WARREN, nominated by Dwight D. EISENHOWER, *chief justice* 1954–69. Warren wrote the Court's opinion in the landmark civil rights case BROWN VS. BOARD OF EDUCATION OF TOPEKA.

John Marshall Harlan (1899–1971), nominated by Dwight D. Eisenhower, served 1955–71.

William J. Brennan (1906–97), nominated by Dwight D. Eisenhower, served 1956–90.

Charles E. Whittaker (1901–73), nominated by Dwight D. Eisenhower, served 1957–62.

Potter Stewart (1915–85), nominated by Dwight D. Eisenhower, served 1959–81.

Byron J. White (1917–98), nominated by John F. KENNEDY, served 1962–93.

Arthur J. Goldberg (1908–90), nominated by John F. Kennedy, served 1962–5.

Abe Fortas (1910–82), nominated by Lyndon B. JOHNSON, served 1965–9.

Thurgood MARSHALL, nominated by Lyndon B. Johnson, served 1967–91.

Warren E. Burger (1907–95), nominated by Richard M. NIXON, *chief justice* 1969–86.

Harry M. Blackmun (1908–), nominated by Richard M. Nixon, served 1970–94.

Lewis F. Powell (1907–), nominated by Richard M. Nixon, served 1971–87.

William H. Rehnquist (1924–), nominated by Richard M. Nixon, has served from 1972, *chief justice* since 1986. Rehnquist

presided over the IMPEACHMENT trial of Bill CLINTON.

John Paul Stevens (1920–), nominated by Gerald FORD, has served from 1975.

Sandra Day O'CONNOR, nominated by Ronald REAGAN, has served from 1981.

Antonin Scalia (1936–), nominated by Ronald Reagan, has served from 1986.

Anthony M. Kennedy (1936–), nominated by Ronald Reagan, has served from 1988.

David H. Souter (1939–), nominated by George BUSH, has served from 1990.

Clarence Thomas (1948–), nominated by George Bush, has served from 1991.

Ruth Bader Ginsburg (1933–) nominated by Bill CLINTON, has served from 1993.

Stephen Breyer (1938–), nominated by Bill Clinton, has served from 1994.

SUBJECT INDEX

The references in this index are to headwords in the Dictionary.

Entries may appear more than once under different subject headings.

Most subjects in this index are broken down into secondary themes indicated by **bold italics**. In most cases these secondary themes follow an alphabetical order, though in the case of the **Battles** category, the listing of themes is chronological by conflict; and in the **Biographies**, **Foreign relations**, **Political history** and **Women's history** categories, the listing of themes is chronological by period, followed by alphabetical by theme.

African-American history

Biographies: Ralph Abernathy; Muhammad Ali; Ella Baker; Benjamin Banneker; Stokeley Carmichael; Richard Davis; Frederick Douglass; W.E.B. Du Bois; Medgar Evers; Marcus Garvey; Fanny Lou Hamer; Patricia Roberts Harris; Jesse Jackson; Martin Luther King; Thurgood Marshall; James Meredith; Jesse Owens; Asa Philip Randolph; Hiram Revels; Paul Robeson; Jackie Robinson; Sojourner Truth; Harriet Tubman; Denmark Vesey; Booker T. Washington; Ida B. Wells-Barnett; Malcolm X.

General: Atlanta Exposition Speech; Black Power; buffalo soldiers; Civil Rights Movement; Detroit riot; graduate school cases; Great Migration; Harlem Renaissance; Jim Crow; lynching; Mississippi Freedom summer; Plessy vs. Ferguson; Scottsboro boys case; sharecropping; Springfield lynch riot; Tuskegee syphilis scandal; Watts riot.

Organizations: African Methodist Episcopal church; Black Panther Party; Congress of racial equality; Lowndes County Freedom Organization; Mississippi Freedom Democratic Party; National Association for the Advancement of Colored People; National Urban League; Nation of Islam; Niagara Movement.

Slavery and emancipation: abolition; Black codes; Contrabands; Davis Bend experiment; emancipation proclamation; exodusters; field order 15; forty acres and a mule; freedmen; gradual emancipation; Kansas–Nebraska act; manumission; Quok Walker case; Reconstruction; Nat Turner's revolt; sharecropping; underground railroad.

SLAVERY is a headword within the dictionary.

See also subject headings CIVIL RIGHTS MOVEMENT, RECONSTRUCTION and SLAVERY within this appendix.

American Revolution

Biographies: John Adams; Sam Adams; Ethan Allen; Benedict Arnold; Aaron Burr; George Rogers Clark; John Dickinson;

Benjamin Franklin; Horatio Gates; Alexander Hamilton; Patrick Henry; John Jay; Thomas Jefferson; John Paul Jones; Marquis de Lafayette; James Madison; Thomas Paine; Timothy Pickering; Paul Revere; Betsy Ross; George Washington.

Causes: Administration of Justice Act; American Board of Customs Act; Boston Port Bill; Currency Act; Declaratory Act; Dunmore's Proclamation; Intolerable Acts; Massachusetts Government Act; Proclamation of 1763; Quartering Acts; Quebec Act; Republican ideology; Stamp Act; Sugar Act; Tea Act; Townshend Revenue Act; vice-admiralty courts; virtue.

Organization of government: antifederalists; Annapolis Convention; Articles of Confederation; Confederation Congress; Constitutional Convention; Continental Congress; Declaration of Independence; federalism; *Federalist Papers*; Mount Vernon Conference; Northwest Ordinance; Ordinance of 1785; Virginia Statute for Religious Freedom.

Mediation: Carlisle Peace Commission; Olive-Branch petition.

Military issues: Cincinnati, Society of; Conway Cabal; Hessians; Minutemen; Morristown Mutiny; Newburgh Conspiracy; Revolutionary War; Valley Forge.

Popular protest: Boston Massacre; Boston Tea Party; Committees of Correspondence; *Common Sense*; Continental Association; *Gaspee,* burning of the; *Liberty* riot; Loyalists; Massachusetts Circular Letter; non-importation agreements; Paxton Boys; Regulator movements; Shays's Rebellion; Sons of Liberty; Suffolk Resolves; Stamp Act Congress; united empire loyalists.

AMERICAN REVOLUTION AND REVOLUTIONARY WAR are headwords within the dictionary. *See also* subject headings BATTLES; BIOGRAPHIES; BOOKS, PAMPHLETS, NEWSPAPERS AND JOURNALISM and TERRITORIAL EXPANSION within this appendix.

Battles

Revolutionary War: Bemis Heights; Bennington; Brandywine Creek; Bunker Hill; Camden; Charleston, siege of; Chesapeake Capes; Fort Stanwix; Fort Ticonderoga, US capture of; Germantown; Lexington and Concord; Long Island; Monmouth Court House; Paoli; New York City, British occupation of; Oriskany; Philadelphia, British occupation of; Princeton; Quebec, US campaign to capture; Saratoga, British surrender at; Savannah, British capture of; Sullivan's campaign; Trenton; White Plains; Yorktown, British surrender at.

War of 1812: Chippewa; Fort Toronto, US capture of; Lake Champlain; Lake Erie; New Orleans; Thames river; Tippecanoe Creek; Washington DC, British destruction of.

Pre-Civil War: Alamo; Buena Vista; Chapultepec; Monterrey; San Jacinto; Vera Cruz.

Civil War: Antietam; Atlanta; Chancellorsville; Chickamauga; Chattanooga; Cold Harbor; Fort Donnelson and Fort Henry, battles of; Fort Fisher, capture of; Fort Sumter, attack on; Franklin; Fredericksburg; Gettysburg; Manassas; Mobile Bay; *Monitor vs. Virginia*; Nashville; Peninsular campaign; Petersburg; Rich Mountain; Seven Days' battles; Shenandoah Valley campaigns; Shiloh; Spotsylvania Court House; Vicksburg, siege of; Wilderness.

Between US forces and Native Americans: Creek War; Fallen Timbers; Horseshoe Bend; Little Big Horn; Red River War; Seminole Wars; Sioux Wars; Winnebago War.

World War I: Meuse–Argonne offensive; St Mihiel offensive.

World War II: Bataan; Bulge; Coral Sea; Corregidor; D-Day landings; Guadalcanal campaign; Iwo Jima; Midway; Okinawa; Omaha Beach; Pearl Harbor, Japanese attack on; St Lô offensive; Tarawa Atoll.

Vietnam War: Ia Drang Valley; Khe Sanh, siege of; Operation Cedar Falls; Operation

Rolling Thunder; Tet offensive.

REVOLUTIONARY WAR, WAR OF 1812, MEXICAN WAR, SPANISH-AMERICAN WAR, WORLD WAR I, WORLD WAR II, KOREAN WAR, VIETNAM WAR and PERSIAN GULF WAR are headwords within the dictionary.

Biographies

American Revolution: John Adams; Sam Adams; Ethan Allen; Benedict Arnold; Aaron Burr; George Rogers Clark; John Dickinson; Benjamin Franklin; Horatio Gates; Alexander Hamilton; Patrick Henry; John Jay; Thomas Jefferson; John Paul Jones; Marquis de Lafayette; James Madison; Thomas Paine; Timothy Pickering; Paul Revere; Betsy Ross; George Washington.

Jacksonian America: John Calhoun; Peggy Eaton; Andrew Jackson; Richard Mentor Johnson.

Assassins and other criminals: John Wilkes Booth; Al Capone; Charles Guiteau; Lee Harvey Oswald.

Authors, inventors and educationalists: Horatio Alger; George Bancroft; Benjamin Banneker; Alexander Graham Bell; Rachel Carson; W.E.B. Du Bois; Thomas Edison; Daniel Coit Gilman; Cyrus McCormick; Samuel Finley Breese Morse; Noah Webster; Eli Whitney; Wilbur and Orville Wright.

civil rights campaigners: Ralph Abernathy; Ella Baker; Stokeley Carmichael; Cesar Chavez; Medgar Evers; Ernesto Galarza; Fanny Lou Hamer; Jesse Jackson; Martin Luther King; James Meredith; Malcolm X.

Explorers, pioneers and environmentalists: Daniel Boone; Rachel Carson; Davy Crockett; John Charles Frémont; Charles August Lindberg; Zebulon Pike; Gifford Pinchot; Brigham Young.

Industrialists and financiers: Andrew Carnegie; Henry Ford; J. P. Morgan; John D. Rockefeller.

Journalists, publishers and broadcasters: Charles Coughlin; Horace Greeley; William Randolph Hearst; Henry Robinson Luce; Joseph Pulitzer; Victoria Claflin Woodhull.

Jurists: Louis Brandeis; Salmon Chase; David Davis; John Marshall Harlan; Oliver Wendell Holmes; Charles Evans Hughes; John Jay; John Marshall; Thurgood Marshall; Sandra Day O'Connor; William Howard Taft; Roger Taney; Earl Warren.

Law enforcement: J. Edgar Hoover; Allan Pinkerton.

Military leaders: Omar Bradley; John Burgoyne; Ambrose Burnside; George Rogers Clark; Mark Clark; Henry Clinton; Charles Cornwallis; George Custer; Patrick Ferguson; Horatio Gates; Ulysses Grant; Joseph Hooker; Sir William Howe; Thomas 'Stonewall' Jackson; Joseph Johnston; Marquis de Lafayette; Robert E. Lee; Douglas MacArthur; George McClellan; George Meade; George Patton; Matthew Perry; John Pershing; Winfield Scott; Philip Sheridan; William Sherman; Frederick von Steuben; Zachary Taylor; William Westmoreland.

Native Americans: Joseph Brant; Cochise; John Collier; Geronimo; Alexander McGillvray; Osceola; the Prophet; John Ross; Sacajawea; Sitting Bull; Tecumseh.

Politicians and statesmen: Dean Acheson; Spiro Agnew; Madeleine Albright; John Peter Altgeld; Albert Beveridge; James Blaine; John Breckinridge; William Jennings Bryan; John Calhoun; Joseph Cannon; Salmon Chase; Henry Clay; Jefferson Davis; Eugene Debs; Bob Dole; Stephen Douglas; Michael Dukakis; John Foster Dulles; Geraldine Ferraro; John Charles Frémont; James William Fulbright; Barry Goldwater; Al Gore; Patricia Roberts Harris; Alger Hiss; Cordell Hull; Hubert Humphrey; John Jay; Hiram Warren Johnson; Richard Mentor Johnson; Edward Kennedy; Robert F. Kennedy; Jeane Duane Jordan Kirkpatrick; Henry Kissinger; Marquis de Lafayette;

Robert M. LaFollette; Alf Landon; Huey Long; Eugene McCarthy; Joseph McCarthy; George McClellan; George McGovern; Robert McNamara; George Marshall; Walter Mondale; George Norris; Frances Perkins; H. Ross Perot; J. Danforth Quayle; Hiram Revels; Nelson Rockefeller; Dean Rusk; William Henry Seward; Al Smith; Edwin Stanton; Thaddeus Stevens; Adlai Stevenson; Henry Stimson; Norman Thomas; George Wallace; Henry Wallace; Tom Watson; James B. Weaver; Daniel Webster.

Presidential candidates: James Blaine; John Breckinridge; William Jennings Bryan; Aaron Burr; Henry Clay; Eugene Debs; Bob Dole; Stephen Douglas; Michael Dukakis; John Charles Frémont; Barry Goldwater; Horace Greeley; Charles Evans Hughes; Hubert Humphrey; John Jay; Robert F. Kennedy; Robert M. LaFollette; Alf Landon; Eugene McCarthy; George McClellan; George McGovern; Walter Mondale; H. Ross Perot; Winfield Scott; Al Smith; Adlai Stevenson; Norman Thomas; George Wallace; Henry Wallace; Tom Watson; James B. Weaver Daniel Webster; Victoria Claflin Woodhull.

Presidents: John Adams; John Quincy Adams; Chester Arthur; James Buchanan; George Bush; Jimmy Carter; Grover Cleveland; Bill Clinton; Calvin Coolidge; Dwight D. Eisenhower; Millard Fillmore; Gerald Ford; James Garfield; Ulysses S. Grant; Warren Harding; Benjamin Harrison; William Henry Harrison; Rutherford B. Hayes; Herbert Hoover; Andrew Jackson; Thomas Jefferson; Andrew Johnson; Lyndon B. Johnson; John F. Kennedy; Abraham Lincoln; William McKinley; James Madison; James Monroe; Richard Nixon; Franklin Pierce; James Polk; Ronald Reagan; Franklin D. Roosevelt; Theodore Roosevelt; William Howard Taft; Zachary Taylor; Harry S. Truman; John Tyler; Martin Van Buren; George Washington; Woodrow Wilson.

Reformers and campaigners: Jane Addams; Susan Brownell Anthony; Clara Barton; Elizabeth Blackwell; Amelia Bloomer; Carrie Chapman Catt; Dorothea Dix; Frederick Douglass; Elizabeth Gurley Flynn; William Lloyd Garrison; Marcus Garvey; Emma Goldman; Julia Ward Howe; Helen Hunt Jackson; Mary 'Mother' Jones; Florence Kelley; Lucretia Mott; Carry Nation; Alice Paul; Jeanette Rankin; Hillary Rodham Clinton; Eleanor Roosevelt; Margaret Sanger; St Elizabeth Anne Seton; Anna Howard Shaw; Elizabeth Cady Stanton; Lucy Stone; Francis Townsend; Sojourner Truth; Harriet Tubman; Booker T. Washington; Ida B. Wells-Barnett; Victoria Claflin Woodhull.

Sports and entertainment: Muhammad Ali; Phineas Taylor Barnum; Buffalo Bill; Walt Disney; Jesse Owens; Elvis Presley; Paul Robeson; Jackie Robinson; Babe Ruth; Jim Thorpe.

Trade unionists: Richard Davis; Eugene Debs; Samuel Gompers; Jimmy Hoffa; John L. Lewis; Terrence Powderly; Asa Philip Randolph.

Books, pamphlets, newspapers and journalism

Common Sense; Federalist Papers; Letter from Birmingham City Jail; Letters from a Farmer in Pennsylvania; The Liberator; Miscegenation: The Theory of the Blending of the Races; muckrakers; *Notes on the State of Virginia; The Passing of the Great Race; The Shame of our Cities; South Carolina Exposition and Protest; The Theory of the Leisure Class; Uncle Tom's Cabin;* yellow journalism.

NEWSPAPERS is a headword within the   dictionary

Civil Rights Movement

Activists: Muhammad Ali; Ella Baker; Cesar Chavez; Medgar Evers; Ernesto Galarza; James Meredith; Malcolm X.

Background: Brown vs. Board of Education; citizens' councils; graduate school cases; Jim Crow; Plessy vs. Ferguson.

Campaigns: Albany desegregation campaign; Birmingham desegregation campaign; freedom riders; Greensboro sit-in; Little Rock school desegregation battle; March on Washington; Mississippi freedom summer; Montgomery bus boycott; Operation Breadbasket; Selma Freedom March.

Concepts and statements: affirmative action; black power; comparable worth; de facto segregation; 'I have a dream' speech; *Letter from Birmingham City Jail*.

Leaders: Ralph Abernathy; Stokeley Carmichael; Cesar Chavez; Jesse Jackson; Martin Luther King.

Legislative response to: Boynton vs. Virginia; bussing; Civil Rights Acts of 1957, 1960, 1964, 1968, 1970; Harper vs. Virginia Board of Elections; Heart of Atlanta Motel vs. US; Swann vs. Charlotte-Mecklenberg Board of Education; Voting Rights Act.

Organizations: Black Panther Party; Congress of Racial Equality; Lowndes County Freedom Organization; Mississippi Freedom Democratic Party; National Association for the Advancement of Colored People; Southern Christian Leadership Conference; Student Non-Violent Coordinating Committee.

CIVIL RIGHTS MOVEMENT is a headword within the dictionary. *See also* subject headings AFRICAN-AMERICAN HISTORY and BIOGRAPHIES within this appendix.

Civil War

Background: abolition; bleeding Kansas; border states; Brooks–Sumner incident; Christiana riot; Compromise of 1850; the Confederacy; Davis resolutions; Kansas–Nebraska act; Lecompton constitution; Mason–Dixon line; New York City draft riot; presidential election of 1860; slave power; Wilmot proviso.

Conclusion: Appomattox Court House; *River Queen* peace talks.

Diplomatic history: *Alabama* claims; Trent affair.

Military issues: Andersonville; contrabands; the draft; March to the Sea; Peninsular campaign; Quantrill's raiders.

Politics and government during: Conscription Act; Copperheads; Emancipation Proclamation; Ex Parte Merryman; Ex Parte Milligan; Gettysburg Address; ironclad oath; Legal Tender Acts; Abraham Lincoln; Peace Democrats; presidential election of 1864; Radical Republicans.

CIVIL WAR and RECONSTRUCTION are headwords within the dictionary. *See also* subject headings BATTLES, BIOGRAPHIES, CONSTITUTIONAL DEVELOPMENT AND TERMINOLOGY, RECONSTRUCTION and SLAVERY within this appendix.

Cold War

Bay of Pigs invasion; Berlin blockade; Berlin Wall Crisis; Central Intelligence Agency; Central Treaty Organization; Communist Control Act; containment; Cuban missile crisis; détente; Dies Committee; domino theory; John Foster Dulles; Eisenhower doctrine; Forward Strategy; Korean War; McCarran Act; Joseph McCarthy; McCarthy hearings; Marshall Plan; military-industrial complex; New Look defense policy; North Atlantic Treaty Organization; NSC-68; Potsdam Conference; red-baiting; Reykjavik Conference; rollback; Rosenberg trial; Smith act; Southeast Asian Treaty Organization; Strategic Defense Initiative; Truman doctrine; U-2 incident; Yalta Conference.

COLD WAR is a headword within the dictionary. *See also* subject heading SOCIAL PROTEST AND REFORM within this appendix.

Constitutional development and terminology

Annapolis Convention; Articles of Confederation; Bill of Rights; concurrent majority; Congressional Reconstruction; Connecticut Compromise; Constitution of the United States; Constitutional Convention; Double jeopardy; electoral college; Electoral Count Act; Founding Fathers; impeachment; implied powers; judicial review; loose constructionism; pocket veto; popular vote; Primary Elections; ratification; Reconstruction Acts; secession; separation of powers; states' rights; strict constructionism.

The text of the Constitution, The Bill of Rights and the Thirteenth, Fourteenth and Fifteenth amendments appear in Appendix 1. The FIRST AMENDMENT and all subsequent amendments are headwords within the dictionary.

Economic history

Agricultural and industrial development: crop lien; Coca-Cola and Pepsi; Federal farm loan act; McDonalds; National Reclamation Act; Pacific Railroad Act; Panama Canal: *Report on Manufactures*; Route 66; Rural Electrification Administration; sharecropping; Tennessee Valley Authority; trusts.

Boom and bust: baby boom; Black Friday; Depression of 1837; Depression of 1893; Great Depression; Hoovervilles; Panic of 1857 ; Panic of 1873; Panic of 1907; Wall Street Crash.

Fiscal and monetary: Bank of the United States; Bland–Allison Act; Bretton Woods Conference; Deposit Act; Emergency Banking Relief Act; Federal Reserve System; Free silver; Gilded age; gold standard; greenbacks; Independent Treasury Act; Legal Tender Acts; money trust; J. P. Morgan; *Report on the Public Credit*; Resumption Act; savings-and-loans crisis; Sherman Silver Purchase Act; silver–gold controversy; specie; Specie Circular; supply-side economics.

Regulation: Black–Connery Bill; Charles River Bridge vs. Warren bridge; Clayton anti-trust act; Dingley Tariff; Mann Elkins Act; Emergency Relief and Construction Act; Federal Reserve System; Federal Trade Commission; Gibbons vs. Ogden; Granger Laws; Hawley–Smoot Tariff; Hepburn Act; income tax; Interstate Commerce Act; legal-tender cases; McCulloch vs. Maryland; McKinley Tariff Act; McNaury–Haugen Bill; Munn vs. Illinois; National Industrial Recovery Act; National RecoveryAdministration; North American Free Trade Agreement; Northern Securities Company vs. US; Pujo hearings; Reconstruction Finance Corporation; Sherman Anti-Trust Act; Tariff of abominations; tariffs; Wilson–Gorman Tariff Act.

See also subject headings GOVERNMENT AGENCIES AND BUILDINGS, NEW DEAL and SUPREME COURT VERDICTS within this appendix.

Foreign relations

Revolutionary period: Carlisle Peace Commission; Franco-American Alliance; Genêt's mission; Jay–Gardoqui negotiations; Jay's treaty; Paris, treaties of.

Early national period: Adams–Onis treaty; Bayonne decree; Embargo Act; Ghent, treaty of; impressment; Macon's Bill Number 2; Nootka Sound crisis; Quasi-War; San Jacinto, treaty of; San Lorenzo, treaty of; XYZ affair.

Antebellum period: Bear Flag revolt; Cahuenga, treaty of; *Caroline* affair; Guadalupe-Hidalgo, treaty of; Kanagawa, treaty of; Mexican War; Oregon border crisis; Right of deposit; San Ildefonso, treaty of; Slidell mission; Webster–Ashburton treaty.

Civil War: *Alabama* claims; *Trent* affair.

Cold War: Anzus treaty; Atlantic Charter; Berlin blockade; Berlin Wall crisis; Containment; Cuban missile crisis; Détente; Eisenhower doctrine; Forward stategy; U-2 incident.

Annexations, interventions and invasions: Cuba; Dominican Republic; Grenada; Guam; Iranian hostage crisis; Lebanon; Mexico; Panama; Philippines; Puerto Rico; Siberia.

Conferences: Casablanca; Dumbarton Oaks; Paris Peace Conference; Paris peace talks; Potsdam; Quebec; Reykjavik; Teheran; Washington Naval Conference; Yalta.

Organizations: Central Treaty Organization; League of Nations; North Atlantic Treaty Organization; Organization of American States; United Nations; Southeast Asian Treaty Organization.

Policies and doctrines: Carter doctrine; dollar diplomacy; fourteen points; good-neighbour policy; isolationism; Kellogg–Briand pact; Ludlow resolution; 'mad dog' strategy; Monroe doctrine; Neutrality Proclamation; Nixon doctrine; open-door policy; Platt amendments; Roosevelt corollary; War Powers Act.

Wars: Korean War; Mexican War; Persian Gulf War; Revolutionary War; Seven Years' War; Spanish-American war; Vietnam War; War of 1812; World War I; World War II.

TERRITORIAL EXPANSION is a headword within the dictionary. *See also* subject headings BIOGRAPHIES, COLD WAR, TERRITORIAL EXPANSION, VIETNAM WAR, WORLD WAR I and WORLD WAR II within this appendix.

Government agencies and buildings

Central Intelligence Agency; Congress; Federal Bureau of Investigation; Federal Deposit Insurance Corporation; Federal Emergency Relief Administration; Federal Reserve System; Federal Trade Commission; National Aeronautics and Space Administration; National Security Council; Office of Strategic Services; Pentagon; Supreme Court; White House.

See also subject heading NEW DEAL within this appendix.

Hispanic-American history

Aztlan; Braceros; Cesar Chavez; chicano; Ernesto Galarza; La Huelga; La Raza Unida; Zoot suit riots.

Immigration

Chae Chan Ping vs. US; Chinese Exclusion Act; Contract Labor Act; Emergency Quota Act; National Origins Act; nativism; People vs. Hall; Smith Act; Workingmen's Party.

IMMIGRATION is a headword within the dictionary.

Labor history

Biographies: Richard Davis; Eugene Debs; Elizabeth Gurley Flynn; Emma Goldman; Samuel Gompers; Jimmy Hoffa; Mary 'Mother' Jones; John L. Lewis; Terrence Powderly; Asa Philip Randolph.

General: baby boom; cowboys; eight-hour movement; Great Migration; Haymarket riot; Ludlow massacre; Triangle Shirtwaist Factory fire; yellow-dog contract.

Government initiatives and legislation: Adamson (Eight-Hour) Act; Commission on Industrial Relations; Fair Labor Standards Act; Landrum–Griffin Act; National Industrial Recovery Act; National Labor Relations Board; Norris–LaGuardia Act; Public Works Administration; Taft–Hartley Act; Wagner Act.

Organizations: American Federation of Labor; American Railway Union; Civilian Conservation Corps; Civil Works Administration; Congress of Industrial Organizations; craft unions; industrial unions; Industrial Workers of the World; Knights of Labor; Molly Maguires; National Labor Union; National War Labor Board; United Mine Workers of America; Workingmen's Party; Works Progress Administration.

Strikes: coal strike of 1902 ; coal strike of 1946 ; Coeur d'Alene miners' strike; Homestead steel strike; La Huelga; Lawrence textile strike; Pullman strike; rail strike of 1877; sit-down strikes; steel strike of 1919.

Supreme Court verdicts: Adair vs. US; Bailey vs. Drexel Furniture Company; Danbury hatters' case; Duplex Printing Press Company vs. Deering; In Re Debs; Lochner vs. New York; Muller vs. Oregon; National Labor Relations Board vs. Jones and Laughlin Steel; United Steel Workers of America vs. Weber.

Native American history

Biographies: Joseph Brant; Cochise; John Collier; Geronimo; Alexander McGillivray; Osceola; the Prophet; John Ross; Sacajawea; Sitting Bull; Tecumseh; Jim Thorpe.

Government policy towards: Cherokee Nation vs. Georgia; Dawes Severalty Act; Indian Claims Commission; Indian Removal Act; Trail of Tears; Wheeler–Howard Act; Worcester vs. Georgia.

Institutions: Carlisle Indian School; reservations.

Military history: Black Hawk War; Creek War; Fallen Timbers, battle of; Fetterman massacre; Horseshoe Bend, battle of; Little Big Horn; Pontiac's War; Red River War; Sand Creek massacre; Seminole Wars; Sioux Wars; Winnebago War; Wounded Knee, massacre at.

Nations: Apache; Arapaho; Cherokee; Cheyenne; Chickasaw; Choctaw; Comanche; Creek; Five Civilized Tribes; Hopi; Iroquois Confederacy; Kiowa; Mohawk; Nez Percé; Pueblo peoples; Seminole; Seneca; Shawnee; Shoshoni; Sioux; Zuni.

Organizations: American Indian Movement; Wounded Knee protest.

Religion: Ghost Dance; peyote cult.

Treaties: Fort Jackson; Fort Laramie; Fort Stanwix; Greenville; Indian Springs; Medicine Lodge; New Echota.

TERRITORIAL EXPANSION is a headword within the dictionary.

New Deal

Agencies: Agricultural Adjustment Administration; Civilian Conservation Corps; Civil Works Administration; Commodity Credit Corporation; Farm Credit Administration; National Recovery Administration; Public Works Administration; Reconstruction Finance Corporation; Resettlement Administration; Rural Electrification Administration; Tennessee Valley Authority; Works Progress Administration.

Background: bank holiday; brains trust; dust bowl; fireside chats; Great Depression; the hundred days; Okies; Wickersham report.

Legislation: Banking Act; Black–Connery Bill; Emergency Banking Relief Act; Emergency Relief and Construction Act; Emergency Relief Appropriation Act; Fair Labor Standards Act; Hatch Act; National Industrial Recovery act; Social Security Act; Wagner Act.

Political history: court-packing controversy; First New Deal; good-neighbor policy; the hundred days; New Deal coalition; presidential election of 1932; Franklin D. Roosevelt; Schecter Poultry Corporation vs. US; Second New Deal; United States vs. Butler.

NEW DEAL is a headword within the dictionary. *See also* subject heading BIOGRAPHIES within this appendix.

Political history

Early national period: Alien and Sedition Acts; Fries's rebellion; Hartford Convention; Kentucky Resolutions; Neutrality Proclamation; Whiskey Rebellion; XYZ affair.

Jacksonian America: Maysville Road veto; nullification crisis; Specie Circular.

Gilded Age: Omaha Platform; populism; Pendleton Act; progressivism; silver–gold controversy.

Campaigns and slogans: 'Cross of Gold' speech; Fair Deal; Great Society; Log Cabin and Hard Cider campaign; New Deal; New Freedom; New Frontier; New Nationalism; presidential elections of 1800, 1860, 1864, 1876, 1912, 1932, 1948, 1960, 1968, 1972; Square Deal; Wade–Davis Manifesto; War on Poverty.

Controversies: Bork confirmation hearings; court-packing controversy; 'corrupt bargain' of 1824; Crime of '73; Peggy Eaton; McCarthy hearings; Parker confirmation hearings; Sacco and Vanzetti case; savings-and-loans crisis; silver–gold controversy; Warren Commission; Yazoo land fraud.

Parties and factions: Albany Regency; Americans for Democratic Action; antifederalists; Anti-Masonic Party; Barnburners; Bourbons; Communist Party of the USA; Constitutional Union Party; Democratic Party; Democratic-Republicans; Dixiecrats; doughface; Equal rights party; Farmer-Labor Party; Federalist Party; fire-eaters; Free Soil Party; Grand Army of the Republic; Granger movement; Greenback Party; Half-Breeds; hayseed socialists; Hunkers; Know Nothing Party; La raza Unida Party; Liberal Republican Party; Liberty Party; Loco-focos; Moral Majority; Mugwumps; National Republicans; National Union Party; National Women's Party; Peace Democrats; People's Party; Progressive Party; Prohibition Party; Quids; Radical Republicans; Redeemers; Republican Party; Socialist Party of America; Stalwarts; Union Party; Whig Party; Women's Peace Party; Workingmen's Party; Yippies.

Scandals: Crédit Mobilier scandal; Iran–Contra scandal; Lewinsky scandal; Teapot Dome scandal; Tuskegee syphilis scandal; Tweed ring; Watergate scandal; Whiskey Ring; Whitewater affair.

Terminology: Bloody shirt; Brains Trust; Concurrent majority; Congressional Reconstruction; Contract with America; Copperhead; Filibuster; first party system; Founding fathers; free silver; gerrymandering; The hundred days; kitchen cabinet; Mason–Dixon line; pocket veto; military-industrial complex; New Deal coalition; populism; Primary Elections; progressivism; Reagan Democrats; red baiting; Redemption; Red Scare; Rollback; second party system; secret ballot; slave power; smoke-filled room; solid south; spoils system; Tammany Hall; third party system; war hawks.

Political thought

American System; antifederalists; Domino theory; federalism; *Federalist Papers*; free-soil ideology; Jacksonian democracy; Jefferson-

ian democracy; Kentucky resolutions; Lockean thought; populism; progressivism; Redemption; Republican ideology; Rollback; social Darwinism; supply-side economics; Virginia resolutions; virtue; Webster–Hayne debate.

See also subject headings AMERICAN REVOLUTION, BIOGRAPHIES, CIVIL RIGHTS MOVEMENT, CIVIL WAR, CONSTITUTIONAL DEVELOPMENT AND TERMINOLOGY, NEW DEAL, RECONSTRUCTION, SLAVERY, SOCIAL PROTEST AND REFORM, and SPEECHES AND CATCHPHRASES within this appendix.

Reconstruction

Agencies: Freedmen's Bureau.

Background: Colfax massacre; contrabands; crop lien; Field Order 15; forty acres and a mule; freedmen; Jim Crow; Andrew Johnson; Ku Klux Klan; Memphis riot; New Orleans riot; Redeemers; Redemption; Scalawags.

Legislation: Civil Rights Acts of 1866, 1875; Enforcement Acts; Ku Klux Klan Act; Reconstruction Acts; Tenure of Office Act; Wade–Davis Bill.

Politics and government during: black codes; Black Republicans; bloody shirt; carpetbaggers; Compromise of 1877; congressional Reconstruction; Fifteenth Amendment; Fourteenth Amendment; ironclad oath; Joint Committee on Reconstruction; Presidential election of 1876; presidential reconstruction; Proclamation of Amnesty and Reconstruction; Proclamation of Reconstruction; Radical Republicans.

Supreme Court verdicts: civil rights cases; slaughterhouse cases; Texas vs. White; United States vs. Reese.

RECONSTRUCTION is a headword within the dictionary. *See also* subject headings AFRICAN-AMERICAN HISTORY, BIOGRAPHIES, CIVIL WAR and POLITICAL HISTORY within this appendix.

Religion, cults and beliefs

African Methodist Episcopal church;

Christian Science; Everson vs. Board of Ewing Township; Ghost dance; Mormons; Nation of Islam; Oneida commune; peyote cult; Second Great Awakening; Social gospel; transcendentalism; unitarianism; Virginia Statute for Religious Freedom; Brigham Young.

Science, technology and education

Apollo program; Atomic Energy Commission; barbed wire; Alexander Graham Bell; Rachel Carson; *Challenger* disaster; Thomas Edison; ENIAC; Henry Ford; Daniel Coit Gilman; Lewis and Clark expedition; Cyrus McCormick; Morrill (Higher Education) Act; National Aeronautics and Space Administration; National Defense Education Act; national parks; Newspapers; radio and television; railroads; time zones; Noah Webster; Eli Whitney; Wilbur and Orville Wright.

Slavery

Abolitionist movement: abolition; African Methodist Episcopal church; American Antislavery Society; American Colonization Society; *Amistad* mutiny; John Brown; Salmon Chase; Frederick Douglass; William Lloyd Garrison; raid on Harper's Ferry; Thaddeus Stevens; *The Liberator*; Sojourner Truth; Harriet Tubman; underground railroad.

Legal status of: Abelman vs. Booth; Connecticut Compromise; Constitution of the United States; Dred Scott vs. Sandford; Fugitive Slave Act; Thirteenth Amendment; Quok Walker case.

Political history: bleeding Kansas; Compromise of 1850; Davis resolutions; Emancipation Proclamation; Freeport Doctrine; Gag Rule; Kansas–Nebraska Act; Lecompton constitution; Liberty Party; Lincoln–Douglas debates; Missouri Compromise; Ostend Manifesto; personal liberty laws; Wilmot Proviso; Thaddeus Stevens.

Resistance: Christiana riot; Nat Turner's Revolt; Denmark Vesey.

Terminology: contrabands; exodusters; freedmen; gradual emancipation; manumission; slave power.

SLAVERY is a headword within the dictionary. *See also* subject headings AFRICAN-AMERICAN HISTORY, CIVIL WAR, POLITICAL HISTORY and RECONSTRUCTION within this appendix.

Social protest and reform

Biographies: Ralph Abernathy; Jane Addams; Muhammad Ali; Susan Brownell Anthony; Ella Baker; Clara Barton; Elizabeth Blackwell; Amelia Bloomer; William Jennings Bryan; Stokeley Carmichael; Carrie Chapman Catt; Cesar Chavez; Richard Davis; Eugene Debs; Dorothea Dix; Frederick Douglass; W.E.B. Du Bois; Medgar Evers; Elizabeth Gurley Flynn; Ernesto Galarza; William Lloyd Garrison; Marcus Garvey; Emma Goldman; Samuel Gompers; Horace Greeley; Fanny Lou Hamer; Julia Ward Howe; Helen Hunt Jackson; Jesse Jackson; Mary 'Mother' Jones; Florence Kelley; Martin Luther King; John L. Lewis; Huey Long; Eugene McCarthy; George McGovern; James Meredith; Lucretia Mott; Carry Nation; Alice Paul; Terrence Powderly; Asa Philip Randolph; Jeanette Rankin; Paul Robeson; Eleanor Roosevelt; Margaret Sanger; Anna Howard Shaw; Elizabeth Cady Stanton; Lucy Stone; Francis Townsend; Sojourner Truth; Harriet Tubman; George Wallace; Booker T. Washington; Tom Watson; James B. Weaver; Ida B. Wells-Barnett; Malcolm X.

Events: Boston massacre; Chicago convention riots; Detroit riot; Fries's Rebellion; raid on Harper's Ferry; Haymarket riot; Homestead steel strike; La Huelga; Kent State antiwar protest; March on Washington; Montgomery bus boycott; Selma Freedom March; Seneca Falls Convention; Watts riot; Wounded Knee protest.

Legislation: Adamson Act; Bonus Bill; Civil Rights Act of 1866; Civil Rights Act of 1875;

Civil Rights Act of 1957; Civil Rights Act of 1960; Civil Rights Act of 1964; Civil Rights Act of 1968; Civil Rights Act of 1970; Dawes Severalty Act; Dependent Pension Act; Emergency Relief Appropriation Act; Enforcement Acts; Equal Rights Amendment; Fair Labor Standards Act; Freedom of Information Act; GI Bill of Rights; Homestead Act; Hyde Amendment; Ku Klux Klan Act; Medicaid; Medicare; Pure Food and Drug Act; Social Security Act; Volstead act; Voting Rights Act; Webb–Kenyon Interstate Liquor Act; Wheeler-Howard Act.

The FIRST AMENDMENT and all subsequent amendments are headwords within the dictionary

Organizations: Abraham Lincoln Battalion; American Antislavery Society; American Civil Liberties Union; American Indian Movement; American Woman Suffrage Association; Anti-Saloon League of America; Antiwar Movement; Bonus Army; Communist Party of the USA; Congress of racial equality; Coxey's Army; Farmer-Labor Party; Grand Army of the Republic; Industrial Workers of the World; jayhawkers; Knights of labor; Lowndes County Freedom Organization; Mississippi Freedom Democratic Party; Molly Maguires; Niagara Movement; National American Woman Suffrage Association; National Association for the Advancement of Colored People; National Labor Union; National Organization for Women; National Woman's Party; National Woman Suffrage Association; Oneida commune; Socialist Party of America; Southern Christian Leadership Conference; Student Non-Violent Coordinating Committee; Women's Christian Temperance Union; Women's Movement; Workingmen's Party; Yippies.

Suppression of: blacklist; Dies Committee; J. Edgar Hoover; McCarthy hearings; Allan Pinkerton; Red Scare; Schenck vs. US.

Terminology: abolition; affirmative action; comparable worth; eight-hour movement; Gun control; Levittowns; Gay Rights; Great

Society; Medicaid; Medicare; muckrakers; populism; progressivism; Prohibition; social gospel.

See also subject heading AMERICAN REVOLUTION within this appendix.

Speeches and catchphrases

'Arsenal of Democracy'; Atlanta Exposition Speech; 'Checkers'; 'Crisis of Confidence'; 'Cross of Gold'; forty acres and a mule; Gettysburg Address; 'Go West, young man, and grow up with the country'; 'House Divided'; 'I have a dream'; inaugural addresses; 'The only good Indian is a dead Indian'; 'Say it ain't so Joe'; Uncle Sam; 'Win one for the Gipper.'

Sport and Entertainment

Muhammad Ali; Phineas Taylor Barnum; baseball; Buffalo Bill; Walt Disney; Hollywood; jazz; Jesse Owens; Elvis Presley; radio and television; Paul Robeson; Jackie Robinson; Babe Ruth; spectator sports; Jim Thorpe.

Supreme Court verdicts

Abortion: Hodgson vs. Minnesota; Roe vs. Wade; Thornburgh vs. American College of Obstetricians; Webster vs. Reproductive Health Services.

Civil rights: Baker vs. Carr; Boynton vs. Virginia; Breedlove vs. Suttles; Brown vs. Board of Education; Civil rights cases; Ex Parte Merryman; Ex Parte Milligan; Ex Parte Yarborough; graduate school cases; Harper vs. Virginia Board of Elections; Heart of Atlanta Motel vs. US; Meritor Savings Bank vs. Vinson; Miranda vs. Arizona; Oregon vs. Mitchell; Plessy vs. Ferguson; Regents of the University of California vs. Baake; Skinner vs. Oklahoma; slaughterhouse cases; Swann vs. Charlotte-Mecklenburg Board of Education; United States vs. Cruikshank; United States vs. Reese.

Commerce: Charles River Bridge vs. Warren

Bridge; Gibbons vs. Ogden; legal-tender cases; Munn vs. Illinois; Northern Securities Company vs. US; Santa Clara County vs. Southern Pacific Railroad; Schecter Poultry Corporation vs. US; Standard Oil Company of New Jersey et al. vs. US; Swift and Co. vs. US; United States vs. Butler; United States vs. E.C. Knight; Wabash, St Louis and Pacific Railroad vs. Illinois.

Constitutional issues: Chisholm vs. Georgia; Dartmouth College vs. Woodward; Fletcher vs. Peck; McCulloch vs. Maryland; Marbury vs. Madison; Texas vs. White; US vs. Reese.

Free speech and religion: Abrams vs. US; Everson vs. Board of Ewing Township; Schenck vs. US.

Immigration: Chae Chan Ping vs. US.

Labor: Adair vs. US; Bailey vs. Drexel Furniture Company; Danbury hatters' case; Duplex Printing Press Company vs. Deering; In Re Debs; Lochner vs. New York; Muller vs. Oregon; National Labor Relations Board vs. Jones and Laughlin Steel; United Steel Workers of America vs. Weber; Youngstown Sheet and Tube Co. vs. Sawyer.

Native Americans: Cherokee Nation vs. Georgia; Worcester vs. Georgia.

Slavery: Abelman vs. Booth; Dred Scott vs. Sandford.

Women's suffrage: Minor vs. Happersett.

Territorial expansion

Bear Flag Revolt; Black Hawk War; bleeding Kansas; border ruffians; Bozeman Trail; Cahuenga, treaty of; George Rogers Clark; US attempts to annex Cuba; East Florida; frontier thesis; Gadsden Purchase; Homestead Act; Lewis and Clark expedition; Louisiana Purchase; manifest destiny; Mason–Dixon line; Mexican War; Missouri Compromise; Northwest Ordinance; Northwest Territory; Oklahoma land rush; Ordinance of 1785; Oregon border crisis; Oregon Trail; Zebulon Pike; Proclamation of 1763; Sycamore Shoals, treaty of;

Transylvania Company; West Florida; Wilderness Road.

Trials

Sacco and Vanzetti; Scopes trial; Scottsboro boys case.

Vietnam War

Events (*see also* subject heading BATTLES in this appendix): Operation Cedar Falls; US operations in Cambodia; Christmas bombing; US operations in Laos.

Opposition to: Antiwar Movement; Chicago convention riots; Kent State antiwar protest.

Terminology: Agent Orange; bodycount; domino theory; the draft; fragging; Kissinger initiative; 'mad dog' strategy; MIAs; My Lai massacre; Operation Chaos; Paris peace talks; Pentagon Papers; search and destroy; Tonkin Gulf Resolution. VIETNAM WAR and ANTIWAR MOVEMENT are headwords within the dictionary.

See also subject headings BATTLES, BIOGRAPHIES and COLD WAR within this appendix.

Women's history

American Revolution: Betsy Ross.

Jacksonian America: Peggy Eaton.

Abortion: abortion; Hodgson vs. Minnesota; Hyde Amendment; Roe vs. Wade; Thornburgh vs. American College of Obstetricians; Webster vs. Reproductive Health Services.

African-American: Ella Baker; Fanny Lou Hamer; Sojourner Truth; Harriet Tubman; Ida B. Wells-Barnett.

Civil rights: comparable worth; Equal Rights Amendment; Meritor Savings Bank vs. Vinson; National Organization for Women; Women's Movement.

Civil rights campaigners: Ella Baker; Fanny Lou Hamer.

Jurists: Sandra Day O'Connor.

Native Americans: Sacajawea.

Politicians and statesmen: Madeleine Albright; Geraldine Ferraro; Patricia Roberts Harris; Jeane Duane Jordan Kirkpatrick; Frances Perkins.

Reformers and campaigners: Jane Addams; Susan Brownell Anthony; Clara Barton; Elizabeth Blackwell; Amelia Bloomer; Carrie Chapman Catt; Dorothea Dix; Elizabeth Gurley Flynn; Emma Goldman; Julia Ward Howe; Helen Hunt Jackson; Mary 'Mother' Jones; Florence Kelley; Lucretia Mott; Carry Nation; Alice Paul; Jeanette Rankin; Hillary Rodham Clinton; Eleanor Roosevelt; Margaret Sanger; St Elizabeth Anne Seton; Anna Howard Shaw; Elizabeth Cady Stanton; Lucy Stone; Women's Christian Temperance Union; Victoria Claflin Woodhull.

Suffrage: American Woman Suffrage Association; Minor vs. Happersett; National American Woman Suffrage Association; National Woman's Party; National Woman Suffrage Association; Seneca Falls Convention; women's suffrage.

ABORTION, WOMEN'S SUFFRAGE and WOMEN'S MOVEMENT are headwords within the dictionary. *See also* subject headings BIOGRAPHIES, LABOR HISTORY and SOCIAL PROTEST AND REFORM within this appendix.

World War I

Committee on Public Information; the draft; Espionage Act; Fourteen Points; League of Nations; Meuse–Argonne offensive; National War Labor Board; Paris Peace Conference; John Pershing; Selective Service Acts; St Mihiel offensive; Versailles, treaty of; War Industries Board; Women's Peace Party; Woodrow Wilson; Zimmermann telegram.

WORLD WAR I is a headword within the dictionary.

World War II

Battles: Bataan; Bulge; Coral Sea; Corregidor; D-Day landings; Guadalcanal campaign; Iwo Jima; Midway; Okinawa; Omaha beach; Pearl Harbor, Japanese attack on; St Lô offensive; Tarawa Atoll.

Biographies: Omar Bradley; Mark Clark; Dwight Eisenhower; Douglas MacArthur; George Marshall; George Patton.

Conclusion: Hiroshima and Nagasaki, bombing of; Manhattan Project.

Outcome: baby boom; Cold War; GI Bill of Rights; Potsdam Conference; Yalta Conference.

US policy during: ABC-1 agreement; 'Arsenal of Democracy' speech; Atlantic Charter; Casablanca Conference; the draft; Four Freedoms; Lend-Lease Act; Quebec Conferences; Japanese-Americans, relocation of; Selective Service Acts; Teheran Conference.

WORLD WAR II is a headword within the dictionary.

FURTHER READING

Few modern nations have been the subject of such intensive historical investigation as the United States of America. One could fill a fair-sized library solely with works covering the American Civil War. The following list of further readings is highly selective, but chosen with users of *Cassell's Dictionary of Modern American History* in mind.

The development of recent historiography has left readers seeking a general narrative account of the history of the USA less well served than those seeking further information about a particular topic or theme. Brogan, Hugh, *The Longman History of the United States of America* (London and New York, 1999) and Jones, Maldwyn A., *The Limits of Liberty: American History 1607–1980* (New York and Oxford, 1995) provide the best recent overviews of the broad sweep of American history. Acting on the assumption that there is much to be learned from disagreeing with an author, I would also recommend two broad surveys that reflect particular political outlooks. Zinn, Howard, *A People's History of the United States: From 1492 to the Present* (London and New York, 1996) is written from a left-wing perspective, while Johnson, Paul, *A History of the American People* (London, 1997) reflects the interests and concerns of a conservative radical. Although often disavowing claims to be providing 'grand narrative', a number of

authors have argued that a struggle to define and extend liberty, freedom and equality provides the driving force behind American history. This overarching theme has been pursued in two particularly thought-provoking surveys: Pole, J. R., *The Pursuit of Equality in American History* (Berkeley and Oxford, 1993) and Foner, Eric, *The Story of American Freedom* (New York and London, 1998). Many recent works argue that America's essence as a nation has been defined by a collision of cultures from which white Americans seized a cultural ascendancy while African-Americans and native peoples emerged bloodied but unbowed. See Countryman, Edward, *Americans* (New York and London, 1996) for an introduction to this approach. For valuable treatments of immigration and white ethnicity, see Jones, Maldwyn A., *American Immigration* (Chicago and London, 1960), Reimers, David M., *Ethnic Americans: A History of Immigration and Assimilation* (New York, 1982) and Thernstrom, Stephan, ed., *The Harvard Encyclopedia of American Ethnic Groups* (Cambridge, Mass., and London, 1980).

Excellent single-volume accounts of the American Revolution can be found in Countryman, Edward, *The American Revolution* (New York and London, 1985) and Bonwick, Colin, *The American Revolution* (London, 1991). For a more detailed but still highly readable survey, see Middlekauff, Robert, *The Glorious Cause* (New York and Oxford, 1982). Maier, Pauline, *American Scripture: Making the Declaration of Independence* (New York, 1997) and Beard, Charles A., *An Economic Interpretation of the Constitution of the United States* (rep. New Brunswick, NJ, 1998) provide stimulating accounts of the forces that lay behind the drafting of the documents defining America's identity as an independent nation. An advanced overview of the legacy of the American Revolution can be found in Wood, Gordon S., *The Radicalism of the American Revolution* (New York and London, 1992). Elkins, Stanley and McKitrick, Eric, *The Age of Federalism: The Early American Republic, 1788–1800* (New York and Oxford, 1993) offers a magisterial survey of the development of party politics in America. Brown, Roger H., *The Republic in Peril: 1812* (New York and London, 1964) charts the role played by partisan politics in provoking the USA's second war with Britain.

Wilentz, Sean, *Chants Democratic: New York City and the Rise of the American Working Class* (New York and London, 1984) and Sellers, Charles, *The Market Revolution* (New York, 1991) detail the emergence of the urban working class and an increasingly commercial economic culture in the 19th-century USA. McCormick, Richard L., *The Second American Party System: Party Formation in the Jacksonian Era* (New York, 1966) and Watson, Harry L., *Liberty and Power: The Politics of Jacksonian America* (New York, 1990) assess the political consequences of social change in the Jacksonian era. Howe, Daniel Walker, *The Political Culture of the American Whigs* (Chicago and London, 1987) studies the era from a non-Jacksonian perspective.

The literature on slavery is enormous. Kolchin, Peter, *American Slavery: 1619–1877* (New York and London, 1995) provides the most accessible survey of the development of the USA's 'peculiar institution'. Three of the best studies of life under slavery are Genovese,

Eugene D., *Roll, Jordan, Roll: The World the Slaves Made* (New York, 1974), Berlin, Ira, *Slaves Without Masters* (New York, 1974) and Blassingame, John W., *The Slave Community: Plantation Life in the Antebellum South* (2nd rev. edn, New York, 1979). Stampp, Kenneth M., *The Causes of the Civil War* (New York, 1991) illuminates the ways in which the continuing existence of slavery produced an 'irrepressible conflict'. Collins, Bruce, *White Society in the Ante-bellum South* (London, 1985) treats the lives of the majority non-slaveholding southern white population.

Although thousands of books describing aspects of the Civil War and Reconstruction are currently in print, two titles are indispensable for further study – McPherson, James M., *Battle Cry of Freedom: The American Civil War* (New York and Oxford, 1988) and Foner, Eric, *Reconstruction: America's Unfinished Revolution* (New York, 1988). Each contains an authoritative bibliography.

The Oxford History of the American West (New York and Oxford, 1994) offers a useful introduction to its subject. For an account which challenges long-standing assumptions, see Limerick, Patricia, *The Legacy of Conquest: The Unbroken Past of the American West* (New York and London, 1987). For an overview of relations between settlers and native peoples in the era of westward expansion, see Nobles, Gregory H., *American Frontiers: Cultural Encounters and Continental Conquest* (New York and London, 1998).

Wiebe, Robert H., *The Search for Order, 1877–1920* (New York and London, 1967) provides an excellent introduction to the history of the 'Gilded Age'. Goodwyn, Lawrence, *The Populist Moment: A Short History of Agrarian Revolt in America* (New York and London, 1978) and Kazin, Michael A., *The Populist Persuasion: An American History* (Ithaca, NY, and London, 1998) provide provoking assessments of America's 'hayseed socialists'. Woodward, C. Vann, *Tom Watson:*

Agrarian Rebel (rep. New York and Oxford, 1963) links the populists' failure to the politics of race. Woodward, C. Vann, *The Strange Career of Jim Crow* (3rd edn, New York, 1974) and Williamson, Joel, *The Crucible of Race: Black–White Relations in the American South since Emancipation* (New York, 1984) assess the construction of racial segregation in the south. Link, Arthur S., and McCormick, Richard L., *Progressivism* (New York, 1983) and Hofstadter, Richard, *The Age of Reform: From Bryan to FDR* (New York, 1955) provide introductions to the Progressive reform movement in northern cities. LaFeber, Walter, *The Cambridge History of American Foreign Relations Volume II: The American Search for Opportunity, 1865–1913* (Cambridge and New York, 1993), Williams, William Appleman, *The Tragedy of American Diplomacy* (2nd edn, 1972) and Hunt, Michael H., *Ideology and US Foreign Policy* (New Haven, Conn., 1987) introduce the USA's rise to the status of a world power and its acquisition of overseas possessions. Knock, Thomas J., *To End All Wars: Woodrow Wilson and the Quest for a New World Order* (New York, 1992) explores the links between Wilsonian foreign policy and domestic political culture.

The best introductions to the politics of the interwar years are Leuchtenburg, William E., *The Perils of Prosperity* (Chicago, 1958) and Parrish, Michael E., *Anxious Decades: America in Prosperity and Depression, 1920–41* (New York, 1992). Terkel, Studs, *Hard Times: An Oral History of the Great Depression* (New York and London, 1970) captures the atmosphere of the Depression era. Badger, Anthony J., *The New Deal: The Depression Years, 1933–1940* (London, 1989) provides an excellent introduction to its subject and a useful bibliography. Dallek, Robert, *Franklin Roosevelt and American Foreign Policy, 1932–1945* (New York and Oxford, 1979) provides a well-received account of US foreign policy prior to and during World War II. The military history of the war is

covered in Dear, I.C.B and Foot, M.R.D., ed, *The Oxford Companion to the Second World War* (New York and Oxford, 1987).

A useful overview of the Cold War is provided by Mason, John W., *The Cold War: 1945–1991* (London and New York, 1996). Further detail is provided in Young, John, *The Longman Companion to the Cold War and Detente, 1941–91* (London, 1993). Kennedy, Robert F., *Thirteen Days: The Cuban Missile Crisis* (London, 1969) illuminates one of the most dramatic moments of the Cold War. Herring, George C., *America's Longest War: The United States and Vietnam, 1950–75* (2nd edn, New York, 1986) offers a standard introduction to its subject.

The best single volume overview of US history since 1945 is provided by Chafe, William H., *The Unfinished Journey: America Since World War II* (3rd edn, New York, 1995). Cook, Robert, *Sweet Land of Liberty? The African-American Struggle for Civil Rights in the Twentieth Century* (London and New York, 1998) provides a sure-footed introduction to the Civil Rights Movement. Other standard accounts of the Civil Rights Movement include Branch, Taylor, *Parting the Waters* (New York, 1988) and Garrow, David J., *Bearing the Cross: Martin Luther King and the Southern Christian Leadership Conference* (New York, 1986). Morgan, Iwan W., *Beyond the Liberal Consensus: A Political History of the United States Since 1965* (London, 1994) traces the political fall-out from the collapse of the organized Civil Rights Movement.

Students and general readers can approach the study of American history in the same manner as professional historians: namely, by reading and questioning primary texts. The following primary texts have been reprinted by mass- market companies such as Penguin and specialists houses such as the Library of America, usually in formats that include an introductory essay and select bibliography. (Rather than direct readers to specific editions, I have identified the works themselves and their authors where necessary.) *The Autobiography of Benjamin Franklin* provides an unsurpassed insight into life in colonial America and the origins of the American character. *Notes on the State of Virginia*, written by Thomas Jefferson, offers frank views on racial inequality and a fascinating insight into the influence of Enlightenment thought in America. *The Federalist*, a series of essays written by Alexander Hamilton, John Jay and James Madison under the pseudonym Publius, and often marketed under the title *The Federalist Papers*, offer a classic defense of the US Constitution. *The Autobiography of Frederick Douglass* and the *Narrative of Sojourner Truth* illuminate the abolitionist movement.

Thomas Wentworth Higginson's *Army Life in a Black Regiment* and Ulysses S. Grant's *Personal Memoirs* provide two very different perspectives on the Civil War. Equally varied are the views on 19th-century African-American history and culture laid out by Booker T. Washington in *Up From Slavery* and W.E.B. Du Bois in *The Souls of Black Folk*. Students interested in the Progressive era should read Jane Addams's *Twenty Years at Hull House* and Jacob Riis's *How the Other Half Lives*. In their different ways Betty Friedan's *The Feminine Mystique* and Haley, Alex, ed., *The Autobiography of Malcolm X* provide unrivaled points of departure for studies of the social upheavals of the 1960s and 1970s.